CONTENTS

LIST OF FIGURES

LIST OF TABLES

ACKNOWLEDGEMENTS

It is customary to thank one's partner last, by stating the book could never have been finished without their help. I will break with tradition and thank my partner at the beginning, as in this case it is literally true. I abandoned the project on more than one occasion and Helena rescued it from the bin, smoothed my ruffled feathers, and set me back on the road again. Thank you. My Mum, as ever, was a pillar of support and belief.

Over the years, a huge number of people have helped me. Especially in the various universities, museums, and libraries I worked in. I wish I had kept a record of all your names, I am sorry I didn't. Thank you all. All the staff and students of the British Museum outstation at Shoreditch were especially supportive over many years and I am grateful to you all.

The Department of Archaeology, University of Southampton, supported my research by the award of two grants for illustrative work.

David Keen, Hannah Fluck and David Underhill-Stocks read all, or most, of earlier drafts. Their advice was very valuable. A number of people read chapters in early form: Chris Stringer, Rob Hosfield, Nick Ashton, Anne O'Connor, Rebecca Scott, Simon Parfitt, Derek Roe, John Gowlett, Robin Dunbar, Will Roebroeks. I greatly appreciate them giving up their time, and I took on board most of what everyone said.

A huge vote of thanks goes to Penny Copeland, who created most of the figures. Without her skill and cheerful professionalism the book would have been a lesser work. Thanks.

Figure acknowledgements

The following figures were reproduced with kind permission.

Figure 1.1A   Pointed, cleaver, and ovate from Ashton *et al.* 1992a, plate 67/3228; plate 52/3200; Figure 11: 22, 3. Trustees of the British Museum. Cordiform drawn by John Wymer, Wymer 1999, figure 4. Wessex Archaeology.

Figure 1.1B   Thinning flakes from McNabb *et al.* 1996, Figure 10, Sussex

Archaeological Collections, volume 134. Sussex Archaeological Collections and the Sussex Archaeological Society.

Figure 1.2   Ashton *et al.* 1992a, Figure 11.7, 3 and 4. Trustees of the British Museum.

Figure 1.3   Ashton *et al.* 1992a, Figure 1.8,1; 11.8,6; 11.18,1. Trustees of the British Museum.

Figures 2.1 and 2.2   Lorraine Lisiecki.

Figure 2.5   Bridgland 2001, Figure 3.7. The Lithics Studies Society and David Bridgland.

Figures 2.7   Bridgland 1994, Figure 4.3. Springer Science and Business Media, and David Bridgland.

Figures 2.9A and 2.9B   Bridgland 1994, Figures 2.2 and 3.2. Springer Science and Business Media, and David Bridgland.

Figure 2.10A   Bridgland and Schreve 2001, Figure 5. Balkema for Taylor and Francis.

Figure 2.10B   Modified and used with permission of David Bridgland and Andy Howard

Figure 2.11A   Bridgland and Schreve 2001, Figure 3. Balkema for Taylor and Francis.

Figure 2.11B   Westaway *et al.* 2006, Figure 13. Elsevier

Figure 3.1   Bridgland 1994, Figure 5.17. Springer Science and Business Media, and David Bridgland.

Figure 3.6   Wenban-Smith and Bridgland 2001, Figure 1. The Prehistoric Society.

Figure 3.7   Conway *et al.* 1996, Figure 8.1. Trustees of the British Museum.

Figures 3.8 and 3.9   McNabb 1996b, Figures 4, 5, 6. *Antiquity* Publications Limited.

Figure 3.10   Conway *et al.* 1996, Figure 16.10. Trustees of the British Museum.

Figure 3.12   Ashton *et al.* 1998, Figure 4.32. Trustees of the British Museum.

Figures 4.3A and 4.3B   Clayton 2000, Figure 8. Preece and Parfitt 2000, Figure 2. The Quaternary Research Association.

Figure 4.4   Lee *et al.* 2004, Figure 8. Elsevier.

Figures 4.5 and 4.6   Wymer 1999, Figures 44 and 61. Wessex Archaeology.

Figures 4.7 and 4.8   Maddy *et al.* 2000, Figures 1 and 4. Elsevier.

Figure 5.2   Maddy and Bridgland 2000, Figure 1. Elsevier.

Figure 5.3   Wymer 1999, volume 2, map 6. Wessex Archaeology.

Figure 5.5   Wymer 1999, Figure 34a and 34b. Wessex Archaeology.

Figure 5.9   Ashton *et al.* 2005, Figure 35. The Prehistoric Society.

Figure 6.4   Schreve *et al.* 2002, Figure 15. Elsevier.

Figure 7.1   Wymer 1999, Figures 26, 27, 31. Wessex Archaeology.

Figure 7.3   Wenban-Smith 1995, Figure 28. The Quaternary Research Association.

Figure 7.4   Wymer 1999, Figure 34e and 34f. Wessex Archaeology.

Figure 8.3   Byrne 2004, Figures 4 and 5. Elsevier.

Figure 10.1   Warren 1924a, plate 5. Essex Naturalist and Essex Field Club.

Figure 10.2   Warren 1922, Figure 1 and Figure 2. The Prehistoric Society.

Figure 11.1   Warren 1932, Figure 5. Essex Naturalist and Essex Field Club.

Figure 13.1   Dunbar 2003, Figure 2. Annual Reviews www.annualreviews.-org

Figure 13.2   Wilson 1988, Figure 1. World Archaeology/Routledge for Taylor and Francis.

Figure 13.3   Smith 1916, Figures 29–36. The Society of Antiquaries

Figure 13.4   Gowlett 2005, Figure 4.5. Routledge for Taylor and Francis.

Table acknowledgements

Table 2.1   Bridgland *et al.* 2001, Table 1. John Wiley & Sons Limited.

Table 8.1   Falguères and Bahain 1997, Table 1. Elsevier.

Table 10.1   Daniel 1975, Figures 2 and 4. Modified with kind permission of Duckworth.

Table 10.2   Smith 1911b. Tables on pp. xii and 11, modified with kind permission of Trustees of the British Museum.

LIST OF ABBREVIATIONS

AA	amino-acid
AAR	amino-acid racemisation
BGS	British Geological Survey
BM	British Museum
CF-bF	Cromer Forest-bed Formation
DSC	deep sea cores
EFA	external flaking angle
ESR	electron spin resonance
IFA	internal flaking angle
IPH	Institut de Paléontologie Humaine
kya	thousand years ago
kyr	thousand years
LPMT	Lower Palaeolithic Microlithic Tradition
MAZ	mammal assemblage zones
MI	marine isotope
MIS	marine Isotope stage
MPR	Middle Pleistocene Revolution
mya	million years ago
myr	million years
OD	Ordnance Datum
OIS	Oxygen Isotope Stage
OSL	optically stimulated luminescence
PCT	prepared core technology (Levallois)
TERPS	The English Rivers Project Survey

INTRODUCTION

Most books will tell you that the Clactonian is an Old Stone Age or Palaeolithic culture. It is an association of similar stone tools, but is mostly defined by the lack of one very special tool type, the handaxe.

This book has a number of complementary aims, but first and foremost its purpose is to demystify the earlier part of the British Palaeolithic. Perhaps more than any other period in archaeology, the study of early human societies in the Palaeolithic is inherently multi-disciplinary. Apart from the traditional study of stone tools, Palaeolithic archaeologists have to inform themselves about geology, climatology, anthropology (cultural and physical), as well as social theory, statistics, and a host of biological disciplines. It is this blending of diversity that many archaeology students find so off-putting. Especially the geology; why should we do this? We are archaeologists not geologists; we study people not places. The reason is that Palaeolithic archaeology must describe as well as explain.

To understand the people who lived in these long vanished landscapes we must understand how those landscapes came to be, and critically, *how they affect our ability to describe and explain ancient human society*. When a Neolithic or Bronze Age archaeologist stands on top of a cliff, they see the world more or less as people in later prehistory did. Granted, there will be important differences. The forests and villages will be long gone, but the river valleys and hills will still be there. This is a powerful aid in beginning to understand the relationship between physical and social landscapes. But this luxury is denied to the Palaeolithic archaeologist. The great ice sheets have waxed and waned many times over the last half a million years, destroying and reshaping the physical landscape.

And in this lies another one of the problems with Palaeolithic archaeology that some students have difficulty with. The sense of remoteness and the lack of anything intuitively familiar can make the Palaeolithic seem quite alien. The Neolithic in Britain lasted about 2,500 years; the Bronze Age about 1,000 years. In that time people were born, lived their lives, died, and were sometimes buried with their possessions. They were *Homo sapiens*, living social lives that we can begin to comprehend, in a world we can more or less appreciate. Combined, the Neolithic and Bronze Age represents 0.5 per cent of the British prehistoric record. But the Palaeolithic (Lower Middle and Upper) represents just over 98 per cent, and the Lower and Earlier Middle Palaeolithic, the subject of this book, about 73 per cent. That is a period of nearly 700,000 years, spanning at least five ice ages. This is the time of Homo antecessor, Homo heidelbergensis and the early Neanderthals. Would we see these species as part of the human family, or as strangers living in a strange land? I suspect the latter. That is why the multidisciplinary nature of Palaeolithic archaeology is so important. The geography of these lost worlds helps us to put the rivers back onto the blank map; pollen analysis and the study of seeds can restore the forests and open plains, the archaeological sites tell us where hominins lived, the mammals, molluscs and beetles flesh out the woods and open spaces with a rich ecological diversity, and from the deep sea cores and the ice beneath the polar caps we can reconstruct the changing nature of ice age climate.

The Palaeolithic is remote, but it need not be incomprehensible. Once students of archaeology realise why and how all the various bits of the jigsaw puzzle fit together, the archaeology of this time becomes much more familiar. The all-important job of deconstructing and critiquing data and theory is made more enjoyable when you understand how your piece of the puzzle is relevant to others around it. So this book will attempt to make the earlier Palaeolithic in Britain more readily accessible by delivering a big picture approach.

This book will be more than just a physical and social geography of the Lower and Earlier Middle Palaeolithic. I want students of archaeology to be aware of many of the unseen forces that affect how we interpret this very ancient past. Many of the physical techniques used to reveal the ancient world are scientific. They confer an apparent objectivity to the whole process of discovery and interpretation. But advances in social theory have made it clear, that while objective data about the world can be derived from these methodologies, how we interpret that data can be subject to very powerful social influences. These often lie below the level of conscious recognition. The practice of science is not quite as objective as we sometimes believe it to be. I want students to be conscious of this important aspect.

As a social science, archaeology (and indeed science itself as a social practice), is subject to periodic shifts in its core beliefs. These follow changes in the way contemporary society uses knowledge to understand itself. So interpretations of the past move through phases which reflect changes in academic fashion. I have been studying the Clactonian and the British Lower Palaeolithic for more than 20 years, and of late I sense the pendulum is beginning to swing back towards more traditional cultural interpretations. The Clactonian can be presented as a discreet and carefully bounded phenomenon. When something is so conveniently packaged, it can project a powerful impression of distinctiveness. After a while that distinctiveness seems self-evident. Thus empowered, the reality of something's true nature is rarely questioned. I believe this underpins cultural explanations of the Clactonian.

So another reason for wanting to write this book is to simply set the record straight as to what the Clactonian is, and more especially what it is not. If my guess is right and cultural interpretations are coming back into vogue, then students of archaeology and those from other cognate disciplines will be able to evaluate the evidence for a culturally independent Clactonian for themselves.

After more than two decades of studying the Clactonian, I am embarrassed to say I have no new brilliant insights or startling revelations to offer that will explain everything. What I do have is the unshakeable belief that ancient human behaviour was complicated. In their own way, these ancient lives were as complex as our own today. Simple cultural dichotomies and neatly pigeon-holed interpretations that tie up all the loose ends will never help us understand the intricate and variable behaviour of creatures for whom no direct analogues now exist, and whose lives were shaped by environmental niches which have long since vanished.

The structure of the book

The book is divided into two Parts. Part I will look in detail at the Clactonian in its British Lower Palaeolithic context. Chapter 1 describes what the Clactonian is, and some of the archaeological concepts which affect the way we interpret it. It will also briefly describe the hominin occupation of Europe prior to the time of the Clactonian. This will set the broader archaeological scene. In the remainder of the first section of the book we will go on to place the Clactonian in its physical context. In Chapter 2, the latest geological interpretations are introduced, and how and why they are relevant to understanding the physical world in which hominins lived are explained. In Chapter 3, the evidence for the sites said to be Clactonian is evaluated, and we ask whether any of them are really robust enough to support the concept of an independent Clactonian culture. Chapters 4–7 will present the physical geography of the Lower and Earlier Middle Palaeolithic in Britain. The Clactonian sites from Chapter 3 will be placed into their physical and environmental setting. In Chapter 8, we will briefly discover some of the European evidence for stone tool industries said to be similar to the Clactonian and the lessons of Part I will be reviewed in Chapter 9.

In Part II, we will look in greater detail at the Clactonian itself. In Chapters 10 and 11, its development as a historical concept is considered. These chapters describe the changes in interpretive fashion mentioned above. Chapter 12 will look at the very essence of the Clactonian – the stone tools. A question is asked: What is it about these artefact assemblages that warrant them being thought of as a separate culture? In Chapter 13, we will look at some of the theories that have been put forward to explain hominin behaviour in the Lower Palaeolithic. Do any of these ideas help us understand the Clactonian? How might the external world described in Part I have affected the way hominins organised their social lives and social behaviour? The epilogue will briefly restate the position on the Clactonian as a social phenomenon.

I do want to make one point very clear. This book is not about me providing answers. It is about providing readers with enough information to make their own minds up, at least about what the most significant questions should be. At the same time I hope it will clarify the sometimes impenetrable nature of British earlier Palaeolithic studies.

Part I

WHERE, WHAT AND WHEN
The Clactonian in its broader context

1

STRANGERS IN A STRANGE LAND
The Clactonian problem, outlined and defined

We must begin by defining some concepts that will be important to our understanding of just what the Clactonian is. These are the concepts of *assemblage*, *assemblage type*, and *assemblage tradition* as used in Palaeolithic archaeology. The various descriptive terms are detailed in Box 1.1. For the purposes of this book, the artefacts in question are stone tools.

Box 1.1 The interpretation of assemblages in the British Lower and Earlier Middle Palaeolithic

Archaeological assemblage. Defined by the presence of a series of significant features or attributes present in a body of artefacts. All the artefacts will possess this attribute. An assemblage may also be defined by a number of different shared significant attributes. The significance is chosen by the archaeologist. The significance usually reflects the archaeologist's belief that these features were also important to the original makers. (On occasion the significance may be something that is purely of relevance to modern archaeological dialogues.) The significant attribute may be a specific type of artefact, whose presence or absence confers a particular status. Alternatively, particular technological, or stylistic features on the artefacts may be chosen as the criteria for distinguishing an assemblage. Whatever is chosen as important will serve as a 'boundary' in physical/psychological space and time, as it will serve to unite one collection of archaeological artefacts, and distinguish it from another that does not possess these attributes.

Archaeological assemblage type. A series of archaeological assemblages whose similarities suggest a common understanding of practice. These similarities will be the shared attribute, or attributes, that defined a single assemblage. The label 'assemblage type' will therefore serve to distinguish one set of assemblages from another set. Strictly

---

speaking, no spatial or temporal limits are required in defining an archaeological assemblage type. But, in practice, some geographical boundaries and a broad temporal contemporaneity are implied because of the requirement of a common understanding between the groups making the individual assemblages.

Archaeological tradition. This label is applied when an assemblage-type can be shown to have a clear temporal depth. In other words, the common understandings of practice persist over a span of time. At the very least, this persistence implies several generations worth of time, sufficient to perpetuate shared knowledge between, say, grandparents and grandchildren or great-grandchildren. So an arch-aeological tradition should be recognised, at the very least on a centennial scale.

These three ways of looking at groupings of artefacts represent a long-standing archaeological framework that would have been familiar to most practitioners of archaeology in the past century. They remain the primary methodology for understanding culture in Palaeolithic archaeology.

Assemblages from secondary contexts. These have been transported by a river, and deposited when the river's power to move sediment diminished. Artefacts from this type of context can still be classified as archaeo-logical assemblages on the basis of shared significant attributes. A secondary context may contain two distinct archaeological assemblages, identified on the basis of dissimilar attributes. In such a case the river will have swept different assemblages from its banks. The distinctiveness of the indicator attributes will be critical in these cases. Another variation on this is the presence of two assemblages in a gravel deposit in very different physical condition. In this case, the analyst has chosen to privilege artefact appearance as a primary filter of interpreting assemblage character. One group of artefacts will be more rolled/transport damaged than the other. The other assemblage will show little or no damage. An assumption of such an interpreta-tion would be that the more rolled assemblage was older as it had been in the river longer. If the rolled and unrolled assemblages were identical in all other respects, an analyst might interpret these as older and younger assemblages from the same assemblage type. This might be taken as evidence of a tradition as the assemblage type is displaying clear time depth. On the other hand, if there were differences between the two assemblages, the analyst may choose to interpret them as two different assemblages possibly belonging to two different assemblage types of different ages.

Much of the archaeology recovered from British Middle Pleistocene sediments comes from fluvial contexts, especially gravels. Excavations in such deposits represent key-hole samples from what are potentially spatially extensive sedimentary bodies. The limits of the excavation are usually determined by practical considerations (how long can we dig for, and how much can we expose and properly record during that time?). This usually means that excavators do not know the true limit of a horizontal scatter of material, or the extent to which an artefact-rich body of sediment will extend beyond the edges of a trench/site. Without the certainty of establishing the edges of an occupation horizon, or how big a gravel bed is, we can never be certain that our excavations are sampling the true extent of the diversity of material that would have been present at the site. This is a common problem in all archaeology.

The Clactonian is a series of stone tool assemblages that all share one common feature – they all lack a particular type of tool and the evidence of its manufacture. This is the handaxe, and some examples are shown in Figure 1.1A to illustrate some of the variation present in these tools.

Handaxes are often called bifaces (I will use both terms in this book) as they are bifacially thinned and shaped. This means they are worked on both upper and lower faces. To achieve this, the knapper has carefully reduced the volume (thinning) above and below a pre-conceived midline (the edge of the tool). At the same time the knapper shaped the handaxe to transform the tool's edge into a cutting edge around all or most of the artefact. Handaxes can be made in a number of different ways, but as the thinning and shaping proceed, the kinds of flakes that are removed can become quite distinctive. Thinning flakes are the bi-product of the process of thinning and shaping and can be as diagnostic of the presence of handaxes as the actual handaxes themselves. Some examples are shown in Figure 1.1B. It is quite conceivable that a small excavation could locate its trenches at points where no handaxes were present, but the site could still be identified as having a handaxe assemblage on the basis of a few thinning flakes.

Thus, Clactonian sites/assemblages are all identified on the basis of a complete lack of handaxes or thinning flakes. The name derives from the town of Clacton-on-Sea, Essex, where British assemblages of this type were first extensively described. The cultural label given to assemblages with handaxes is the Acheulean, after St Acheul (now a suburb of Amiens) in northern France.

At the next level of interpretation, similar assemblages are grouped together into assemblage types. This is an explanatory framework designed to include all the sites which have similar assemblages and impose on them

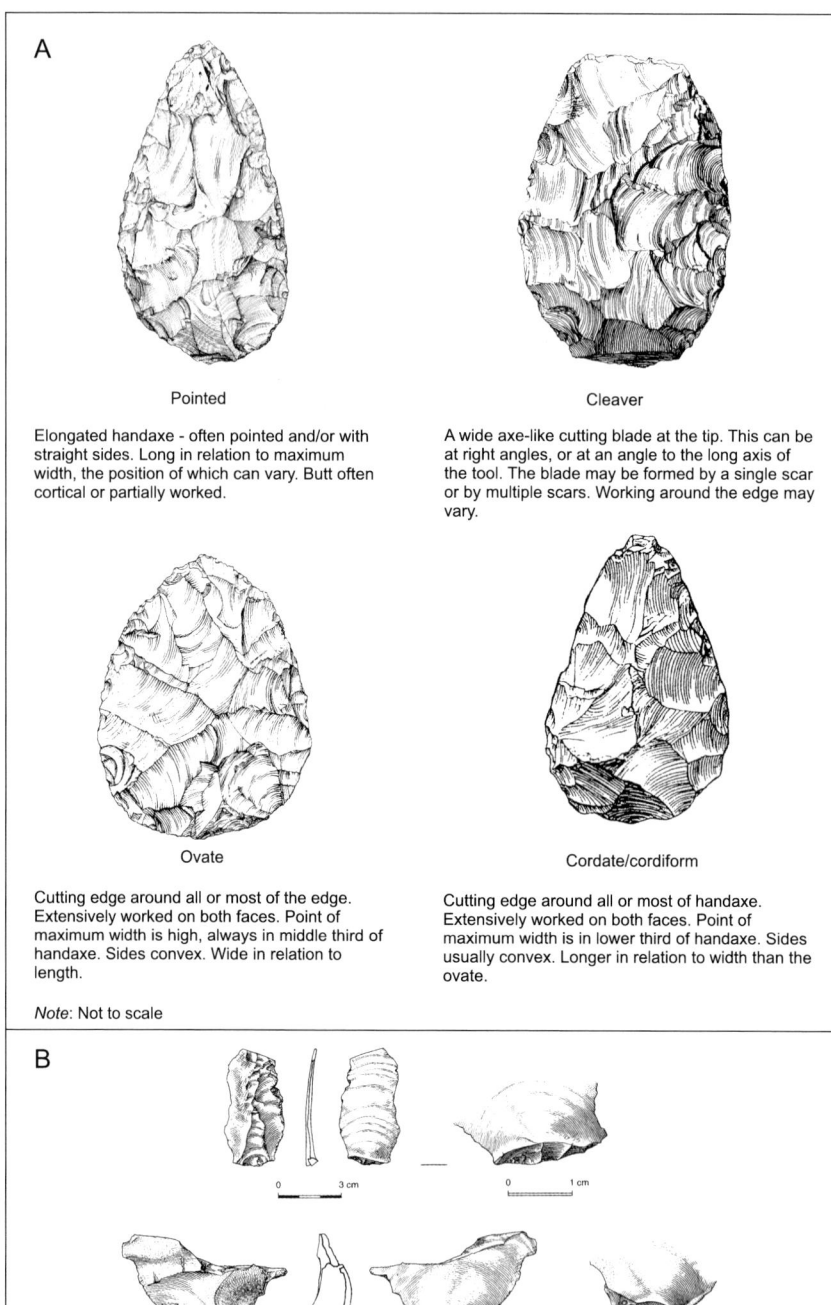

A

Pointed

Elongated handaxe - often pointed and/or with straight sides. Long in relation to maximum width, the position of which can vary. Butt often cortical or partially worked.

Cleaver

A wide axe-like cutting blade at the tip. This can be at right angles, or at an angle to the long axis of the tool. The blade may be formed by a single scar or by multiple scars. Working around the edge may vary.

Ovate

Cutting edge around all or most of the edge. Extensively worked on both faces. Point of maximum width is high, always in middle third of handaxe. Sides convex. Wide in relation to length.

Note: Not to scale

Cordate/cordiform

Cutting edge around all or most of handaxe. Extensively worked on both faces. Point of maximum width is in lower third of handaxe. Sides usually convex. Longer in relation to width than the ovate.

B

0   3 cm

0   1 cm

0   3 cm

0   1 cm

Figure 1.1 Characteristic artefacts of the Acheulean/handaxe phenomenon. A – some common handaxe or biface types. Pointed, ovate, and cleaver from High Lodge. B – thinning flakes (from Neolithic site of Harrow Hill, Sussex).

Note: For each thinning flake the butt is shown greatly enlarged. Note the lack of clear points and cones of percussion on the thinning flakes' butts (see Chapter 12 for detailed explanation). All illustrations used with permission.

a common explanation for their distinctive similarity. For most of the last century the common explanation was a cultural one. Clactonian assemblages all lacked handaxes because the hominins that made these assemblages did not know how to make them. That knowledge was not a part of their cultural heritage – the full repertoire of knowledge hominins could pass from one generation to the next. Handaxes, on the other hand, were a part of the cultural heritage of the Acheulean. The Clactonian was usually referred to as a non-handaxe (or non-biface) assemblage type.

So if the Clactonian assemblage type is defined negatively, by the lack of something, what then does it have? It has cores, flakes, and flake tools, that are identical to the ones found in the Acheulean assemblages. These are described in more detail in Chapter 12. Put briefly, cores are nodules of rock, usually flint, that are knapped. This is the process of striking a rock with a hammer stone. What comes off is a sharp-edged flake. What is left in your hand is the core. This will have a concave flake scar on its surface where the flake came off. Cores are usually knapped for many flakes and will be defined by a number of intersecting negative flake scars. Some examples of cores are shown in Figure 1.2.

Because of their sharp edges, flakes can be used as they are, and the most suitable ones selected for cutting or scraping activities. Alternatively, the flake may be retouched. This means its edge has been carefully shaped with a hammer stone to make a durable edge that will not blunt so quickly. Some examples are shown in Figure 1.3. Some flakes are flaked again, in other words, have another flake taken off from their edge as if they were cores. These are called flaked flakes and are also shown in Figure 1.3. The Clactonian is composed of these cores, flakes, retouched tools and flaked flakes. The problem is that these all appear in Acheulean assemblages, except that there are handaxes and their thinning flakes as well.

We now approach the crux of the Clactonian problem. I will illustrate it with a hypothetical example. Imagine a group of Acheulean hominins moving across the landscape in search of food. Some of them carry handaxes, some of them carry wooden spears. Quite by chance they come across a sick rhinoceros on a river bank. It has collapsed but is not yet dead. No other predators or scavengers have seen the rhino yet. They quickly kill it. Those with spears take up defensive positions around the carcass. They will warn of approaching danger and keep other scavengers at bay. Those with handaxes set to work to butcher the carcass. Those without handaxes forage around the area and find nodules of flint which they quickly knapp to make some sharp flakes to help in the butchery, especially in slicing through the thick hide. The group is large and aggressive enough to ward off other predators and scavengers and so they have the time to methodically butcher the carcass. All of the group take turns, snacking as they go. They save some meat for later. As evening approaches, it is time to move on. They have successfully defended their prize for many hours. Once they have

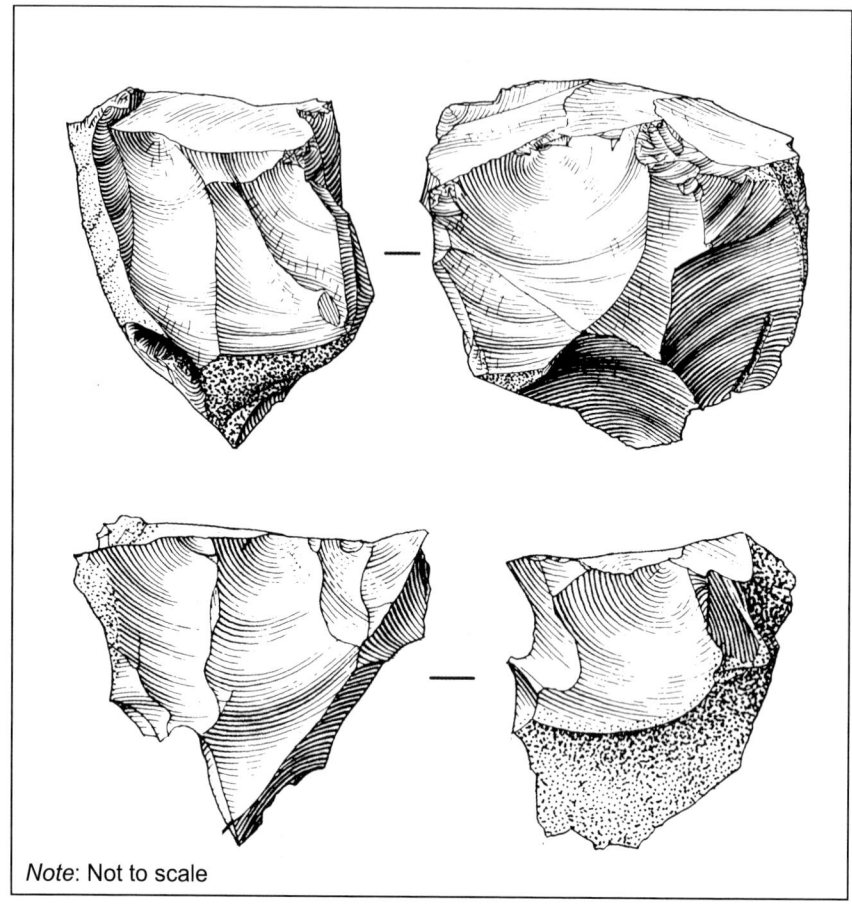

Note: Not to scale

Figure 1.2 A selection of hard hammer-struck cores.

Note: Note the negative flake scars – the concave beds left by detached flakes. From High Lodge. Used with permission.

gone what is left? A butchered rhino carcass, and a handful of cores, flakes and flake tools. They took their handaxes away with them. So although they were an Acheulean group, the 'cultural' signature left on the ground was unambiguously Clactonian. Unless some of the handaxes were lost, discarded, or broken and re-sharpened, there would be no way of identifying the site as an Acheulean one.

This imaginary scenario illustrates a particular point. Given that cores, flakes, flake tools, and flaked flakes are common to all Lower Palaeolithic assemblages, are we justified in identifying an assemblage type solely on negative evidence? In effect, much of the theory and methodology that

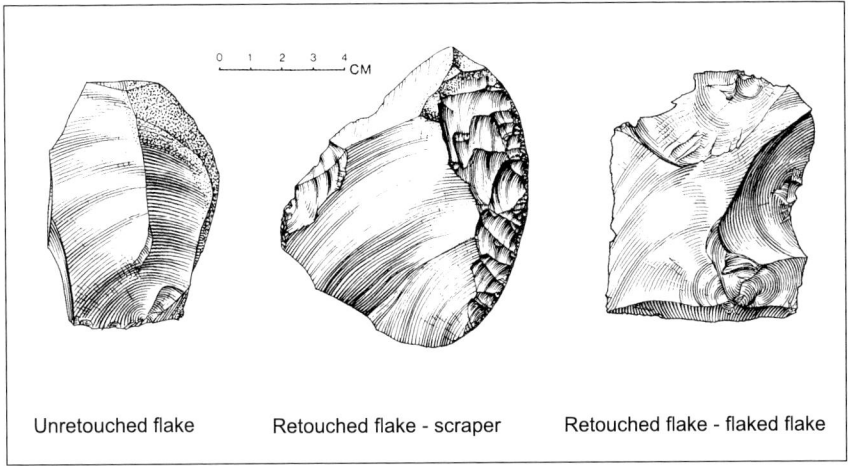

| Unretouched flake | Retouched flake - scraper | Retouched flake - flaked flake |

Figure 1.3   A selection of flakes and retouched flakes from High Lodge.

Note: Used with permission.

underpins the recognition of distinct assemblages, and thus cultural identity, is not effective in every situation.

Supporters of an independent Clactonian would respond by saying I am over-simplifying the situation and ignoring a very particular body of data, and they would be right. To explore this, I must introduce two other arch-aeological concepts, primary and secondary context. If our rhino butchery site was buried by fine grained sediment emplaced by gentle water flow, then the site would be completely undisturbed and all the remains would be exactly as they were left. The site would be in primary context. However, let us imagine a stream became established over a part of the site and some of the artefacts were washed away. Alternatively, the associations between individual stone tools and bones were changed as a minor flood, or heavy rainstorm shunted material about. The site could now, arguably, be described as being in a disturbed primary context. For sites on river banks or on gravel bars, this was a common occurrence.

What about the material that was washed away? These artefacts were entrained into the river and transported as part of the river's bedload. They came to rest when the power of the river to continue transporting its bedload diminished. This could be because the river itself was no longer flowing so strongly. Alternatively, the inside of meander bends, or troughs in the river bed itself could temporarily affect the river's carrying capacity, resulting in deposition. Even a fallen tree could be a focus for deposition. Later, the river may have re-exposed the artefacts and washed them further downstream again.

Many Lower Palaeolithic sites are collections of artefacts from fluvial sediments that were clearly derived from elsewhere. These are called secondary context sites – see Box 1.1. As can be imagined, a primary context site can reveal much about hominin behaviour from the patterns and associations between artefacts and bones. The behavioural information from secondary context sites is more limited. The majority of sites used to establish the cultural independence of the Clactonian are secondary context sites.

Supporters of the Clactonian would now remind me that it is the sheer quantity of artefacts at these secondary context Clactonian sites that really define them as distinctive non-handaxe assemblages. This is a very good argument. It goes like this. Clactonian sites/assemblages are large, in most cases, many hundreds of artefacts, in some cases, many thousands. They either represent a large body of hominins staying at a place for a brief period, or one group/small groups visiting the same place over many hundreds of years. Either way, the large size of the assemblage should sample the full range of the knapping practices of the hominins who visited that locality. Since no trace of handaxes or thinning flakes are present in these large secondary context assemblages, they must therefore sample a *long-term behavioural pattern* in that particular area. They must represent an assemblage type which shows time depth, or, in other words, an archaeological tradition.

This is an excellent argument, but we should be cautious. I would remind Clactonian fans that a small number of classic handaxes and thinning flakes have actually been found in large Clactonian assemblages. They are securely provenanced to these deposits (McNabb 1992b; 1996b). Their circumstances of discovery are described in more detail in later chapters. When I was younger I made much out of these, but I now realise I was wrong to do so. Clactonian supporters would very quickly remind me that these few Acheulean artefacts only mean that at some time during the accumulation of the huge numbers of cores and flakes at Clactonian sites, one or two individuals made or used and then lost a few classic handaxes or thinning flakes. They do not contradict the overpowering non-handaxe archaeological signal from these sites.

True! But I would continue the argument by further reminding Clactonian supporters that the number of *excavated* Clactonian sites is relatively few. The cultural concept of the Clactonian was established on the basis of large collections of artefacts, from secondary context sites, which were collected in a very unsystematic way – called selected assemblages. It was not uncommon for early twentieth-century collectors to keep only those artefacts they considered significant. This would result in a very biased view of hominin behaviour.

In a carefully controlled archaeological excavation, all the artefacts are kept. It is from excavations that we get a realistic picture of assemblage richness and character. But we have to bear in mind that these are still 'keyhole' excavations, sampling only a tiny proportion of the relevant deposits. The tradition that great exposures of gravel at Clactonian sites never contained any handaxes is ultimately just that, unsubstantiated tradition. It was perpetuated by word of mouth to support cultural interpretations, and was unsupported by *extensive and frequent excavations* in available deposits.

Let me make one thing clear at this point. I do not dispute the existence of large numbers of cores and flakes from Clactonian sites, nor the absence, or virtual absence in some cases, of handaxe technology at these sites. Nor do I dispute the fact that this pattern of behaviour must have persisted for a certain period of time – although frustratingly we don't know how long. What concerns me is whether or not we are justified in applying cultural explanations to this kind of patterning in the data.

This, then, is the Clactonian dilemma. Is the dominance of cores and flakes a genuine product of learned cultural behaviour? Is an archaeological tradition really the same thing as a cultural tradition?

Basic archaeological and geological background

Figures 1.4 and 1.5 give the archaeological and chronological framework for the sub-division of time in the Palaeolithic (the name for the traditional archaeological framework based on stone tool cultures), and in the Pleistocene (the name for the geological framework based on changes in the Earth's climate and its effect on landscape and ecology). Archaeologists love to divide things up into threes, usually applying labels like early, middle and late; or lower, middle and upper. The Palaeolithic is no exception. The term itself actually means Old Stone Age to distinguish it from the Mesolithic which is the Middle Stone Age, and Neolithic or New Stone Age. These are late nineteenth- and early twentieth-century labels and just how relevant they really are is a moot point. The Mesolithic in western Europe is traditionally seen as a period when modern humans lived in hunter-gatherer societies, some sedentary, others not. They were loosely linked by common ideas of tool use, but this varied from place to place. The succeeding Neolithic was the period during which sedentary communities began to use ceramics more extensively, made polished stone axes, and engaged in agriculture and animal husbandry.

The Palaeolithic in western Europe is divided into three phases. The Lower Palaeolithic spans that period of time from the earliest hominin occupation of Europe, up to the appearance of Levallois/Prepared Core Technology (sometimes abbreviated to PCT – this is explained below). The Lower Palaeolithic is the time of the Acheulean and the Clactonian. This huge period of time, spanning more than 700,000 years in Britain, and perhaps as much as 1.2 million years in Europe, is the period of at least three different hominin species: *Homo erectus*, *Homo antecessor*, and *Homo heidelbergensis*. The hominin record will be discussed in more detail in the next section.

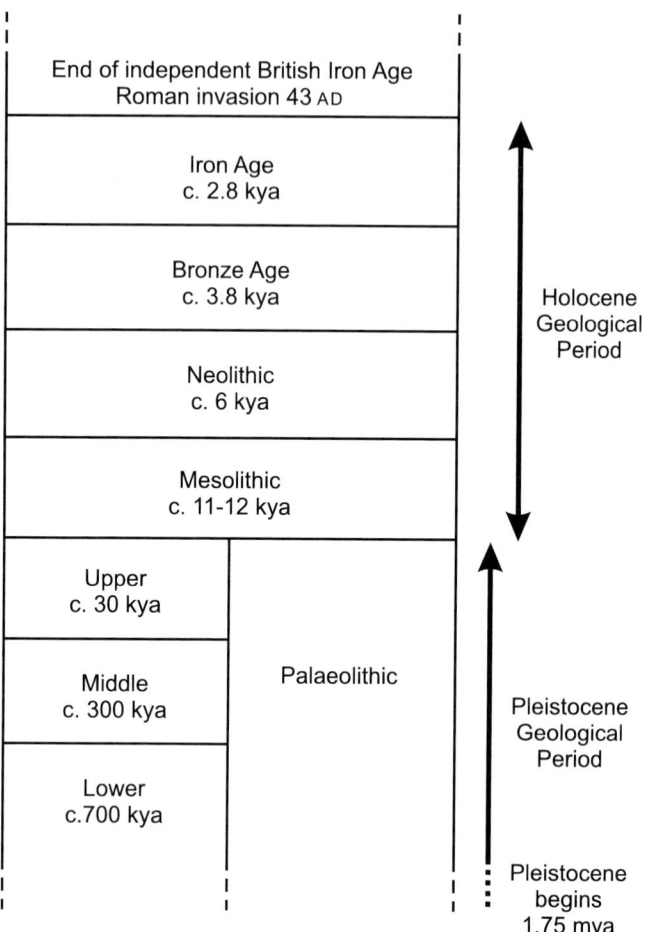

Figure 1.4 The sub-periods of the British Prehistoric framework.

Note: Dates are in thousands of years ago (kya), or in millions of years ago (mya).

The Middle Palaeolithic represents a period when new types of stone tools, and new ways of making them appeared. The handaxe of the Lower Palaeolithic began to diminish in importance. A new way of making tools emerged and is often called Prepared Core Technology – PCT. It is also called Levallois, after a site in the suburbs of Paris where it was first recognised. It represents a very different way of thinking about tools and their manufacture (Schlanger 1996). Cores have carefully shaped surfaces, from which particular types of flake are removed. Where and when Levallois first appeared in Europe is a much debated topic. Did it spread into Europe from Africa with migrating hominins? Was it independently invented in different

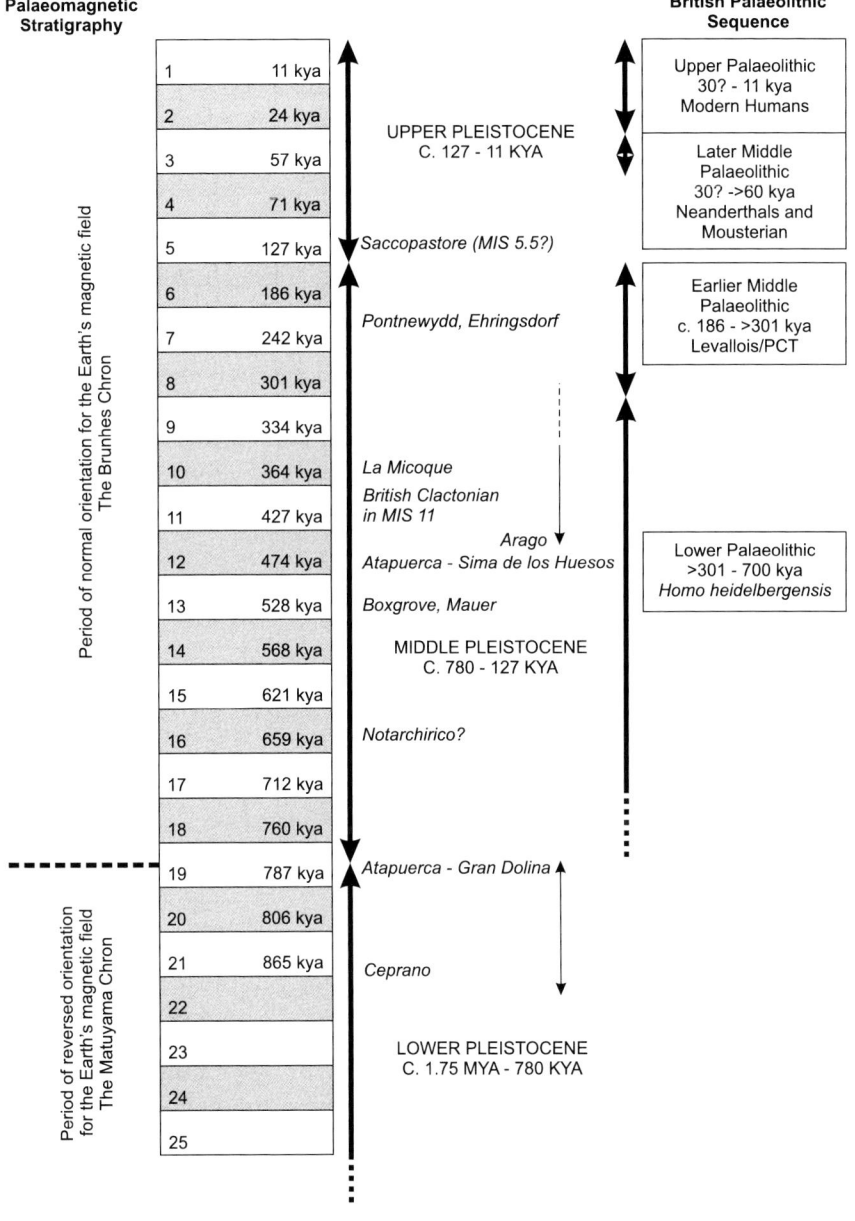

Figure 1.5 The archaeological and geological sub-divisions of the Pleistocene in Britain, set against the marine isotope (MI) sequence. Glaciations = even numbers; interglacials (warm periods) = odd numbers.

places and at different times, perhaps evolving out of the local Acheulean? We do not know.

The Earlier Middle Palaeolithic begins in Britain about 300,000 years ago; the Later Middle Palaeolithic begins about 60 kya and is the time of the Neanderthals. Their material culture was called the Mousterian. Some Neanderthal/Mousterian groups continued to use PCT, while others did not. In Britain, there is a clear demarcation between the Earlier and Later Middle Palaeolithic. The demarcation is a period when Britain was abandoned by hominins for over 100,000 years. Those that reoccupy Britain in the Later Middle Palaeolithic are Neanderthals. On the Continent, where no abandonment occurred, the dividing line between the two sub-periods is much more difficult to gauge.

At some time around 40,000 years ago anatomically modern humans, *Homo sapiens*, first appear in the European record. Their appearance in Europe was one of many such migrations of modern humans into Europe. They overlapped with the Neanderthals for as much as 10,000 years, though how much real contact there was between the two species is much debated. Modern humans finally replaced the Neanderthals about 30,000 years ago, or a little after this date. From this point on, Europe was only inhabited by moderns. This is the period of the Upper Palaeolithic. Just when modern humans arrived in Britain is a much debated topic. I have taken a date of about 30,000 years ago as a best guess.

It is important to grasp that the Pleistocene is not a completely different period of time. The Palaeolithic framework and the Pleistocene framework are complementary, just different ways of dividing up the same time period by focusing on different lines of evidence, human in the former, and the natural world in the latter. The Pleistocene itself begins at 1.75 million years ago, and ends about 11,000 years ago. During this period the Earth gets colder; this is the period of the ice ages when the polar ice caps expanded during glaciations, and contracted during interglacials. The Pleistocene is also divided into three: Lower, Middle, and Upper. The boundaries were originally set by the disappearance of certain key animal species, and their replacement by new ones, thus signalling major changes in environment. Since the 1950s, new kinds of data have been used to fix these boundaries. One such is palaeomagnetism. It is based on reversals in the direction of the Earth's magnetic field, and a detailed history of these fluctuations has now been achieved (see Klein 1999, for a review). The palaeomagnetic boundaries marking divisions in the Pleistocene are shown in Figure 1.5. An excellent review of the use of palaeomagnetism as a dating technique is given in Walker (2005).

For the remainder of this book, I will use the following conventions for discussing periods of time expressed in years. If, for example, an occupation at a site lasted for 10,000 years, I will use the convention 10 kyr, or if a period of time lasted for 10,000,000 years, I will use the convention 10 myr.

Here, a length of time is being described in years. On the other hand, if a site is dated to 10,000 years ago, I will use the convention 10 kya, or 10 mya if something was dated to that many million years ago. Here a specific age is being expressed in years. Another important chronological label that I will use from this point on is MIS (marine isotope stage). These are the subdivisions of Pleistocene time and climate represented in Figure 1.5. Each subdivision represents a glacial (cold) or an interglacial (warm) phase of the Pleistocene climate of the earth. The subdivisions are recorded in deep sea cores. This will be explained in more detail in Chapter 2.

Who made the Clactonian?

Before we look at this question, let us answer a related one. What is a hominin? I have used this term a number of times already. All living creatures are arranged in a hierarchical taxonomy based upon their evolutionary relationship with each other. Labels like genus and species refer to a particular level in that taxonomy. The old expression hominid that may be familiar to some readers applied to a taxonomy based upon skeletal similarities and differences. Modern humans were believed to share a close relationship with chimpanzees and gorillas on the basis of their skeletal morphology. Hominid referred to ancestors and cousins of the human species, after the split from the gorillas and chimps.

But in recent years molecular biology/DNA has changed this. Humans and chimps do share a recent common ancestor, but we do not share a recent common ancestor with the gorilla. Genetics has demonstrated this lineage split off from the common ancestor of humans and chimps long ago. The term hominin has been introduced to accommodate these new relationships (Wood and Richmond 2000). This is shown in Figure 1.6. Today the expression hominid refers to the higher primates (chimps, gorillas, orangutans, our ancestors and extinct cousins, and ourselves), while hominin just refers to those genera which evolved after the split with the chimps. In the taxonomical hierarchy the level of sub-tribe has two divisions, the Australopiths (which incorporates a number of genera, *Australopithecus*, *Ardipithecus*, *Paranthropus* – all of which are extinct distant African cousins to ourselves), and the Hominans, which includes our own genus *Homo*. Below the level of genus is the species – we are *Homo sapiens*. In this book the only hominin species we will encounter are those within our own genus *Homo*. I will use the term hominin to mean ancestors or relatives within genus *Homo*.

As far as the Lower and Earlier Middle Pleistocene in Europe is concerned, there are three hominin species that we need to discuss: *Homo erectus*, *Homo antecessor* and *Homo heidelbergensis*.

Homo erectus/ergaster was one of the earliest hominins ever discovered (Boaz and Ciochon 2004; Shipman 2001). Its remains are found in Asia

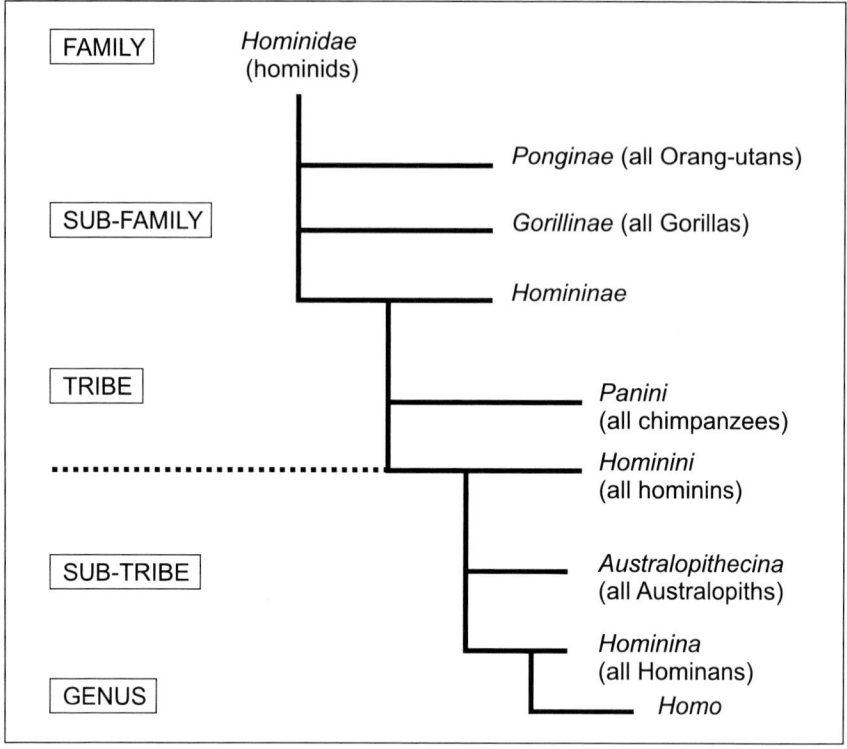

Figure 1.6 Hominin phylogeny.

Note: Everything below the dotted line can be considered a hominin, and post-dates the split between the last common ancestor of all the hominins and the chimpanzees.

and South-East Asia (China, Java), as well as north, east and southern Africa. In recent years there has been a tendency to split the species into two. *Homo ergaster* is the name given to earlier African examples of the species, and the name *Homo erectus* is retained for the Asian and South-East Asian specimens (see Manzi 2004 and Rightmire 1998, for excellent reviews). Naturally this is hotly disputed and there is no consensus of opinion on which is the most appropriate course to follow, splitting or lumping together.

A remarkable series of fossils have come from the site of Dmanisi in the Republic of Georgia (Figure 1.7). The fossils date to c. 1.7 mya (Gabunia *et al.* 2001; Rightmire *et al.* 2006). This makes them contemporary with H. *ergaster* in Africa. At the time of writing there are three skulls with their mandibles, another skull, a large mandible, and a number of post-cranial bones (Lordkipanidze *et al.* 2005; Rightmire *et al.* 2006). These fossils were originally assigned to *Homo ergaster* (Gabunia and Vekua 1995). But most commentators on these remains emphasise the amount of diversity present

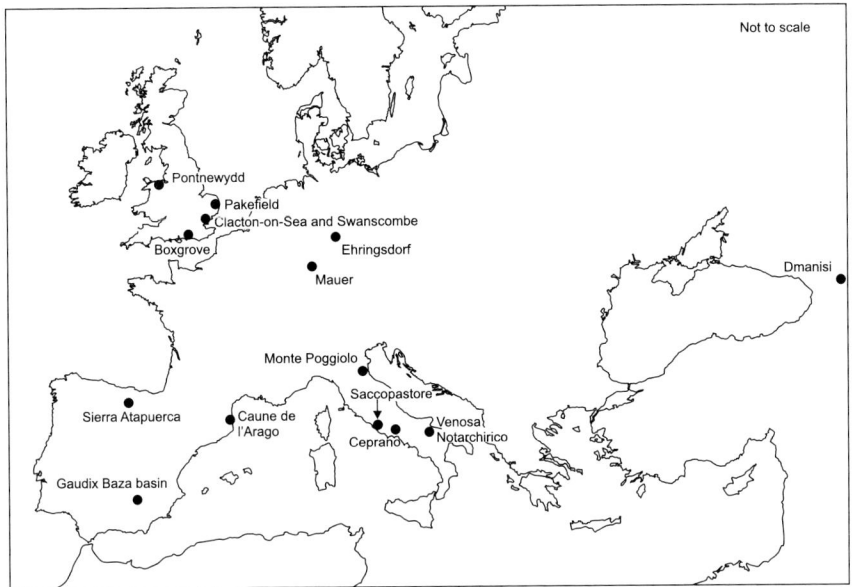

Figure 1.7 Map of selected early hominin occupation sites in Europe.

in the fossils. Some have traits that are more similar to a very ancient form of African hominin, *Homo habilis* (*sensu lato*), dated between < 2.0 and 1.6 mya (Conroy 2005). For a species of *Homo* less than 2.0 million years in age, the Dmanisi fossils do show many primitive characteristics that are quite surprising. They also have very small brains for *Homo* of this age, especially when compared to classic examples of contemporary *Homo ergaster*. Rightmire and colleagues have argued that the variability is a reflection of the age of the fossils. They are right at the beginning of the *Homo ergaster* lineage, and individuals still show features inherited from their immediate evolutionary ancestors.

The large mandible noted above is so unlike any of the other fossils, it has been attributed to a new species *Homo georgicus* (Rightmire *et al.* 2006). Giorgio Manzi has suggested (2004) that all the fossils from Dmanisi should be grouped with this species and that it was *H. georgicus* that migrated out of Africa. In the Far East, it developed into Asian and South-East Asian *Homo erectus*. The African *Homo ergaster* stayed in Africa continuing its own line of evolutionary development. This flies directly in the face of the consensus opinion that African *Homo erectus/ergaster* was the world's first hominin coloniser. For the moment it would seem safer to continue to interpret these fossils as *Homo ergaster*, with the large mandible possibly belonging to a different species (Rightmire *et al.* 2006), but this may change as more specimens are discovered.

21

Stone tools were present in the Dmanisi deposits. They represent cores and flakes, but whether they should be associated with H. *ergaster/erectus*, H. *georgicus*, or both, remains unclear.

Homo *antecessor* was discovered at the Trinchera Gran Dolina in the Sierra de Atapuerca in northern Spain, see Figure 1.7 (Bermúdez de Castro *et al.* 1997; Carbonell *et al.* 1995). The locality is a vertical fissure in-filled with sediments that were exposed when a railway cutting sliced through the limestone in which the fissure developed. In fact, there are a number of Early and Middle Pleistocene faunal and archaeological sites in the Sierra. Several levels are present within the Gran Dolina sediments. The lowest layers, 1 and 2, represent sediments from an enclosed cave. Using palaeomagnetism, researchers located the Early/Middle Pleistocene boundary (dated to c. 780 kya, see Figure 1.5 and Table 8.3) in layer TD7. It was from the layer directly below this, layer 6, also called the Aurora Stratum, that the fossils of Homo *antecessor* were discovered (Bermúdez de Castro *et al.* 2004). So the Trinchera Dolina hominins have to be older than 780 kya. Initially more than 80 fragments of hominin were identified, including a partial face. It was on the basis of this modern-looking face (at least compared to Homo *erectus* and Neanderthals) that H. *antecessor* was identified as a new species. The mid-facial region did not project out as much as in earlier hominins. What has caused most of the controversy surrounding this fossil was that the partial face belonged to a juvenile, perhaps 10–11½ years old. Young faces change considerably as they grow, and many researchers felt that a new species should be established on a fully adult specimen.

More recently a partial mandible has been recovered from TD6 and assigned to H. *antecessor* (Carbonell *et al.* 2005). The gracile bone is the left half of the jaw, and may belong to a female who died between 15 and 18 years of age. This important discovery will do much to reassure those who were uncertain about the reality of H. *antecessor* as a species. Comparison of the jaw with other fossils has suggested a rather surprising interpretation. Its closest affinities are not to African species at all, but to the classic Homo *erectus* populations of the Far East (ibid.). It is possible that H. *antecessor* may be the descendant of an early migrant from Africa which established itself outside the African continent and then began to spread throughout Eurasia. Flakes and cores were present in level TD6, but no handaxes.

In 1994, a skull cap was found at Ceprano in Italy, see Figure 1.7. It was originally described as Homo *erectus* (Ascenzi *et al.* 1996; Clarke 2000). It is dated to between 800 and 900 kya. Its supporters are confident of this age because the stratigraphy in the sedimentary basin within which Ceprano occurs is very well understood (Manzi *et al.* 2001; Manzi 2004). If Ceprano's association with Homo *erectus* is correct, it would be the only example from Europe discovered. (There are claims for later Middle Pleistocene examples at Vértesszölös in Hungary and Bilzingsleben in Germany, but these are more lilkely to be Homo *heidelbergensis*, given their post-MIS 12 age.) This in itself is not necessarily problematic as the number of European Early Pleistocene hominin finds is very small, so others may await discovery. But Manzi (2004) has suggested that the Ceprano skull cap should be considered as an adult example of H. antecessor. Given its date, this is a very reasonable suggestion. No artefacts were found with the Ceprano skull cap, but a number of slightly older archaeological sites are present in the Ceprano basin which lack handaxes (see below; ibid.).

A particular behavioural pattern has been associated with H. antecessor, cannibalism. Many of the human remains from TD6 have cut marks from stone tools, a result of the tool accidentally marking the bone during de-fleshing. The interpretation of the discoverers is that this represents dietary cannibalism.

Homo heidelbergensis: this species was named in 1908 (Rightmire 1998) on the basis of a jawbone found at Mauer near Heidelberg, see Figure 1.7. The Mauer jaw is dated to MIS 13 (see Figure 1.5; Bischoff et al. 2003), as is the Boxgrove tibia (Roberts and Parfitt 1999). The fossils from Arago (Figure 1.7) in the south of France are MIS 12 and therefore date to the time of the Anglian glaciation in Britain (474–427 kya; Bischoff et al. 2003). The Sima de los Huesos is another locality at Atapuerca (Figure 1.7). Its hominin sample was originally dated to c. 300 kya. Recently (ibid.) they have been re-dated to between 400 and 500 kya.

The site is a deep vertical shaft at the end of a long passage within a cave. Some researchers assume the bodies were deliberately interred here (i.e. thrown down the shaft for whatever reason). However, the hominin bones were found associated with large numbers of cave bear bones, so another entrance may have existed in Pleistocene times and the base of the shaft could have been a bear's den. Over 50 per cent of the hominin remains show some sort of carnivore damage, but this is mostly from lion and fox (Bermúdez de Castro et al. 2004). Over 4,000 pieces of fossil bone have been recovered, comprising a minimum of 28 hominin individuals. This is the largest sample of H. heidelbergensis yet discovered. Their cranial and post-cranial anatomy shows that they are ancestral to the Neanderthals whose earliest representatives are (arguably) from Ehringsdorf in Germany, Pontnewydd in Wales in MIS 7, and Saccopastore in Italy in MIS 5.5 (see Figures 1.5 and 1.7). A single stone tool has been discovered from the Sima, a handaxe. The excavators doubt that this was a casual loss and cite its presence as supporting evidence for the bodies having been delib-erately thrown down the shaft. In other words the handaxe was also deliberately 'interred'. There are no cut marks from stone tools on any of these remains.

The above discussion on H. heidelbergensis concentrated on the earlier representatives of this species. After the Anglian glaciation (= MIS 12, see Figure 1.5), the scale of hominin occupation in Europe seems to have expanded considerably (Roebroeks 2001), and the post-Anglian fossil sample is consequently much larger. After MIS 12, only *H. heidelbergensis* is present in Middle Pleistocene Europe. But naturally things are not so straightforward. The problem lies with the degree of morphological variability between different specimens, especially the skulls. *H. heidelbergensis* is often referred to as a dustbin taxon. This is a label for a group of hominins united largely by geographical and temporal limits but showing considerable diversity in many features. The diversity may be sufficiently great to suggest that later Middle Pleistocene *H. heidelbergensis* is actually not one, but two or more quite different hominin species. At present, there are no answers to these questions. Many palaeo-anthropologists see *Homo heidelbergensis* as a single but very variable species. This is often described as a polymorphic species.

If there is little agreement on the integrity of individual hominin species, imagine the mayhem present in attempting to work out their phylogenetic relationships (i.e. the ancestor–descendant family tree). I have attempted to summarise some of the complexity in Figure 1.8. I must emphasise this is not my attempt at producing a hominin phylogeny. It is simply an attempt to show some of the relationships suggested by various researchers. It does not claim to be anywhere near comprehensive.

The earlier time range

A fairly straightforward interpretation would go something like this. Some time not long after the speciation event that led to *Homo ergaster/erectus* originating in Africa c. 1.8 mya, this species began a series of dispersals at different times throughout Eurasia. The fossils in Dmanisi, Ceprano, and in China and South-East Asia, are evidence of this. In Europe, *H. erectus* evolved into *H. antecessor* and/or *H. heidelbergensis*. In Africa, *H. erectus* evolved into *H. rhodesiensis*, which for our purposes we will take as the African equivalent of *H. heidelbergensis*.

But alternatives to such a simple view have already been suggested. On the one hand, *H. antecessor* may be a purely Eurasian species, having evolved outside of Africa. Could the fossils from Dmanisi be the ancestors of *H. antecessor* – a small-brained species which left Africa while *H. ergaster* stayed on? Or, as suggested by Rightmire and colleagues, are the Dmanisi fossils part of a geographically widespread, but quite variable, *H. ergaster* population emanating from Africa? The earliest members of the genus *Homo* so far discovered are dated to between 2.4 and 2.3 mya; the earliest *H. ergaster* date to about 1.8 mya. If Rightmire *et al.* are correct, then *H. ergaster* may have begun range expansion very early in its evolutionary history. So Dmanisi might well be a group of *H. ergaster* who were part of this species' earliest migrations out of Africa. The truth is, we have too little evidence to tell one way or another. This is why Figure 1.8 has so many pathways marked 'or'.

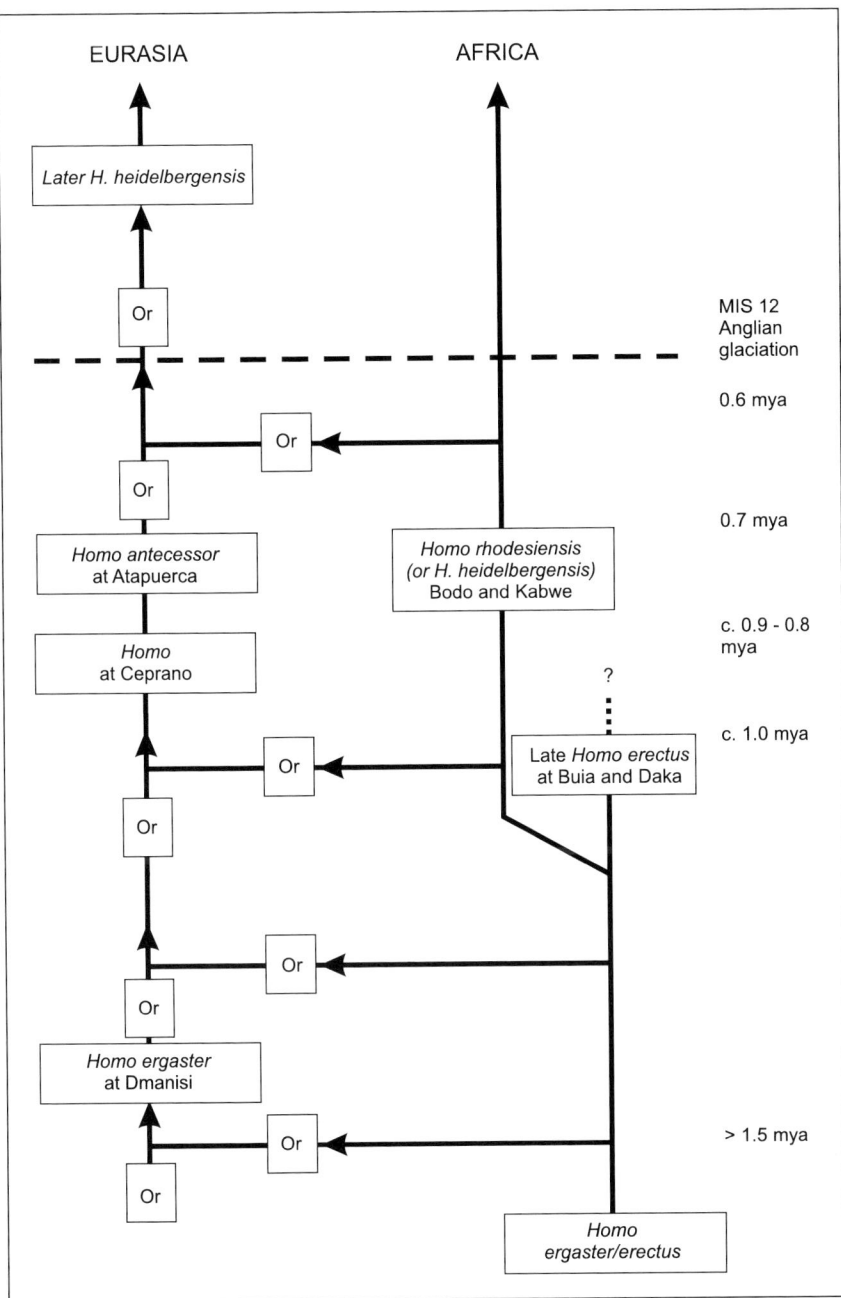

Figure 1.8 A number of possible geographical ancestor/descendant relationships for Middle Pleistocene *Homo*.

The later time range

Those scientists who believe in a single polymorphic species of Homo heidelbergensis would argue that only one speciation event occurred during this period, it took place some time just before or just after 1.0 mya, and H. heidelbergensis, or its African equivalent Homo rhodesiensis, was the result. At some point before c. 780 kya, a population of this new species migrated from Africa into Europe. In this scenario the hominins from Ceprano and Gran Dolina are variations on the H. heidelbergensis theme. However, the postulated affinities of H. antecessor to the Asian fossil sample suggest that a straightforward scenario such as this is unlikely.

Homo ergaster in Africa appears to continue with little major evolutionary change as the specimen of late H. erectus/ergaster from Daka (Bouri) in Ethiopia suggests (Gilbert et al. 2003, and references therein). This is dated to about 1.0 mya. Nevertheless, the specimen does show some differences when compared with its earlier Homo ergaster ancestors. This could mean one of two things. On the one hand, these later H. ergaster populations represent a direct link between earlier H. ergaster and the late Middle Pleistocene African hominins like those found at Bodo and Kabwe. Or, these differences are the natural trajectory of Homo erectus in Africa prior to this species becoming extinct. In which case, H. heidelbergensis/rhodesiensis in Africa represents a speciation event away from the H. erectus line before it died out.

In Europe, either H. antecessor develops into H. heidelbergensis and then into the Neanderthals, or it is replaced in Europe by Homo heidelbergensis who migrates from Africa some time after 780 kya and replaces (or absorbs) the old H. antecessor stock. This later position would explain why there are no H. antecessor fossils in Europe after, say, 600 kya, and why handaxes appear in such abundance in the archaeological record from about this time onwards. In other words, the handaxe originated in Africa and was carried into Europe by Homo heidelbergensis, which then developed into the Neanderthals in Europe. Researchers following this interpretation would have no problem with any number of later Middle Pleistocene migrations out of Africa, as these would all be H. heidelbergensis.

In a diagram like Figure 1.8, where there are as many 'or' pathways as there are hominin species, it is clear that new data are desperately needed to clarify the situation. On Figure 1.8 I have added a dotted line to mark the time of the Anglian/MIS 12 glaciation. This is taken as the division between the earlier Middle Pleistocene and the later Middle Pleistocene. After this time a number of H. heidelbergensis fossils begin to show some of the features that will characterise their descendants, the Neanderthals. Some scientists would like to see these later populations of H. heidelbergensis as examples of the earliest Neanderthals.

I have gone into some detail over hominin phylogeny as it will have a bearing on the earliest occurrence of non-handaxe assemblages in the

Figure 1.9 The Swanscombe skull.

European archaeological record, and therefore some bearing on the Clactonian. This will be described in the next section. For our purposes we may assume that the Clactonian in post-Anglian Britain was a product of *Homo heidelbergensis*, and we will further assume for the moment that this is the only hominin species present in Europe at this time. Directly relevant to this is the Swanscombe skull from the Upper Middle Gravels at the Barnfield Pit, Swanscombe, see Figure 1.9. This was associated with handaxes. Only two parietals and an occipital were found (papers in Ovey 1964). There are no grounds at present for believing the Clactonian and Acheulean were made by different hominin species.

The archaeological evidence for the earliest occupation of Europe

In Figure 1.10, the basic scheme presented in Figure 1.8 is reproduced, this time only presenting the archaeological information. It makes one very immediate point. Assemblages with and without handaxes are a persistent feature of the whole of the African Early and Middle Pleistocene record.

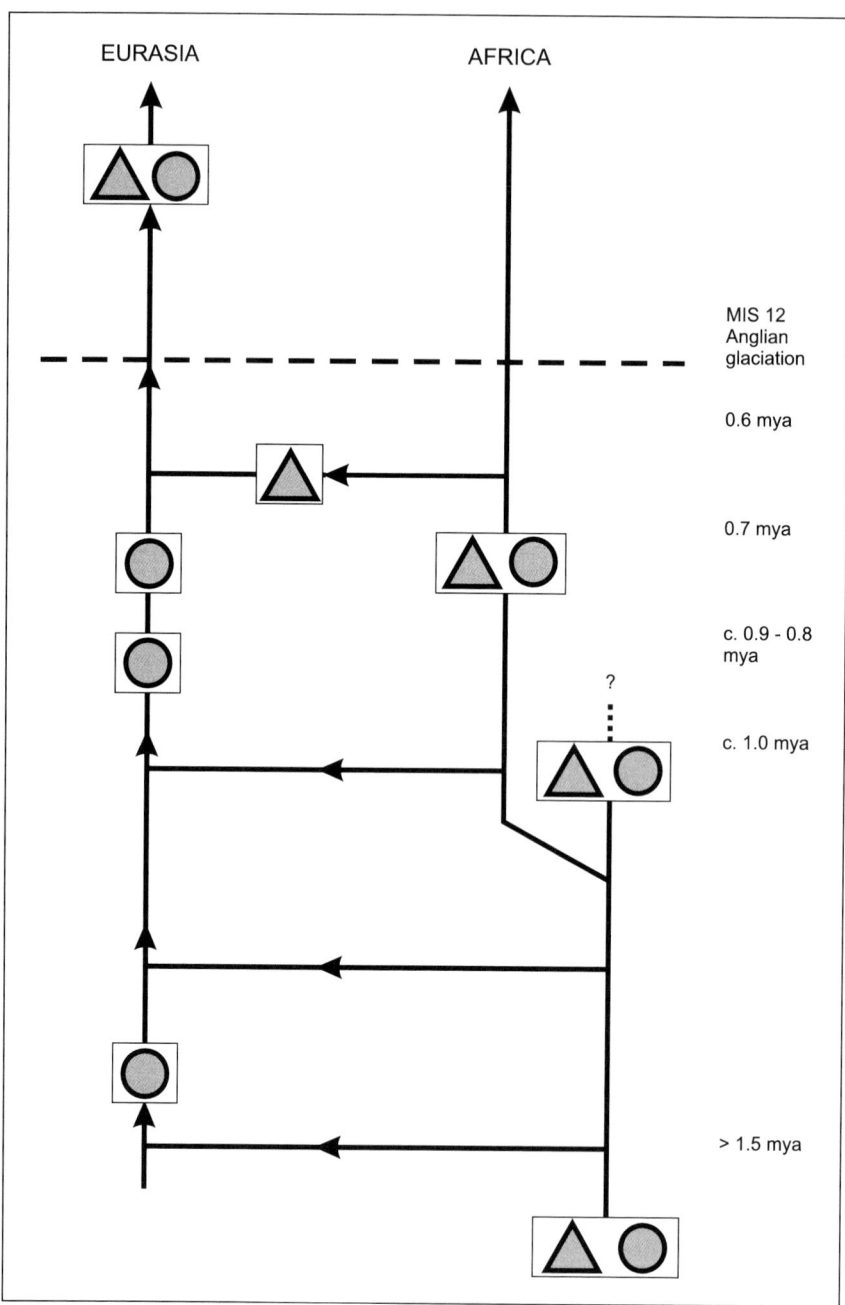

Figure 1.10 A number of possible links between hominins, sites and archaeological assemblage types in Middle Pleistocene Europe and Africa. Key: △ = handaxe assemblages; ○ = non-handaxe assemblages.

Note: See Figure 1.8.

In Africa, the earliest assemblages so far discovered, the Oldowan, are non-handaxe in character. They date back to as much as 2.6 mya (Domínguez-Rodrigo *et al.* 2005). At Olduvai Gorge, Oldowan Industries are present until c. 1.4 mya (lower part of Middle Bed II) when they are replaced by Developed Oldowan assemblages (Leakey 1971; McNabb 2005). These are essentially a continuation of the Oldowan technology but with a small number of handaxes added to the tool kit, and an increased emphasis on some of the other Oldowan tool types (Leakey 1971). Interestingly, the definition of Developed Oldowan (ibid.) allows for the presence of a few classic handaxes without compromising the essential non-handaxe character of the assemblage, in contrast to the Clactonian in Europe which, by definition, can have none. This serves to reinforce a basic point that archaeological assemblages are a result of modern archaeologists imposing their ideas on the past. This theme will be developed in Chapters 10 and 11.

The hominins at Dmanisi are only associated with flakes and cores (Gabunia and Vekua 1995; Gabunia *et al.* 2001), though the assemblage is small. Claims are also made for other non-handaxe assemblages in the Caucasus that are broadly contemporary (Gabunia 2000; Tappen *et al.* 2002). Elsewhere, a series of archaeological sites in Syria and Israel support a relatively early hominin migration (Bar-Yosef 1994; Ron and Levi 2001; Ron *et al.* 2003), so an early migration up the Rift Valley by African tool-making hominins is quite possible. Other early Oldowan like assemblages are present at Ain Hanech in Algeria (Sahnouni *et al.* 2002). But the handaxe makers were not far behind. The earliest Acheulean handaxe sites in Africa emerge between 1.7 and 1.4 mya, and the Acheulean is relatively wide-spread throughout Africa from about 1.4 mya onwards (Clark 1994). The site of 'Ubeidiya in Israel is dated to 1.4 mya. It shows a series of alternating handaxe and non-handaxe assemblages (Bar-Yosef and Goren-Inbar 1993), but its earliest assemblage appears to be a handaxe one (Bar-Yosef and Belfer-Cohen 2001). At the Evron quarry in western Galilee dated to between 1.0 and 0.78 mya (Ron *et al.* 2003), there is a handaxe assemblage (though the handaxes were not found in the excavation, Tchernov *et al.* 1994). At the Israeli site of Gesher Benot Ya'aqov (Goren-Inbar and Saragusti 1996; Saragusti and Goren-Inbar 2001) a handaxe assemblage is present which shows remarkable similarities to contemporary African assemblages both in the appearance of the handaxes and in the technology used to make them. The site is dated to more than 780 kya.

At Atapuerca, H. *antecessor* is associated with a small collection of flakes and cores. The excavators have suggested that the Aurora stratum may date to as much as MIS 21 (see Figure 1.5, Table 8.3). The lowest deposits at Gran Dolina with archaeology are layers 3, 4, and 5, with a few cores and flakes in each, dating to MIS 22 (> 865 kya). The Sima del Elefante, another locality at Atapuerca, has a small collection of flakes in its lower levels and these are dated to c. 1.0 mya (Bermúdez de Castro *et al.* 2004; Parés *et al.* 2006). But it is difficult to reconstruct the true character of these assemblages because they are so small. Elsewhere in Spain there are two early archaeological sites that also lack handaxes, Fuentenueva-3 and Barranco León 5 in the Guadix-Baza basin in southern Spain (Gibert *et al.* 1998; 2001). These sites, with cores, flakes and retouched flake tools, are often called the Orce sites; they are shown on Figure 1.7. There has been considerable debate as to the age of these assemblages (Roe 1995; Navarro *et al.* 1997; Oms *et al.* 2000). More recent studies have shed light on this. Gibert and colleagues (Gibert *et al.* 2006) suggest, on the basis of correlations between different species of small mammal, that the site is comparable to Dmanisi in age, though just a little younger. They also note that precise dating is very difficult in the Guadix-Baza basin.

There are claims for early non-handaxe assemblages in Italy, the most famous of which is Monte Poggiolo dated at c. 0.8 mya, but there are concerns over just how reliable the dating really is (Villa 2001). There are core and flake assemblages present in the Ceprano basin which pre-date the skull cap and may date to 900 kya (Manzi 2004). In Britain, the earliest site with evidence of hominins is Pakefield in Suffolk (Parfitt *et al.* 2005), see Figure 1.7. Here unambiguous flakes and a core have been recovered from sediments which may date to MIS 17. The insect and beetle fauna (Coope 2006) from the site suggest hominins were exploiting resources along the banks of a large and mature river, meandering across a wide flood plain. There were old cut-off loops with still water plants and local micro-environments on the floodplain. Animal carcasses were occasionally present on the river bank. Dung beetles attest to the presence of large herbivores. The climate was a warm temperate one. Mean July Figures were between 17 and 23°C, a Mediterranean-like climate (Parfitt *et al.* 2005). This site proves hominins had penetrated north of the Alpine barrier before 650 kya, perhaps tracking the north-westward expansion of Mediterranean-like conditions in this interglacial.

On the face of it, here is a small but consistent body of evidence suggesting the presence of non-handaxe-making hominins in western Europe just prior to, and just after 1.0 mya; and even earlier if the recent dating of the Guadix-Baza basin is correct. At Atapuerca the core and flake assemblage is directly associated with *H. antecessor*. But are these non-handaxe assemblages part of an inherited Oldowan-like tradition, descended from African or Eurasian hominins? Could they be legitimately called Oldowan, or even early Clactonian? Were they perhaps ancestral to the Clactonian? At present it is impossible to answer any of these questions. It is worth emphasising these are usually small assemblages of a few flakes and cores. Consequently, it is difficult to confidently associate them with any assemblage type. For the moment it is safest to leave the cultural implications of these assemblages in a suspense account.

For those who suggest *Homo heidelbergensis* migrated into Europe from Africa some time after 700 kya, or that there were a number of such movements, the age of the oldest biface in Europe is critical. The earliest dated handaxe assemblage that I know of comes from the Italian site of Notarchirico (Piperno *et al.* 1998), see Figure 1.7. This is dated to c. 650 kya. The interest of this site also lies in the inter-digitation of handaxe and non-handaxe assemblages stratified one above the other. This may represent occupation over many hundreds of years or more. In this sense the site resembles 'Ubeidiya (see above). But just as with 'Ubeidiya, the earliest assemblage from the site is a handaxe one.

From this time onwards we see handaxes appear more frequently in the European record. What is the explanation for this? There were a number of pulses of African and Eurasian fauna into western Europe beginning just before the Pliocene/Pleistocene boundary at 1.75 mya. Between 1.0 and 0.5 mya there were further migrations of African fauna into Eurasia (Turner 1992). If *H. heidelbergensis* was migrating into Europe, it may well have been as part of the broader movement of fauna out of Africa. Alan Turner (ibid.) notes the appearance of various African carnivores in European mammal assemblages after 1.0 mya, such as the lion, the leopard and two forms of hyaena. These would have been rivals with whom early *Homo* was in direct competition. If they moved westwards to take advantage of new opportunities, hominins could well have moved with them following the herds. Turner's data show another major change in the carnivore community at c. 500 kya.

This, then, is the hominin and archaeological background to the later Middle Pleistocene in which the Clactonian occurs.

2

GEOLOGICAL AND OTHER FRAMEWORKS

> A theory is a good theory if it satisfies two requirements: It must accurately describe a large class of observations on the basis of a model that contains only a few arbitrary elements, and it must make definite predictions about the results of future observations.
>
> (Hawking 1988: 9)

Introduction

In this chapter I will explore the links between climate, environment, and the creation of river terraces. Why? Because the major Clactonian sites are almost all in secondary contexts, usually the gravel deposits of river terraces. The sites are accumulations of cores and flakes that record the activity of hominins upriver of the site. In some cases these artefacts may have travelled far, in others they will be very local, perhaps coming from only a few hundred metres away. Understanding how and why river terraces form will play an important part in helping us to interpret these assemblages. But more than this, relating the development of river terraces to climate change, will enable us to begin to place the Clactonian, and the earlier Palaeolithic in Britain in a meaningful chronological framework.

I will begin by describing the deep sea core record. It is through this that we have come to appreciate the complexity of climate change during the Pleistocene. I will then go on to describe the orbital forcing mechanisms that play an important role in triggering the patterns of climate change seen in the deep sea cores. Terrestrial effects related to orbital forcing will also be discussed. I will then link all of this to the great spreads of gravel and other sediments that form river terraces.

The record of the deep sea cores (DSC)

In sea water there are tiny creatures called foraminifera. They build their shells (tests) out of the minerals and nutrients in sea water. These substances contain oxygen which also gets built into the shells. Among the various isotopes of oxygen in sea water are two called oxygen sixteen (^{16}O) and oxygen eighteen (^{18}O). When these animals die their skeletons fall to the sea bed and become incorporated within the basal mud. As more sediment is deposited, the micro-organisms become buried. As the process is constant, DSCs preserve a continuous record of the rain of forams (as they are called for short) onto the gradually accumulating ocean bed. For our purposes a DSC is a continuous record of the changing relationship between ^{16}O and ^{18}O in the skeletons of the forams at different depths in the core. But how does this help us understand climate change?

^{16}O is isotopically lighter than ^{18}O, it has two less neutrons. The key point is that ^{16}O is more susceptible to evaporation than ^{18}O, especially in colder climates, because cold air cannot absorb the heavier isotope as easily. During a glaciation more of the lighter isotope is evaporated from the oceans as moisture and carried away by the winds that transfer precipitation northwards to the ice fields. These consequently become enriched in ^{16}O. The flip side of this is that the oceans are enriched in ^{18}O. It is important to note that the heavier isotope is still subject to evaporation in a glaciation, just less so.

As the ice sheets melt in an interglacial, ^{16}O is returned to the ocean, and the normal balance between the two is re-established. The forams which are building their shells from ocean water will reflect these changes. During glaciations their skeletons will be relatively enriched with ^{18}O, while in an interglacial the balance between the two will be more even. In the early days of this research it was thought that there was a strong correlation between isotopic composition and temperature. While a correlation does exist, various factors make it very difficult to measure. Today the isotopic balance of oxygen in the oceans is taken as a proxy for the *volume* of water in the oceans. A high ^{18}O count in foram shells in a DSC indicates a time of low sea level, a glaciation, because the water (and a lot of the ^{16}O in it) has been drawn up into the ice sheets. Conversely, a more even ratio between the two is taken to imply high sea level, and consequently interglacial conditions.

Figure 2.1 shows an MIS curve. It was created from 57 different DSCs, combined to give a continuous DSC record stack spanning 2.0 myr (Lisiecki 2005; Lisiecki and Raymo 2005). One thing the core makes very clear is the cyclic nature of climate change. Pliocene and Pleistocene climate is characterised by a see-saw pattern of glacials and interglacials. Each glaciation is given an even number, and each interglacial an odd number. Glacials are represented by troughs on the curve, while the warm interglacials are represented by peaks. These are the marine isotope stages (MIS) that were introduced in Figure 1.5. After the Brunhes/Matuyama boundary (the position of the Lower Pleistocene/Middle Pleistocene transition based on palaeomagnetic evidence), there have been 9 periods of glacial-like cold and 10 warmer periods, see Figure 1.5.

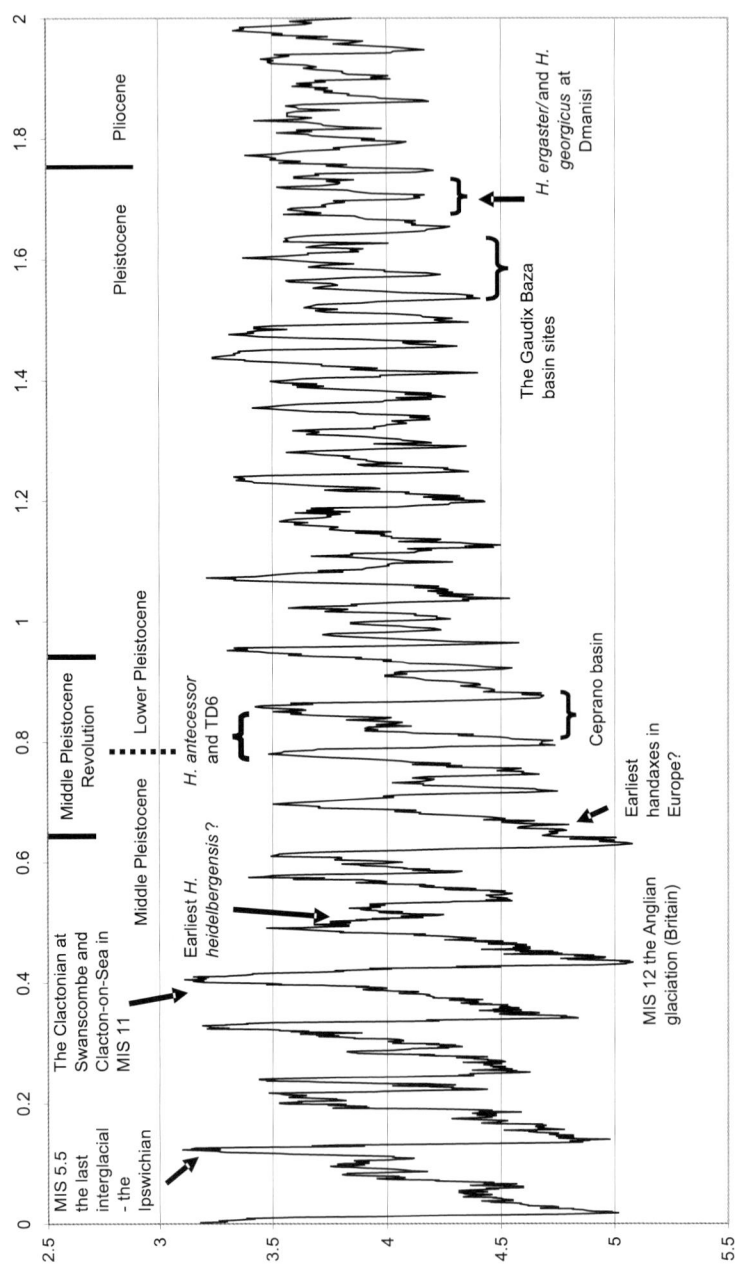

Figure 2.1 Deep sea core record of glaciations (troughs) and interglacials (peaks) for the Pleistocene.

Note: Data used with permission.

Some readers may be more familiar with the term Oxygen Isotope Stage, abbreviated to OIS. The reason I am using MIS in this book is that in recent years deep ice cores, drilled from the Antarctic and Greenland ice caps, have also been contributing detailed climate curves. These also use oxygen isotopes to distinguish between different climatic cycles. But the oxygen isotope signal from ice cores is slightly different from that in the basal muds on the sea floor (though the basic pattern of recorded climate change is similar). So to distinguish between the two signals, MIS is used to indicate the oxygen isotope signal from the marine record.

One other thing that the curve in Figure 2.1 shows is a shift in the wavelength (width between the peaks) and amplitude (height and depth) of the glacial interglacial cycle. In other words, as we move into the Middle Pleistocene the glacial–interglacial cycles are becoming longer, and the temperature differences between them becoming greater when compared to earlier cycles – this is particularly noticeable for the glacials which become much colder than their Early Pleistocene predecessors. This shift is called the Middle Pleistocene Revolution (MPR), or sometimes the Middle Pleistocene Transition. It marks a shift in the orbit of the Earth, from a circular orbit around the sun to an elliptical one. This will be explained in more detail in the next section.

Since the early 1970s there has been a lot of work on the theory behind the DSCs as well as advances in technology and the practical work of recognising glacial–interglacial boundaries in the cores. One development concerns the labelling of sub-stages. The DSCs have shown that there are minor reversals in climate within the broader glacial and interglacial periods. Stadials are cold phases in an interglacial, while interstadials are warm phases in a glaciation. Initially these were labelled with letters. For example, MIS 5 had five sub-stages. MIS 5a was the most recent and this was a warm phase; MIS 5e was the oldest and this too was a warm phase. MIS 5e is the equivalent of the Ipswichian – the name given to the last interglacial before the present one, see Figure 2.2. More recent practice has been to number them, for example, 5a becomes 5.1; 5e becomes 5.5. This brings the numbering of sub-phases into line with the main MI stages. Warm peaks will always be odd numbers, cold troughs will be even numbers, and the higher the decimal, the older the sub-stage. The existence of stadials and inter-stadials raises a particular question, how warm does it have to be to qualify for an interglacial, and how cold for a glaciation? Some of the peaks and troughs on Figures 2.1 and 2.2 are not counted as full glacials or interglacials. This is a subject that climate scientists are still debating.

The complexity of determining an accurate climatic record is exemplified by the case of the last glaciation, known as the Devensian in Britain. On the basis of well-established radiocarbon dates, and a well-researched mammal record, the Devensian is taken to last from MIS 5.4 until the end

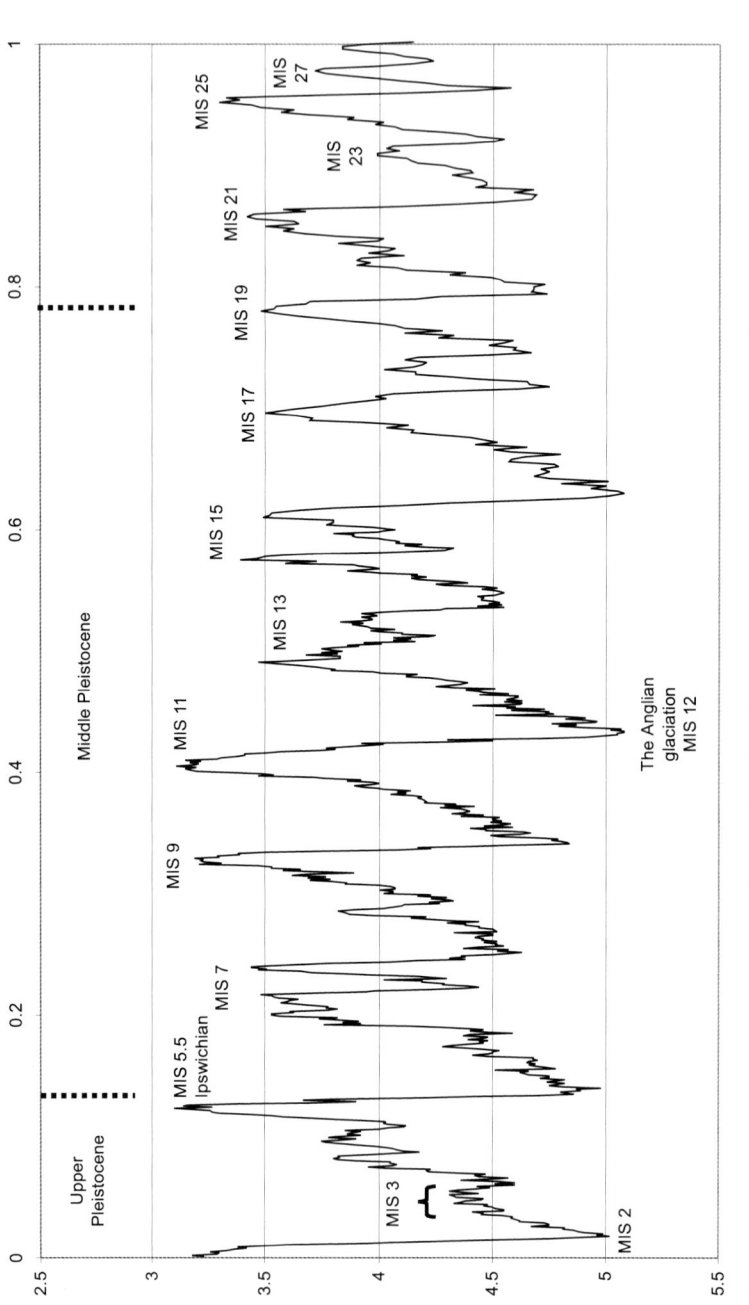

Figure 2.2 Deep sea core record showing glacial–interglacial cycle with marine isotope stages (MIS) for the Middle Pleistocene.

Note: Data used with permission.

of MIS 2, see Figure 2.2. Where does that leave the period from MIS 5.4 to 5.1? These should be fully interglacial (i.e. all of 5 should be an interglacial as it is an odd numbered stage), but as seen in Figure 2.2, the climate is showing a gradual decline between sub-stages 5.4 and 5.1, with warm peaks that nowhere near approach the oxygen isotope ratios of earlier interglacials (MIS 7, MIS 9, MIS 11). On the other hand, stage 5.5 is a sub-stage yet it is considered to be a full interglacial. This is not so surprising given the strength of its peak. MIS 3 should be an interglacial – but it is not warm enough. What does all this mean? Is the last interglacial–glacial cycle (5.5 to end of 2) somehow different from all its predecessors? Alternatively were all interglacial–glacial cycles like this, but the resolution of the DSCs is just not precise enough to pick this up because these cycles are so much older? The simple answer is that we do not know as yet.

Whichever way geochronologists ultimately decide to subdivide the DSC record, it remains a vitally important reflection of the dynamic nature of Pleistocene climate. For fuller treatments of this, see Jones and Keen (1993), Lowe and Walker (1997), and Walker (2005).

Astronomical theory and orbital forcing

This is the theory that major changes in the Earth's climate are related to changes in the Earth's orbit around the sun, as well as how it spins on its axis. Changes in the position of the Earth, relative to the sun, determine how much radiation (called insolation) different parts of the Earth's surface will receive, at different times of the year. This has an effect on the length of the seasons and how warm or cold they are. This in turn is linked to the persistence of snow cover and the build-up of ice. Persistent ice accumulation over many decades can lead to the conditions favourable to the onset of a glaciation. Bradley (1999) makes it clear that the total amount of radiation received by the Earth does not change very much even when the orbit of the Earth does change. *The real effect is a redistribution of energy across the seasons.*

Right at the outset it must be stated that while most researchers are agreed that there is a cause and effect link between the Earth's orbital and axial changes, and climatic shifts, exactly how this link manifests itself is disputed. The various orbital forcing mechanisms, although cyclical (i.e. they follow a repetitive cycle), have had different influences on the Earth's climate at different times. When the cycle is repeated, the effect on the climate is often different the next time round because other boundary conditions have changed. So although why climate may change is relatively well understood, the specifics of how it does so in each case are still debated. Excellent summaries are to be found in Bradley (1999); Jones and Keen (1993); and Lowe and Walker (1997).

There are three major astronomical effects on climate. The first is the *orbital eccentricity* of the Earth, see Figure 2.3. At times the Earth's orbit

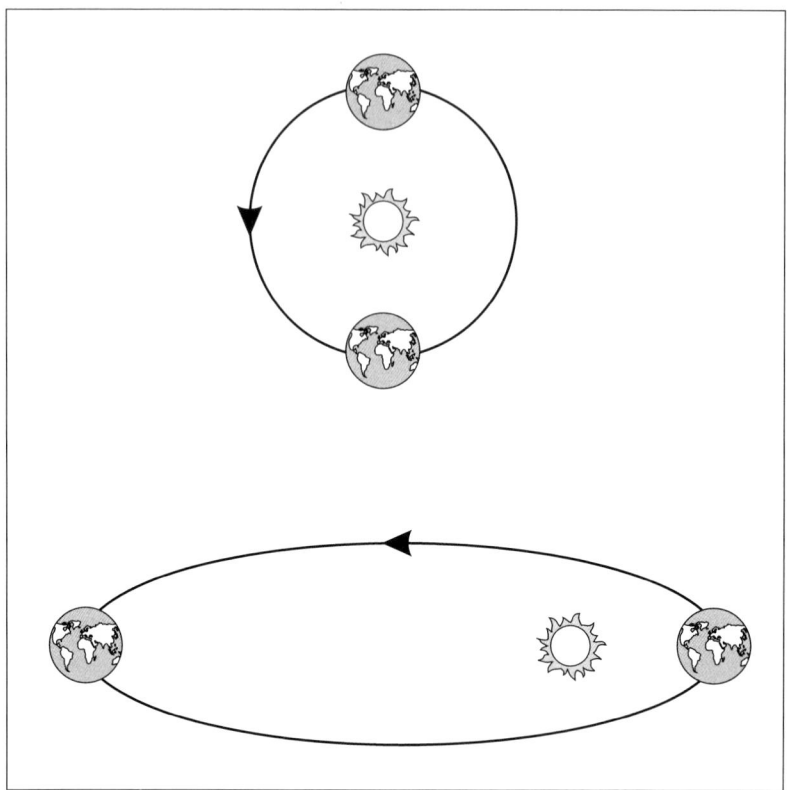

Figure 2.3 Orbital eccentricity.

around the sun is nearly circular, so the distance between the two is almost the same all of the time. One summer will be very much like every other, and each winter more or less the same as the last. At other times the orbit is an ellipse. When the Earth is at its closest to the sun in the elliptical orbit, it is said to be in perihelion. When at its furthest, it is in aphelion. Although at first this might seem to be a very critical parameter, research suggests that by itself this is the weakest of the three main astronomical influences.

Many scientists are beginning to believe that *precession* is a more important orbital forcing mechanism. Precession is the appearance that, over time, the seasons will occur at different times of the calendar year. The shift is not appreciable on a human timescale though. It is suggested that precession has a greater effect than orbital eccentricity on redistributing insolation over the northern hemisphere. In northern hemisphere summers, the Earth is tilted toward the sun. In winter, the northern hemisphere is tilted away, so less surface area is exposed. But the axis of rotation of the Earth is not fixed. As the Earth spins around on its axis, the axis itself is shifting its position. In fact it wobbles like a child's spinning top, see Figure 2.4a. It takes about 27 kyr to complete one full revolution of the wobble. It is the circle that the axis describes that is known as precession. (At different points along the circle the axis will point to a different star constellation than it did at the same time of year many thousands of years previously, giving rise to the Earth's movement through the different houses of the zodiac.) This means that as the line of the axis approaches the point where it is furthest away from the sun, the summer tilt of the northern hemisphere towards the sun will expose less of that hemisphere's surface. Consequently, less insolation will reach the higher latitudes. It is the solstices (summer longest day; winter shortest day) and equinoxes (point at which length of day/night is same in spring and autumn) which actually move or

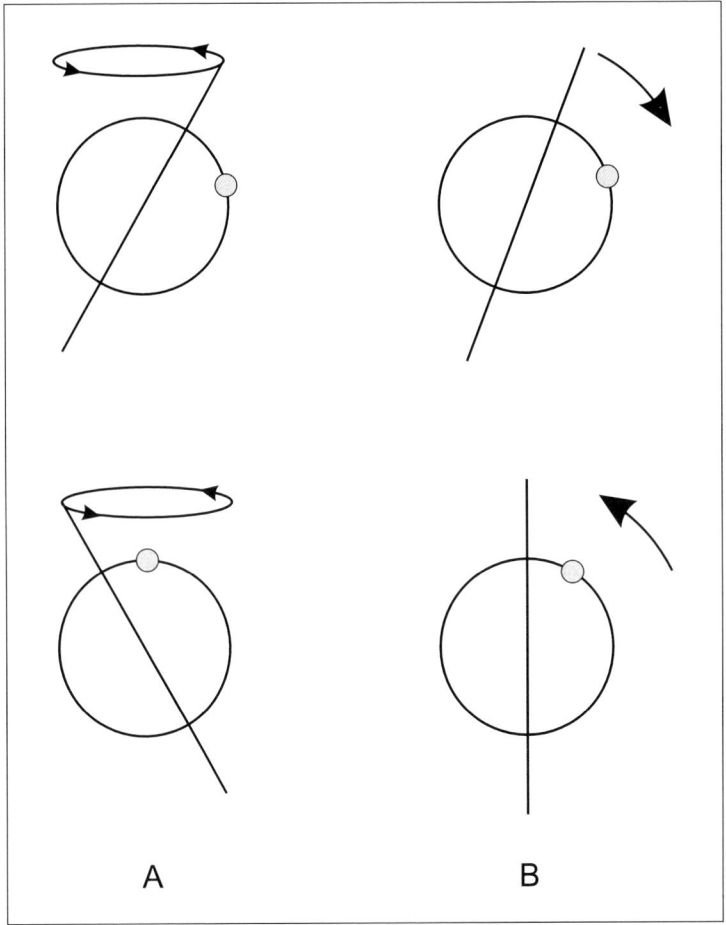

Figure 2.4 A precession of the Earth's axis. B Obliquity of the Earth's axis.

precess, thus dragging the seasons (of which they are the mid-points) with them.

One final factor is important, the *obliquity of the ecliptic*. While the Earth is wobbling around its axis, the angle of the axis itself changes slightly, see Figure 2.4b. The angle is measured in relation to the imaginary plane described by the Earth as it travels along its circular or elliptical orbit. The shift is some 3 degrees of tilt, and takes about 41 kyr to move to its maximum position and back again. The effects of obliquity are most marked in the higher latitudes. Increase the tilt and the amount of surface area exposed to radiation is increased in the higher latitudes. It also affects the intensity of the difference between winter and summer in the higher latitudes, by affecting how much summer and winter daylight time there is. Or put another way, increase the tilt of the axis and more radiation is received by the high latitudes because the days are longer. Summer midday sun will be stronger. Reduce the tilt, and if other conditions are right, snow cover will persist in high latitudes.

But how can these three conditions actually affect climate? The first to suggest a link was a Scot called James Croll, but it was the brilliant Serbian mathematician and geophysicist Milutin Milankovitch who worked out the precise details. His mathematical calculations predicted just when the budgets of solar radiation would be at their strongest and at their weakest by calculating the position of the Earth in relation to the sun at different times in the Quaternary. In effect, predicting the onset of glacial and interglacial conditions. He also believed that position on the surface of the Earth was critical. For Milankovitch, the key zone was between 60° and 70° N. Within this zone, when the tilt of the Earth's axis was at its greatest, orbital eccentricity was high, and the northern hemisphere summer coincided with aphelion, then conditions were conducive to the build-up of glaciers. The overall reduction in summer insolation in this zone was not enough to melt the winter snow. Eventually snow cover would be persistent all the year round.

Milankovitch's theories were popular when they first appeared as they predicted the cyclic nature of glacials and interglacials. During the 1940s and 1950s, Milankovitch's ideas fell out of fashion. It was not until the 1970s that they were resurrected. This was because of the acceptance of the DSC record as a genuine reflection of changes in world climate. Once DSCs could be dated, it was realised that periods of glacial and interglacial climate coincided with the changes in the insolation values that Milankovitch had predicted for major climatic changes. What is more, as the number of DSCs that were drilled increased, it became evident that the same broad pattern of change was present in each of the cores, so these changes were truly global.

Atmospheric and oceanic circulation

In the past 20 years scientists have realised that the influence of the orbital forcing mechanisms on local conditions can vary because of the interplay of different elements within the total climate system on each other. Two of the most important climatic sub-systems are atmospheric and oceanic circulation. Others include atmospheric gases such as carbon dioxide and methane, the amount of dust in the atmosphere, and changes in the extent of ice cover. Ice is highly reflective. The more ice there is, the more heat will be radiated back into space. These systems, and others, locally interact with each other and affect one another. This localised interplay determines just how effective the influence of the three orbital forcing mechanisms will be. Scientists have become aware that in many cases critical thresholds in one or more local climatic sub-systems must be overcome before Milankovitch scale events can take effect.

It has also become apparent from studying the last glaciation that there are sub-Milankovitch climate changes which can occur on millennial and centennial (or even sub-centennial) scales. These are not the same as the stadials and interstadials that were described above and which were clearly present in the DSCs. These are much shorter events. It is only through the greater scale of resolution present in the ice cores that these sub-Milankovitch events have been identified (Lowe and Walker 1997). For the last glaciation these are often called Dansgaard–Oeschger events after their discoverers. They represent rapid reversals in climate. They may be affected by orbital forcing, but are more likely to be a product of feedback loops in local physical systems (e.g. oceanic current flow) reaching critical thresholds. One of the biggest problems in Quaternary climatic research, as already alluded to, is that the really detailed climate records are confined to the last interglacial–glacial cycle. This is the period for which the most evidence has survived. Although hotly debated, many scientists now accept that these millennial scale sub-orbital rapid climate shifts were a common feature of earlier glacial–interglacial cycles (McManus *et al.* 1999).

Atmospheric circulation is directly affected by insolation levels. If the equator is receiving more solar radiation, then the higher latitudes are not. Insolation gradients between high and low latitudes (i.e. higher in one and lower in the other) are reflected in parallel temperature gradients. Higher low latitude temperatures will attract high pressure weather systems toward the equator where ocean surface area is considerable, resulting in higher evaporation rates. Low pressure systems over high latitudes will then attract the moisture rich winds which will release precipitation as snow over the land masses. Studies have shown this pattern to be prevalent during periods of Pleistocene ice growth (Bradley 1999: 41f.). In warmer interglacial phases the high latitudes receive more energy so the gradient between the low and high latitudes is less pronounced. High pressure systems are shunted north, evaporation is reduced, so the power of the circumpolar air circulation currents is not so great, moisture transfer northwards is reduced.

Ocean currents are an important conduit for the transfer of heat from the equatorial regions into the northern latitudes. Shallow surface Atlantic ocean currents flow northwards at a temperature of about 10° C. In the winter months, to the south of Iceland, these waters begin to sink as their salinity level (density) increases in the cooler more northerly waters. These deeper and more saline waters then flow southwards at a temperature of about 2° C. The heat loss is transferred into the atmosphere and can represent about 25 per cent of the equivalent annual budget of radiation for the Atlantic northwards of 35° of latitude (Lowe and Walker 1997). Interrupt or cut off this thermohaline circulation and a critical source of heat to the northern latitudes is lost or reduced sufficiently to have an important effect on local and regional climate sub-systems. Production of cold saline deep-water is generally lower in glacials and higher in interglacials (if the last cycle is anything to go by). So the conveyor belt, as it is known, runs slower during a cold phase or perhaps stops all together. As the Earth passes into an interglacial phase, the conveyor runs up again.

Once again the situation isn't that clear-cut. As the last glaciation came to an end, and the conveyor was presumably restarting, it was interrupted on a number of occasions. The key to why this happened is melt waters from glacial retreat. As the climate improved, there was a break-up of the ice pack and the creation of fleets of icebergs – called Heinrich events. The icebergs began to melt, releasing into the sea vast quantities of cool fresh water which had fallen as snow. The result was a slowing down of the conveyor and a return to much colder conditions for a short period during each Heinrich event. There were many such Heinrich events during the final stages of the last glaciation. This is a good example of how local feedback can influence the effects of external (i.e. orbital) climate-driving mechanisms. Just as scientists are beginning to accept millennial scale Dansgaard–Oeschger events as a common feature of pre-MIS 5.5 climatic cycles, evidence is also growing in support of Heinrich events being not uncommon prior to the last glaciation. McManus et al. (1999) note that ice sheet calving can be associated with periods of glacial–interglacial transition, and vice versa. They may even be associated with the shift to stadials and inter-stadials.

Naturally what I have presented above is an oversimplification of the reasons for climate change. I have also only dealt with a few of the major effects that orbital forcing can have on regional terrestrial systems. Most of the details of the interplay between these various climatic systems, and the different scales they operate at, are hotly debated. Nevertheless, there is clearly a link between orbital forcing, the global distribution of annual insolation budgets, and the effect of this on regionally significant terrestrial climate systems. This would be the same for the Pleistocene, as it is today. The next link we must forge is that between terrestrial climate change (i.e. the differing MI stages), and its effect on rivers and their terraces, since it is within these deposits that we find the Clactonian sites. One model is particularly relevant here, that of David Bridgland. The model directly links terrace development to the MIS curve and to large-scale climate change as preserved in the DSCs. The model was developed on the Lower Thames Valley which is where the majority of the Clactonian sites are located.

David Bridgland's model of river terrace development

Until very recently the relationship between rivers and climate was taken to be fairly straightforward. In a glaciation sea level dropped. Rivers flowing out to sea had further to go to reach their new coastlines. The result was downcutting as the river eroded a new lower flood plain along which it could flow out to sea. The old flood plain, now left high and dry above the river, became a terrace. In the succeeding glaciation the cycle would be repeated. So the development of the staircase of river terraces along the side of a valley was directly controlled by climate, and terraces formed under cold conditions. But it has recently been recognised (Bridgland and D'Olier 1995) that this model is too simple. Every time a glacial period caused a drop in sea level, the river would simply re-occupy its old re-exposed valley from the preceding cold period. There would be no need for it to repeatedly re-cut its downstream bed. Lengthening of the river in such circumstances would be likely to cause aggradation (deposition) and not downcutting (Bridgland pers. comm.).

Rivers are hideously complicated things with local conditions affecting different stretches of the river in very different ways, which is why no two rivers are identical. Fortunately though, broad patterns of similarity do exist. What research has now shown is that uplift of the land is the major cause of river incision (Maddy et al. 2000; 2001; Maddy and Bridgland 2000; Westaway et al. 2002; 2003). What causes this? The most important mechanism is crustal thickening. In periods of low erosion, sediment is deposited off-shore on the continental shelf where the brittle Upper Crust is thicker. The Upper Crust inland, under the eroding upland areas, is thinner, so a pressure gradient exists. Semi-molten rock from the Lower Crust is forced inland from below the continental shelf because of the pressure gradient. However, since erosion levels are low, the amount of crustal material moving inland is also low, so there is a rough balance between the two.

But when erosion increases, this equilibrium is disturbed. This is at times of climatic transition, in particular that from glacial to interglacial. As more and more sediment is deposited on the continental shelf, the base of the Upper Crust here advects downwards because of the increased pressure of sediment. There is a corresponding move upwards in the base of the Upper Crust inland, beneath the eroding upland area. So the pressure gradient becomes ever greater. As a result, more crust from beneath the continental shelf is forced landward, and the crust beneath the eroding inland area gradually thickens. The net result of all this is uplift of the area where erosion is occurring. In addition, sediment unloading will contribute to uplift. The removal of sediment from the eroding areas will take a huge weight off the surface of the land. The land surface will begin to rise, bouncing back like a mattress regaining its shape. This will add to the net uplift.

So the role of climate in uplift, and consequently in river terrace formation is evident, as is the inter-related character of all these processes. Climate drives erosion.

But climate has another critical role to play. The slow rise of the land isn't enough by itself to induce the kind of river incision that will lead to major terrace formation. The land will also be rising during the interglacial (although not as much as during those periods of high inland erosion), and the bulk of available evidence demonstrates that the vast majority of river terraces are not formed during temperate periods. What climate does is to influence soil, vegetation, and water supply, and these in turn affect the erosive potential of rivers in uplifting areas.

The work of Dave Bridgland, Darrel Maddy and Rob Westaway suggests that a river will cut down through its old flood plain and create a new lower flood plain at the transition from a glaciation to an interglacial. Figure 2.5 shows the model of river development. In this period of climatic transition the first two phases of river development occur. The glaciers have receded and the land is slowly rising. The climate is not yet warm enough for plants to have extensively re-colonised the slopes of river banks as the permafrost thaws. The slopes adjacent to the river are therefore prone to erosion, as are the banks themselves. The amount of sediment and water entering the rivers is considerable. It is the lack of vegetation that is the key here. The mere fact of un-vegetated surfaces increases erosion enormously (D. Keen, pers. comm.). Additionally, this is a period of heavy rainfall and frequent storms before the weather systems settle down during the coming interglacial. Water will also be released from the melting permafrost. The net discharge of water is consequently very high. It is the high levels of erosion at this time that results in the rapid increase of deposition offshore on the continental shelf. This triggers the downward advection of the base of the brittle Upper Crust beginning the process of increased crustal thickening.

The net result of the combination of uplift and the quantity of water entering the rivers is downcutting through the old floodplain. This is left as a terrace on the valley side. Prior to the interglacial itself (Figure 2.5 – phase 3), a proportion of all this eroded material is deposited over the base

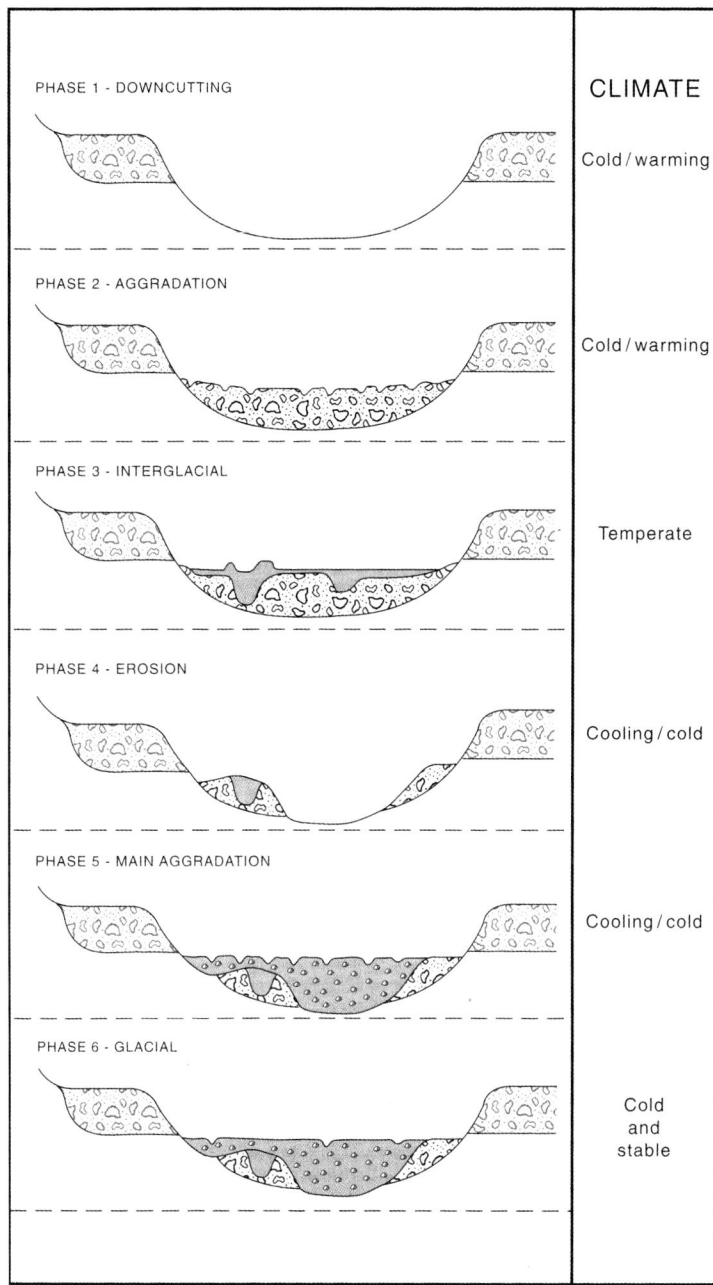

PHASE 1 - DOWNCUTTING   CLIMATE

                                         Cold / warming

PHASE 2 - AGGRADATION

                                         Cold / warming

PHASE 3 - INTERGLACIAL

                                         Temperate

PHASE 4 - EROSION

                                         Cooling / cold

PHASE 5 - MAIN AGGRADATION

                                         Cooling / cold

PHASE 6 - GLACIAL

                                         Cold
                                         and
                                         stable

Figure 2.5 Six-stage developmental model of river terrace formation according to David Bridgland.

Note: Used with permission.

of the new channel in its middle reaches and the higher parts of its lower reaches (Figure 2.5 – phase 2). So at the base of every flood plain there will be a thin veneer of aggraded material dated to still cold or cool climatic conditions.

In the interglacial (Figure 2.5 – phase 3), the erosive power of the stream is much reduced. Slopes will be stabilised by vegetation. Water supply will be generally steady. The effects of torrential rainfall would be reduced. Mostly the river would be depositing finer grained material such as silts and sands. Erosion and deposition will be largely confined to within the channel, and the re-working downstream of pre-existing channel sediments. Over-bank flooding will occasionally deposit fine-grained sediments away from the channel margins. At the end of the interglacial this changes. There may be initial erosion due to unstable conditions (Figure 2.5 – phase 4), but as the climate cools, more vegetation dies off and slopes become bare. Freeze thaw action accelerates slope disintegration. This adds to the amount of material being entrained within the river. Storms are more frequent as the climate becomes more unstable. Flood events will be frequent and more powerful. The valley sides, now free of the binding influence of vegetation, will be eroded more quickly and the river will widen its floodplain. The result of all this erosion and sediment input is the deposition of large amounts of material on the river bed in Figure 2.5 – phase 5. Erosion may remove quantities of the interglacial sediments and incorporate them into the bed-load too. Phase 5 sees the aggradation of considerable amounts of material over, or in place of, the interglacial sediments. In Figure 2.5 – phase 6 the glaciation is in full swing, erosion and deposition are at a minimum.

What is important to remember about the Bridgland model is that a terrace is effectively a sandwich, see Figure 2.6. The lower slice (Figure 2.6 – phases 1 and 2) comprises cold or cool climate sediments from the end of the old glaciation and the switch to the interglacial. In the middle is the interglacial filling of the sandwich (Figure 2.6 – phase 3). The upper slice is the cold to cooler sediments of phases 4 and 5. In geological terminology each individual terrace is called a formation (Bridgland 1995). In turn, these are made up of a number of members. In the schematic model in Figure 2.6, each of the three subdivisions is a member. In turn, each member can be further divided into a series of beds. A member may be composed any number of beds. The individual beds within the members may be separated by minor erosion phases.

This model was developed on the deposits of the Lower Thames Valley, and how the model applies to the deposits is laid out in Table 2.1. Here the phases of the model are applied to the different aggradations which go by the names of the sites where they are most clearly represented. Table 2.1 shows that in the Lower Thames Valley there are four main terraces or formations: the Boyn Hill/Orsett Heath, the Lynch Hill/Corbets Tey, the

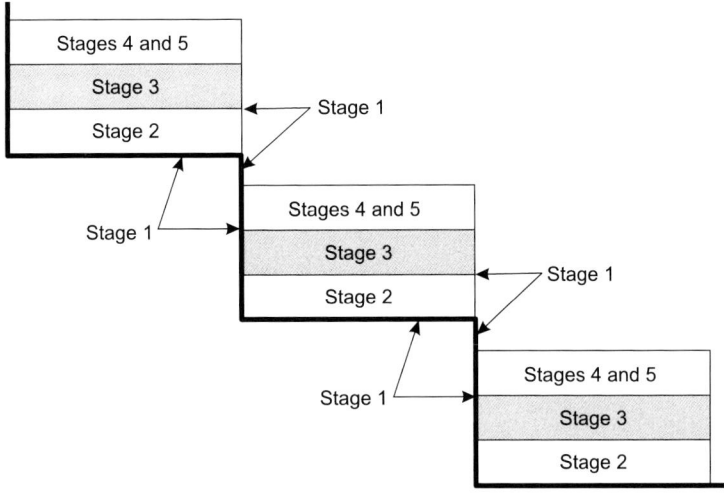

Position in glacial/interglacial cycle	Climate	Bridgland terrace model phase
End of interglacial and earliest phases of glaciation	Cool	4 and 5
Interglacial	Warm	3
Glacial/interglacial transition	Cool	1 and 2
Glacial maximum (pleniglacial)	Cold	6

Figure 2.6 Relationship of stages in Bridgland's terrace model to climate.

Note: Three hypothetical terraces show the relationship of the different stages to each other and to the previous terrace.

Taplow/Mucking, and the Kempton Park/East Tilbury Marshes formations. The name before the forward slash refers to the name given to the terrace upstream of London, in the Middle Thames Valley. The name after the forward slash is the name given to the same terrace, but downstream of London, in the Lower Thames Valley proper. I will return to this in more detail in Chapters 4 to 7. Each of the formations can be seen to be divided into the three members alluded to above. Table 2.1 also shows how different sections of the river can have their own local member labels, even

Table 2.1 The fluviatile formations of the Middle and Lower Thames and the members (individual tripartite divisions) that comprise them

Name of formation in Middle Thames	Name of equivalent formation/member in Lower Thames	Name of equivalent deposits in Southend area	Name of equivalent deposits in area of Dengie peninsula	Name of equivalent deposits in Clacton area	Stage in Bridgland model
Kempton Park Formation	East Tilbury Marshes upper gravel	Submerged	Submerged	Submerged	4+5
	Trafalgar Square interglacial deposits	Submerged	Submerged	Submerged	3
	East Tilbury Marshes lower gravel	Submerged	Submerged	Submerged	2
					6+1
Taplow Formation	Mucking upper gravel	Submerged	Submerged	Submerged	4+5
	Aveley Interglacial deposits	Submerged	Submerged	Submerged	3
	Mucking lower gravel	Submerged	Submerged	Submerged	2
					6+1
Lynch Hill Formation	Corbets Tey upper gravel	Barling Gravel	Dammer Wick Gravel	Submerged (Cudmore Grove Gravel)	4+5
	Purfleet Interglacial deposits	Shoeburyness Channel interglacial deposits	Burnham Channel interglacial deposits	Cudmore Grove interglacial deposits	3
	Corbets Tey lower gravel	Shoeburyness Channel Gravel	Burnham Channel Gravel	Submerged	2
					6+1
Boyn Hill Formation	Orsett Heath upper gravel	Southchurch Gravel	Asheldham Gravel	Mersea Island/ Wigborough Gravel	4+5
	Swanscombe Interglacial deposits	Southend Channel interglacial deposits	Asheldham Channel interglacial deposits	Clacton Channel interglacial deposits	3
	Orsett Heath lower gravel	Southend Channel Gravel	Asheldham Channel Gravel	Basal Clacton Channel Gravel	2

Note: The earliest post-diversion formation/terrace, the Black Park Formation will be buried below the Boyn Hill/Orsett Heath Formation. It will be found below the various lowest members of this formation at different points in the Lower Thames Valley, for example, below the Southend Channel Gravel in that area, or the Asheldham Channel Gravel on the Dengie peninsula.

Source: Table modified after Bridgland et al. (2001). Table 1, with additional data from Bridgland, pers. comm. Used with permission.

though they preserve different portions of the same continuous deposit. So, for example, in phase 2 of Bridgland's model of terrace development (see Figure 2.7), in the Lower Thames Orsett Heath Formation, we find the Orsett Heath lower gravel. Further downstream, at Southend, the same aggradation is called the Southend Channel Gravel. Further downstream again, phase 2 of the Bridgland model is given the label Asheldham Channel Gravel, after a site where a continuation of the same gravel unit is preserved on the Dengie peninsular. Figure 2.7 shows the Lower Thames Valley terrace staircase in diagrammatic form based on Table 2.1.

So Bridgland's model links climate change, at the scale of Milankovitch/ MIS cycles, with more localised climate driven geomorphological changes. The effects of these large-scale climate changes on local sequences are easily appreciated in this model. The river terraces contain artefacts, swept off the banks of the rivers, and entrained within the river's bedload. Terraces develop down the sides of their river valleys like a staircase. The older the terrace, the higher up in the staircase it is. Many of the archaeological sites that this book is concerned with are contained within these old floodplain gravels.

This model provides a chrono-stratigraphic sequence for the Lower and Middle Thames, and as such it provides a robust framework which can be tested by the application of dating techniques such as optically stimulated luminescence (OSL), amino-acid racemisation (AAR), electron spin resonance (ESR) and other dating techniques that are applicable to the Pleistocene. I have not included a separate section on dating techniques as those applicable to the Pleistocene have been thoroughly reviewed by Mike Walker in a recent book. Readers interested in the nitty gritty details of various applications can consult his book (Walker 2005). For my purposes it is only necessary to state a site has been dated, and, where necessary, note the technique used.

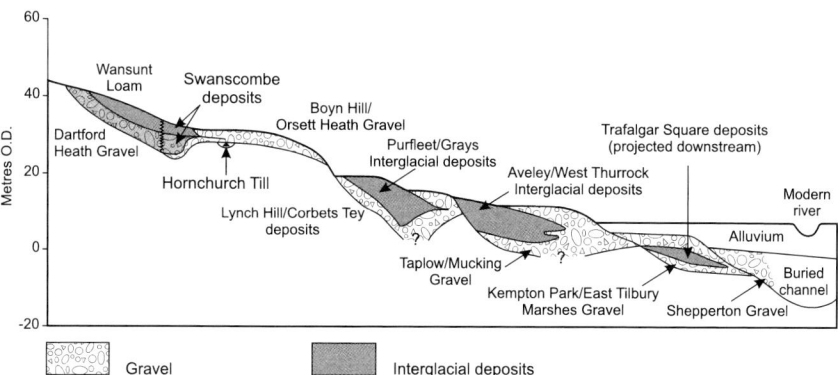

Figure 2.7 Schematic of terrace sequence for the Lower Thames Valley.

Note: Used with and modified with permission.

But it must be stated that Bridgland's interpretation of how a terrace forms, and his chrono-stratigraphic sequence of the Lower Thames, is only one possible interpretation of this river's history, and it is not one that has found universal acceptance. For example, the Cambridge geologist Phil Gibbard has produced a very different interpretation of the Thames Valley sequence not based not upon the MI sequence (1985; 1995; Gibbard and Lewin 2002). Geologists like Gibbard make a very salient point. Without independent dating techniques it is impossible to fit deposits of terrestrial gravel and finer sediments into specific MI stages. The only really effective methodology is palynology – pollen analysis, where pollen is preserved in fine-grained temperate sediments. However, palynology gives a radically different sequence to that in the MI sequence. After the Anglian, and before the Devensian, it can only demonstrate the presence of two interglacials, an earlier Hoxnian, and a later Ipswichian. By definition these have to be separated by a glaciation – the Wolstonian (often referred to as the Wolstonian stage). This sequence is shown in Figure 3.3. Compare this figure to the more complex MI sequence in Figure 1.5. Evidently any geochronological interpretations of river terraces which use such contrasting frameworks will be very different.

Additionally, there is much debate as to whether the Bridgland model can be successfully applied to every British river. As we shall see in later chapters, there are some rivers which appear to dispense with phase 2 of the model and have interglacial sediments sitting directly on the eroded surface of the newly cut flood plain. In some cases, phase 4 of the model is not evident. A good example of this complexity is illustrated in ongoing research by Rob Hosfield and colleagues (Hosfield, pers. comm.). The River Axe flowing through Dorset and Devon, which we will look at in later chapters, has what is known as a fill terrace system. The terraces are formed by sediment deposited in the river valley and through which the river has cut when it eroded its new floodplain. Some 20 kilometres to the west is the River Exe, also in Devon, but its terraces are known as strath terraces. A combination of factors (including tough bedrock and a thick constantly replenished bedload of sediments difficult to erode) prevents the river downcutting, even when other rivers in the area have responded to external forcing mechanisms (the Bridgland model) and begun to incise. Instead the river erodes laterally creating a wider than usual floodplain. Only when one or more of the controlling factors change (such as reduction in deposition of durable sediment combined with increase in erosive potential of the river) does the river begin to finally downcut. What is left is a strath terrace, a relict of an over-widened valley whose terrace may be bedrock, or just a thin veneer of sediment. Strath terraces present challenges for dating as the terraces themselves can significantly lag behind the external forcing mechanisms that are forming terraces in other rivers. So here we have two Middle Pleistocene rivers, flowing at the same time, and relatively close to each other, yet with very different terrace histories. Outside of Britain there are a number of major European rivers which have been interpreted in a very different way. An excellent example is the Somme river of northern France, with its suite of archaeologically rich Middle Pleistocene terraces. Pierre Antoine and colleagues (Antoine *et al.* 2000; 2003) have postulated that downcutting of each Somme terrace occurred rapidly during the early glacial phase of each climatic cycle. Antoine *et al.* (2000) construct their model on the basis of sedimentology, stratigraphic relationships, chrono-metric dating, and floral and faunal evidence. These data do not present a pattern that is easily accommodated by Bridgland's model.

I follow Bridgland's work in this book because his writings specifically engage with the archaeological record, and his interpretations therefore contextualise the Clactonian sites. His work also accepts the complexity of Pleistocene climate as represented in the DSCs, and its effect on river terrace development. But readers should be aware of the intense ongoing debate concerning how rivers should be interpreted (see Hosfield and Chambers 2005b, for an excellent review). There is little agreement as yet, and it may well be that Bridgland's model, while applicable to the Lower Thames Valley, is less useful elsewhere.

The geographical framework used in this book

This is a convenient point to introduce the approach I will take (most of the time) in describing the archaeology of the Clactonian in its later Middle Pleistocene geological and geographical context. This framework con-textualises the Clactonian sites which are described in the next chapter, as well as the four period-based chapters (Chapters 4 to 7) that follow.

I have chosen to present information by concentrating on the major river valleys for which recent research has established a chrono-stratigraphic record that can be related to the MI stages. The comparison of the chrono-stratigraphic position of the various formations and members in these dif-ferent river systems is presented in Table 2.2. For many of the smaller rivers this type of chrono-stratigraphic data is not yet available. I am aware that in following this approach I am ignoring or sidelining some important Palaeolithic sites, as well as downgrading certain river systems which may have been important to Palaeolithic hunters (and some modern geologists). Where necessary, I will move out of the river valleys to discuss key sites elsewhere.

For most of the period-based chapters I will take an anti-clockwise tour around Britain. I will begin with the Thames, and take each of the three regions of that river in turn. The Upper Thames is taken to be that stretch of the river from its source to the Goring Gap, see Figure 2.8. The Middle Thames is that stretch of the river from the Gap to the River Lea, a north bank tributary flowing through London. I will also, where necessary, look

Table 2.2 The correlations between different geological members and formations in different river systems in relation to the glacial–interglacial cycle as shown in the MI sequence of the deep sea cores

MIS	Stage name	Upper Thames	Middle Thames	Lower Thames	Trent *1	Trent *2	Severn	Warwickshire Avon	Solent *3
1	Holocene	Alluvium	Floodplain	Tilbury alluvial deposits	Terrace and floodplain	Floodplain	Alluvium	Alluvium	Alluvium
late 2	Devensian	Northmoor Gravel	Shepperton Gravel	Shepperton Gravel	Holme Pierrepont Allenton S+G Beeston S+G	Holme Pierrepont S+G Scarle S+G	Power House T1 Worcester T2	T1 T2	
4–2				Upper East Tilbury Marshes Gravel			Holt Heath T3	Wasperton T3	St Leonard's Farm gravel – upper
5.4– 5.1		? Upper Eynsham Gravels – locally	Isleworth Upper Kempton Park						
5.5	Ipswichian	Eynsham Gravels	Brentford	Trafalgar Square Peckham	Crown Hill Beds	Fulbeck S+G		New Inn (Eckington)	? Pennington IGD ? Stone Point IGD
6		Stanton Harcourt Gravels	Lower Kempton Park Upper Taplow	Lower East Tilbury Marshes Gravel Upper Mucking Gravel	Borrowash S+G Egginton Common S+G	Balderton S+G	Kidderminster Station T4	Cropthorne T4	Pennington Lower Gravel St Leonard's Farm Gravel – lower Milford-on-Sea
7	Aveley/West Thurrock Interglacial	Stanton Harcourt Channel IGD		Aveley IGD West Thurrock IGD		Thorpe on the Hill beds		Ailstone Strensham	Hordle/Stanswood Bay (MIS= 7.2)
8		Lower Summertown-Radley – locally Upper Wolvercote – locally	Lower Taplow Upper Lynch Hill	Lower Mucking Gravel Upper Corbets Tey Gravel (2)	Ockbrook S+G Etwall S+G	Whisby Farm S+G	Bushley Green Gravels T5	Pershore Gravels T5	Downton/Tom's Down

MIS	Purfleet	?Wolvercote Channel IGD		Purfleet-Grays IGD			Bushley Green IGD	?Pershore IGD	Beckton Farm (MIS= 9.2)
9								?Pershore IGD	
10		Wolvercote Gravel	Lower Lynch Hill Upper Boyn Hill	Lower Corbets Tey Gravel (1) Upper Orsett Heath Gravel			Spring Hill T6		Old Milton
11	Swanscombe Interglacial	?Wolvercote Channel IGD		Swanscombe and Clacton IGD					
12		Hanborough Gravel ?Wallingford fan gravels	Lower Boyn Hill Black Park Gravel Winter Hill	Lower Orsett Heath Gravel Black Park below Orsett Heath level St Osyth	Eagle Moor S+G Findern Clay Oadby Till Thrussington Till	Eagle Moor S+G Skellingthorpe Clay	Woolridge T7 (= Anglian outwash)		Mount Pleasant
13									Setley Plain (MIS= 13.2)
14									
15									
16									

Notes: (1) – equivalent of Little Thurrock Gravel

(2) – part of which will be equivalent to Botany Gravel at Purfleet

Trent *1 – Trent (above Nottingham) and lower Dove and Derwent

Trent *2 – from Newark to Lincoln

Solent*3 – terraces between the Avon and the Test

IGD – interglacial deposits

S+G – sands and gravels

T – terrace

Sources: Based on Wymer (1999); Bridgland et al. (2004); Bridgland, pers. comm.; Bridgland et al. (2001); Westaway et al. (2006)

Figure 2.8 Map of selected British rivers discussed in the text.

at sites in the Kennet Valley. The Lower Thames is from the Lea to the estuary. The terrace sequence for the Lower Thames has been presented in Figure 2.7; that for the Upper Thames and Middle Thames is presented in Figures 2.9A and 2.9B respectively.

From the Lower Thames, I will move northwards into East Anglia. In this rich Lower Palaeolithic landscape I will discuss a number of sites related to river terraces (Figure 2.10A), as well as those related to lakes and estuaries.

After East Anglia, I will move westwards to that part of England bounded by the Chiltern Hills in the south and the southern portion of the Trent basin in the north. Although there are many rivers draining this area, I will focus on the Nene and the River Great Ouse. Emphasis will be on relating this area, and East Anglia, to the Lower Thames Valley sequence.

In the Midlands, I will concentrate on the drainage basin of the Trent

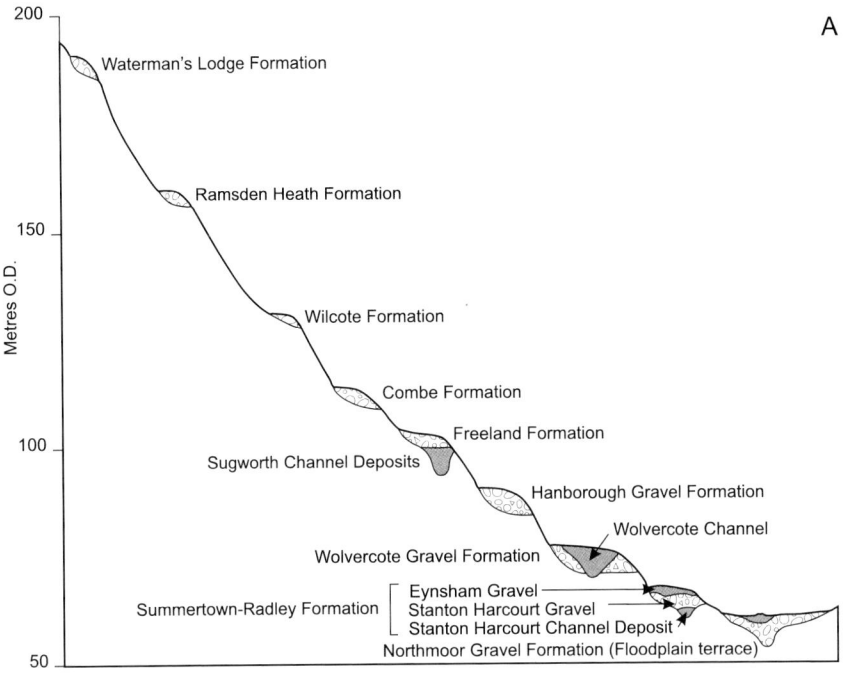

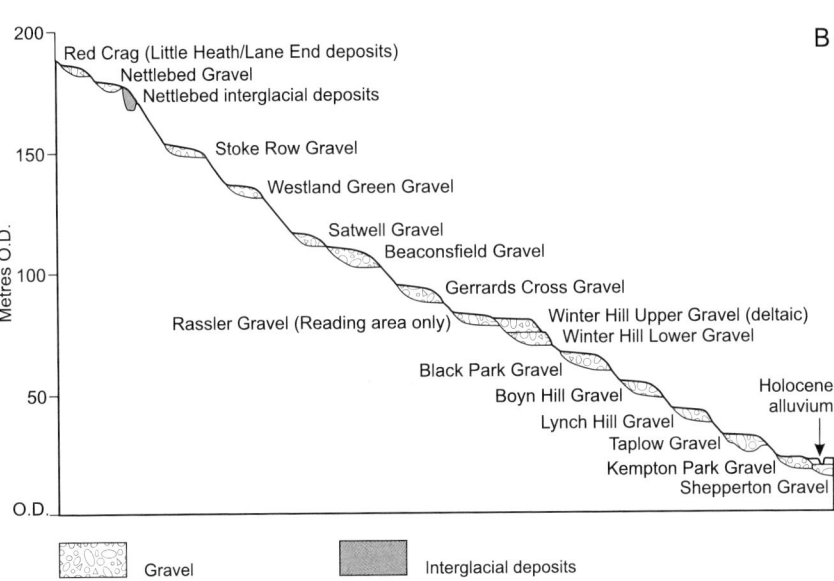

Figure 2.9 A: Schematic of terrace sequence for the Upper Thames Valley. B: Schematic of terrace sequence for the Middle Thames.

Note: Used with permission.

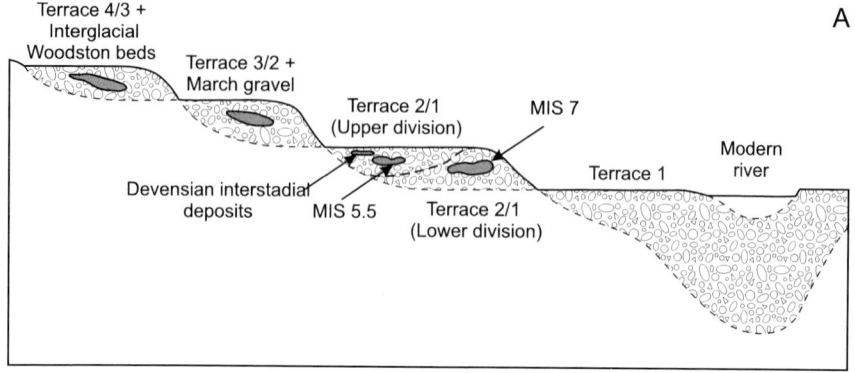

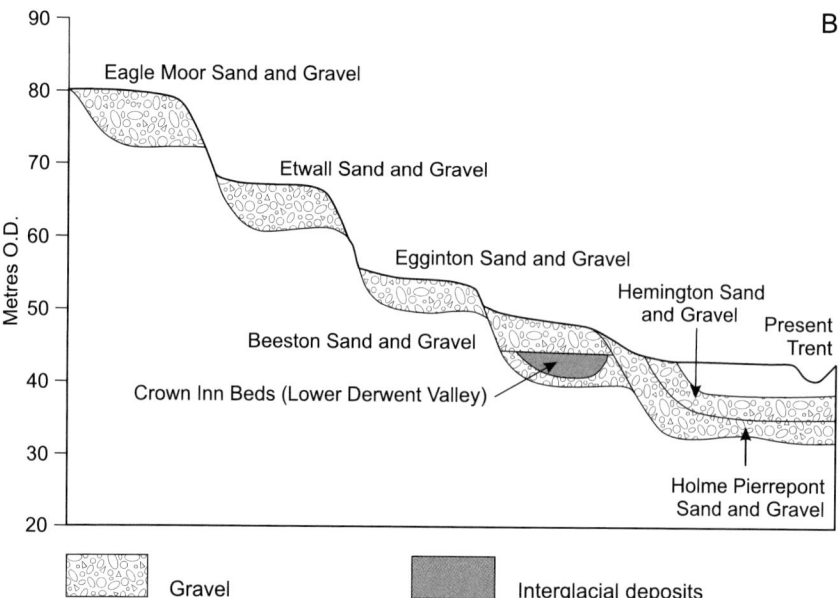

Figure 2.10 A: Schematic of terrace sequence for a typical East Anglian river. B: Schematic of terrace sequence for the Trent

Note: Used with permission.

(Figure 2.10B). In the west of Britain I will only concentrate on the Severn–Avon system (Figure 2.11A).

Moving southwards, I will focus on the Dorset River Axe when appropriate, but for the most part I will only concentrate on the Solent river basin system (Figure 2.11B). I will also look at the Kentish Stour to the east of the Thames Valley when necessary.

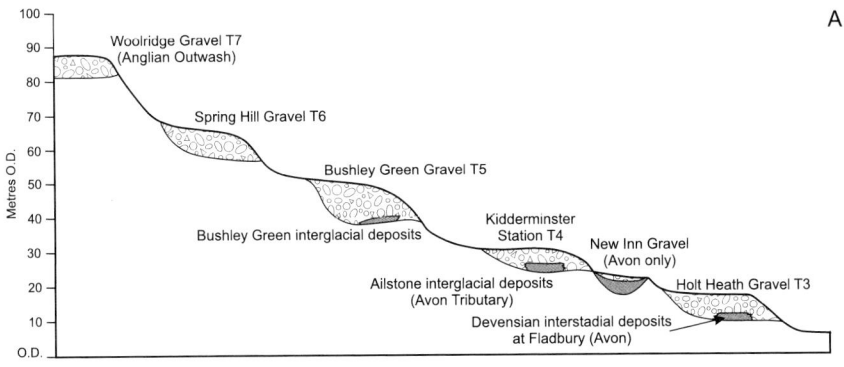

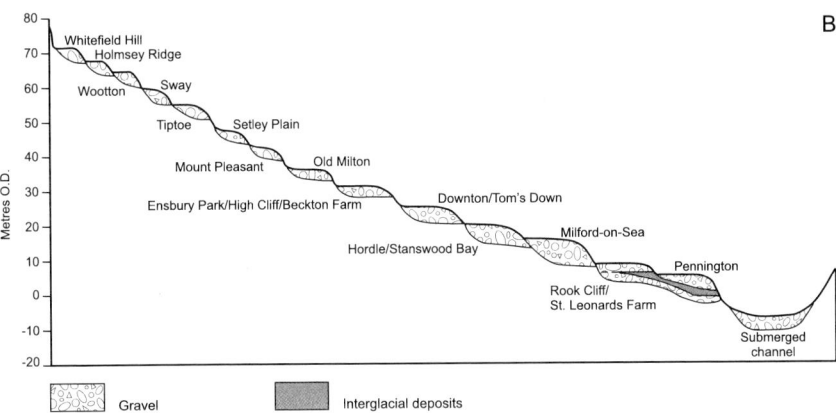

Figure 2.11 A: Schematic of terrace sequence for the Severn–Avon rivers. B: Schematic of terrace sequence for the Solent river.

Note: Used with permission.

The mammalian framework

Before closing this chapter there is one further type of evidence I would like to introduce, that of Pleistocene fauna, and, in particular, the data provided by the large and small mammals. This has traditionally been a critical line of evidence in chrono-stratigraphic studies of the Middle Pleistocene. Animal lineages evolve by natural selection (Mayr 2001). The appearance of new lineages as well as the extinction of old ones can provide important potential marker points. At face value, mammals should provide a time- and environment-sensitive barometer that could reinforce other chrono-stratigraphic analyses. Naturally there are problems. Rates of evolutionary change are not constant, and absence from a specific location need not imply extinction. Some local populations may become extinct long before the species does. Additionally, mammal specialists have to infer what ancient environments were like by projecting the modern tolerances and habitat preferences of extant species back into the past. The preferences of extinct species can only be guessed at by analogy. Nevertheless, faunal analysis represents a critical line of evidence in reconstructing ancient environments and in chrono-stratigraphic studies. An excellent introduction is presented in Klein (1999).

In a paper in 1989, Andy Currant suggested a grouping of particularly important mammal lineages in a time-progressive sequence (Currant 1989). Each group corresponded with a specific time period, and was based on a collection of sites whose mammal assemblages were more akin to each other than those in the other groups. Needless to say, these were not the only animals present at the sites in each group, merely the most significant chronologically. What was important about this paper was that it did not attempt to shoehorn the groups into the pollen-based terrestrial sequence of two post-Anglian interglacials that was still in vogue at that time. Nor did it attempt to align the groups with MI stages, although it did recognise the complexity in climate history that the DSC record represented.

More recently, Danielle Schreve (2001) has re-examined the faunas of the British later Middle Pleistocene and identified significant groupings of animals that she calls mammal assemblage zones (MAZs). Five post-Anglian MAZs were identified, which she linked to the MI sequence. These were the Swanscombe MAZ (MIS 11); the Purfleet MAZ (MIS 9); the Ponds Farm MAZ (early MIS 7); the Sandy Lane MAZ (late MIS 7); and the Joint Mitnor Cave MAZ (MIS 5.5). The scheme clearly lends itself to Bridgland's chrono-stratigraphic model of the Lower Thames terrace sequence.

The potential of using mammal data is highlighted by the possibility of distinguishing distinct sub-phases within an interglacial. Schreve's data have suggested that two MAZs can be identified in MIS 7, the Ponds Farm MAZ which corresponds to the earlier part of the interglacial, and the Sandy Lane MAZ which belongs in the later part. Figure 2.2 does show a major stadial present within the climatic history of this interglacial. But whether these MAZs can be directly related to the MI sub-stages remains to be seen. One interesting result of dividing up the faunal assemblages of MIS 7 is the different character of the two sub-stages. The earlier Ponds Farm faunal assemblage is a more enclosed woodland fauna, while the Sandy Lane fauna is characteristic of more open conditions. Important corroboration for aspects of this model are provided by data from molluscs (Keen 2001).

In the same vein as Schreve's MAZs, Andy Currant and Roger Jacobi (2001) provide a similar assessment of the faunal assemblages of the last interglacial (MIS 5.5) and of the subsequent stages within the Devensian glaciation (MIS 5.4–2). Together these two papers provide a modern and comprehensive history of the British faunal record from the late Middle Pleistocene onwards. One important aspect of Currant and Jacobi's work concerns the occupation of Britain after MIS 6. It has long been suggested that hominins were absent from the last interglacial (MIS 5.5). One of its characteristic mammals is the hippopotamus. No artefacts have ever been securely associated with MIS 5.5 faunal assemblages containing hippo. In fact, no hominin remains, or artefacts, have ever been found associated with any securely dated MIS 5.5 faunal assemblages. After exhaustive research identifying faunal assemblages of distinct climatic phases post-dating MIS 5.5, Currant and Jacobi have suggested that hominins were absent from Britain for the whole of the period from MIS 6 down to late MIS 4. This suggests that Britain was abandoned by hominins for well over a 100 kyr. Lithic artefacts only begin to be associated with faunal remains again in late MIS 4 and early MIS 3, when it can be assumed their makers were the Neanderthals of the Later Middle Palaeolithic (see Chapter 1).

One of the most significant aspects of recent mammal research has been the development of what has become known as the 'vole clock'. Evolutionary change is much slower in larger mammals compared to smaller ones, in particular shrews, voles, and other small rodents. As individuals, these animals live short and energetic lives, and consequently any changes in morphology resulting from natural selection will occur quickly. Most of the really significant evolutionary changes seen in small mammals have occurred in their teeth as these creatures have adapted to changing habitats. One lineage that has proved particularly important is that of Mimomys savini, an extinct form of water vole. Its molars possess roots, and a particular occlusal (the biting surface of the tooth) pattern. Some time between 600 and 500 kya (Klein 1999), the molars of this species underwent a distinct change and became rootless. From this time onwards their molar teeth would grow continuously throughout the life of the animal. This change is considered significant enough to represent a speciation event and the name given to the vole with rootless molars, the lineal descendent of Mimomys savini, is Arvicola terrestris cantiana. This species is the ancestor of the modern water vole Arvicola terrestris terrestris. The difference between these latter two is in the thinning of the enamel on portions of the molars over time.

The timing of the Mimomys–Arvicola transition has been worked out on evidence from small mammal assemblages from German and Dutch Middle Pleistocene sites (Preece and Parfitt 2000) which can be securely located in time by other dating techniques. An application of this to British pre-Anglian stratigraphy is presented in Figure 4.2, and discussed more fully in Chapter 4. Another important lineage that undergoes change is the narrow-nosed vole Microtus gregaloides. This evolves into Microtus gregalis. This transition is somewhat later than Mimomys–Arvicola, but nonetheless is complete by the beginning of the Anglian glaciation. This latter transition may be a way of distinguishing between the two pre-Anglian temperate phases that occur within the *Arvicola* zone. M. *gregaloides* is present in the earlier temperate phase, while M. *gregalis* is present in the latter. This will also be discussed further in Chapter 4. Schreve (2001) suggests that post-Anglian changes to *Arvicola* can be identified in MIS 11, 9, and 7 by changing thicknesses in molar enamel. The vole clock has been particularly important in determining the age of some of the earliest hominin sites in Britain.

3

THE CLACTONIAN SITES IN THEIR PHYSICAL CONTEXT

The old river in its broad reach rested unruffled at the decline of the day, after ages of good service done to the race that peopled its banks, spread out in the tranquil dignity of a waterway leading to the uttermost ends of the earth. We looked at the venerable stream not in the vivid flush of a short day that comes and departs forever, but in the august light of abiding memories.

(Conrad 1973: 6)

Introduction

In this chapter I will take a critical look at the archaeological sites that have been labelled Clactonian. My purpose here is to determine which, if any, of these sites merits the title of a non-biface assemblage. From this we will be able to assess the strength of the arguments that are marshalled in favour of a non-biface Clactonian assemblage type or tradition.

The Clactonian sites in MIS 11

Clacton-on-Sea

Clacton does not represent one site, rather it is a series of localities with archaeology, fauna, or other Pleistocene environmental data. The various sites are located on the map in Figure 3.1. The localities sample some 3 km along the foreshore and hinterland between Lion Point and the location of the West Cliff foreshore site, just to the south-west of Clacton Pier. On geological and faunal grounds these localities are considered to be broadly contemporary.

Detailed site histories have recently been published in Wymer (1985), Bridgland (1994), and Bridgland et al. (1999), so here I will briefly set the scene for each locality. After initial observations on the geology (Brown 1838) and archaeology (Kenworthy 1898), it was Hazzledine Warren who

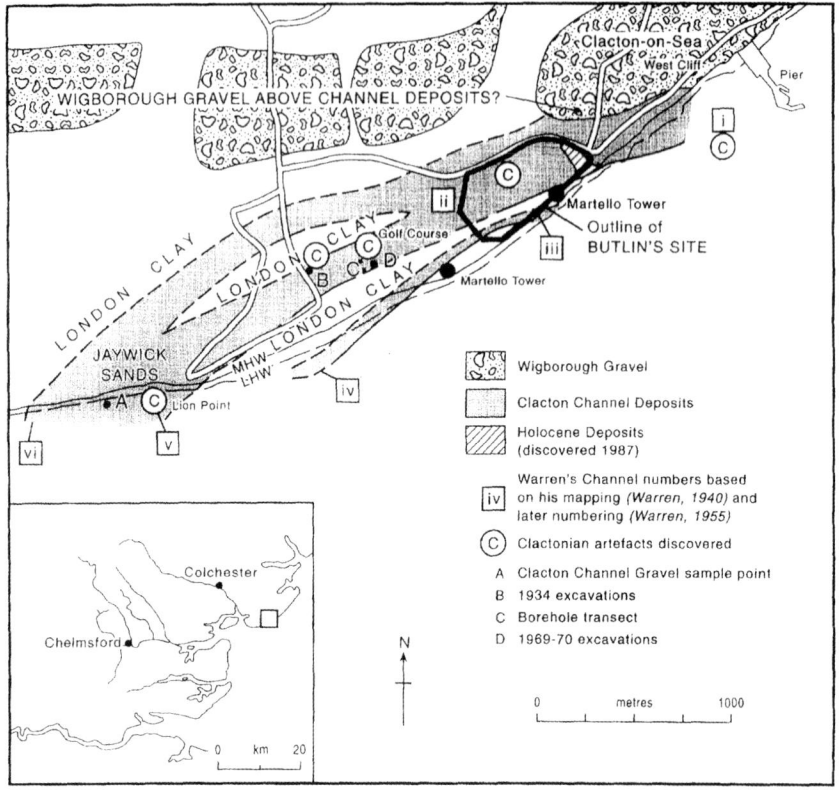

Figure 3.1 The various archaeological localities at Clacton-on-Sea.

Note: Used with permission.

began to systematically observe geological exposures (see Chapters 10 and 11; Warren 1923), and collect artefacts (Warren 1922), finally coining the term Clactonian (Warren 1926) to describe the non-handaxe assemblage type he believed was present at Clacton. Warren's early work was centred on the West Cliff locality, where he observed exposures on the foreshore and in the adjacent cliffs, especially after storm erosion. He later expanded his collecting activities to Lion Point where again he collected from low tide exposures of the buried Pleistocene channel (Warren 1932). Warren believed that a series of five buried Pleistocene channels could be identified between Lion Point and the West Cliff exposures (see Figure 3.1). Two of the channels, iii and iv, represented separate points along a single smaller channel which was later in date than the Clacton Channel, and related to the River Colne (Bridgland *et al.* 1999). The remaining channels are actually different points along the length of a single major river channel which

Warren identified with the Thames (Warren 1932; he originally believed it was a silted up tributary of the main river).

Clacton-on-Sea – West Cliff

This was Warren's original collecting locality (which he called channel i). A schematic section is shown in Figure 3.2. Both his first major publication on the stratigraphy at Clacton (1923), and his final definitive paper (Warren 1955) described the sequence at the West Cliff. The significance of this location was it retained the most complete sequence of deposits from the whole of the Clacton area. The Clactonian industry and the fauna and other types of environmental evidence were found in the basal deposits, the Lower Freshwater Beds. These were mostly flinty gravels in a sticky clay matrix. These were overlain by the Upper Freshwater Beds which were mostly sands and clays. Together the Freshwater Beds were about 11 m

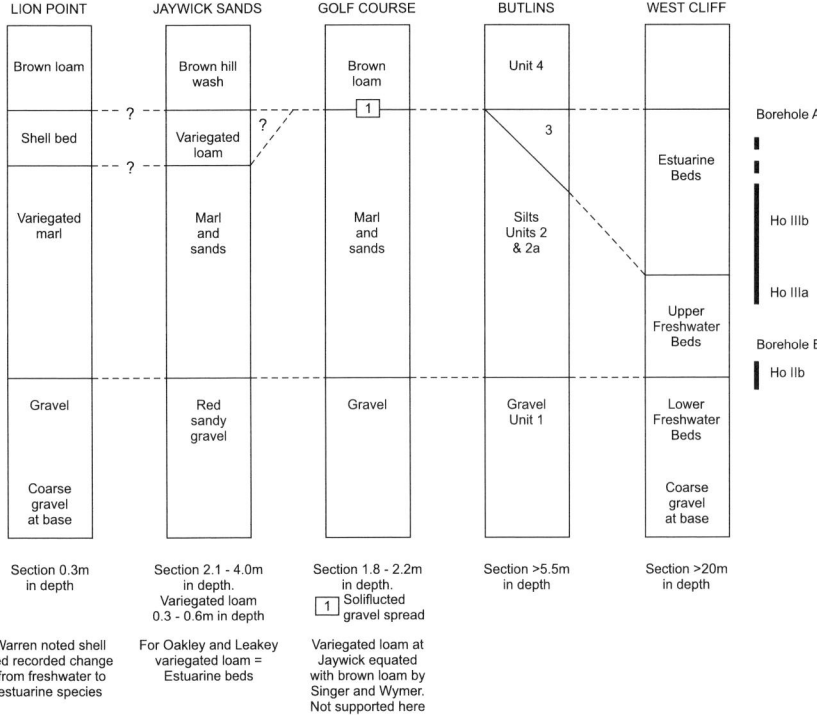

Figure 3.2 Comparative stratigraphic sequence for the various archaeological localities at Clacton-on-Sea.

Note: Horizontal and vertical relationships not to scale. Diagram is intended to clarify unit relationships and nothing else. Pollen data from boreholes at West Cliff shown to right of section.

deep. These were overlain by the Estuarine Beds, which were up to 9 m of clays and sands which contained occasional lenses of freshwater shells in the lower portion. These beds indicated that sea level had risen and that the lower reaches of the river at Clacton had become part of the Thames estuary. Fuller descriptions of the stratigraphy are to be found in Warren (1955), Wymer (1985), Bridgland (1994) and Bridgland *et al.* (1999).

Warren (1932) believed that the gravels at West Cliff were an extension of the same gravels present at Lion Point, in other words, the Lower Freshwater Beds were present at both sites; the river's course described an arc between the two places. At Lion Point erosion and compression of the sediments had reduced the sequence to less than 0.5 m in depth. However, at the West Cliff the full depth of deposits were preserved. One significant difference between the two locations was that the Freshwater Beds at the West Cliff contained abundant organic remains. So prevalent was one species that the Lower Freshwater Beds at the West Cliff had become known as the *Elephas antiquus* gravels – the elephant beds. Also plant remains, seeds, and even logs of wood were described by Warren (1923). His explanation for why they should occur here and not at Lion Point was that the curve between the two sites represented a meander bend with material accumulating in the apex of the bend at the West Cliff (Warren 1932).

It was from the West Cliff that the first pollen diagram for the British Middle Pleistocene was published (Pike and Godwin 1953), generated from the evidence of two bore holes. Borehole A, on the cliffs above the beach, sampled the estuarine deposits throughout their full depth and into the first metre of the underlying Upper Freshwater Beds, see Figure 3.2.

Pollen analysis was introduced briefly in the last chapter. It was a major chrono-stratigraphic tool in the 1970s and 1980s prior to the wide-scale acceptance of the DSCs. Its supporters advocated the recognition of only two post-Anglian/pre-Devensian interglacials. Each interglacial went through a set sequence of development, as plants, grasses and trees re-colonised the freshly de-glaciated landscape. The broad sequence of development was the same for each interglacial – see Figure 3.3A, and was for the most part identified on the basis of tree (arboreal) pollen. But there were important differences between the three interglacials. Particular tree species may have been well represented in one, but poorly represented in another; some tree species dominated their forests at different times in different interglacials. Thus it was in the detail that different interglacials could be distinguished from each other.

Pollen analysis also provided a powerful relative dating technique for placing archaeological assemblages within specific sub-divisions of an interglacial. According to the pollen data, the sediments from the boreholes at Clacton-on-Sea dated to the Hoxnian interglacial, Figure 3.3B. The detailed pattern of forest development for the Hoxnian is set out in Table 3.1. This

A

Early glacial	Herb dominated
Post-temperate pollen zone IV	Birch-pine forest
Late temperate - pollen zone III	Mixed deciduous - coniferous forest
Early temperate - pollen zone II	Deciduous forest
Pre-temperate - pollen zone I	Birch-pine forest
Late glacial	Herb dominated

B

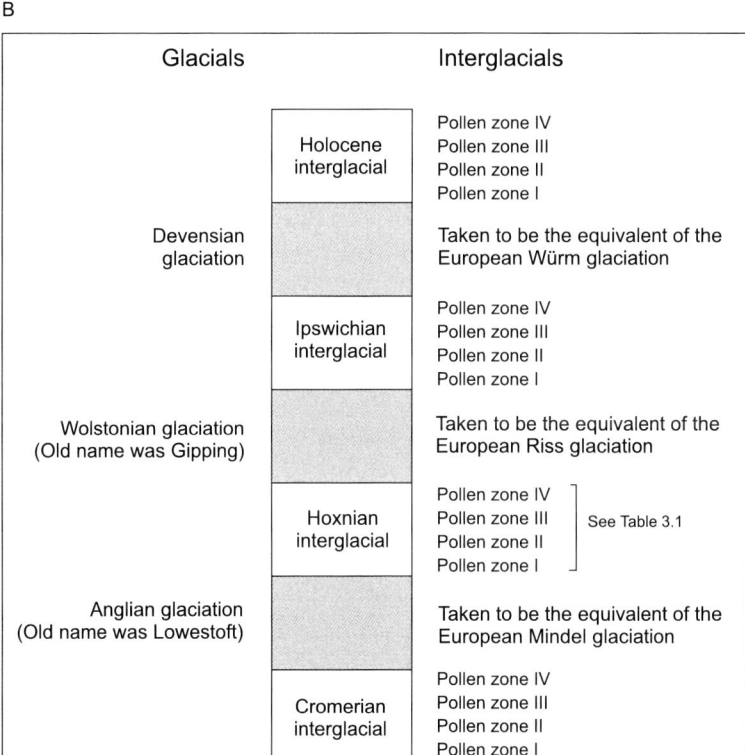

Figure 3.3 The traditional terrestrial pollen-based sequence as promoted during the 1970s and early 1980s. A is the basic development of forest common to all interglacials. B the glacial–interglacial sequence of the traditional terrestrial pollen-based sequence.

Table 3.1 A generalised interpretation of the pollen diagram for the Hoxnian interglacial as it would have been understood in the 1970s and early 1980s

Stage name	Stage designation	Environment – forest development	Clacton	Swanscombe	Hoxne
Wolstonian (originally called Gipping)	G		? park tundra		Upper Industry? ▲
Post Temperate	Ho IV		Coniferous forest (open) Pine and birch woodland	Upper Middle Gravels ▲	Upper Industry? ▲
Late Temperate	Ho III	IIIb	Fir increasing	West Cliff Estuarine Beds **A** ↑	Lower Middle Gravels ▲	↑ ? Lower Industry ▲ ↓ ?
		IIIa	Deciduous and yew woodland	Upper Freshwater Beds ↓		
Early Temperate	Ho II	IIc	Grassland (NAP) Deciduous and yew woodland			A handaxe with Ho IIc pollen adhering ▲
		IIb	Alder and oak forest	Base of Upper Freshwater Beds at West Cliff, and top of Lower Freshwater Beds ●	**B** ↑ ↓ Lower Loam ● Lower Gravels ● ↓ ?	
		IIa				
Pre-Temperate	Ho I		Pine and birch woodland Coniferous forest	Golf Course marl ●	Solifluction at base of Lower Gravels? ●	
Late Anglian (originally called Lowestoft)	L		? park tundra	Golf Course gravel ●		

Notes: Circles indicate Clactonian artefacts, triangles indicate handaxes. Hoxne Upper Industry was never successfully located in the system. A + B = West Cliff boreholes. NAP = non-arboreal pollen phase – period of extensive East Anglian deforestation. Table is still broadly applicable to temperate portion of MIS 11 in today's framework of interpretation. However, there are doubts about Golf Course being late Anglian or Ho I/Pre-Temperate

was worked out in the 1970s. Although the three sites in Table 3.1 would today be dated to MIS 11, the pattern of forest development is still valid.

The Estuarine Beds were assigned to pollen zone III, the Late Temperate, see Table 3.1. This gave a precise age within the interglacial for the sea level rise that created the Estuarine Beds (early in pollen sub-zone IIIb). The portion of the Upper Freshwater Beds sampled by borehole A in the cliff was dated to the earlier phase of the Late Temperate (pollen zone IIIa). The second bore hole (B) was drilled on the foreshore, and it sampled the lower part of the Upper Freshwater Beds (Bridgland *et al.* 1999), and possibly the top of the Lower Freshwater Beds (Turner and Kerney 1971). Its pollen spectra suggested these deposits belonged in pollen zone IIb. Since the Clactonian was mostly associated with the Lower Freshwater Beds it too was equated with pollen zone IIb.

Taken together, the environment of the Freshwater Beds indicated warm and fully temperate conditions with an abundant large mammal fauna including elephant, rhinoceros, bovid and deer, all inhabiting a wooded river bank.

Hazzledine Warren's notebooks, curated in the British Museum, make it clear that a small number of handaxes can be associated with the Freshwater Beds (Wymer 1985; McNabb 1992b; 1996b). The evidence for this takes the form of three entries describing bifaces found on the foreshore at West Cliff between 1911 and 1914. In two cases the bifaces are described by Warren as having been recovered from the *Elephas antiquus* gravels. The third is presumably an equivalent of those artefacts at Lion Point that Warren catalogued as being found further up the beach but which were derived from the Clacton Channel deposits (see below). Despite the abundant environmental remains, the archaeology at the West Cliff site is in secondary context, the stone tools have been derived from elsewhere, although in most cases they need not have come from very far away.

The Freshwater Beds and the Estuarine Beds are interglacial deposits and therefore represent phase 3 of Bridgland's model.

Clacton-on-Sea – Butlins Holiday Camp

This has been fully described by Bridgland *et al.* (1999) – the site is shown on Figure 3.1. The sediments investigated are situated close to the southern bank of the main channel, and parallel the situation at the Golf Course c. 1 km to the south-west (see below). The Pleistocene deposits were revealed in deep drainage trenches dug by developers building on the site of the old holiday camp. Unit 1 (see Figure 3.2) at the base of the sequence represented a sandy gravel which was associated with the Lower Freshwater Beds. It contained flint artefacts and fauna. It was overlain by unit 2, a silt and clayey-silt deposit with many shells in its lower sections. Some were bivalves with both halves still articulated as in life. This was equated with the Upper Freshwater

Beds. Unit 3 were the Estuarine Beds, which were only represented in one corner of the site. They were orangey clayey silts. The base of this layer, which was eroded into unit 2, was a lag deposit of comminuted shells. Unit 3 was interpreted as the feather edge of the Estuarine Beds. Unit 4 was a stiff brown clay which may have been a solifluction deposit (sediment that has sludged down slope usually indicating cold conditions), originating from the adjacent bank. Alternatively, it may represent the in-situ alteration of the upper parts of the Clacton Channel deposits by pedogenesis (soil formation). It is probably a lateral equivalent of the brown clays that overlie the Golf Course, Jaywick Sands and Lion Point to the south-west (see below).

The main significance of these investigations was their position part way between the two classic areas of West Cliff and Lion Point. The remnant of the Estuarine Beds in the sediments at the east end of the site demonstrated that this deposit originally extended well beyond the area of the West Cliff, but it has been eroded away. The investigations also provided information on the MIS 11 rise in sea level noted above. These data contradict those of Pike and Godwin's borehole A; the data from Butlins suggest the marine transgression may be somewhat earlier – pollen zone Ho IIc/IIIa rather than early in IIIb (Bridgland, in Bridgland *et al.* 1999).

The archaeology from the site is identical to that from the Golf Course described below. There were no bifaces present (Wymer, in Bridgland *et al.* 1999). Beds 2, 3 and 4 may have been subjected to cold climate periglacial conditions. In other words after the temperate sediments had accumulated, there was at least one period of intensely cold climate before the whole site was completely buried.

This site probably samples the river's gravel bed at the southern margin of the channel (see Figure 3.1).

Clacton-on-Sea – Golf Course Site

This site represents the only locality at Clacton which has in-situ archaeological material exposed in area excavations. It was excavated in 1969 and 1970 by John Wymer and Ronald Singer (Singer *et al.* 1973). The sedimentary sequence at the Golf Course was relatively simple (see Figure 3.2). At the base was just under a metre of sandy gravel with artefacts and bones, and this was overlain by what the excavators described as a marl, which is a calcareous (rich in calcium carbonate) silty clay. These two deposits represent the Lower and Upper Freshwater Beds respectively. A localised patch of gravel overlay the marl and contained bones and artefacts. It was c. 10–20 cm thick and probably represents a wedge of soliflucted material that spread over the marl's surface from the adjacent bank. This was overlain by a brown fissile clay.

The excavators suggested that hominins temporarily occupied the surface of a gravel bar adjacent to the river bank. They made and used stone tools on this gravel surface and then left them behind when they moved on. The stone tools were very fresh in appearance, and distributed mostly in the upper part of the gravel. More rolled and damaged flintwork was spread evenly throughout the depth of the gravel. Since the location was attractive to animals coming down to the water's edge to drink, the excavators suggested that animal trampling pushed fresh artefacts down into the body of the gravel. There were Clactonian artefacts in the marl as well as the gravel, and these were in all probability derived from the gravels. Refitting flintwork between the surface of the gravels and the marls supported this. For the excavators this represented a single site in disturbed primary context.

The in-situ character of the flintwork from the Golf Course site was based, primarily, on two pieces of evidence:

- high proportion of unrolled flintwork;
- unrolled flintwork concentrated near top of gravel.

Further support for the in-situ character of the assemblage was offered by:

- microwear;
- refitting artefacts.

Condition of the artefacts at the Golf Course site

The system of assessing artefact condition was based on work done by John Wymer (1976), and represented one of the first attempts to quantify the damage that fluvial transport could inflict on a flint artefact. Wymer concentrated attention on the arêtes or ridges between flake scars on flakes and cores. If there were small facets or pits on the ridges, then these were interpreted as the result of clast collision within the river. If the pits were in excess of 2 mm in size, the artefact was *very rolled*; between 1 and 2 mm, the artefact was *rolled*; if pits were present but no bigger than 1 mm the artefact was *slightly rolled*; if the arêtes were slightly worn but not pitted, then the piece was *sharp*; and if the arêtes were as fresh as when first knapped, the artefact was in *mint* condition. Wymer's data for artefact condition in the gravel is presented in Figure 3.4A. It is clear from the figure that there are many more unrolled artefacts than rolled ones, and that the frequency of artefacts drops dramatically with increased depth. Wymer argued that the unrolled artefacts were the disturbed remains of the in-situ site, while the rolled artefacts represented an older phase of occupation in the vicinity, the artefacts from which became incorporated in the gravel as the river migrated over its flood plain.

Work by Harding *et al.* (1987) showed that experimental bifaces, placed in a gravel river at times of high flood, could be transported up to 100 m, and lose over a centimetre from their entire circumference through attrition damage. However, the arêtes were only slightly damaged – they would

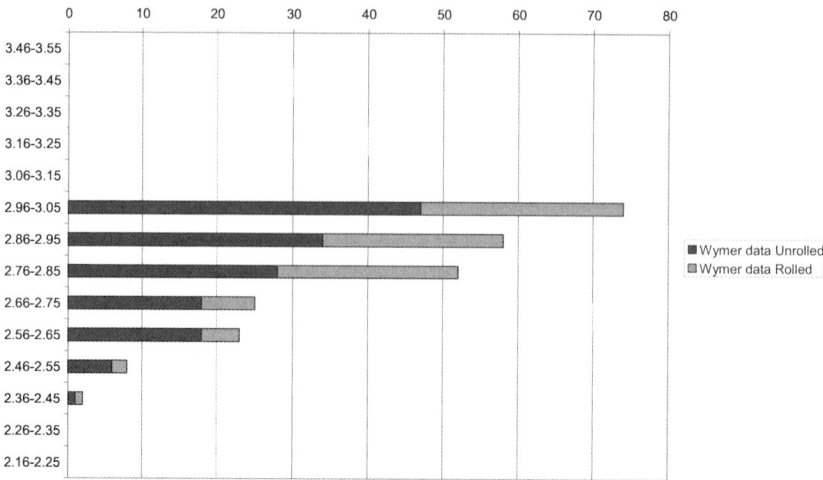

A   Frequency of rolled and unrolled artefacts in Lower Freshwater Beds at Golf Course Clacton-on-Sea

Note: n = 242, artefacts from centre of site between eastings 48 and 58 and northings 18 and 25.

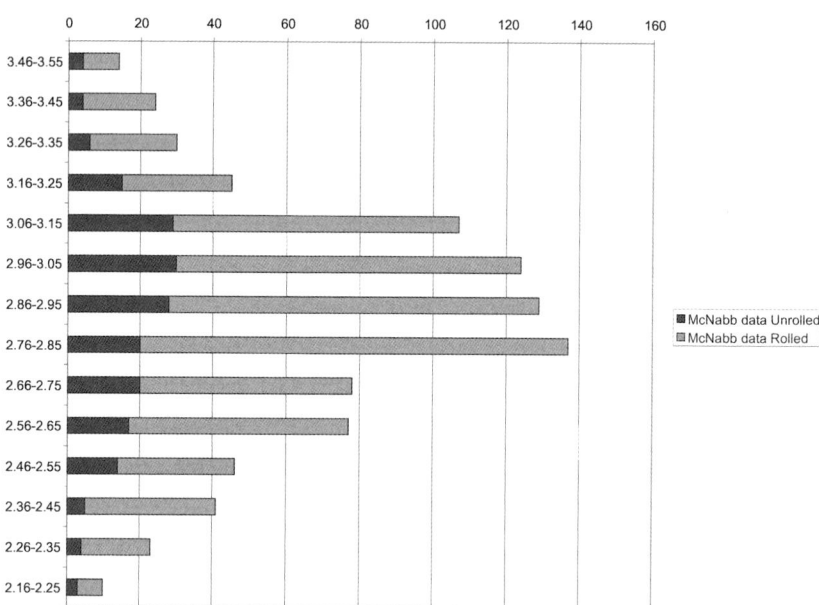

B   Frequency of rolled and unrolled flint artefacts in Lower Freshwater Beds at Golf Course Clacton-on-Sea

Note: n = 885, artefacts from whole of site.

Figure 3.4 Artefact condition at the Golf Course site, Clacton-on-Sea.

Note: Vertical scale is in units of 10 cms calculated above sea level (OS datum = 0.0 m OD). In 3.4A Wymer's mint and fresh categories for artefact condition have been grouped together as unrolled. His remaining categories have been grouped together as rolled.

have been classed as sharp or slightly rolled. Subsequent work by Rob Hosfield and Jenny Chambers (Chambers 2003; Hosfield and Chambers 2005a) has shown just how complicated this process can be. The original experiments were done on handaxes. Their edges would have been artificially shaped during manufacture. So chipping of the edge as a result of transport damage would be hard to see. Unretouched flakes and cores have no such shaping and any transport damage that occurred would be visible on the artefact's edge.

The system I employed when analysing the Golf Course site was slightly different to that of Wymer. If the edges of the flint artefact showed no evidence of damage, then the piece was unrolled. If the edges showed patches of continuous or semi-continuous edge damage, often abrupt and/or irregular in size and appearance, then the piece was considered to be rolled. No further subdivision was made within this category, given the results from the Harding et al. experiments. The data for condition following this system are presented in Figure 3.4B. Wymer restricted his analysis to the centre of the site, whereas I used all the available artefacts from the gravels. The horizontal surface of the gravel bar in Figure 3.4 is in the interval 2.96–3.05 m OD, this was what Wymer used as the gravel surface for his study. The artefacts above this in Figure 3.4 represent those in the thin gravel veneers that clung to the sloping sides of the channel. The data from my study clearly show that the frequency of rolled material is much greater than suggested by Wymer's methodology. Furthermore, the concentration of unrolled material in the upper part of the unit is nowhere near as apparent.

So what does this mean? I do not dispute the presence of in-situ flintwork. The refitting of cores to flakes (Keeley 1980; Wymer 1985) proves this. Nor do I dispute that activity occurred on the gravel's surface, again the refits demonstrate this along with the evidence of microwear on some of the stone tools (Keeley 1980). What I do dispute is the interpretation that the Golf Course was a single disturbed primary context site. My interpretation is as follows.

Hominins had moved up and down the river bank utilising the surfaces of gravel bars for a considerable period of time as the rolled artefacts in the Golf Course gravels indicate. These gravels were constantly being moved downstream by the river as it reworked its deposits within the confines of its own channel. This explains the relatively continuous frequency of rolled and unrolled artefacts distributed through the depth of the gravels. In my opinion, the data do not support the interpretation of a large disturbed primary context site. Singer and Wymer located their trenches at a point where a few cores and flakes were knapped on the gravel's surface. A 'background noise' of secondary context flintwork, in varying conditions, was already present throughout the gravel. The experimental work of Kathy Schick well illustrates the dangers of making too much of a few refits (Schick 1986: 276). The cores and flakes are evidence of one or more fleeting visits by small groups of hominins to an active gravel surface prior to that surface being buried. This was not one specific site, but the accumulation of many. Circumstantial evidence for this is present in the form of a small number of flakes which show patination – a surface discoloration on a flint which results from exposure to the elements. These pieces must have lain on the gravel surface for some time before being incorporated into the gravel and moved downstream as the flood plain underwent reorganisation. A few of these pieces show more recent re-flaking. In other words, they were old artefacts that had been re-exposed, picked up, and then flaked again. Such a scenario as this would also explain why chips (pieces = < 20 mm in length) are present, but in small numbers, 61 were identified in this study from the gravel. Schick's work (ibid.) demonstrates that thousands of chips should be present.

The Golf Course assemblage comprises cores and flakes, with no evidence of classic handaxes or of thinning debitage. One possible non-classic handaxe is present (Singer et al. 1973: Figure 19, No. 52) – but this is an enigmatic piece. Non-classic handaxes will be explained in more detail when discussing Swanscombe, below.

Rather than one site frozen in time, the Golf Course is a snap-shot of a resting-moment in a dynamic fluvial environment.

Finally, there is plenty of evidence for cold climate activity in the Golf Course sediments, though just how many periods of cold conditions are represented is open to debate. At least one episode must post-date the deposition of the marl as a large ice wedge cast penetrates the whole depth of the marl and most of the gravel. The soliflucted gravel on the marl surface may date to this time as well. On the channel bank the London Clay bedrock and the marl were contorted together. But is this a post-marl MIS 11 stadial, or the onset of the MIS 10 glaciation? We simply do not know.

Clacton-on-Sea – Jaywick Sands

The 1934 excavations here were published in 1937 by Kenneth Oakley and Mary Leakey (Oakley and Leakey 1937). A series of seven test pits were excavated from the northern bank of the palaeo-channel towards the centre of the river. Two further test pits, and the foundation trenches of a house nearby were also investigated. In addition, a bore hole survey extended the investigations across the whole width of the Clacton Channel. For our purposes the stratigraphy has been broken down into three major units which are presented in Figure 3.2. A series of higher loams (hill-wash), the equivalent of the brown loams found elsewhere, overlay variegated loams (equated with the Estuarine Beds by the excavators), in turn overlying marls, and sands which were the equivalent of the Upper Freshwater Beds. A basal reddish coloured gravel represents the Lower Freshwater Beds, the equivalent of the gravel at the Golf Course, Butlins and at the West Cliff.

The archaeology represents rolled flakes and cores from the channel. There was no extensive spread of flintwork on the gravel surface, or on the nearby river bank. Jaywick Sands therefore samples a purely secondary context situation. The flakes and cores form part of the river's bed load, the sweepings from more distant sites. The situation here resembles that of the Butlins site, artefacts in secondary context, evenly distributed through the depth of the Lower Freshwater Beds.

No handaxes came from the basal gravels, just cores and flakes. Two observations are important here. The first is that cold climate activity had affected the sediments while the channel was being infilled. Lumps of clay, presumably from the bank, were found mid-stream in the equivalent of the Upper Freshwater Beds. Oakley and Leakey suggest they would have to have been semi-frozen in order to get into the stream and not be subsequently broken up or dissolved. If so, these may provide circumstantial evidence for cold climate activity while the Upper Freshwater Beds were accumulating. Second, they note that the gravels they excavated (i.e. the top of the Lower Freshwater Beds) were smaller than those seen on the Lion Point foreshore and on the foreshore at the West Cliff. They argued that these latter sites sampled deeper portions of the Lower Freshwater Bed channel.

Clacton-on-Sea – Lion Point

Warren had been observing the foreshore at Lion Point since 1911, although he did not publish it in any detail until 1932. This was the site of his channel v, see Figure 3.1. It is important to remember when studying Warren's own illustration of Lion Point (1932: Figure 4) that this is not a vertical section, but the sloping foreshore as well as the section behind it. The Pleistocene deposits are still exposed today at very low tide where they outcrop beneath the modern beach. These exposures were more readily accessible in Warren's day as the modern sea defences have changed the pattern of long shore drift and encouraged the build-up of sand. The stratigraphy is shown in Figure 3.2. Once again the gravels at the base represent the Lower Freshwater Beds, and the marls represent the Upper Freshwater Beds. A variegated marl with shells at the base was suggested by Warren to be a remnant of the Estuarine Bed.

Archaeologically, one particular feature of Lion Point is of interest. Warren's notebooks make it clear that he divided the foreshore into distinct zones, see Figure 3.5 (McNabb 1992b), much as he did with the West Cliff localities. Those artefacts in his collection marked Gr were picked up in situ from the channel gravel itself. Those marked Clacton Lion Pt or Cl. L.P., or variations on these, were all derived from the in-situ gravels, but were found further up the beach deposited there by wave action. The important point about artefacts marked with these labels is that Warren was certain they came from the in-situ Clacton Channel deposits. A further zone s-b (storm

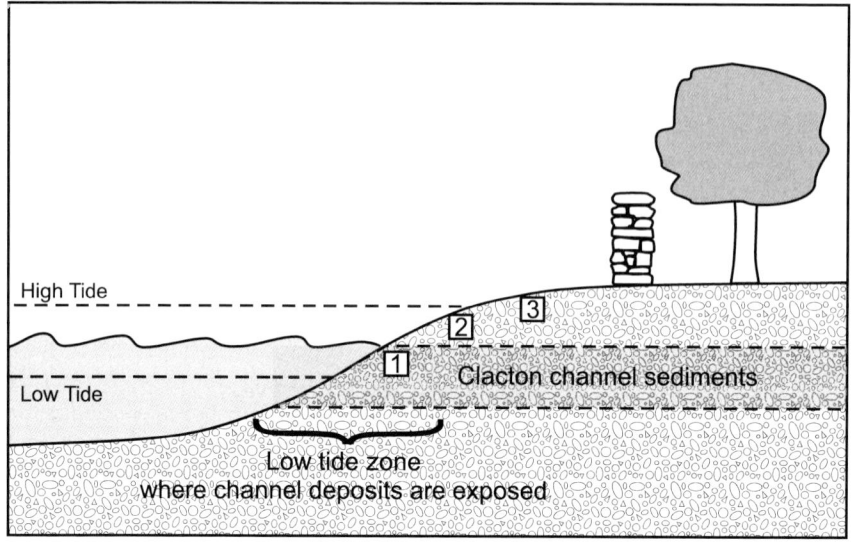

Figure 3.5 Cross-section through Lion Point showing different artefact recovery zones of Hazzledine Warren.

Notes: 1 – Clacton Channel sediments, in-situ recovery. 2 – further up the beach. A number of different labels were applied to this zone over the years. Artefacts from here derived from channel sediments. 3 – storm-beach. Highest zone. Artefacts from channel shunted up here by highest tides and storm conditions.

beach) represented artefacts derived from the in-situ gravels which had been shunted up to the top of the beach, near the sea wall, by wave action associated with heavy storms.

The illustrated Clactonian artefacts from Warren's 1932 paper on Lion Point (Warren 1932: Figure 5; artefacts curated in the British Museum), and those from the definitive 1951 paper (Warren 1951, all figures; artefacts curated in the Natural History Museum) clearly indicate that Warren considered that artefacts from all of these zones came from the in-situ gravels. In other words, he was collecting Clactonian artefacts from all the way up the beach.

What makes these artefact labels all the more interesting is that there are two non-classic bifaces marked Clacton Lion Pt in the Warren collection in the British Museum. The notations on the pieces, the provenance details in the notebooks, and Warren's acceptance of material from the same area of the beach as being Clactonian (and with identical artefact markings), make it certain that these non-classic bifaces came from the buried Clacton Channel gravels. In addition, a classic biface can be securely provenanced to the Lion Point Channel gravels (McNabb 1992b; 1996b). It was recovered by a Lieutenant Gordon Walker in 1944. A letter by Walker to the curator of the Ipswich museum makes it clear that the biface was found 'on the site of the Clacton Channel'. Other possible handaxes from the foreshore are discussed by Wymer (1985).

Warren used the Lion Point material in his definitive 1951 paper on the Clactonian. The site represents the middle of an ancient river channel and is therefore in secondary context. All the artefacts have been derived from elsewhere. As Oakley and Leakey (1937) suggested, the Lion Point locality may represent a deeper part of the channel than their Jaywick Sands site (or the Golf Course and Butlins sites) and this may have implications for the perception of the Clactonian as an assemblage of large cores and flakes, see Chapter 12.

Relationship between the Clacton localities

How should we think of Clacton-on-Sea and its various archaeological localities? Received wisdom suggests that the Thames river which flowed through Clacton-on-Sea, and deposited the sands and gravels just described, was a single channel river (although at Clacton it split around a hump of London Clay toward the middle of its course, see Figure 3.1). The sections and bore hole data of Oakley and Leakey, and Singer and Wymer, show that it was a river that was persistently shifting its channel, and cutting and re-cutting its own deposits at least in its higher units (Upper Freshwater Beds), and along its margins. Local access to the water's edge may well have been via temporary gravel bars at the edge of the channel. Experimental knapping scatters put down at various points on the surface of gravel bars (Schick 1986; Harding et al. 1987; Chambers 2003; Hosfield and Chambers 2003; and references therein) have demonstrated that material can be buried by gravel, re-exposed, or transported away by flood events. Over hundreds of years, visits to a locality by flint knapping hominins would build up a prodigious quantity of cores and flakes and other debitage which would be variously buried, or on the move, as the river continuously re-organised its floodplain.

So what about the different sites, should we think of them as all being broadly contemporary as, for example, the identification of all the gravels in Figure 3.2 as Lower Freshwater Beds implies? This is where palynology comes in. The pollen evidence from the Lower Freshwater Beds on the West Cliff foreshore suggested an age within pollen zone IIb, a sub-phase of the Early Temperate (see Table 3.1). However, the pollen from the Golf Course site gravels was studied by William Mullenders (in Wymer 1974). These results suggested that the gravel here was earlier. They found evidence for a cold climate existing when the gravel was laid down, and further suggested that the marl was from the Pre-Temperate pollen phase. But there are problems with the use of pollen at the Golf Course site (Turner 1985), and significantly, the mammal remains from the gravels are fully temperate. The most parsimonious explanation is that the cold climate pollen signal from the Golf Course is wrong. On the basis of this, phase 1 of Bridgland's model (downcutting) is represented by the channel itself, but phase 2 of the model is absent (removed by erosion – or perhaps too far downstream). All the gravels at Clacton and the various marls and loams (the combined fresh-water beds) aggraded under fully temperate conditions (pollen zone II) as the mammalian and molluscan evidence suggests. These are the equivalent of phase 3 of Bridgland's terrace model. Sites may differ in age somewhat within this Early Temperate pollen zone, but then the sites record a con-tinuum of occupation along the river bank throughout this period via snap-shots of different parts of the gravels at slightly different times.

Despite the presence of a few non-classic bifaces, and one or two possible classic ones, the overwhelming majority of the artefacts from Clacton are all cores and flakes. In that the gravels must have aggraded over a period of time, and evidence of handaxe technology is for the most part absent, there appears no reason to doubt that a non-handaxe assemblage type is represented in the Lower Freshwater Beds at the various localities at Clacton-on-Sea.

Swanscombe – Barnfield Pit

The Barnfield Pit is another of the corner stones in the arguments supporting an independent Clactonian tradition. There are vast numbers of flint artefacts from this quarry in north Kent: handaxes, thinning flakes, cores, hard hammer flakes and retouched flake tools. But from the Clactonian levels at the base of the sequence only one confirmed (and possibly one other) record of an Acheulean handaxe exists. The long sequence of sediments at the site, the archaeological succession, and the discovery of three refitting fragments of a hominin skull, transformed this quarry into a world-renowned arch-aeological site. Comprehensive site histories have recently been published by Bridgland (1994) and especially Conway et al. (1996). Figure 3.6 shows the location of the Barnfield Pit in relation to some of the other famous quarries in the area that have produced archaeological material.

Figure 3.7 shows a schematic representation of the Barnfield sequence. It is divided into three broad phases. The earliest phase is composed of the Lower Gravels (Ia–Ic) and Lower Loams (Id–Ie). They represent the sedi-mentary infill of a wide single channel river along its southern bank. At the very base of the Lower Gravels are coarse and poorly sorted patches of gravel (Ia) resting on the Thanet Sand bedrock. Bernard Conway (1996b; 1996c) interpreted these as being the first aggradation in the newly cut channel. As a solifluction unit they may have been deposited under cold conditions, but the mammals recovered from them were temperate. They were originally more extensive within the channel's base. They were mostly eroded away by the river before the deposition of the bulk of the Lower Gravels (Ib) were laid down within the channel. These are an upward fining sequence (the size

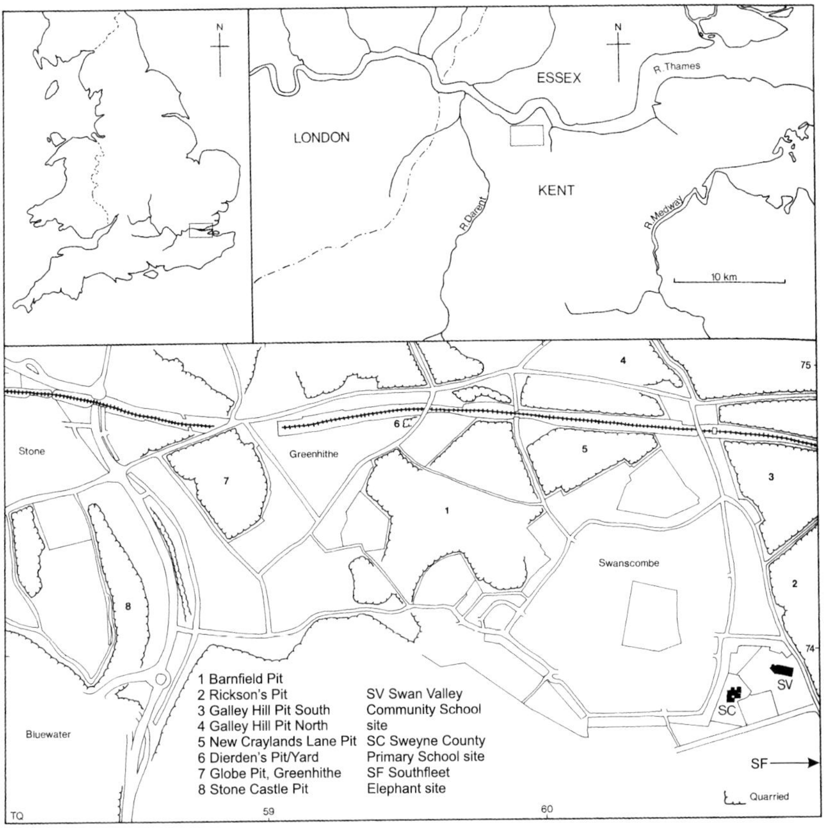

Figure 3.6 Map of pits and quarries in Swanscombe area.

Note: Used with permission.

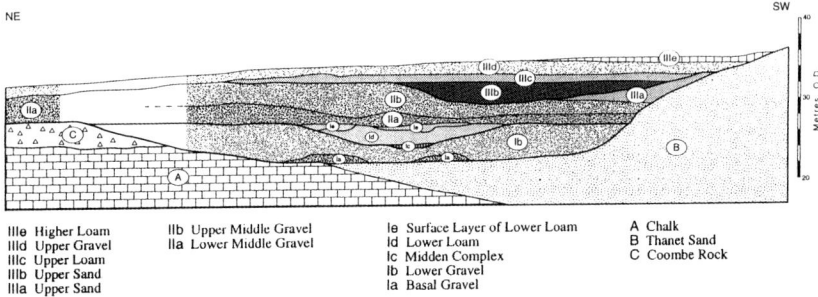

Figure 3.7 Cross-section of deposits in the Barnfield Pit, Swanscombe.

Note: Used with permission.

of the clasts get smaller as you move up the profile) indicating the river was gradually losing its power to transport heavy items. There is one break in the depositional sequence in the middle of the Lower Gravels representing an unknown period of time when the river stopped depositing gravel.

The gravels were laid down in a temperate climate as the fauna and pollen indicate (Kerney 1971; Schreve 2001). Hubbard (1982) suggests this is pollen zone IIb of an interglacial (see Table 3.1), but the usefulness of the pollen profile from the Barnfield Pit is not without its critics (Turner 1985). At the top of the Lower Gravels is what the excavators called the midden (Ic). They interpreted this as a collection of bones which were hominin food refuse, but examination of the bones and the flint tools suggested they were damaged and rolled as a result of transport. In reality, the midden is almost certainly a natural deflation and scour surface (Ashton and McNabb 1996a; Currant 1996).

The Lower Loam (Id) was composed of over-bank silts and sands. It represents the river in a quiet phase when it had lost its erosive power and was only depositing fine sediments. The loams probably represent a marshy environment, possibly in a meander loop, with periodic drying out leaving temporary land surfaces across which small streams ran and eroded shallow channels. This deposit was also laid down in a fully temperate climate as the pollen and fauna indicate. Hubbard (1996) suggested that the Lower Loam should also be associated with pollen zone IIb of the interglacial. So the Lower Gravels and Lower Loams were broadly contemporary with the Lower Freshwater Beds at Clacton. The surface of the Lower Loam (Ie) was a soil horizon indicating that a stable land surface existed here for some time. At some point prior to the deposition of the Middle Gravels proper, a thin film of gravel was laid over the open land surface. Remarkably, the footprints of animals were preserved in the gravely surface, even skid marks where animals had slipped (Davis and Walker 1996)

The Clactonian artefacts at Swanscombe were found in the Lower Gravels and Lower Loams, especially the former. These were recovered by amateur collectors such as R. H. Chandler, and A. T. Marston (see Chapters 10 and 11), as well as by professional archaeologists and geologists. (The proceedings of various learned societies are full of descriptions of field trips to Swanscombe, they usually ended up having a cream tea or beer at a local hostelry!) The majority of the literally thousands of cores and flakes were collected. A small number of handaxes have been found in the Lower Gravels (probably not more than two), as well as a handful of handaxe thinning flakes (letters in the Marston archive of British Museum; Marston 1942; 1996; McNabb 1996b). The only pieces that survive are those illustrated in Figure 3.8. We can be certain of the provenance of the biface – the black ovate – because its finder, A. T. Marston, had another reason to make sure of its context. He believed, mistakenly, that a later erosion event had removed much of the Lower Loam and Lower Gravels leaving a deep

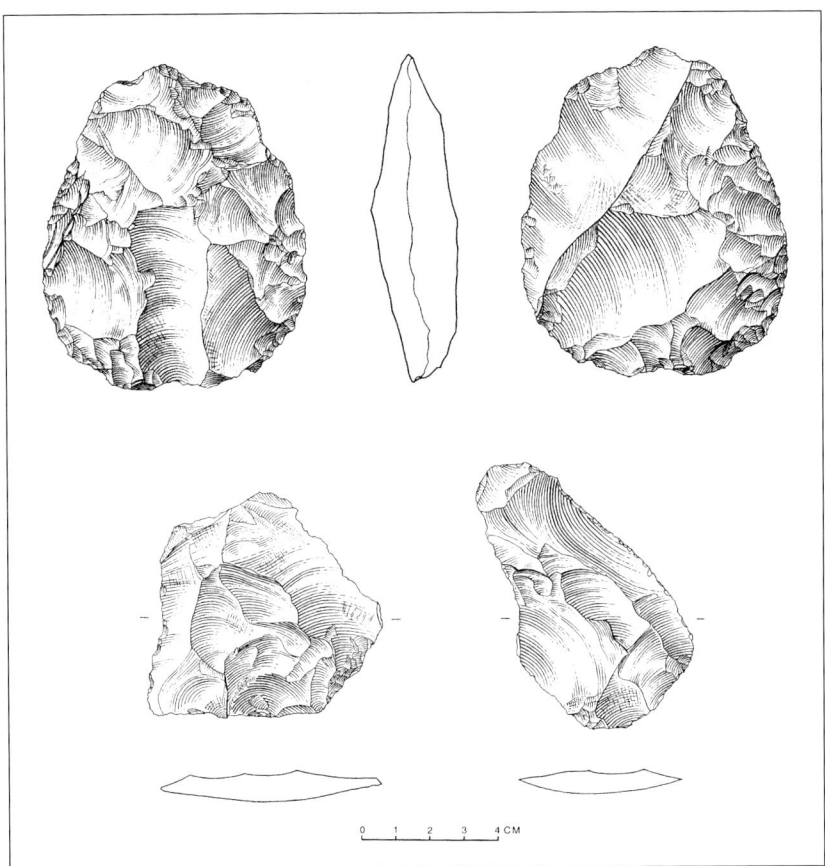

Figure 3.8 Above, the black ovate from the Lower Gravels, Barnfield, Marston collection, British Museum. Below, two thinning flakes from the Lower Gravels (museum box marked with a query), Marston collection, British Museum.

Note: Used with permission.

channel. Finding the black ovate at the base of it was an important piece of evidence for dating his channel, as he believed, to a post-Clactonian time. Now we know such a channel did not exist (Chandler 1942; McNabb 1996b), and his careful descriptions of digging the handaxe out from in-situ gravel actually describe him digging the artefact out of undisturbed Lower Gravels. When I was younger, I made a lot out of this discovery. I now believe I was wrong to have made so much out of it. I still maintain this handaxe (and the thinning flakes with it) do come from the base of

79

Lower Gravel, but it is one of only two provenanced classic handaxe in the Clactonian deposits.

If the black ovate was recovered from where Marston said it was, is it possible that it was trans-located downwards from higher deposits when solution activity dissolved the underlying chalk and, locally, the Acheulean rich Middle Gravels slowly collapsed into a solution hollow (Conway 1996b). Solution is evident elsewhere in the pit (Dewey 1959; Wymer 1964). There is a possibility that it occurred close to section F where Marston discovered the black ovate. There are minor faults in the Upper Middle Gravels in Conway's section G (Conway 1996b), at the north-eastern end of what was, effectively, the same section that Marston observed. Conway argued these were a result of tensions in the sediments on the camber of a solution hollow. If so, the solution hollow lay to the south or north of the section at this point. It is important to note that this is the only evidence in this area for anything resembling solution activity, *and the deposits directly below the Upper Middle Gravels in section G were completely undisturbed.* Other sections cut by Conway, further along the line of Marston's section F (towards the ancient bank of the river), showed absolutely no evidence of faulting or disturbance of the deposits at all. This is especially so for the centre of the old section where Marston found the black ovate (see sections J–K/KA in Conway 1996b). So although solution activity is well attested to in the pit, it cannot be invoked to explain the presence of the black ovate at the base of the Lower Gravels in Marston's section F. What about this second handaxe? A letter in the Marston archive of the British Museum about the black ovate, refers to this second biface and describes it as stained brown in colour. It remains to be identified in the Marston collection.

But the black ovate (and the thinning debitage) at the base of the Lower Gravels change very little. The remainder of the flintwork from the Lower Gravels and Lower Loams comprises cores, flakes, and retouched tools with not a whiff of Acheulean technology anywhere. But if classic handaxes are virtually absent, there are non-classic handaxes present.

In 1994, Nick Ashton and I suggested that handaxes represented a single continuum encompassing a range of different shapes and forms (Ashton and McNabb 1994). On the one hand were those classic handaxes we are all familiar with from illustrations in the archaeological literature. At the opposite end of the continuum is the non-classic handaxe. On these bifaces a variable amount of bifacial thinning and shaping has modified an edge but has not shaped the tool as a whole to produce an immediately recognizable outline shape.

Figure 3.9 illustrates a few of them. The artefact from the Dewey collection was catalogued as a chopping tool, a good example of the power of prevailing interpretation influencing observation. The small non-classic piece from the Waechter excavations was excavated from the top of the Lower Gravel. The provenance of this artefact has also been hotly disputed (McNabb 1992b).

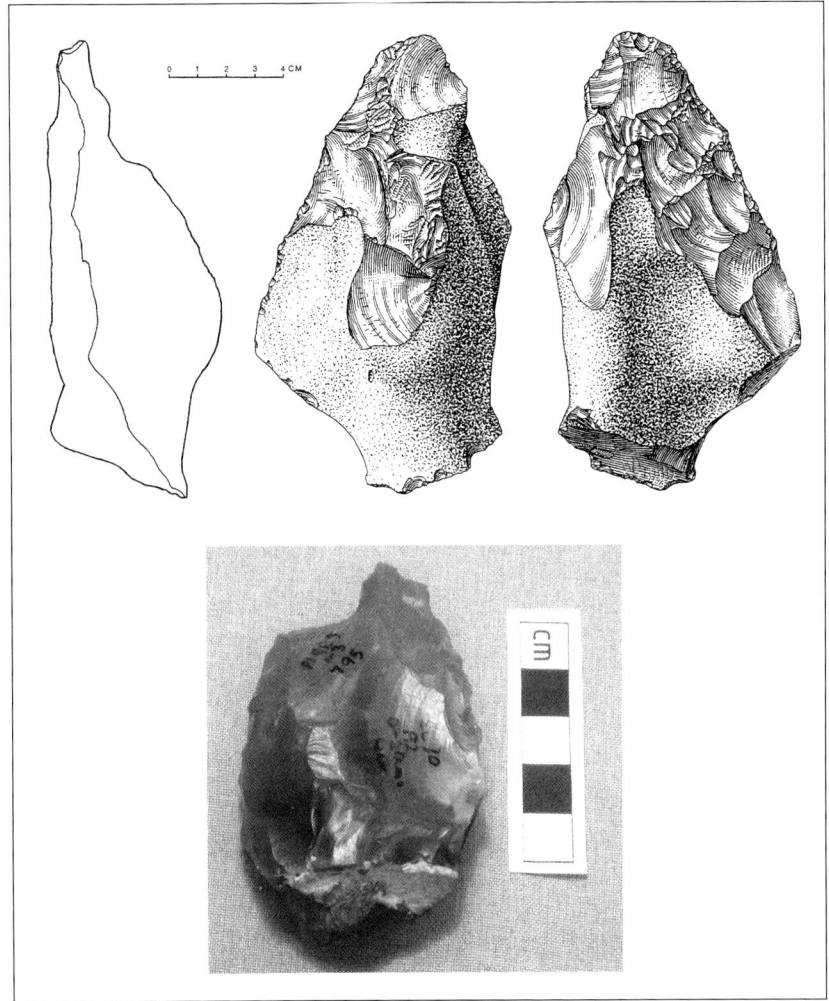

Figure 3.9 Non-classic handaxes from the Lower Gravels, Barnfield Pit, Swanscombe.

Notes: Line drawing is from the Dewey collection. British Museum. Used with permission. Photograph is of non-classic excavated *in-situ* from top Lower Gravels, Waechter excavation.

Nevertheless, it was excavated *in situ*, and its provenance is clearly marked on the artefact (*contra* the later confusions of Waechter and Newcomer in the latter's reply to Ohel in 1979, see Ohel 1979a). It is in identical condition to other artefacts so marked, and, critically, the only patch of Lower Middle Gravel from which it could have conceivably fallen onto the surface during the excavation was noted by the excavators to be archaeologically sterile

(McNabb 1992b; 1996b). This artefact I also made a lot out of, erroneously interpreting it as a classic handaxe which it evidently is not. This is an example of my own wish to find handaxes in Clactonian deposits influencing my judgement. The piece is a non-classic handaxe and fits in with other such examples from Clactonian and Acheulean sites elsewhere.

With one exception, the flintwork from the Lower Gravels and Lower Loams is in secondary context. This exception is the knapping floor in the Lower Loam. The excavators in 1970 came across a concentration of very sharp-looking flakes and debitage on a horizon they interpreted as an ephemeral dry land surface. The marshy environment that was the Lower Loam may have dried up, perhaps just for one summer. Mark Newcomer refitted a number of the flakes back together (Waechter et al. 1970). Nick Ashton and I later reconstructed what had happened here, see Figure 3.10 (Ashton and McNabb 1996a). Up to a maximum of nine different flint nodules were brought to the site. Some had already been knapped before they arrived. One nodule was knapped and its core subsequently removed,

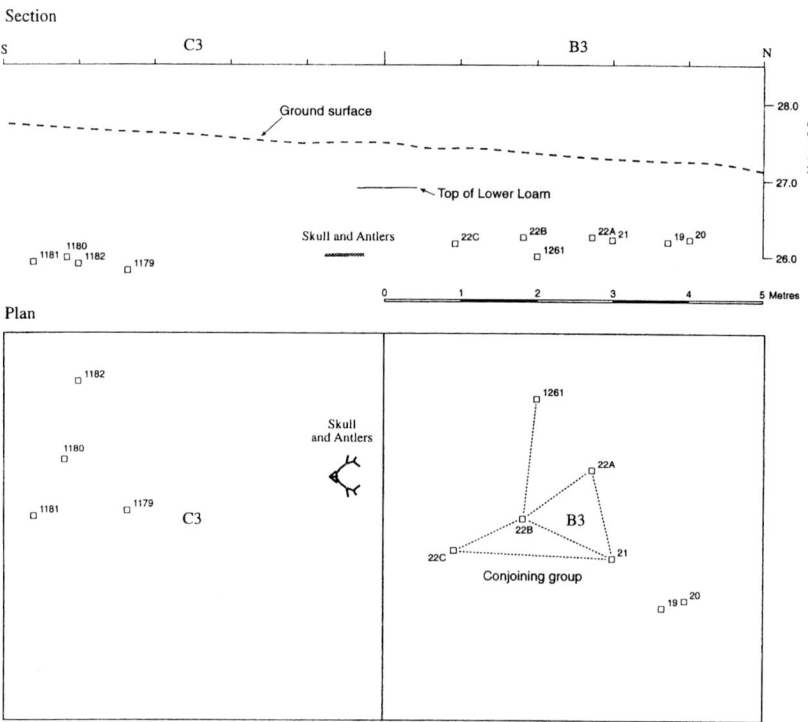

Figure 3.10 Plan of Lower Loam knapping floor. C3 and B3 are excavation square numbers.

Note: Used with permission.

and then a second nodule was knapped directly on top of the first. The core for this one was taken away as well. Close by, other nodules were knapped; one of them (complex 20) had two refitting groups of flakes with a gap of about 30 cm between them. Tentatively we postulated that flakes and debitage had fallen either side of the knapper's thigh. Not many of the flakes had been retouched into tools, but one large flake did have the characteristic damage pattern associated with its use as a wedge. One edge of the flake had been crushed, while the other had been battered by something – as if it had been hammered. Apart from a few fragments of broken-up bone, the only fauna associated with the knapping floor was the skull and antlers of a large species of extinct fallow deer (*Dama dama clactoniana*). It is purely speculation, but if you wanted to butcher the carcass of an adult deer with a large wrack of antler, detaching its head would make the task much simpler. Hammering a large sharp flake through the bones of the neck would get the job done.

As Figure 3.7 shows, the channels of Stage I were buried by the deposits of Stage II. It is from these deposits we get the Acheulean at Barnfield. These deposits extended well beyond the limits of the former channel and are true terrace deposits, a result of the river aggrading gravels and sands across a wide floodplain. The Lower Middle Gravels (IIa in Figure 3.7) are interpreted as being deposited in a braided stream environment with a number of thread-like channels criss-crossing the floodplain. The pollen, if reliable, suggests an open grassy environment next to the river. The fauna, pollen, and molluscan evidence imply the Lower Middle Gravels were laid down in a temperate climate, and should be associated with pollen zone IIIb of the Late Temperate phase, making these gravels comparable with the Clacton Estuarine Beds, see Table 3.1 (also Kerney 1971).

In this layer for the first time appear examples of what is called the Rhenish fauna. These are a suite of fluvial molluscs of mainland European origin which are believed to migrate down the Rhine and made their way into the Thames system. This implies a period of lowered sea level and a reconnection between the two rivers. A number of researchers have sought to link the appearance of the Acheulean with the Rhenish fauna, implying a hominin migration up river valleys. The Rhenish fauna is also noted at Clacton-on-Sea in the Estuarine Beds (although they first appear near the top of the Upper Freshwater Beds). But at Clacton they are not associated with handaxes.

Curiously the handaxes from the Lower Middle Gravels tend to be quite small and pointed (Wymer 1964), quite different from those in higher deposits. Perhaps the knappers were forced to make their handaxes on the smaller gravel pebbles that formed the bedload of the flood plain. The Upper Middle Gravels (IIb in Figure 3.7) represent mostly sands which show evidence of extensive small-scale channelling. The fauna and pollen suggest interglacial conditions, but slightly cooler than the underlying deposits. Acheulean handaxes were common in the Upper Middle Gravels and it was here that the three portions of the Swanscombe skull were discovered (see Figure 1.9).

Stage III represents a series of deposits that, near their base (IIIa–b in Figure 3.7) suggest a return to cold conditions. These cold climate sands, channelling, and ice wedge casts have been interpreted by Conway (1996c) as being evidence of full glacial conditions, making the Upper Loam (IIIc in Figure 3.7) part of a later interglacial. Bridgland (1994; Bridgland and Schreve 2001) sees no evidence for this, and equates the whole of the Swanscombe sequence with the Boyn Hill/Orsett Heath stage, a view point tentatively supported here. Nick Ashton and colleagues (pers. comm.) have suggested that the end of MIS 11 may be a complicated period, with climate switching between temperate and cool conditions, and back again, as the interglacial came to an end. The cold climate sediments (III a–b in Figure 3.7), and the temperate Upper Loams may reflect this. There are records of handaxes being present in the Upper Loams (Waechter 1973; Roe 1981b).

The importance of the Swanscombe fluvial interglacial deposits is that they record almost the full history of the interglacial that succeeded the Anglian glaciation (Bridgland 1994; contra Conway 1996c). They are thus MIS 11 in age. The Clactonian is restricted to the Lower Gravels and Lower Loams. The Lower Gravels Channel will have been cut in the late-Anglian/earliest MIS 11 period which would be phase 1 of Bridgland's terrace model. The patches of cold climate solifluction gravels identified by Conway (phase Ia in Figure 3.7) may well represent the earliest aggradation under cold or cool climate conditions – phase 2 of Bridgland's model, but like the Golf Course, the fauna is a warm one. So it is perhaps more parsimonious to interpret them as interglacial in character. The bulk of the Lower Gravels and the Lower Loams are unequivocally interglacial as the molluscs and fauna indicate (Kerney 1971; Schreve 2004a). This would be phase 3 of Bridgland's river terrace model. In fact, all of the Barnfield sequence is interglacial. Evidence for cold climate stages within this sequence would therefore equate with cold phases within MIS 11. There seems no reason to doubt that the Lower Gravels/Lower Loams are the upstream equivalent of the Lower Freshwater Beds, and at least the lower part of the Upper Freshwater Beds at Clacton. Similarly, the Middle Gravels are the upstream equivalent of the Estuarine Beds at Clacton, as the molluscs indicate, at least for some part of this period. Gravel was being deposited in this part of the river while the lower stretches became an estuary as the sea level rose. Nor is there any reason to doubt that the higher parts of the Barnfield sequence reflect the declining climatic conditions of the end of MIS 11, phases 4 and 5 of Bridgland's model.

Swanscombe – Rickson's Pit (NGR TQ 608742)

The location of this site is shown in Figure 3.6. It was originally described by Dewey (1930; 1932; 1959), and later by Burchell (1934) and Tester (1985) among others. Probably the most reliable observer was Dewey who visited the pit on a semi-regular basis. His observations are followed here, while those of Burchell are not. In my opinion, Burchell over-interpreted what he saw, affording minor sedimentary units the status of major depositional events. Dewey, a trained and experienced geologist, familiar with the area, visited the pit many times and his descriptions of the sections at the western end of the pit are clear and unambiguous. (Independent confirmation of Dewey's observations are presented in Chandler 1932.) At the base of the sequence was a coarse gravel overlying chalk, see Figure 3.11, and above the gravel a white sandy unit with localised concentrations of shells – the shell bed. Overlying this was an evenly bedded sand, in turn overlain by gravels and sands with cross-bedding. The sequence was capped by a deposit described as hill-wash.

Excavations were conducted in the lowest gravel in 1934 by Louis Leakey, but they were never published. This gravel was considered by Dewey to be an extension of the Lower Gravels Channel at Barnfield Pit. The stone tool

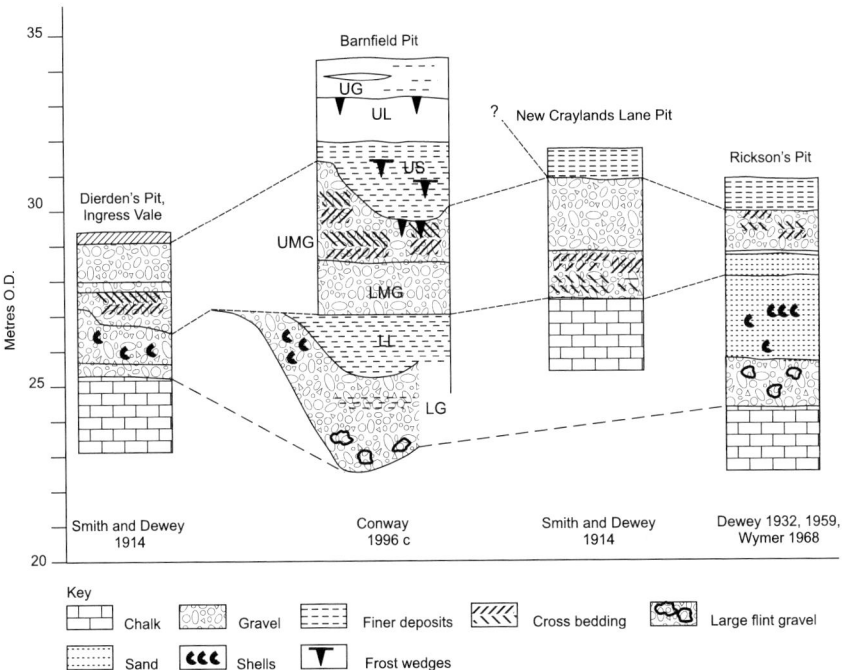

Figure 3.11 Schematic sections from selected pits in the Swanscombe area – see Figure 3.6.

assemblage recovered did not contain any handaxes further strengthening its association with the Barnfield Lower Gravels Channel. The industry from this basal gravel is considered Clactonian. Caution should be exercised with this assemblage. Although excavated, Ohel (1979a) noted a bias towards larger artefacts, suggesting some selectivity in what was kept. The higher deposits contained handaxes, some on ephemeral land surfaces (Dewey 1959) whose descriptions are strongly reminiscent of similar surfaces noted by Marston in the Upper Middle Gravels at Barnfield (Marston 1937). The dating of the site is plagued by the use of artefact typology (for example, Waechter 1973) which results in chronological gymnastics, not helped by the confusion Burchell created. There appears no *a priori* reason to doubt the majority of the Rickson's sequence is anything other than MIS 11, and that the lowest gravel, and archaeologically sterile shell bed above it, are downstream extensions of the Barnfield Lower Gravels Channel. (It is possible that Dewey's (1930; 1932) shell bed at the top of the Lower Gravels takes the place of the Lower Loam, which was local to the Barnfield.)

Before leaving Rickson's Pit it is important to note that in the Marston collection from this site, curated in the British Museum, there are a small number of unambiguous handaxe thinning flakes (no more than eight) that were collected by Marston from the lowest gravel at the site. A number are clearly soft hammer. But again, these are not enough to dispute the basic archaeological signal from the site – the predominance of cores and flakes.

The Southfleet Road elephant butchery site, Swanscombe

This important new Clactonian site awaits full publication. An interim report (Wenban-Smith *et al.* 2006) provides a preliminary interpretation. An elephant carcass occurred in an organic rich horizon within a grey clay (unit 3 at the site). About 100 artefacts, consisting entirely of flakes and cores were found associated with the partial carcass – a portion of the skeleton had been destroyed during commercial working adjacent to the site. There is no reason to doubt that the artefacts, found in and among the bones, were not directly associated with the carcass and represent a butchery event. Whether the hominins who knapped there actually killed the animal has yet to be established.

To the south of the carcass, and at a slightly higher level was a further scatter of artefacts, more than 1,500. This larger scatter may also be broadly contemporary with the carcass. One suggestion is that the scatter sits on slightly higher dry ground adjacent to a more waterlogged area within which the elephant died. This assemblage is also a core and flake assemblage with no trace of handaxes or their manufacture.

What makes this non-handaxe site so interesting is the preliminary interpretation of its stratigraphic context. It is in the Ebbsfleet Valley, which was a south bank tributary of the Thames, joining the main river just to the east of Swanscombe. The altitude of the knapping scatters, and the sedimentary character of the grey clay, suggest it is contemporary with the Lower Loam at nearby Barnfield Pit. It may have been part of a zone of complicated sedimentation which developed at the confluence of the Ebbsfleet tributary and the main eastward flowing Lower Gravel/Lower Loam Channel. On the basis of molluscs and pollen, the grey clay would date to the Early Temperate phase of the MIS 11 interglacial, which fits with a correlation with the Lower Loam at Barnfield, 1.5 km to the north-west.

Beneath the grey clay is a sand unit (unit 2 at the site) with 'sparse' artefacts, and below that a chalk-rich sand which also has a few artefacts. The excavators speculate on whether these too are Clactonian assemblages spanning the late Anglian and Pre-Temperate phases of the interglacial (see Table 3.1). In my opinion, based on the interim report, there are too few artefacts to confirm a Clactonian non-biface assemblage. At the very least, these data suggest a limited presence of hominins in the Swanscombe area, earlier in the interglacial.

Above the grey clay there is a fluvially bedded gravel with abundant bifaces, but little manufacturing debitage (or any other type of debitage for that matter). This unit (unit 5 at the site) is tentatively correlated with the Lower Middle Gravels at Barnfield and has a height range of between 26.0 m and 28 m OD. The range fits well with that seen for the Middle Gravels elsewhere in the vicinity (Figure 3.11).

The significance of this superb discovery remains to be fully assessed. The excavators suggest (Wenban-Smith et al. 2006, 481 and Table 2) that it provides confirmation of the existence of the Clactonian as a non-handaxe cultural tradition, occupying a significant portion of the earlier part of the MIS 11 interglacial. I believe this is premature. It certainly suggests that the sequence seen at Barnfield and Rickson's is a locally significant one, namely, a Lower Gravel/Lower Loam Channel which is virtually devoid of handaxes, followed by the deposition of flood plain sands and gravels, with handaxes, onto a locally significant erosion surface at about 27 m OD (although this varies between 26 and 28 m OD), see below.

Relationship between the Swanscombe localities

Just as at Clacton, the various archaeological sites in the immediate vicinity of Swanscombe represent snap-shots of a lost Pleistocene landscape. Figure 3.11 shows the details of the sections from a series of critical Swanscombe localities, their locations are shown on Figure 3.6. The line at c. 27 m OD reveals a locally significant erosion surface (surface E4 of Conway 1996c, although his broader 'regional' interpretation of its significance is not supported here). It coincides with the surface of the Lower Loam at the Barnfield Pit which was a palaeosol (ibid.), indicating an open land surface. The other two sites in the immediate vicinity of Barnfield Pit, Dierden's

Pit/Ingress Vale, and the New Craylands Lane Pit support this. There is no reason to suppose that the deposits below 27 m at these sites are not part of the Lower Gravels/Lower Loam Channel (Barnfield stage I of Conway in Figure 3.7).

This presents an interesting conundrum as far as Dierden's Pit is concerned. In Figure 3.11 the observations of Smith and Dewey (1914) are reproduced. These were based on section cutting in these deposits by them. They found flakes and cores in the shell bed, and within the base of *erosive* pockets of loam cut into it. No handaxes were found. But earlier reports by Stopes (1899), among others (e.g. Newton 1901), are adamant that handaxes were found in the shell bed at Dierden's, some by Stopes himself, and that the shell bed here extended down from 26.82 m OD to 23.8 metres OD. This would have made the handaxes in the shell bed a lateral equivalent of the Barnfield Lower Gravel. Dewey, who observed extensive sections in Barnfield Pit, in later years described the upper part of the Lower Gravels at Barnfield as a shell bed (Dewey 1932; 1959). The two pits are only some 600 metres away from each other, and the contrasting observations are difficult to reconcile. On the basis of the local significance of the 27 m OD erosion surface, I will take the shelly upper part of the deposits at Dierden's and the upper part of the Lower Gravels at Barnfield, as being lateral extensions of the *same* deposit – namely, the top of the Lower Gravels Channel. For the moment I have followed Smith and Dewey, taking their point that the non-handaxe assemblage that they recovered was done so under controlled conditions.

New Craylands Lane Pit has chalk at about 27 m OD (Smith and Dewey 1914), suggesting that the Lower Gravels/Lower Loam Channel was confined to the south of here. At the downstream site of Rickson's, the equivalent surface is slightly higher than their postulated upstream equivalents at Barnfield. This minor difference is put down to an uneven erosive contact with the succeeding Middle Gravels over the floodplain in the Swanscombe area. To the south, fieldwork by Francis Wenban-Smith (Wenban-Smith and Bridgland 2001) has shown that the Middle Gravels (with handaxes) at the Swan Valley Community School site are benched onto local bedrock (chalk and Thanet Sand) at about 27 m OD, so the Lower Gravel/Lower Loam Channel cannot be present here either. As noted above, the erosive contact on which rests the Lower Middle Gravels at the Southfleet site varies between 26 and 28 m OD.

Above the 27 m OD bench the different pits tell a consistent story; sands and gravels, with extensive cross-bedding, are deposited all over the area. These represent phase II of Conway's Barnfield sequence, and are the equivalent of the Middle Gravels from that pit. The geological mapping of the Boyn Hill/Orsett Heath outcrop shows that terrace deposits attributed to this phase were laterally extensive, passing well beyond the limits of the underlying Lower Gravels/Lower Loam Channel. Wenban-Smith's work at the Swan

Valley school, cited above, demonstrates that Middle Gravels are present here, so the flood plain represented by the Middle Gravels was extensive. Handaxes are associated with most of these units, in contrast to the deposits below the 27 m bench where they are infrequent or absent. These cross-bedded sands and gravels were deposited in a braided river environment with extensive channel migration, involving the cutting and re-cutting of floodplain sediments. Bones and stone tools will have been reworked across the floodplain for centuries. The higher units in the Barnfield sequence (Conway's stage III, Figure 3.7) are only preserved in the immediate vicinity of Barnfield Pit, erosion having removed them from elsewhere.

Does what we can construct of the MIS 11 landscape at Swanscombe, and the archaeology associated with it, provide enough reason to support the presence of a non-handaxe tradition in earlier MIS 11? Yes. Despite the occasional handaxe or small clutch of thinning flakes, the excavated material is dominated by cores and flakes. As at Clacton, the two Lower Gravels Channel localities at Swanscombe (Barnfield and Rickson's) preserve a depth of sediment in which a consistent archaeological signal is present, consistent over an unspecified period of time. The interpretation of the Southfleet elephant butchery site fully supports this, confirming the local significance of this pattern, and the local significance of the 27 m. OD erosion surface.

I have no doubt that the Acheulean material in the Lower Gravels is correctly provenanced to these deposits. The challenge, as with Clacton, is to explain its presence in these gravel beds – as opposed to just trying to explain it away by disputing its provenance.

Barnham St Gregory, Suffolk (NGR TL 875787)

The traditional significance of Barnham St Gregory was that interglacial sediments were stratified above glacial till, and within these temperate deposits Acheulean bifaces were stratified above Clactonian cores and flakes. This was one of the only two sites in Britain where this sequence was proved by excavation. There have been three controlled excavations here; by Paterson (1937; 1942), John Wymer (1985), and by the British Museum (Ashton et al. 1998). A detailed history of investigations prior to the British Museum project are described elsewhere (McNabb 1998).

The geological sequence is schematically illustrated in Figure 3.12. A deep channel was cut in the chalk probably by Anglian outwash as the MIS 12 glaciers began to recede. The channel, nearly 20 m deep, was infilled with sands and gravels (unit 1, Figure 3.12). These were overlain by a chalky diamicton (unit 2, a diamicton is a structureless deposit which shows no evidence of the process by which it was deposited) which was later interpreted as Lowestoft (= Anglian) Till. A channel was eroded into this till up to 13.5 m in depth which began to fill with fine-grained silts and clays (unit 5).

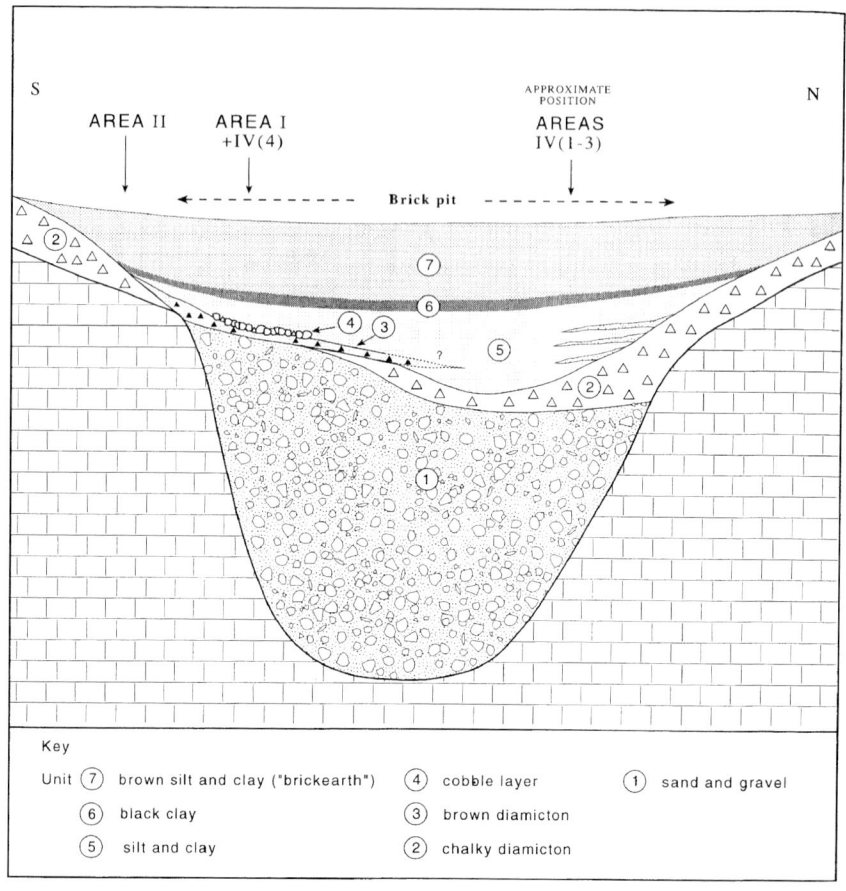

Figure 3.12 Schematic cross-section of Barnham St Gregory, British Museum excavation.

Note: Used with permission.

The suggestion is that this began to occur soon after the disappearance of the ice, and these sediments record the beginning of the transition to more temperate interglacial conditions.

As the channel/depression filled up, there was bank collapse along its side (at Area I) which led to the formation of the brown diamicton (unit 3) on the south side of the channel. There was a lag gravel or cobble layer (unit 4) overlying this. The cobble layer was winnowed by running water which removed most of the finer elements of the gravel leaving a very resistant well-consolidated band of cobbles. Within this, and on its surface, were Clactonian artefacts. These came from the British Museum's excavation in Area I, which was adjacent to the trench excavated by Wymer in 1979

(1985), and just to one side of where Paterson located his area excavation in the early–mid-1930s (Paterson 1937). The geological interpretations of the BM team therefore contextualise all the other excavations at Barnham. Overlying the cobble layer was a yellow silty sand (unit 5e) which passed laterally back into the centre of the channel – Area III. It was from this area, in sediments roughly contemporary with unit 5e, that faunal, molluscan and pollen evidence was recovered which indicated these sediments had aggraded during the Early Temperate zone (pollen zone II) of an interglacial. The artefacts on the surface of unit 4, and within unit 5e, were thus broadly contemporary with this.

On top of the silts and clays of unit 5 a soil developed (unit 6) representing a period of time when the river had dried out, or the main channel had shifted its position. This soil could be traced in sediments along the southern bank (and elsewhere). It was associated with Acheulean handaxes and with thinning flakes (Areas I and V), and represents the basis upon which the older stratigraphic observations of Acheulean overlying Clactonian were made. The whole sequence was overlain by colluvial loams (mixtures of sand or silt in various proportions that were not laid down by a river, but mostly emplaced by the wind or surface runoff). This is unit 7, the brown silts and clays – the brickearths of older authors, from which traditionally most of the handaxes came.

But the excavations of the BM revealed that the archaeological situation was much more complicated than a simple Acheulean/Clactonian super-positioning. In Area IV.4 some 50 m to the east of Area I and along the same southern margin of the channel, a lateral extension of the cobble band (unit 4) was identified, overlain by a less sandy equivalent of unit 5e and a more weakly developed extension of the palaeosol – unit 6. Within the cobble band here was an Acheulean assemblage of flakes from the manufacture of possibly three handaxes, as well as a single small handaxe, which was also recovered. How is this to be explained? The basic breakdown of the data is simplified in Table 3.2. Both rolled and fresh cores and flakes are found in both areas throughout the depth of the cobble band, and from its surface. So, however the cobble band was originally emplaced, by fluvial activity, solifluction from the adjacent bank, or a bit of both, the deposit developed over time incorporating older rolled flintwork as well as episodes of knapping contemporary with the top of the unit. Table 3.2 also shows that rolled artefacts associated with handaxe manufacture are present within the cobble band in Area IV.4 too. Although there are only 27 of them, and they are not excessively rolled, they nevertheless demonstrate that as the cobble band developed, there was at least some handaxe manufacture prior to the unrolled handaxe debitage associated with the top of the cobble band in Area IV.4.

Wenban-Smith (1998) has questioned the contemporaneity of the two areas, suggesting they could be separated by some time, with the cobbles of

Table 3.2 Stratigraphy at Barnham in relation to presence or absence of rolled or fresh artefacts

Deposits	Area I		Area IV.4		Area IV.4	
	Cores and flakes		Cores and flakes		Handaxes and/or thinning flakes	
	Rolled	Unrolled	Rolled	Unrolled	Rolled	Unrolled
Palaeosol (unit 6)						
Yellow silty sand (unit 5e)	+	+				
Surface of cobble band (unit 4)	+	+	+	+		+
Within cobble band (unit 4)	+	+	+	+	+	+

Notes: Presence is indicated by a cross, absence by empty cell. Shaded cells indicate no artefacts present. A single unrolled handaxe was present in unit 6 Area I – not indicated on table.

Source: Data from Ashton et al. (1998).

Area I buried when the cobbles of Area IV.4 were an exposed surface. In my opinion, this is unfair on the data, asking of them a level of precision they simply cannot provide and then using the impossibility of an answer to deny the contemporaneity of the two assemblages. The plain facts are that handaxes, cores and flakes were being knapped while unit 4 was aggrading. When the cobble band finally became a stable surface, handaxes continued to be made at Area IV.4, while cores and flakes were knapped in Area I.

The rolled cores and flakes, and handaxe debitage, may attest to some-what older occupation at the site. Mark White (2000), while accepting the contemporaneity of all the fresh material, has suggested that the presence of the older rolled cores and flakes supports the presence of an earlier Clactonian assemblage. This is an intriguing suggestion, but as the data in Table 3.2 suggest, such a clear-cut dichotomy is not possible. In my opinion, there are hints that a few Acheulean implements were actually present in the Area I cobble band as well. Paterson's excavations were adjacent to the British Museum's Area I. From the surface of the cobble band, and just below it (Paterson's industries D and E) there are a number of pieces I interpreted as thinning flakes (McNabb 1992a). Additionally, an otherwise un-provenanced biface found by Mrs R. Caton is described as being scratched (Paterson 1937), very suggestive of it having come from the cobble band where similar scratched flintwork is present (see also Ohel 1982).

Nick Ashton (Ashton et al. 1998) has suggested an alternative explanation for the archaeological pattern at Barnham, one that avoids cultural explanation altogether. He proposes a landscape and resource exploitation model. It relies on the behavioural variability of hominins reacting to a landscape that was changing over time. The channel's gravely banks represented a constant supply of raw material for knapping. Activities requiring sharp edges and retouched flake tools were carried out on these surfaces. Some activities called for bifaces, and these too were made out of the gravels along the edge of the river. The presence of rolled and fresh material on and in the gravels implies that the resources at the channel's margin were exploited over a long period. In time the gravel banks became buried and this resource was denied to the hominins. Rather than take themselves to the raw material and make tools, it was necessary now for the hominins to take the raw material and tools to the job. In the upper part of the sequence bifaces either appear as isolated tools left on the landscape (one isolated handaxe in the palaeosol unit 6 – of Area I), or as a few handaxe thinning flakes (Area V). These are the signatures of a more mobile use of technology and one that could be adapted to many uses, as well as repaired or re-sharpened with a minimum of effort. This is the sort of technology one would resort to if access to the 'quick and dirty' resource of a gravel bed had been lost.

Barnham has provided important clues to the Clactonian debate. It demonstrates that traditionally interpreted Clactonian and Acheulean sites were broadly contemporary (at least here) and both occupied the same kind of environment in fully temperate conditions. Additionally, Area I presents an interesting parallel with the Golf Course site at Clacton. Old and fresh flintwork was incorporated within an aggrading gravel deposit. This was overlain by finer sediment. There was sufficient power in the stream to lift some of the material off the surface of the gravel and incorporate it within the finer sediment. Both sites have refits between the finer sediment and their gravel surfaces. In effect, both sites sample a long-term hominin engagement with a particular ecological niche – the river bank, except at Barnham that engagement was more variable than at Clacton. Another parallel is that between Barnham and the Barnfield Pit where a small handaxe presence appears contemporary with a much larger core and flake one. At the very least Barnham shows that the relationship between Acheulean and Clactonian sites is more complicated than earlier generations suspected.

Since the gravel at Barnham is not a terrace gravel, it is not really appropriate to attempt to place this site within the Bridgland terrace model. However, since the site is MIS 11, and the archaeology in the gravels appears to date from the equivalent of the Early Temperate pollen zone, then a broad contemporaneity with the Lower Gravels/Lower Loam at Barnfield, and the Lower Freshwater Beds at Clacton is not unwarranted. This will be further discussed in Chapter 5.

Clactonian Sites later than MIS 11

All of the sites described in this chapter so far have been dated to MIS 11. In this next section I will look at a small group of sites which are later in time than those described above. These represent part of the Lynch Hill/Corbets Tey Formation (see Table 2.1 and Figure 2.7). In terms of the Bridgland model this is the second terrace of the post-Anglian Thames and represents the incision at the transition from the MIS 10 glaciation to the MIS 9 interglacial. The incision cut through the sediments of the Boyn Hill/Orsett Heath Formation in the centre of the Thames channel and left remnants of them isolated as a terrace along the sides of the valley.

Globe Pit at Little Thurrock

Once again we return to the Lower Thames Valley, to its northern bank just to the east of London. During the latter part of the nineteenth century and the earlier part of the twentieth, extensive brickearth deposits (fine silts and clays that were literally quarried for brick making), stretching from near Purfleet across to Little Thurrock, were excavated, mostly by hand, for commercial purposes. This great spread of brickearth was known as the 'Grays Brickearths' in the older geological literature (Carreck 1976; Bridgland 1994), and was part of the northern feather edge of the Middle Pleistocene Thames channel. Recent research indicates that at least two extensive brickearth deposits were actually present, one earlier in age than the other, but which were not distinguished as such by the original investigators. At West Thurrock (see Chapter 7) is a remnant of brickearth dated to MIS 7. This belongs to the Taplow/Mucking Formation (see Table 2.1). At the Globe Pit, Little Thurrock, is the remnant of a brickearth spread that belongs in the Lynch Hill/Corbets Tey Formation, and dates to MIS 9.

John Wymer's excavations in the early 1950s (Wymer 1957) formally identified Little Thurrock as a Clactonian site. There have been two further controlled excavations since then (Snelling 1964; Bridgland and Harding 1993), and a number of important sections have been cut and described by Bernard Conway (Conway 1970; Wymer 1985), and Richard West (1969) among others. It was West who first suggested that the Little Thurrock brickearth should, on palynological grounds, be interpreted as an extension of those at West Thurrock, Ilford and Aveley (now interpreted as MIS 7 deposits). However, for West, all these brickearths were Ipswichian/MIS 5.5 in age. Full site histories are presented in the references already cited.

Geologically there are two contrasting interpretations of the stratigraphy of Little Thurrock. They are summarised in Figure 3.13. Figure 3.13A shows the general relationship between the deposits at the site. The brickearth overlies a gravel which contains the Clactonian artefacts. The gravel is benched into the local Thanet Sand bedrock which overlies chalk. Debate concerns the exact relationship between the gravel spread at c. 15 m OD in which the Bridgland/Snelling/Wymer excavations occurred, and a lower gravel at c. 6 m OD recorded by West and by Conway and Hart in the late 1950s and 1960s. Are they the same gravel or two different ones? In one interpretation, Figure 3.13B (Conway 1996a; Wymer 1985), the two gravels are considered as distinct and non-contemporary units, each aggraded onto its own bench. However, solifluction has occurred and material from the

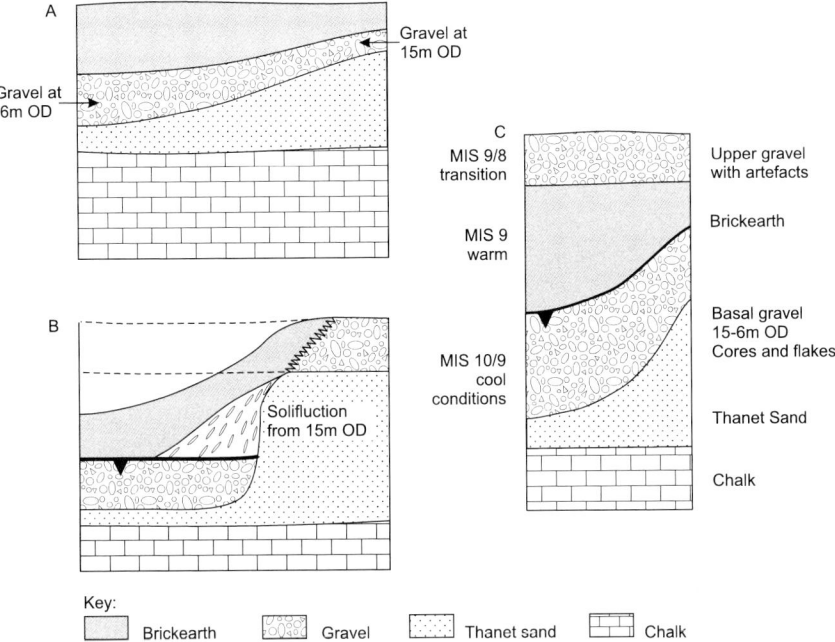

Figure 3.13 Contrasting interpretations of depositional sequence at Little Thurrock. A: generalised sequence; B: according to Conway and Wymer; C: according to Bridgland.

higher bench has sludged down the erosion slope between the two, blanketing the slope. On the lower terrace Conway recorded the presence of a land surface at the top of the gravel. There were fossil ice wedge casts, indicating cold climate activity, penetrating down from this surface.

This interpretation is contested by Bridgland (1994; Bridgland and Harding 1993) whose excavations specifically targeted the slope between the gravel at c.15 m OD and the lower gravel at c. 6.0 m OD. Bridgland posited a single sequence of bedded gravels and sands, Figure 3.13C. Bridgland and Harding (1993) robustly asserted that the gravel 'is bedded, and therefore cannot be soliflucted'. The bedding, they argue, is evidence of fluvial deposition and indicates that the gravel at 15 m OD and that at 6 m OD are part of a single and continuous sheet of gravel that thins out northwards as Figure 3.13A shows. I support the interpretation of Bridgland and Harding (ibid.). I worked as part of Bridgland's excavation team, and was able to observe the bedded nature of the gravels in person.

The traditional Clactonian assemblage from the site is present in the higher portion of the gravels at c. 15 m OD. It was from here that Wymer, Snelling, and Bridgland all recovered portions of an assemblage that lacked handaxes or thinning flakes. (I do not agree with Phil Harding's interpretation of a thinning flake present in the Bridgland excavations. The artefact also had slight patination not apparent on the other artefacts, ibid.: 278.) Conway (1996a) discovered artefacts from beneath the land surface with its frost wedges at c. 6.0 m OD. In situ, within the gravel, he recovered what he interpreted as two classic bifaces (Conway 1996a: Figures 1 and 2a). There were flakes associated with the bifaces. Unfortunately this material is now lost so we can only go on Conway's illustrations. From these I would tentatively agree with Mark White (2000) that the first biface is actually a non-classic, and that judgement on the other should be suspended for the moment.

In many respects Little Thurrock is similar to Jaywick Sands. Both sites are channel margin localities, and the archaeology is all in secondary context having been derived from elsewhere; the archaeology is part of the bedload. Most of it is small in size, probably reflecting its location at the channel margin. Whether there are two gravels or only one at Little Thurrock does not really matter, both gravels are part of the Lynch Hill/ Corbets Tey Formation. The non-handaxe character of the assemblage at 15 m OD is not in any doubt, and the presence of a non-classic handaxe lower down proves little since they also occur in Acheulean assemblages. In my opinion, there is a single wedge-shaped body of gravel at Little Thurrock, the thin end of the wedge tapering out to the north near the ancient river's bank (Figure 3.13C). The erosion surface and ice wedge probably represent a minor cold phase at the end of Bridgland's phase 2, prior to the deposition of the interglacial brickearth. The gravel contains the sweepings of channel margin occupation somewhere upstream. These were hominins who made cores and flakes and non-classic handaxes. The assemblage is evidently a non-biface one, but does it contribute to establishing a non-handaxe assemblage type? I am less certain, the reason being it is hard, with a channel margin sediment, to establish any real sense of time depth; Jaywick Sands is similar. I have my doubts about Little Thurrock.

Applying the Bridgland terrace model to the site raises an interesting point. After the new Corbets Tey/Lynch Hill floodplain was cut (phase 1 of the terrace model) near the glacial–interglacial transition, the gravel was emplaced at the base (phase 2). This is the single spread from 15 m down to 6 m as interpreted by Bridgland. This would date to late MIS 10 or earliest MIS 9. If we assume that the archaeology is contemporary with this, then Little Thurrock provides clear evidence for hominin occupation in cold or cool climatic conditions at least in stage 2 of the terrace model. At Swanscombe and Clacton, this was equivocal at best. Other evidence for this will be presented in later chapters. The erosive surface noted by Conway with ice wedges could date to this phase. The temperate stage of the terrace model would be the MIS 9 brickearths, see Figure 3.13C. Phases 4–5 of the Bridgland model are no longer readily apparent at this site because modern industrial and urban expansion has removed so much of the original deposits. But this was not always the case. Kennard (1904; 1916) described a higher gravel overlying (and by implication later than) the brickearth. It lay in a channel cut into the brickearth. This had been quarried away by the 1960s, but Conway was able to identify a remnant (his middle gravel) and confirm the observations of Kennard (Conway 1996a: Figure 3; see also Wymer 1985: 310; Bridgland and Harding 1993: 280). So stages 4 and 5 of Bridgland's terrace model were present at Little Thurrock. Kennard famously described a side scraper from this deposit, it is actually a transverse scraper (personal observation).

Lower Gravels at Cuxton (15 Rochester Road)

Cuxton is a site on the left bank of the River Medway, see Figure 2.8. The terraces of this river are variously preserved in its lower and upper reaches and contain important Palaeolithic sites. Bridgland (2003) has attempted a reconstruction of the Pleistocene history of the river and its relationship with the Thames Pleistocene terraces. The Medway was a right-bank tributary of the Thames for much of its history.

Recently, Mark White (2000) has suggested that the non-handaxe assemblage from the lower gravels at the Rochester Road site (Cruse et al. 1987) be interpreted as a Clactonian assemblage, relating to the Corbets Tey/Lynch Hill Formation – or at least its equivalent in this river valley (Bridgland 2003). Cuxton has a large Acheulean assemblage from the Rectory site (Tester 1965) over the road from the Rochester Road locality. The two sites are undoubtedly part of the same gravel spread, with the Rectory site somewhat higher (its base on chalk is c. 3.0 m higher than the chalk underlying the Rochester Road site 30 m away). The gravels at the Rochester Road site represent deposition in a braided river environment. There are two gravel deposits (each composed of a number of gravel/sand beds), separated by an erosion horizon. Handaxes are present in the upper gravels along with cores and flakes. There are cores and flakes in the lower gravels but handaxes are absent. Paul Callow, who studied the artefacts (Callow in Cruse et al. 1987), was adamant that the lower assemblage should not be considered as Clactonian, though on the basis of the data he presented, Mark White (2000) was unable to understand why. To my mind, the reason is clear. Apart from bifaces and their thinning flakes, the cores and flakes, and flake tools in any Acheulean assemblage will be the same as those from any Clactonian site (or at least the same range of variability will be present, McNabb 1992a; McNabb and Ashton 1995). The lower gravel assemblage at Rochester Road is 118 artefacts, excavated from about 5.5 m^3 (and the lower two sandy beds were not excavated in entirety). Given the similarity between the flake and core elements of the Acheulean and Clactonian, this is too small an assemblage, recovered from too small an area to confidently describe it as Clactonian. At best, it shows a hominin presence from the times of the earliest infilling of the Corbets Tey/Lynch Hill flood plain in the Medway Valley.

The altitude of both of the Cuxton Acheulean sites presents a problem for Bridgland's reconstruction of them as Corbets Tey/Lynch Hill equivalents in the Medway. The top of the Pleistocene gravels at Cuxton do not coincide with the projected surface height of the Corbets Tey/Lynch Hill Terrace in this area. They are too low by c. 8 m. They are better associated with the surface of the Binney Gravel which is the top of the next terrace down – equivalent to the Taplow/Mucking Formation, see Table 2.1. Bridgland argues that this implies the real surface of the Cuxton gravels has been truncated by erosion and the top is now missing. In fact, the archaeology at Cuxton would fit equally as well in the lower terrace. There are particular types of core called simple prepared cores (explained in detail in Chapter 7) present in the Acheulean assemblage from the Rectory site (personal observation) and from the Rochester Road site (Cruse et al. 1987: Figure 4.2a). As will be described in Chapter 6, these first begin to appear at the end of the time period represented by the Lynch Hill/Corbets Tey Formation (see Table 2.1). So the Rectory and Rochester Road sites could fit into either terrace. If it proved to belong to the lower terrace, it would make the identification of the lower gravels at Rochester Road as Clactonian even more unlikely.

Greenlands Quarry at Purfleet

The various Middle Pleistocene archaeological sites at Purfleet are justly famous: Greenlands and Bluelands quarries, Botany Pit and Esso Pit. These sites from the north bank of the Lower Thames Valley, downstream of Little Thurrock, contain sediments dated to the Lynch Hill/Corbets Tey Formation, see Table 2.1. What makes them important is that between them they preserve a complete record of the development of this terrace; mammals, molluscs, pollen, other biological evidence, and archaeology, are all preserved in a sequence of stratified sediments. Recent work (Bridgland et al. 2003; Schreve et al. 2002) has done much to clarify the relationship between the deposits in the different pits. A fuller discussion is presented in Chapter 6.

In terms of the Clactonian, the significance of Purfleet is the presence of archaeology at the base of the sequence. In Greenlands Pit, coombe rock (a cold climate chalky sludge considered to be the result of broken-up chalk moving down a slope under saturated condition) sits on top of chalk bedrock (see Table 6.1). Above this is a gravel bed, called the Little Thurrock Gravel Member, between 40 and 50 cm in depth. It was aggraded under cold conditions. Schreve et al. (2002) interpret it as a downstream equivalent of the gravels at Little Thurrock which underlie the brickearth there. So it would be MIS 10/9 in age and represent the first aggradation of the river in the newly cut Lynch Hill/Corbets Tey channel in this area (phase 2 of

Bridgland's terrace model). In the two lowest units at Greenlands, the Little Thurrock Gravel and the shelly gravel above it, there were cores and flakes that Mark White (in Schreve *et al.* 2002) has suggested might represent a Clactonian assemblage.

The recent work at Greenlands exposed a section nearly 14 m long. The lower beds were exposed for 6 m. No handaxes or thinning flakes were found. But as White fairly points out, the density of finds in these lower levels is very low; there were ten artefacts in the recent excavation from these two units, and in all only 50 artefacts have ever been excavated that can be safely attributed to them (White, in Schreve *et al.* 2002: 1455). In my opinion, this is too small a sample to interpret as Clactonian; this is a similar problem to that noted at Cuxton. The difference here is that there were too few artefacts over too wide an area. (There may actually be a handaxe from these lower beds. Wymer (1985) asserts that Palmer (1975) found one handaxe in the shelly gravel above chalk in Bluelands. Schreve *et al.* equate the shelly gravel at Bluelands quarry with their shelly gravel from the adjacent Greenlands quarry – the two deposits are at similar heights.)

What these data do make clear is that hominin occupation began close to the MIS 10/9 transition.

Other sites labelled Clactonian

There are a number of other sites which are often described as Clactonian or which have the label Clacton-like applied. They are almost always small assemblages in secondary context and from limited exposures. There are a number in East Anglia (Wymer 1985), especially along the Essex coast where Victorian collectors described elephant beds. They may or may not be contemporary with Clacton-on-Sea, and will not be discussed in any more detail here.

One site which does deserve mention is Rainbow Bar, Hampshire. This enigmatic site in the Solent estuary is a gravel bar exposed at low tide, located at the point where the River Meon enters the estuary. Geologically, the site is a mystery. Does its gravel belong to a Pleistocene Meon, and thus represent a terrace from this Solent tributary? Alternatively, are these deposits part of a Solent river terrace which would have paralleled the modern shore line? At present there is not enough information to even speculate. The site was first discovered by a local collector, Chris Draper, in the 1950s (Draper 1951), and more recently has been diligently observed by Brian Hack, who has amassed a large collection of artefacts (1998; 1999; 2000; 2004; 2005). Draper and Hack both suggested that Lower Palaeolithic artefacts were present at the site, Draper suggesting that the cores and flakes represented a Clactonian element. There are reports of handaxes (Hack 2004), and of Levallois (Draper 1951; in my opinion, this is not a Levallois artefact – personal observation). While I cautiously support Draper and Hack's contention that Lower Palaeolithic flintwork is present in the Rainbow Bar assemblage, confidently distinguishing it from the later prehistoric material on the bar is currently impossible. Cores and flakes, identical to those at other Lower Palaeolithic sites, are present in the assemblage, however, they occur in a bewildering variety of physical conditions. There are even two non-classic handaxes. Selecting out a Lower Palaeolithic element, let alone a Clactonian one, would be nigh-on impossible. Mesolithic material is clearly present in the form of a tranchet axe (Draper 1951; Jacobi, pers. comm.), and this kind of core and flake working is attested to elsewhere in the Mesolithic. There is blade working present that may be Upper Palaeolithic, Mesolithic or later prehistoric in age. For the moment, Rainbow Bar must remain a frustrating mystery.

Conclusion

In Part II of this book I will argue that the interpretation of the Clactonian as a cultural phenomenon was a product of the historical development of Palaeolithic archaeology in Britain. I will also argue that the existence of a non-handaxe cultural tradition has never been established by reference to a data set or methodology independent of the historical debate about the Clactonian. In this chapter I have described the sites which directly contributed to that debate, and attempted to place them in their broader geo-chronological setting. What, then, has a detailed look at the Clactonian sites revealed?

1   In my opinion, a secondary context site should have a minimum of 500 artefacts, and ideally 1,000 in order to justify the label non-handaxe assemblage. Why? Secondary context assemblages can be fairly said to represent a random sample of activities/technologies within an area upstream of the site. An assemblage of 1,000+ artefacts will reflect a number of bank side occupations over an unknown period of time. Differences in condition (rolled vs unrolled) demonstrate that transport will have occurred over varying timescales. A large assemblage should therefore sample the full spectrum of activities present at a locality over a particular length of time. It is not unreasonable to suppose that this would reflect centennial timescales at the very least.
2   Clacton and Swanscombe demonstrate the presence of a single flint working technology that occurs in a single well defined geological context.
3   At the Barnfield Pit the passage of time is clearly revealed in the nature of the gravels. They are an upward fining sequence reflecting the ever decreasing power of the river to transport large clasts. There is even a pause in deposition when, for an unspecified period of time, the river

ceased to aggrade. At Lion Point and the West Cliff at Clacton, Warren noted largish cobbles at the base of the river channel. The excavators of the Golf Course and Jaywick Sands noted finer gravel near the top.

If we combine these observations with the previous two points, then I would suggest we have a physical mechanism for identifying the existence of a non-handaxe tradition at a site that does not refer to the simple presence of cores and flakes, and then resorts to historical debate to empower their interpretation. Where a single technology is present at a secondary context site, and where the artefacts display a wide spectrum of physical conditions, and when the artefacts occur in a geological context that shows the passage of time, then I would argue that the evidence reveals a genuine continuity in hominin behavioural practice at that site – an archaeological tradition.

4 Localities at Clacton and Swanscombe have evidence of the presence of handaxe makers in the area in the form of one or two classic handaxes or a handful of thinning flakes. I robustly defend their provenance. These present an interesting set of possibilities in terms of hominin geographies, but do not compromise the overall interpretation of these sites as non-handaxe assemblages.

5 The makers of handaxe and non-handaxe assemblages can, locally, occupy the same ecological niche, as demonstrated at Barnham, and at broadly the same time.

6 Just to underline the point once more, the Barnfield Pit and Rickson's Pit at Swanscombe represent two non-handaxe assemblages – different points along the same channel. The Southfleet site, also a non-handaxe locality, is probably contemporary with them. Lion Point and the Golf Course site at Clacton-on-Sea also represent non-handaxe assemblages. These also sample distinct points along the same channel. The pollen evidence suggests the Swanscombe and Clacton sites are broadly contemporary (at least they all occur in the Early Temperate pollen zone (IIb?) of MIS 11). There is a genuine Acheulean presence at these sites, but it is a very minor one. These sites confirm the presence of a non-handaxe assemblage type, at least in MIS 11. Little Thurrock may represent a further non-handaxe assemblage, dating to the MIS 10/9 transition, or early MIS 9, but the issue of establishing time depth remains a concern (as it does with the Southfleet site!).

4

HOMININ OCCUPATION IN THE CROMERIAN COMPLEX AND IN THE EARLY PART OF THE ANGLIAN GLACIATION

Chronology and background

In this chapter I will review the evidence for the earliest occupation of Britain. The question that should be kept in mind when reading this chapter is, do the non-handaxe assemblages reviewed here provide a link between those mentioned in Chapter 1 and the Clactonian assemblages described in Chapter 3, which will be placed in their broader context in the next chapter? Would this justify the belief in a long-lived European non-handaxe tradition? I will return to this at the end of the chapter.

The interglacial before the Anglian glaciation in the traditional pollen-based terrestrial sequence was called the Cromerian. This was introduced in the last chapter, see Figure 3.3. As with all of the warm periods in this pre-DSC framework, the Cromerian was recognised by its own unique pollen signature. This was supported by a series of mammal species present in pre-Anglian deposits that did not appear after that glaciation, such as an extinct form of bison (*Bison schoetensacki*), an extinct species of elk (*Alces latifrons*), and an extinct species of rhinoceros (*Dicerorhinus etruscus*). This is now split into two: *Stephanorhinus etruscus* is the name given to earlier Middle Pleistocene forms, *Stephanorhinus hundsheimensis* is the name given to later forms that pre-date the Anglian – they may eventually prove to be the same species (Stuart 1982; D. Schreve, pers. comm.). Following the seminal work of Richard West (1980), the Cromerian interglacial was divided into four phases each of which represented a pollen based sub-stage (Figure 3.3) tracking the progress of the interglacial as it developed. As with the interglacials that succeeded the Anglian, the Cromerian in this scheme was interpreted as a single unbroken temperate phase. As far as the archaeology of the Cromerian was concerned, much of the debate from the 1960s to the 1980s concerned the following research agendas:

1   Establishing the presence in Britain of an Early Acheulean industry from sites like Kent's Cavern in Devon, and elsewhere.
2   The possibility that the handaxe, core and flake/flake tool assemblages from High Lodge were pre-Anglian.
3   Whether or not Westbury-sub-Mendip, Somerset (which was accepted as pre-Anglian) had true artefacts or not.

Linked to these was the question of when was Britain first occupied by hominins.

The fauna from Westbury also raised the worrying spectre of a more complicated bio-stratigraphic sequence than the pollen data allowed: were the mammals from the site genuinely suggesting an extra warm phase between the end of the Cromerian and the start of the Anglian? How could that be accommodated within the sequence?

The global climatic pattern for MIS 13, and the beginning of the Anglian in MIS 12, is shown in Figure 2.2. The sites discussed in this chapter are shown on the map in Figure 4.1. This is not a comprehensive list of sites from this period, only those mentioned in the text.

The critical area in Britain for investigating the Cromerian is the East Anglian coastline of Norfolk and Suffolk. Here sediments are being continuously exposed by marine erosion along 80 km of coastline (Parfitt 2005; Parfitt et al. 2005). Sections of this huge stretch of exposed deposits are known as the Cromer Forest-bed Formation (CF-bF), which is now known to encompass many temperate and cold climate phases of the Pleistocene. What are preserved in the cliffs are a series of glacial outwashes and glacial tills. As a glacier moves over the land, it erodes the surface it passes over. All this material is carried along at the base of the glacier. When it melts, this material, now compacted, is left behind as a till. Glacial outwash is the release of more of this scoured material, usually in the form of sands and gravels, as the glacier melts. Tills and outwashes can be left behind when a glacier finally melts, or when it retreats temporarily, for example, during an interstadial. In addition to these, there are temperate fluvial/estuarine deposits relating to a number of now vanished pre-Anglian rivers that flowed across East Anglia. Overlying the CF-bF are the sediments of the MIS 12 Anglian glaciation, represented by more tills and glacial outwashes.

As cliff exposures, these are laterally extensive sections making the relationship between different deposits easier to identify, at least in theory. So the stratigraphic relationship between the pre-Anglian deposits and those of the Anglian should be simple and directly observable. Naturally it isn't as simple as that.

West (1980) based his work on the terrestrial pollen framework that was introduced in Chapters 2 and 3. He identified one site in particular, West Runton, as a stratotype for the Cromerian interglacial. A stratotype is a geological deposit which acts as a reference section for all other deposits

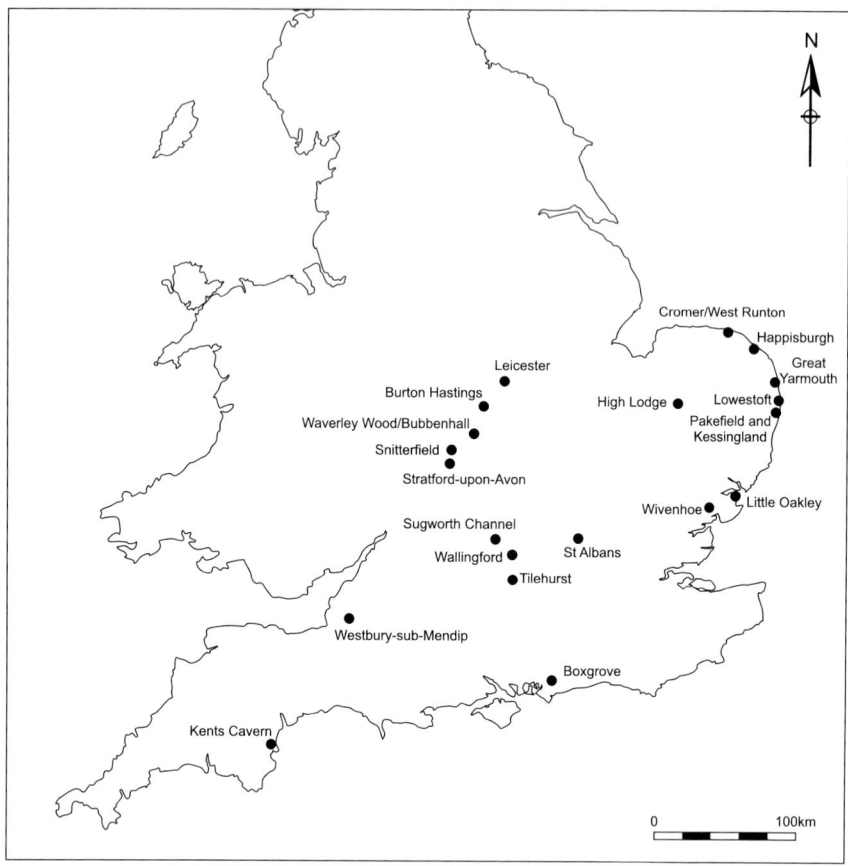

Figure 4.1 Map showing selection of sites discussed in Chapter 4.

belonging to the same geological unit or period. He then identified a series of sites along the East Anglian coastline that he believed fitted into the four sub-divisions that represented the pollen sub-stages of the Cromerian inter-glacial. However, a number of other researchers were suggesting that the deposits in some of these sites did not represent Cromerian sub-stages. Rather, they dated to completely different temperate phases than that pre-served in the stratotype; in effect, different interglacials. The small mammal record and the DSCs were suggesting that lumping all the temperate deposits in the CF-bF into one interglacial, called the Cromerian, was a vast oversimplification. In Chapter 2, the vole clock was briefly introduced. This was the evolutionary development of certain lineages of small mammal into new species. One of the problems of lumping all these sites into a single temperate period was that there was not enough time for *Mimomys savini* to evolve into *Arvicola terrestris cantiana* in just one pre-Anglian interglacial.

The most recent papers on the CF-bF (Preece and Parfitt 2000; Stuart and Lister 2001; Parfitt et al. 2005) have abandoned much of the old system. Instead sites in the CF-bF are simply placed into one of five successive faunal groups. This is the format followed in Figure 4.2, a framework based on mammalian evidence. Localities discovered in the future with suitable bio-stratigraphic evidence will presumably be compared to the framework, and either assigned equivalence with one phase, or used to refine the framework itself by adding additional phases. As the authors of Figure 4.2, Richard Preece and Simon Parfitt, are at pains to note, it remains to be

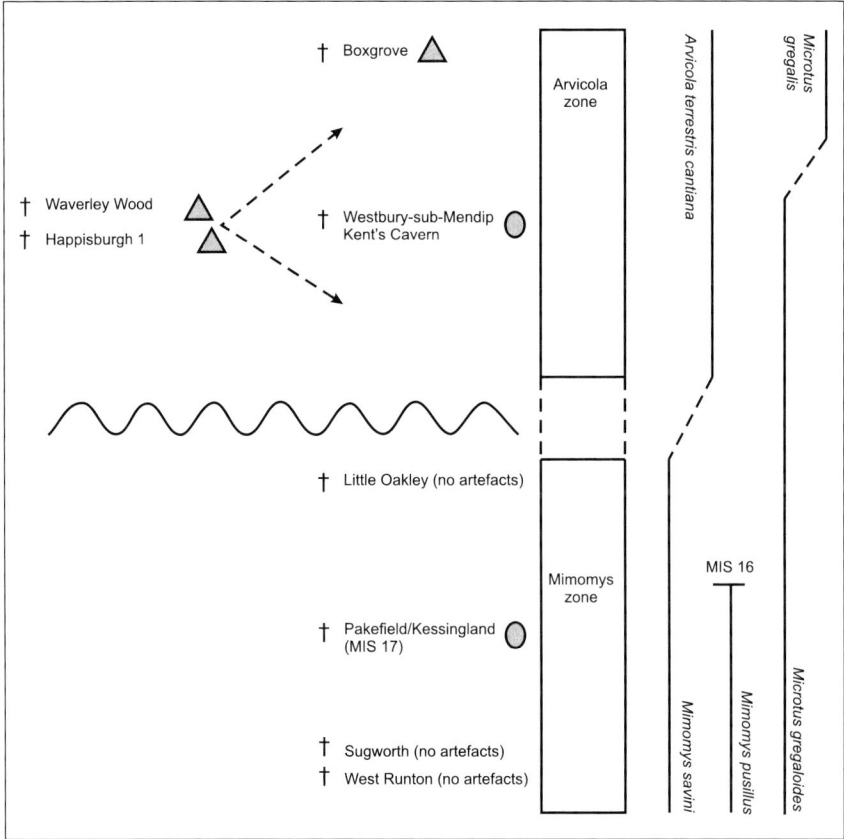

Figure 4.2 Schematic showing five chrono-stratigraphic faunal groups, named after sites of discovery, in pre-Anglian deposits in Britain. Critical small mammal indicator species also shown. Most recent at the top.

Notes: Triangles indicate presence of handaxes, ovals indicate cores and flakes only. Cross indicates normal magnetic field direction, indicating inclusion in Brunhes Chron.

Source: Data from Preece and Parfitt (2000) Preece and Parfitt (n.d.) Coope (2006).

established whether these sites are fully interglacial or interstadial in character. Some of them may belong to the same temperate phase while others belong to completely different ones. This is very much work in progress. The small mammal evidence which underlies much of this framework is supported by data on molluscs (Preece 2001) and large mammals (Stuart and Lister 2001). Critically, it will be important to tie the sites in Figure 4.2 into the chrono-stratigraphic histories of the rivers and tills (Rose *et al.* 2001; Lee *et al.* 2004) whose sediments are also exposed along the East Anglian coast, as well as further inland. But this is proving exceptionally difficult.

Why is it so difficult? In the mammalian groups set out in Figure 4.2, *Mimomys* is present in the three earliest groups, and its descendant, *Arvicola*, is present in the most recent two. The evolutionary change from one to the other must take place in the time range between the second and third groups, counting backwards in time. At Cromer on the Norfolk coast (Parfitt *et al.* 2006) there are three glacial tills beautifully preserved in the sea cliffs. The oldest is the Happisburgh Till. There is also the Runton/ Becton Till, and the Walcott Till. This last is an equivalent of the famous Lowestoft Till and so definitely MIS 12/Anglian in age. In fact, all three were once thought to be different pulses of ice advance in the Anglian glaciation (Parfitt *et al.* 2005). At Happisburgh, the deposits underlying the Happisburgh Till contain *Arvicola* and handaxes, and so should date to MIS 13 (or perhaps 15) – but certainly within the Arvicola zone. But geologists have thrown a spanner in the works (Lee *et al.* 2004). They claim that the Happisburgh Till is evidence of a previously unrecognised glacial advance in MIS 16, so the deposits under the Happisburgh Till would have to be MIS 17 or earlier. But the mammal people cannot accept this. The magnetic polarity of the sediments at the sites in the three early *Mimomys* groups is normal. So these must date from after the Brunhes/Matuyama boundary at c. 780 kya in MIS 19 (see Figure 1.5). This means that all three *Mimomys* faunal groups, and the transition to *Arvicola*, would have to happen between MIS 19 and MIS 17. The mammal people assert that there is just not enough time for this to happen.

For the moment, the term 'Cromerian Complex' is given to the time period encompassed by the different mammal groups in Figure 4.2, and which appear in sediments of the CF-bF along the Norfolk and Suffolk coasts. The sediments within this long stretch of coastline will date from a number of different pre-Anglian MI stages, and will have been laid down by different rivers flowing at different times and at different points along what is today's coastline. It is probable that the sediments of more than one glacial phase are also present in the sequence. Sorting out the chrono-stratigraphic relationships of these deposits will be a huge task that will take many years.

Regional geographies

The Midlands and into East Anglia – the Bytham river

I would normally begin the regional geographies with the Thames Valley because of the importance of this critical sequence. However, for this chapter, it is more appropriate to begin in the Midlands with the one of the great vanished rivers of Britain.

Figures 4.3A and 4.3B show the reconstructed course of the Bytham across East Anglia and the Midlands respectively. Prior to MIS 12 the Bytham river represented one of the most important drainage systems in Britain. Its existence has only been realised in the past decade or so. The river had a long history but most of the sediments that recorded this were destroyed when the river itself was destroyed by the Anglian glaciers. Today remnants of its deposits are found beneath Midlands and East Anglian tills, and other sediments. Its source is unknown, though Rose *et al.* (1999) suggest that for part of the river's history its headwaters were in Wales, and Wymer (1999) suggests that it flowed past the western slopes of the Chiltern Hills as its course took it north-east into the Midlands. In East Anglia in the Early Pleistocene, it may have been a left-bank tributary of the pre-diversion Thames, though in the earlier Middle Pleistocene the two rivers were separate at least for that stretch of their courses that took them across East Anglia (Lewis 1998; Rose *et al.* 1999).

In East Anglia something of the river's long history has been preserved in a series of deposits now known as the Bytham Group (Lee *et al.* 2004). This is a series of different geological members, either represented by individual layers at different sites, or as groups of closely related layers – see below and Figure 4.4. Geologists have found it difficult to relate the different members to each other in a single stratigraphic succession. The problem is that many individual members are geographically distant from each other, so linking them is sometimes problematic.

Another point of discussion is just how much of the pre-Anglian drainage pattern survived the MIS 12 glaciation (see below). After the Anglian ice had retreated, many stretches of the old Bytham valley in the Midlands and East Anglia, although mantled in till, still represented low-lying linear depressions in the landscape. Some post-Anglian rivers occupied stretches of the ancient Bytham's course.

In the Midlands, the Bytham flowed north-eastwards in a valley between Stratford and Leicester, see Figure 4.5. This section of the Bytham valley survived the Anglian glaciers, though now it lies buried beneath later sediments. However, the post-Anglian drainage pattern that established itself in this part of the old valley was completely different to that of the vanished Bytham. In the southern portion of this part of the valley, the precursor of the modern River Avon was established by at least MIS 9 or possibly MIS 10

A

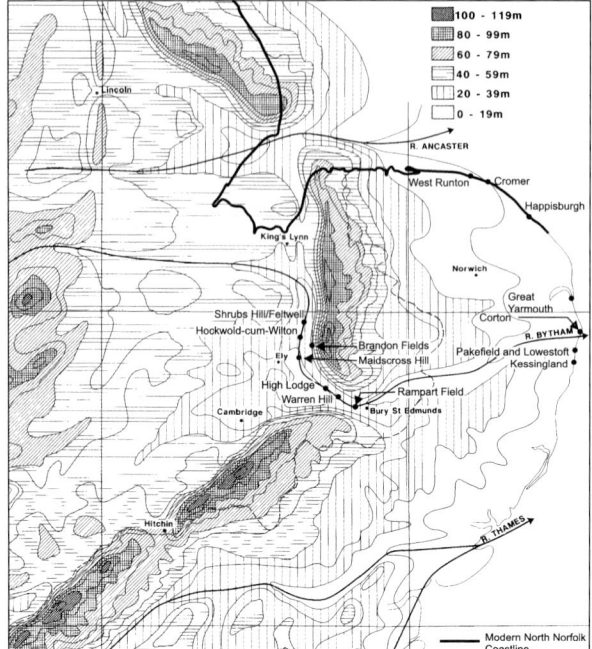

B

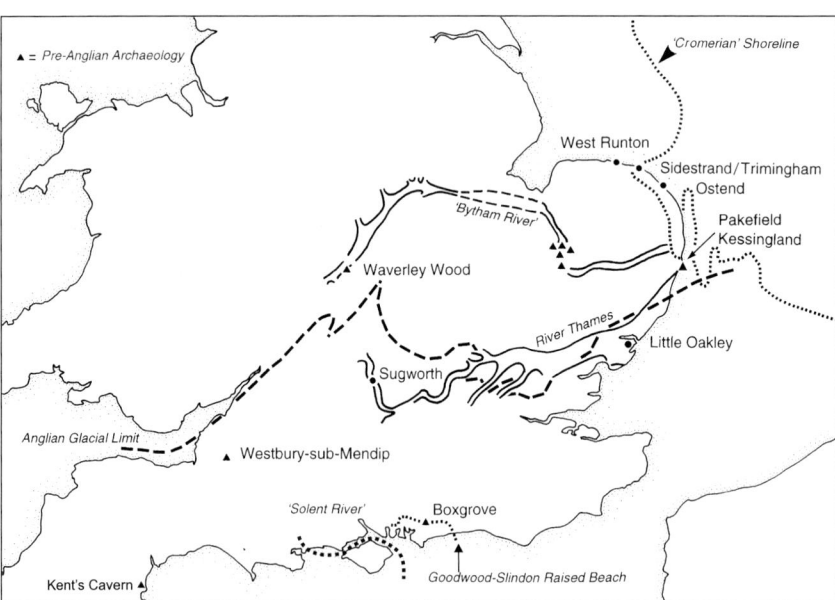

Figure 4.3 A: Hypothetical reconstruction of the topography of pre-MIS 12 East Anglia. B: The course of the Bytham river across the Midlands and into East Anglia.

Notes: Triangles indicate position of pre-Anglian archaeological sites. Images used with permission.

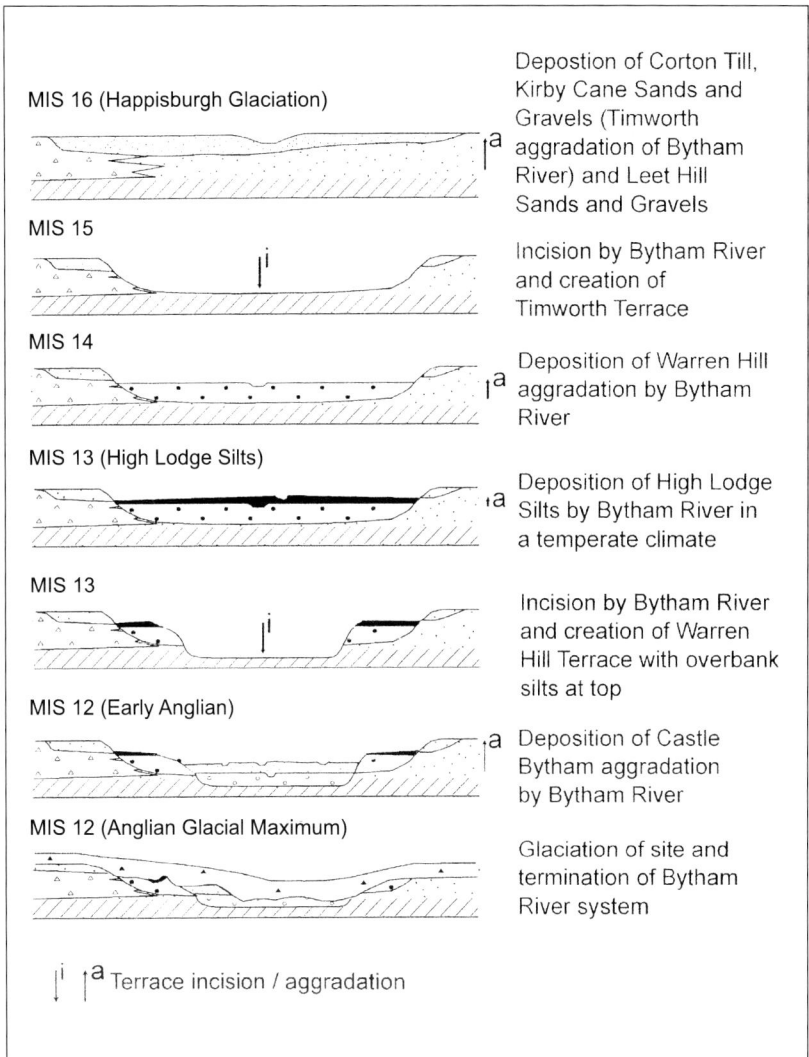

MIS 16 (Happisburgh Glaciation)

Depostion of Corton Till, Kirby Cane Sands and Gravels (Timworth aggradation of Bytham River) and Leet Hill Sands and Gravels

MIS 15

Incision by Bytham River and creation of Timworth Terrace

MIS 14

Deposition of Warren Hill aggradation by Bytham River

MIS 13 (High Lodge Silts)

Deposition of High Lodge Silts by Bytham River in a temperate climate

MIS 13

Incision by Bytham River and creation of Warren Hill Terrace with overbank silts at top

MIS 12 (Early Anglian)

Deposition of Castle Bytham aggradation by Bytham River

MIS 12 (Anglian Glacial Maximum)

Glaciation of site and termination of Bytham River system

Terrace incision / aggradation

Figure 4.4 Schematic of the developmental history of the terraces and deposits of the Bytham river as promoted by a number of geologists.

Note: Used with permission.

(see Figure 2.8; Maddy et al. 1995; Wymer 1999). This river ran in the opposite direction to the Bytham, flowing toward the south-west where it became the Warwickshire Avon. In that part of the Bytham's old course near Leicester, the precursor of the modern River Soar flowed in a north-easterly direction, following the old Bytham drainage line, but then

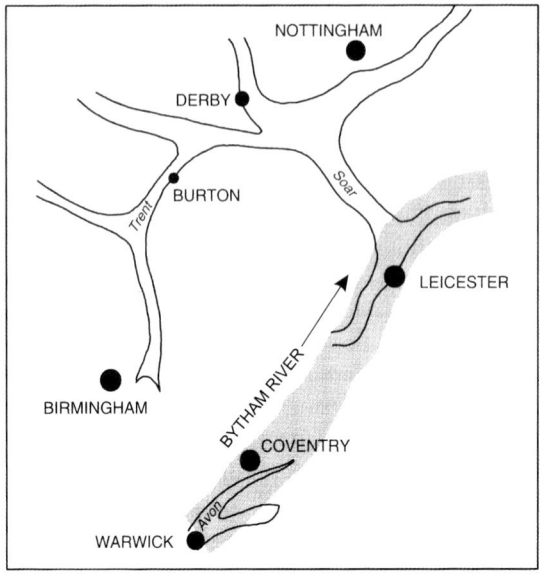

Figure 4.5 Sketch map of the former Bytham river drainage, compared to that of major modern rivers in the Midlands.

Note: Used with permission.

abandoning it by turning north where it was confluent with the Wreake, and then to the south bank of the Trent. The relationship between the Midlands deposits and those in East Anglia are shown on the cross-section in Figure 4.6. Clast lithology (rock type of individual gravel pebbles) indicates that quartzite gravel, derived from Midlands bedrock, was an important component of the Bytham's bedload, and its presence in gravel sections aids in the identification of Bytham sediments in East Anglia where locally

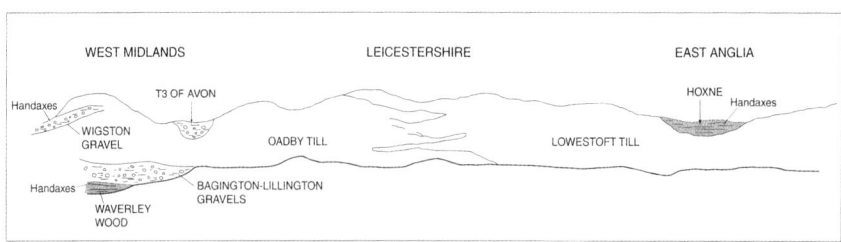

Figure 4.6 Schematic cross-section of the relationship between major depositional units in East Anglia and in the Midlands.

Note: Used with permission.

derived gravels are usually of flint from the underlying chalk. The south-eastward-flowing Bytham's course near Bury St Edmunds, see Figure 4.3A, is now occupied by the north-westerly-flowing River Lark (Lewis 1998), and the Lark seems to occupy much of the older river's course in this section of its valley. East of Bury, the Bytham turned from a south-easterly course to a more easterly one. Today this portion of the drainage line is occupied by the eastward-flowing River Waveney (Figure 2.8).

In Figure 4.4 a series of schematic cross-sections show the development of the terraces of the Bytham river. The scheme is based on the work of Lee et al. (2004) and remains controversial, as does their dating of the individual stages. What the figure really shows is the complexity of this river's history; how it was evolving over time, and how the terraces were a combination of diverse sedimentary units/members. Different inter-glacial and glacial sediments were incorporated in the terraces, so each had a complex depositional history of its own. Lee et al.'s conception of the river's development is very different from the Bridgland model (downcut-ting occurs in interglacials and gravel aggrades in glacials). How various stages and members relate to one or more of the bio-stratigraphic phases in Figure 4.2 remains to be seen.

At the site of Waverley Wood Farm Pit at Bubbenhall in Warwickshire (Figures 4.1 and 4.3B), three organic channels underlie various members of the Bytham Group (in this part of the river's course they are formally referred to by their local name of Baginton Sand and Lillington Gravel, these being individual members in the Baginton Formation). The oldest of the channels may be separated from the later two by a whole glacial period (Meijer and Preece 1995). The overlying sand and gravel members repre-sent the floodplain of the Bytham. In turn, these are overlain by an Anglian till. AAR dates suggested an age of MIS 15 for these channel sediments (Bowen et al. 1989). But small mammal data shows that Arvicola is present in the limited mammal assemblage. Resolving the precise dating of Waverley Wood will depend on whether or not the channels do date to different interglacials, or from different phases of the same one, as well as whether the Arvicola zone should be confined to MIS 13, or could include MIS 15 (or at least part of it). At least part of the channel complex (the later part) is likely to date to MIS 13 and is in the Arvicola zone.

Originally three handaxes and two flakes were recovered from the site, the handaxes and one of the flakes being found on the floor of the pit and therefore not in context (Shotton and Wymer 1989). One of the flakes (in quartzite) did come from the base of one of the channels. More recent work (Lang and Keen 2005; Keen et al. 2006) has since recovered more andesite bifaces, and established a clear presence of quartzite handaxes at the site, also from the channels (Lang and Keen 2003). In-situ artefacts can now be provenanced to the highest and to the lowest of the channels (Lang and Keen 2003; Keen et al. 2006). These artefacts clearly indicate the presence of hominins in the Bytham valley before the Anglian, possibly a long time before it. What is more, they demonstrate occupation well in land from the coast. Wymer (1999) and Keen *et al.* (2006) suggest that the andesite bifaces may have been carried by hominins for some time before they were lost or discarded. They are made from an andesite tuff which is found in the Lake District. On the other hand, there are clasts of andesite found within the local gravels (ibid.), so it is possible they were made from river clasts found occasionally in the region. There are a small number of andesite handaxes from other sites in the Midlands (Lang and Keen 2003; 2005), and most of them are associated with Bytham river deposits. There are also flint handaxes from Waverley Wood. Since the nearest flint sources lie far to the east and to the south, these artefacts may well have been brought into the area by hominins. Beetle evidence for the middle channel reveals how complex the climatic signal from the site is (Coope 2006). It records a climate gradually getting colder, with a temporary reversion, near the top of the channel infill, to warmer conditions.

As noted, the Waverley Wood organic sediments are overlain by sand and gravel members which are part of the Baginton Formation. In turn, these are overlain by a glacial till, the Thrussington Till equated with the Anglian. That glacial ice moved south along the valley of the Bytham is demonstrated clearly by the deposits at Snitterfield, just to the north of Stratford (Maddy and Lewis 1991). Here sediments that are the equivalent of the Baginton Formation are overlain by sands, silts and clays that are the result of pro-glacial ponding as the Bytham flowed up against the advancing ice front further upstream, forming a pro-glacial lake. There is another such lake in the Midlands at Wolston, known as Lake Harrison; Shotton (1953) believed that these were actually different parts of a single huge lake! The Snitterfield deposits chart the course of a right-bank tributary of the main Bytham river.

No archaeology was discovered with the Snitterfield deposits, but there is associated with another Anglian till, the Oadby Till (Figure 4.6). The Midlands are critically important for understanding the Anglian glaciation. There are a number of tills, and other glacial deposits that indicate the Anglian ice front advanced and retreated on a number of occasions within the time span of the Anglian glaciation. The Thrussington Till mentioned above represents an early advance. The Oadby Till represents a later one. To the north-west of Coventry a series of bifaces were discovered in the vicinity of Burton Hastings and Wolvey by a local collector (R. Waite, see Saville 1988). These are mostly surface finds scattered over a number of different locations, but have come from the underlying gravels in this area, the Wigston Gravels (see Figure 4.6). Since they are surface finds, it is assumed that they have been derived from the upper parts of the Wigston Gravels. These Wigston Gravels are part of an outwash plain of sands and gravels that developed in front of the Anglian Oadby glacier. Any artefacts in the

Wigston Gravels have to date to before the Oadby Glacier itself, as they will have been picked up by the ice and then deposited by melt water in the outwash. The artefacts were a mixture of handaxes and debitage in flint and in quartzite. This indicates the presence of hominins slightly to the north-west (presumably) of the Bytham's main valley. There are no other pre-Anglian archaeological sites in the Midlands which can be securely related to the Bytham.

The sands and gravels of the Bytham river in western East Anglia contain a number of archaeological sites. A group of five sites are identified as having potential Bytham river deposits on the presence of quartzites within their gravel. The five sites are located on the long southward stretch of the river prior to the south-eastward curve that would take it into what is now the modern River Lark. Shrubb Hill and Feltwell (Figure 4.3a; Wymer 1985) have a number of bifaces in a wide variety of conditions, some of which are very rolled (Wymer 1999). What is curious about Shrubb Hill is its height. It is a little over 1.2 m above sea level, and is therefore much lower than the sites associated with the Bytham further downstream. Wymer suggests a number of factors that may be responsible for this, including subsidence of the Fen area in which the site is located. Alternatively, it may be on a low and so later terrace of the Bytham, the higher sites being on earlier terraces (Wymer 2001).

Situated some 6 km to the east is Hockwold-cum-Wilton (Figure 4.3A; Wymer 1985). This is at 18 m above sea level. It is a much smaller assemblage but the range of biface types complements those at Shrubb Hill and Feltwell. A proportion of the Hockwold bifaces are also rolled. At Maidscross Hill, Lakenheath (Figure 4.3A; ibid.), another gravel with a quartzite component is present, but this site attains a height of some 30 m above sea level. The same range of bifaces appears to be present and again there is a rolled and worn component to the assemblage. At about 30 m OD is the Brandon Fields Pit at Brandon (Figure 4.3A), on the east side of a gravely ridge running at right angles to the direction of flow of the local river, the Little Ouse. Biface and flake tools are reported from the gravels (ibid.), which were here noted to be quite rich in quartzite and other non-local rocks, and from which a number of the implements had been made. As with the other sites, the range of biface types, and the condition they were in, are comparable.

The next set of Bytham sites are today associated with the drainage of the River Lark, or on high ground close to this valley. Three of these sites have Lower Palaeolithic artefacts, but there are other sites within the Lark drainage that do not have any archaeology associated (Wymer 1985; Bridgland et al. 1995b; Lewis 1998).

High Lodge, Mildenhall (Ashton et al. 1992a) was the subject of intensive investigations during the 1960s, and then again in the late 1980s (the historical context of this is described in Chapter 11 and Table 11.2). In effect, the sediments at High Lodge preserve a portion of the flood plain of the Bytham river during MIS 13 (ibid.). The fauna associated with the artefacts, and the sedimentology of the clays within which the archaeology occurs, imply a temperate environment and a slow-moving or still body of water. The beetles and insect evidence (Coope 2006) suggest the site was a reedy marsh that dried out in the summer months. There were meadows nearby, and if a tree line was present, it was some distance away.

The clays contain a primary context assemblage of cores and refitting flakes, as well as flake tools and a number of well-made scrapers. Biface making was evidently carried out somewhere close by on the flood plain, as a thinning flake was also found in the clays during the 1960s excavations. As Anglian glaciers entered the area, a great raft of this clay, containing the refitting knapping scatters within it, probably already in a frozen state, was gouged out of the flood plain and carried along within the body of the moving ice sheet. On melting, the glacier deposited the clays, probably still in a semi-frozen state and still with undisturbed archaeology, onto a basal lodgement till.

Above the clays a considerable quantity of sands and gravels were then deposited which contained bifaces. These too are probably remnants of the artefact litter that hominins left behind on the Bytham flood plain. Presumably these were swept up by the ice from another part of the flood plain (or perhaps were originally from deeper in the channel below the clays) but were not drawn into the glacier in blocks of frozen sediment. Finally, a flow deposit (the so-called upper till) was laid down on top of the gravels. This was the detritus from the surface of the glacier, which swept down over the other deposits as its leading edge was melting.

The artefacts from the clays are in mint condition, while the bifaces from the sands and gravels above are in a mixed condition, though most are quite fresh. High Lodge is the only substantial core and flake assemblage from pre-Anglian deposits that even remotely approaches the criteria discussed in the last chapter for a non-handaxe assemblage. But it has the thinning flake noted above, and scrapers of this kind (see Figure 1.3) are not present in Clactonian assemblages. Whether this site should or should not be interpreted as a Clactonian assemblage is a matter of personal opinion. I believe the scrapers merely reflect the complexity of hominin behaviour practised at various points on the Bytham's floodplain.

Warren Hill (Figure 4.3A; Bridgland *et al.* 1995b; Lewis 1998) is another famous site in the British Lower Palaeolithic. As with Swanscombe, it has an artefact count in the thousands. Useful histories are given by Wymer (1985) and by Roe (1981b). Although sections in the gravel exposures from here were observed by various people, very little was written on the site. One of the most detailed reports (Solomon 1933) interpreted the gravels as glacio-fluvial outwash. This was on the basis of a general tumbled appearance to the gravel, and the presence of chalk clasts which would not have survived prolonged fluvial transport. This interpretation became the commonly accepted one. The glaciation responsible was thought to be a post-Anglian one. However, recent work in the pit has revealed the sequence in more detail. The gravels overlie a sand unit, in turn, overlying chalk (Bridgland *et al.* 1995b). The conclusion of the recent investigations was that while the gravel certainly was unusual, it was not outwash but fluvial in origin. There is a notable quartzite component in the gravel, and with the exception of chalk clasts, the gravels do not contain the normal lithologies present in other Anglian outwash deposits in the area (*Rhaxella* chert and Jurassic limestone – ibid.).

Most of the artefacts were recovered by quarry men. It is assumed, probably correctly, that they originate within the gravel, although Wymer (1985: 90ff.) notes early reports of the presence of other beds. Solomon (1933) divided the artefacts up into discrete groupings based on visible condition. Roe (1981b) using slightly different criteria, confirmed that division within the artefact set was possible. A rolled assemblage of mainly pointed bifaces was distinct from a fresher series. Bridgland *et al.* (1995b) suggest that it may be valid to distinguish between the fresher ovates and the more worn/rolled ovates. At present, it may be safer to just infer that a genuinely older assemblage of more worn bifaces is interspersed with a fresher series. Lee *et al.*'s (2004) controversial dating of the Bytham's terraces has suggested a possible date for this site in MIS 14 (Figure 4.4), which might make the more rolled handaxes MIS 15. Simon Lewis (pers. comm.) prefers a stage 12 date for the gravels, thus dating the handaxes to sometime (probably) within MIS 13.

At the nearby site of Rampart Field, Icklingham (Figure 4.3A; Bridgland *et al.* 1995b), a similar situation is present. Although this site only has a small number of artefacts associated with the gravels, these gravels lack the features normally associated with Anglian outwash. They are therefore interpreted as fluvial sediments of the Bytham group.

One interesting point to emerge from the above discussion is the frequency with which rolled artefacts occur in the same deposits as fresher ones. The assumption here is that unrolled/slightly rolled artefacts are broadly contemporary with their deposits. The more damaged artefacts may well be much older.

East Anglia, the Norfolk and Suffolk coastline

A more detailed reconstruction of East Anglia before the arrival of the Anglian glaciers was presented in Figure 4.3A. Pre-Anglian sediments are contained within the CF-bF, as noted at the beginning of this chapter. It is worth re-emphasising that the different sedimentary units and beds that make up this Formation span a number of different interglacial–glacial cycles.

The West Runton Freshwater Bed may well represent a right-bank tributary of the Ancaster river (Figure 4.3A; Clayton 2000; Rose *et al.* 2001). The molluscs (Preece 2001) and sediments imply a slow-flowing river. These sediments with *Mimomys* (Preece and Parfitt 2000) are among the oldest Cromerian Complex sites that can currently be fitted into the sequence in Figure 4.2. The Ancaster is believed to have flowed across what is now the north Norfolk coast after emerging from the Ancaster Gap which gives it its name (though *in-situ* sediments relating to it have yet to be identified there).

Geographically, Pakefield and Kessingland (Figure 4.3A) are near Lowestoft. Pakefield was discussed in Chapter 1. Flakes and cores, but no handaxes, have been discovered in sediments that contain *Mimomys*. A minimum age of MIS 17 is suggested for this site (Parfitt *et al.* 2005). Section drawings presented by Parfitt *et al.* (ibid.: Figure 3) show these temperate fluvial sediments are stratigraphically below other sediments associated with the Bytham river. Whether or not these early MIS 17 interglacial deposits are early Bytham sediments, or part of a different river remains to be seen. Hamblin and Moorlock (1995) show the Bytham floodplain (i.e. the width of the valley, not the river itself) as stretching from Great Yarmouth to just south of Lowestoft. Anthony Stuart and Adrian Lister (2001) have suggested that the site of Corton a few kilometres to the north (and also between Great Yarmouth and Lowestoft) is contemporary with Pakefield and Kessingland, and that the three sites sample points along the same floodplain. Corton's stratigraphic succession is very similar to that of Pakefield/Kessingland.

With the exception of Pakefield, Figure 4.2 shows that early hominin occupation of Britain was confined to the *Arvicola* zone as exemplified by Boxgrove and Westbury. Very few of the East Anglian coastal sites have produced archaeology. One of the first to do so is Happisburgh (locality 1) almost half-way between the Ancaster and the Bytham. Here several handaxes and flakes have been found beneath the Happisburgh Till which may make them very old indeed (Lee *et al.* 2004). But caution is necessary. As noted earlier in this chapter, the mammal evidence from the site suggests a more recent date, within the *Arvicola* zone. For the mammal specialists either the identification of the Happisburgh Till at Happisburgh is wrong (i.e. it is actually a different till), or the dating of the glaciation it represents is wrong – too old. On the evidence of the beetle and insect faunas, Coope (2006) suggests that Happisburgh 1 and Waverley Wood may be contemporary. They both have very similar suites of beetles, even the exotic components are very similar. Happisburgh appears to have been a marsh. Dung beetles attest to the presence of larger mammals along the river's margins. Coope (ibid.) suggests Happisburgh is too far up the coastline to be related to the Bytham. So perhaps it represents another river midway between the Ancaster and the Bytham along which handaxe-making hominins were definitely moving in pre-Anglian times. These later pre-Anglian rivers could well represent the route of entry into eastern England for hunters moving westward across the dry land of the North Sea bight as Wymer (1999) has noted.

The Thames Valley and its tributaries

During part of the Early Pleistocene the headwaters of the Thames were probably in Wales, but by the Middle Pleistocene the river had been captured by more southerly drainages and rose in the Cotswolds, near to where it now rises. As Figure 4.7 shows quite clearly, the course of the river in the Middle Pleistocene, particularly in its lower stretches, was very different from that of today. The Upper Thames is taken to be that stretch of the river from its source to the Goring Gap. This is the passage through the cretaceous chalk of the Chiltern Hills. The Middle Thames is the stretch from the Goring Gap to the Thames' confluence with the River Lea, and the Lower Thames is from the Lea to the estuary. From Figure 4.7 it is evident that the course of the Thames across East Anglia had been gradually moving southwards like a door swinging on its hinge. In effect, the lower reaches of the Bytham river in Figure 4.3A flowed over an area that the Thames had already abandoned in its migration southwards.

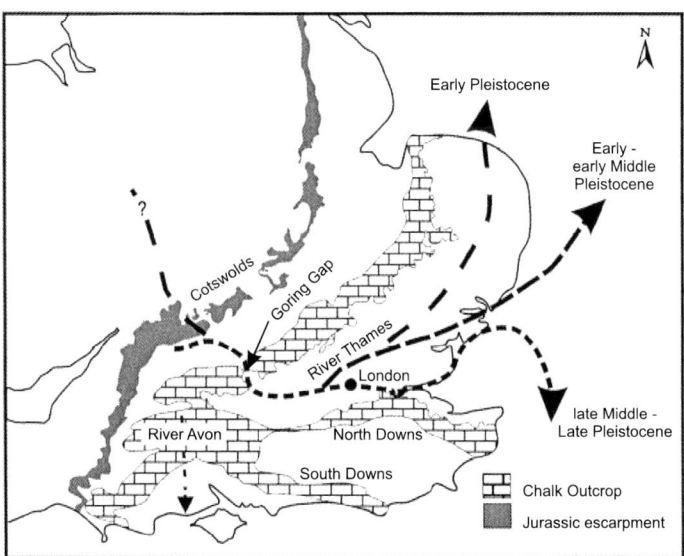

Figure 4.7 Schematic reconstruction of the history of the Thames river across East Anglia.

Note: Dotted lines indicate different courses of the river. Used with permission.

Figure 4.8 gives some idea of the changes in Middle Pleistocene geography initiated by the advancing Anglian ice sheets to the south and west of East Anglia. We have already seen that the whole of the Bytham system, and the other East Anglian rivers whose sediments are found along today's coastline were over-ridden by the Anglian ice and destroyed. Just prior to the arrival of the glaciers, the course of the River Thames was as follows. It flowed through the Goring Gap into the Middle Thames area as it does today. Once in the Middle Thames area, the river then turned roughly north-eastwards and flowed through the Vale of St Albans, and then on toward the East Anglian coast. Across East Anglia, these pre-diversion

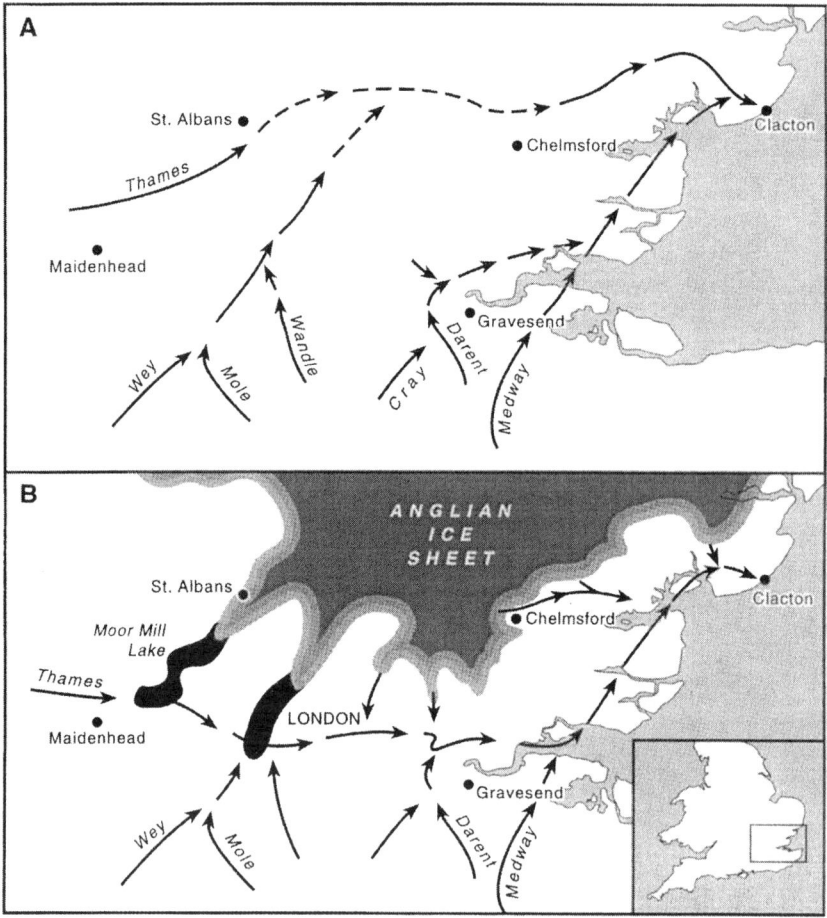

Figure 4.8 The courses of the Thames and Medway rivers (A) before and (B) during/after the MIS 12 diversion of the Thames.

Note: Used with permission.

Thames deposits are collectively termed the Kesgrave Group. Figure 4.8 details what happens next. Much of this part of the story is the work of Cambridge geologist Phil Gibbard (1979; 1985). Two large lobes of ice on the south-western margin of the glacier dammed the Thames, the westernmost lobe overrunning the Vale of St Albans completely. The Thames now flowed into a huge pro-glacial lake called the Moor Mill Lake. A second lake was located to the east. Although no one quite knows why, the Moor Mill was breached and a vast quantity of water flowed eastwards along a spillway which was formed by the enormous outpouring of water. The water flowed into the eastern lake. At some point the eastern lake also burst its banks and a huge volume of water was again released. This time it flowed into a small pre-existing east–west valley which was deepened and widened to become what we know today as the Lower Thames Valley.

Sadly, there is nowhere in the Upper Thames, or upper part of the Middle Thames, where former pre-diversion deposits are well preserved. In these stretches of the river the floodplain tends to be narrow, and later erosion and deposition have resorted the gravels of earlier aggradations. So the identification of a pre-Anglian occupation of the Upper and Upper Middle Thames Valleys is difficult. This must surely be a major reason why Wymer's (1999) extensive survey of the British Lower Palaeolithic was unable to identify a single substantial Cromerian site with archaeology throughout the whole of this stretch of the Thames. In the Upper Thames there is only one site, the Sugworth Channel (see Figures 4.1 and 4.2 and 2.9A; Wymer 1999) that dates to this period. In fact, a series of rich organic channels were discovered here. The evidence from the mollusc and mammal faunas, and the pollen, suggests the site is similar in age to the West Runton Freshwater Beds (Preece and Parfitt 2000). Mimomys was present, but unfortunately archaeology was not.

Within the proximity of Goring Gap itself, there is an intriguing location that preserves evidence of early Anglian or pre-Anglian occupation. The Wallingford fan gravels (Table 2.2) represent the sweepings of the slopes of the Chiltern Hills, moved down slope by solifluction. There are a number of sites within these gravels and they contain handaxes (Wymer 1999). Further upslope, these gravels interdigitate with gravels of the Winter Hill Terrace (Figure 2.9B; Horton et al. 1981). This is an extensive and thick spread of gravels in the Middle Thames that dates to the coldest phase of the Anglian (Table 2.2; Gibbard 1985), the period of lockdown when cold climate conditions would almost certainly have precluded hominin occupation. As a solifluction deposit that interleaves with the Winter Hill gravels, the archaeology contained within the fan gravels must be at least as old, or older than the gravels themselves. As the sweepings of adjacent slopes (Wymer 1999), the artefacts provide evidence for occupation of high ground and low-lying hills, in this case, the Chilterns, in the pre-Anglian or early Anglian at the latest.

Once through the Goring gap and into the Middle Thames, the evidence of occupation in the Thames during this period virtually vanishes. A number of localities within the Middle Thames have produced artefacts from soliflucted deposits, but were these genuinely from pre-Anglian surfaces? Others have come from high level gravels, but as Wymer (1999) points out, it is difficult to know whether these artefacts are really associated with the upper part of these deposits, or reworked into the gravels' surfaces in later times. At Tilehurst, just south of the Gap, a series of artefacts have been found in just this situation (ibid.). The artefacts are associated with a patch of gravel over 100 m OD. The gravel is Gerrards Cross Gravel considered by Gibbard (1985) to be older than the Winter Hill Gravel (Figure 2.9B). It too is an Anglian aged deposit (or possibly late Cromerian). The problem here is that only a few of the handaxes came from within the gravels, the remainder were surface or near surface finds. Other occasional surface finds are present on high ground elsewhere, and on Winter Hill Terrace surfaces in this western section of the Middle Thames, but the same problems affect these finds too.

This situation is perpetuated in the former Lower Thames Valley in the pre-diversion course across Hertfordshire and East Anglia. From Figure 4.8 it is clear that the ancient floodplain of the Thames traversed a considerable area. This is the area where we find the Kesgrave Group of deposits. Yet not a single biface has ever been found in these deposits, in fact, artefacts of any description are virtually non-existent (Wymer 1999). The site of Little Oakley, Essex, has Thames deposits of pre-Anglian age and faunal remains (see Figure 4.2). Its location was just upstream from the Thames' pre-Anglian confluence with the northward-flowing Medway (see Figure 4.8; Bridgland 1994; Preece 2001; Preece and Parfitt 2000). The river here was large and swiftly flowing. In Figure 4.2 the site is placed near the *Mimomys*/*Arvicola* boundary. The reason for this is that a number of the *Mimomys* teeth have no roots, so this may be a transitional population. Sadly, no artefacts are associated with the site.

Another pre-diversion site is Wivenhoe, the last fluvial terrace of the Thames in its old course before the river's diversion. The site is close to Little Oakley, and represents the next step down in the Thames terrace staircase in this area. Unfortunately it has no mammal or mollusc evidence so it cannot be fitted into the scheme presented in Figure 4.2. Bridgland (1988; Bridgland et al. 1988) equates this site with the Gerrards Cross Gravel in the Middle Thames that was present at Tilehurst. This would make it late Cromerian or early Anglian in date. There are two small flakes from the Wivenhoe deposits which were found in situ (Bridgland 1988), but in my opinion this is not enough evidence to establish a hominin presence in the pre-diversion Thames in this part of the valley – they may not even be hominin-struck flakes. The next step down in the terrace flight from Wivenhoe is the St Osyth/Holland Gravels (Table 2.2). These are equated by Bridgland (1988) with the Winter Hill Terrace of the Middle Thames. They represent outwash and melt waters flowing along the former course of the Thames during the period when the glaciers had overridden the Vale of St Albans.

The south-bank tributaries of the Thames

One of the sites mentioned in early discussions of pre-Anglian occupation (Roe 1981b) is Farnham Terrace A. Much of the evidence for an early or pre-Anglian date rests on the height at which this terrace is located. Farnham Terrace A sits on the high ground above the modern River Wey with its flight of later terraces on the south side of the valley. The high plateau behind has been cut by more recent rivers and streams. Incised into this plateau is a channel, the Boundstone Channel. Oakley (1939) considered it to contain the sweepings of ancient land surfaces adjacent to the river when the Boundstone Channel was an active river meandering across its flood plain at this height, and prior to the cutting of the Wey terraces in the valley as seen today. If this is true, then it implies a very high antiquity for the deposits in the channel.

Slightly lower is a second channel, the Gravel Hill Channel considered to be of a similar age. Today the Wey sweeps southwards at a point somewhat to the north-east of Farnham. However, in pre-Anglian times it continued to flow north-east in at least part of what is the modern valley of the River Blackwater (and is sometimes known here as the Farnham river). So the palaeo-geography of this river was very different from that of today. Roe (1981b) summarising the contextual difficulties associated with Terrace A artefacts, noted that much of the original evidence for ascribing such an early date was based on artefact typology. However, the position and altitude of the channels, if they are genuine early Wey deposits, do rather imply an ancient date.

Although a number of south- and north-bank tributaries of the Thames will have existed in pre-Anglian times, reconstructing their courses and identifying sedimentary units that were associated with these ancient river courses is as difficult as it is in the main valley.

Outside of the Thames Valley

Westbury-sub-Mendip

Pioneering work by Bishop (1974) suggested, on the basis of the mammalian fauna, that not only was the site pre-Anglian in age, but that it represented a temperate episode in between the Cromerian as understood in the 1960s and 1970s, and the succeeding Anglian glaciation. The publication of the long-awaited Westbury monograph (Andrews et al. 1999) has done much to clarify the questions that have surrounded this site since the Natural History Museum began its programme of excavations in 1976. The site is a limestone cave on the southern slopes of the Mendip Hills. It was almost certainly never a hominin habitation. Rather, the cave was in-filled with a series of sediments washed in from the surface, among which were artefacts. Another big question surrounding this site concerned whether or not the artefacts were genuine (see Roe 1981b, for a review).

The raw material at the site is loosely described as flint. The difficulty in determining whether these pieces are real artefacts is a result of extensive natural modification to their surfaces. They have been modified by a process known as cortication (Jill Cook, in Andrews *et al.* 1999). Not yet fully understood, this process involves the removal of the chalcedony cement which binds the various microscopic constituents of flint together (microskeletons and inorganic precipitates known as lepispheres). The flint becomes very brittle. In places, the chalcedony cement is re-crystallised, giving the raw material a whitish appearance. During the process surface features are altered, so any diagnostic signs of knapping become difficult to see. In short, although the artefacts were clearly associated with a pre-Anglian fauna, it was by no means certain they were artefacts.

Cook's detailed analysis of the pieces concludes that they are fragments of naturally fractured flint (ibid.). Scrutiny of the accompanying illustrations supports this conclusion with one, or possibly two exceptions. However, Schreve, Currant, and Stringer (in Andrews *et al.* 1999) note that not all archaeologists support this interpretation. The question then to be answered is, how does flint which does not naturally occur in the Mendips find its way into a subterranean cavern? One possibility is from a Cretaceous aged rock cap that once covered the site but has now been eroded away. But as Cook notes, there is little evidence for this. The question of how natural flints entered the cave system remains unresolved, and the nearest flint sources are on the west of Salisbury Plain. However, chert deposits, which are similar to flint and originate within limestone, are present on the central Mendips. Occasional artefacts resembling handaxes in chert have been found in the parish of St Cuthbert Out (Brian Hack, pers. comm.). These may well may have come from a relatively local chert source. One unambiguous cut mark is present on a red deer metacarpal from the cave, and four other possible examples were noted. This represents 0.1 per cent of the analysed bone assemblage. So humans may not have been too common in the vicinity of the cave's entrance, but they were definitely there. Their limited presence should not be too surprising as the cave was a carnivore den on more than one occasion.

More important than the archaeology is the long and complex record of climatic change preserved in the fossil remains. In fact, it is now recognised that not one but two pre-Anglian temperate phases are present in the stratigraphic sequence. On the basis of indicator species of known climatic tolerance, these two warm phases had temperatures as warm or warmer than today. This implies fully interglacial conditions. Two cold phases separate these. The relationship of Westbury to the other rich Cromerian faunal sites is still actively debated; does the site represent a distinct climatic phase, or do some of the warm and cold episodes equate with others in Figure 4.2? For the moment, we do not know, but once again the voles are able to shed some light on the problem. The site has *Arvicola* and therefore falls comfortably within that zone. It also has the tundra vole *Microtus gregaloides* which suggests that Westbury is earlier in the *Arvicola* zone.

Kent's Cavern

This site is justly famous as one of the localities involved in what became known later as the 'Antiquity of Man' debate (van Ripper 1993). Investigation at the site had a long pedigree before William Pengelly began his 16-year programme of excavation in 1865 (see Evans 1872; 1897; Straw 1996, for good introductions). This was one of the sites where humanly made artefacts were found in definite association with the bones of long extinct animals, in contexts where both were clearly contemporary, and of high antiquity. The deposits they were found in were sealed by undisturbed stalagmite floors. Roe (1981b) notes that modern confusion over the stratigraphy prevented the acceptance of the Lower Palaeolithic tools from the basal part of the sequence as having been found in a secure context. This was resolved by Campbell and Sampson (1971). Recently the site has been investigated by researchers interested in the formation of the cave, and the nature and dating of the various infills (Proctor and Smart 1989; Proctor *et al.* 2005).

Beneath the Cave Earth which contains Upper and Middle Palaeolithic artefacts, is the Crystalline Stalagmite, a flowstone deposit which Proctor *et al.* (2005) assert ceased to form at about 115,000 BP. One intriguing suggestion by Straw (1996) is that a substantial earth tremor re-opened the cave and brought the long phase of Crystalline Stalagmite development to an end. In places, this deposit is over 3.5 m thick. It accumulated in a long depositional hiatus when the cave was a closed system with no openings to the outside world. This hiatus may have lasted some 250,000 kyr. The Crystalline Stalagmite was originally extensive throughout the cave system. This implies that the deposit below has to be at a very minimum c. 350,000 kya. This age has recently been confirmed by a large-scale dating programme in the cave (Proctor *et al.* 2005).

The deposit beneath the Crystal Stalagmite is the Breccia, a multiple event debris flow unit, possibly laid down under cold conditions and which contained a bear-dominated fauna and a small number of bifaces and flakes that were found by Pengelly *in situ*. This age of > 350,000 years ago validates the identification of Cromerian indicator species such as the cave bear

Ursus deningeri, which is not known after the Anglian in Britain (Cook and Jacobi 1998), and which is found throughout the Breccia. Cook and Jacobi (ibid.) suggest that the teeth of *Homotherium*, a pre-Anglian sabre tooth cat, were found by chance by much later hominins and removed into another part of the cave. Here they became incorporated in the much later Cave Earth. The sediments that were indurated to form the Breccia entered the system through openings which are today located at the back of cave. In terms of age and position within the Cromerian Complex, this site is difficult to locate as it lacks the substantial vertebrate fauna of some of the other pre-Anglian locations. On the basis of preliminary observations made by M. Bishop (in Cook and Jacobi 1998), there is a similarity between the bear fauna from Kent's and that from Westbury-sub-Mendip. This has been supported by further analysis (Proctor *et al.* 2005). Tentatively, the two sites are placed in a similar age bracket.

Cook and Jacobi (1998) describe a number of the Breccia artefacts in detail, including the bifaces, and a small number of flakes and possible cores. Proctor *et al.* (2005) emphasise the fact that although the handaxes are usually given prominence, flakes were the most common artefact type, and some are retouched. The bifaces, of which 15 are securely provenanced to the Breccia (Cook and Jacobi 1998), are thick in cross-section and show a minimum of flaking and shaping. There are excellent illustrations of some of them in Roe (1981b, Figure 4.4). A few would class as trihedral (thick with triangular cross-sections) on some African typologies; one was made from a natural flake, the remainder on slabs and thick blocks. Cook and Jacobi (1998) make it clear that the form of the nodule has significantly influenced the final outline shape and overall morphology of the finished artefact. The knapping strategies involved in their manufacture reflect expedient approaches to the problem of bifacially flaking thick blanks with wide and obtuse angles between the faces. This has led, erroneously, to an appearance of crudity and the notion of primitive knapping abilities. This simplicity in appearance was part of the reason they were ascribed to an Early Acheulean cultural phase (Roe 1981b). The suggestion that they are similar to other pre-Anglian 'crude' bifaces from higher terraces of the River Somme in northern France, labelled Abbevillean, remains to be tested. However, not all the bifaces appear crude, some would class as ovates, extensively thinned with a cutting edge all the way around.

A feature of note is the condition of these artefacts. They have undergone the same process of cortication noted on the Westbury artefacts. These, however, have not lost their percussion features and there is no doubt of their status as artefacts. However, they have also undergone staining, a process of discoloration of their surface by exposure to iron rich minerals in ground water. The staining is not uniform on all the artefacts, some being visually very different from others. It has led to the suggestion that, along with the evidence of transport damage on margins, the Breccia artefacts

124

may be rather older than the deposit they occur in. They may have lain exposed on land surfaces and/or been transported by water prior to their being incorporated in the debris flows emplaced within the cave. Proctor *et al.* (2005) note that evidence of condition is variable, so the artefacts may not all belong to a single contemporary assemblage.

Boxgrove

For many researchers this is the jewel in the British Lower Palaeolithic crown. A primary context pre-Anglian site for which so much environmental and archaeological information is available, it is astonishing. Indeed, Boxgrove has provided a unique window on conditions just prior to, as well as just after, the onset of the Anglian glaciation.

Boxgrove is not so much one site, as a scatter and patch network of activity debris spread over several hundred metres. The deposits show a stratified sequence of fossilised land surfaces, each a small part of a much more extensive land surface stretching away for kilometres east and west of the site. Dominating the landscape was a steep chalk cliff, up against which were banked the Slindon Sands (Roberts and Parfitt 1999), which represent a near-shore marine deposit from a high sea-level event. The Slindon Sands grade upwards into the Slindon Silts. These represent sedimentation in an area away from the open sea. They are interpreted as inter-tidal mud flats. Occupation of these temporary dry land surfaces is indicated by in-situ flint scatters from unit 3b. From this level a number of finds were made; a bone percussor, limb bones of red deer smashed open by hammer stones, a knapping scatter from repairing the broken tip of a biface (sufficiently undisturbed that the position of the knapper's leg was picked out by a line of debitage).

A remarkable discovery in the slightly higher unit 4b was the horse-butchery site. The excavators (Roberts and Parfitt 1999; Pope and Roberts 2005) argue convincingly for a group of hominins bringing nodules of flint from the nearby cliff (c. 40 m away), conducting the initial knapping to make bifaces at one spot, and then finishing the bifaces off a few metres away. These were then used to butcher a horse carcass. The numbers of cut marks on the bones suggest that the group butchering the animal had sufficient time to dismember the whole carcass; at the very least pro-active carcass defence is implied. Although the cut mark evidence from the whole of unit 4b is strongly inclined toward horse bones, other animals also display evidence of butchery, including bear, rhino, deer, giant deer and wolf. Presumably not all were hunted.

In time, the inter-tidal mud flats gave way to an open grassy plain as the sea receded further from the cliff line. Unit 4c represents a palaeosol imposed on the surface of the Slindon Silts. It was a major dry land surface and is interpreted as a largely tree-less grassy plain over which herds of grazing mammals were roaming. Somewhere in the vicinity, forest was also present. On the basis of its soil micromorphology, the surface may have been open anywhere between 20 and 100 years. It is from here that most of the archaeology and fauna were recovered. At one point along this land surface a spring was responsible for a localised waterhole. It was from these freshwater deposits that a hominin tibia identified as *Homo heidelbergensis* was recovered. In the main, the mammal evidence argues for temperate but cooler conditions.

What is remarkable about the knapping behaviour of the Boxgrove hominins is the deeply conservative nature of what they made. For the most part, ovate handaxes were made. The thinning and shaping were done with carefully prepared soft hammers (Pitts and Roberts 1997). Examples of these were recovered from the waterhole sediments. The handaxes look remarkably similar in shape throughout the whole Boxgrove sequence; tranchet finishes (a flake taken off the tip to produce a razor-sharp edge) also appear throughout. What is notable, through its absence, is core working. Retouched flake tools are effectively confined to the waterhole where cutmarks on the bones imply carcass processing.

Unit 4b and unit 4c indicate extensive areas of treeless open ground. Across this landscape hominins did little other than move flint nodules and partially finished bifaces around, produce finished bifaces, repair them (Austin 1994) and butcher carcasses. It should be stressed that the excavators do not consider any of the 'sites' on any of the land surfaces to be living places, these may have been elsewhere, perhaps above the cliff line.

Overlying the Slindon Silts are the sediments of the Eartham Formation. These represent a shift toward terrestrial-dominated deposition with sediments being inputted from the hill slopes to the north of the cliff. These sediments, and higher deposits, buried the cliff during periglacial conditions. The basal sediments of the Eartham Formation preserve evidence for the onset of much cooler conditions than before. The later deposits in the Eartham Formation are fully glacial in origin. However, it is clear from the finds of isolated bifaces, as well as refitting scatters, that hominins were occupying the area well into the much colder conditions of the early Anglian. In this sense the artefacts in the Eartham Formation parallel those from the Wallingford fan gravels, and may be contemporary in the broadest sense. This is an important insight into the environmental tolerances of *Homo heidelbergensis*; this was a creature able to survive in much colder conditions than previously supposed. European evidence supports this (Roebroeks et al. 1992). As Figure 4.2 shows, the site falls squarely in the *Arvicola* zone, and since it has the narrow-skulled *Microtus gregalis* it is later in time than Westbury.

The erstwhile Solent river

Another one of the lost rivers of England, the Solent was the major drainage channel of the Hampshire basin during the Pleistocene. Terraces associated with the Solent are present in a strip from Bournemouth to Portsmouth, some 60 km. These parallel the modern coastline. However, the evidence for Solent terrace gravels is found as far inland as Wimborne Minster and Brockenhurst. This is because the Solent, a west-to-east-flowing river, had been migrating southwards from the Early Pleistocene. Much of the New Forest is underlain by the Solent's staircase of gravel terraces. In its final phase the river flowed through a large valley which ran out from today's Poole Harbour and around the north of the Isle of Wight. A high chalk ridge connecting the Isle of Purbeck to the Needles on the Isle of Wight formed the southern flanks of the valley. At some point in the Middle or Late Pleistocene this ridge was breached, and subsequent coastal erosion has formed the Solent estuary and Isle of Wight as we know them today. Westaway *et al.* (2006) believe the breach to have initially occurred in MIS 6. The Milford-on-Sea gravel (Table 4.1) is suggested to be the last flood-plain of the Solent before the river was beheaded and the chalk ridge breached. During MIS 6 the major left bank tributaries, the Frome, Stour and Avon, continued to flow into the old Solent valley between Poole and Hengistbury Head/Christchurch, but now flowed from east to west down this length of the old Solent's course and passed through a small breach in the chalk ridge as a single river to connect with la Manche, the Channel river, further south. The Solent itself found new headwaters in local streams to the east of its former confluence with the Avon. During the last inter-glacial, MIS 5.5, high sea levels entered the breach in the chalk ridge and drowned the old Solent valley to the west of the Isle of Wight. High sea levels also drowned the Solent valley to the east and north of the Isle of Wight, this area becoming an estuary for a much truncated Solent river. The Isle of Wight may not have become an island proper until later in the Late Pleistocene, as during MIS 5.5 Westaway *et al.* (ibid.) tentatively propose that the island was connected to the mainland by a narrow isthmus connecting the northwest of the island to a stretch on the mainland between Milford-on-Sea and Hengistbury Head. Needless to say, this whole scenario remains deeply contentious.

There are a host of difficulties associated with the reconstruction and dating of the Solent's Pleistocene terrace sequence. Different sections of it have been mapped using different systems of describing terraces. Add-itionally, its north bank tributaries (see Figure 2.8; modern-day Frome, Piddle, Stour, Avon, Test, Itchen, Meon) were also mapped differently. Excellent introductions to the Solent are to be found in Allen and Gibbard (1993), Wymer (1999), Bridgland (2001), Bates (2001), Hosfield (2005), and Briant *et al.* (2006). A good general introduction to the Pleistocene geology and archaeology of the region is Wenban-Smith and Hosfield (2001).

Needless to say, almost every aspect of the reconstruction of the Solent is hotly disputed. The interpretation of the Solent's Middle Pleistocene history that I have chosen to follow is a new one and may prove to be quite controversial. It is that proposed by Westaway et al. (2006). I am using this because it presents a detailed and integrated interpretation of the main Solent channel, as represented by the gravel terraces between the Avon and the Test (see Figure 2.8), as well as the tributary valleys. This scheme will be subject to much debate. One of its more controversial elements is the use of archaeology as a means of dating. Westaway and colleagues believe handaxe assemblages with high numbers of twisted edges signify MIS 11 (following White 1998c), and that the first occurrence of Levallois is dated to MIS 9/8. They have used these as tie points to help date terraces that contain these types of data. Another dating technique used is predictive uplift modelling. This relies on predicting the rate of uplift a terrace should have experienced at different times in the Pleistocene (see Chapter 2). From this are generated a series of predictions as to various possible heights for the terrace. The rate of uplift and height of each 'model' are indicators of the age of the terrace. The actual height is then noted, and the most appropriate model/date chosen. For the moment, the framework remains the first large-scale attempt to produce a basin-wide approach to interpreting the Solent, and will be used here. The various terraces and their ages for the sequence in the western Solent are presented in Table 4.1.

The archaeology from the Solent is subject to the same difficulties of artefact provenance noted for the Middle Thames. When dealing with just a few artefacts, usually found on or near the surface, you can never be sure that they are not later intrusions which have become incorporated within the surface of the unit. John Wymer faced this difficulty when amassing the data for The English Rivers Project Survey (abbreviated to TERPS; Wessex Archaeology 1992; Wymer 1999). I have used these data to construct Table 4.1. The artefact totals refer to those sites in the TERPS data where artefacts may be clearly provenanced to a single gravel terrace. Sites where two terraces are present in the vicinity of a find, or where brickearth overlies a gravel are omitted. For this reason, the totals in Table 4.1 are likely to be underestimations of actual counts (compare Table 4.1 to the data in Hosfield 2005).

The British Geological Survey's (BGS) remapping of the Stour terraces, and this river's confluence with the Solent in the vicinity of Bournemouth (Bristow et al. 1991), divided the terraces into three groups. Terraces 14–11 represented gravel deposits that had been laid down by the Solent as it flowed eastwards, and its floodplain crossed the area that would later be incised by the Stour to form its modern valley. Terraces 10 and 9 represented gravel deposits that were related to the time the Stour began to cut

Table 4.1 Solent basin chrono-stratigraphic framework as suggested by Westaway et al. (2006)

MIS	Stour Valley Terraces 14–11 = Solent River Terraces 10–9 = Solent/Stour Terraces 8–1 = Stour River	Avon	Main Solent channel terraces
14	T 13a/Ambersham 2/0		
13		T 8 (MIS = 13.2) 8/0	Setley Plain (MIS = 13.2) 1+/0
12	T 12/Sleight 290/1	T 7 807/0	Mount Pleasant 0/0
11			
10	T 11/Gravel Hill 15/1	T 6 10/0	Old Milton 208/2
9	T 10/Ensbury Park (= MIS 9.2) 286/7	High Cliff Gravel (MIS = 9.2) 8/0	Beckton Farm (MIS = 9.2) 0/2
8	T 9/West Southbourne 44/1	T 5 4/0	Downton/Tom's Down 0/0
7	T 8/Knighton Lodge (= MIS 7.2) 1/0		Hordle/Stanswood Bay (MIS = 7.2) 15/0
6	T 7/2nd Lower Taplow 0/0	T4 1/0	Milford-on-Sea 7/0

Notes: T = terrace. Figures in bottom right hand refer to approximate artefact counts from the terraces; handaxes before the forward slash, Levallois after it.
Source: Data from Westaway *et al.* (2006) and Wessex Archaeology (1992), Bristow *et al.* (1991).

its current valley but could not be precisely related to either river. Terraces 8–1 were related to the Stour's depositional history within its modern valley. If Bristow *et al.*'s interpretation is right, and the dating proposed in Table 4.1 also correct, then the modern Stour did not incise its valley until quite late in the Middle Pleistocene. Most of the terrace flights for the Solent and its tributaries have not been directly dated. An important exception to this has recently been made by Rebecca Briant and colleagues (Briant *et al.* 2006) using OSL to fix the age of two terraces, the Stanswood Bay and the Pennington Upper Gravels (too recent to be shown on Table 4.1). For the Stanswood Bay Gravel they generate an age between MIS 8 and MIS 7.2, which is a fair match with that inferred by Westaway *et al.* in Table 4.1.

On the face of it, the evidence for a pre-Anglian occupation of the Solent is poor. The evidence amounts to one record of a handaxe being found in the equivalent of the Setley Plain gravel dated to MIS 13, and one further report of handaxes being found in the same gravel. There is a small group of artefacts from terrace 8 of the Avon which would date to the same interglacial. There is no particular reason to discount these, though the two handaxes from a Stour terrace dated to MIS 14 are probably intrusive.

The evidence for occupation in late MIS 13, or possibly earlier MIS 12 is, however, better. The pits at Corfe Mullen in the Stour Valley, especially the Railway Ballast Pit (sometimes called the Ballast Hole by earlier writers), produced a large body of artefacts from gravel mapped by the BGS as terrace 12 (Calkin and Green 1949; Roe 1981b; Bristow et al. 1991). On Westaway et al.'s dating, this would equate to MIS 12. The handaxes from here are often referred to a pre-Anglian date on typological grounds (Wymer 1999, and especially Roe 2001).

Unfortunately, earlier researchers observed that the artefacts from the Railway Ballast Pit came from close to the terrace bluff (slope), and could therefore represent much later artefacts that became incorporated within the gravel as it sludged down the slope of the bluff. However, a number of these early observers (e.g. Bury 1933) make it clear that artefacts were found within the main body of the gravels as well. Green (1947), and Calkin and Green (1949), note that many of the Railway Ballast Pit implements came from on, and within, a white clay (actually a clayey silt) at the base of the sequence underlying both terrace deposits and the bluff. Such a deposit seems to me to be more consistent with fluvial deposition than slope process. Cautiously then, there is a case to be made for some of the Corfe Mullen artefacts being in situ. The Corfe Mullen Pits account for almost all of the terrace 12 artefacts from the Stour; 289 of the 290 handaxes in Table 4.1 come from Corfe Mullen. The presence of a single Levallois flake here seems anomalous and should probably be disregarded as a surface intrusion.

Cogdean's pit, to the east of the Railway Ballast Pit is also mapped within terrace 12 by the BGS. Calkin and Green (1949) and Green (1947) suggested that artefacts within this pit came from a small tributary channel incised into the body of terrace 12. The channel was later in date and so were the handaxes contained within it. They were mostly found in gravel which owed its provenance to slope processes more than anything else. Whether these artefacts were from a later tributary can no longer be established. However, the BGS map a tongue of slope-derived gravel running through this part of the terrace, just where Calkin and Green located their solifluction filled channel (unless the BGS just followed these older descriptions?).

High numbers of handaxes are also recorded for the Avon in terrace 7. Maddy et al. (2000) and Westaway et al. (2006) date this terrace to MIS 12 on the basis of crustal uplift rates. As at Corfe Mullen, the high numbers of artefacts reflect a few very productive sites such as Woodgreen and Bemerton (ibid.). Away from these, the rate of finds drops off dramatically.

On the basis of the evidence presented, I would cautiously accept the premise that hominins were in this section of the Solent basin in pre-Anglian times. To the east of Southampton, the broad expanse of Solent terrace gravels has no records of pre-Anglian finds being made.

Conclusions to the pre-Anglian and early Anglian occupation phase

In this chapter I have concentrated on the river valleys, but there is no reason to suppose that high ground and interfluves were not occupied. Wymer (1999) describes handaxes from Plateau Gravels, High Level Gravels, Chalk and Clay with Flints deposits. So hominins were not restricted to just the valleys themselves. But since most of these records are only individual finds, they are impossible to date and may belong to any phase of the Lower Palaeolithic.

It will be fairly evident that Clactonian sites, following the criteria laid down for their acceptance in Chapter 3, do not exist in the pre-Anglian or early Anglian. The only real candidate is High Lodge, but its scrapers do not occur in the Swanscombe or Clacton gravels. Also missing from this phase is any evidence of sites with high numbers of cores and flakes, but only a few clearly contemporary handaxes or thinning flakes. The British pre-Anglian and early Anglian are dominated by hominins who were handaxe makers.

Returning to the question I posed at the beginning of this chapter, it is clear that a non-handaxe tradition did not persist from the time of the earliest occupants (Pakefield) into post-Anglian times. My reading of the data is that when we do see non-handaxes assemblages in Britain in secure contexts, they are a new phenomenon. This is the subject of the next chapter.

5

HOMININ OCCUPATION JUST BEFORE, DURING, AND JUST AFTER MARINE ISOTOPE STAGE 11

The Swanscombe Interglacial

Introduction

This chapter concerns the period of time spanning late MIS 12 which is the end of the Anglian glaciation, the interglacial that followed – MIS 11 – often called the Swanscombe Interglacial, and the return to arctic conditions at the beginning of MIS 10. This is the period traditionally associated with the Clactonian – the first temperate phase after the retreat of the Anglian glaciers. In the terrestrial pollen-based framework this was the Hoxnian interglacial, see Figure 3.3 and Table 3.1.

Research has demonstrated that a number of the sites that would have traditionally been called Hoxnian actually belong in MIS 9. The reason for this is that the pollen signatures of MIS 11 and 9 are quite similar. This will be discussed in more detail below. On the Bridgland terrace model, the period of time discussed in this chapter is the Boyn Hill/Orsett Heath Formation, and this is shown in Figure 2.7 and Table 2.1. The main sites discussed in this chapter are shown in Figure 5.1.

In this chapter I will attempt to place the Clactonian sites described in Chapter 3 into a local and regional framework of significance. From this I hope that readers will be able to judge for themselves whether there is good evidence for an independent Clactonian assemblage type/tradition.

The late Anglian and the MIS 12/11 transition

In the last chapter we looked at the events surrounding the formation of the Lower Thames Valley as it is known today. A great mass of water flowed into a small pre-existing valley, when the banks of an ice dammed lake burst (Figure 4.8). The erosion from the passage of this water certainly created what we now know as the Lower Thames Valley. But it also affected parts of the Middle Thames as well, since the waters will have flowed along part of this reach too. The first post-diversion aggradation in the Middle and Lower Thames is the Black Park Terrace composed of the Black Park Gravel. This Black Park Terrace is not a terrace as we understand it from the Bridgland

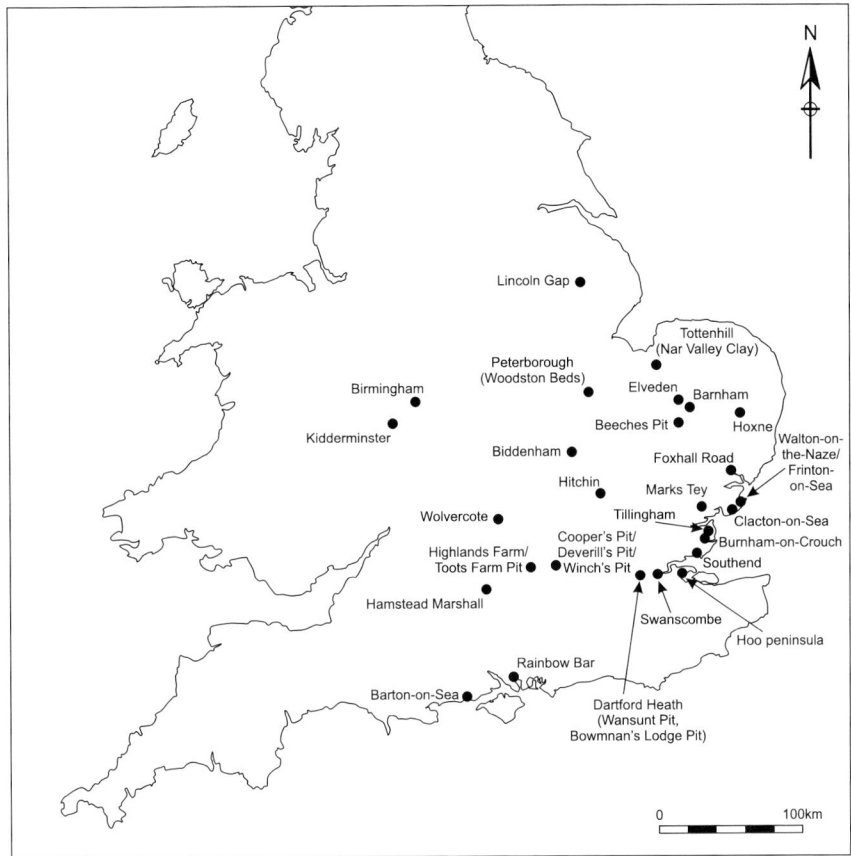

Figure 5.1 Map showing selection of sites discussed in Chapter 5.

model. It will be recalled from Chapter 2 that fluvial terraces are a response to the complex relationship that exists between climate and uplift. The Black Park Terrace was formed by the dynamic flow from the pro-glacial lakes bursting their banks. In effect, this gravel has been dumped onto the valley floor by torrential floods and subsequently resorted and redistributed by the Black Park River Thames. This explains two features about this terrace. First, it is not a very big one, especially when compared to the lower terraces which are proper climate/uplift driven features, see Figure 5.2. It may have taken as little as 15,000 years to fully aggrade (Ashton and Lewis 2002). Second, the surface slope of the Black Park Terrace from the Middle into the Lower Thames is very steep, much more so than in a normal terrace. Somewhere between London and Dartford Heath it actually passes below the level of the next youngest terrace, the Boyn Hill/Orsett Heath Terrace, see Figure 5.2 and Table 2.1. Normally it would represent a higher step in the terrace

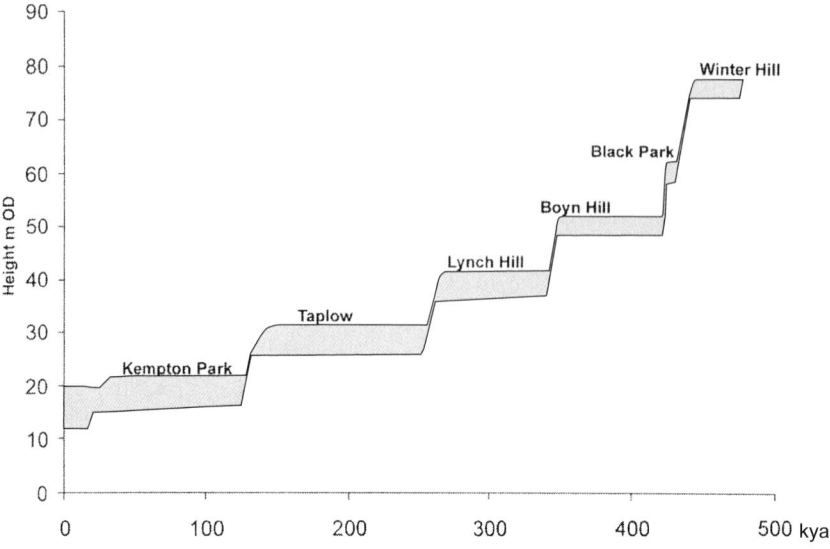

Figure 5.2 Comparison of relative extent of Middle Thames terraces based on duration of Formation and height above sea level.

Note: Used with permission.

staircase preserved along the side of the valley. Instead it is subsumed somewhere underneath the Boyn Hill/Orsett Heath Terrace surface. For this reason any Black Park Terrace sites to the east of London are now lost (but see alternative view by Gibbard below).

In the last chapter it was noted how difficult it was to find any convincing sites which indicated early Anglian occupation of the Thames Valley. But in the late Anglian the situation is different. There is a good deal of evidence to suggest hominins were present along stretches of the Middle Thames and along some of its tributaries. The Kennet (Figure 2.8) is a tributary that flows into the Middle Thames at Reading. Along its southern flanks are the Silchester Stage Gravels which Gibbard (1985) argues are an equivalent of the Black Park Terrace in the main Middle Thames Valley. There are a number of finds of handaxes associated with these gravels (Bridgland 1994; Wymer 1999) but not all are necessarily from within the gravels. There is one substantial site that is contemporary with the gravels – Hampstead Marshall. Wymer (1999) notes at least 23 handaxes from here, and others have been found in the same deposits further east along the Kennet Valley. Wymer (1968) notes that most of these handaxes are rolled, suggesting they have been derived from elsewhere. Although the Silchester Stage gravels are the sweepings of ancient land surfaces, the only other gravel spread the handaxes could have been derived from is the

Winter Hill Gravels (Figure 2.9B). These date to the coldest part of the Anglian and have no certain archaeology associated with them. Despite the evidence of transport damage, it is possible to suggest that the Silchester Stage artefacts are genuinely contemporary with the late Anglian.

Today the Thames flows through Reading. In the late Anglian, the river ran further to the north-east and occupied what is now an abandoned channel known as the Caversham Ancient Channel, see Figure 5.3. Wymer (1968; 1999) notes a number of localities within the Caversham Channel deposits which contain archaeology definitely associated with the Black Park Gravels. Of these the Highlands Farm Pit (Wymer 1956; 1961; Bridgland 1994) is the most notable. Some 4 metres of gravel contained cores, flakes, and handaxes. Highlands Farm is one of the sites for which a Clactonian element has been proposed. The early work on the site was by Treacher *et al.* (1948) who noted that the vast majority of artefacts were handaxes; only a few flakes (and a single core) could be assigned to the Clactonian. They noted a wide variety of handaxe forms and explicitly stated that all types occurred in every imaginable condition and were evenly distributed throughout the gravels (Treacher *et al.* 1948: 137). Wymer's excavations in the late 1950s,

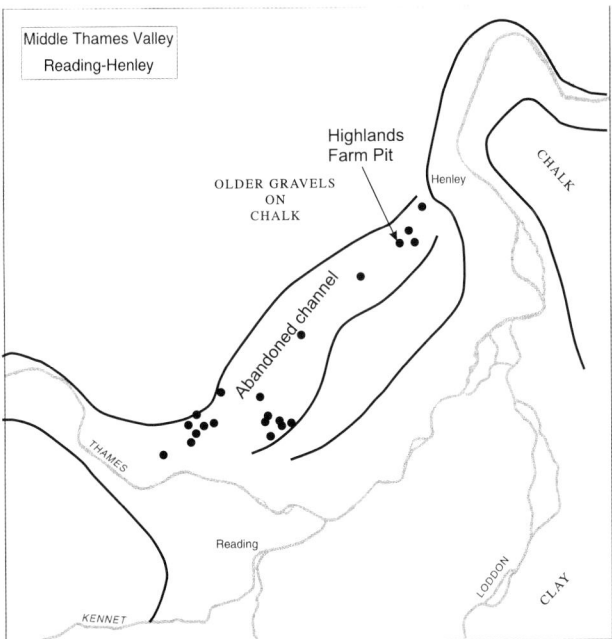

Figure 5.3 Map showing position of Caversham Channel and a selection of Black Park Terrace sites.

Note: Modified and used with permission.

and the work of other collectors significantly increased the number of cores and flakes, which probably went largely unrecognised by the quarry men in Treacher's time (Wymer 1956; 1961). These were readily interpreted as a Clactonian element. The TERPs data (Wessex Archaeology 1996) record some 3,000 flakes from the site and 250 cores.

Wymer noted (1961: 20) that a proportion of the better-made handaxes were in much fresher condition – and these were given a Middle Acheulean label. The Middle Acheulean was a typological concept based on well-made handaxes, usually ovates and cordiforms. It represented a stage of technological advancement in Acheulean material culture; thinning on handaxes was extensive and more controlled than in the Early Acheulean, and done with a soft hammer. Nevertheless, the Treacher data make it clear that the full range of conditions was present on *all* artefacts, and Wymer himself (1956) noted that a number of the so-called better-made handaxes were in a rolled condition. His 1968 data, slightly reworked, are presented in Table 5.1. They make the point only too clearly, there are no grounds for separating one type of handaxe from the remainder on the basis of condition alone.

Table 5.1 Lithic assemblage composition for Highlands Farm, Caversham Channel

Description	Wymer's types (1968)	Mint/sharp	Rolled
Cores	A, B, C, variations on these + chopping tool	7	89
Handaxes – little to no shaping, sometimes pointed	D, E, DF, EF	27	93
Pointed and shaped with straight sides (or slightly concave)	F, FG, FM	2	1
Pointed and shaped with convex sides	G, GJ, GK, DG, DK	1	4
Flat, carefully shaped, with convex sides – ovates and cordiforms	J, K, HK, JK, JH, KN, KH	59	56
Cleavers	H, GH	1	7
Ficron – markedly elongated, pointed and well shaped, with pronounced concave sides	M		
Bout coupé	N – flat butted cordate		
Broken and unfinished handaxes and rough-outs	Broken and unfinished handaxes and rough-outs	20	10
Thinning flakes	Thinning flakes	71	27
All retouched flake tools	All flake tools	16	70
Levallois or simple prepared cores	Levallois or proto-Levallois	1	4

Source: Data adapted from Wymer (1968).

Today, of course, we know that handaxe makers also knapped cores for flakes and modified some of them into flake tools, so there are no grounds for identifying a distinct Clactonian assemblage from Highlands Farm. In the 1980s, Boxgrove and High Lodge conclusively demonstrated the existence of well-made ovate and cordiform handaxes at pre-Anglian sites, so the whole concept of a typologically defined Middle Acheulean phase is not appropriate. Handaxe shape has no temporal significance. The most parsimonious explanation of the pattern seen at Highlands Farm is that the Caversham Channel deposits preserve evidence of a lengthy period of occupation in the late Anglian. A wide variety of handaxe forms were made, including a small number of cleavers. Wymer (1999) proposed a late Anglian inter-stadial to explain the Caversham occupation and its date, ruefully admitting there was no real evidence for it. But as we saw in the last chapter, the evidence from Wallingford and Boxgrove implies *Homo heidelbergensis* was adapting to colder or cooler conditions so it is not necessary to postulate a distinct late-Anglian interstadial.

Further evidence of late Anglian Black Park Terrace occupation is much more equivocal as it concerns sediments in the Lower Thames Valley. As noted above, to the east of London the steep slope of this terrace has carried it below the level of the Boyn Hill/Orsett Heath Terrace. But this is not accepted by all. Phil Gibbard (1985) has made a very robust case for the Dartford Heath Gravels, immediately east of London, being Black Park Terrace, while Bridgland (1994) has argued in favour of them being Boyn Hill/Orsett Heath. The controversy remains unresolved. Of interest to us are two observations made by the geologist Henry Dewey (1959) who noted the following:

- There were channels cut into the bedrock underlying the Dartford Heath Gravels. They were present beneath Pearson's Pit on the east side of the Heath. These channels were cut to the same level as the Lower Gravels Channel at Barnfield Pit, Swanscombe, some 8 km downstream to the east. They were probably an upstream equivalent of the Lower Gravels Channel. No handaxes were reported from these buried channels.
- The Dartford Heath Gravels that overlay the channels at Pearson's Pit had handaxes in them. Wymer's suggestion (1968) that they come from the top of the gravels is predicated on condition and not observation; Dewey makes it clear that the handaxes came from the top as well as the base of the gravels.

If Bridgland is correct and the Dartford Heath Gravels are Boyn Hill/Orsett Heath Formation deposits, then they equate with the handaxe rich Middle Gravels at Swanscombe which overlie the Lower Gravel channel (see below and Figure 3.7). They would date to well within MIS 11. But if Gibbard's suggestion is right, then the Dartford Heath Gravels are late MIS 12, and so link the handaxe makers in the Middle Thames with those in the Lower Thames. The suggestion is intriguing, but as yet cannot be proven. Its relevance to the Clactonian is that Mark White (2000) has argued that only Clactonian knappers are present in Britain at the MIS 12/11 boundary and in the earlier phases of the interglacial. The late Anglian age of the handaxes in Pearson's Pit would be a serious challenge to this hypothesis. I will return to Dartford Heath below.

The presence of hominins in the Lower Thames Valley in the late Anglian or at the glacial–interglacial transition was suggested by Wymer (1974) for Clacton-on-Sea, and by Conway (Conway *et al.* 1996) for the Lower Gravels at Swanscombe. These transitional deposits would be the equivalent of the second stage of Bridgland's terrace model. The MIS12/11 date of these deposits was discussed in Chapter 3. I find no convincing evidence to support a hominin presence at the Golf Course, Clacton, at the MIS 12/11 transition. I would cautiously suggest the same for the Barnfield Pit, but the evidence here is more equivocal. There are temperate mammals/molluscs associated with each of these supposedly transitional cold climate gravel beds. The most parsimonious explanation of the data is that these deposits date to some time within the interglacial.

Sadly, there is nowhere else in Britain that preserves archaeological evidence dated to the late Anglian or the transition to MIS 11.

MIS 11 – the Swanscombe Interglacial

Hominin occupation in MIS 11 shows considerable diversity in terms of the types of environment and resources exploited. Wymer (1999) notes occupation in major and minor river valleys, on the freshly exposed till plains of East Anglia, on the higher ground of the Downs and in a variety of localised situations; lakes and ponds, braided stream beds, marshes, etc. On the basis of pollen analysis, it seems that the interglacial rise in sea level (or at least the attainment of its maximum height) occurred rather late, in pollen zone III (Table 3.1, but the evidence from the Butlins site discussed in Chapter 3 may contradict this). If there was a late sea-level rise, Britain could well have been connected to the continent for a considerable portion of the interglacial – the land bridge would have been a range of low lying hills across the modern Straits of Dover (the Dover–Artois hills, with lower ground extending north-east into the North Sea Basin and south-west into the English Channel). Major British rivers would have flowed eastwards, across the modern East Anglian coast, continuing across low lying country as they had done in pre-Anglian times, skirting the northern edge of the Dover–Artois hills. This scenario is just one possibility, and others are introduced later in this chapter.

The preceding section argued for the presence of hominins in the late

Anglian. While it is possible hominins were present across the glacial–interglacial transition as well, for the moment the evidence is equivocal. Most of the sites for which we have data, and these are the Clactonian sites, suggest occupation in pollen zone II of the interglacial, the Early Temperate (see Figure 3.3, Table 3.1). At this point the interglacial would be in full swing. In my opinion, there is no conclusive evidence of Clactonian knappers present in the Pre-Temperate pollen zone of MIS 11, though hominins may well have been present (for example, the small numbers of flakes from the base of the Southfleet elephant site, or the rolled assemblages from Barnham and the Golf Course). This early Clactonian presence is the climatic and physical background of Wenban-Smith's (1998) explanation of the Clactonian. He has argued that the Clactonian is a response by hominins to differences in the availability of raw material for knapping. Hominins found an abundance of flint raw material in the new unforested landscapes of the earlier part of MIS 11. They did not need to make handaxes until the more heavily forested phases later in the interglacial made good quality flint harder to find. Handaxes were thus a strategy used by mobile hunter-gatherers to combat unpredictable resources. There is nothing inherently wrong with this as an explanation (especially on a local scale). But if we remove Swanscombe and Clacton from the list of sites associated with the MIS 12/11 transition, as well as the Pre-Temperate pollen zone (which would equate with the earliest part of MIS 11), then it would seem that unequivocal Clactonian occupation of Britain is not evident until Early Temperate pollen zone IIb. In other words, when the mixed oak forests were already well established in the landscape.

The alternative, implied in Mark White's scenario (2000; White and Schreve 2000), is the movement of culturally distinctive Clactonian hominins from, or across, the dry land areas of the southern North Sea. They entered Britain by moving along the river valleys. Certainly the only two sites for which a distinct Clactonian could possibly be argued in MIS 11, Clacton and Swanscombe, are confined to one river valley, the Thames, and only to its lower reaches at that. Acheulean hunter-gatherers followed later and occupied the river valleys formerly inhabited by the Clactonian knappers. Finally, the late rise in sea level stranded the migrants.

In principle, it is not unreasonable to speculate that a number of hunting groups may have had inter-seasonal ranges that were confined to the British land mass, while others, moving along river valleys that were confluent with major European rivers, would have had ranging patterns that took them much further afield. Whether or not they were culturally distinct from each other is another matter.

Regional geographies of the Swanscombe Interglacial

The Thames Valley – the Upper and Middle reaches of the river

After the Black Park Terrace, the next terrace in the flight is the Boyn Hill/ Orsett Heath Formation, see Figures 2.7 and Table 2.1. In the Middle Thames, the Formation is called the Boyn Hill Terrace. Downstream in the Lower Thames the same terrace is the Orsett Heath Terrace.

In neither the Upper Thames nor Middle Thames are interglacial deposits preserved which can be related with confidence to the Swanscombe Interglacial. What sites there are, represent collections of artefacts, usually handaxes, recovered by nineteenth-century collectors, from gravel deposits. These deposits represent various members within the Boyn Hill/Orsett Heath Formation – but relating them specifically to interglacial conditions has proved difficult.

There are surprisingly few Boyn Hill/Orsett Heath sites in the Upper Thames. The Wolvercote Channel deposits (Table 2.2) are discussed in the next chapter, but they may date to MIS 11 – the jury is still out on this (Bridgland, pers. comm.). There are temperate mammal remains in sediments believed to have been washed out from the Lower Hanborough Terrace which is considered to be late MIS 12. This would make these deposits MIS 11 (at least their reworking into their present position would be a result of melt at the MIS 12/11 boundary). However, there is continued discussion of the age of this terrace, and it may well be that the whole of the Hanborough Terrace is MIS 12, in which case, any fauna would likely date to MIS 13 (Bridgland pers. comm.). The resolution of this must await further research.

The classic Middle Thames area for Boyn Hill/Orsett Heath sites is the stretch between Reading and Iver, where the Thames makes a series of sweeping bends and the Boyn Hill/Orsett Heath and succeeding Lynch Hill/Corbets Tey Terraces have been left clearly separated (this is particularly so for the stretch between Maidenhead and Iver). Some very important Boyn Hill/Orsett Heath handaxe sites are found all along this part of the river's course, sites such as Toot's Farm (Caversham), Winch's Pit, and the celebrated Cooper's and Deverill's Pits.

Wymer's (1968) extensive review of the Middle Thames sites contained details of the frequencies of individual handaxe types from many of the sites, following his own typological approach to handaxe classification. This was simplified in Table 5.1 for the Highlands Farm site in the Caversham Channel. This format is repeated in Figure 5.4. I have used those sites from Wymer's (1968) book with more than 20 handaxes, and which can be clearly assigned to a specific terrace in the Middle Thames in the TERPs data (Wessex Archaeology 1996). Sadly only four sites from each of the Black Park and Boyn Hill Terraces were suitable, although this does provide a

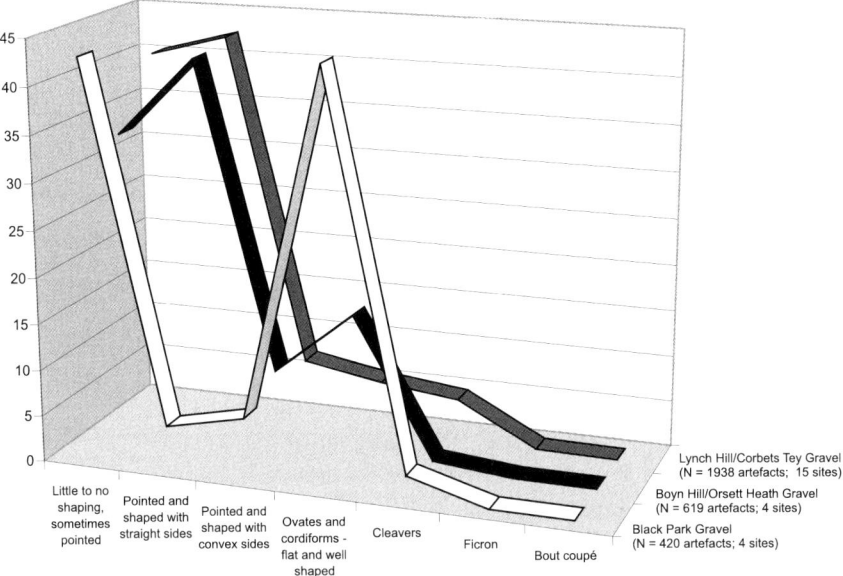

Figure 5.4 Frequency of occurrence of different types of handaxe from Black Park, Boyn Hill and Lynch Hill Terraces of the Middle Thames.

combined sample of over a thousand handaxes. There is quite a marked difference between the two terraces. In the Black Park Gravels, pointed handaxes with clear attention to shaping (whether with straight or convex sides) are markedly infrequent. Instead the assemblages are dominated by a mixture of poorly shaped bifaces and the flatter types, the well-made ovates and cordiforms of Wymer's handaxe system. In this respect the data are similar to the pre-Anglian sites of Boxgrove, High Lodge and Warren Hill, which also have a strong presence of this particular morphology. The flatter ovate and cordiform morphologies are present in the Boyn Hill/Orsett Heath Middle Thames, but in much smaller numbers – here the pointed and well-shaped handaxes with straight sides predominate. It would be fascinating to explore this pattern in more detail. What does it reflect, Victorian collecting habits, sample biases, different erosion and depositional patterns of the river, or is it a genuine trend in what hominins were making?

But it is clear from the sites in the Boyn Hill/Orsett Heath Formation, that no Clactonian assemblages are present in the Upper or Middle Thames, they are exclusively Acheulean. This in itself is an interesting observation. This interglacial is supposed to be the classic time period for Clactonian hunter-gatherers. Core and flake assemblages are clearly present in the Lower Thames in the Early Temperate pollen zone. Yet in over 150 years of quarrying, not a single Clactonian site has come from the Middle Thames. Of course it is not impossible that one or more such sites did exist. The lack of handaxes may have resulted in these sites being missed by quarrymen who had their sights focused on handaxes (and profit!). But the curious fact still remains, there are no Clactonian sites in the Boyn Hill/Orsett Heath occupation phase in the Upper or Middle Thames Valley.

The Lower Thames Valley

Bridgland's river terrace model was primarily developed on sites from the Lower Thames Valley which explains why it is particularly suited to the sites discussed below. The palaeogeography of the Lower Thames during the time of the Boyn Hill/Orsett Heath Formation is shown in Figure 5.5. What the map depicts is the river flowing eastwards. The modern estuary would not have existed because the coast lay much further east. Across this low-lying dry land area the river took a dramatic left turn after being joined by the northward-flowing Middle Pleistocene Medway. The combined Thames/Medway flowed northwards (up the modern Essex coast) until it reached the vicinity of Clacton-on-Sea when it took a right-hand turn and flowed eastwards once more. Here it re-occupied part of its old pre-diversion course.

The age of the Dartford Heath deposits have already been discussed. I will support the view of Bridgland (1994) that they date to the Boyn Hill/Orsett Heath Formation, but the case is far from proven. Bridgland (pers. comm.) has suggested that the channel noted under the Dartford Heath Gravels at Pearson's Pit on the east side of Dartford Heath (see above),

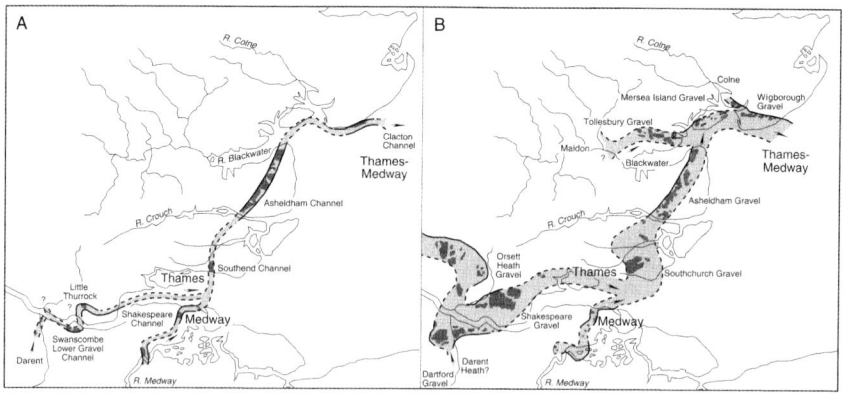

Figure 5.5 The Lower Thames Valley during the development of the Boyn Hill/Orsett Heath Formation. A the interglacial channel; B the mapped gravels overlying the channel, stages 4 and 5 of Bridgland's terrace model.

Note: Used with permission.

and which is believed to be the upstream equivalent of the Swanscombe Lower Gravels Channel (Dewey 1959), may be the MIS 12/11 incision of his model's first stage. He implies the deep and earlier Black Park Terrace incision was located elsewhere (further north on the floodplain) and has now been buried, or removed by later downcutting of the valley. This hypothesis allows us to accept a simple heuristic model which overcomes some of the difficulties in tying the Dartford Heath sequence to that of Barnfield Pit Swanscombe (Bridgland 1994, for a good review of this; see Chapter 3 for a full description of the Swanscombe sequence). This is shown in Figure 5.6.

Both localities have large channels at the base of their sequences. Above these are terrace gravels emplaced by the Thames while it flowed in a braided stream environment. This would be the Dartford Heath Gravel itself, and the Middle Gravels at Barnfield Pit. They sweep over and bury the channel features. Both of these floodplain gravels have temperate fauna associated (elephant teeth at the base of the Dartford Heath deposits, and a full interglacial mammal and mollusc fauna at Barnfield).

At the Wansunt Pit, Dartford Heath, is a channel cut into the Dartford Heath Gravels, the Wansunt Channel (Chandler and Leach 1912; Leach 1913; Smith and Dewey 1914). It contains a temperate sediment, the Wansunt Loam. At Barnfield (Figure 3.7), there is a channel cut into the top

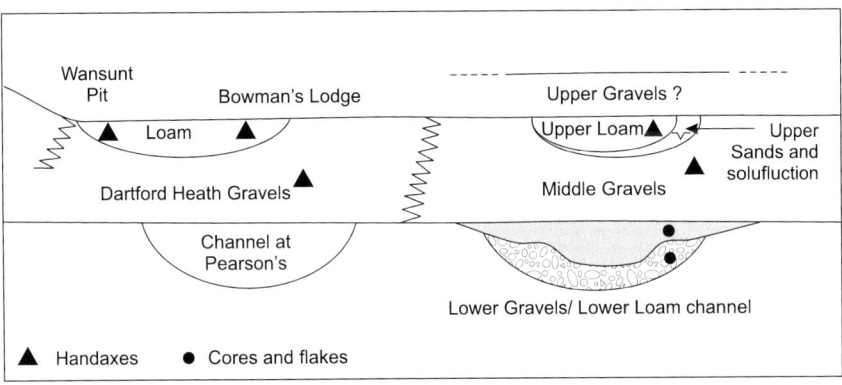

Figure 5.6 Schematic cross-section of the relationship between Barnfield Pit, Swanscombe and Dartford Heath.

Note: The two basal channels, at Dartford Heath and the Barnfield Pit, represent incision at the MIS 12/11 transition. These would represent stages 1 and 2 of the Bridgland terrace model. The infill of the channels and the gravels above them (Dartford Heath Gravels and Middle Gravels) represent aggradation in the MIS 11 interglacial, so these would equate with stage 3 of Bridgland's model. The Upper Loam at Barnfield Pit is a temperate deposit separated by a cold phase (Upper Sands and solifluction) from the earlier temperate Middle Gravels. It is unclear whether the Upper Loam represents the continuation of the MIS 11 interglacial, or represents climatic fluction at the end of MIS 11 and the MIS 11/10 transition.

of the Middle Gravels and also infilled with a temperate sediment, the Upper Loam (Conway 1996c).

However, although the Upper Loam Channel has a temperate infill, the channel itself was cut under cold climate conditions prior to the warm phase (Figure 3.7, units IIIa and IIIb). There is evidence that the Upper Middle Gravels were deposited in an environment that was already becoming much cooler. I would support the interpretation that the Wansunt Channel at Dartford, and the Upper Loam Channel at Barnfield are contemporary and part of the same channel (see especially Wenban-Smith and Bridgland 2001). The brief cold phase responsible for the erosion of this channel may have been an interstadial within late MIS 11, or perhaps it reflects the perturbation of climate that may characterise the end of the MIS 11 interglacial (Ashton, pers. comm.).

The return to cold conditions at the end of the interglacial is represented by the Barnfield Upper Gravels (Figure 3.7). What appears to be missing at Barnfield is the bulk of this terrace's gravels attributable to stage 5 of Bridgland's river terrace model. Perhaps the Upper Gravel is a remnant, but this doesn't seem very likely. They are also absent from Wansunt and the nearby site of Bowman's Lodge too. Some of the higher portions of the Dartford Heath Gravel may represent a local development of this stage.

There is archaeological logic to this simple sequence. Unfortunately no artefacts were recovered from the Pearson's Pit basal channel, although it is possible a core and flake industry was present but went unrecognised by the quarry men who found the handaxes in the gravels above. Dewey (1959) recorded handaxes coming from the Dartford Heath Gravels overlying the Pearson's Pit Channel. On the simple model in Figure 5.6 this tallies well with the records of handaxes coming from the Middle Gravels at Barnfield. The Wansunt Loam also contains handaxes (Chandler and Leach 1912; Smith and Dewey 1914). Across the road from the Wansunt Pit is Bowman's Lodge which also has a loamy deposit overlying Dartford Heath Gravel. There are handaxes at the interface between the gravel and the loam (Tester 1951; 1976). It is an assumption that the loams at the two sites are the same deposit (see Bridgland 1994, for a review of these arguments). Other than the presence of handaxes in the Wansunt Loam and Upper Loam at Barnfield, the archaeology is not much help here, but Roe (1968) did tentatively include the Upper Loams in his group VI (sites with more pointed ovates), which also included Bowman's Lodge. Although the Bowman's Lodge handaxes did not display any evidence of twisted edges, these are present in the Wansunt Loam handaxes, as well as on bifaces from the Upper Loams at Barnfield Pit. At both sites they occur more often than is seen in other contemporary MIS 11 sites (Roe 1968; Wymer 1968; Waechter 1973; and especially White 1998c).

Before moving downstream of Swanscombe it is worth reiterating that the Lower Gravels Channel at Barnfield and its extension at Rickson's Pit

(Chapter 3) do contain one or two classic handaxes or their debitage. From the British Museum's Marston collection, Barnfield Pit, there is the black ovate, as well as a few thinning flakes (Figure 3.8). These latter have a question mark next to their provenance on the box they are kept in. I firmly believe, but cannot prove, that long ago a British Museum curator added the question mark to the provenance on the box label. The black ovate was marked Middle Gravels Erosion Stage so it did not contradict cultural expectations (see Chapter 3 – the handaxe was one of Marston's proofs for the existence of the deep channel he believed he had discovered). But the thinning flakes were not so marked, and consequently they ran counter to expectations. From Rickson's Pit there are a few thinning flakes in the Marston collection from the lowest gravels – there is no query next to their provenance. While I am convinced of the Lower Gravels provenance of all of these examples of Acheulean technology, it must be clearly stated that they in no way change the otherwise overwhelming predominance of cores and flakes/flake tools at these localities.

Downstream of Greenhithe/Swanscombe there are no significant archaeological sites from the MIS 11 Thames until Clacton-on-Sea, see Figure 5.5. However, important geological localities are present in eastern Essex, representing deposits of the combined Thames/Medway. They are the interglacial deposits within the Southend Channel and the Asheldham Channel (see Table 2.1). At Southend, handaxes occur in gravels which overly the channel sediments (Wymer 1999). An important exposure of the Thames/Medway is at East Hyde, Tillingham (Roe 1999). These have been revealed through small exposures and bore holes, so detailed description must await opportunities for excavation. It is suggested that at the base of each channel are gravel deposits which equate with (at least in part) the MIS 12/11 transition, followed by gravels dating to the earlier part of the interglacial, as at Swanscombe and Clacton. Succeeding these deposits are finer sediments representing full interglacial conditions. Artefacts have not been found as yet.

These channel exposures are critical for the Clactonian debate as the discovery of handaxes in their basal deposits would place Acheulean hunter-gatherers in the early MIS 11 Thames/Medway Valley between Clacton and Swanscombe. But for the moment no artefacts have been recovered. At the very least this suggests that not every stretch of the river was occupied by hominins. On the other hand this may only reflect the lack of larger-scale excavations.

On the Hoo peninsular south of the Thames/Medway confluence is the Shakespeare Channel, a Medway equivalent of the main Thames channel (Bridgland and Harding 1984; Bridgland et al. 2001; Bridgland 2003). The channel has no archaeology, but the gravels that overlie it, the Shakespeare Gravels, do. Bridgland and Harding (1984) optimistically identified an Acheulean and Clactonian component as coming from the gravels. This latter is based on the presence of one flake and one core which is insufficient evidence, in my opinion.

Further downstream we come to Clacton-on-Sea. As noted in Chapter 3, Clacton is a number of different archaeological localities. Of these, Lion Point and the Golf Course assemblages are the only two big enough, in my opinion, to sustain the notion of a local non-handaxe assemblage-type. The pollen from the West Cliff locality (Pike and Godwin 1953) fixed the Clactonian there to the Early Temperate pollen zone of the interglacial, pollen zone IIb, see Table 3.1 (Turner and Kerney 1971). The marine transgression was in pollen zone III, as indicated at Clacton by the Estuarine Beds.

It is likely that the Thames had been connected to the Rhine for some time before the beginning of estuarine conditions at Clacton since Rhenish molluscs are present near the top of the Upper Freshwater Beds (see Figure 3.2; and they are present at the top of the Lower Loam too, Kerney 1971). It will be recalled from Chapter 3 that the Rhenish molluscan suite was a fauna of freshwater snails thought to have migrated upstream from mainland Europe when the Thames and the Rhine were connected. The exact timing of this is interesting, and impacts upon Mark White's suggestion (2000) that Acheulean hunters occupied Britain in the latter part of the Early Temperate pollen zone (pollen zone IIc on Table 3.1 – from this point on, there are no Clactonian sites in MIS 11). Rhenish molluscs suggest that a link between the Thames and Rhine existed, and that by implication the North Sea bight must have been exposed for the two rivers to flow across and meet. Hominins could easily have used the Rhine–Thames corridor to move westwards into Britain. But MI data suggests sea-level rise at the beginning of interglacials is rapid. This leaves us with a number of competing scenarios:

- The land bridge was intact and the North Sea coast was still to the north of where Clacton is today. The Thames was a left bank tributary of the Rhine. The course of the Thames perhaps skirted the northern edge of the Dover–Artois hills. Clactonian hunters arrived first. Later, and with the North Sea coastline still some way to the north, the Rhenish molluscs migrated up the Thames, as Acheulean hunters were doing the same.
- There was a limited opportunity for crossing over into Britain before the rising sea levels rendered Britain an island. Clactonian hunters crossed over prior to this. This scenario requires there be no evidence of this sea-level rise preserved in any of the sites we possess today. Subsequently, there was a temporary drop in sea level, during which a Thames–Rhine reconnection occurred. Acheulean hunters now migrated into Britain. The land bridge lasted only until the return to full interglacial sea levels. The Estuarine Beds at Clacton mark this later rise. But as David Keen (pers. comm.) has pointed out, this isn't very likely.

The Rhenish molluscs are fully temperate, if they migrated up the Thames, it was in interglacial conditions.

- There were a number of rises and drops in MIS 11 sea level, but for a variety of reasons this evidence is difficult to identify.

For the moment, it is not possible to suggest which, if any, of the above possibilities is correct. To the east of Clacton-on-Sea, the MIS 11 Thames passes under the modern Essex coastline and is now buried by marine sediments. Wymer (1985) notes exposures near Walton and Frinton that may well represent further Pleistocene channels, or a continuation of the main Thames channel, but their relationship to the Clacton deposits cannot be securely established. Another correlative of the Swanscombe/Clacton gravel channel may be at Burnham-on-Crouch (Bridgland, in White 2000).

East Anglia in MIS 11 and afterwards

Turning northwards from the Thames Valley it is frustrating not to be able to directly link the Lower Thames Valley sequence with the sediments of the East Anglian hinterland that lies to the north-east of it. When the ice sheets retreated, they left an undulating till plain. It is likely that some drainage patterns re-established themselves in former courses where the till merely blanketed the old valley sides. In other cases whole new drainage patterns will have developed following the topography of the till surface. Many East Anglian MIS 11 sites are lakes developed in kettle holes where dead ice (ice trapped within the lodgement till by the retreating glacier) eventually melted, causing collapse of the overlying till surface. These formed deep and wide hollows that subsequently filled with water to become lakes. These sites are particularly important as they became reservoirs for a some-times near continuous pollen rain. At Hoxne (West 1956) and Marks Tey (Turner 1970), the pollen record covers much of the vegetational history of the interglacial. These small lakes may have been a common feature of the new post-Anglian landscape in Norfolk and Suffolk.

Barnham St Gregory has been described in detail in Chapter 3. The point to reiterate here is that this was one of the only two British Lower Palaeolithic sites in Britain where the traditional relationship between an early Clactonian and a later Acheulean was demonstrated stratigraphically; the other was Barnfield Pit. Excavations by the British Museum (Ashton *et al.* 1998) in the area of the older excavations (Area I) did indeed confirm a large core and flake assemblage. While the British Museum excavations found no Acheulean in Area I (but see Chapter 3 for my own observations on this), handaxes and thinning flakes were present some 50 m to the east in Area IV.4 in the same unit – the cobble band. Questions of con-temporaneity between the two assemblages were discussed in Chapter 3, as has the suggestion by Mark White that rolled cores and flakes in Area I preserve evidence of an older Clactonian assemblage which predates the contemporary fresher flintwork of Areas I and IV.4. Nick Ashton's shifting resource exploitation model is a much more parsimonious explanation than a simple culturally based behavioural dichotomy. Shifts in the character of material culture tracked changes in the availability of flint as a resource for tool making. Changes in technology, paralleling changes in the sedimentation regime, can be readily seen at the site.

Recent work at Elveden (Ashton *et al.* 2005) has considerably expanded upon the original work of Paterson (Paterson 1942; Paterson and Fagg 1940). The site retains evidence of knapping on a marginal lag gravel as fluvial conditions gradually replaced a small body of still water, possibly lacustrine in origin. This is another example of one of those small lakes in the till plain noted above. A heuristic sequence is presented in the schematic diagram in Figure 5.7. The pollen places the earlier lacustrine phase in the pre-temperate zone of an interglacial (Ho I). The interglacial is MIS 11. There is an ostracod in these deposits that becomes extinct during this interglacial. The upper part of the lacustrine sequence was deposited during fully temperate conditions, probably pollen zone II – Early Temperate. It is not possible to place the archaeology, which is in the higher fluvial deposits, into a specific zone of the interglacial, but the fauna and molluscs are fully temperate so an association with Ho II is likely.

Over time, there are changes in the character of the artefacts. These

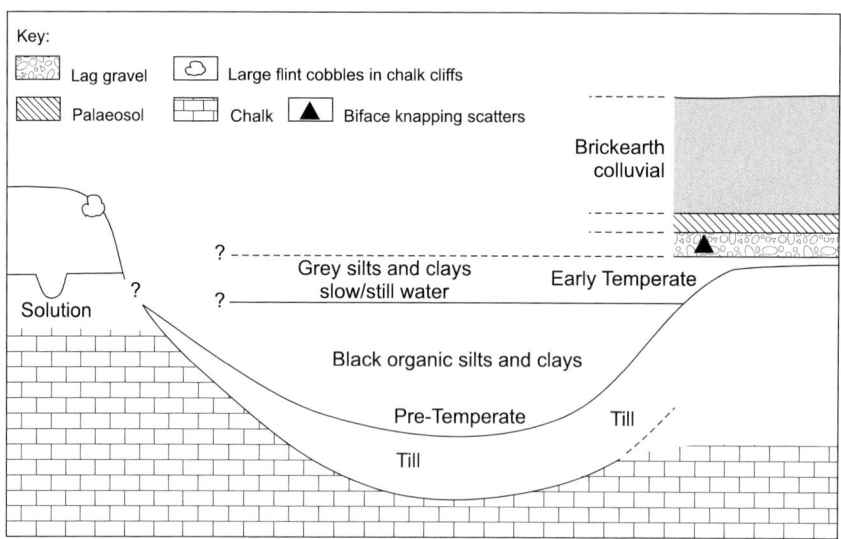

Figure 5.7 Schematic cross-section of British Museum excavation at Elveden.

Source: Data from Nick Ashton, pers. comm.

reflect shifts in the availability of flint as the lag gravel became buried by the colluvial brickearths. Hominins had to rely on flint from low chalk bluffs exposed at the side of the river. This is another variation on Ashton's resource availability model pioneered at Barnham, but in this case applied to a purely Acheulean site. Importantly, this site demonstrates Acheulean knappers making cores and flakes at the same spot as they practised the initial stages of biface manufacture. This is implied at Barnham Area IV.4, but at Elveden there is no Clactonian to confuse the picture. As the excavators note, the sequence at Barnham is phenomenally similar to that at Elveden. It is quite possible that the two sites are contemporary and that a single channel connects the two sites together, but this remains to be proved. Certainly the behavioural responses to changes in the local landscape were very similar, an important point of convergence between a group of hominins making cores and flakes at one locality, and handaxes at the other – unless, of course, this was the same group!

Beeches Pit (Wymer 1985; Gowlett and Hallos 2000; Preece et al. 2000; 2006) is another important MIS 11 location, only a few kilometres away from Barnham and Elveden. The site has in-situ Acheulean biface manufacturing episodes associated with a fully interglacial climate. It also has the earliest evidence of fire in Britain, see below and Chapter 13. A simplified stratigraphy is presented in Figure 5.8. There are two archaeological areas, AH and AF, both of which have handaxes and core working associated. At AH, occupation appears to have been associated with a small standing pool of water whose sediments have been designated as unit 3, and are divisible into a number of sub-units.

The lowest layer (3a) has molluscs associated with the early part of an interglacial. Layer 3b has the earliest archaeology at the site. On the basis of terrestrial molluscs, it may well relate to the Lower Loam at Swanscombe (Preece et al. 2000). This makes the layer 3b Acheulean at Beeches Pit the earliest post-Anglian handaxe-making horizon in Britain. If confirmed, this would attest to an Acheulean presence in Britain within the same phase of the MIS 11 interglacial as the Clactonian to the south in the Lower Thames Valley, something that has already been suggested for Barnham. There is also a hearth in this level.

Layer 3 was overlain by a tufaceous unit (layer 4). Preece et al. (2000; 2006) suggest the tufaceous sediments are the equivalent of the Lower Middle Gravels at Barnfield, again on the basis of terrestrial molluscs. A provisional correlation between Beeches Pit, Swanscombe, Elveden and Barnham has recently been suggested by Richard Preece and colleagues (Ashton et al. 2005: Figure 35). This is the first real link between East Anglia and the Thames Valley; it is shown in Figure 5.9. However, it should be pointed out that this does not imply direct contemporaneity. There could be many hundreds of years separating the Lower Loam knapping floor and the making of bifaces around a hearth in Beeches Pit. Nevertheless, it

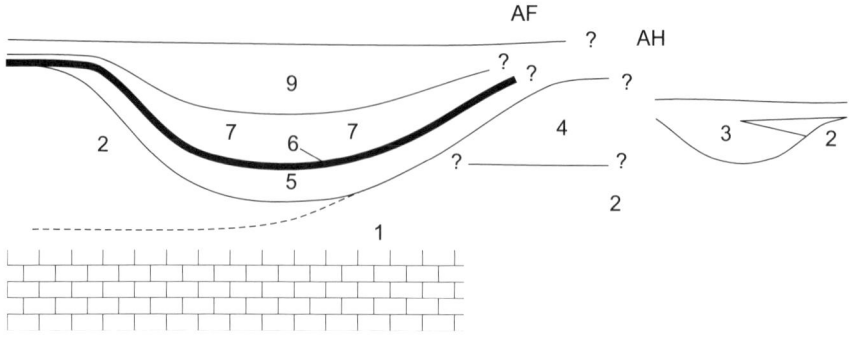

Figure 5.8 Schematic cross-section of Beeches Pit.

Source: Data from Preece *et al.* (2000); Preece *et al.* (2006).

Notes:
1 Till deposited on chalk
2 Fluvio-glacial deposit, probably outwash. Possibly deposited in a small body of standing water in an outwash channel.
3 Silty clays with molluscs and vetebrate fauna deposited in a small body of standing water/ marsh. A deposit of 2 has slipped off the side of the feature. Molluscs indicate Early Temperate pollen zone – possibly equivalent with Barnfield Lower Loam. Hearth feature.
4 White creamy silty clay – 'tufa'. Molluscs suggest temperate deciduous forest. Possibly equivalent of the Lower Middle Gravels at Barnfield.
5 Grey brown silts and clays – temperate mature woodland.
6 Black horizon with bone, sediment, and flints, all burnt. Localised downslope slipping of deposits into channel. Cold climate. Hearth in AF may have slumped into channel from bank.
7 Calcareous silty sand with a possible palaeosol on top. Cold climate.

Layers 5, 6 and 7 are channel deposits.

8 Very localised deposit of cover sand not shown.
9 Mass movement deposit covering sequence.

certainly implies contemporaneity on a geological time scale, and most of Palaeolithic archaeology is a dialogue carried out at this very scale.

Area AF (Figure 5.8) samples the bank of a larger channel feature. The archaeology here is later than AH as the occupation was probably on the surface of layer 4. Artefacts are present within the sediments of layer 5, and layer 6 is a mass movement deposit of bones, flints, sediments, and organic materials that have been burnt (some are present in the upper part of layer 5). John Gowlett, the archaeological excavator of Beeches Pit, believes almost all of unit 6 to be a deposit of hearth debris – material swept off the hearths which accumulated like a fan downslope of the hearth. Other researchers disagree and interpret this extensive channel fill deposit as the residue of natural forest fires.

The archaeology demonstrates handaxe making, core and flake working, and the presence of flake tools. Some of the handaxes have been moved into

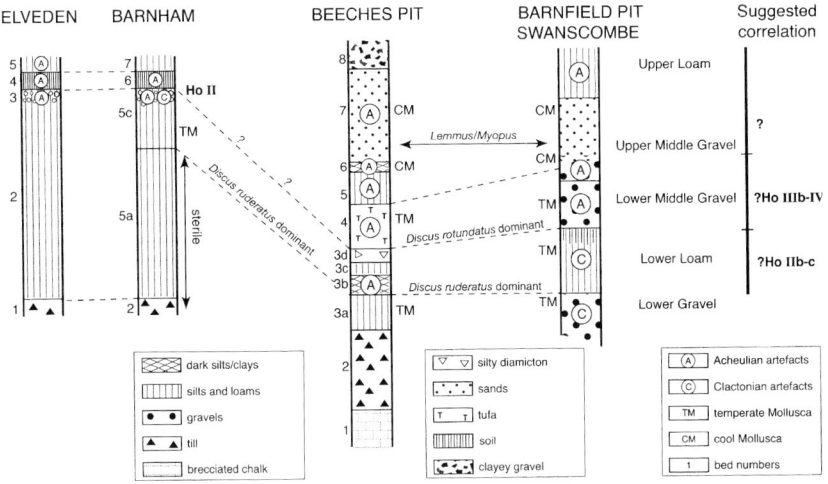

Figure 5.9 A reconstruction of the relationship between selected East Anglian MIS 11
             sites and Barnfield Pit, Swanscombe.

Source: Based on the work of Richard Preece and colleagues

Note: Used with permission.

the immediate area, having been made elsewhere (Hallos 2005). Others
were made on the spot. Hominins clearly came back to this place on a
number of occasions, as two hearths in AF appear to have been stacked one
on top of the other. Flintwork appears arranged around the margin of these
hearths. In addition to the evidence for the controlled use of fire, and all that
implies, the relighting of fires would be good evidence for the reuse of
specific locations in the landscape. Since the Beeches Pit site would have been
surrounded by forest, and perhaps only approached by game trails, then we
may have an example of the targeting of a location along a known trail.

    The site of Hoxne is one of the most celebrated Lower Palaeolithic locali-
ties in Britain, with a pedigree extending beyond Prestwich and Evans
(Wymer 1983 and 1985, for historical significance) to John Frere (1800).
Major excavations were conducted at the site in 1972–74 and 1978 by
Ronald Singer and John Wymer for the University of Chicago (Singer et al.
1993). The dating of the site, and the allocation of the archaeology to
specific pollen sub-stages within the Hoxnian during the 1970s and 1980s
were shown in Table 3.1. Bowen et al. (1989) considered the site to date to
MIS 9 on the basis of amino-acid ratios. Recently Schreve (2001) has placed
the mammal assemblage in MIS 11.

    More recent fieldwork at the site (Ashton et al. n.d.; Lewis et al. 2000)
has concentrated on re-opening sections and sampling sediments in
order to increase the environmental database and re-appraise stratigraphic

151

relationships. This new work has radically re-interpreted the sequence (Ashton *et al.* n.d.). This is summarised in Figure 5.10. The most important implication of this new work is that Stratum C is now recognised as a cold climate deposit as it was originally reported by Clement Reid, one of the sites earliest investigators. West (1956) erroneously believed it to date to the Late Temperate interglacial pollen zone – IIIb. Deposits of this sub-zone appear to be absent from the area of the investigations, and the IIIb-like pollen in Stratum C may have been derived into it from the local destruction of these units. As yet, it is not possible to state whether stratum

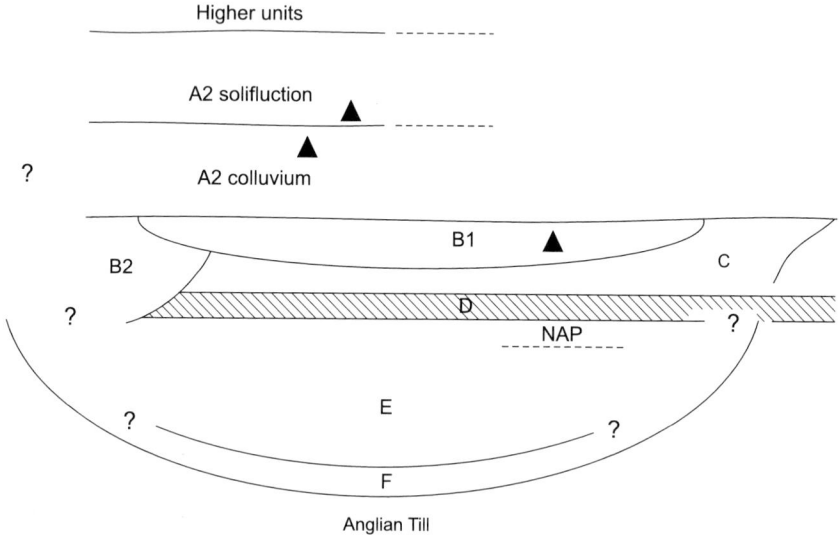

Figure 5.10 Schematic cross-section of Hoxne.

Source: Data from Nick Ashton, pers. comm. Based on work of Nick Ashton, Simon Lewis, Simon Parfitt and colleagues.

Notes:
F   Cool late glacial?
E   Temperate/interglacial lake clays, pollen zones Ho I – Ho IIc
NAP Non-arboreal pollen phase, a period of open treeless landscape.
D   Peat horizon, alder carr developing during temperate conditions, pollen zone Ho IIIa

Hiatus – Pollen zone Ho IIIb?

C   Cold climate deposit with derived temperate pollen from missing units attributable to Ho IIIb
B2   Fine sands and chalky gravel – fluvial. Geological bed 4 of Singer *et al.* Climate warm. Middle Industry, probably not *in situ*.
B1   Bedded sands, silts and clay. Fluvial. Temperate climate with cool winters. Lower Industry at base.
A2   Colluvium – sandy clay unit. Equivalent of geological bed 5 of Singer *et al.* Temperate climate? Upper Industry *in situ* at top = archaeological layer 7 of Singer *et al.*
A2   Solifluction – flint gravel – coarse sandy matrix. Equivalent of geological bed 6 of Singer *et al.* Derived Upper Industry at base. Archaeological layer 6 of Singer *et al.*
Higher units cold climate.

C is a cold phase within MIS 11, or actually represents the MIS 10 glaciation. It is entirely possible that Stratum C is the equivalent of the cold
climate Upper Sands at Barnfield. Whichever proves to be the case, the
archaeology at Hoxne clearly post-dates this cold period, and the full MIS
11 interglacial conditions that preceded it.

Two primary context archaeological assemblages are present at Hoxne
(Figure 5.10). The Lower Industry was found in the fluvial sediments of
Stratum B1, laid down during a temperate climate. The Upper Industry was
in situ in a layer termed Stratum A2 colluvium. Upper Industry artefacts,
derived from Stratum A2 colluvium, were present in the colder climate
solifluction gravels known as Stratum A2 solifluction

Lewis et al. (2000) interpret the distribution of the flintwork from the
Lower Industry as being a result of fluvial 'stretching' along the bed of one
of the river channels that succeeded the lake. That the assemblage is in near
primary context is demonstrated by occasional refits, and the very fresh
condition of the cores, flakes, bifaces and associated manufacturing debitage
(personal observation). If one was to extract the bifaces and the thinning
flakes from the assemblage, the remainder would have a very Clactonian
appearance – cores and hard hammer flakes identical to those found at
Swanscombe and Clacton, all made in the same way. Some aspects of the
flake tool component are also very similar. For example, a large flake has
been used as a wedge, identical to the one on the Lower Loam knapping
floor at Barnfield Pit. The numbers of thinning flakes in the Lower Industry
indicate that bifaces were being thinned and shaped at the site. Mark
White (1998a) has demonstrated that the hominins who made the Lower
Industry had to bring flint nodules to the site in order to knap them The
nearest source of flint may have been several hundred metres away.

In and among the fresh cores and flakes, and the equally fresh handaxes
and their debitage, is a small but significant component of rolled cores
and flakes. As with Barnham and the Golf Course, this suggests an earlier
hominin presence in the vicinity. It may be a telling point that this rolled
core and flake material has never been interpreted as Clactonian. Why?
Wrong place and wrong time!

Stratified above the Lower Industry is a small collection of artefacts
labelled by Singer and Wymer as Middle Industry. This was recovered from
their Bed 4, which is the equivalent of the channel labelled B2 on Figure
5.10. The Middle Industry was thought to be that discovered by Frere. This
is based on a large flake in a very distinctive mottled type of flint found at
this height and very similar to the flint Frere's handaxes were made from.
Ashton (pers. comm.) does not believe the Middle Industry is a distinct
assemblage, he suggests it may have been derived from elsewhere.

The Upper Industry, also a biface assemblage, is located at the top of
Stratum A2 colluvium and is associated with warm conditions. This is
the second in-situ industry at the site. In the re-interpretation (Ashton et al.

n.d.), the sandy clays of this unit are not fluvial but colluvial. The Upper Industry is located near the top of the layer. The Upper Industry (distributed through a number of distinct geological sub-horizons and therefore in all probability a series of near contemporary smaller assemblages) is noted for the frequency of scrapers present, suggesting processing activities were important here. Elements of the Upper Industry have been derived into a soliflucted deposit. This is the derived Upper Industry of Stratum A2 solifluction.

The handaxes in the Upper Industry are dissimilar to those in the Lower Industry which are more ovate and cordiform (Singer et al. 1993). Those in the Upper Industry are more pointed and elongated – perhaps another example of the flexibility of Ashton's resource variability model. There is also a wide variety of outline shapes and of degrees of finish in the Upper Industry.

One other East Anglian primary context site should be discussed, Foxhall Road, Ipswich. At this site, clays and silts accumulated in either a smallish basin or in a narrow river channel connecting deeper pools, that gradually silted up with fine sediments (Wymer 1985; see especially White and Plunkett 2004). The MIS 11 date is inferred on the basis of the whole sequence of deposits lying on Anglian Lowestoft Till. White and Plunkett have managed to reconstruct the 1903–1905 excavations by Nina Layard in astonishing detail, based on the rediscovery of her site records. Two occupation surfaces were present near the base of the sequence. In a disturbed context handaxes were recovered from the surface of a red gravel, possibly the bank of the stream. Stratigraphically slightly below this, but broadly contemporary, were a series of lithic scatters on the surface of a grey clay. This may have been a temporary dry land surface in the pools/channel feature. The higher banks provided some shelter from the wind. Layard discovered a series of artefact clusters, in one case associated with what was almost certainly a hearth. This is a primary context Acheulean location, one to which handaxes were brought ready made. I will discuss this site further in Chapter 13.

It is frustrating not to be able to directly relate any of these East Anglian sites to those in the Lower Thames Valley. It is equally frustrating not to be able to relate any of them to the rivers of East Anglia and the terrace gravels that identify their Middle Pleistocene courses. It is a sobering thought that the comprehensive TERPs data, summarised by Wymer in 1999, were not able to place a single archaeological site from an East Anglian gravel terrace in a secure MIS 11 context. So, on Figure 2.8, for the rivers Wensum, Yare and Waveney which drain to the sea, and the westward draining Nar, Lark, and Little Ouse river, and the northward draining Cam, no sites from the Swanscombe Interglacial can be identified. How is this so? There are gravel terraces aplenty and stone tools within them. Sadly it is the usual story. Many handaxes are surface finds so they may have just worked their way into the top of the gravel's surface. In some cases, many gravel spreads cannot be related to particular terraces with confidence. In other cases terraces cannot be distinguished from each other (in East Anglia they are low lying and tend to run into each other so that the steps in the terrace staircase cannot be easily recognised – see Figure 2.10A). Additionally, most of the terraces do not contain interglacial sediments sandwiched between colder climate ones as in the terraces of bigger rivers. This means diagnostic molluscs, mammal bones and other environmental indicators will be absent.

Wymer (1999) notes another problem. During the 1970s and 1980s it was received wisdom that only two major ice sheets affected Britain in the Middle and Late Pleistocene. The Anglian ice sheet left till which blanketed East Anglia and the Midlands, but the Devensian (MIS 5.4 to MIS 2) glaciers did not penetrate as far south as East Anglia. So, all the tills in Norfolk, Suffolk, and Essex were Anglian/MIS 12 by default. But evidence has been growing that the situation is not that simple. Darrel Maddy and colleagues have shown that ice was present in MIS 6 in the Severn Valley at Birmingham and Kidderminster. In the valley of the river Nar, the Lower Tottenhill Gravels (see below) have been recognised as outwash from a glacier, that may date to MIS 10, 8, or possibly 6, although the first two are more likely. So, was there actually more than one post-Anglian pre-Devensian ice advance into this region? If this is the case, how far south did the ice come? What effect will it have had on the East Anglian drainage patterns – perhaps the rivers of East Anglian have only a short history of terrace development, post dating an MIS 10, 8, or 6 ice advance? All these factors contribute to our inability to identify archaeological sites in East Anglian river terraces.

Non-archaeological sites are present, many providing vital environmental and palaeo-geographical data; and many important handaxe sites are also present in the region but they cannot be securely provenanced (Wymer 1985).

And the Clactonian? None.

The Midlands in Boyn Hill/Orsett Heath times

Before moving into the Midlands proper, we should examine the evidence for MIS 11 hominin occupation in the considerable region to the west of East Anglia, the region bounded by the southern Midlands to the north, and the Chiltern Hills to the south. Only one location is known for archaeological remains that date to this period.

Just north of the scarp slope of the Chilterns there are a number of sites that date to this interglacial. They are located within the Hitchin Gap – see Figure 4.3A. This is a throughway cut into the Chilterns Escarpment by sub-glacial erosion during the Anglian (Hopson *et al.* 1996). In the succeeding Swanscombe Interglacial, this would have been a landscape not dissimilar to the freshly de-glaciated East Anglian till surface. A series of small lakes formed in kettle holes and a large lake filling the Hitchin Gap centred on the modern town (Boreham and Gibbard 1995, and references therein). Pollen analysis from the sediments associated with the lacustrine infillings of these lakes suggests that they occupied the Pre-Temperate and Early Temperate phases of MIS 11. The lakes may have persisted until pollen zone IIc, at which point they became dry land surfaces. Older sources describe a number of units overlying the lake deposits. One of them was sometimes called the *Chara* marl, it was overlain by gravel and then brickearth (the base of the brickearth was often just described as a gravelly brickearth). While there is circumstantial evidence that a few handaxes were found in the marl (Hopson *et al.* 1996; Oakley 1947), Clement Reid who excavated the deposits (Reid 1897), described handaxes as coming from the gravel. So it is not possible to relate the archaeology to the MIS 11 interglacial lake sediments, only to the fluvial phase that suc-ceeded the lake (Ashton *et al.* n.d.). There was a wealth of archaeology present. Earlier authors (Oakley 1947; Smith 1931) describe mint condi-tion bifaces and scrapers, even hammer stones! These were probably *in-situ* horizons.

One tantalising possibility can be mentioned here, though there is no actual evidence for it. The Hitchin channel (Hopson *et al.* 1996) was a sub-glacially formed channel, infilled with tills and other deposits. It runs north from Hitchin for at least 40 km toward Huntingdon and into the River Great Ouse drainage (see Figure 2.8). It does not contain any inter-glacial MIS 11 sediments, but as Lewis (1998) noted for East Anglia, many rivers utilised the linear depressions of these tunnel valleys to re-establish their courses. All the terraces around Hitchin are probably Devensian in age (Hopson *et al.* 1996), but it would be fascinating to know whether such a Middle Pleistocene river existed. It would have directly linked the Chiltern high ground with the River Great Ouse catchment, and so the Midlands to the north, and the East Anglian till plains to the east. The Hitchin Gap could have represented a through route from the London Basin northwards.

Sadly though there are no sites that can be associated with MIS 11 anywhere in the drainages of the River Great Ouse or the Nene (Figure 2.8). This is frustrating as handaxes are evidently present within their terrace gravels (Wymer 1999). One site that may be MIS 11 is the prolific site of Biddenham, Bedfordshire, on the highest terrace of the Great River Ouse (Harding *et al.* 1992, and references therein). However, there is some debate as to whether this site, with its many handaxes, belongs in MIS 11, or in MIS 9. Tentatively I will accept a date of MIS 9 and discuss this site in the next chapter.

Although Palaeolithic sites of Swanscombe Interglacial age are not pres-ent in this area to the south of the Midlands, non-archaeological sites

provide important palaeo-environmental and palaeo-geographical information. It has been suggested that the River Nene ran into a broad fjord-
like embayment during this interglacial. The famous Woodston beds of
Peterborough (Horton *et al.* 1992) are placed in pollen zone II of an interglacial, see Figure 5.11. Basally, fluvial gravels give way to finer fluvial
sediments. These in turn are overlain by estuarine deposits. These estuarine
deposits would represent the south-west corner of the embayment. These
are overlain by fluvial gravels associated with terrace 3 (highest) of the
Nene terraces at Peterborough. In the north-east corner of the supposed
embayment there are the Nar Valley Clays, which also represent estuarine
deposits, closer to the estuary's mouth. No archaeology is recorded from
these MIS 11 estuarine deposits.

Currently the Woodston beds are thought to be MIS 11 on the basis of
mammals (Schreve 2001) and pollen (Thomas 2001). But opinions and
evidence are divided. The crux of the problem is that the top of the estuarine Woodston Beds are over 14 metres OD. This means that the sea level
responsible for them was also at this height at its maximum. But this is far
too low for MIS 11, since the maximum sea level for this interglacial was
much higher than this. The evidence from the Nar Valley suggests a sea
level of up to 23 m OD or more. On the other hand determining just what
local sea level was in an interglacial is difficult to judge. This whole area
adjacent to the Fens has also experienced subsidence since the Devensian.
Tentatively, the MIS 11 date for the Woodston beds is accepted here.
Wymer (1999) suggests that they were once much higher but have been
eroded, and the evidence of the Peterborough type section (Figure 5.11)
makes this very clear.

Elsewhere I have speculated (McNabb 2006) whether or not a robust
Nene/River Great Ouse flowing into an estuary penetrating this far inland
would have presented a formidable barrier to hominins moving out of East
Anglia, or northwards from the lakes and streams of Hitchin. Perhaps the
easiest (or first encountered) route into Britain was along the palaeo-valley
of the Thames as it flowed eastwards toward the Rhine. If the Nene estuary
and its rivers were a significant barrier to further movement west or north,
then hominins arriving in Britain via this route may have been restricted to
the equivalent of a south-eastern province. In that case, occupation of the
northern Midlands might have been by hominins who by-passed these
more southerly routes of entry. Hominins who occupied the area to the
north of the Thames/Rhine palaeo-valley could have taken advantage of
the eastward-flowing rivers which would have crossed what is today the
Lincolnshire coast. The modern River Trent flows from south to north
across western Lincolnshire (Figure 2.8), but in post-Anglian times it
flowed eastwards through the Lincoln Gap (although just when is of course
hotly disputed, see Wymer 1999, for a summary). Other rivers may have
done the same. But all this of course is purely speculation.

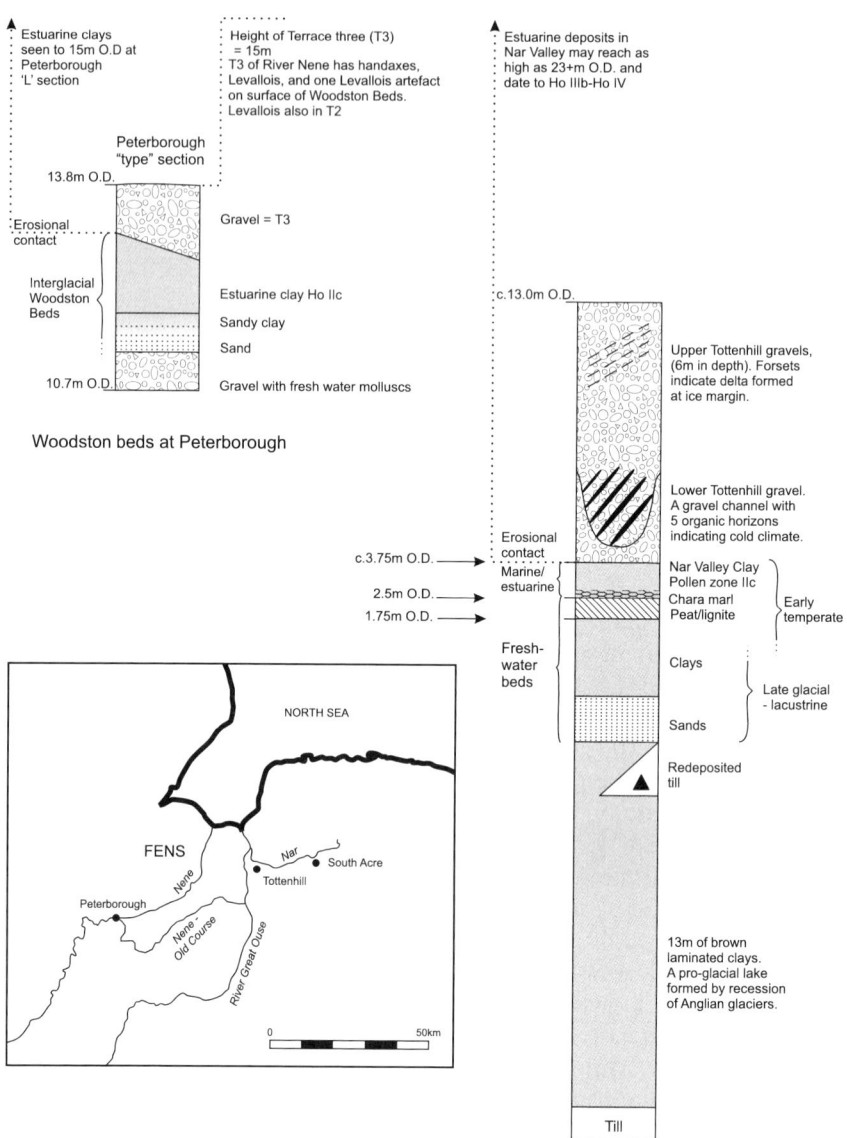

Estuarine clays
seen to 15m O.D at
Peterborough
'L' section

Height of Terrace three (T3)
= 15m
T3 of River Nene has handaxes,
Levallois, and one Levallois artefact
on surface of Woodston Beds.
Levallois also in T2

Estuarine deposits in
Nar Valley may reach as
high as 23+m O.D. and
date to Ho IIIb-Ho IV

Peterborough
"type" section

13.8m O.D.

Erosional
contact

Gravel = T3

Interglacial
Woodston
Beds

Estuarine clay Ho IIc

c.13.0m O.D.

Sandy clay

Sand

10.7m O.D.

Gravel with fresh water molluscs

Woodston beds at Peterborough

Upper Tottenhill gravels,
(6m in depth). Forsets
indicate delta formed
at ice margin.

Lower Tottenhill gravel.
A gravel channel with
5 organic horizons
indicating cold climate.

Erosional
contact

c.3.75m O.D.

Marine/
estuarine

2.5m O.D.

1.75m O.D.

Nar Valley Clay
Pollen zone IIc

Chara marl

Peat/lignite

Early
temperate

Fresh-
water
beds

Clays

Late glacial
- lacustrine

Sands

Redeposited
till

NORTH SEA

FENS

Nar

South Acre

Tottenhill

Nene

Peterborough

Nene
Old Course

River Great Ouse

0   50km

13m of brown
laminated clays.
A pro-glacial lake
formed by recession
of Anglian glaciers.

Till

Nar Valley sequence at Tottenhill

Figure 5.11 The relationship between the Nar Valley clays near Tottenhill and the
Woodston Beds at Peterborough.

In the Midlands, within the valleys of the Soar, Wreake and Trent (see Figure 2.8) sediments of this period are particularly lacking. Later sands and gravels in these valleys, post-dating MIS 11, can be placed with some confidence in a terrace sequence and fitted into the MI chronology (Table 2.2 and Figure 2.11; Wymer 1999). However, not a single Swanscombe Interglacial site is known. This may provide further circumstantial support for the presence of an ice sheet in MIS 10 or 8 that eradicated earlier deposits, though part of the problem in the Midlands may reflect more modern factors. In the south-east of England there was a long tradition of amateur collectors, most of whom lived in or near London and visited a relatively small number of famous pits on a semi-regular basis. The gravels sat on top of chalk which was being extensively quarried for London's insatiable urban expansion. But the equally rapid urbanisation of the Midlands was more widespread, there were fewer collectors in relation to the size of the area they had to cover.

The rivers of the west

The Warwickshire Avon, Figure 2.8, drains the central part of the southern Midlands Yet within the long stretch of this river not a single site can be placed in the Swanscombe Interglacial. This is the same for the Severn. Much of its valley did not exist before the Anglian (Maddy et al. 1995) and both valleys appear to have long flights of terraces which may date back only as far as MIS 10 (Figure 2.11a and Table 2.2).

There are temperate sediments at the base of some of the Severn and Avon terraces, but these post-date the Swanscombe Interglacial and are discussed in later chapters. On the face of it, the Severn and Avon system should potentially be another Lower Thames Valley; long rivers providing access for hominins ranging inland, and a clear flight of terraces up the sides of the valleys. Yet the amount of Middle Pleistocene archaeology present in both valleys is minimal. What Lower Palaeolithic archaeology there is, is largely confined to single discoveries of bifaces in the lower terraces (Wymer 1999; Lang and Keen 2005). It is further possible that many of the bifaces found on the Avon terraces may not date to the terraces on which they were found. They may have originally been derived from Bytham river sediments which underlie the gravels of the higher terraces, and were entrained into these later terrace gravels when erosion cut through the pre-Anglian deposits (Lang and Keen 2005; David Keen pers. comm.). It is quite possible that the paucity of artefacts means that the west was genuinely not a major route of entry into Britain during the Lower Palaeolithic. We just don't know.

The South

The Solent continued to flow in its valley as it did in pre-Anglian times, and remained the main drainage artery for the Hampshire basin.

No MIS 11 interglacial deposits remain within the Solent river basin, but in the main reach of the valley, the terrace dated to the first post-Anglian glaciation (MIS 10), the Old Milton Terrace, contains a number of sites with artefacts provenanced to this gravel spread (Table 4.1). As such, these may be the sweepings of the eroded MIS 11 floodplain. But as with Corfe Mullen in the last chapter, the majority of the artefacts in Table 4.1, for the reach between the Avon and the Test, come from one site, in this case, the cliffs at Barton-on-Sea. Nearly two hundred handaxes have been recovered from the scree slopes below the eroding gravel cliffs. There are two Levallois pieces from the collection. Westaway et al. (2006) argue that in fact there are two separate terraces here, subsumed within the original mapping of the Old Milton Gravel. They suggest the Levallois dates to the later terrace – their Beckton Farm Terrace. A number of the handaxes from the eroded cliff tops have twisted edge profiles which suggests an MIS 11 age (ibid.; White 1998c). These would relate to the slightly higher and older segment of this area of cliff line, the Old Milton Gravel as mapped by Westaway and colleagues. However the use of handaxes with twisted edges as a dating technique remains deeply controversial. So despite the lack of MIS 11 interglacial sediments, there are some grounds for accepting a hominin presence in the main Solent Valley in the Swanscombe Interglacial.

The Hampshire Avon could have been an important Solent tributary for hominins. As Wymer (1999) notes, it leads up almost into the catchment of the Kennet and so nearly into the Middle Thames. In its higher reaches it has no terraces as it is confined within a narrow valley. However, in its lower reaches terrace gravels are present and individual terraces can be distinguished. It seems likely that MIS 11 occupation was present here as well, though relating the numbered terraces to the MIS chronology has not yet been done with any confidence. Terrace 7 of the Avon is dated to the Anglian, and shows a sizeable collection of handaxes, although true to form, a large proportion come from just one site, in this case Wood Green (Westaway et al. 2006). I would not be surprised if at least some of the spreads of gravel mapped as terrace 7 turn out to be MIS 11 or 10. Bridgland (in Westaway et al. 2006) notes a number of Avon sites with deposits that may relate to different terraces. Table 4.1 indicates a hominin presence in the Stour as well at this time, but the finds from this tributary were more evenly distributed across a number of different localities.

All of these localities throughout the Solent system are secondary context Acheulean sites, so what of the Clactonian? Rainbow Bar is the only possible candidate for a Clactonian site. It was discussed in Chapter 3. The site cannot be tied into the MI chronology, or the terrace sequence for the Solent.

Although Palaeolithic artefacts are probably present, the site is mixed and it is not as yet possible to distinguish between earlier and later prehistoric artefacts with any confidence.

Conclusions for hominin occupation in late MIS 12/MIS 11/and early MIS 10

This phase lasts from the late Anglian, through the Swanscombe Interglacial (c. 75,000 years in duration) and into the MIS 10 glaciation. Hominins were certainly present in the late Anglian, but whether they were present in any numbers at the MIS12/11 transition, and in the earliest part of the interglacial (pollen zone I on Table 3.1) is far from certain.

There are numerous sites from the Early Temperate pollen zone when the forests would have been at their most extensive. There seems no reason to believe that hominins were not present from that point on until the end of the interglacial and possibly across the transition into MIS 10.

However, hominins do not appear to have been everywhere. For hominins moving north across the la Manche Valley, the modern south coast would have represented the beginning of high ground. The Solent valley, and its tributaries, would have been an important route of entry into the game-rich woodlands beyond, the same for those hominins moving west across the dry land of today's southern North Sea. Major river valleys would have represented easy access into rich new lands. But the north of England and the Midlands may have been only sparsely populated. Likewise, the Severn and Warwickshire Avon may reflect only occasional visits by hominins simply because they were not coming into Britain from the west. By contrast, the south-east of Britain appears to have been relatively densely populated. The access route provided by the Thames will have played a part in this.

But what of the Clactonian in the interglacial with which it is traditionally associated? Only two sites with non-handaxe assemblages really qualify for the label Clactonian: Swanscombe (three contemporary localities) and Clacton (two or three contemporary localities). They also qualify for the label assemblage-type. I am persuaded that these sites, with their overwhelming numbers of cores and flakes, were the product of hunters who migrated into Britain in the Early Temperate phase of the interglacial. They were using the Thames corridor. These sites conform to the definition of an archaeological tradition. But I am not yet persuaded that these sites represent a persistent cultural tradition. Why are there so few Clactonian sites, and why are they geographically and temporally confined to one river valley, apparently in one particular phase of this interglacial? Barnham, Elveden and Beeches show that handaxe makers were present at broadly the same time in East Anglia, and Barnham shows they were exploiting the same environments. There may even have been a few handaxe makers in the vicinity of Swanscombe and Clacton. I wish I had even a few answers for the many questions that surround the Clactonian in the Swanscombe Interglacial.

6

HOMININ OCCUPATION JUST BEFORE, DURING, AND JUST AFTER MARINE ISOTOPE STAGE 9

The Purfleet Interglacial

Introduction

This period comprises the end of MIS 10, the MIS 9 interglacial, which is sometimes called the Purfleet Interglacial, and the return to glacial conditions in MIS 8. In terms of Dave Bridgland's model for the Lower Thames (Table 2.1, Figure 2.7) this would be the Corbets Tey Formation, and its upstream continuation in the Middle Thames – the Lynch Hill Formation.

One of the difficulties about placing sites within MIS 9 has been distinguishing them from sites in MIS 11. In the Thames this is done mostly on the altitude of the site above sea level. The height is compared to the estimated heights of the different terraces at that point, and the site is then associated with whichever terrace has the closest altitudinal match. But away from river valleys, distinguishing between sites, especially those with lake sediments, has proved far more difficult. Effectively these types of site both share the classic Hoxnian pollen profile of the traditional sequence (Figure 3.3).

This has led to a rethink of the pollen data (Thomas 2001), and it has now been suggested that MIS 11 and 9 shared a very common floral history. There are, however, subtle differences between the two. For example, the Non-Arboreal Pollen phase (NAP) in pollen zone IIc of the Swanscombe Interglacial in East Anglia is absent from the Purfleet/Grays Interglacial. Thomas suggests that it is too localised an event to be reproduced in both Interglacials, and is therefore a real indicator of difference between the two temperate events. In MIS 11, the maximum interglacial sea-level rise was achieved late in the interglacial, in pollen zone III (but see discussion on Butlins site in Chapter 3 for a possible exception to this). In the Purfleet/Grays Interglacial it occurs earlier, in pollen zone II (Roe 1999). The particular character of the Rhenish mollusc fauna at the top of the Lower Loam at Swanscombe and in the Upper Freshwater Beds at Clacton is also a good MIS 11 indicator. This fauna is absent in MIS 9 (though some of the species which go to make up the Rhenish fauna are found in MIS 9, see Keen 2001). The fluvial mollusc *Corbicula fluminalis* only appears later on in the

MIS 11 interglacial, but is present early in the MIS 9 interglacial (Bridgland *et al.* 2001).

MIS 9, like MIS 11, was a high sea-level interglacial relative to MIS 7 and 13. This is shown in Figure 2.2. It will be recalled that the DSC curve is a proxy record of global ocean volume. Sea levels approached those of today (Aldhouse-Green 2001). Figure 2.2 shows that the warmest peak of the interglacial is at the beginning, with a relatively swift fall off towards much cooler interglacial conditions. Not included in what is interpreted as the interglacial proper is the temperate spike after MIS 9 (Figure 2.2). Although a clear recovery in climatic conditions, it is just not warm enough to be included in the interglacial (using sea level as a proxy for climatic amelioration). It is equivalent to MIS 5.3 and 5.1, which are the beginning of the last glaciation, the Devensian.

Sites that can be clearly attributed to this occupation phase, and to MIS 9 in particular, are few. Those mentioned in the text are shown on Figure 6.1. Evidence from Barling (Bridgland *et al.* 2001), and from Hackney in north London, suggest a climate with winters much the same as today but with summers that were warmer by several degrees (Green *et al.* 2006).

The MIS 10/9 transition

There are no archaeological sites that can be placed within the late glacial phase, but there is good evidence for a hominin presence in Britain across the glacial–interglacial transition. This evidence is confined to the Lower Thames Valley.

The site at the Globe Pit, Little Thurrock, is a Clactonian site and was described in detail in Chapter 3. It represents the feather edge of the northern bank of the Lynch Hill/Corbets Tey Thames river. The gravel which underlies the Grays Brickearth at this site (Figure 3.13), and which contains the artefacts, represents stage 2 of the Bridgland terrace model. No *in-situ* occupation of the bank is present, but the cores and flakes, and non-classic handaxes, represent sweepings from the river margin somewhere upstream. All the artefacts are rolled but not excessively, so the assemblage samples activity from the general area of the site. In all three excavations (Wymer 1957; Snelling 1964; Bridgland and Harding 1993), which produced over 670 artefacts under controlled conditions, no convincing examples of classic handaxes or thinning flakes have been discovered. Erosion and ice wedges underlying the Grays Brickearth probably relate to the glacial–interglacial transition which is stage 2 of Bridgland's terrace model. White (2000) has suggested that Little Thurrock represents the first return of hominins into the Thames Valley after the MIS 10 glaciation, and as with the Swanscombe Interglacial, these were a culturally distinct Clactonian. Acheulean hominins followed later in the interglacial. Cultural interpretations notwithstanding, the size of the Little Thurrock assemblage strongly

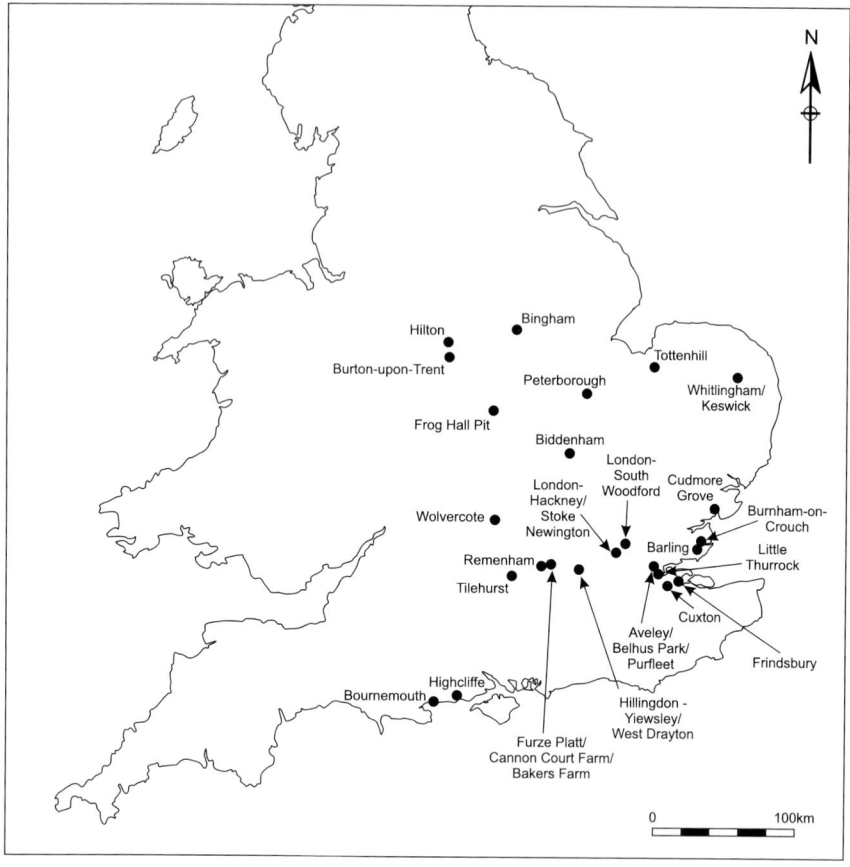

Figure 6.1 Map showing selection of sites discussed in Chapter 6.

suggests that the spectrum of activities undertaken in the vicinity of the site did not include handaxe manufacture. As noted in Chapter 3, this is a viable candidate for a Clactonian assemblage, though its channel-margin location, and the inability to demonstrate time depth for the assemblage leave me uneasy about this site's Clactonian status.

The interglacial deposits from Purfleet are described in more detail in the next section. Recent multidisciplinary work (Schreve *et al.* 2002) has clarified many aspects of the complicated Pleistocene sequence in this area, see Table 6.1. Two adjacent quarries at Bluelands and Greenlands have basal sediments that have been equated with the MIS 10/9 transition as defined here. Section cleaning by Suzanne Palmer (1975) in Bluelands identified a basal gravel (her bed 18) sitting on chalk. The precise correlative of this unit was not present in the Bluelands sections cut in the recent investigations, but was present in the adjacent Greenlands quarry, where it was

Table 6.1 Depositional sequence at Purfleet, Greenlands Pit

Unit	Description	Depositional environment	Local environment	Climate	Archaeology	MIS	Correlation with Schreve et al. – Bluelands	Correlation with Palmer 1975 at Bluelands	Correlation with Botany Pit
8	Botany Gravel	High energy deposit	Open ground?	Cold	Rolled handaxes (Levallois from nearby pits)	8	←	Beds 6 and 7?	Basal gravel at Botany Pit
7	Grey-brown silty clay	Decalcification removed evidence of bedding		Warm		9/8?	4.5 m of horizontally bedded sandy gravel from high energy braided river	Bed 8	
6	Bluelands Gravel	Higher energy deposit, layer of flint cobbles	Open ?	Warm-cool	Handaxes and thinning flakes – Acheulean. 2 cores resemble simple prepared cores	9		Bed 11?	
5	Greenlands shell bed	Large slow flowing river with sand flats	Mixed woodlands	Warm	flakes	9			
4	Silty clay	Mud flats alternating with sand banks. Local scouring from faster flow	Mixed oak woodlands with adjacent open areas	Warm	←	9	Silty clay – finely layered		

(Continued overleaf)

Table 6.1 Continued.

Unit	Description	Depositional environment	Local environment	Climate	Archaeology	MIS	Correlation with Schreve et al. – Bluelands	Correlation with Palmer 1975 at Bluelands	Correlation with Botany Pit
3	Shelly gravel	High energy river, bars in braided network	Adjacent marsh, woodlands and grasslands	Warm	Cores and flakes (c. 10) with no handaxes	9	Basal gravel with temperate shells	17?	
2	Little Thurrock gravel	Deposited away from the channel's edge		Cold?	Clactonian ? →	10	Missing from Bluelands	18?	
1	Coombe Rock			Cold		10	Coombe rock		

Source: Based on Schreve et al. (2001). With additional data from Wymer (1985) and Palmer (1975).

termed the Little Thurrock Gravel Member (bed 2 of Schreve *et al.* 2002, see Table 6.1). The excavators attribute this gravel to a cold climate. In both the Purfleet quarries, flakes were rare at this level. Wymer (1985) speculated on the possibility that this gravel at Purfleet, and the gravels beneath the Grays Brickearth at Little Thurrock were the same but decided on technological and typological grounds that they probably were not. The implication of Schreve *et al.*'s work is that they were indeed contemporary and broadly relate to the MIS 10/9 transition. Mark White cautiously suggests the lower units at Purfleet are Clactonian, but in my opinion the assemblage is far too small to be certain, c. 50 artefacts from Palmer and the more recent investigations combined (see Chapter 3). However, the small assemblage does indicate that hominins were here as well as at Little Thurrock, some 6 km downstream before the onset of fully temperate interglacial conditions.

Regional geographies for MIS 9

The Upper and Middle Thames Valley

The equivalent of the Lynch Hill/Corbets Tey Formation in the Upper Thames is the Wolvercote Formation composed of a basal gravel (MIS 10, Wolvercote Gravel), followed by the interglacial Wolvercote Channel deposits, and an overlying gravel (the Upper Wolvercote Gravel, see Figure 2.9A and Table 2.2). The basal gravel has been interpreted as outwash, although Maddy and colleagues (Maddy *et al.* 1991) have shown that its composition is no different from the higher fluvial Hanborough Terrace of the Boyn Hill/Orsett Heath Formation or earlier. So it should be thought of as a river-lain deposit.

The archaeology was located in gravels and finer deposits at the base of the interglacial Wolvercote Channel. It was almost certainly a primary context-site with tools being made on the gravel bars or beaches of a substantial river channel, although some of the larger handaxes may have been imported (White 1998a). The site is most notable for the presence of plano-convex handaxes (D-shaped in cross-section) that have been made on large flakes. These are characterised by markedly narrowed and elongated tips. These have at times been equated with late Acheulean Micoquian assemblages in Europe which have similar types of very flat pointed handaxe (Roe 1981b, and references therein). It is important to note that other smaller and less 'refined' bifaces were also present within the assemblage (Wymer 1968), and the plano-convex handaxes should be seen in the context of a generally pointed handaxe assemblage. True plano-convex bifaces are relatively few in number (Ashton 2001).

The site's MIS 9 date should cast considerable doubt on a late Acheulean/ Micoquian association, but as Roe notes (1981b), it is the fact that a number of the plano-convex handaxes were found together that is important.

Was this handaxe morphology a cultural choice? Did the hominins want to make these kinds of handaxes and so deliberately chose flake blanks that would help them achieve this? An equally plausible explanation for this association is a purely technological one. Given that the local gravels appear to have been devoid of a constant supply of readily knappable flint, there may have been an emphasis on maintaining the handaxes that could be made at the site, as well as those imported from elsewhere. The emphasis on working tips, and the plano-convex shape itself, have been argued to be a result of a specific re-sharpening strategy (Ashton 2001). Ashton argues they were trying to maintain their equipment in an area where it was difficult to make new bifaces or replace old ones? This is the only site in the Upper Thames Valley that can be confidently placed in MIS 9.

Moving into the Middle Thames Valley, the situation changes. The Lynch Hill/Corbets Tey Terrace is reputedly the richest archaeological terrace in the Middle Thames, possibly reflecting a greater hominin population than in Boyn Hill/Orsett Heath times. This has been challenged by Nick Ashton and Simon Lewis (2002). They argue that the pattern is actually reversed when you take into account the way artefacts have been recovered. There has been more quarrying and urban development on this terrace, so no wonder more artefacts have been found. In Table 6.2, and Figure 6.2 which has been generated from Table 6.2, I have adapted their methodology, using TERPs data. Using a slightly different data set, Figure 6.2 confirms the pattern suggested by Ashton and Lewis. The Black Park Terrace has a relatively low artefact density, which is unsurprising given how little of it

Table 6.2 Data for Middle Thames Valley on occurrence and frequency of sites and artefacts within terrace gravels from different formations within the Middle Thames

Terrace/ Formation	Approximate number of sites	% of terrace affected by human impact	Presence of Levallois	Artefact density per square kilometre	Duration of terrace as aggrading flood plain
Black Park	27	0.84		20.8	15 kyr
Boyn Hill	48	20.67		67.9	75 kyr
Lynch Hill	133	27.04	Cores = 21 Flakes = 273	51.3	160 kyr
Taplow	41	12.70	Cores = 2 Flakes = 5	3.9	110 kyr
Kempton Park	10	41.44	Flakes = 1	0.1	112 kyr

Notes: Sites included were those clearly associated with one gravel formation. Sites in brickearth, or from brickearth overlying gravel were omitted. Percentage of terrace affected by human impact taken from Ashton and Lewis (2002) calculated as urban growth + quarrying/terrace area. Black Park data includes Silchester Stage gravels. Lynch Hill includes London equivalent, the Hackney Gravel. Data taken from Wymer (1999); Wessex Archaeology (1996); Ashton and Lewis (2002).

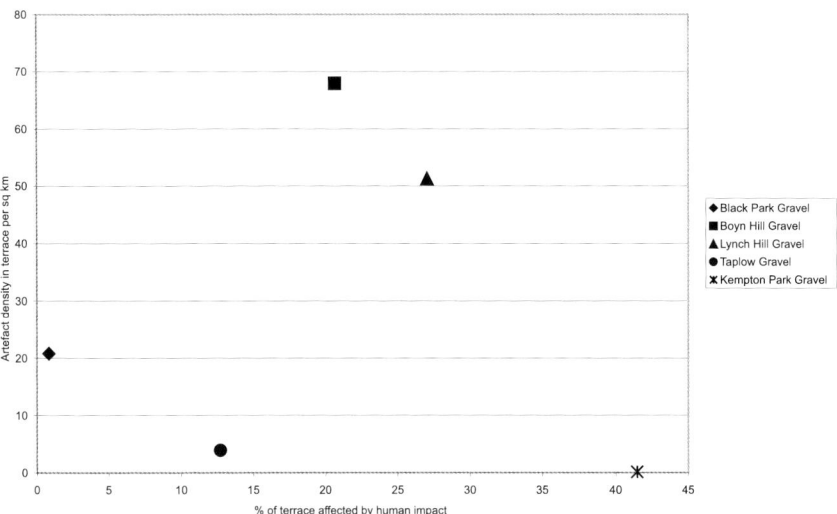

Figure 6.2 Comparison of the amount of modern disturbance (horizontal axis) affecting the Middle Thames terraces, with their archaeological richness (vertical axis).

has been developed/exists. The Boyn Hill and Lynch Hill Terraces show a greater degree of disturbance, so not surprisingly these provide the highest frequencies of sites and artefacts. They are also bigger terraces and took longer to aggrade. Figure 6.2 puts paid to the belief that the Lynch Hill is the terrace with the most evidence of occupation. While the Middle Thames Lynch Hill does have more sites and more artefacts, these data show the Boyn Hill Terrace to be proportionally richer when human impact and the spatial extent of the terrace are taken into account.

The drop in relative frequency between the Boyn Hill and the Lynch Hill was taken by Ashton and Lewis to indicate a declining population; fewer hominins revisiting Britain when the land bridge was open at the start of each interglacial. The low frequency for the Taplow Terrace represented a population crash. In the case of the Kempton Park Formation, the low values are not surprising. As the lowest terrace, this would be expected to be the most heavily disturbed as human expansion moved away from the river in post-Roman times. More artefacts will have been lost from here than anywhere else. Moreover, between MIS 6 and MIS 4 Britain was abandoned so the low artefact values for the Kempton Park gravels are unsurprising. However, I suspect that the pattern in Figure 6.2, and that in Ashton and Lewis's data, is nothing to do with hominin population. It is more to do with an uneven pattern of collecting on the part of early researchers; a few zealous collectors, concentrating on known pits with high productivity. It is perhaps significant that similar studies (Hosfield 2005), in other areas, do not support this pattern.

The handaxe typology data for the Middle Thames, discussed in the last chapter, show a marked similarity between the Boyn Hill and Lynch Hill Terraces, in contrast to the Black Park Terrace, see Figure 5.4. Both have very high frequencies of pointed handaxes, either unshaped, or shaped with straight sides. What is different about the sites from this terrace is the lower proportion of flat ovate and cordiform-shaped handaxes. The sample size is a respectable one, over 1,900 handaxes from 15 sites so there should be grounds for confidence in the pattern. As noted in Chapter 5, trying to explain that pattern is more difficult. Is this a collecting bias, or a real reflection of hominin behaviour? We just don't know.

There is complete absence of any PCT/Levallois from the earlier terraces, see Table 6.2. In a century and a half of collecting, from those sites securely provenanced to Lynch Hill Gravels (not brickearth sites or sites in brickearths overlying Lynch Hill Gravels), Levallois is largely confined to this terrace, and shows only a minor presence in the later ones. But what is not clear is whether the Levallois artefacts from the Lynch Hill Gravels in the Middle Thames, actually come from the gravels themselves (i.e. were contemporary with the formation of the terrace), or come from near the surface, or on the surface, and could actually post-date the formation of the terrace. This is the contention of Ashton et al. (2003), who highlight how desperately little secure contextual information there is for Levallois coming from the main body of the Lynch Hill Gravels.

Some quarries in this terrace were vast, others barely meriting the name of pit. Cannoncourt Farm, at Furze Platt, is a celebrated site and is known for some of the largest bifaces ever found in the British Lower Palaeolithic. The site may well have been in near primary context (Roe 1968) as many of the bifaces were in excellent condition. The bifaces were found mostly by the gravel diggers during quarrying, hence the preponderance of these over other kinds of artefact. It is frustrating not to have any idea of the original quantity and character of the cores, flakes, and flake tools that may have been present, let alone the frequency of other handaxe types. The site is notable for small quantities of cleavers. On the opposite side of the river, and in the same gravel, the site of Baker's Farm has considerably more cleavers associated, but here there are reports of a small Levallois component within the assemblage. Despite the concerns of Ashton et al. (2003) described above, in principle, there is no real reason why there should not be Levallois/PCT at the end of the interglacial or at the MIS 9/8 transition. Levallois is present at 23 of 133 Lynch Hill sites that can be firmly associated with gravel from this terrace, in other words 17 per cent (this figure is drawn from TERPs data and refers to only those sites clearly stated to be associated with gravel from this terrace; Stoke Newington, the Hillingdon pits, and sites marked brickearth above gravel were omitted). The main body of the Lynch Hill Gravels should equate with stage 5 of Bridgland's river terrace model, and so, in theory, date to the end of MIS 9 or the transition to glacial conditions. But the point about the security of proven-ance is an important one; do these artefacts come from within the gravel or at its surface? With older sites, where artefacts were collected by workmen, we cannot be sure.

There are sites in the Middle Thames tributaries that may also be referred to the gravels of this period. Wymer (1999: 80ff.) notes that in the Lynch Hill equivalent gravels of the Loddon, a south-bank tributary of the Thames joining the main river between Henley and Reading, there are a small number of Levallois artefacts. From the main river, Ashton *et al.* (2003) have re-evaluated those Levallois pieces from the famous sites of Yiewsley and West Drayton (Hillingdon) that can be provenanced. While the Lynch Hill Gravels contain handaxes, many rolled, the Levallois is in a much fresher condition and can be traced to the surface of the gravels. It may well be signif-icant that as yet no Levallois artefacts have been found in any unambiguous MIS 9 interglacial deposits, but then sites of this age are difficult to find in the Thames.

Only one site from the Middle Thames remotely approaches being called Clactonian. This is the enigmatic assemblage from Remenham. It has never been given this label because of the association of two handaxes (Wymer 1968). It also falls below the minimum threshold of 500 artefacts necessary for a Clactonian site. Given the size of the assemblage in relation to the evidence for handaxes, it certainly qualifies for a locality where core and flake working dominated activities. The core and flake assemblage came from the filling of two solution hollows some 2.7 m apart. The lithics were patinated white and their condition/visual appearance was very distinctive. In the sandy and bedded gravels between the solution hollows at least two handaxes have been found in rolled and stained condition (Wymer 1968; 1999), their appearance quite different from the flakes and cores in the solution hollows. Wymer explains the site as follows. The cores and flakes came from a land surface higher up in the bedded gravels. This surface was subject to solution as, locally, the underlying chalk dissolved and artefacts ended up in solution hollows. Erosion later removed the land surface altogether, taking the rest of the artefacts away with it, at the same time as truncating the top of the solution hollows. Deposition then recommenced with more sandy bedded gravel being laid down over the site. There are three flakes from within the solution hollows whose physical appearance is more like that of the handaxes from the bedded gravel. In addition, there are a number of retouched pieces in the assemblage from the solution hollow that look later prehistoric – one with a tang (Reading Museum collection). This suggests that the site is disturbed.

The label Clactonian is also sometimes applied to the site of Grovelands Pit, Tilehurst Road, in Reading. Handaxes and fauna were recovered together from the base of a gravel. As shown in Figure 6.3, the site is rather different from most of the Middle Thames Lynch Hill sites in that it has a more

171

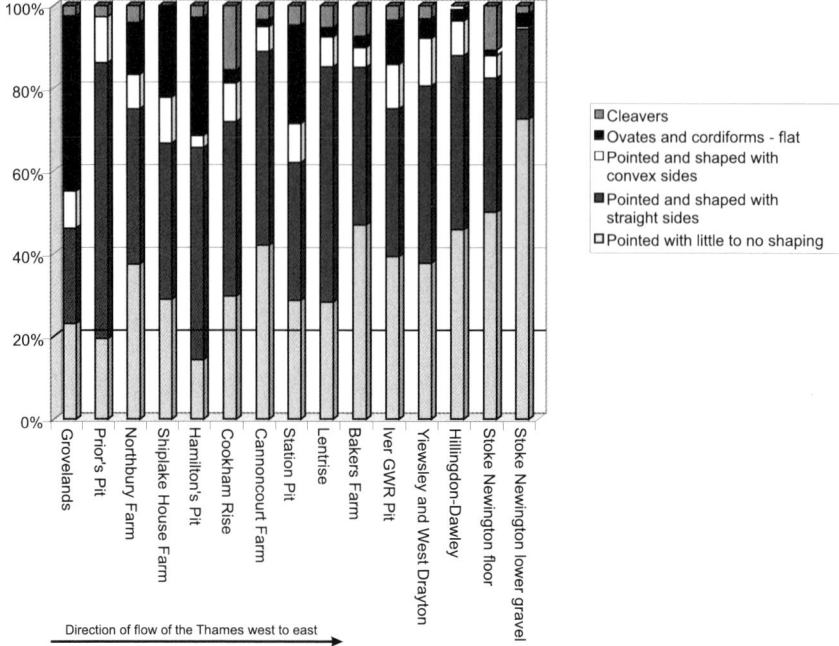

Figure 6.3 Percentage of occurrence of different types of handaxe at selected sites along the Middle Thames Valley in the Lynch Hill Terrace.

Note: Figure omits two ficrons from Cookham rise.

even frequency of pointed and ovate/cordiform type handaxes. But it was the cores, flakes, and especially the flake tools and scrapers that attracted most attention. They have been referred to as Clactonian. These were supposedly less rolled than the majority of the handaxes. However, the variability in condition in all artefact classes is quite marked (personal observation). Wymer (1968: Figures 56 and 57) illustrates a selection showing flaked flakes and High Lodge-type scrapers. These in themselves should really preclude Grovelands from being called Clactonian because these types of scraper do not occur in Clactonian assemblages (see Chapter 12). They are noted to occur in some assemblages where handaxes are present in small numbers such as Hoxne Upper Industry, or perhaps at High Lodge. The Grovelands site may be another example of *Homo heidelbergensis'* behavioural flexibility, and a warning to modern archaeologists about the inappropriateness of either/or cultural dichotomies.

In the vicinity of the River Lea, the boundary between the Middle and Lower Thames regions, there are two sites that may be placed securely within the Purfleet/Grays Interglacial. Stoke Newington was first described by Worthington Smith (Smith 1884). The site is actually a series of localities in and around Abney Park Cemetery and Stoke Newington Common (see Wymer 1968, for a plan). The sequence established by Smith is as follows. A basal gravel contained rolled bifaces near the base and at the top. Locally this gravel is the Hackney Gravel, which was laid down by the River Lea. This river was (and is) a northern tributary of the Thames. The Hackney Gravel is Lynch Hill in age. Above the gravels were finer silts and sands presumably representing interglacial environments. Within these, Smith located his famous 'floor', which he believed to be a single and very extensive land surface. In all probability this was a series of discrete but ephemeral dry land surfaces on an aggrading marshy floodplain. It is likely that at least some of the sites were primary context activity locations, and may have been broadly contemporary. Smith's meticulous observations, his collecting, and his extensive refitting of artefacts were years ahead of his time. There were handaxes, flake tools, cores, debitage, hammer stones and even anvil stones present on some of the floor exposures.

The floors occur near the base of a deposit of silts and sands, a brickearth locally known as the Highbury Silts and Sands. Bridgland (1994) dates the brickearths at Stoke Newington to MIS 9, and therefore a part of the Lynch Hill/Corbets Tey Formation. Gibbard (1995) argues they are younger. Smith (1884) noted that, in places, the overlying brick earth had been contorted, often pushed into sections of the floor itself. This may well be post-interglacial cold climate activity dating to MIS 8.

An important environmental site in Hackney, north London (Green et al. 2006), related to the River Lea, provides tentative evidence that the archaeological horizons at Stoke Newington date to earlier in MIS 9. Wymer's typology charts for the floor (1968: 302ff.) do not show any unambiguous Levallois artefacts, and Worthington Smith (Smith 1884) does not illustrate any. There is a single example in the underlying Lynch Hill Gravels but in the absence of other evidence this seems unlikely. The various 'floor' exposures suggest this was a location to which hominins returned on a number of occasions.

To the east of Stoke Newington is the site of South Woodford, in the Lynch Hill/Corbets Tey equivalent of the terraces of the River Roding. The site lies on the west bank of this northern tributary. Full descriptions are provided by Wymer (1985) and more recently by Mark White and colleagues (White et al. 1998). The site is important for several reasons. The first is the variety of handaxe shapes present. Although there are only four handaxes, they are all quite different, and one of them could easily be classified as a cleaver. This variability in handaxe shape, present at a single site, was pointed out for MIS 11 sites in the previous chapter. Some of these pieces may well have been broken during use and then had to be repaired by thinning and re-shaping. Second, the site is in near primary context, and it is probable that it was an activity location where butchery and carcass dismemberment occurred on high ground overlooking the valley. There is use damage and possibly microwear on the artefacts (see White *et al.* 1998, for full discussion). The broken handaxe tips from the site, and the breaks and damage on the handaxes, are all consistent with accidents occurring during carcass processing. If this is the case, then the site may represent a single episode or short-term stay at one place.

The Lower Thames Valley

Readers should re-familiarise themselves with the various channels and overlying gravel members that go to make up the Lynch Hill/Corbets Tey Formation shown in Table 2.1. A reconstruction of the Lower Thames Valley in MIS 9 is presented in Figure 6.4. The interglacial channel is shown as well as the more extensive gravel spreads (stage 5 of the terrace model) that overlie the channel. It is evident that the nature of the floodplain has changed since MIS 11 times. The river now no longer flows up what is the eastern margin of modern Essex and then through Clacton. Rather, it swings east near Burnham-on-Crouch. A tributary, the Blackwater–Colne, as represented by the Cudmore Grove Channel, flows southward to meet it. The implication of this is that the estuary is now much nearer to the modern Lower Thames estuary than it was in MIS 11.

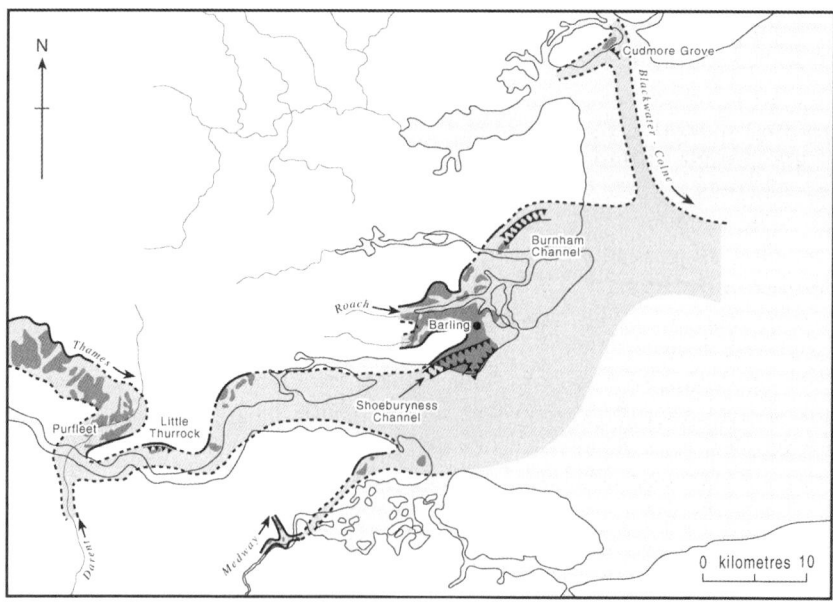

Figure 6.4 The Lower Thames Valley floodplain during the time of the Lynch Hill/ Corbets Tey Formation.

Note: Used with permission.

The sedimentary sequence at Purfleet (Table 6.1; Schreve *et al.* 2002), whose basal sediments have already been discussed, is undoubtedly the most important site in the Lower Thames Valley for this period. It records the full history of the interglacial from the MIS 10/9 transition through to the MIS 9/8 transition in a series of gravels and finer sediments that contain archaeology as well as faunal and floral remains. The interglacial sediments begin with a shelly gravel (bed 3). This unit and the succeeding two form the Purfleet Member, the result of deposition under fully temperate conditions and representing a variety of local woodland and open environments.

As noted above, the frequency of artefacts in the lowest beds was limited. Whether the continued paucity of artefacts in the interglacial deposits reflects infrequent occupation cannot be assessed. Hominins may have just chosen not to frequent this particular section of the river for some reason or other. The succeeding two layers (6 and 7) represent the transition between the temperate Purfleet Member and the cooler/cold climate Botany Member (layer 8) which will be discussed in more detail at the end of this chapter. The bulk of the archaeology from the site comes from unit 6, the Bluelands Gravel. Flakes, cores, and a small number of retouched pieces (a side scraper, end scraper and a flaked flake) represent the hard hammer core working in the assemblage. One handaxe made on a flake, and a handful of thinning flakes attest to the Acheulean character of the assemblage. Mark White, who interpreted the lithics, makes it clear that there are good grounds to consider the assemblage as a single entity, perhaps representing occasional sweepings into the river of ephemeral bankside occupations in the immediate vicinity.

Another site in the vicinity of Purfleet and Little Thurrock is Belhus Park (Wymer 1985; 1999). This site demonstrates a distinctive MIS 9 mammal signature (Schreve 2001). Belhus Park was discovered during the construction of road works. Interglacial deposits contained a cleaver, and a small number of bifaces were found in the overlying gravels. Wymer (1985) suggests that the bifaces came from nearby surfaces contemporary with the interglacial beds.

On the reconstruction of the Lower Thames floodplain in Figure 6.4 it will be seen that the eastward-flowing Thames, in the left of the figure, curves back on itself in a broad sweep at Purfleet. Then it resumes its eastward direction. The river is flowing around a huge outcrop of chalk known as the Purfleet anticline. In effect, the river flows in a Z shape pattern. Bluelands and Greenlands are on the eastern bank. The anticline is located on the inside corner of the lower bend. During Orsett Heath times the area would have been a broad floodplain. It was with the downcutting in Corbets Tey times that the chalk was exposed. With each further downcutting episode the anticline became higher as more chalk was exposed by erosion. (Bridgland *et al.* 1995c, and pers. comm.). However, Gibbard

(1995) has argued that the river's flow direction to the south-west implies that sediments here were a product not of the Thames but of a tributary stream, the Mar Dyke, which today flows into the main river nearby. Bridgland argues this stream only developed later. In any event, the presence of the chalk hill would have been a prominent feature in the floodplain. Just how much flint was exposed in the bankside river cliffs of chalk is not known – probably a lot. Certainly at Purfleet occasional large cobbles of flint were present in the river bed (White, in Schreve *et al.* 2002) from which cores and flake blanks for handaxes could be made.

East of Purfleet, sediments of the River Thames dating to this period are present intermittently along the northern bank of the modern Thames. Wymer (1985; 1999) notes handaxes as coming from the terrace gravels, but not in any profusion. Presumably these gravels represent stage 5 of the Bridgland model. As Figure 6.4 and Table 2.1 show, near Southend the interglacial channel (Bridgland stage 3) turned north-east to form the Shoeburyness Channel, and then turned eastwards via the Burnham Channel. The modern River Colne flowed southwards as a northern/left bank tributary of the Thames, confluent with the main river somewhere off today's Essex coast.

At Cudmore Grove some of these early Colne deposits are preserved at the Cudmore Grove Channel Site on Mersea Island. (There are three Pleistocene sites on Mersea Island. The one under discussion here is formally termed the Cudmore Grove Channel Site. Within the space of a kilometre, and also on the foreshore, are the Cudmore Grove Hippopotamus Site, and the Cudmore Grove Restaurant Site. Both of these are later in date.) None of these buried channels in the MIS 9 floodplain have produced substantial amounts of archaeology. There is a single flake from the basal gravel of the Cudmore Grove Channel Site (which would equate with stage 2 of Bridgland's terrace model, though it may well have come from the base of the interglacial stage 3 deposits – Bridgland, pers. comm.). Gravels from stage 5 of Bridgland's terrace model overlie parts of these MIS 9 interglacial channels (Bridgland *et al.* 2001); the Barling Gravel (overlying the Shoeburyness Channel), the Dammer Wick Gravel (overlying the Burnham Channel), and the Cudmore Grove Gravel (overlying the Cudmore Grove Channel Site) do have records of handaxes coming from locations in the vicinity of where these gravels are mapped. Wymer (1985) notes a number provenanced to the Barling Gravel, enough to suggest that hominins were present in this part of the river valley towards the end of the interglacial or at the interglacial–glacial transition.

Upstream of its confluence with the Thames, the Medway has a series of deposits mapped as terrace gravels that Bridgland (2003) interprets as being equivalent to the Lynch Hill/Corbets Tey Formation. In the Lower Medway, the Stoke Gravels and the Grain Gravels are Medway equivalents of the Barling Gravel but they have yielded no archaeology. Upstream it is difficult to correlate the Lower Medway with the Upper Medway for a number of reasons (ibid.), and Lower Palaeolithic sites are few. Cuxton lies in the Medway Gap separating the two areas. This site was discussed in Chapter 3. The Acheulean site at the Rectory has large pointed handaxes and a few simple prepared cores. Lower down the valley side, c. 30 m away from the Rectory is the Rochester Road site (Cruse *et al.* 1987) with Acheulean over-lying a small Clactonian assemblage (White 2000). I suggested in Chapter 3 that this lower assemblage is too small to be a Clactonian assemblage. One of the cores from the higher part of the gravels at the Rochester Road site (Cruse *et al.* 1987: Figure 4.2a), also bears a striking similarity to the simple prepared cores described by White and Ashton (2003) from Frindsbury and from Purfleet (see below). Bridgland associates these deposit with the Stoke/Grain gravels downstream. As seen in Chapter 3 this gravel unit is actually 8 m too low to be included in the Stoke/Grain Terrace. Its height agrees more closely with the surface of the next terrace down, that of the Binney Gravel, which is a correlative of the Taplow/Mucking formation. Bridgland has suggested that the top of the Stoke Terrace has been eroded away. But it is worth re-stating that archaeologically, there is absolutely no reasons why Cuxton should not be in the lower formation.

East Anglia

Sadly the rather gloomy state of affairs from the last chapter continues in this one. Not a single archaeological site with a decent quantity of artefacts can be firmly placed in this hominin occupation phase from the north-east-flowing Nene and River Great Ouse, or the westward- and north-west-flowing Nar, Wissey, Little Ouse River, Lark or Cam (see Figure 2.8). This is particularly frustrating since the site of Biddenham, Bedfordshire, men-tioned in the previous chapter, is particularly rich in artefacts. The artefacts come from gravels which are part of the highest terrace of the River Great Ouse. But do they date to MIS 11 or 9? Evans (1872; 1897) figures a series of large acutely pointed handaxes. There have been claims of 'proto-Levallois' artefacts (Roe 1981b), but these remain to be substantiated. Recent work at the site (Harding *et al.* 1992) confirmed the artefacts were coming from near the base of the gravels. A date within this occupation phase is reasonable, but by no means certain.

The situation is the same for the rivers Wensum, Yare, and the Waveney which all flow eastwards to the sea. There are terraces and handaxes and other artefacts aplenty, but either they cannot be related to each other, or they cannot be dated. Wymer (1999) asserts people were almost certainly present in East Anglia in this occupation phase, but where, when and how many is unknown. Part of the frustration concerns the inability to precisely provenance some very important sites. For example, in the Yare drainage are the sites of Whitlingham Sewage Farm, and Keswick. These are handaxe rich sites, both with unusually high numbers of cleavers, and in a gravel at c 15 m. OD. They are very similar to each other and must surely be contemporary, perhaps part of the occupation of braided streams along the same river bank (Wymer 1985 and references therein). The artefacts are either unrolled or only slight rolled. These are large assemblages but they lack Levallois.

Another complication with East Anglian terraces concerns the presence of Levallois itself. The Lower Thames Valley demonstrates the possible association of Levallois with handaxe-making hominins at the end of MIS 9 (see below). The possibility of this was raised for the Middle Thames too. The East Anglian river valleys have a number of sites which contain handaxes and Levallois, seemingly together, and in physically similar condition. But are they Earlier or Later Middle Palaeolithic in age? Many of the Levallois artefacts in the low-lying terrace gravels of East Anglia may date to the Later Middle Palaeolithic/Mousterian of MIS 3 and be a product of the Neanderthal re-occupation of Britain. These could have been incorporated into lower terrace gravels along with older handaxes as a result of erosion and re-deposition in the Devensian (MIS 5.4–2).

As was noted in the previous chapter, there is as yet no consensus of opinion on whether the estuarine Nar Valley Clays and the Woodston Beds are contemporary (either MIS 11 or 9), or date to different interglacials, see Figure 5.11. In the last chapter I tentatively agreed with those who have dated the Woodston Beds to MIS 11. The Nar Valley in East Anglia would represent the north-eastern corner of any marine embayment, and the Woodston Beds in the Nene Valley near Peterborough would, presumably, be close to the southern/south-western corner. There is no reason to suppose that the embayment and proto-Nene were not present in this occupation phase as well as the previous one, despite this interglacial having a lower sea level than MIS 11.

Wymer (1999) notes a Levallois flake from the surface of the Woodston Beds. This is difficult to date because the age of the Third Terrace, the highest Nene terrace which directly overlies the Woodston Beds, is unknown. Horton et al. (1992) illustrate the only section (Peterborough Type section) where the relationship between the interglacial beds and the terrace gravels was seen. This shows the Third Terrace eroded into the underlying Woodston Beds (Horton 1992), suggesting a possible hiatus existed between the two deposits. Wymer (1999) suggests that Levallois and handaxes were swept off a land surface on the top of the Woodston beds. The land surface was an old one, and its archaeology considerably post-dated the Woodston Beds by as much as 100 kyr. He also noted that this interpretation was speculative. The suggestion is a good one though. The possibility of a considerable lapse of time between the MIS 11 estuarine deposits (if such they are?), and the overlying third terrace gravels is supported at Tottenhill, see Figure 5.11 (Ventris 1996). Here the Nar Valley Clays are overlain by the Lower Tottenhill Gravel. This is considered to be a glacial deposit, and implies a glacier must have been present in this area some time between MIS 11 and the Devensian. The Upper Tottenhill Gravels may well be glaciogenic as well. There may have been much post-MIS 11 rearrangement of the landscape and erosion in the vicinity of the hypothesised Nene embayment prior to the imposition of the later Middle Pleistocene terraces along the rivers flowing into the embayment.

There are artefacts from gravels within the fluviatile sequence of the Nar Valley. They may be contemporary with the period when estuarine conditions in this north-eastern corner of the great embayment were giving way to gravel depositing rivers (Wymer 1999).

The Midlands

It's the same story here too. The main drainage across the Midlands is the River Trent and its associated tributaries (see Figure 2.8). South of the Midlands, there is not a single site in this whole area with evidence of primary context occupation, though important geological and palaeontological sites that can be associated with the Purfleet Interglacial do exist. One such example is Frog Hall Pit, Warwickshire (Keen *et al.* 1997). Here a channel is infilled by a cold stage gravel, overlain by an organic temperate deposit that is dated to MIS 9. The environmental data from the temperate sediments suggest the early part of an interglacial, and importantly demonstrates a climate showing more continentality than today. This means shorter and hotter summers and longer and cooler winters. That summers were at least warmer than today is supported by the environmental evidence from Hackney (Green *et al.* 2006). Frog Hall Pit exemplifies the difficulties of distinguishing between MIS 11 and 9 especially when pollen signatures between the two interglacials are so similar (Thomas 2001).

In the last chapter I speculated that the absence of Swanscombe Interglacial sediments in the Trent (Figure 2.10b and Table 2.2) may have been circumstantial evidence for a post-Anglian glaciation in this area. The frequency of artefacts in relation to those deposits that can be provisionally dated, and placed in a terrace sequence, are given in Table 6.3. It underscores the absence of identified sediments and archaeology from the first two post-Anglian hominin occupation phases. It is only in the Trent Valley from just east of Burton-on-Trent, to just west of Bingham, that it is possible to identify dateable terrace sediments with archaeology. The majority come from the MIS 8 Etwall Sand and Gravel. It is impossible to know which stage of the Bridgland model these deposits would relate to, but if they are stage 5, as most substantial gravel units should be, then they may represent artefacts/gravels reworked into this terrace from earlier in MIS 9 or late MIS 10. The frequency of artefacts can be seen to be quite low in

179

Table 6.3 The formations/terraces of the River Trent, above and below the Bingham/Nottingham area

	Trent from west of Burton-on-Trent to just east of Bingham				Trent from Newark to Lincoln			
Terrace	Handaxes	Levallois	Other stone tools		Terrace	Handaxes	Levallois	Other stone tools
Floodplain deposits	2	1	1		Floodplain deposits	1		1
Hemington Terrace	1							
Holme Pierrepont S+G	2		2		Holme Pierrepont S+G			
Allenton S+G	22		35		Scarle S+G			
Beeston S+G								
Crown Hill Beds					Fulbeck S+G	1		
Borrowash S+G	7		1+		Balderton S+G	7		1
Egginton S+G								
					Thorpe on the Hill Beds	1		
Ockbrook S+G	44		91+		Whisby Farm S+G			
Etwall S+G								
Eagle Moor S+G	1?				Eagle Moor S+G			

Source: Data from Wymer (1999); Wessex Archaeology (1997); Howard and Knight (2004).

Notes: Reach from Burton to Bingham includes relevant data from lower Dove river. S+G = sands and gravels.

Table 6.3. But it should be remembered that there are other gravel deposits, with artefacts in this region, that cannot be associated with a dated terrace but may well belong to this or the preceding occupation phase. Most of the artefacts in the Etwall Sand and Gravel come from a few pits around the village of Hilton. This in itself should warn against simply assuming an absence of evidence is evidence of absence.

The West

The same gloomy picture persists in the west of Britain in the areas drained by the Severn and the Avon rivers (Figure 2.8 and Table 2.2), repeating the picture found in MIS 11. Darrel Maddy and colleagues (Maddy et al. 1995; Wymer 1999; Bridgland et al. 2004) note the relationship between the Bushley Green Gravel of the Severn Valley, and terrace 5 of the Avon Valley (Figure 2.11a). At the base of both of these are temperate beds containing fossils. Those below the Severn's Bushley Green Gravel have been dated by amino-acid racemisation to MIS 9, and by inference so are the temperate sediments beneath Avon terrace 5, the Pershore interglacial deposits. The gravels above these units are therefore dated to MIS 8 (also Lang and Keen 2005).

There is no in-situ archaeology associated with these temperate beds or with the overlying cold climate gravels (although the degree of commercial exploitation is nowhere near the scale of that in the south or south-east of England). The TERPs data (Wessex Archaeology 1994; 1996) recorded no Palaeolithic archaeology within the Severn–Avon system for the lateral equivalents of terrace 5, that could equate with MIS 9 artefacts that had been reworked into the overlying MIS 8 gravels. However, Lang and Keen (2005) do record a small number of artefacts that can be related to Terrace 5 equivalents in both rivers. The number is small – only four handaxes. In addition to the chrono-stratigraphic interpretations, the work of Maddy and colleagues mentioned above has suggested that standing ice was not present in either valley during the glaciations of MIS 10 or 8 (but it must be said the jury is still out on this question). As we saw in the last chapter, there is no real reason why people should not have been inhabiting these broad river valleys as they were elsewhere.

The South

As noted in previous chapters (see Figure 2.11b and Table 4.1), terraces 10 and 9 of the Stour date to a time when this river was beginning to incise its modern valley, though whether these terraces were laid down by the ancient Solent, or the Stour remains uncertain (Bristow et al. 1991). BGS geological mapping (ibid.) implies that only with terrace 8 and below can fluvial aggradations be confidently associated with the modern Stour. So the Purfleet Interglacial may have seen the beginning of dynamic changes in the Pleistocene landscape of the Solent basin.

The deposits of this interglacial represent an important basin-wide marker horizon. Westaway *et al.* (2006; Table 4.1) suggest terrace 10 of the Stour, and the Ensbury Gravel of the same river, terrace 9 of the Hampshire Avon, and the High Cliff Gravel at Highcliffe, also an Avon deposit, and the Beckton Farm Terrace of the main Solent channel are all contemporary. They date to MIS 9.2, a cold phase toward the end of the Purfleet interglacial. So these terraces all formed within the interglacial, and their contained archaeology may well date from the interglacial as well. If artefact totals are anything to go by, then occupation of the valley in this period may have been prolific. This is especially so in the Stour – but these totals really reflect the presence of a few exceptionally rich sites. The totals would have been larger but I have omitted the King's Park and Queen's Park pits at Boscombe, Bournemouth, because there is some uncertainty as to whether they are associated with terrace 10 or 9. They are also very rich handaxe sites, and contain Levallois. Westaway and colleagues suggest it is with this MIS 9 group of terraces that Levallois makes its first appearance in the Pleistocene record of the Solent. The occasional finds on higher terraces must have been intrusive into their gravels. It must be said that although the absolute frequency of Levallois/PCT is not high, there is an increase in this technology in MIS 9.

The complete lack of finds associated with the main channel in Table 4.1 is not a genuine absence. It reflects the difficulty of adapting the BGS geological mapping which was used by TERPs to plot out find spots, to the reinterpretation of the deposits presented by Westaway *et al.* (2006). In the last chapter it was noted that the cliffs at Barton-on-Sea, which had been formerly mapped as one terrace, in fact, contained two terraces, the lower and younger one being the Beckton Farm Terrace with which the two Levallois pieces were more properly associated. Undoubtedly a number of the handaxes found at Barton-on-Sea will date to the Beckton Farm Terrace as well. At Highcliffe, the High Cliff Gravel dates to the Purfleet Interglacial. It is an extension of the Avon terrace sequence, presumably close to where that tributary joined the main river. It too contains handaxes eroded from terrace gravels at the tip of the cliffs and recovered from gravel scree at the base.

The transition from interglacial to the beginning of glacial conditions in MIS 8

For the end of the period of hominin occupation encompassed by late MIS 10, MIS 9, and early MIS 8, we return to Purfleet, and the sediments at the top of the sequence here (Table 6.1). The topmost deposit at Greenlands is the Botany Gravel, named after the basal gravel in the Botany Pit c.1.5 km to the west. Although classic Levallois material was not found at Greenlands or

Bluelands, Mark White (in Schreve *et al.* 2002) noted the presence of classic Levallois flakes in a continuation of the Botany Gravel at the nearby Armor Road extension site. The upshot of all this research is that it now appears quite definite that classic Levallois technology was being made by hominins in the Purfleet area in late MIS 9 or in early MIS 8. In the Middle Thames Valley it was not as clear-cut as this. We saw that while Levallois was associated with the Lynch Hill Terrace there, pinning down its exact provenance was difficult. In principle, and on the basis of the above, there is no reason why some of the Middle Thames Levallois should not be associated with the end of the Purfleet Interglacial and/or the beginning of the MIS 8 glaciation.

In terms of the great Z-shaped bend the Thames took at Purfleet, the Botany Pit itself represented a locality a little downstream of Bluelands and Greenlands, and on the opposite (western) side of the river. Although excavated, the Botany Pit site was never properly published. Wymer (1968) provides some detail. A large number of ordinary cores were recovered (>100) as well as hard hammer flakes, described as in the hundreds. Only 10 to 15 handaxes were found and no thinning flakes. Botany Pit was therefore a site to which handaxes may have been brought and then discarded. The published descriptions suggest a large riverbank location where hominins probably made use of flint outcropping from nearby chalk cliffs. The site is clearly disturbed, but the artefacts may well come from the immediate vicinity of the site; most of the damage on the artefacts was probably incurred when 'torrential' floodwaters swept the artefacts off the chalk bank and into gravels and sands at the river's margin (Wymer 1968). This explanation invites comparison with recent excavations near the Esso Pit (Bates *et al.* 1998), where handaxes and flakes were found in a comparable location also adjacent to a chalk cliff.

Some 200 metres to the east of the sections cut by Schreve *et al.* at Greenland's Pit, the very feather edge of the Thames' channel is present in sections cut in Stoneham Lane (Bridgland *et al.* 1995c). No occupation site was found on the bank here. Over the whole period of time that this area was visited by hominins, some areas were clearly more attractive as foci for activity than others, and raw material availability clearly played a big part in this. In the final phase of occupation at Purfleet, cold conditions pertained, and the landscape may have been rather open. Clearly chalk cliffs were still exposed in parts of the river's reach here, and flint readily available. The Purfleet Anticline, and the nearby smaller Beacon Hill would have represented vantage points from which to survey the open floodplain. So these sites demonstrate a specific targeting of flint rich bankside locations where nodules were presumably eroding out of the chalky banks. Elsewhere there is evidence for movement up and down the river's banks, as the light scattering of flintwork in the marginal gravels indicates. But clearly not everywhere was occupied.

In classifying the material from the basal gravel at Botany Pit a number of researchers have used the term 'proto-Levallois'. Precise definitions of proto-Levallois are a little difficult to find but it seems to apply to cores and flakes that show rudimentary centripetal or parallel flaking (bipolar from two opposite ends of the core, or unipolar from just one end), and significantly, involves some faceting or preparing of the striking platform. In effect, these pieces show some of the technological features that are required to make Levallois/PCT, but do not show the extensive use of them on individual cores and flakes. So they 'look a bit like' classic Levallois pieces without actually being so. More recently, Mark White and Nick Ashton (2003) have tackled this issue by looking at the artefacts from Botany Pit (Snelling collection, British Museum). In a very cogently argued article they define proto-Levallois in terms of parallel flaking with detachments made from surfaces which have only a minimum of preparation or maintenance, if any. The similarity to Levallois is that the detachments are made parallel to a fixed margin, and come from a single surface (this is explained in more detail in Chapter 12). There was no attempt here to control the shape of the preferential removals or to maintain the flaking face (i.e. through careful preparation or re-preparation). Rather than proto-Levallois, they call them simple prepared cores. Additionally, at Botany Pit there are ordinary flake cores as well as discoids (these different core types are also described in more detail in Chapter 12). They note a similar occurrence of simple prepared cores at the enigmatic site of Frindsbury on the Medway (Cook and Killick 1922–1924) which might, by implication, be of the same date.

It is worthwhile restating that at broadly the same time as this intriguing simple prepared core material was being knapped, classic Levallois was being made, as were handaxes – all within the same environment. As would be expected, a background noise of core and flake production, and some flake tools, accompanies these assemblages, but no grounds exist to separate these cores and flakes out as part of a distinct Clactonian.

The introduction of Levallois/PCT at the interglacial–glacial transition is an interesting observation. Was the 'new' technology brought by hominins who were now able to traverse the re-exhumed Dover–Artois hills as the sea level dropped in response to climatic deterioration? Does it arrive late at Purfleet, but is present earlier elsewhere, for example, in the Middle Thames? Or perhaps it is genuinely earlier in the south of England as the occasional finds in the Solent Valley terraces suggest (see Chapter 5 – if these are really PCT and in context)? These are all questions that cannot as yet be answered.

In Chapter 3, a channel at the top of the Grays Brickearth at Little Thurrock was described. Its existence now can only be inferred from the observations of early twentieth-century researchers. In theory, this could be broadly contemporary with the late interglacial occupation of Purfleet, although notably there were no Levallois pieces. It would represent stages 4 and 5 of Bridgland's terrace model.

To conclude this section I will briefly return to the Solent Valley again. Table 4.1 shows that MIS 8 is represented in the Stour, and the Avon by a small number of find spots in these two tributaries. To which part of the glaciation they belong we do not know. They may represent the sweepings of MIS 9 occupation from the Solent's destroyed Purfleet Interglacial flood-plain. Alternatively, they may represent sporadic occupation at the beginning or end of MIS 8.

Conclusion for hominin occupation in late MIS 10/MIS 9/early MIS 8

The archaeology of this period is a rich and varied one, even though sites are scarcer by comparison with MIS 11. Only a single site matches the requirements for being called Clactonian, and that is Little Thurrock. Hominins were clearly around from early on in this period, actually at the glacial–interglacial transition. With the exception of Little Thurrock the period is dominated by Acheulean assemblages, although fixing many of them at a particular point in the interglacial period is difficult. Only Remenham has a large core and flake component, but this is accompanied by a small handaxe element. The site may be disturbed. Purfleet is every bit as important as Swanscombe in the higher and older terrace. Its significance is greatly enhanced by the ability to place it in a localised landscape which shows variability in use of the natural resources present.

The introduction of PCT/Levallois is a critical benchmark in the British Lower Palaeolithic. It signals a profound change in the way stone tools were thought about and made – the beginning of the Earlier Middle Palaeolithic. It impacts on a number of ways in which we interpret the behaviour of Homo heidelbergensis. If nothing else, PCT may imply changes in the social nature of learning since this is a complicated technique which surely must require some level of instructional learning. There may be changes in the way people were using the landscape and engaging with resources as well. The targeting of specific chalk cliffs with flint nodules eroding out was probably deliberate, and may have represented a 'traditional' or remembered resource drawing hominins back year after year. This may well explain the pattern that we will see for Levallois sites in the next chapter. Many researchers believe Levallois to represent a curated technology (White and Pettitt 1995) which implies forward planning and a deeper ability to think strategically than was manifested in the Acheulean.

Is Levallois a new technology that handaxe makers invent and then disseminate in southern Britain, or is it brought in by new groups of H. heidelbergensis who have undergone a significant behavioural adaptation which is reflected in new material culture? One fruitful line of research would be the recognition of just when Levallois points appear in the British Pleistocene record. These are a fundamentally important tool form. They are a deliberate weapon technology, the first in the Palaeolithic record in Britain. Whether they were used as spear tips for throwing, or as hand-held stabbing weapons, Levallois points must mark a fundamental change in the way people went about acquiring food – principally meat. The Acheulean (and the Clactonian too for that matter) is an on-the-ground, hand-held processing technology (as well as one for the manufacture of other organic tools). But Levallois points represent a shift to composite hunting weaponry. There is evidence for wooden spears in the European Lower Palaeolithic (Oakley et al. 1977; Thieme 2005) but they were untipped – just a sharpened wooden point. We cannot actually guarantee they were used for hunting and used as thrown projectile weapons (McNabb 2000), hominins may well have conceived of them in a very different way. However, once tipped with a stone point, the message is quite clear. Levallois points appear absent from the time of the Purfleet Interglacial.

7

HOMININ OCCUPATION JUST BEFORE, DURING, AND JUST AFTER MARINE ISOTOPE STAGE 7

The Aveley Interglacial

Introduction

The archaeology of this period is described as Earlier Middle Palaeolithic. The introduction of PCT/Levallois to Britain at the end of the last occupation phase, at least at Purfleet, is a departure from the Lower Palaeolithic way of life of the makers of the Acheulean and Clactonian assemblage types. Andy Currant and Roger Jacobi's (2001) hypothesis that Britain was abandoned in MIS 6, and not re-occupied until late MIS 4, neatly divides the Middle Palaeolithic into two parts (see Chapter 1). The Earlier Middle Palaeolithic (EMP) is the subject of this chapter, from late MIS 8 until earlier MIS 6 and the abandonment. The interglacial – MIS 7 – is called the Aveley/West Thurrock Interglacial, or sometimes the Stanton Harcourt Interglacial. The incidences of Levallois at the end of MIS 9, or early MIS 8, make it clear that the beginning of the EMP should really be placed there. Once again it is assumed that hominins migrated south before the height of the MIS 8 glaciation, and only returned with the reintroduction of plants and animals some time in late MIS 8.

There are three basic types of Levallois: centripetal (often called radial), laminar (or parallel/blade), and convergent (or Levallois point technology). Examples are shown in Figure 7.1. The key to the whole concept of PCT is that the knapper prepares a *single* surface from which preferential flakes (i.e. the desired end product) are detached (Chazan 1997; White and Ashton 2003). This is the Levallois flaking face. It is the removal of flakes, blades or points from this prepared and carefully maintained surface that makes these artefacts Levallois. In the system of describing assemblages that will be presented in Chapter 12, these are cores with a single fixed flaking face as well as a fixed margin.

At the end of the last chapter I speculated on whether Levallois points were present in that occupation phase, with all the changes in social learning and communal hunting practices that might be implied. There was no certain evidence. They are certainly present in the time period covered by this chapter.

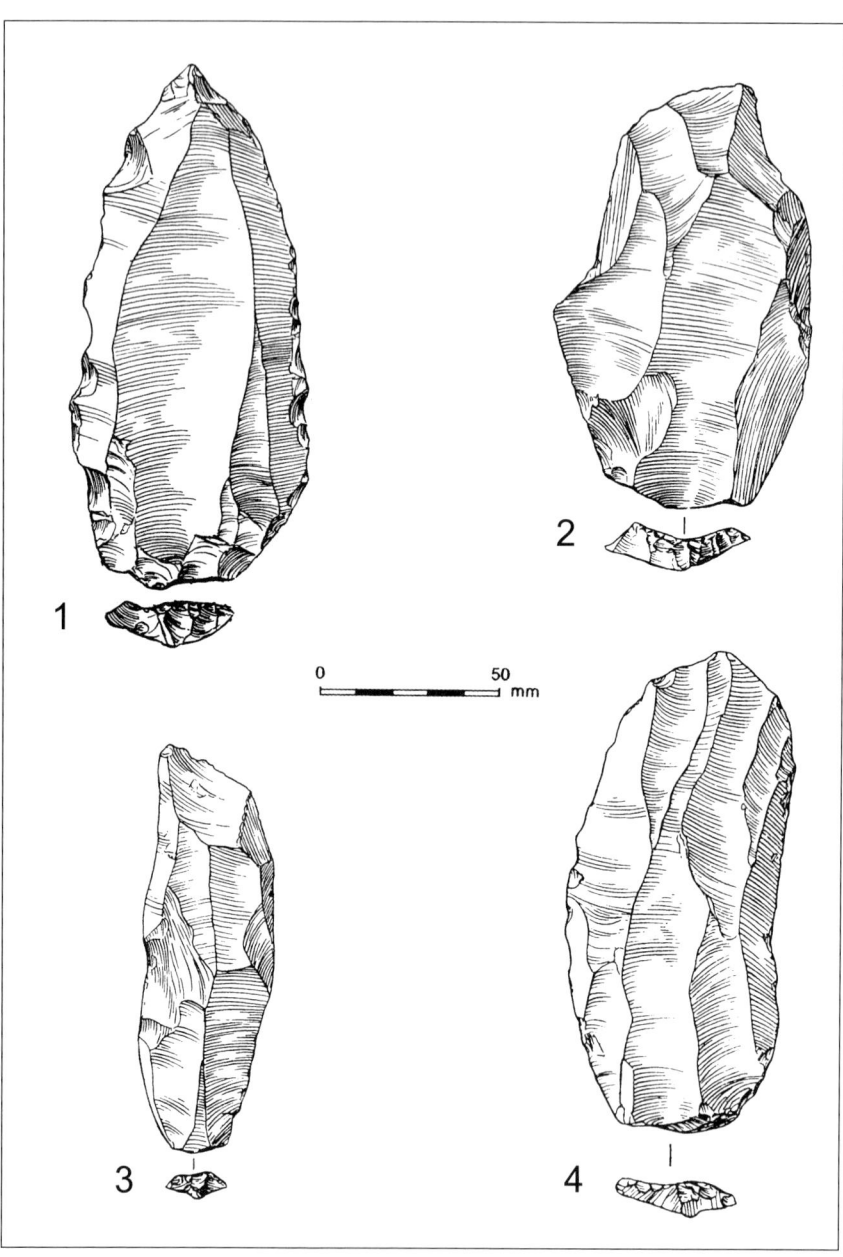

Figure 7.1 Different types of Levallois/PCT. 1 convergent/pointed; 2 flake made by centripetal Levallois; 3 Levallois blade (length is × 2 maximum width); 4 flake blade (length is still × 2 maximum width, but piece is wide), note the laminar (blade-like) removals on dorsal.

What was the nature of the relationship between handaxe makers and those who practised PCT? We do not know. On the one hand, if PCT developed out of the Acheulean, handaxe makers could have continued to make their traditional tool kits as well (they need not have used PCT all the time). Alternatively, it has been suggested that once PCT appeared, the incidences of handaxe manufacture decline, so Levallois may have been introduced by a new people who no longer used handaxes. On the other hand, perhaps the indigenous Acheulean knappers simply dumped their old technology in favour of a new one, when they encountered the spread of new ideas and/or new peoples? Rebecca Scott (pers. comm.) has argued that the hominins who made and used PCT preferred the flexibility that the new technology offered. Perhaps Britain was occupied by two broad cultural groups competing for resources and expressing their distinctiveness through different technological repertoires? This type of explanation merely reprises the Clactonian/Acheulean conundrum of preceding occupation phases. It is important to remember that ordinary flake cores, flakes, and flake tools, continued to be made.

There is no Clactonian in this occupation phase, and no claims have ever been made for its persistence into the Earlier Middle Palaeolithic. I decided to include this chapter in the book as it rounds off the story of the earlier Palaeolithic occupation of Britain, prior to its long abandonment beginning in MIS 6.

The location of a number of the sites mentioned in the text are shown in Figure 7.2. MIS 7 is a low sea-level interglacial (Aldhouse-Green 2001), so the land bridge may have been open for some time at the beginning of the interglacial. The DSC curve in Figure 2.2 shows an early warmer peak followed by two cooler temperate phases. The earlier warm peak may be reflected in higher sea levels in MIS sub-stage 7.5, not much lower than today's levels, but then declining after this. In terms of Bridgland's terrace model, late MIS 8, MIS 7, and early MIS 6 form the period of time covered by the Taplow/Mucking Formation of the Middle and Lower Thames Valleys shown in Figure 2.7 and Table 2.1. Aldhouse-Green (2001) suggests that the low sea level of this interglacial may have dragged the $0°C$ isotherm (the boundary between oceanic and continental climates) further west. On the one hand, any hominins adapted to more oceanic environments may well have migrated west into Britain tracking the shift in their preferred habitats. At the same time, hominins adapted to more continental climates may also have been tracking westwards as their range of preferred habitats began to expand into new areas.

So, did the new technology arrive with big game hunters from the continental interior with its longer and harsher winters? Were they following in the wake of more traditional Acheulean hominins better adapted to greater (oceanic) seasonality, and for whom a mixture of scavenging and hunting medium-sized game was more suitable? The precise relationship

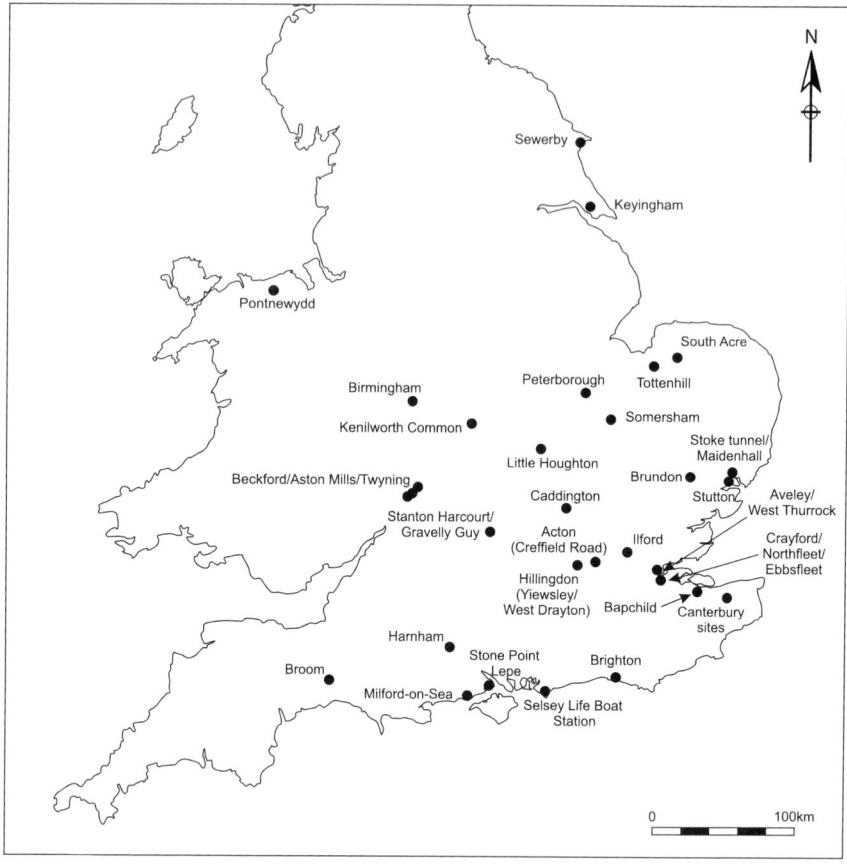

Figure 7.2 Map showing selection of sites discussed in Chapter 7.

between PCT and handaxe technology is one of the most important research questions for this period of hominin occupation.

The MIS 8/7 transition

The archaeological signal from the glacial–interglacial transition is a distinctive one. There is a small group of sites, within a relatively small area in the Lower Thames Valley that are similar to each other, especially in choice of location.

The site of Baker's Hole is an internationally famous one. Much confusion over its location, once thought completely lost to quarrying, has been dispelled by detailed research on the collections and archives by Francis Wenban-Smith (1995). A summary of previous interpretations is presented by Bridgland (1994). The site is not part of the Thames Valley proper, but represents a series of sediments aggraded within a small south-bank tributary of the Thames, the Ebbsfleet. Collecting by Spurrell (1883) revealed a very rich site, with waste flakes present by the 'cartload', see Figure 7.3. Later, some 150 m to the south-east, Reginald Smith (1911a) described a similar locality. These two sites have become known as Baker's Hole, but are sometimes also described as the Northfleet sites. Although local particulars differ, the two locations show a remarkable degree of similarity. Spurrell (1883) noted artefacts to lie on a gravel and were overlain, at least in parts, by coombe rock. Smith's (1911a) slightly more ambiguous description implies that the artefact horizon at his site was at the base of the coombe rock (or at least this is the currently held understanding), and the artefacts were also overlain by it (Bridgland 1994). The gravel underlying Spurrell's site may simply imply it was further away from the channel margin than Smith's site, and the coombe rock sludged out beyond the limit of the bank.

Recent research, as well as the original publications, make it clear that both were primary context knapping floors, quite possibly an extension of the same one. Smith's site has refits (Wenban-Smith 1995). Both had bifaces present, and the bifaces and Levallois elements came in unrolled and rolled conditions. All three types of Levallois were present. Most authors suggest that flint was being directly grubbed out from nearby chalk cliffs, hence the sheer quantity of artefacts. The differential condition and patination on both Levallois artefacts and the handaxes may imply that these sites were a consistent focus of repeated activity over a long period of time. One potential problem with assessing the relationship between the handaxes and the Levallois from here is that Smith's paper on the site used a collection of artefacts made by the quarry manager over a number of years. Some of the artefacts may have come from deposits overlying the coombe rock (Smith 1911a; Rebecca Scott, pers. comm.). Sites D and E in Figure 7.3 now preserve all that remains of the once locally extensive coombe rock deposits. Current interpretation suggests that coombe rock could only form during a glacial period, in the case of Baker's Hole, the end of MIS 8. Stadials would not be cold enough for it to form.

At the Lion Pit Tramway Cutting, West Thurrock, a similar knapping floor has been discovered (Bridgland 1994; Bridgland and Harding 1995). Adjacent to a chalk cliff, a basal channel gravel contained a PCT assemblage in disturbed primary context. The lack of smaller chips and flakes clearly indicated that the site had been winnowed by moving water, however, the presence of refitting artefacts, in particular, flakes which fit back on to their cores, indicated that the larger artefacts from the site were undisturbed. Collections were made from here by Hazzledine Warren, the great champion of the Clactonian (Chapters 10 and 11). Only one formal excavation has been conducted (Bridgland 1994), and at that only a small strip of the knapping floor was accessible. It was, however, very productive and fully

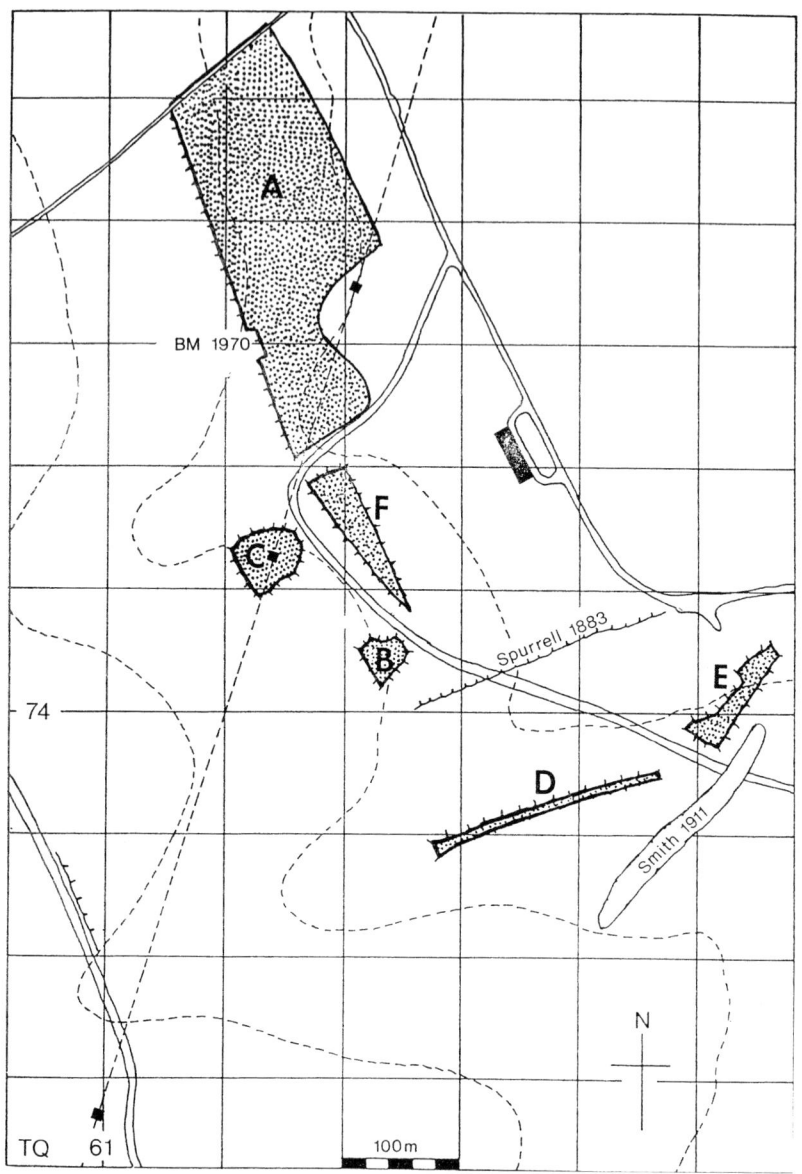

Figure 7.3 Map of Baker's Hole and Ebbsfleet Valley sites. The Baker's Hole/
Northfleet coombe rock sites of Spurrell and Smith are shown and dated.
Areas with letters in upper case represent extant deposits. Burchell's main
Ebbsfleet Valley site was site B.

Note: Used with permission.

confirmed previous interpretations. Radial and laminar Levallois were present on the floor (Bridgland and Harding 1995). Some cores show the use of convergent preparation to help shape Levallois flaking faces (Rebecca Scott, pers. comm.), suggesting the manufacture of Levallois points. No bifaces were recorded from the excavation; a single example was discovered by Warren. This is assumed to have come from the gravel. As with Baker's Hole, the site was adjacent to a chalk cliff, and flint may have been available here, although Harding (Bridgland and Harding 1995) notes that much of the gravel is nodular in character and this may have provided a source of suitable raw materials as well.

The in-situ knapping floor from Stoneham's Pit at Crayford, is often described as being located on the surface of the gravels that underlie the brickearths at this site (Chandler 1916; Bridgland 1994; Wymer 1999). If so, it would date to the MIS 8/7 transition – phases 1 and/or 2 of Bridgland's terrace model. It is clear that implements did indeed come from the gravel's surface and within it (Chandler 1916; Kennard 1944). Kennard suggests this was a landsurface. However, the actual Levallois knapping floor of Spurrell came from within the brickearth (Rebecca Scott, pers. comm.; White et al. 2006). This implies that the knapping floor is an interglacial site so it will be described in more detail in the next section.

An important discovery was made at Harnham, to the south of Salisbury (Whittaker et al. 2004). Here in a small tributary valley of the Avon a preserved fossil landscape was identified. OSL and AAR dating techniques suggest an age of about 250 kya toward the end of MIS 8. Handaxes, cores, and flakes, and flake tools were recovered on the Pleistocene land surface and associated with butchery remains. Importantly, no Levallois was present. It is tempting to posit this site being broadly contemporary with Broom on the River Axe.

The Axe (Figure 2.8) is not a river we have visited in earlier chapters. The dating by OSL is based on new work at the site by Rob Hosfield (Hosfield and Terry 2000; Hosfield and Chambers 2002), who attempted to place the existing handaxe collections from the site in a more secure chrono-stratigraphic context. The dating suggests occupation in late MIS 8 (Rob Hosfield, pers. comm.).

The major collector here was Charles Bean. He collected in the 1930s and 1940s from Pratt's Old and Pratt's New Pits on either side of Holditch Lane (Green, C.P., 1988; Marshall 2001). The artefact assemblage is large, over 1,000 handaxes, some rolled while others are fresh. They were made of flint and chert. There are reports of three Levallois artefacts. The stratigraphy at the first pit to be dug at the site, the Railway Ballast Pit, is relatively simple. More than 8 metres of gravels are divided into a lower 'flinty' gravel, and an upper 'cherty' gravel. Separating the two, locally, was a clay/silt unit. The gravels are considered to be cold climate, and the product of braided streams, while the clay/silt is a temperate sediment (Shakesby and Stephens 1984). The broad stratigraphic sequence is repeated in the Holditch Lane Pits (see section by T. T. Paterson, in Hawkes 1943).

Shakesby and Stephens (1984) argued that the majority of the unworn handaxes came from a single horizon at the top of the lower flint-dominated gravels. This has been cast into doubt by the recent excavations which failed to find any evidence of an extensive 'floor' horizon. Hosfield and colleagues argued that the archaeology is distributed through a gradually aggrading floodplain that is constantly being reworked. Detailed analysis of a sample of the handaxe collections failed to find any significant differences between the handaxes in a worn condition, and the fresher ones (Marshall 2001), suggesting that the hominins were doing much the same thing, in the same way, over a long period of time.

This is an important locality if artefact frequency is anything to go by, but one where Levallois was seemingly unimportant. Hominins adapted to local conditions by producing large quantities of chert handaxes. Marshall (2001) argues that the frequency of artefacts supports the belief that Acheulean society was tethered to places where resources were available or abundant. The Railway Ballast Pit to the south, and the Holditch Lane pits to the north, are either side of the Blackwater, a small stream that runs into the Axe river next to the site. Today it is little more than a minor brook, but if its valley is anything to go by, it was formally much more substantial. Irrespective of whether the gravel sheets were deposited by the Axe, the Blackwater, or both, the former Blackwater/Axe must have cut into these gravel spreads and revealed a flood plain rich in high quality knapping clasts. This leaves us with three possible interpretations:

1   Here at Broom, an Acheulean community, present in late MIS 8, was associated with a reliable raw material source. The presence of rolled and fresh artefacts implies this pattern of occupation persisted in this area for some time. In other words, they were perpetuating the old Lower Palaeolithic way of life. There was little incentive to adopt new technologies as the resources available were plentiful and ever present. The three Levallois pieces, if genuine, might suggest at least occasional forays through the area by more mobile groups of hunters.

2   Rather than be tethered to one place, perhaps this was a logical spot to revisit for mobile Acheulean hunter-gatherers moving up the Axe valley, or using the Blackwater and other tributaries to penetrate the dissected high ground flanking either side of the main valley. The Axe itself would have made a convenient corridor for hominins moving inland from the la Manche valley. The rolled component of the assemblage suggests this access corridor had been a familiar one for a long time.

3   Wymer (1999) has noted that at the confluences of major streams there are very often huge aggregations of artefacts. Is this because at

such locations the carrying capacity of rivers change and these places become natural zones of deposition? This would explain both the huge quantity of gravel as well as the high artefact frequency. Such locales would have been advantageous camping grounds or hunting stands for early hominins, and natural foci for activity. However, we still need to explain the lack of Levallois at the site.

Broom and Harnham raise the fascinating possibility of the survival of hominins perpetuating the old Lower Palaeolithic lifestyle just before the beginning of the Aveley Interglacial. We have already seen that Levallois makers were present at the MIS 8/7 transition in the Lower Thames Valley. At Broom and Harnham there were handaxe makers with very little use, if any, for Levallois. Is it possible that the Broom assemblage was made by Acheulean hominins who weathered out MIS 8 in the la Manche valley and northern France, re-occupying the high ground north of the la Manche valley when conditions began to improve? Was Harnham the result of a similar group ranging up the Hampshire Avon from the Solent valley in search of game on the higher ground of the Wessex Plateau?

Regional geographies for MIS 7

Can MIS 7 be subdivided into discrete periods?

Recent work by Danielle Schreve (2001; 2004b), building on that of Andy Currant (1989) was described in Chapter 2. She distinguishes between the fauna associated with the four post-Anglian interglacials on the basis of key faunal groups, as well as the presence or absence of particular indicator species. As Figure 2.2 shows, there are three temperate peaks within this interglacial, the oldest (7.5) being considerably warmer than the other two. Schreve has suggested that there is a marked difference between the earlier and later animal populations of the Aveley Interglacial. The earlier phase she terms the Ponds Farm MAZ; the later one is the Sandy Lane MAZ.

The Ponds Farm sub-phase is characterised by straight-tusked elephant, horse, and red deer, also warmth-loving creatures such as the European terrapin (they require temperatures of 18°C or more for their eggs to hatch). They indicate a generally warmer and more forested environment. The later Sandy Lane phase is characterised by a mammoth and horse-type fauna indicative of more open conditions. Schreve suggests this is a response to a period of reconnection to the Continent during a stadial (possibly MIS 7.4), allowing for the migration into Britain of new animals such as the woolly rhino, and a species of jungle cat. Other species do not return; fallow deer apparently do not migrate back across the land bridge in the Sandy Lane sub-stage. This is the only post-Anglian interglacial in which mammoth occurs. The mammoth is one of the more dominant species in the Sandy Lane sub-phase. Those that appear in this sub-phase are a variant on the early Middle Pleistocene *Mammuthus trogontherii*. There are two forms of these later Middle Pleistocene *M. trogontherii*. Both are descendants of the earlier type, but one is slightly smaller, and its molars have less plates forming the tooth. This latter form is often called the Ilford mammoth-type. Both variants are present in the Sandy Lane phase and lived side by side (at least their remains can occur in the same deposits). Mammoth is present in late MIS 8 deposits, but then apparently disappears in the Ponds Farm phase of the interglacial, only reappearing in the Sandy Lane MAZ. It is important to note that they occur in temperate deposits, so they are not solely an indicator for cold climate as is sometimes thought (this is the later type of mammoth, *M. primigenius* which dates to the Devensian)

The Upper and Middle Thames Valley

In the Upper Thames the only site that may be confidently attributed to the MIS 7 interglacial is that at Stanton Harcourt. The site is correlated with the lower part of the Summertown-Radley Terrace of the Upper Thames in the Oxford region (Figure 2.9a and Table 2.2), and is famous for the prodigious number of mammoths that have been recovered from the interglacial sediments. (There are a number of pits dug into this formation. The Stanton Harcourt Interglacial channel is in Dix's Pit at Linch Hill – not to be confused with the Lynch Hill Terrace of the Middle Thames.) The Ilford type of mammoth is common. The interglacial sediments occupy a wide channel cut into the basal London clay. *Corbicula fluminalis* is present within the deposits so an MIS 7 (or earlier) age is implied. This mollusc is not present in the British Pleistocene record in deposits younger than MIS 7 (Keen 1990; 2001). But the amount of archaeology present is small – less than ten pieces coming from the interglacial deposits themselves. Among these were handaxes, one fresh Levallois core and some flakes. The Levallois core and fresher flakes may be contemporary with the faunal remains. Significantly, the handaxes are rolled (Rebecca Scott, pers. comm.), the implications of which will be described below.

More handaxes have been found in the overlying cold climate Stanton Harcourt Gravels. Bridgland (1994) suggests the cold climate Stanton Harcourt Gravels, when deposited, truncated the upper parts of the interglacial channel deposits (and therefore its banks) and so entrained the archaeology within the basal part of these later gravels. Less than 1 km to the north-west of Dix's Pit is the Gravelly Guy Pit (Scott and Buckingham 2001). This is an exposure within the Stanton Harcourt Gravels and a number of handaxes have come from here. Their situation dates them to late MIS 7 (or perhaps to the MIS 7/6 transition). Scott and Buckingham suggest the artefacts from the base of this gravel actually date to the interglacial.

Several researchers (MacRae 1988; Wymer 1999; Hardaker 2003) make the intriguing suggestion that this far up the Upper Thames Valley flint only occurs as small derived nodules usually damaged and unsuitable for knapping. Large flint bifaces must have been transported into the area. The nearest viable flint sources are those on the Chilterns some 20 km to the south. In particular, one such biface from Stanton Harcourt is the third largest ever discovered in Britain (Wymer 1999). As a substitute for flint, quartzite pebbles were frequently used in the Upper Thames for making handaxes, and for producing flakes from cores (Hardaker and MacRae 2000; Hardaker 2003). A plentiful supply was present in the gravels of the Evenlode valley, transported south from the Midlands. Elsewhere, the evidence for hominins in this part of the Thames Valley is sparse.

In the Middle Thames Valley though, the situation is different. The sedimentary deposits of this period in the Middle Thames form the Taplow Terrace/Formation. The area around Hillingdon, west London, in particular at Yiewsley and West Drayton, was a particularly rich one for Levallois material. All of the archaeology was discovered during quarrying and no controlled excavations took place when the gravel and brickearth pits were in production. A basal gravel (Collins, 1978, labelled it the Warren Gravel – the equivalent of the Lynch Hill Terrace gravel discussed in the last chapter) was overlain by a locally present loam (fine grained deposit which Collins terms the Warren Loam), then a solifluction gravel and coombe rock, and finally a brickearth. Artefacts were present in the lower gravels, in the solifluction/coombe rock, and in the overlying brickearths. The majority of the Levallois is reported to have come from the brickearth, or from the junction between the solifluction gravels and the brickearth (ibid.). All three type of PCT are represented; very little of it has been retouched.

Ashton et al. (2003) have argued that the only artefacts that can be unambiguously associated with the Warren Gravel are handaxes which would date to the time of the Lynch Hill Formation. They also argue that the Levallois from the Yiewsley and West Drayton sites that can be accurately provenanced, sits on the terrace surface, buried by the solifluction gravel/coombe rock. The implication is that the Levallois post-dates the terrace surface by a considerable period of time. Consequently, the Levallois is thought to date to late MIS 8 or within MIS 7. The upper brickearths are mapped as part of the Langley Silt Complex. This great mantle of fine-grained deposits of different ages is spatially extensive, and covers a number of terraces in the eastern half of the Middle Thames Valley (Gibbard 1985; Wymer 1994).

Brickearth also blankets a rich Levallois site at Creffield Road, Acton, London. It too was mapped as Langley Silt Complex. As with the Hillingdon assemblages, the Levallois here sits on these earlier Lynch Hill equivalent gravels. A Mousterian date has been suggested for this site, but this seems unlikely (White and Jacobi 2002). Many British Later Middle

Palaeolithic/Mousterian sites are characterised by the presence of the *bout coupé* – a biface type characteristic of the British Mousterian and so made by Neanderthals. For the few *bout coupé* that have been found in the vicinity, there is no secure contextual information to identify which deposits they came from.

At the junction of the brickearth with the underlying Lynch Hill gravel, a 'floor' was discovered by John Allen Brown (Brown 1887). There is an excellent summary in Wymer (1994; see also Wymer 1968). Ashton and colleagues (2003) argue the same stratigraphic relationship pertains here as in the Hillingdon pits. The only securely provenanced artefacts that come from the Lynch Hill Gravel are handaxes (but see White *et al.* 2006). The Levallois artefacts sit on or above the Lynch Hill Terrace surface, so there are no grounds for associating them with these earlier gravels.

The whole area around Creffield Road appears to have been one where Levallois was knapped on the surface of this gravel, presumably it represented a stable (and apparently regionally extensive?) land surface. The artefacts from the different locations sample a continuum of occupation and are in a variety of conditions, some very fresh while most are slightly worn (Rebecca Scott, pers. comm.). In effect, this is a similar situation to Stoke Newington described in the last chapter – a locality revisited by hominins on many occasions. Fresh Levallois material is present in the brickearth too. The Levallois artefacts appear to be mainly of convergent and laminar types, many retouched. There are few Levallois cores and those present have been exhaustively knapped (Rebecca Scott, pers. comm.). It is possible that this was an activity area to which finished artefacts were brought (Wymer 1968; White and Jacobi 2002). White and Jacobi suggest that some of the convergent points arrived at the site hafted, implying this was a hunting stand. Alternatively, as it is situated on the higher slopes of the valley, it may have been a 'tooling up' location, where hunters came to repair equipment and collect new cores and flakes before returning to the hunt in the valley below (White *et al.* 2006).

The Lower Thames Valley

The downstream equivalent of the Middle Thames Taplow Terrace in the Lower Thames is the Mucking Terrace/Formation.

The Thames floodplain during this occupation phase, and the overlying gravel aggradations that bury the interglacial river channel (i.e. stage 5 of Bridgland's terrace model), are shown in Figure 7.4. For this section we return to the sites of Baker's Hole, Crayford, and West Thurrock. The deposits related to the glacial–interglacial transition at these sites, and which were described above, are overlain by MIS 7 interglacial sediments.

At Baker's Hole, these are the Ebbsfleet Channel deposits. As noted elsewhere, the Ebbsfleet was a south-bank tributary of the Thames, confluent

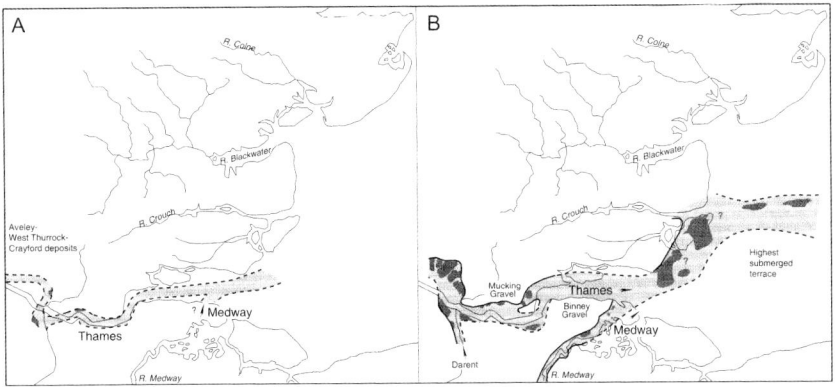

Figure 7.4 The Lower Thames Valley during the development of the Taplow/Mucking Formation. A: the interglacial channel. B: the mapped gravels overlying the channel which represent stages 4 and 5 of Bridgland's terrace model.

Note: Used with permission.

with it just to the east of Swanscombe. The 'Ebbsfleet Channel deposits' is a label applied to the temperate sediments that overlie the coombe rock at a series of locations a few hundred metres to the west of the Spurrell and Smith sites mentioned earlier, see Figure 7.3. The name Ebbsfleet is preferred for these deposits as the temperate sediments here represent channel infill by this tributary. Table 7.1 presents a rationalisation of the often conflicting deposit descriptions and labels used by various researchers. At first glance the sequence (from Site B in Figure 7.3), looks like its deposits should encompass the whole of the Taplow/Mucking Formation, but this is not the case. Nevertheless, a long period of time is indicated as the sediments record transitions between warm and cold conditions. A number of researchers have described the Ebbsfleet deposits (see Bridgland 1994; Wenban-Smith 1995, for full histories).

The Levallois material is confined to beds 2–4, Table 7.1. Above this, there is a change in the character of the assemblage as the frequency of Levallois material drops off dramatically. This has been established by the researches of Rebecca Scott (pers. comm.). She suggests that from bed 5 and above (i.e. from the fully interglacial temperate beds and onwards), the archaeology is dominated by rolled Acheulean. The handaxes in both the lower and upper parts of the sequence are in a visibly different condition to the fresher Levallois artefacts in units 2–4. The implication of her work is that the two groups of artefacts were made at different times. She suggests hominins targeted the area for Levallois production while the gravel banks and beaches of the Ebbsfleet river provided a source of flint nodules for knapping. The river was continuously eroding its banks and flint was present

Table 7.1 The depositional sequence for the Ebbsfleet Valley

Bridgland 1994	Wenban-Smith (1995)	Burchell	Artefacts present (Wymer 1968)	Rebecca Scott, pers. comm.
Bed 12 Cryoturbation Bed 11 Sandy fluvial brickearth Bed 10	Solifluction	Upper trail/C.R. Uppermost Loam Cailloutis (thin gravel bed) Lower trail/C.R.	Scrapers and handaxes, and crude cleaver. Thinning flakes	
Bed 9 Cryoturbation				
Bed 8 (decalcified at top) (Bed 7 Upper Coombe Rock difficult to link to Burchell here)	Calcareous loam	Calcareous loam		
Bed 6 Freshwater silts	Temperate silts	Temperate Beds (Upper Loam?)	Handaxes, scrapers, facetted flakes	No Levallois present. Handaxes worn
Bed 5. Silt or brickearth. Loessic silt is incorporated into channel infill from sides of channel. Periodic bank collapse causes gravel from bed 4 and coombe rock to interdigitate with bed 5 at channel's margin. May originally have been a lower fluvial (= Burchell's Lower Loam) and upper colluvial (= Burchell Middle Loam) separated by lag gravel extension from bank (bed 4). Palaeosol? at top (5a) – possibly cold climate unit.	Middle loam	Upper Middle Loam Middle Coombe Rock Lower Middle Loam Lower Loam?	Handaxes, scrapers, prismatic blade cores	No Levallois present Handaxes worn

Bed description		Stratigraphy	Artefacts	Notes
Bed 4. Gravel. Blankets the sloping side of the channel's edge on western side of section at site B. May originally have spread out toward centre of channel as a lag over lower part of bed 5, but can no longer tell. No longer possible to establish its relationship with gravels in bed 2 because intervening bed 3 absent.	Solifluction gravel	Melt-water gravels above Ebbsfleet Channel bank		Levallois present at site B in gravels overlying sloping channel banks. Worn handaxes also present
Bed 3. Coarse sand – not present in site B – possibly quarried away Bed 2. Coarse gravel	Fluviatile gravels	Lower Loam ? Lowermost Loam Lower Gravels Melt-water gravels at base channel	Flakes and flakes with facetted platforms. Levallois flakes and pointed Levallois flakes Handaxes Scrapers and retouched flakes Prismatic blade cores	Levallois present. Some Levallois pieces bifacially thinned like handaxes. Levallois mostly fresh. Very few handaxes, they are more worn than Levallois
	Coombe Rock			

Source: Data from Bridgland (1994); Wenban-Smith (1995); Wymer (1968); and Rebecca Scott, pers. comm.

in the gravels, and perhaps in the coombe rock. But within the banks of the river there were handaxes from much older deposits. These had been incorporated in the bankside sediments through earlier phases of erosion and solifluction. These became mixed in with the fresher Levallois material on the gravel surface. When the temperate sediments (bed 5 of Bridgland and above) buried the gravels, the Levallois makers moved on looking for a new raw material source. In the meantime the river continued to erode the older Acheulean artefacts out of its banks and incorporate them in the still aggrading MIS 7 sediments. The difference in condition between handaxes and Levallois was noted for Stanton Harcourt as well.

Is it possible to place the Ebbsfleet interglacial channel deposits in either the Ponds Farm or Sandy Lane sub-phases? In her recent re-evaluation of the MIS 7 fauna noted above, Danielle Schreve (2001; 2004b) identified an absence of mammoth in the earlier part of the interglacial. It is, however, clearly present in the Sandy Lane MAZ, representing the more open environments of this later phase. Mammoth is present in beds 4 and 6 of the Ebbsfleet Channel sequence (Table 7.1), as well as in bed 2 near the base. Schreve suggests that the temperate deposits at Ebbsfleet, as well as Crayford and West Thurrock, should date to the Sandy Lane sub-phase, and makes the intriguing suggestion that the earlier Ponds Farm sub-phase deposits are missing at all three sites (Schreve, pers. comm.). Perhaps these sediments were never deposited at these locations, or they were eroded away during MIS 7.4. If so, this would mean that a considerable hiatus was present between the MIS 8/7 coombe rock and gravels at the base of these sites, and the temperate sediments that overlie them. It would also mean that a lot of the earlier MIS 7 archaeological signal (i.e. that associated with the Ponds Farm) was missing from the Lower Thames Valley.

A critical interglacial site is that of Stoneham's Pit at Crayford which was another discovery of Spurrell (1880a; 1880b). Here a chalk cliff appeared to have accumulated a scree slope of gravel directly underneath it. Jill Cook (1986) describes the gravel as flint rubble and Spurrell asserts that the nodules of flint knapped by the hominins came from this scree. As with Baker's Hole, this was an exceptionally rich site. Spurrell managed to refit a number of artefacts into a series of discrete groups of conjoining artefacts. One of these represented a virtually complete core (see Oakley 1972, plate 2). However, at this site, no bifaces seem to have been present (ibid.) that could be related to the knapping floor. The technology is often described as laminar, aimed at the production of Levallois blades and (fortuitously?) pointed blades (compare Mellars 1974 with Cook 1986). No mention is made of convergent or radial Levallois techniques being present. Rebecca Scott (pers. comm.) has argued that the blades are actually fortuitous. Removing long thin detachments was the only way to successfully approach the initial flaking of elongated nodules such as those that occur at the site. She makes the cogent point that the blades from the refitting cores were left behind by the knappers. Instead a number of broader flakes from deeper in the knapping sequence of these cores were removed. The refitting suggests these are from properly constructed Levallois flaking faces. The cores that were abandoned on the floor were unambiguously Levallois and not blade-like. Although tradition places this knapping floor at the junction between the basal gravels and the overlying brickearth, Scott's research suggests that the floor is more properly associated with the interglacial brickearths (see also White *et al.* 2006). As noted above, Schreve (pers. comm.) dates this site to the Sandy Lane phase of MIS 7.

There is no record of archaeology present in the temperate deposits overlying the knapping floor at West Thurrock, but artefacts would certainly appear to have been present higher up in the brickearths at Crayford (Kennard 1944; this reference has a marvellous anecdote about forgers of Palaeolithic tools that is well worth reading). Both handaxes and cleavers were present, as were Levallois points, some of them retouched to accentuate the point. Aveley, the type site for the fauna from this interglacial, has a small collection of artefacts. A few have come from the lower deposits, attributable to the Ponds Farm MAZ, while another handful have come from the higher units which equate with the Sandy Lane MAZ. As White *et al.* (2006) point out, these few artefacts at least demonstrate that there was a hominin presence earlier in MIS 7 in the Lower Thames Valley. The brickearths at the Uphall Road pit, Ilford, (Oakley and Newcomer 1978; Wymer 1968; and especially Bridgland 1994: 256ff.) produced a small number of Levallois pieces (*contra* Newcomer), and a handaxe thinning flake. A Levallois point was retouched at the tip in an identical manner to that illustrated by Kennard from the Crayford Brickearth. Elephant and mammoth remains have been found in great numbers in the Uphall Pit interglacial sediments. The presence of mammoth should suggest that the Uphall Road brickearths equate with the Sandy Lane MAZ.

East Anglia

As we have seen in earlier chapters, once away from the Thames Valley with its well-researched and clearly defined terrace staircase, identifying the interglacial filling in the terrace sandwich of Pleistocene rivers becomes more difficult. Many finds of Levallois implements are either surface finds or isolated discoveries of one or two cores or flakes. In such circumstances it is difficult to know whether these are MIS 7, or MIS 3 and so Mousterian.

Two particularly important sites are at Brundon, and Stoke Tunnel/ Maidenhall. The latter (Layard 1912; 1920; comprehensive summary in Wymer 1985) represents a series of exposures in a very extensive bone bed known as the Stoke Bone Bed. This is a widespread feature continuing on for at least a kilometre to the south of the initial site of discovery. The bones represent a number of animals, mammoth, horse, bear, red deer, giant deer, auroch and lion among others. The bones accumulated in locally variable clay, darkly organic in places. None of the bones were noted to be cut marked and it is highly unlikely that the deposit is a result of hominin action. Indeed, if the numbers of finds are to be believed, hominin inter-action with the bones was limited, at least in the areas where observations and excavations were conducted. Only a few artefacts were discovered that could be directly associated with the bone bed, but some of these were Levallois in character. Wymer (1985) notes that the deposits infilled a hollow or channel associated with a steep cliff formed from the clay bed-rock. He postulated that if more substantial Palaeolithic remains were to be located, they would lie along the banks of the bedrock where hominins may have come to exploit a natural death trap. In his own excavations at the site, Wymer (1985) recovered the remains of a single mammoth, whose bones were somewhat scattered, but whose feet were still articulated (Wymer 1999: 142, for photograph) leading him to suggest the mammoth had become mired in the deposit. The bones of a wolf were associated with the mammoth. Schreve (2004b) dated this site to the Sandy Lane stage of MIS 7.

Brundon represents a complicated series of deposits seemingly banked up against the side of the valley of the Suffolk Stour river (Moir *et al.* 1939; Wymer 1985; White *et al.* 2006). The artefacts occur at the base of stratum 3. Only a handful were in sharp condition, but Levallois and non-Levallois appeared to occur in the same range of conditions, rolled and sharp. The Levallois demonstrates the presence of radial and laminar techniques. Bifaces of cordiform aspect were associated, but no true *bout coupé* have been recorded which would have definitely implied a later, Mousterian, age for the Levallois. Wymer (1985) notes that some of the handaxes were made on Levallois flakes, and a cleaver was also present. The pieces illustrated by Reid-Moir in the original report show non-PCT flake cores and well-made scrapers of the High Lodge type. Although the assemblage cannot be *in situ*, it may nevertheless have a certain degree of contextual integrity, at least in the sense of being a palimpsest that dates to MIS 7. The gravels of bed 3 are underlain by a clay which contains *Corbicula fluminalis* and therefore have to date to MIS 7 or earlier. Mammoth and horse are present but the Ipswichian indicator, hippopotamus, is not. Schreve (2001; 2004b) places the site in her Sandy Lane mammal assemblage zone. In general, there seem good grounds to attribute this site to the Aveley/West Thurrock Interglacial, and interpret it as sweepings down slope from a possible primary context loca-tion higher up the valley side. There is evidence that artefacts from higher deposits at the site have been incorporated in the assemblage somehow (Rebecca Scott, pers. comm.), but with caution the dating of the secondary context Levallois assemblage to MIS 7 can be accepted.

There are no other undisturbed sites or rich assemblages of artefacts in secondary context in East Anglia that can be related to MIS 7. Some of the isolated discoveries do, however, cast light on the ranging habits of Levallois makers. They occupied the river valleys as at Barnham Heath and elsewhere, but also moved out of the valleys and ranged across the interfluves and intervening high ground as a small number of finds in the vicinity of South Acre show. The pits here are mapped as lying in a dry valley that connects the till plateau to the east with the Nar Valley (Sainty and Watson 1944; comprehensive reviews in Wymer 1985 and 1999). The artefacts are in solifluction deposits, implying that they were moved down slope quite possibly off the plateau. A fair number of hard hammer struck flakes and non-PCT cores led some of the early workers to suggest a Clactonian element to the assemblage, but this only reflected the prevailing culture-historical paradigm. Handaxes, thinning flakes, High Lodge-type scrapers, and Levallois cores and flakes were present. In more recent years, PCT has been identified in the valley gravels of the Nar, so hominins in this period may have moved between the valley bottoms and the adjacent uplands, quite possibly using the dry valleys as access corridors.

On the Suffolk Stour, downriver of the Brundon site, there are two local-ities with Levallois that are likely to be within the late MIS 8/MIS 7/early MIS 6 age bracket. At Stutton, the Stutton Brickearth, has revealed one fresh handaxe made on a flake and a Levallois flake. The brickearths overlie a gravel, from which downstream, at the modern estuary, rolled bifaces have been recovered. Wymer (1999) notes the association of a distinctive mammoth and horse fauna, and a radiometric date not inconsistent with MIS 7 for the brickearth.

Elsewhere there are numerous find spots where Levallois/PCT occur as isolated finds or as a few pieces associated with other artefacts. Distinguish-ing between Earlier and Later Middle Palaeolithic PCT has always been difficult, especially for artefacts in secondary context and with no other diagnostic artefacts in association. A challenging suggestion has been put forward by Mark White and Roger Jacobi (2002). They suggest that the Neanderthals of the British Mousterian/Later Middle Palaeolithic were not Levallois makers (or at least made it infrequently). They were more focused on bifacial technologies like the *bout coupé* handaxe, and flake tools. This is an intriguing suggestion. If it was true, it would mean that the vast majority of Levallois found in south-eastern Britain would date to the Earlier Middle Palaeolithic. Our ability to confidently map the ranging patterns of Levallois hunters would be greatly enhanced. The suggestion is preliminary, and will need rigorous testing, but if true, it would be a major step in clarifying hominin behaviour in this period.

It would also impact heavily on suggestions by Ashton and Lewis (2002) that hominin population levels had crashed in MIS 7. In the two preceding chapters I suggested that their data actually reflected the ranging patterns of Victorian and Edwardian amateur archaeologists and artefact collectors. Rebecca Scott (pers. comm.) takes this further. In noting that Levallois is a technology geared towards sustainability and productivity, and that hominins were no longer tethered to raw material-rich tie points in the landscape, she argues that this new behavioural pattern will directly affect the visibility of sites in the landscape. The big sites like Baker's Hole and Crayford were provisioning localities for groups who then dispersed, taking their Levallois equipment with them. Out on the hunt there were small locations for artefact repair, 'tooling up' and re-provisioning. There were locations were tools were lost or damaged during use. In all, fewer sites with smaller artefact frequencies. Not a drop in population, but a change in archaeological visibility based on a change in behaviour.

The Midlands

Before discussing the Midlands proper, I will examine the region between the northern escarpment of the Chiltern Hills and the southern limits of the Trent's drainage basin, beginning with the Chilterns themselves.

The site of Caddington near Luton in the Chiltern Hills is one of the most famous Palaeolithic sites in Britain, and one of a series of Acheulean localities discovered and investigated by G. Worthington Smith, and described in his remarkable book *Man the Primeval Savage* (Smith 1894). The sites represent, in all probability, primary context activity locations where biface making and core reduction occurred on the edges of standing bodies of water. Today the sites are associated with brickearth deposits, in many cases a result of aeolian and colluvial deposition along dolines (linear features composed of a series of surface depressions that are a result of the dissolution of the underlying chalk bedrock). Within these depressions standing water pools developed, becoming a focus for plant and animal communities. The Chiltern brickearth sites are thoroughly reviewed by Avery *et al.* (1982), Sampson (1978), and White (1997). These sites are scattered all over the Chiltern Hills. They have proved remarkably difficult to date and may belong anywhere between MIS 11 and 7. However, White does note that a strong case can be made for these sites being placed toward the end of an interglacial.

The Cottages site (Site C) at Caddington is probably the best known. Here a primary context Acheulean occupation horizon was discovered by Worthington Smith in 1890 (Smith 1894; Sampson 1978). For the next two years he collected artefacts with the aid of the brickearth quarrymen. The working faces passed beyond the limits of the Acheulean floor in 1895 (Sampson 1978). Quarrying at site C continued intermittently. Eight years after the Acheulean site was worked out, the quarry faces passed over what is described as a primary context Levallois floor (ibid.). Smith's markings on the artefacts show that between December 1903 and January 1906 Levallois cores and flakes were being found by Site C quarry men from this floor. Almost no other information is available on this exposure; it lay some

100 metres away from the Acheulean floor at site C, and in the 'same circumstances'. Roe (1981b) describes and illustrates some Levallois from Caddington. He makes the intriguing observation that cores of the type White and Ashton (2003) labelled as simple prepared cores are present (though it is not clear whether the PCT he describes comes from the Site C floor or the later discovered Levallois floor; Sampson and colleagues are adamant there was no Levallois from the main Cottages site). As with the other Chiltern brickearth sites, Caddington is undated. On the basis of the information presented here, a late MIS 9 date is possible, but inclusion in the latter part of the Aveley/West Thurrock Interglacial might be more appropriate.

To the north of the Chilterns there is clear evidence of Levallois-making hominins present in this area, in both river gravels and interglacial deposits. The valley of the River Great Ouse, which flows north-eastward into the Wash (Figure 2.8), has a number of Levallois sites, though these are all isolated finds, or a handful of artefacts at best. Some come from slightly higher terraces, and on this evidence alone may date to MIS 7. There are over 20 sites with Levallois mapped in the terrace gravels of the River Great Ouse that roughly stretch between Bedford and Earith, and it is unlikely that all would be intra-Devensian. One site that appears to be MIS 7 in age is Somersham, based on the presence of *Corbicula fluminalis*. Suggestions of an MIS 5.5 Ipswichian date would therefore appear unlikely for this site. Wymer (1999) notes a small number of Levallois flakes from within the temperate sediments. It is possible that this site could date to MIS 9, but as was noted in the previous chapter, no Levallois has as yet been unequivocally associated with MIS 9 temperate deposits, only at the end of the interglacial. For the moment an MIS 7 date for this site is probably safest. The molluscs from the interglacial deposits have a brackish (salty) component, and the deposit appears to have been laid down under tidal conditions. So at least here the makers and users of Levallois technology were exploiting a tidal/estuarine environment. If this is the case, then tidal conditions must have penetrated quite far inland; perhaps the successor of the Nene embayment hypothesised in the last two chapters persisted into the Aveley Interglacial.

Some quite rich Levallois sites are to be found in the valley of the Nene (see Figure 2.8). In the upper reaches of the valley there is no well-developed flight of terraces, the further upstream you go, the more the terraces merge into each other. However, lower down in the valley the situation is different. Over 30 Levallois artefacts have come from Hick's Pit near Peterborough from within terrace 3 gravels (which overlie the earlier Woodston Beds – see Chapter 6 and Figure 5.11), and also from terrace 2 gravels, in particular at Baker's Pit at Woodston, where Levallois artefacts, handaxes and retouched flakes are recorded. But as was noted in preceding chapters, the age of these terraces in the Nene has not been established – though they must post-date MIS 11 and possibly MIS 10.

Recently, Bridgland and Schreve (2001) have attempted to fit the terraces from this area, and those from the East Anglian rivers that flow into the Wash, into Bridgland's terrace model. They isolate the difficulty with doing this, and at the same time explain why these rivers developed only a few terraces compared to the Thames or Solent. Unlike their more famous cousins, these rivers did not rejuvenate (i.e. cut down to a new floodplain level in stage 1 of Bridgland's terrace model) with every glacial–interglacial cycle. In some cases later cycles are cut into the same terrace as earlier ones, see Figure 2.10A. This area is slowly subsiding, and this overcomes the sediment-driven uplift that was discussed in Chapter 2. Bridgland and Schreve imply that terrace 2/1 on the River Cam (which contains MIS 7 deposits) is the equivalent of terrace 1 on the River Welland. This is shown schematically in Figure 7.5. Both the Welland and the Nene have three terraces, and if a correlation between Nene terrace 2 and Welland terrace 1/Cam terrace 2/1 could be supported, then this would at least place the Levallois sites in the Nene terrace 2 within the late MIS 8/MIS 7/early MIS 6 age bracket. Particularly so if terrace 2 has Ipswichian deposits overlying these beds as they assert is the case in the Cam – there were no hominins in Britain in MIS 5.5.

The Nene does have another interesting site that may date within this occupation phase. At a gravel pit near Little Houghton, outside of Northampton, a fossil waterhole was discovered (Smith 1995). Remains of elephant, bison, and woolly rhino, were associated with a 50 m-wide depression in the underlying clay. A linear feature interpreted as an animal track way was noted leading into the watering hole. Environmental

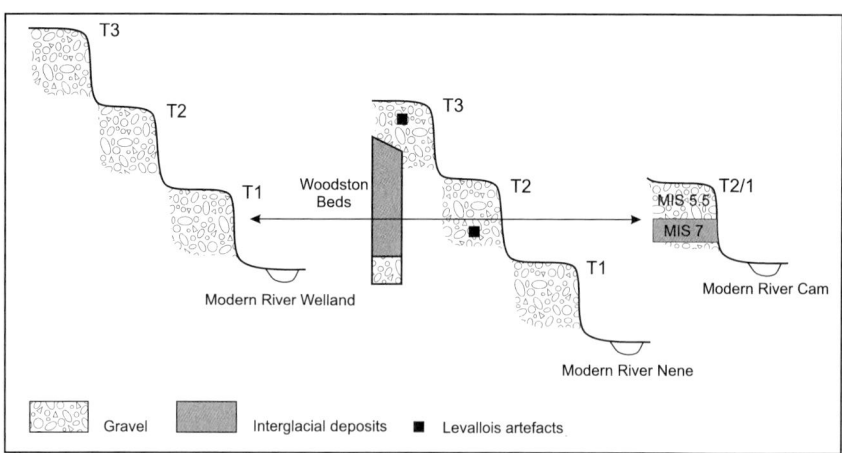

Figure 7.5 Schematic comparison of East Anglian terraces.

Note: The arrowed line indicates terrace 1 of the Welland, terrace 2 of the Nene, and the lower portion of terrace 2/1 of the Cam are considered contemporary.

indicators suggested a cool climate. The dating is ambiguous, but an inter-stadial date in a pre-Devensian cold period is indicated; there is mammoth reported from the site. A date somewhere within this occupation phase is not implausible. A few handaxes have been found in the immediate vicinity, but not directly associated with the waterhole feature.

Once into the Midlands proper the picture becomes bleaker. As noted in preceding chapters, the major drainage line of this part of the Midlands is the Trent and its principal south-bank feeder streams, the Soar and the Wreake (Figure 2.8). To the south-west are the drainages of a number of rivers in the vicinity of Birmingham. Yet in all this huge area, the TERPs project (Wessex Archaeology 1997) recorded less than five Levallois arte-facts, and some of these may not even have been Levallois! But, if the evidence of terraces is anything to go by, then hominins were present during the late MIS 8/MIS 7/early MIS 6 occupation phase. In recent years, gravel deposits of the Trent and its tributaries, formerly not considered as fluvial, have been re-interpreted as proper river terrace gravels. Although only provisionally dated (Howard and Knight 2004, for an excellent review), upstream of Nottingham (see Tables 2.2 and 6.3), the Etwall Sand and Gravels are dated to MIS 8 and the Egginton Common Sand and Gravels are dated to MIS 6. Both contain bifaces, cores, and flakes. If the MIS to terrace associations in Table 6.3 are substantiated, then sediments equivalent of the Thames Valley Taplow/Mucking Formation should span the end of the Etwall Gravel and the beginning of the Egginton Gravel. So, at least some artefacts in the latter terrace ought to date from this occupation phase.

It is possible that the Taplow/Mucking equivalents in the Trent have dropped out of geological sight, fallen below the levels of the more recent terraces (as with the Black Park Terrace in the Lower Thames, Chapter 4). The Beeston Sand and Gravel is dated to MIS 5 or 4 and from its gravels, bifaces, flakes, and cores have been recovered (Posnansky 1963; especially Howard and Knight 2004). Since the terrace dates to a time when no people were present in Britain, these artefacts must be a result of the reworking by the Trent of higher terrace gravels. Many of the artefacts are heavily rolled. Logically these ought to come from the Egginton Terrace. Yet there remains the singular fact that there is virtually a complete absence of Levallois from this region (Table 6.3). Hominins appear to have been present, but they were not making Levallois. Can the interpretation that Levallois hunters were not staying long in one place for any length of time adequately explain this pattern? On the face of it, this seems unlikely. The dearth of Levallois would appear better explained by a genuine absence of hunters using PCT in this part of Britain – or perhaps at best only making occasional forays into *terra incognita*.

East of the Trent, the only drainages that have recorded Pleistocene archaeology within their gravel deposits are the Rivers Slea and Witham. The TERPs data do not record a single Levallois artefact for this area. North of here there are two records of Levallois artefacts. The Levallois core from Sewerby may be later prehistoric in date, and there are concerns as to its provenance (Wymer 1999). A Levallois flake is said to come from the Kelsey Hill Gravel near Keyingham north of the Humber estuary. The gravels here are of an unusual nature, being the sweepings of a number of different surfaces and brought together in the gravels of a sub-glacial river. When the glacier melted, the gravels were left as a ridge. The gravels are rich in *Corbicula fluminalis* implying that the glacier could not have been younger than MIS 6 – because it will have swept up older interglacial deposits containing *Corbicula* which could only date, at their latest, to MIS 7 (Keen 2001). If genuine, this is the furthest north Levallois making and using peoples got, but it remains to be substantiated. It may also be evidence for a post-Anglian but pre-Devensian glacial advance, as was noted at Tottenhill.

The West

One reason sometimes put forward to explain the lack of a substantial Levallois presence in the north and in the west is that PCT technology required the presence of abundant high quality flint. Many of the older conceptualisations of PCT implied it was wasteful of raw material – a big nodule to make a single flake or point. In such an interpretative framework, occupation would almost have to be restricted to southern Britain and the areas of chalk bedrock. This view of Levallois has been shown to be false. As noted above, Levallois technology is really about productivity and sustainability. In addition to this, the link to large high quality flint nodules has also been dispelled. The site of Pontnewydd in North Wales clearly demonstrates this argument is untenable.

This site, excavated between 1978 and 1995 (Aldhouse-Green 1998), is a critically important one for a number of reasons. It is certainly MIS 7 in age, and occupation may also occur in early MIS 6 (ibid.); it contains hominin remains (teeth); it extends the geographical limits for known Middle Palaeolithic occupation into upland areas and into western Britain/North Wales; there are important observations on the nature of tool behaviour (Green 1984; Green, S. H. 1988). It is located in an upland area in the valley of the river Elwy, a tributary of the River Clwyd, which flows north to the sea up the Vale of Clwyd. The slopes of the Elwy/Clwyd confluence provide a dramatic vantage point over the low lying ground of the Vale of Clwyd. Was this a location where one or more groups of hunters making hunting expeditions north and west stopped; or had the site a deeper significance, a fixed place in the mental and physical landscapes of Levallois-making peoples to which they constantly returned (Aldhouse-Green 2001)?

As with most caves, Pontnewydd itself was never occupied, though there might have been occupation near the entrance. Activity was focused in the area above the cave entrance near to a cliff face. Debris from tool making, and the tools themselves have been washed into the cave through holes in the roof to become incorporated, along with bones, in the cave sediments. These Main Cave deposits preserve evidence of hominin activity early in MIS 7, possibly the Ponds Farm MAZ, or just after it (see below). The artefacts occur in the Intermediate Complex (250–225 kya) and in the overlying Lower Breccia (225 kya). The artefacts in the former are probably intrusive from the latter. The site's director, Stephen Aldhouse-Green, suggests much of the occupation may have been in the cold phase of MIS 7.4, see Figure 2.2). The New Entrance suggests a second and later period of occupation for which preliminary dates between 214 kya and 179 kya have been produced (Aldhouse-Green 2001). These span the later two temperate peaks and perhaps the beginning of the succeeding glaciation. This in itself is a significant discovery since it suggests that the memory of a favoured observation point may have persisted in a particular hominin group (alternatively, a vantage point was self-evident to any new visitor to the area).

The same handaxe and Levallois assemblage is present in the Main Cave assemblage and in the New Entrance. One of the most significant features of the site is the raw material usage (Newcomer 1984; Green, S. H. 1988). Flint is present, but in very small quantities, and the tools and cores in flint are of small size, the cores being worked almost to exhaustion. Not surprisingly none of the bigger tools are made out of this rock. The most commonly occurring rocks are of volcanic origin. The critical observation here is that all of the major Levallois forms present at the site (convergent and radial) occur in each of the more common rock types, and a few are made out of the less common raw materials – suitable sedimentary rocks and even basalt! A similar variety of use is seen in the production of bifaces and the occasional cleaver. The point here is that irrespective of what rock types tools were being made of, there was an invariance in what was made. The conceptualised end product transcended all other factors. The Levallois technique was imposed on any rock that can be knapped. This is a point brought out by Aldhouse-Green who posits Levallois as dependent not upon an abundance of flint, but rather an abundance of any raw material from which tools could be made.

In this light, the sources of rock become important. Aldhouse-Green noted that in the Upper and Lower Sands and Gravels, the units directly underlying those with the stone tools, cobbles of most of the volcanic rock types used to make the tools are present in the gravels. As well, natural flint is present in small quantities, in the form of small gravel clasts. Was the attractiveness of the location in part due to a traditional memory of a convenient source of raw materials associated with an excellent vantage point for hunting? Did hunters visit the Elwy/Clwyd valleys because they knew they could provision themselves by quarrying out nodules from the sediments in the floor of the cave? Importantly, the handaxes and

Levallois appear to be in the same range of conditions. They may well be contemporary.

In the drainages of the Severn and Warwickshire Avon, there is little evidence for the presence of Levallois-making hominins during this period, though it seems difficult to believe they were not present if they made it as far north-west as Pontnewydd. The TERPs data (Wessex Archaeology 1996), and Lang and Keen (2005) record very few sites for the Warwickshire Avon with Levallois material (there are few enough without Levallois as it is), and none for the Severn in its gravel terraces upstream of the estuary. At Beckford (south of Bredon Hill) and Kemerton (Aston Mills), a single Levallois core and flake at each site occur with bifaces within terrace gravels (Wymer 1999). Combined, the biface count from these two sites is over 40 (Lang and Keen 2005). But the terrace is number 2 of the Avon drainage, and is dated to the Devensian glaciation. Radiocarbon dates from other sites in terrace 2 indicate an age of c. 38,000 years ago suggesting that at least some of these deposits may be broadly contemporary with Neanderthal occupation. Conversely, these artefacts may predate this time and be a result of the reworking of older sediments into Devensian terraces. Lang and Keen record other handaxe locations within this terrace. There is a single Levallois flake from Kenilworth Common in the Dunsmore Gravel, on the southern outskirts of Coventry further up the Avon Valley. The possibility of pre-Devensian Levallois sites is suggested by two Levallois artefacts from Twyning (Wymer 1999). The terrace here is number 4 in the Avon system and is dated to MIS 6. This may represent a limited presence of Levallois hunters later on in the Aveley Interglacial. There were 10 or more handaxes and flakes found elsewhere in this same gravel. Lang and Keen (2005) record a handful of other handaxe sites from terrace 4.

The grand total of PCT from this huge river valley hardly represents a horde of Levallois-using people moving up the Avon to wrest the Midlands plateau from indigenous biface makers! Once more, does an absence of evidence imply that this was genuinely not a route for hominins?

The South

In the Solent basin, terrace 8 of the Stour, known as the Knighton Lodge Gravel, is dated to MIS 7.2, as are its main channel correlatives, the Hordle and Stanswood Bay gravels, see Table 4.1. There is a clear hominin presence, but nothing like that seen in MIS 9 and 8. Why the decrease? A fall in population as Ashton and Lewis (2002) would argue? Perhaps it reflects the lack of extensive commercial quarrying, or the lack of a small number of artefact rich pits. We just don't know. It is frustrating to have so few sites in these deposits. Westaway et al. (2006) date these terraces to MIS 7.2, so they could potentially contain archaeology that was contemporary, or nearly so, with occupation in the Solent basin during the earlier part of the Aveley interglacial. Terraces 7 and 4 of the Stour and Avon respectively, equate with the Milford-on-Sea Terrace in the main channel. The gravels of the Milford-on-Sea Terrace represent the last floodplain of the Solent before the major changes in MIS 6 that will behead the river's upper course (see Chapter 3). A few artefacts come from a small number of sites here. Those from Milford itself are, like the higher Barton Cliffs, recovered from scree slopes at the bottom of the gravel cliffs.

Much debate surrounds the existence of organic deposits in the Solent area that may date to MIS 7. These are the Stone Point organic beds (Bates 2001; Bridgland 2001), considered by Bridgland and Schreve (2001) to be from the earlier part of the interglacial. Sadly there are no artefacts *in situ* within them. However, Westaway *et al.* (2006) note that there are difficulties in assigning these organic deposits to MIS 7 – they may well be last interglacial/MIS 5.5 in age. For the moment they remain in a suspense account.

Elsewhere in this erstwhile drainage basin a few other Levallois artefacts are present which cannot be confidently related to the terrace sequence.

To the east of the Solent terraces the Norton raised beach correlates with the Black Rock raised beach visible in the cliffs at Brighton. This continuous buried cliff line represents the south coast in MIS 7, probably toward the eastern end of it (Hutchinson 1998; Parfitt *et al.* 1998). Occasional handaxes occur in its deposits so hominins were occupying the coastline to the east of the Solent basin. In between these two areas, there is an interglacial channel at Selsey Life Boat Station, which contained in addition to flora and fauna, one Levallois core *in situ* (Rebecca Scott, pers. comm.). There is *Corbicula fluminalis* in these deposits so they must be at least MIS 7 in age, or earlier (see papers in Murton *et al.* 1998 for fuller discussion).

The South-East

There are a number of sites in the drainage of the Kentish Stour (see Figure 2.8) which are noted to contain Levallois, in particular, sites in Canterbury, on terrace 2, and on the higher terrace 3 (Wymer 1999; and papers in Murton *et al.* 1998). This is another river that we have not looked at before now. There is considerable debate as to how old these terraces really are. Wymer tentatively equates the gravels at Sturry (a suburb of Canterbury) with the Wolstonian Complex, and the terrace 2 gravels overlain by 'brickearth', to an interglacial within this period. In our terms, this would equate with late MIS 8/MIS 7/early MIS 6. At the site of Wear Farm (Bridgland *et al.* 1998), Chislet, just over 9 km away from Canterbury, terrace 2 gravels of the Stour were overlain by fine-grained loamy deposit with *Corbicula fluminalis* giving a minimum age of MIS 7. So the gravels beneath would have to be MIS 7 or earlier. It is tentatively suggested that, by extension, the brickearths overlying terrace 2 at Canterbury are therefore the same age.

This implies that terrace 2 find localities in Canterbury, such as Vauxhall Pit and St Stephen's Pit, may sit on terrace surfaces buried under a fluvial MIS 7 loam. The gravels of terrace 2 may also date to the late MIS 8/MIS 7/ early MIS 6 occupation phase.

Levallois finds are few. Some caution must be exercised as Mousterian *bout coupé* handaxes have been found in gravel deposits in the area, so some of the Levallois here may be a product of much later Neanderthal occupation, if Neanderthals actually did make Levallois in Britain. (A true *bout coupé* is said to have come from St Stephens Pit, but see White and Jacobi (2002) for discussion of the uncertainty surrounding its exact provenance.)

Just to the north of the city, Sturry is also known for rich handaxe sites. The artefacts come out of terrace 2 gravel, which is overlain by only a thin smear of brickearth (at least at the Homersham's pits, Dewey and Smith 1925; Roe 1981b; Smith 1933). Earlier twentieth-century observers reported that a lower zone of reddish gravel in which handaxes occurred, was overlain by a further zone of gravels from which Levallois was reported. Rebecca Scott (pers. comm.) has suggested that only a single unambiguous Levallois artefact is present, and this was from the lower reddish gravel. The assemblages from the lower zone and the middle zone are otherwise identical. A third zone, near the top of the gravels contained handaxes similar to those in the nearby Fordwich site. These artefacts, for which an early date is sometimes claimed (White 1998b), are from a disturbed deposit on a higher terrace, and may have been reworked into the top of the terrace 2 gravels in semi-frozen rafts of deposit moved under periglacial conditions.

The site of Bapchild is away from the Stour, but in the vicinity of its headwaters. It may well represent the remains of an *in-situ* Levallois knapping locality (Dines 1928; 1929; Roe 1981b). Radial Levallois occurred in soliflucted chalk and gravels, the material having been sludged down slope. Cores and flakes were present and a few retouched tools. But handaxes were absent from the assemblage and there is no other way of dating the site. Attribution to this occupation phase must be tentative.

The transition from interglacial conditions to the beginning of the glacial conditions in MIS 6

Unfortunately there are no archaeological sites that can be fitted into this time period.

Conclusions for the late MIS 8/MIS7/early MIS 6 occupation phase

Ashton and Lewis (2002) proposed that this was an occupation phase with a relatively low population level, certainly the lowest of the three post-Anglian interglacials. But the evidence does not necessarily support such an interpretation. Where abundant raw materials are present, then we see large sites. Away from these, the frequency and magnitude of sites drop dramatically, but this may be due to a particular pattern of occupation. An emerging consensus on the nature of Earlier Middle Palaeolithic technology suggests it was geared to mobility, and perhaps the sparseness of evidence elsewhere reflects this – small bands of highly mobile hunters moving across a diverse landscape with a stone tool kit adapted to big game hunting, tool repair and core productivity. Such groups may have wintered at sites like Pontnewydd. If the hunters were following herds of large or medium-sized grazing herbivores, they may have covered huge distances during the annual migrations, and visited known factory sites on a yearly basis to provision individuals and groups for the long annual cycle of movement. But there is still the question of the handaxes. A different technology practised by a different people; at Broom, the survival of an older way of life? Did the Levallois hunters gradually replace the handaxe makers, or did they arrive to find a land from which the handaxe makers had all but disappeared? These questions remain to be answered.

8

THE EUROPEAN SCENE

In my opinion the dating of the British Clactonian clearly shows that there were periods when the hominids in Britain did not make classic handaxes: . . . and [this] may require a radically different explanation from many other non-handaxe explanations.

(White 2000: 37)

Introduction

When Mark White wrote those words, he had four scenarios in mind within which the Clactonian, as a British non-handaxe assemblage, could be set within the context of similar European assemblages:

1   There were very early European non-handaxe assemblages that date to the earliest occupation of Europe (see Chapter 1). The Clactonian knappers were the descendants of these early colonists.
2   There were areas of Europe where handaxes were either very rare or were completely absent. Non-handaxe sites within such geographical areas were part of a regionally significant occupation pattern. The non-handaxe-making groups may or may not have been descended from the non-handaxe makers in (1).
3   In regions where handaxes were made, there were periods of time when they were not made at all.
4   In regions where handaxes were made, there were sites where handaxes were not made, but these locations were surrounded by sites where handaxes were being made at the same time.

It is important to note here, as White makes clear, that these four options *describe* the possible context of British and European non-handaxe assemblages, but they are not explanations as such. It is worth reiterating the question confronting Clactonian scholars; can we establish the existence of one of these patterns from the data available to us? Or, in other words, can we establish the existence of a genuine non-biface archaeological assemblage type, for which temporal depth would allow us to attach the label archaeological tradition, thereby implying there must be some form of socially significant mechanism which perpetuates the pattern?

On the face of it, the first two options would establish a good case for believing in socially/culturally validated lines of intergenerational learning – a cultural tradition. However, the second two seem to me to be more appropriate to the Clactonian as an assemblage type in Britain. The fourth proposition described the British Clactonian more effectively.

In this chapter I will look at the evidence for the existence of a non-handaxe assemblage type in Europe. The aim of this chapter is to determine whether or not precise parallels to the Clactonian exist, and then determine whether or not those parallels, or lack of them, allow us to chose between one of White's interpretations.

Non-handaxe assemblages in Europe

France

It is clear that there is no shortage of sites which lack handaxes. On the French coast at La Pointe-aux-Oies, Wimereux, see Figure 8.1, there are a series of gravel deposits on the shore exposed at low tides. The gravels contain cores and flakes, although cores predominate because of differential collecting biases (Tuffreau and Antoine 1995). The material is rolled and patinated from white and yellowy, to reddish brown. The variety in condition and surface appearance may suggest that a number of chronologically distinct assemblages are present (Tuffreau 1971). The material is believed to have been eroded from a marine gravel at the base of the cliffs, and other abraded artefacts may have been derived from higher fluvial gravels related to the estuary of the river Slack. The marine deposits here may be very old, there are records of *Mammuthus meridionalis*, a very ancient mammoth > 1.5 myr in age. The situation and recovery invite comparisons with Lion Point and Rainbow Bar. However, much work needs to be done on dating the cliff sediments, and Tuffreau and Antoine (1995) note that handaxes, or at least proto-bifaces, are present in the collected assemblage from the foreshore.

Further down the coast, the mouth of the Somme river represents access into a valley system that has played an important part in the history of Palaeolithic archaeology (van Ripper 1993). The valley boasts an impressive number of Middle Pleistocene sites (Tuffreau and Antoine 1995), see Figure 8.1, which are located within a well-researched and dated terrace sequence (Bates 1993; Antoine *et al.* 2000). At Abbeville, there are handaxe sites which may be as old as MIS 16 or 15 (Bridgland *et al.* 2006), and others which date to MIS 14 or 13. The earliest occupants in this part of France were clearly handaxe makers (Tuffreau *et al.* 1997). This compares

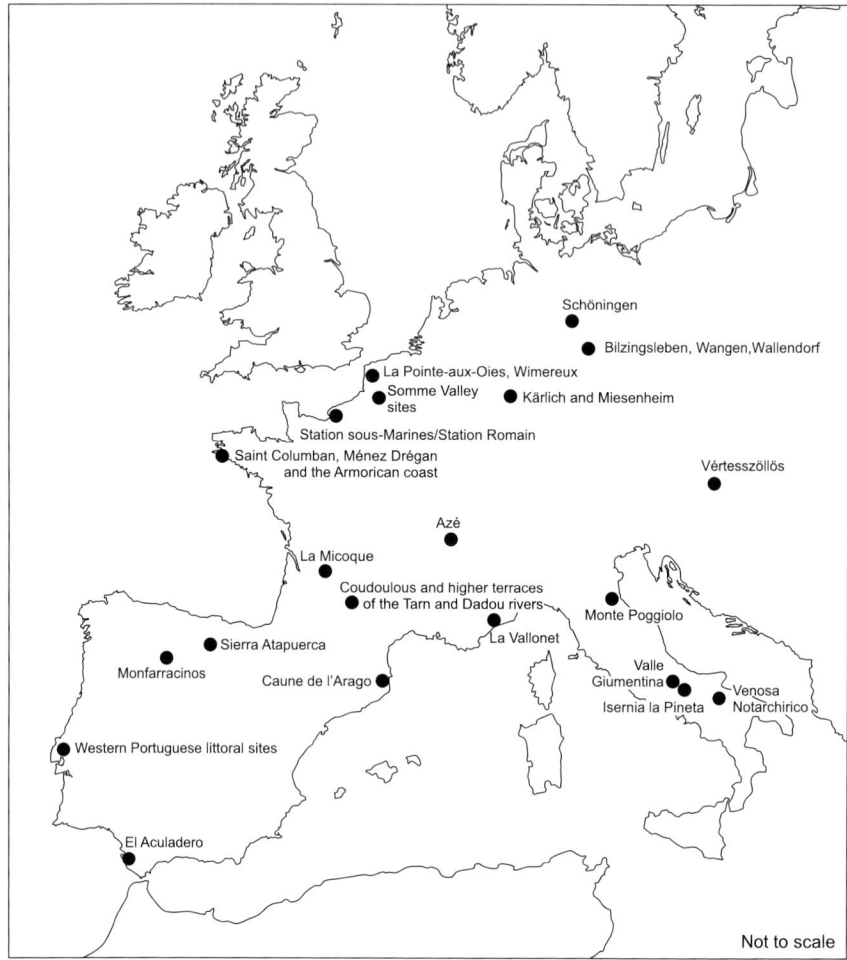

Figure 8.1 Map of Europe showing selected sites discussed in Chapter 8.

well with British evidence for an early handaxe-making population at sites like Boxgrove probably in MIS 13. The handaxe makers are well attested to within the *Arvicola* zone, see Chapter 4 (Roberts and Parfitt 1999; Lee *et al.* 2004; Preece and Parfitt n.d.). In post-Anglian times, handaxe sites are also present in the Somme, in MIS 12–11 at Saint Acheul, and at the Cagny sites (MIS 12–9) on the River Avre, a tributary of the Somme. Yet in all the years of research in this critically important river basin, not one single large convincing non-handaxe assemblage has been discovered. On the face of it, Clactonian-like sites are absent from this valley.

Further to the west at the mouth of the River Seine (Figure 8.1), are the Stations sous-Marines, reported to be Clactonian, and the Station Romain –

218

an Acheulean site. The sites are on the foreshore to the north of the entrance to Le Havre, and are today buried by modern beach accumulation. The Abbé Breuil (1932) identified these localities as being Clactonian. Although this was not universally accepted (reviewed by Lechevalier, in Ohel and Lechevalier 1979), Breuil's views predominated. Reappraisal of both the stratigraphic context, and the artefacts, makes it clear that a small number of handaxes and rough-outs were present within the assemblages from the 13 or so 'stations' on the foreshore (Ohel and Lechevalier, 1979). These researchers interpret all the stations as part of a continuum of Acheulean activity on the marine littoral, with the possibility of spatially distinct activity areas. It is assumed that the artefacts originated from a submerged Seine terrace now below the level of low tide. Wave action eroded the terrace gravels, and the artefacts were washed up onto the modern beach line to become trapped in between larger rocks. It should be noted, however, that gravels cap the adjacent cliffs, and cliff collapse is much in evidence. The sites are undated, but the presence of Levallois, and even blades, would at least suggest a time later in the Acheulean period, if the sites are not contaminated by later Prehistoric artefacts.

Staying with the coast, a series of sites on the Armorican peninsular, and north-western Atlantic coast of France, appear to fit the bill as far as non-handaxe industries are concerned, see Figure 8.1. However, some caution may be necessary as the sites are often described as having 'few to no' handaxes. These sites are grouped collectively under the name Colombanien (Monnier and Molines 1993). In general, the Acheulean in Brittany appears rather sparse. Sites are usually represented by single handaxes found in river valley contexts. While occasional handaxes are found along the southern coast of Brittany (ibid.: Figure 1), most of the coastal sites along the southern Armorican littoral are Colombanien (ibid.; Hallegouet et al. 1992). They represent unifacial and bifacially worked beach cobbles, and retouched tools made on flakes. Denticulates and retouched notches form the bulk of the flake tool inventory. When handaxes are found on the Armorican peninsula they are usually in the north

The sites are found on the modern shore line in fossil beach deposits where the hominins exploited the locally available beach materials. The high instances of typological choppers (unifacially flaked cobbles), and notches and denticulates, suggest caution as these can be easily reproduced by attrition in a dynamic seashore environment. At sites like these where artefacts are recovered from high energy gravels, archaeologists have to be particularly careful. These tool forms can be easily reproduced by natural clast-collision. The term geofact is often applied to such morphologies to highlight their potential natural origin. But a clear hominin presence is indicated by ordinary cores and flakes. Bifaces appear to be genuinely infrequent.

Dating the Colombanien sites has proved difficult, but ages between MIS 13 and 10 are suggested (Monnier and Molines 1993; Monnier 1996). The relationship of these sites to the isolated Acheulean handaxes discovered inland is problematic, as many of these cannot be dated either. Does this mean the Colombanien is a genuine culturally distinct group confined to, and conditioned by, the resources available in the coastal areas where they lived? Or is the Colombanien what Acheulean knappers made when they came to the coast? It is not possible to tell as yet. A single handaxe is reported from the type site of St Colomban. However, at the site of Ménez Drégan (Monnier, pers. comm.), a collapsed sea cave which has been carefully excavated, a non-handaxe assemblage is present in a layer provisionally dated to MIS 11, and again in a higher layer provisionally dated to MIS 9. One thing is clear, that along the Armorican coastline in the later Middle Pleistocene, assemblages with few or no handaxes were definitely being made.

Across northern France to the east of the Armorican coast and Brittany, the pattern is different. Here, especially centred on the Paris basin, are Acheulean sites characterised by varying percentages of Levallois. They are flint dominated, and many possess bifacially thinned and shaped cleavers. They are grouped under a loose umbrella term, the Northern Acheulean. Rolland (1986) implies their 'regional identity' is related to their location on the great loess plains of the north, as well as their proximity to abundant quantities of good quality flint as evidenced in the high incidence of Acheulean quarry sites found. Svoboda (1989) suggests the flint-based Northern Acheulean extends eastwards right across northern France and into the North European Plain. Paola Villa (1983) has indicated caution should be exercised in accepting this Northern Acheulean facies. It is based on a series of old collections, many recovered by quarrymen earlier in the last century, or from highly selected assemblages amassed by collectors from the same period. How real a pattern it represents remains to be established by extensive excavation. But no continuing non-handaxe assemblages have ever been reported.

Slightly to the south of this Northern Acheulean area, across mid-France and moving eastwards, Svoboda (1989) suggests a somewhat different character to Acheulean assemblages. In this zone the extensive use of quartzites has produced a different Acheulean variant. These would be the sites found within the Central European Highlands (eastern France, Germany, and into Bohemia, see discussion on southern France below). One potential non-handaxe assemblage is found on terrace D of the river Creuse, a Loire tributary. Here the Pont-de-Lavaud pebble tool site has the rare distinction of being radiometrically dated; 10 ESR dates give an average date of 1.03 mya (Bridgland et al. 2006).

Moving south along the French Atlantic coast, Acheulean sites are present within the river valleys of the coastal plain, but become scarcer as one moves inland. East of Bordeaux, in particular along the Dordogne and Vézère valleys, are some of the most famous Palaeolithic sites in Europe. Of particular importance to us is La Micoque (Figure 8.1). At the top of the stratigraphic sequence, see Table 8.1, is a handaxe assemblage. The

Table 8.1 Contrasting interpretations for the archaeological levels at the rock shelter site of La Micoque

Archaeological layer	Abbé Breuil's interpretation in the early 1930s	D. Peyrony's interpretation in the late 1930s	F. Bordes' interpretation in the late 1960s	Modern interpretation of dating and artefact analysis
6	Micoquian	Micoquian	Micoquian	Micoquian MIS 9?
5	Tyacian	Tyacian	Acheulean meridionalis	Acheulean meridionalis MIS 10?
4	Tyacian	Mousterian	Pre-Mousterian	Middle Palaeolithic MIS 10
3	Clactonian	Tyacian	Pre-Mousterian	Middle Palaeolithic MIS 10
2	Clactonian	Tyacian	Not determined	Not determined
1	Clactonian	Not determined	Clactonian or Acheulean	Not determined MIS 11?

Note: Modern dating and archaeological interpretations based on work of J. M. Geneste, J. P. Texier, P. Bertran, H. P. Schwarcz, R. Grün, C. Falguères, J.-J. Bahain, and H. Saleki

Source: Modified after Falguères *et al.* (1997, table 1). Used with permission.

handaxes are elongated, carefully shaped, and pointed, often called lanceo-lates. The site has given its name to an assemblage type characterised by these kinds of bifaces – the Micoquian, spanning the late Acheulean time bracket. (In central and eastern Europe the cultural label Micoquian is often applied to later assemblages of handaxes and bifacial tools that date to the end of the Mousterian and the Neanderthal occupation of Europe.)

Beneath this were two layers with non-handaxe assemblages that were given the cultural label Tyacian by the Abbé Breuil (Breuil 1932; Falguères and Bahain 1997; Texier and Bertran 1993). No precise definition was ever provided by Breuil, but the impression given was that this was an industry fashioned on small and poorly made flakes, with few well-made scrapers, and high incidences of notched and denticulated pieces. There was some limited preparation of striking platforms as well. The Tyacian was later noted at other sites with comparable assemblages, such as Fontéchevade, in the Rissian levels at Pech de l'Azé II, and Sainte-Anne-d'Evenos (Movius 1948a; Bordes 1968). Breuil (1932) considered the Tyacian to have developed out of the Clactonian cultural stream and argued it gave rise to the Mousterian. He argued the Clactonian was present in the lowest layers at La Micoque. In the most recent revisions of the lithic assemblages from the site (Falguères

221

and Bahain 1997, for summary), the Tyacian as a label has been dropped altogether. Handaxes are now known from the two levels designated within layer 5 (now described as Southern Acheulean – see below), and a few are present in layer 4 (Laville *et al.* 1980).

The Tyacian as a discrete entity has suffered shifting fortunes (Cook *et al.* 1982; Falguères and Bahain 1997; Rolland 1986) as Breuil's views fell from favour and interpretive fashion changed. This is reflected in Table 8.1. A re-working of the southern French pre-Mousterian non-handaxe phenomenon was suggested by Lumley (1975) who coined the term Evenosian to explain Tyacian-like assemblages at Fontéchevade, Sainte-Anne-d'Evenos, and the lower levels of the Caune de l'Arago at Tautavel (see below), but this term does not seem to have gained widespread acceptance either.

Rolland (1986) has argued that the assemblages from La Micoque levels 3 and possibly 4 do represent a discrete phenomenon within the site. The industry is represented by small short flakes. They are struck from the sides of long elongated cores, often using two adjacent detachments. This gives the cores and flakes a singular appearance. Notches and denticulates are well represented, but scrapers are not. (While this aspect of Rolland's interpretation is supported here, his belief in the African genesis of the technique and its transitional status leading toward the early Mousterian is not.) In effect, the assemblage from La Micoque 3 is one dominated by a particular core reduction technique, which produces distinctive-looking flakes. (Laville and colleagues (1980) assert that well-made scrapers were present in layer 3, similar to those from High Lodge! This presumably explains why for these authors, layers 3 and 4 are best described as Mousterian.)

As noted above, a number of researchers have commented on the similarity between La Micoque's lower layers and those of other sites such as Fontéchevade layer E, the lower layers at Baume-Bonne, and des Tares, to name but a few (Rigaud and Texier 1981; Cook *et al.* 1982; Rolland 1986, *inter alia*). But differences exist between all of them, in some cases between different types of tools, in others between different kinds of scraper retouch or choice of flake blank for retouching. Rolland (1986) suggests in some of these cases raw material quality and availability will have influenced their character.

Villa (1983) has highlighted the inter-assemblage variability in the Tyacian assemblages in southern France. But the dating of these assemblages is difficult. Many can only be dated by reference to layers that have accumulated under cold conditions (recognised on geological grounds). Most of this type of dating work was done in the 1960s and 1970s when it was believed that sedimentation in caves was a product of cold climate activity (Laville *et al.* 1980). Layers recognised as having been formed in glaciations were then fitted into an accepted sequence of stadials and interstadials within different glaciations, Relating such 'sedimentological' dating to the MIS curve is difficult without absolute dating techniques, which cannot always to applied to these sediments. La Micoque layers 3 and 4 were considered to be 'early Rissian'. This would place them somewhere in the middle part of the period encompassed by the Lynch Hill/Corbets Tey and Taplow/Mucking Formations of the Thames. La Micoque, Baume-Bonne, Fontéchevade and other French non-handaxe assemblages in mid-France were thus younger than the British Clactonian.

More recently radiometric dating (Falguères and Bahain 1997) has placed layers 3–5 from La Micoque in MIS 10. They may be broadly contemporary with some of the earliest dates for the important site of Orgnac 3 (Moncel et al. 2005: Table 1), which has a few bifaces, but which sees a gradual transition from a core, flake, and flake tool-dominated assemblage to one marked by Levallois (Moncel 1996). Interestingly, the PCT element at Orgnac first appears at the end of MIS 9, and the beginning of MIS 8 (Moncel et al. 2005), just as in the Lower Thames Valley. So the question here is, do the La Micoque and Orgnac 3 levels represent localised expressions of a (mostly) non-handaxe assemblage type, or are handaxe makers adapting to local circumstances? This of course is the Clactonian conundrum in a nutshell. These lower layers at La Micoque are unlikely to be explained by Mark White's first proposition, outlined at the start of the chapter, as there is no evidence of a long-lasting non-handaxe tradition in this part of France. (Unfortunately few if any caves in the limestone regions retain earlier Pleistocene sediments. The older sediments were removed when the later Middle Pleistocene sediments were emplaced.) One interpretation is definitely inappropriate, that encompassed by White's second proposition. These sites are often surrounded by Acheulean localities.

So the pattern is a complicated one. The non-handaxe assemblages from south-west France are best described by White's propositions 3 and 4. There are sites which clearly deserve the label Acheulean. There are other sites, or specific levels within them, which either lack handaxes altogether, or have a very small number of them. Interpretations vary considerably as to whether these should or should not be called Acheulean, Tyacian, or something else. On the other hand, the Tyacian appears difficult to sustain as a separate assemblage type, let alone as a tradition (irrespective of the occasional biface). Many French researchers do not regard the non-handaxe assemblages as belonging to a discrete assemblage type. They are seen as part of a general later Middle Pleistocene trend that will ultimately lead to various facies of the Mousterian. In other words a gradual shift towards assemblages dominated by flake tools with varying emphasis on scrapers, notches and denticulates with an ever increasing emphasis on Levallois.

In Figure 8.2, Villa (1983) has condensed the views of François Bordes. The map depicts his interpretation of the different regional cultural traditions found across France and northern Spain. The areas are loosely defined, and cultural exclusivity is not implied; for example, Tyacian sites could be found within the Languedoc-Roussillon province, as well as in the Tarn and

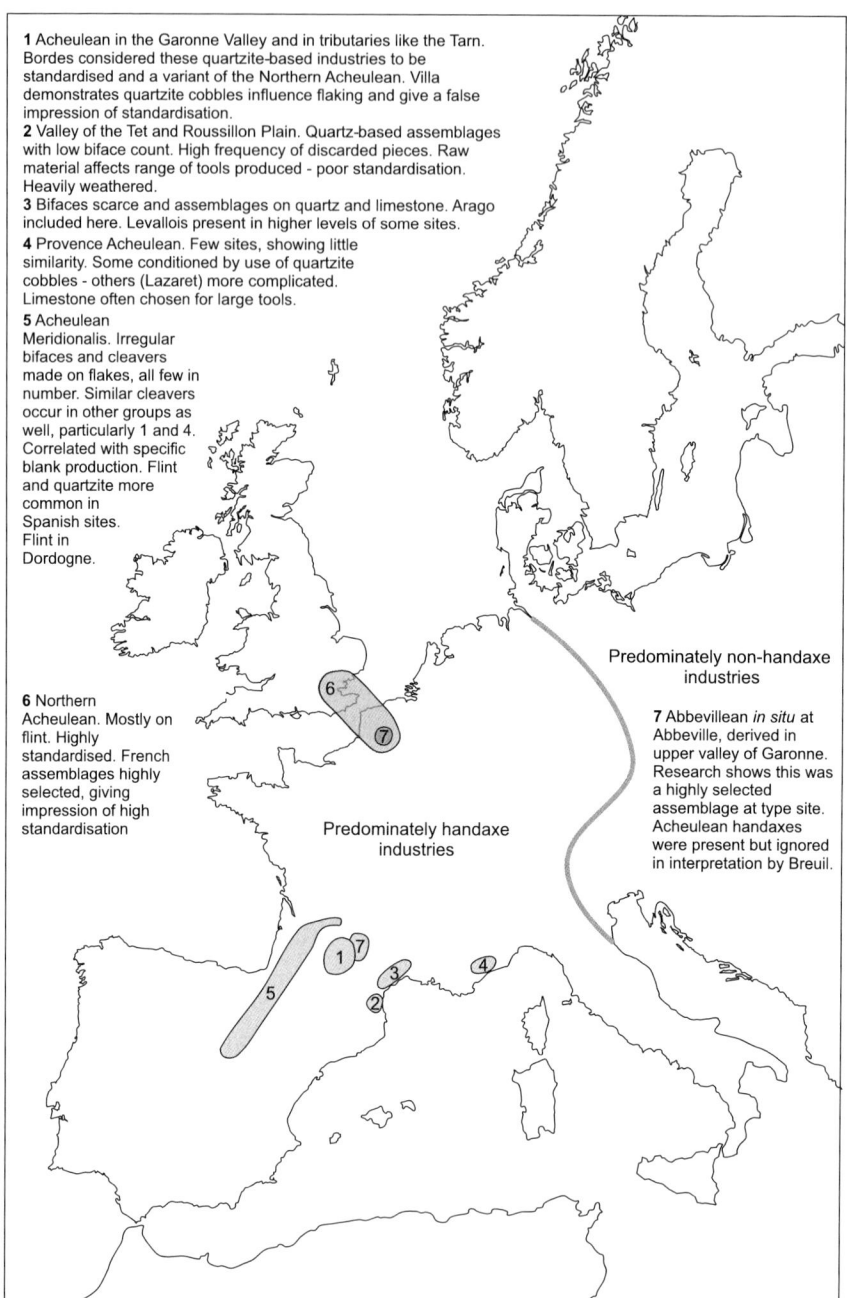

1 Acheulean in the Garonne Valley and in tributaries like the Tarn. Bordes considered these quartzite-based industries to be standardised and a variant of the Northern Acheulean. Villa demonstrates quartzite cobbles influence flaking and give a false impression of standardisation.

2 Valley of the Tet and Roussillon Plain. Quartz-based assemblages with low biface count. High frequency of discarded pieces. Raw material affects range of tools produced - poor standardisation. Heavily weathered.

3 Bifaces scarce and assemblages on quartz and limestone. Arago included here. Levallois present in higher levels of some sites.

4 Provence Acheulean. Few sites, showing little similarity. Some conditioned by use of quartzite cobbles - others (Lazaret) more complicated. Limestone often chosen for large tools.

5 Acheulean Meridionalis. Irregular bifaces and cleavers made on flakes, all few in number. Similar cleavers occur in other groups as well, particularly 1 and 4. Correlated with specific blank production. Flint and quartzite more common in Spanish sites. Flint in Dordogne.

6 Northern Acheulean. Mostly on flint. Highly standardised. French assemblages highly selected, giving impression of high standardisation

Predominately non-handaxe industries

7 Abbevillean *in situ* at Abbeville, derived in upper valley of Garonne. Research shows this was a highly selected assemblage at type site. Acheulean handaxes were present but ignored in interpretation by Breuil.

Predominately handaxe industries

Figure 8.2 Map showing the distribution of regional variations on the Acheulean and other Middle Pleistocene archaeological cultures as postulated by Bordes and colleagues

Source: Data from Bordes (1968); Villa (1983); Laville et al. (1980); Kozlowski (2003).

Garonne province where many Acheulean sites show a similarity to the northern 'classic' Acheulean.

The *Acheulean meridionalis* or Southern Acheulean tradition is poorly defined, but implies a loose grouping of Acheulean sites characterised by the presence of flake cleavers and very low incidences of Levallois. It was noted above that to the south of the northern classic variant (Figure 8.2), raw material begins to make its mark on tool production. Many Southern Acheulean sites demonstrate their knappers making extensive use of local, and imported, quartzites. Handaxes tend to be more crude in appearance than their northern flint counterparts, less well shaped and less well finished. The flake tools show more Upper Palaeolithic types such as burins and end scrapers (Villa 1983). The Southern Acheulean is found in the Iberian peninsular, south-western France (and claims for it are made in Italy), and it may even be related to North African Acheulean assemblages. The quartzites, and the quartzite flake cleavers lend these assemblages an African appearance.

Rolland (1986) asserts that the Southern Acheulean cannot be considered a uniform cultural group or regional facies, as the degree of variability present between assemblages is too marked (for example, it incorporates his version of the Tyacian – La Micoque layer 3 and possibly 4). This is a point that is also forcibly made by Villa (1983). She argues the degree of inter-site variability is so great, and the effects of local raw material conditioning so strong, that the concept of a Southern Acheulean tradition cannot be accepted. Dating the *Acheulean meridionalis* is equally difficult. On the basis of sedimentological/geological dating, many of these sites were dated to Riss III. This was the last cold stage of the equivalent of the Wolstonian glaciation of the traditional British sequence. As a late Middle Pleistocene phase, this might roughly equate with MIS 8 or 6 in modern terms, but these kind of correlation are fraught with difficulty.

There are a number of open air sites and rock shelter sites in the Valley of the Garonne and its tributaries, that have claims for large assemblages of cores, flakes, and core tools but few handaxes (Tavoso 1976; Jaubert and Servelle 1996). These do not fit a Tyacian cultural label at all. These sites, like Coudoulous 1 (see Figures 8.1 and 8.2) on the confluence of the Célé and the Lot (a Garonne tributary), and the open-air sites on the higher terraces of the Tarn (another right-bank tributary), and the Dadou, share similarities with the Colombanien sites. They have large collections of unifacially worked choppers and core tools, many with only a few detachments restricted to one part of the blank. They were recovered from cobble-rich gravels. While many of the unifacial artefacts may be open to doubt, more likely to be geofacts, hominins clearly exploited these gravels when the rivers ran at these heights. Dating is difficult, but some of these localities may be older than MIS 12.

French researchers assiduously avoid cultural labels like the Clactonian for these sites, preferring to see these assemblages as facies of the Acheulean with a few, or no handaxes at all. In some cases they are vaguely defined as a Pre-Acheulean (Jaubert and Servelle 1996). Many of the sites for which an Acheulean label is given, are sometimes referred to as Older Acheulean (Villa 1983). This differentiates them from the later Middle Pleistocene Southern Acheulean just described. As the name suggests, these are thought to be much older in date, but just how much older is anyone's guess. Once again, the character of these sites is a reflection of the type of raw materials available, quartzite river clasts. Villa (1983) notes this has greatly affected the type and appearance of many of the handaxes, giving them a cruder look. This in turn has influenced the dating of the sites, as handaxe typology is the only real method of fitting them into any kind of chronological sequence.

South-eastern France cannot easily be subsumed within a generalised Southern Acheulean tradition. Acheulean sites are much scarcer in the Rhône basin than further west. To the north of this basin, on the slopes of the eastern Pyrenees, some 80 m above the Verdouble river is the Caune de l'Arago (see Figure 8.1). This is a critically important site for exploring the possibility of a non-handaxe tradition in southern France (Byrne 2004). What makes it important is its long sequence of repeated occupations throughout the Middle and Upper Pleistocene. Its main chrono-stratigraphic and typo-technological characteristics are shown in Table 8.2, and the relationships between raw material and tool production are shown in Figure 8.3. Occupation is present in MIS 14 (the lowest levels have yet to be excavated) and continues to MIS 3. Raw material procurement strategies remain the same throughout this long sequence. The focus is on the intensive exploitation of local rocks (see Figure 8.3), but there is a clear exotic component as well (Wilson 1988). The most frequent rock types are quartz and quartzite available from local alluvial sources within the immediate vicinity of the cave. In every level, the largest flakes were picked out for retouching, and the best raw materials (flint/chert) were worked by centripetal discoidal techniques; limestone was usually reserved for pebble tools. Scrapers were more often than not produced on good quality flints and quartzites, while notches and end scrapers were made on poorer crystalline raw materials. Wilson (1988) notes that some of the raw materials can be provenanced to sources some 30–35 km away from the site. She describes the relationship in this way:

> The minimum range of exploration and exploitation of the region that this represents is the same for each occupation layer within the cave, and covered an area of about 65 by 30 km. In fact the Arago material is not so much the evidence of occupation of this cave only, as evidence of occupation (or use) of the entire region, just by chance preserved at Arago.
>
> (ibid.: 377ff.)

Table 8.2 Chronological and stratigraphic sequence at Arago in relation to aspects of lithic technology

Ensemble	Unit	Marine isotope stage	Nature of occupation	Estimate of territory size	Bifaces present	Selected features of lithic assemblages
V	A	4				High ratio of tools to unmodified flakes, notches frequent, no pebble tools, no bifaces
	B					
IV	C	7–8				
III	D	12	Long term			Transitional layer, intensive knapping mostly discoids
	E		Long term		Yes	Bipolar frequent, angular debitage, diverse tool kit, pebble tools more frequent, notched tools more frequent
	F		Seasonal, spring to summer	Smallish, concentrate on one biotope, mostly hunt sheep	Rare and atypical	
	F/G		Short-term stay	Small concentrate on local area, hunt wild sheep and horse, musk ox	No	
	G		Large family group for 1 year or more	Very large, hunting mostly horse wild sheep and wild goat	Present in small numbers	

Continued overleaf

Table 8.2 Continued

Ensemble	Unit	Marine isotope stage	Nature of occupation	Estimate of territory size	Bifaces present	Selected features of lithic assemblages
II	H	13				Scrapers frequent, discoidal working infrequent, tool blanks large, flaking not intensive, pebble tools rare
	I		Long term			
	J		Seasonal, autumn	Large territory, hunting mostly red deer and fallow deer		
I	K	14	Single/short term			
	L		Male hunting party, very short stay c. < 2 weeks	Single local biotope exploited, almost exclusively hunt reindeer		
	M		Single/short term			
	N					
	O					
	P					
	Q				yes	
	R					
	S					

Source: After Byrne (2004) and Lumley et al. (2004).

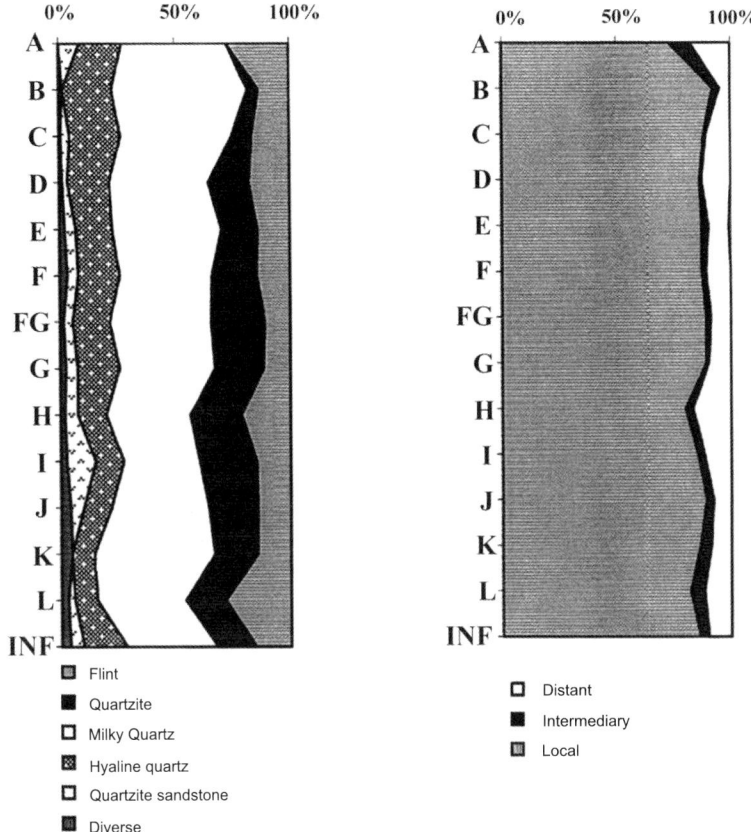

Figure 8.3 Raw material usage from the Caune de l'Arago.

Note: The left-hand diagram shows the use of specific rock types in the cave, and changes in their frequency over time. Vertical axis indicates layers – INF (lower layers) at base, A at top. Right-hand diagram shows percentage of rock types used that were local compared with those from a more distant source. See Table 8.2. Used with permission.

Importantly, no sharp cut-off was present between the Lower and Middle Palaeolithic levels. There was a steady decline in flake size over time with a corresponding increase in discoidal flaking. In other words, there was no sharp distinction between non-handaxe phases, single layers with handaxes, and the appearance of the Middle Palaeolithic. This is very much in line with French scholarship which, on the whole, favours sequences of local evolution and not distinct cultures succeeding each other (e.g. Orgnac 3 above). While more flakes at Arago were turned into tools in the higher layers, the only real qualitative change was the increase in the frequency of notches over scrapers in the Middle Palaeolithic levels at the top of the sequence (Byrne 2004). But the basic message of raw material usage, technology and typology was one of long-term stability and continuity over time.

Bifaces are present in level Q and intermittently in levels E–G in ensemble III which is the equivalent of the Anglian glaciation. The typological and technological stability cross-cuts environmental and climatic change, as do the main activities carried out within the cave; tool manufacture and carcass processing, see Table 8.2, Lumley *et al.* (2004). Clearly the presence of bifaces makes little difference to what hominins did, or how they did it. Byrne (2004) notes that under such circumstances cultural explanations are inappropriate. Her explanation focuses on the stability of the raw material resources and the broader procurement system. As long as they don't change, the broad assemblage character doesn't need to either. It should be noted that such an explanation is very different from arguing that strong lines of social learning strait-jacketed the production of material culture. Arago demonstrates the critical importance of sites with long sequences of occupation. These kinds of site are the only true litmus for quantifying behavioural variability, and assessing the viability of culturally based explanations. Single occupation layers at sites can often serve to distort the true character of hominin occupation in a region.

Recently, the genuineness of the stone tools from the cave site of La Vallonet (Figure 8.1; Lumley *et al.* 1963) has been called into question (White 1995; Roebroeks 2001). Many of the core tools were unifacial choppers made on rounded cobbles. It now appears that these were natural fractures made by pressure loading from overlying sediments, and which entered the cave through a vertical chimney. They derive from Miocene pebble beds which overlie the cave. As an Oldowan-like chopper/chopping tool assemblage, this was one of the few sites that would have supported Mark White's first proposition as it was considered to be typologically very old, possibly Lower Pleistocene.

Far to the north of Arago, in a tributary of the Saône river, the site of Azé (Figure 8.1) has a non-handaxe industry that may well be the result of a one-stop or short-term occupation. Other non-handaxe sites are present in the area (Amiot 1993). Azé is dated to the Mindel-Riss interglacial or the early Riss. The stone tool assemblage was made on cobbles and blocks of flint, many from the local river, and chert blocks broken off from the cave walls. The researchers who published the site (Moncel *et al.* 2001) were reluctant to discount a cultural explanation for the assemblage. It is a curious mixture of apparent raw material determination on the one hand, and expedient response to large cobbles from the local stream on the other. The flint was not in the best of conditions, and the flint tools were more heavily and invasively retouched than the chert ones. Some of the flint tools may have been re-sharpened. This suggests some pressure on raw material quality or availability. On the face of it, that would explain why chert torn from the shelter walls was also used as a raw material for making flakes and flake tools. Yet many of the cores in flint were far from exhausted and could have sustained further flaking – so this doesn't square with a raw material problem. In my opinion, the 'expedient' explanation for this assemblage, suggested as one possible interpretation by the excavators, is a better explanation that a cultural one. Flint cobbles and nodules in the stream may have been variable in quality, and the best of them were brought into the cave and more extensively knapped. Good quality flint flakes would naturally be more intensively worked. Those of a quality sufficient for reuse would be re-sharpened, as this would save going down to the stream to hunt for more suitable cobbles. The majority of the chert chunks were only expediently retouched to form tools – again this can be explained by a least effort approach during a brief one-stop occupation of the site.

The Iberian peninsula

Across the Pyrenees and into Iberia the situation is different (see major reviews in Santonja and Villa 1990; Carbonell and Rodriguez 1994; Raposo and Santonja 1995). The major drainage basins of the Iberian peninsula run from east to west and drain the central highlands. In nearly every area quartzite is an important, if not the major, component of the bed load of rivers. The larger rivers and their tributaries have acquired terrace flights with up to 20 or more individual terraces; in some cases up to 150 m above the modern rivers (Raposo and Santonja 1995). In other systems a more modest 8–10 terraces are recorded. Artefacts fashioned on the quartzite cobbles and pebbles from these alluvial terraces form the bulk of the Iberian Lower Palaeolithic record. Most sites therefore represent secondary context open localities, either on terraces surfaces, or from within the body of the terrace itself. Non-handaxe assemblages in these situations share familiar problems to those from the southern French river terraces; small assemblages, non-diagnostic tools, selected artefacts that may be natural, and the ever present uncertainty in dating. Monfarracinos (Figure 8.1) and Toro in the Douro Valley, are good examples, possibly dating to the early Middle Pleistocene. Bridgland et al. (2006) note a number of non-handaxe sites which could, potentially, have very early dates. The sites are on high terraces of tributaries of the Duero and Tagus rivers. A possible very early Acheulean site is San Bartolomé de Las Abiertas in the 60 m terrace of the Sangrera, a tributary of the Tagus. This terrace is thought to be the equivalent of terrace 13 in the main valley, within which the Brunhes-Matuyama boundary is located. However, a considerable degree of clarification would be necessary to refine this relationship.

Breuil and Zbyszewski (1942–1945) studied assemblages from raised beaches along the Portuguese littoral (Figure 8.1) of the Estremadura area, claiming them to be manifestations of Early Pleistocene pebble tool cultures. Whether or not many of these surface finds are genuine artefacts is still hotly debated. Many may be geofacts. Other localities may represent genuine accumulations of artefacts, or at least contain some real artefacts. Further to the south, but still associated with the coastal plain, more of these pebble artefact sites are found along river valleys in the hinterland of Seville. El Aculadero in Southern Spain (Figure 8.1) has upwards of 22,000 artefacts, but it is likely that most of these are geofacts. It remains to be seen whether the non-handaxe character of these open-air exposures represents a genuine expression of cultural learning. It is equally possible to argue that the small fluvial pebbles would not allow the manufacture of anything other than cores and flakes (Raposo and Santonja 1995). François Bordes tacitly admitted that his celebrated typology list was of a more local (i.e. Dordogne) significance when forced to simplify it in order to make it applicable to the assemblages from El Aculadero (Querol and Santonja 1983). The non-handaxe sites here may cover a considerable time span, though again precise dating is very difficult.

One aspect of these sites does invite comparison. The occurrence on the Iberian littoral of localities exploiting cobbles and pebbles (marine beach in the case of the Estremadura sites, and fluvial in the Cadiz region), is reminiscent of the Colombanien. On the face of it, hominins used what raw materials they could find wherever they could find them.

Just when the earliest handaxes appeared in Iberia is an open question. The oldest date from a secure context is from Atapuerca, see Table 8.3 and Figure 8.1. The higher levels at Trinchera Dolina (TD 11 and 10) have core and flake assemblages resembling Middle Palaeolithic ones because of the presence of centripetal flaking (Mallol 1999). These date to an interglacial, either MIS 11 or 9. In the nearby Trinchera Galeria, levels 10 and 11 contain handaxes and are broadly contemporary with the same numbered units from Trinchera Dolina (Carbonell and Rodriguez 1994). Recent redating of the nearby Sima de los Huesos site, with the remains of possibly 28 individuals in a deep vertical shaft within the cave, has placed the hominin assemblage anywhere between 400 kya and 500 kya (this is a best guess scenario based on an infinite radiometric date of >350 kya – Bischoff et al. 2003). A single handaxe has been found associated with the hominin remains.

Italy

Moving westwards to the Italian peninsula, there is a strong cultural tradition to archaeological interpretation. This has led to a tendency to see Lower Palaeolithic assemblages as either Acheulean or Clactonian (or sometimes Tyacian) depending on the presence of handaxes (Bietti and Castorina 1992). Early sites without handaxes are best exemplified by Monte Poggiolo, Isernia la Pineta and Venosa-Notarchirico (Mussi 1995; Milliken 1999;

Table 8.3 Chrono-stratigraphic and archaeological sequence at Trinchera Gran Dolina in the Sierra Atapuerca, Spain

Trinchera Dolina level	MIS	General climate	Local climate	Stone tools present	Details of lithic strategies employed
11	11 or 9	Interglacial	Warm, moist local valleys, pine and oak forest.	Yes	Cores and flakes. TD10a has 300+ artefacts. Cores and flakes.
10	→	→		Yes	Standardisation and centripetal flaking. Middle Palaeolithic-like. Local raw materials. Levels 10 and 11 are stratigraphically equivalent to levels 10 and 11 in nearby Trinchera Galeria which has handaxes.
9					
8	TD8b = MIS 13 or 15		Cold, moist, some forest		
	TD8a = MIS 18	Glacial			
7	Brunhes/Matuyama boundary here in MIS 19		Cold	Yes	
6	MIS 21	Interglacial with fluctuating humidity	Drier and more open	Yes	300+ artefacts, cores and flakes mostly small. Unstandardised. Mostly on flint. Denticulates, scrapers, other non-diagnostic retouched tools. All raw materials locally available.
			Dry and open		
			Becoming drier, valleys humid	Yes	
5	MIS 22	Dry and cold – continental climate	Transition cold-warm. Still continental.		
4	→	→	Dominated by arid steppe species.	Yes	Small number of cores and flakes. Quartzite from local sources. Unstandardised.
3			Some forest.	Yes	
2	Enclosed cave				
1	Jaramillo in this unit				

Source: Data from Antoñanzas and Bescós (2002); Carbonell and Rodriguez (1994); Mallol (1999). Dating based on Antoñanzas and Bescós.

Villa 2001). These are shown on Figure 8.1. There are a number of claims for other early non-handaxe sites, but there are either uncertainties concerning their age, the nature of their assemblages, or the provenance of their assemblages (Mussi 1995; Roebroeks and van Kolfschoten 1995).

The site of Monte Poggiolo is provisionally dated to the Lower Pleistocene, dates of 800–900 kya are normally quoted on the basis of palaeomagnetism and ESR dates on quartz grains (Milliken 1999; Villa 2001), but there are uncertainties surrounding these dates. The deposit within which the artefacts occur is interpreted as a fluvial deltaic fan, which accumulated when the Adriatic coast was nearer than it is today (c. 40 km away), and the southern reaches of the great Po valley were still drowned by the sea.

The stone tool assemblage is made on flint pebbles from the fan gravels. Cores and flakes are common, while retouched tools are rare (Mussi 1995 notes the presence of proto-handaxes!). While a hominin presence is clear, some caution is warranted as there are a large number of pebbles and cobbles with single removals and flakes with wholly cortical dorsal surfaces which can denote natural percussion in a clast-dominated sediment. No classic handaxes appear to have been present. All commentators note that the clasts from the gravel were small, usually less than 10 cms and most flakes are less than 6 cms. For the moment, it is better to consider Monte Poggiolo as a site where hominins exploited a readily available source of raw materials, which may not have been conducive to regular handaxe production. It remains to be established how early in date the site actually is.

Isernia is another site with a disputed early date. Potassium-argon dating on volcanic crystals of sanidine produced an age of c. 736 kya, and palaeomagnetic studies have produced a reversed field direction suggesting an age within the Matuyama (see Figure 1.5; Mussi 1995; Milliken 1999; Villa 2001). But the fauna suggests a later age. The small mammals contain an *Arvicola* fauna, with evidence of it being an assemblage earlier in this genera's history. More recently (data reviewed in Roebroeks 2001) a consensus age of about 600 kya appears to be emerging for the site, and this has been confirmed by a new series of radiometric dates (Coltorti *et al.* 2005).

There are four excavated archaeological levels, each with a non-handaxe assemblage. The horizons have been interpreted as living floors, or in some cases habitation floors (Milliken 1999), though this is not accepted by all researchers. Bone accumulations are substantial, some of them showing cut marks and intentional breakage; a few flakes have microwear. In some cases the artefacts number in the thousands (although just how much of this is debris below 2 cms is not clear). There is a small retouched element, many of the tools are denticulates, although they may actually be cores, the end result of intensive re-flaking. The artefacts are in flint (or chert) and limestone, both of which were available locally. The limestone seems to have been mostly in the form of pebbles which were used for the removal of a few flakes. It is possible that, as with Monte Poggiolo, some of these are natural. Again, as with Monte Poggiolo, the raw material is rather small. The flint comes from natural slabs usually less than 8 cms in length, and the average length of all the flint artefact types (flakes, debris and cores) is between 2 and 4 cms (Villa 2001). Additionally, the flint is poor quality and prone to shatter, resulting in a high proportion of small flakes and debitage. Raw material size and quality may well be the reason handaxes were not made at this site.

Other assemblages without handaxes are present within pre- and post-Anglian deposits in Italy, but assigning them to a non-handaxe tradition is difficult; assemblages are usually small, on poor quality flint and/or poorly dated. Villa (2001) cogently argues that none of the early non-handaxe assemblages can be associated with an early pre-Acheulean occupation phase (Mark White's scenario 1). Lower Palaeolithic Italy appears to conform more to White's propositions 3 and 4 and its sites therefore resemble those from south-west France.

The Acheulean of Italy contains a curious practice not widely seen elsewhere – the use of bone as a medium for making tools. Sarah Milliken (1999) suggests that at sites like Anagni-Fontana Ranuccio, Castel di Guido, and La Polledrara di Cecanibbio, all early post-Anglian Acheulean sites, the production of bone handaxes was a direct response to raw material inadequacy. So at least in some places it would seem we have clear evidence that the availability of adequate resources did affect the way hominins behaved (possibly resulting in a behavioural response that could characterise a tradition!). The bone handaxes also signal the possibility that much of the complexity in Pleistocene cultural activity may lie just below the surface threshold of *archaeological visibility*; simplistic blanket explanations like cultural dichotomies only serve to hide these ambiguities.

But one site stands out as potentially demonstrating an unequivocal non-handaxe presence. The sequence for Notarchirico is shown in Table 8.4 (Figure 8.1; Piperno *et al.* 1998; see Mussi 1995; Milliken 1999; and Villa 2001, for overviews). A series of biface and non-biface assemblages alternate with each other. The site is in the Venosa basin in the Basilicata region. The basin has been infilled with fluvial sediments, and volcanic sediments from effusive volcanoes up to 20 km away, in particular, the volcano Monte Vulture. At times the basin was dominated by lacustrine environments, when streams were unable to cope with the increase in sedimentation resulting from ash-falls.

The stone tools were made of limestone, siliceous limestone, chert and quartzite. Retouched tools were rather rare in all the levels. In the non-handaxe levels, flint/chert is the most frequently found raw material and flakes predominate. In those levels with handaxes, which are often made on the chert or quartzite, there is a pronounced heavy duty component to the

Table 8.4 Stratigraphic sequence and archaeological associations from Venosa Notarchirico, Italy

Layer	Depositional environment	Are bifaces present?	Associated archaeology and fauna	Date
Alpha	Flowing river with gravel bars	Cores, flakes, and flake tools	c. 950 artefacts	359 +154/-97 (U series on human femur) 500 kya (AA)
A		Yes		
A1	Unstable conditions, bank collapse and solifluction	Yes	c. 40 artefacts. Elephant skull with tools in direct association	
B	River eroding laterally and reworking its channel deposits. Stone pavement = land surface	Yes		
C	Unstable conditions, bank collapse and solifluction. Followed by increased volcanic load	Cores, flakes, and flake tools		
D	River eroding laterally and reworking its channel deposits. Increased volcanic load	Yes		
E	River eroding laterally. Tephra drift heavy	Cores, flakes, and flake tools		
E1				*Arvicola*
Tephra from Monte Vulture 654 kya +/- 11 kya (Ar/Ar) Levels 2.1–2.4 at Notarchirico ash falls in still water. Level 2.4 has similar chemical composition to above Level 2.1, below 2.4, has date of 640 kya +/- 70 kya (TL)				
F	River eroding laterally and reworking its channel deposits. Stone pavement = land surface. Tephra drift heavy	Yes		753 kya +/- 60 kya (TL)
Basal levels only limited excavation				

Source: Data from Piperno *et al.* (1998); Villa (2001); and Milliken (1999).

Notes: Abbreviations for dating techniques as follows. U series = Uranium series; AA = Amino Acid racemization; Ar/Ar = Argon/Argon; TL = Thermoluminescence.

assemblages with core tools and choppers being present, made out of lime-stone. Thick *rabot* (a retouched tool usually on a very thick flake, often called a push-plane), and end scrapers are also present in these assemblages, again made on limestone. Piperno *et al.* (1998) explicitly warn against imposing simplistic cultural explanations on the data. They point out that small excavations and sample sizes influence interpretations, and that these alternating assemblages occur over a relatively short time span, par-ticularly in the lower levels. Within this time span are a series of eruptive events which influence micro-climates and habitats within the Venosa basin. The differences in archaeological assemblages are seen as rapid adap-tive responses by hominins to sudden changes in local conditions, and resource availability (as at Barnham and Elveden – Chapters 5 and 6).

The handaxes from below the 'Tephra of Notarchirico' date to c. 650 kya or older (MIS 16–17). To my knowledge, these are the earliest well-contextualised and dated handaxes from Europe. Also in the basin is the site of Loreto. Two archaeological levels are present, the lower one (A) dated to MIS 13, the higher (B) to MIS 11; but for a single flint/chert handaxe, the assemblage from B would be dominated by flakes and cores made on gen-erally poor quality raw material. As with so many of these assemblages, the retouched tools are denticulates and flaked flakes. Piperno and colleagues (1998) extend the same explanation for assemblage variability to Loreto as well.

A raft of Clactonian sites have been claimed for the Valle Giumentina (Figure 8.1) in the Abruzzo region (Bietti and Castorina 1992). These authors, if I read them correctly, suggest that until quite recently a number of Italian Lower Palaeolithic archaeologists have been working under the assumption that cores, flakes and flake tools were not a constituent com-ponent of Acheulean assemblages. This was reinforced by the observation that many handaxes were made on limestone (or other non-flint-like raw materials), while cores and retouched tools occurred on finer grained flint-like rocks. The implication is that scholars believed different culture groups exclusively chose different raw materials on which to make their tools.

The Clactonian from the Valle Giumentina represents a number of dis-crete layers with no handaxes (layer 33, and the layer grouping 40–42), with one layer in between these two with five handaxes (layer 37), reflect-ing an apparent culturally variable stratigraphy. The local raw material is flint which is used to make all the tools in each layer. The archaeological levels are in deposits dated to the Riss glaciation. This would correspond to somewhere within the Lynch Hill/Corbets Tey to Taplow/Mucking Formations of the Thames, later than the British Clactonian. A strong con-tinuity is present in the non-handaxe elements in each successive layer. Bietti and Castorina (1992) make the salient point that at a number of Acheulean sites in peninsular Italy, the frequency of handaxes is low, often of the order of only one or two examples, such as at Rebibbia-Casal de'

Pazzi, or Venosa Loreto described above (Mussi 1995; Milliken 2001, for a case study which demonstrates this). Small excavations and limited sampling strategies (as at Valle Giumentina) could well miss the true character of many assemblages, particularly if there is a forced reliance on small and poor local raw materials.

So establishing the presence of a genuine cultural non-handaxe tradition, to explain the character of these non-handaxe assemblages remains to be proven.

Central Europe

Moving northwards over the Alps we come into the area that Bosinski (1995) defines as western-central Europe (between the Alps and the North Sea, the Rhine on the west, the Upper Danube to the south-east, the Weser and tributaries to the north-east). Non-handaxe assemblages are evidently present in the archaeological record of the area, but Bosinski's review of the region (ibid.) gives no grounds for believing a non-handaxe assemblage type or tradition exists. Flaked cobbles and pebble tools are claimed from the lower levels of the great Kärlich quarry near Koblenz (see Figure 8.1). If these are artefacts, they would date to, in some cases, 800–900 kya, but many are single cobbles with one or two unidirectional flake scars and as such may be geofacts (Roebroeks and van Kolfschoten 1995). Just prior to the Anglian there is a stronger archaeological signal. Kärlich layer G (MIS 14), and the site at Miesenheim I (MIS 13), both have small collections of artefacts with no handaxes, but again these assemblages are too small to identify them as part of an unambiguous non-handaxe assemblage type (whether it be very local or more regional). Kärlich layer H fits the same picture but has the distinction of representing settlement in a cold environment of MIS 12. In earlier chapters we saw ample evidence for this in the British data set, and indeed, Kärlich layer H may be broadly contemporary with Boxgrove and the Wallingford fan gravels.

The site of Mauer is in the south of this region, associated with an abandoned meander loop of the river Neckar. Although no artefacts were recovered, there was a rich interglacial fauna, including a hominin jaw bone which is the type specimen of *Homo heidelbergensis*. The site is dated to MIS 13 (Bridgland *et al.* 2006).

Post-Anglian assemblages in this area are quite similar to each other, and the Acheulean is well represented at Kärlich-Seeufer (MIS 11). Moving eastwards to the area between the Elbe basin and that of the Saale, in Germany, the pattern is repeated once more (Mania 1991; 1995; Mania and Mania 2005). There is no evidence for a post-Anglian Clactonian-like tradition in the area, and earlier attempts at identifying one (Collins 1969), based on sites like Wangen and Wallendorf (see Figure 8.1), were based on small assemblages; Mania (1991) notes that Levallois is present at

Wallendorf. The eastern German Lower Palaeolithic is dominated by the Acheulean sites of Bilzingsleben (Mania 1995) and Schöningen (Thieme 1997; 2005) (see Figure 8.1), both securely dated to MIS 11 (Schreve and Bridgland 2002). The former has been described as Clactonian and/or Tyacian (but see Cook et al. (1982) for methodological difficulties with applying this definition here).

Recent excavations have considerably expanded the understanding of Bilzingsleben (Mania 1995; Mania and Mania 2005). Earlier descriptions of the assemblage cited the lack of handaxes. It is now evident that handaxes and bifacially shaped points are present at the site (for example, Mania 1995: Figure 5). These tools would look distinctly out of place on a British Clactonian site. These small bifacial pieces at Bilzingsleben are more in keeping with a tradition in central Europe of producing flatter, asymmetric, bifacially thinned and shaped artefacts that characterise the much later central European Micoquian (see above; Debénath and Dibble 1994; Matskevich et al. 2001). Illustrations of some of these points (Otte 2003: Figure 5) strongly resemble classic handaxes, albeit small ones. Non-classic handaxes appear to be present too. Additionally, a number of Keilmesser are illustrated (Brühl 2003: Figures 2–3) from the site. These are bifacially thinned and shaped backed knives – effectively they have bifacial working down one long cutting edge, and a flat back opposite it for holding or running a finger along. The image of a penknife blade, with its back for finger pressure would be appropriate. While not classic Acheulean handaxes in the western European sense, they are nonetheless bifacially thinned and shaped large cutting tools. I would suggest this makes the MIS 11 site at Bilzingsleben a central European Acheulean variant. This 'style' of artefact may well be evidence of a true regional character to tool behaviour in this area; it persists through the Lower Palaeolithic into the Middle Palaeolithic. There is a single example of a bone handaxe from this site as well.

Schöningen is an extraordinary site. Famous for the presence of seven wooden spears, the deposits here have also revealed a possible throwing stick used in hunting, and a series of wooden shafts with deep grooves in one end which may have acted as hafts for slotting in stone tips – the earliest composite tools in Europe (Thieme 2005). The excavators are adamant that this was hunting equipment. In addition they note that the faunal evidence is dominated by horse carcasses with cut marks. Adult males, females, and juveniles were represented. The interpretation is that this was a one-off hunting event where a single herd of horses was trapped (or ambushed) in the shallows of a lake and then killed. The spear, as a distance weapon, would have greatly facilitated this kind of hunting. After the kill came the butchery and processing of the carcasses around a series of hearths. They may even have been drying the meat if the evidence of a forked stick with extensive charring is what the excavators believe it to be. The existence of composite tools is as important as the presence of the spears. This would be the first time such tools have been described in European Lower Palaeolithic contexts, at least to my knowledge. No handaxes are present in this assemblage, but deliberately made points are, not dissimilar to those at Bilzingsleben. Many of the small tools would be of the right size for hafting, especially the points.

An anticlockwise route, taking in northern, central and southern France, Iberia, Italy and the western and eastern halves of north central Europe reveals no evidence for the perpetuation of a non-handaxe tradition that stemmed from an earlier occupation in the Lower Pleistocene or Early Middle Pleistocene (White scenario 1). Nor is there any evidence for the existence of a regionally important pattern of non-handaxe occupation in pre- or post-Anglian times (White scenario 2). But in pre- and post-Anglian contexts there are a number of very good examples of non-handaxe assemblages that fit in with White's scenarios 3 and 4. I suspect scenario 4 would describe the context of most of the non-biface assemblages discussed in this chapter so far. In some cases it is clear that raw material quality and size would have made it difficult, if not impossible, to make bifaces. In other cases, handaxes were present, but in very small numbers. In the majority of cases the sample size is just too small to be able to characterise the assemblage reliably.

Eastern Europe

Moving eastwards we come into a geographical area where, traditionally, archaeologists have postulated the existence of a non-handaxe assemblage type that conforms to one or both of the first two of Mark White's propositions. Non-handaxe sites in eastern Germany, Moravia, Slovakia and Bohemia (modern-day countries of the Czech Republic, the Slovak Republic, and northern Austria and northern Hungary) have been assigned a place in an eastern European non-handaxe cultural tradition that was ultimately derived from an East Asian or African pebble tool tradition (Warren 1951; Kretzoi and Vértes 1965; Bordes 1968). While most authorities would not nowadays accept the existence of an Old World Pebble Tool/Chopping Tool cultural province, or culture stream, the reported non-handaxe character of a number of east European assemblages has led some authorities (Kretzoi and Vértes 1965) to postulate the existence of a distinctive non-handaxe regional industrial type – the Buda industry. The small size of the artefacts in these assemblages (usually < 2–3 cms in length) are as much a hallmark of their character as is the lack of handaxes. The Buda's existence hinges on being able to demonstrate that a wide range of raw material sizes was available, but the hominins deliberately selected only the smaller clasts for knapping – thus exercising a cultural choice in raw material selection. This is addressed below.

Valoch (1995) reviews these sites and supports the non-handaxe character of a number of well-known sites which appear in the literature as key localities. Yet almost all of them are disputed by Roebroeks and van Kolfschoten (1995) on the basis of being surface finds and/or highly selected collections of artefacts coming from secondary contexts. The assemblages are almost always small. In many cases, identifying true artefacts from the background noise of natural fracture is impossible – in other words, the artefacts are geofacts. Even famous sites like Stránská Skála and Přezletice are disputed.

Vértesszölös in Hungary is the key site for the east European Buda industry (Kretzoi and Vértes 1965; Svoboda 1987; Valoch 1995; Dobosi 2003; Bridgland *et al.* 2006). Based on fauna, the site should date to MIS 13, but a number of radiometric techniques suggest a later date, MIS 10 or 9. Kretzoi and Vértes (1965) originally characterised Vértesszölös as a micro-chopper industry. More recently it has been realised that the frequency of micro-choppers is much lower than originally thought (Svoboda 1987; 1989). Jiří Svoboda has argued in favour of the existence of a 'microlithic' Lower Palaeolithic assemblage type, citing Vértesszölös, Bilzingsleben and Arago, among others, as examples. In this incarnation of the Buda phenomenon, it is again the intentional small size of the artefacts that is the main characteristic of the assemblage. A comparison of some of the key points in the argument as well as other data is presented in Table 8.5. He argues that it is an interglacial phenomenon, and implies that the non-standardised nature of these assemblages reflects a greater reliance on organic-wood technology. In the meantime, Acheulean assemblages, which show more standardisation, reflect colder climate adaptations and are more reliant on stone and bone as primary resources for tool making.

The site of Vértesszölös is a modern travertine quarry. These spring deposits built up on terrace 5 of the Pleistocene river Átalér, a tributary of the Danube. The river marks the boundary between a broad flat plain to the west, and a series of low limestone hills and dissected plateaux to the east and north. The terrace flight links the river with these limestone uplands. Springs were common along the margins of the hills. There are three localities at the site. Locality I is the main archaeological site, where a hominin occipital was discovered, and where four discrete archaeological levels were superimposed on each other within the travertine. These were temporary stable surfaces, on which hominins made and used tools during a pause in the deposition of the travertine. Climatic reconstructions suggest the hominins in the first two levels at Locality I enjoyed a warm Mediterranean-like climate. Dobosi (2003) paints a vivid picture of hominins camping in wide shallow basins in the travertine mantle, naturally walled hollows where a fire could be lit and which gave shelter from the wind. Apart from natural shelter, hominins and animals would have been drawn to the locality because of the springs. Locality II was a faunal site, with some archaeology present, Locality III was another knapping site. The artefacts from all three

Table 8.5 Comparison of selected typological, technological and raw material characteristics between Arago, Vértesszölös and Bilzingsleben

Comment	Arago (layers D–G) MIS 12	Vértesszölös MIS 13 (or 10/9)	Bilzingsleben MIS 11
Most frequently used rock raw material	Quartz	Quartz/quartzite	Flint/chert
Other rock raw materials	Chert, sandstone, quartzite, limestone, hornfels, other metamorphic and volcanic rocks	Limestone, various radiolarites and other fine grained rocks, indurated shales	Quartzite, limestone, quartz, jasper Some rocks possibly of moraines
Changes in raw material use over time?	No Differences from layer to layer, but in general proportions of use of different rock types stable over time	No Single occupation site. Although quartz most frequent, it is not most common selection for tool making	No Single occupation. Clear division. Light duty tools = flint. Heavy duty = pebbles of coarse rocks
Are cores very common?	No High percentage of crushing and debris suggest bipolar anvil technique and smashing of pebbles for quartz	No Small sized pebbles worked in very *ad-hoc* way. Smashing of pebbles also	No A few flint cores mostly worked by trimming and crushing.
Are finer raw materials worked differently?	Yes Flint shows finer working Coarser grained rocks used for chopping tools	Yes They are more intensely worked	No Flint shows no real difference in working
Are bigger flakes and cores/core tools present?	Yes Larger flakes always chosen for retouching. Some broken up to make smaller pieces which are retouched	Yes But rare. Bigger 'core tools' also rare	Yes Mostly anvils and a few bigger flakes
Average size or size range	1–4 cms	Mean length < 4cms	Most < 2cms breadth
Clear evidence of intensive working	Variable and related to different raw materials and tool types	Yes Radiolarites, especially red variety, very intensely worked	Yes

Continued

242

Table 8.5 Continued

Comment	Arago (layers D–G) MIS 12	Vértesszölös MIS 13 (or 10/9)	Bilzingsleben MIS 11
More retouching on debris rather than on flakes	Yes	In general, yes – there is more debris. No clear division between cores and cores with retouched edges	Yes
Most common tools	Side scrapers (1st) Notches, denticulates and becs (2nd) Various Upper Palaeolithic types (3rd)	Side scrapers (1st) Notches, denticulates and becs (2nd)	Scraper like edges Notches, denticulates and becs
Do different kinds of retouch (i.e. scraper + flaked flake) combine to make a tool?	Yes	Yes	Yes
Is there a clear pointed element, or tendency toward pointed artefacts made by retouch?	Yes	Yes	Yes
Are bifaces (classic + non classic) present, or any other Acheulean elements?	Yes Occasional, found in more than one layer but mostly in E	No	Yes in bone Non-classics present, also unifaces

Source: Data from Byrne (2004); Gamble (1986); Kretzoi and Vértes (1965); Mania (1995); Schreve and Bridgland (2002); Svoboda (1987; 1989); and Wilson (1988).

localities are very similar in every respect. There is no real change in tool behaviour between each of the stratigraphic levels (personal observation). Hominins returned to the same place time and again, and did the same things in the same way every time they came back. There was also bone present on the archaeological surfaces; some fragments were large > 7–8 centimetres long, some apparently worked into bone tools, but the majority of the bone was small and very fragmentary. At least some of this highly comminuted material may have been smashed by hominins.

The lithic raw material at the site can be placed into three broad groups. Some artefacts were made out of fine-grained limestone (and the occasional piece of travertine). These are mostly cores, made on angular limestone blocks and flakes. The former are rarely more than 6–7 cm in length. However, the overwhelming majority of limestone artefacts are chips (< 2 cms) and small angular chunks, in all probability natural (pers. obs.). Limestone blocks may well have been freely available as scree along the nearby limestone slopes, and as such a concentration on smaller fragments could be construed as deliberate choice on the part of the hominins. Militating against this is the sheer paucity of limestone fragments that are actually knapped – the majority are just unworked angular chunks and small blocks, accompanied by large quantities of small chips and debris. I get the impression that these are the natural background noise of the fragmented local bedrock.

The second group of artefacts are made on quartz/quartzite. Small cores and flakes are present, accompanied by very occasional larger quartzite flakes. Once again, the majority of the quartz/quartzite debitage are chips. This raw material type comes in very rounded pebble form, and was clearly brought up by hominins from the river which was transporting this lithology from further south. Smashing these pebbles on an anvil is a convenient way of creating sharp edges on the pebbles and of occasionally making small flakes. Evidence of anvil technique is clear on many of the flaked quartzite pebble cores. Anvil smashing/flaking of quartz and quartzite pebbles creates a huge quantity of chips and shatter (pers. obs. on experimental pieces), and this probably explains the large number of chips in this raw material type at the site. Accompanying the small coarser-grained quartz/quartzite pebbles were finer-grained clasts, these were knapped into cores, but many were too small to sustain extensive flaking sequences. It was these pieces which contributed to the erroneous belief that Vértesszölös was a micro-chopping tool assemblage. Their infrequency lent the small number of visually distinctive examples a spurious importance. In terms of the choice of quartz/quartzite pebble sizes available to the knappers, the range was decidedly slanted toward the smaller pebbles – or put another way, they chose the smaller sizes because that was predominantly what was available.

The third raw material group represents a diverse range of finer flint-like raw materials. These included indurated shales of varying quality, and various fine-grained radiolarites that formed within the local limestone. The shales and some of the radiolarites (brown coloured) occur in pebble form, and these too must have been brought up from the river. The green radiolarite comes from further afield and this was also brought to the site (András Markó, pers. comm.). A dark red radiolarite was particularly favoured. It is very fine-grained with good knapping properties. It outcrops some 10 kilometres to the north, but red radiolarite (and brown) is present on the slopes of the limestone hills behind the site (pers. obs.). The radiolarites were intensively worked, particularly the red variety, some cores and retouched pieces being only a few centimetres long. Such intense working is normally interpreted as reflecting raw material scarcity, but that does not seem appropriate here. A behavioural explanation is warranted, one more closely allied to raw material transport than culturally mediated size selection (Hannah Fluck, pers. comm.).

The overwhelming impression of the tool behaviour at all three Vértesszölös localities is of hominins bringing good quality stone to places where they flaked it very intensively, and made do with what else was around them. There is no conclusive evidence for deliberate selection of smaller raw materials. A range of raw material sizes was available at different points in the landscape. Some of it could be on the large side, but most of it took the form of small pebbles. The archaeological assemblage reflects this; some larger flakes and cores but the majority of the artefacts are small. The radiolarites may have been small chunks and flakes to begin with as these were being transported from further away, which is why they were so intensively knapped. It can be no coincidence that at the nearby Middle Palaeolithic site of Tata, and at an Epi-Gravettian (Upper Palaeolithic) site in the area, a persistent feature of these assemblages is the use of small pebbles (András Markó, pers. comm.; Moncel 2003).

Conclusion

Evidence for a non-handaxe tradition conforming to either of White's first two propositions is not present in post-Anglian Europe. As yet, I am unconvinced by claims for it in eastern Europe (essentially, proposition 3). More recently there have been renewed attempts to breathe life into the Buda phenomenon (see papers in Burdukiewicz and Ronen 2006). Many sites including Vértesszölös, Schöningen, and Bilzingsleben are included in a Lower Palaeolithic Microlithic Tradition (LPMT). It is clear that many of the sites discussed do indeed have assemblages dominated by small-sized tools. But again it remains to be proven that hominins exercised clear choice preferences. Big flakes and cores are a small but persistent feature of most of these sites. If cultural choice was being practised then, technically, these pieces should not be there at all. Moncel's (2003) argument that the small sizes of flake scars on larger cores reveals the preference for small flakes is refuted by her own observation that many of these are literally core tools, the small scars are retouched working edges emplaced on flake cores. Equally as damning to the idea of an east European cultural non-handaxe province, cultural tradition, or Buda/LPMT, is the sheer paucity of sites on which to build such a concept. Vértesszölös is the only Lower Palaeolithic site in Hungary, and thus in the northern part of the Carpathian Basin. There are precious few Lower Palaeolithic sites elsewhere in the region. To argue the existence of a tradition on such a small sample, and over such a wide area, seems premature.

For me, the most important thing that distinguishes these assemblages from the Clactonian is the sheer frequency of retouched tools, and the presence of intentionally made scrapers. This is very different from the pattern we see in the Clactonian in Britain. Another important difference is the presence of points made by retouch, and by combinations of different kinds of retouch (Svoboda 1987: Figures 2–7). Some may be the accidental convergence of retouched edges, while others are made by retouching one edge to accentuate a natural point (Hannah Fluck, pers. comm.). Artefact illustrations from many sites clearly show that some of these points were deliberately made as pointed implements, the point itself carefully made by retouch. The presence of these points differentiates these assemblages from the British Clactonian, which does not possess anything remotely resembling such an artefact, accidental or otherwise.

There seems good evidence for White's proposition 4, handaxe makers broadly co-exist with those responsible for the non-handaxe assemblages. Whether or not these assemblages reflect particular patterns of social learning remains far from clear. In some cases I think raw material does influence what was made, largely because it constrains choice; but again this cannot be the answer for every site. It is interesting to note how national traditions in scholarship also shape the interpretation of these sites. In some cases a belief in cultural explanations is implicit, while others play this down in favour of continuity and a gradual shift toward the Mousterian. At Bilzingsleben an assemblage with large bifacially shaped cutting tools is clearly present. Although it does not look like a western European handaxe site – it nonetheless is a manifestation of what passes for the Acheulean in central Europe in MIS 11. A differing regional tradition of archaeological interpretation has influenced our perception of the character of a particular regional manifestation of the large cutting tool phenomenon.

Clearly evident from this brief review is the importance of cave sites and long sequences of hominin occupation. These are the only real reflector of long-term change in assemblage character. They are sadly lacking in Britain.

On the whole, the MIS 11 Lower Thames Valley Clactonian sites do conform to the definition of an assemblage type. However, I do not get the sense of a similar assemblage type on mainland Europe. Non-handaxe assemblages are clearly present, but what similarities there are between them, appear to be more a result of natural convergence, stemming from similar circumstances, and the commonality of basic knapping strategies. Explaining different non-biface assemblages appears more to do with differing local circumstances, rather than persistent lines of strong inter-generational hominin learning exchanged between practitioners at geographically distant localities.

For me, the most striking thing about this whistle-stop tour of the European evidence is how dissimilar the British Clactonian is to its supposed European counterparts. Perhaps the most persistent difference is in the retouch. Continental sites show much higher proportions of retouched tools than Clactonian ones do, and there is an emphasis on points and clearly well-made side scrapers that is absent from Clactonian assemblages. Perhaps this is a reflection of the location of the British Clactonian sites since they are all found associated with rivers where abundant raw material was literally at arm's reach.

9

THE STORY SO FAR

This is an appropriate point to look back and draw many of the threads from the preceding eight chapters together. So far I have presented what is, in effect, a physical geography of the British Lower and Earlier Middle Palaeolithic. I also described the model of river terrace development pioneered by David Bridgland, and tried, where possible, to link the hominin signal from these two broad archaeological periods, to the climatically driven river terrace sequence in major British river systems. The approach has been big picture, and top-down. I followed this approach in order to simplify the relationship between Palaeolithic archaeology and Pleistocene geology. However, I have not shied away from presenting a lot of detailed site information, nor have I sidelined complexity. I hope the big picture approach has served to contextualise all this detail by making its relevance clearer.

The Clactonian is traditionally thought of as a non-handaxe assemblage type which can be interpreted culturally as a tradition. I examined this hypothesis by assessing the quality of evidence for each Clactonian site. There are no wholly undisturbed primary context Clactonian assemblages. Only the Lower Loam knapping floor at Swanscombe and the Southfleet elephant site come close. The Golf Course site at Clacton contains a small heavily disturbed primary context knapping episode, whose flintwork is interspersed with other secondary context artefacts. Technically this site therefore has two discrete assemblages. However, its non-biface character is clear, and in terms of its interpretation, a non-biface assemblage label for the whole site is appropriate. The same is true for Lion Point. The West Cliff at Clacton is too small a secondary context assemblage to be confidently interpreted as such, as are the Jaywick Sands and Butlins localities. A small number of non-classic bifaces are associated with these assemblages, and an even smaller number of classic bifaces are recorded from some of them. They in no way affect the non-handaxe character of the Lion Point and Golf Course assemblages. They merely attest to a very limited presence of handaxe makers in the vicinity, but their relationship to the makers of the cores and flakes is currently ambiguous.

The Lower Gravels in their channel at Swanscombe, and its continuation at Rickson's Pit, represent two discrete, but contemporary non-handaxe assemblages. Again, there is a limited handaxe presence in the area indicated by the presence of a few handaxes and a small handful of thinning flakes. The identification of these two sites as non-biface assemblages is not affected by their presence.

Both the Swanscombe and Clacton localities appear broadly contemporary. They both occur in MIS 11, and are associated with a single river, and a particular section of it at that, the Lower Thames Valley. I have disputed the attribution of the Golf Course site to the late Anglian or pollen zone I of MIS 11. The biological evidence suggests it is unambiguously temperate, and I see no grounds not to associate it with the artefacts from Early Temperate pollen zone IIb at the West Cliff. By implication, the other secondary context assemblages which are too small to be confidently identified as non-biface assemblages at Clacton, date to the same phase. While the basal gravel at Barnfield Pit, Swanscombe, may date to the Anglian/MIS 11 transition (I remain to be convinced), the bulk of the Lower Gravels (from eroded base to top) and the Lower Loam are all Early Temperate in age, and most likely pollen zone IIb as well.

On the basis of this broad contemporaneity, and the marked similarity in their stone tools, the non-biface assemblages of Barnfield Pit, Rickson's Pit, Lion Point, and the Golf Course merit the label assemblage type. An appropriate name for this assemblage type would be the Clactonian. Methodologically, what empowers this interpretation is the clear evidence of a single technology at each site which is consistently practised over a period of time. The variable condition of the artefacts, in geological contexts which indicate time depth support this.

Handaxe makers were present in Britain before the Clactonian, and were also (broadly) contemporary with it. This is based on the few handaxes and thinning flakes from the Clactonian sites, as well as the East Anglian evidence which suggests handaxe makers were present in the forests of Early Temperate pollen zone II north of the Thames Valley. I do not believe Barnham was ever a Clactonian site – handaxes were made during the time the cobble band was aggrading, and its excavator's variable resource exploitation model fits the observed relationship between the character of the archaeology and the changing sedimentary regime better than a simple cultural explanation.

The above implies that White's proposition 4, described in Chapter 8, is the most appropriate description, for the Clactonian situation. It consequently brings the non-handaxe assemblage type of Britain, into line with the non-handaxe assemblages of western Europe, but for which an assemblage type interpretation is not appropriate.

If the acceptance of the Clactonian as an assemblage type in Britain is warranted, does this imply it can be further interpreted as a tradition – a cultural tradition identified by specific patterns of intergeneration know-ledge which are linked to a substantiated time depth? This is more dif-ficult. The Clactonian clearly merits the label archaeological tradition, but whether this is the same as a cultural tradition remains to be seen. For the moment my instinct warns me against such an interpretation. I will explore the question of cultural learning patterns in more detail in Part II, and make the point that theorising and informed speculation apart, the stone tool data do not really help us understand this aspect of hominin life at all.

I also accepted Little Thurrock as a non-handaxe assemblage because of the size of the assemblage, although its position at the MIS 10/9 boundary is incongruous, and a non-handaxe assemblage cannot be substantiated in the equivalent downstream deposits at Purfleet. I still harbour some doubts about this assemblage. Like Jaywick Sands, and the Butlins site, the difficulty here is to establish time depth. These are sites at the very feather edge of the Thames channel, and as such we cannot be sure of the time scale they sample. At least with the Lower Gravels and the Golf Course, we could be more certain because we were sampling the full depth of deeper channel deposits.

If we cannot as yet safely interpret the Clactonian as a cultural tradition, how do we explain it? I wish I knew. I still retain sympathy with those explanations that interpret *Homo heidelbergensis* as a creature which exhibited behavioural plasticity. Its local adaptations and responses to environmental cues were situationally variable. I am equally sympathetic to those views which imply that Lower Palaeolithic hominins were in some ways tethered to predictable resources. That the Clactonian was confined to one river valley in one environment (riparian corridor in Early Temperate forest) must be taken into account, as must the sheer volume of knappable flint within that environment. The lack of handaxes on the Lower Thames flood plain might be explained by the sheer embarrassment of raw materials, which simply invalidated the need for bifaces, or any form of behaviour that involved planning depth beyond the immediate job in hand. This was an ecological niche that did not require tool behaviour to be planned out in advance. We could invoke the same explanation for Wimereux, the Le Havre littoral, the Colombanien, and the Iberian littoral sites. Away from the river valleys, the resource base was less certain, and wider-ranging groups may well have had to adapt their relationship to resources. Byrne (2004) argued that at Arago the stability of resources directly influenced the stability of the material culture signal. The conformity of practice seen in the Clactonian assemblage type could certainly accommodate such an explanation.

The few bifaces we do find at Clacton and Swanscombe could have been made by hunters returning to the valley after foraging further afield. But there is something unconvincing in this explanation. These artefacts are an important part of the puzzle. Rather than deny the existence of these handaxes, I think a more exciting challenge will be to try and understand their presence within an otherwise core and flake-dominated archaeological pattern.

It is now time to look in more detail at the Clactonian itself. In Part II I will begin to address the reasons why I do not believe interpreting the Clactonian as a cultural tradition is as yet possible. To begin with I will the explore the reasons why it was interpreted as a culture in the first place, and why that interpretation has persisted. Then I will go on to look at the stone tools that comprise this enigmatic assemblage type.

Part II

WHY AND HOW:
The Clactonian itself

10

A TWENTIETH-CENTURY CHILD

Non-handaxe assemblages from before 1900 to 1950

> We take it for granted now that science has a social responsi-
> bility. That idea would not have occurred to Newton or Gali-
> leo. They thought of science as an account of the world as it
> is, and the only responsibility they acknowledged was to
> tell the truth. The idea that science is a social enterprise is a
> modern one.
>
> (Bronowski 1973: 259)

Introduction

Whatever one's particular views on the significance of theoretical and post-processual archaeology are, it is difficult, if not impossible, to deny many of the profoundly important insights that have accrued through its critique of archaeological practice and interpretation. Theoretical archaeology is a reflection of much broader trends in social theory often lumped under the umbrella term of post-modernism, or in anthropology post-structuralism. Among its most important contributions is the recognition that knowledge, and especially scientific knowledge, are not objective and free from bias, knowledge is socially constructed and socially constituted. In other words, our understanding of the world (and of the facts that help us interpret it) are seen through the tinted spectacles of culture.

It is not that facts about the world do not exist; I think all but the most ardent post-modernists would accept they do. Rather, it is the belief that social values and cultural biases contribute to the assessment of what consti-tutes a fact; social values contribute to the evaluation of knowledge. This has led to a gulf opening up between social theorists and many scientists who still see the practice of science as a universal methodology for establishing truth which transcends any and all cultural biases. The more enlightened practitioners of science explicitly accept the social and personal dimension inherent in the acquisition of knowledge (Bronowski 1973; Gould 2000). An excellent example of this was the study of the 'science' of eugenics that was so popular among 'hard' scientists in the early part of the twentieth century (Gould 1984, for a detailed case study of this). With the benefit of hindsight, it is now only too clear that these studies were a product of social, racial, and class prejudices that were fostered and manipulated by elitist sections within the political and scientific community.

In this chapter and the next I will look in detail at the Clactonian in its historical context. What I will suggest is that our current conception of this phenomenon is a product of the way British and European Lower Palaeolithic archaeology developed throughout the late nineteenth, and twentieth centuries. As such, the Clactonian is a mirror which reflects not only the history of the development of Palaeolithic studies in British archaeology (McNabb 1996a), but also the broader changes in society and the practice of science in Britain throughout the past century.

The concept of culture was one of the earliest theoretical premises in archaeology and its use is as prevalent today as it has ever been. Like modern human cultures, ancient cultures made distinctive suites of material goods and those cultures are recognised in the archaeological record by what they made. The basic methodology of Palaeolithic archaeology has always rested on the description and classification of stone tools.

It was from distinctive patterns within assemblages of stone tools that different Palaeolithic assemblage types or cultures were originally recognised and distinguished from each other. This too has not changed much from the early days of the discipline. If some of our most basic theory has not changed, neither has much of the methodology by which stone tools are analysed. The three pillars upon which stone tool studies are founded are: presence, absence and proportion (frequency of occurrence); and we might add size to this as well. These have always been the basic analytical tools used to describe assemblages of artefacts. This is as true today as it is ever was. But this chapter and the next will show that time and again Palaeolithic archaeologists throughout the last century conflated description with explanation. *The study of the life ways of ancient humans was thus the description of their material culture.* This is not intended as a condemnation, since these researchers were simply following the common assumptions of their times, most of which would have operated at an unconscious level. It is these shared and often unspoken understandings, drawn out of the ether of everyday practice, that are the biases that render knowledge socially constituted.

Lower Palaeolithic research and the Clactonian up to the early 1920s: the industry with no name

The shared assumptions of prehistorians during the first two decades of the twentieth century revolved around a form of 'social Darwinism', a concept that had been integral to the fabric of late Victorian and early Edwardian society (Moore and Desmond 2004). All temporal change had to be inherently progressive. Change over time was a record of development and advancement in both physical and cultural evolution. This was seen as the central message of Darwin's work. (Wrongly, as it happened, Darwin never associated evolutionary change with progress, Mayr 2001.) This fitted the wish list of Victorian society to a T. But development was seen, with a few notable exceptions, as being definitely linear. Only a single line of evolving humanity was mooted, and consequently there was only a single cultural trajectory marching in lockstep with it. Progress in cultural evolution was marked by the ever increasing sophistication of stone tools.

One of the great proponents of this kind of approach was French prehistorian Gabriel de Mortillet. He asserted human development had proceeded through a series of epochs, a not uncommon idea at that time. Each epoch was a universal stage of development through which all humanity had to pass before evolving into the next. He added to and adapted his system many times during his lifetime. This is shown in Table 10.1. It began with an Eolithic period, divided into two epochs when material culture was characterised by the use of conveniently shaped natural stones which could be enhanced when necessary by retouching. This was succeeded by a Palaeolithic period beginning with an epoch in which hominins made crude handaxes which he called Chellean, succeeded by an Acheulean epoch with more advanced ones. This was then replaced by the Mousterian epoch with its emphasis on flake tools instead of handaxes.

But what was critical to de Mortillet's scheme was the belief that each epoch gave rise to the succeeding one. The sum of advances in one epoch were carried through into the next, which was then characterised by the addition of a new item of material culture, or a new and improved variation on an already existing one. Development and change were thus indigenous, cultures were evolving themselves into ever more advanced forms (Collins 1986). The debt to Darwinism here is quite obvious, although it also suggests a blend of Darwinism and Lamarckism (a pre-Darwinian interpretation of the nature of evolutionary change – animals could change

Table 10.1 The changing views on Palaeolithic classification according to Gabriel de Mortillet

De Mortillet's interpretations between 1867 and 1883		De Mortillet's interpretations, 1897	
'Palaeolithic'	Various Upper Palaeolithic cultures	Palaeolithic	Various Upper Palaeolithic cultures
	Mousterian		Mousterian
	Chellean		Acheulean
Eolithic	Thenasian		Chellean
		Eolithic	Puycournian
			Thenasian

Source: Modified after Daniel (1975). Used with permission.

aspects of their form within their own lifetime and pass that change on to the next generation). Cultural change was slow and incremental and paralleled the pace of biological change, what Robin Dennell has aptly called progressive gradualism (1990). The personal influence of de Mortillet was considerable. He was the director of the French national museum at St Germain-en-Laye. Since prehistory and France were then synonymous (a situation most French men and women would still gleefully concur with), his ideas were widely discussed and adopted. Dennell points out that de Mortillet was a reactionary socialist, rabidly anti-clerical, and his political views coloured his archaeological interpretations. He believed that human progress was inevitable and would prevail even when conservative forces within society, like the Church, acted to derail it. His unilinear developmental scheme was a clear indication (to him at least) of the reality of progressive change in nature.

Towards the end of the nineteenth century the French prehistorians had begun to provide detailed refinements to this kind of developmental sequence – especially in the study of the river gravels and river terraces where many of the Palaeolithic stone tools and handaxes were being found. Different types of tool were noted to occur in successive layers of gravel. Particularly important were the river terraces of the Somme Valley near Abbeville and Amiens. Here Victor Commont and others were producing detailed developmental sequences of progressive evolution in material culture. In other words, they were taking big picture approaches like that of de Mortillet and applying them on a smaller scale, looking for evidence of incremental progression at a local level. This was much helped by a significant advance in geological thinking. In 1909, two geologists, Albrecht Penck and Eduard Brückner, produced a framework for ordering the succession of glaciations that they believed had characterised the climate of the Pleistocene. Based upon observations of glacial moraines in the Bavarian and Austrian Alps, they suggested there had been four separate glaciations. Up to this point, many geologists (but by no means all) had held that only one had affected the earth. They called them (from the oldest to the most recent) Gunz, Mindel, Riss, and Würm. They are shown in the left-hand column of Table 10.2. The development of this system was vitally important to the chronology of the Pleistocene, and it became the framework that most Palaeolithic archaeologists would use for the next 50–60 years, fitting their locally based geological and archaeological observations into these glacial and interglacial periods.

In relating stone tools to the concept of progressive cultural evolution as expressed through developments in individual tool types (for the most part handaxes), and then relating this to the four glacial system, French prehistorians developed an important methodological tool. It was grounded in and empowered by evolutionary theory. A crude-looking tool could only come from an older deposit, a more refined-looking one had to be more

Table 10.2 Glacial–interglacial sequence and stage names of Penck and Brückner (1909) compared to other geological and archaeological sequences in use c. 1911

Penck and Brückner	Penck and Rutot	Obermaier	Boule
Würm – 4th glaciation	Various Upper Palaeolithic industries	Mousterian	Mousterian
Riss–Würm – 3rd interglacial		St Acheul in cool conditions Chelles in warm conditions	Chelles (and presumably St Acheul) in 2nd interglacial
Riss – 3rd glaciation	Mousterian	3rd glaciation	2nd glaciation
Mindel–Riss – 2nd interglacial	Chellean (and by implication St Acheul)	2nd interglacial	1st interglacial
Mindel – 2nd glaciation		2nd glaciation	
Gunz–Mindel – 1st interglacial		1st interglacial	1st glaciation – Pliocene
Gunz – 1st glaciation	Pliocene	1st glaciation	$\longrightarrow$

Note: Note blending of archaeological and geological terminology.

Source: Adapted from R. Smith (1911b). Used with permission.

recent. Because development was unilinear, specific types of tool could only be associated with one phase of development and thus with only one period within the fourfold glacial–interglacial system. Just as particular fossils allowed palaeontologists to identify and date the age of rock formations, so archaeological artefacts had become the zone fossils of the gravel deposits of the Pleistocene. Certain tool types became unique cultural markers, and this was known as the type fossil approach. Archaeology, chronology, and geology became synonymous.

Across the channel in Britain, these theoretical and methodological developments were watched with interest and envy. In the opening address to the then newly formed Prehistoric Society of East Anglia (later to become the Prehistoric Society), Dr W. Allen Sturge (Sturge 1908) extolled the virtues of the French prehistorians, lamenting the lack of similar achievements in Britain. His agenda was clear. Developmental sequences of the kind present in France must be present in Britain. It was the solemn and patriotic duty of the British Palaeolithic archaeologist to go out and find them. The honour of King and Empire were at stake! Six years earlier, the newly published guidebook to the British Museum's Palaeolithic collections had specifically bemoaned the fact that a sequence like that in Northern France was not to be had in Britain (Anonymous 1902).

But the fact that little had changed in the intervening years did not imply that work was not being carried out. Legions of amateur collectors regularly launched themselves on the gravel pits of southern England. It was more a comment on the status of the discipline itself. Most of the Palaeolithic archaeology being done in Britain during the first two decades of the twentieth century was undertaken by amateurs, and in a very non-systematic way. One collector, Henry Stopes, was reputed to have something like 80,000 implements in his collection, mostly from gravel pits in the Swanscombe–Erith area of Kent (Hinton and Kennard 1905; Oakley 1952: 282). But most of these were purchased from workmen in the gravel pits and their exact provenance was often unclear. Although amateur, many of these collectors were educated men whose contributions to the discipline were seminal (Roe 1981a; 2003). But without an equivalent of the long Somme terrace sequence, British researches lacked the integrated chronological/stratigraphic/archaeological framework against which local discoveries could be set. Many discoveries were either individual artefacts found in secondary context, or in isolated gravel layers which could not be fitted into a longer sequence. As early as 1905, Martin Hinton and Alfred S. Kennard had pointed out that such a sequence did exist – in the various deposits of the Thames Valley, but perhaps because none of the pits were known to have long unbroken sequences, progress in British Palaeolithic archaeology still lagged behind that of the Continent.

Among the first British Lower Palaeolithic excavations that could be said to be genuinely professional were those of Smith and Dewey in 1912 and 1913 (Smith and Dewey 1913; 1914). Reginald Smith was an archaeologist at the British Museum, and Henry Dewey was a geologist at the then H.M. Geological Survey. Their mission was clear-cut, to find a comparable developmental sequence to that of Commont. The place they were to choose would become one of the most famous Stone Age sites in Britain and indeed in the world: the Barnfield Pit at Swanscombe, Kent (McNabb 1996a, for a more detailed history of this). The discussions that accompanied the reading of each of their reports to the Society of Antiquaries (Anonymous 1913; 1914), are very informative. The novelty of a joint geological and archaeological venture is quite clear from the points raised in discussion, as are issues of national pride and the clear belief that a progressive unilinear sequence would be vindicated.

Not surprisingly, Smith and Dewey found what they were looking for. Their results are summarised in the right-hand column of Table 10.3. Unfortunately the complete sequence they expected to find at Barnfield was not present. What was missing were the well-made white patinated ovate handaxes that French prehistorians attributed to the St Acheul phase. These were present in the adjacent New Craylands Lane Pit. Following accepted practice, Smith and Dewey inserted the missing layers into their sequence. Their work confirmed the Somme Valley progression of Chellean bifaces (pear shaped), overlain by St Acheul (ovates), with Le Moustier (Levallois/flake tools) stratigraphically later.

Smith and Dewey were a little unsure as to what to make of the lowest horizons at Barnfield Pit, the Lower Gravels (see Figure 3.7) where human artefacts were clearly present (cores and flakes), but implements (handaxes) were lacking. The non-biface horizons were assigned to a pre-Chellean phase. In and among the cores and flakes were some elongated nodules with a minimal degree of chipping at one end. These were reminiscent of similar artefacts from the site of Strépy in Belgium. Many researchers were arguing for a number of pre-Chellean cultures in Europe, one of which was called the Strépyan, see Table 10.3. As one member of Smith and Dewey's audience in 1913 remarked:

> [Mr Dale] ... had feared that pre-Chelles implements meant eoliths, and was relieved to find that the series, though nothing but flakes, bore clear evidence of human workmanship in every case. Was it not possible that the absence of implements from the lowest gravel was accidental?
>
> (Dale 1913: 121)

Although Strépy-like tools were present, Smith and Dewey were reluctant to name the whole deposit after this culture. They sat on the fence and just called it pre-Chellean. The focus of their research was unambiguously

Table 10.3 A comparison between Smith and Dewey's 1913 material culture sequence at Barnfield Pit, and two of the classic sequences from northern France established by V. Commont in the Somme Valley, as well as the general archaeological culture sequence of the time

R. Smith's interpretation of basic Lower and Middle Palaeolithic sequence			R. Smith's interpretation of V. Commont's work at Amiens	R. Smith's interpretation of V. Commont's work at Abbeville	R. Smith and H. Dewey's interpretation of Barnfield Pit, Swanscombe
Periods named after type sites	Classification of context (and period/age)	General characteristics of implements	Site-specific character of implements	Site-specific character of implements	Site-specific character of implements
Le Moustier	Caves and rock shelters	Scrapers made on flakes worked on one face	Bluish-white flints, Levallois flakes, few handaxes		
St Acheul	River drift and alluvium	Amygdaloid (almond shaped) handaxes, finely made, often twisted edges	Acheul II. Flat ovate handaxes (limande), also pointed. Small handaxes. Lustrous white patina. Acheul I. Reddish limandes not patinated. Others grey or yellow. Small handaxes. Twisted edges common	Acheul II. One white implement Acheul I. All ovate handaxes. Unpatinated or patinated yellow or reddish-brown. Rarely with twisted edges	Absent in Barnfield but horizon of white patinated handaxes reported by workmen in pit – top of Middle Gravels and/or base Upper Loam
Chelles		Handaxes – pointed or pear-shaped, or flat and oval, coarsely flaked	Pointed handaxes some elongated, some with concave sides (ficron). Thick butts	Chelles handaxe types	Chelles type handaxes in Middle Gravels

Site	Industry / dating	Nature of material	Classification / remarks
Strépy		Nodules, usually flaked at the point – intentionally so	→
Belgium: Mesvin Maffle Reutel	Eolithic of Rutot – implies single phase (no development) found on different terraces	Nodules flaked without preconceived design plan	Early Chelles or Eolithic. Worked or retouched cortical flakes much patinated →
England: Cromer Forest-bed			No implements. Flakes in Lower Gravels. No handaxes, one implement reminiscent of Strépy type but identification of industry was vague →
Kentish plateau	Eolithic of Prestwich – dated by some to mid-Pliocene	Iron-stained natural flints with edges artificially enhanced by minimal chipping. Alternatively, natural edges used	

Note: There was too much disagreement at that time for a consensus view to emerge. The table distils the interpretations of R. A. Smith of the British Museum, Smith (1911b), and Smith and Dewey (1913). The three left-hand columns would have been familiar to most workers of the time.

directed toward the developmental sequence present in bifaces, largely because they were classifiable into stages, and a single and seamless evolution could be traced. It was difficult to plug pre-Chellean artefacts into this because there were no really diagnostic tools to classify, and nothing that looked sufficiently like the ancestor of the biface. Without its own type fossils, the pre-Chellean was difficult to study, categorise, and then compartmentalise. As the whole concern of archaeology at this time was with the description of cultural development, there wasn't really much in the Lower Gravels that you could show to be developing. The Lower Gravel industry was an anomaly because it didn't fit into the prevailing culture theory.

Inherent within a unilinear developmental sequence was the assumption that you could only expect one level of development to be present at any one time, no matter where you looked. Progressive stages were universal and exclusive. This was why Smith and Dewey expected to find a comparable sequence to the Somme Valley in Kent, and consequently did; observation matched the expectation of prevailing theory. But the writing was already beginning to appear on the wall for these kinds of explanation.

In 1912, Henri Breuil, a French cleric, and at that time gifted amateur archaeologist, published one of the most important Palaeolithic papers of the century (Breuil 1912). The Abbé Breuil was already a well-respected researcher. He had conducted ground-breaking work on the painted caves of Spain and France and was at this time concentrating most of his energies on the Upper Palaeolithic. The 1912 paper established the framework for the chronological relationship between the different Upper Palaeolithic cultures whose characteristic tools appeared in successive layers in the limestone caves of southern France and northern Spain. But in this paper, among other things, he argued that cultures were not changing themselves, i.e. evolving in situ. Rather, the cultural succession seen in the different layers in the caves was a result of new people coming into an area and occupying the same places as the previous inhabitants had done. Their material culture formed the next layer in the cave until they in turn were supplanted by newcomers with their own cultural individuality. Here Palaeolithic archaeology was responding to the beginning of changes in prehistory and in archaeology as a whole. At its height in the 1920s, this framework was called diffusionism, but before the First World War it was still a relatively novel idea (Trigger 1989: 151ff.).

It was no wonder that the old system was beginning to be questioned. A number of very substantial cracks in the unilinear one culture/one layer framework had already begun to appear, beginning with the recognition in 1909 that in a northern Spanish cave, the Grotte de Valle, two distinct Mesolithic cultures were present in the same layer. It was Breuil, along with Hugo Obermaier, who made this discovery (Daniel 1975). Obermaier is something of an unsung hero in Lower Palaeolithic research. In 1906 and

1908, he had described an alternation between handaxe and non-handaxe industries in the French Lower Palaeolithic sequence (O'Connor 2003). Obermaier's contribution to the acceptance of non-handaxe assemblages as distinct archaeological cultures in their own right is seminal, but has not been fully appreciated in English-speaking academia (Narr 1979; O'Connor 2003). The intellectual foundations of the Clactonian as a non-handaxe assemblage type had thus been laid even before Smith and Dewey began work at Barnfield Pit.

What made Breuil's 1912 interpretation palatable to his contemporaries was his retention of the idea that only one culture was present at any one time in a geological layer. His interpretation continued to reflect the social Darwinism that underpinned all social/biological interpretation; competition resulted in the strong being able to occupy a site, while the weak were summarily booted out. This highlights a point made earlier, that explanation and description were synonymous. Cultural changes were explained by new arrivals, who presumably won the battle for competitive exclusion. However, once the sequence was described and interpreted in this light, that was it. What happened to the losers? Where did the newcomers come from and how did they develop? These questions were rarely addressed. It is interesting that Smith and Dewey's work, on the eve of war, was a bit of both unilinear evolution and replacement theory. They imply that the Chellean biface makers 'mastered' their craft and in time developed the St Acheul style of biface. There were different phases of development within the St Acheul period indicating progress within the culture itself. However, the succeeding phase – the Levallois/Mousterian, with its special techniques of flint working, was so different it had to be a result of new people coming in and taking over (Smith and Dewey 1913: 202f.). This was the 'Great Game' in miniature, as cultures vied for territory and possession of sites, just as the European Powers were doing on the world stage, hastening the terrible conclusion that was the inevitable consequence of imperial evolution.

In the meantime, what about the enigmatic industry in the Lower Gravels? Here we turn to one of the most remarkable men ever to have graced British Pleistocene studies – Samuel Hazzledine Warren and his patient researches on the foreshore at Clacton-on-Sea. Although he too was an amateur, Warren already had a distinguished reputation as an archaeologist and geologist, and was proving himself to be an acute observer on the practice of science in the post-Victorian era (Oakley 1959; Spencer 1990; O'Connor 2003). By the time Warren began his work at Clacton around 1908, the area already had a history of discoveries (see Chapter 3). When Warren began his collecting along the Clacton foreshore there was, as yet, little commercial or residential development along the sea front (Picton 1912), and even as late as the early 1920s it was still possible to see the ancient river channel's bank in section in the cliff. Warren published a sketch section of this in 1923 and a photograph in 1924, and this is shown in Figure 10.1 (Warren 1923; 1924a). The modern interpretation of the geological sequence at Clacton-on-Sea is described more fully in Chapter 3. One of the more spectacular finds that he made at Clacton was the tip of a shaped wooden artefact, the so-called Clacton spear, which he discovered in 1911 (Warren 1911; Oakley *et al.* 1977; McNabb 1989).

Warren continued the task of collecting and observing the Clacton fore-shore for more than a decade before he was ready to begin publishing (although he did publish a short note in 1912 – O'Connor, pers. comm.). Why he did not publish a detailed description of the flintwork collection that he was amassing earlier is a mystery. He was very active in the archaeo-logical and palaeontological world, and his publication list up to that point was already impressive. He was in the audience when Smith and Dewey gave their paper in 1913 to the Society of Antiquaries. He even commented on it. Perhaps there was no assemblage that he could really compare his with. It would be a decade and a half before Smith and Dewey's pre-Chellean from the Swanscombe Lower Gravels would be identified as belonging to

Figure 10.1 Photograph of foreshore at Clacton-on-Sea taken by Hazzledine Warren in the 1920s.

Note: The elephant beds with Clactonian tools were found in the muds in the foreground exposed at low tide. Used with permission.

the same industry as Warren had found at Clacton. Whatever the reason, he waited until 1922 before publishing a short but detailed note on his discoveries on the Clacton foreshore.

The 1920s and 1930s – what's in a name?

The next two decades have been described by many authors as a golden age for prehistoric research, but it was a time of intense change in almost every aspect of life. The impact of the 1914–1918 War is difficult for us to imagine nowadays. Although it left the allied powers and in particular the British Empire in a position of dominance, it had also effectively brought the age of empires to a close; by 1920, the German, Austro-Hungarian, Ottoman and Russian Empires were no longer a part of the map of Europe. Many hoped that the Great War for Civilisation would pave the way for a new and better world. Although the British class system did not collapse in the aftermath of war, as had been confidently predicted, the working classes had earned on the battlefields a new sense of their own worth. In Britain, the unquestioned status quo of the old order was passing, and in its place was the rising tide of socialism.

There was also a new-found belief in science and its possibilities. Like all wars, the 1914–1918 conflict had proved a fertile crucible for techno-logical innovation. There was a sense that what science could not solve now, it would certainly do so very soon. Modernism had arrived. Scientific and technological achievement forged ahead. Take air travel, for example: by the end of the war the majority of aeroplanes were still canvas, wood and wire, but by the 1930s air travel was becoming commonplace. Flying boats carried the rich from Southampton to Cape Town; airships ferried the very rich across the Atlantic. It is perhaps no wonder, against such a back-ground, that this period has been termed the age of the 'big sequence' by writers like Dennell (1990). This was the period when long-range correl-ations between river terraces, in valleys often separated by thousands of miles and in different hemispheres, were the order of the day. The scale of prehistoric interpretation was living up to the potential of the times! However, many of the pre-war assumptions about culture and cultural development continued to underwrite and empower these long-range big-picture interpretations.

This period began auspiciously. In 1920, the Institut de Paléontologie Humaine (IPH) founded in 1910, opened the doors of its new premises in Paris. Its first director was the hugely influential Marcellin Boule (see, for example, Table 10.2) and the Abbé Breuil was now Professor of Prehistoric Ethnology (Brodrick 1963; see especially Dennell 1990). Although Breuil's main works on the Lower Palaeolithic were still a decade away, he was visit-ing Britain regularly, and by the middle to late 1920s was well acquainted with both Swanscombe and Clacton (Warren 1922; Chandler 1928–29).

Two of his early students at the IPH were Miles Burkitt who studied there in 1913–14, and Dorothy Garrod who attended his lectures in 1922–23. Burkitt went on to teach the first Palaeolithic archaeology course in Britain at Cambridge. Garrod was to become Professor of Archaeology at Cambridge – its first woman professor (Davies and Charles 1999). Breuil's contribution to the emergence of the Clactonian and its subsequent entrenchment in the archaeological consciousness cannot be over-estimated. He was a hugely powerful man, and his students and devotees also became influential. He has been described as the world's first truly international archaeologist.

In 1922, Hazzledine Warren published his first full paper on the Clactonian, describing the results of his collecting activities. The opening remarks of this paper are instructive:

> I obtained a large series [of flints] between the years 1911 and 1916, but their affinities remained an enigma to me until they were examined by the Abbé N. Breuil, who defined them as Mesvinian. When once it had been suggested, one realised that the determination was obviously correct.
>
> (Warren 1922: 1; note Warren's slip in the use of Breuil's initial, which was actually H.)

The Clactonian now had a name – except for the moment it was called the Mesvinian, and Breuil is responsible for Warren applying that name. Following the practices of the day, the stone tools were described as a 'culture'. However, as an assemblage it didn't really look like anything else discovered up to that date. The Mesvinian was discovered in Belgium by Emile Delvaux in the 1880s, and made popular by Aimé Rutot in the late 1890s (O'Connor, pers. comm.). Initially the site at Mesvin was thought to be a single layer with all the artefacts contained in it. Cores and flakes were present, some with prepared platforms (Breuil 1926). What was critically important about Warren's first Clacton paper was it gave the assemblage from Clacton-on-Sea a specific series of tool types that could be recognised at other sites, and that could be compared with pre-existing tool typologies. What Warren described were stone tools made on nodules and river cobbles of flint. They possessed one heavily flaked edge which was supposed to be an ideal cutting/chopping edge. They were called choppers or chopping tools. Some examples from Warren's paper are shown in Figure 10.2. What is more, Warren described different types of chopping tool. So now the assemblage not only had a diagnostic tool type of its own, but that tool type could be subdivided into a variety of forms. There were also distinctive types of retouched flake tools as well. This was the very stuff of classification.

Warren also postulated that the Mesvinian at Clacton may have been ancestral to the later flake-based Mousterian culture. This was a point of

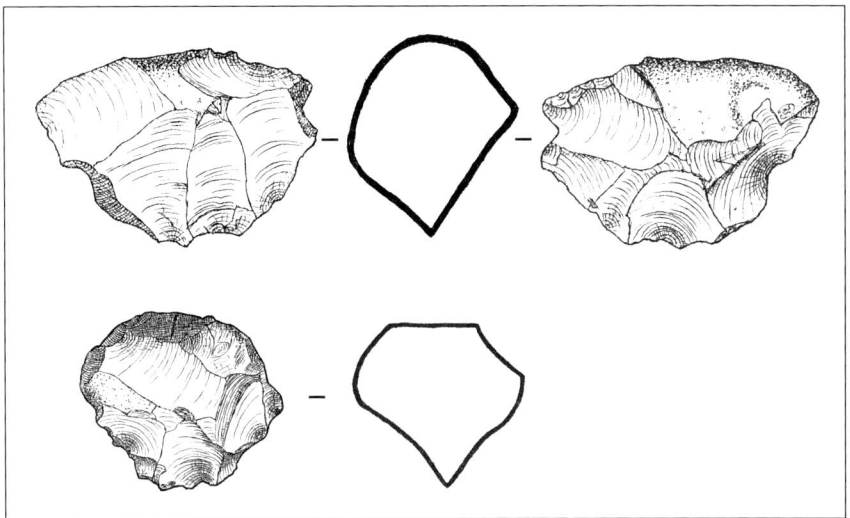

Figure 10.2 Chopping tools from Clacton-on-Sea as published by Hazzledine Warren.

Notes: Used with permission. Notice the working edge with acute angle at the bottom made by alternate flaking. Not to scale.

view he would espouse all his life. It was also one Breuil would favour, and it would be interesting to know whether it was Warren or Breuil who hit on this idea first. A final feature of Warren's first paper on Clacton is one that is highlighted by many historians of the Palaeolithic; Warren believed the makers of the Mesvinian tools and the makers of the bifaces to belong to different but *contemporary* hominin races each producing their own unique brand of material culture. Although the credit for the idea of contemporary 'racial' cultures (it would become known as parallel phyla) cannot go to Warren, he certainly takes it for being the first person to state it explicitly for the British Lower Palaeolithic. Here Warren scores one over Breuil. The Abbé was not fully converted to parallel phyla until the middle of the 1920s (see below).

Warren followed up the 1922 paper on the flint work from Clacton with two on the geology and stratigraphy of the Clacton-on-Sea deposits. His most detailed paper was in 1923, followed by a more simplified version in 1924 (Warren 1924a). The 1923 paper had specialist sections on flora, fruits, rodents, ostracods, molluscs and an elephant jaw. Warren wrote the sections on stone tools, mammals and chrono-stratigraphy himself. His interpretation of the Thames terrace stratigraphy is reproduced in Table 10.4. He argued that the Boyn Hill Terrace of the Thames (at 100ft) contained Chellean artefacts, and that the Taplow Terrace (the 50ft terrace) contained Acheulean artefacts which had developed out of the Chellean. But for part

Table 10.4 Hazzledine Warren's 1923 interpretation of the relationship between the Thames river terraces and archaeological cultural stages

Thames river terrace/phase	Assemblage type – handaxe	Assemblage type – non-handaxe	Climate
Buried channel			Temperate
Ponders End			Arctic
Late Taplow		Mousterian	
Mid Taplow	Late Acheulean	Proto-Mousterian	Colder
Early Taplow and Late Boyn Hill	Early Acheulean + late Chellean	Mesvinian	Temperate
Boyn Hill	Chellean		Warm

Note: The Late Chellean of the Late Boyn Hill Terrace phase was succeeded by the Early Acheulean of the Early Taplow Terrace phase. Although the later succeeded the former, the river ran at almost the same height for part of its course during the two phases.

Source: Modified after Warren (1923).

of its course upstream of Clacton, the deposits of the 100 ft and 50 ft terrace were at very nearly the same height. In addition, the Acheulean in Britain was contemporary with the Mesvinian of Clacton-on-Sea. So Warren provided a relative age, cultural placement and stratigraphic position for his industry in relation to other contemporary stone tool cultures; he then linked those culture streams to independently evolving contemporary racial lineages.

Breuil had been an intermittent visitor to Britain since 1911, and by the time he took up his position in the IPH he was a well-known figure in the British Palaeolithic scene. Brodrick (1963) asserts that it was his position at the Institute that led him to take a keener interest in Lower Palaeolithic research. Up until 1926, however, he did not publish any major observations on the British or Northern French Lower Palaeolithic sequences. It was in this year that he was finally to make a full conversion to parallel phyla (Daniel 1975). Parallel phyla did not immediately sweep away unilinear explanations for culture change; many people resisted strongly (Warren 1924b, for a good summary of the different systems). Daniel also notes that Dorothy Garrod did not completely accept it until 1928 when she gave her presidential address to the Prehistoric Society. In 1926, Breuil signalled his own (initially reluctant?) acceptance of parallel phyla with a paper on the relationship between the Levallois phenomenon, the Mousterian, and biface assemblages. It illustrates some very important points about parallel phyla as an interpretative framework:

- The scheme was still time-progressive. Cultures went through a process of internal evolution as they developed via incremental change.

270

- Each such increment/stage still had its own unique developmental signature, in other words, its own stone tool type fossil.
- By definition, stages were confined to specific sedimentary units, so you could still use individual type fossils to date a layer or fix its stratigraphic position in a sequence (and vice versa).
- Sudden change in archaeological cultures from one geological layer to the next still meant cultural replacement.

In this 1926 paper, Breuil argued that by the beginning of the Würm glaciation (see Figure 3.3, Table 10.2) the Levallois and biface culture streams had fused together to form a new cultural entity, the 'Combe Capelle' type which was characterised by Levallois and biface elements. Explanations of this kind went a long way towards plugging some of the theoretical holes in diffusionist-like interpretations. It provided a mechanism to show how cultures could change, and new cultures appear at sites and in individual layers. Those cultures (i.e. geological layers) which had diagnostic tool types from a number of different cultural phyla were *hybrids*, the products of cultural intermixing, while clear-cut differences between layers were seen as examples of replacement through migration and diffusion. This is an example of the evolution of theory itself, as evidence and explanation were adapted to fit each other.

But when was the name Clactonian first applied? The Mesvinian is mentioned in a footnote to the 1926 Breuil paper. He believed it to be ancestral to the Levallois culture stream. But he now confined the term to the upper parts of the original Belgian Mesvin site. Here were found flakes with proto-Levallois-like faceting and preparation of their platforms. He stated that the lower part of the site (originally unrecognised as a distinct unit) contained a very different-looking industry that was more similar to Clacton-on-Sea (Breuil 1926: 178), *but he did not coin the term Clactonian anywhere in that paper*. That honour goes squarely to Hazzledine Warren who in response to Breuil's footnote added a footnote of his own to a paper that he had already written earlier that year and was proof reading:

> Professor Breuil has stated that the original Mesvinian includes two stages, and he proposes to confine the term to the later stage. The Clacton industry is comparable with the earlier stage for which the name of Clactonian might be adopted.
>
> (Warren 1926: 47)

The main theme of Warren's 1926 paper was the deplorable state of Palaeolithic terminology at that time. The proliferation of cultural labels, unaccompanied by any form of standardised system, was beginning to create difficulties for those who studied the Lower Palaeolithic; worse, it was also beginning to create a rift between geology and archaeology (McNabb 1996a: 38f.).

In 1929, several other Clactonian loose ends were tied up. R. H. Chandler was another of the legion of amateur geologists and archaeologists who spent much of their time stalking the gravel pits of southern England. He was intimately familiar with the Dartford/Swanscombe pits and used to visit the Barnfield Pit at Swanscombe 20 to 30 times a year (Chandler 1942). In 1925, he took the Abbé Breuil around the Barnfield Pit. The party observed the stratigraphy and collected artefacts from the gravels. The Abbé visited again in 1928. As they discussed their finds in the pit he shared his views with the party: 'On this visit the Abbé told me he had found these characteristic flakes in other localities, that he considered them a distinct industry, and, as yet, the industry was without a name' (Chandler 1928–29: 81). This is an interesting passage; either Breuil did not know about Warren's new label (already at least a year old), or at this point he did not think it applicable to what he thought the industry really was. Additionally, it shows that in 1928 Breuil was considering the idea of a cultural entity whose type fossil was a particularly striking looking flake. Chandler (ibid.: 81f. and footnotes) notes that Breuil adopted the name Clactonian in 1929 but considered it a flake-based assemblage type; there were no deliberately made choppers or core tools, only cores for flakes. Chandler, like Warren, did not accept Breuil's interpretation. It is to their credit that they stuck to their guns despite the great man's opposition. Just as Warren had done earlier, Chandler provided a series of distinctive core tool types for his Clactonian at Swanscombe (Chandler 1931), and at the same time consolidated his interpretation by recognising the assemblage in the lowest gravels at Rickson's Pit as being Clactonian as well. Chandler's 1928–29 paper is also important as it was the first time anybody had associated the Lower Gravels at Swanscombe with the newly named Clactonian. Smith and Dewey's collection of pre-Chellean could now be fitted into the expanding framework. Chandler allied himself with the parallel phyla camp and at the same time supported Warren in noting how dissimilar the Clactonian was to the biface phylum and how more like the later Mousterian it was.

One other feature of Chandler's paper is that he split the Clactonian in the Lower Gravels into two groups. One series of artefacts were very worn and rolled-looking and had striations on their surfaces. He suggested that these artefacts had been damaged by glacial action. Since the bulk of his finds were fresh and unstriated, he came to the conclusion that the rolled and striated artefacts were much older than the fresher ones. These more worn artefacts must have been made during a previous interglacial, scratched by the ice of the following glaciation and then deposited in the succeeding interglacial's sediments. More advanced Clactonian knappers, responsible for the unscratched artefacts lived in this later interglacial. In consequence of this, Chandler was the first British author to suggest a time depth for the

Clactonian in print, though this may have been a part of Breuil's thinking already. There is a footnote in Chandler's 1928–29 paper that asserts that Breuil had a similar idea, suggesting the derived series was Mindel in age (see Table 10.2), and the unstriated fresh series Mindel–Riss in age. Chandler, on the other hand, dated the manufacture of the derived series (i.e. the worn artefacts) to the Gunz–Mindel interglacial.

To the best of my knowledge, Chandler (1928–29) also gets the credit for being the first researcher to specifically list the features on flakes that would come to be taken as characterising Clactonian flakes (see Chapter 12). Although Warren does describe these in earlier and later publications, he never placed as much emphasis on them because he believed the Clactonian was mostly characterised by the distinctive chopping tools and core tools made on nodules. Warren also made it clear that these were features that could be found on any hard hammer flake. How much of this was Chandler's own belief, or whether it came from Breuil, is unclear. Probably this was part of the ether of debate.

If the 1920s gave the Clactonian a name as well as a personality, then the 1930s would see it grow into maturity as a world-wide phenomenon, once again as a result of Breuil, who by now was at the height of his fame. But the influence of the Abbé was even more far-reaching. Palaeolithic teaching in Cambridge was now firmly established under Miles Burkitt, who was promoting a pro-Breuil approach to the interpretation of pre-historic sequences. Burkitt had been responsible for Breuil's visit to South Africa in 1925 from which he had returned to the IPH with 3,800 kilos of stone tools for their museum, packed into 54 crates (Brodrick 1963: 149f.). He had identified Clacton-like flakes in the terraces of the Vaal river and elsewhere. The Abbé's biographer, Broderick (1963), makes it abundantly clear that had such a thing as frequent flyer points existed, then this peripatetic cleric would have been able to buy his own aircraft. In 1932, Chandler published his third paper on Swanscombe, in which he described the extent of the Abbé's discoveries of Clactonian; it was present in the Valley of the Kings in Egypt, in the Sahara, in the gravels of the Vaal river, in the 40 m terrace of the Somme, in the Thames Valley and at Clacton in England, as well as Weimar in Germany, Santander in Spain and in Belgium too. All of this was rooted in Breuil's belief that a non-handaxe assemblage could be identified on the basis of a particular stone tool type, namely large flakes with prominent percussion features (described in more detail in Chapter 12). Such flakes were easy to recognise. I have no doubt the simplicity of recognition contributed enormously to the popularity and easy acceptance of Breuil's cultural views.

Between 1931 and 1934, Breuil and L. Koslowski published a detailed archaeo-stratigraphy of the river terraces of northern France, Belgium, and southern England (Breuil and Koslowski 1931; 1932; 1934). Breuil also published a huge paper on the Clactonian itself (Breuil 1932). He listed the features that Chandler had described as characterising a Clactonian flake, adding a few more of his own. Even if he was not the first to describe these, it is the authority of Breuil that firmly fixes them in the consciousness of archaeologists from this point on. Breuil also promoted the concept of Clactonian flakes as being made by the block-on-block, or direct anvil technique. The exaggerated percussion features of a Clactonian flake had to be explained somehow. Breuil believed they were best reproduced, experimentally, by swinging blocks of flint against a rock firmly fixed on the ground. Again, even if he was not the first to say this, the impact of this 1932 paper ensured that the concept became entrenched in the Clactonian literature from this point on. These works, as Dennell (1990) has pointed out, set the agenda for the 1930s and the 1940s. Breuil deliberately promoted a view of slow and minutely incremental change because it was very much in accord with his own conservative and orthodox Catholic views. One of the main reasons why the IPH was set up in the first place was to 'make Darwin safe' for the Catholic right wing. Change was not sudden and dramatic, it was slow and sedate – the contemporary status quo need not be threatened by evidence of a past in which violent upheavals were part of the natural order. The wealthy elite need not fear the inevitability of Bolshevik-like revolts because they were not a natural consequence of progressive change (ibid.).

Breuil's scheme is laid out in Table 10.5. His views had evolved since 1926. The 1932 scheme was far more detailed, with a clearer idea of the kinds of cultural intermixing that occurred between different culture streams in their later developmental phases. As noted earlier, this intermixing of different cultures was an important theoretical development. For Breuil, the engine driving cultural change/fusion was climate. At the beginning of each glacial episode in Europe, the faunas and the hominins would flee south. Here groups from different culture streams would intermingle – different phyla would acculturate. When the glaciers retreated and the humans and faunas migrated north again, each new interglacial phase was populated by humans with a modified culture. In the interglacial, each new hybrid culture would then evolve along its own lines, as well as acculturate with other phyla.

Breuil placed all the big striated flakes from Chandler's derived Lower Gravels series in his Clactonian I phase which was associated with the first warm fauna. This was the Gunz–Mindel interglacial. The Clactonian then underwent a profound development during the Mindel glacial phase achieving its most developed form in the succeeding interglacial. This was the Clactonian proper – of Warren, Smith and Dewey, and Chandler's fresh series. In some parts of Europe (southern France and northern Spain), it was the destiny of the Clactonian to evolve into a rather enigmatic non-biface phenomenon called the Languedocian. In other areas, through the re-defined Mesvinian, the Clactonian would evolve into the Levallois.

Table 10.5 Alternative chrono-stratigraphic sequences produced by the Abbé Breuil in the 1930s

Geological stage name	Geological stage number	Breuil 1932	Breuil 1939
Würm	4th glaciation	Levallois VI–VII	Levallois IV–VII, Levallois V–VII
Riss–Würm	3rd interglacial	Languedocian Acheulean VI–VII; Levallois V, Levallois IV, Levallois III	?Acheulean VI–VII; ?Levallois IV, ?Levallois III; Pre-Würm (cold?)
Riss	3rd glaciation		Acheulean V, Acheulean IV, ?Acheulean III; Levallois II, Levallois I; ?Clactonian II or III
Mindel–Riss	2nd interglacial	Clactonian II Acheulean I–V; Levallois I–II, Mesvinian	?Clactonian II or III
Mindel	2nd glaciation		Acheulean II, Acheulean II, Acheulean I
Gunz–Mindel	1st interglacial	Clactonian I Abbevillean I	Acheulean I; Abbevillean, Abbevillean } Pre-Mindel; Clactonian I, Clactonian I
Gunz	1st glaciation		

Notes: Cultural labels in italics indicate derived assemblages. Notice how in the earlier scheme the crucible of cultural development is mostly in the interglacials, whereas in the later one it is mostly in the glacial periods.

Elsewhere it would evolve into the Mousterian through the Tayacian. As Trigger (1989) has pointed out, the goal of prehistoric research in the 1920s and 1930s was the mapping, in time and space, of these branching cultural variants. The whole project came to be labelled by later researchers as culture-history. The contemporary political agendas of the 1920s and 1930s are often characterised as being obsessed by questions of ethnicity and race (Pringle 2006). The culture-historical project was a reflection of that broader social angst, but expressed through archaeological theory.

From today's perspective, it is clearly an unworkable system, at the very least, too big and too complicated. Flaws were apparent, but glossed over. For example, while the Clactonian goes through only two stages of development up to the Mindel–Riss interglacial, the Acheulean stage experiences five developmental phases in just one interglacial (Table 10.5). This is an excellent example of force fitting. Breuil needed slow incremental change, especially in something as complicated as the evolution of biface form. The Chellean was crude and simple – therefore it was early and so contemporary with the pre-Mindel Clactonian I. The final phases of the Acheulean (VI and VII) were the Micoquian, and since they were interspersed with advanced Levallois, as well as acculturating with the Tayacian, they had to be Riss–Würm in age. Since the Acheulean appeared contemporary with the Clactonian, all five pre-Micoquian Acheulean stages were lumped in the second interglacial. Anne O'Connor (pers. comm.) suggests that parallel phyla had been greeted with horror by many geologists in the middle to late 1920s, as it meant the one zone/one type fossil correlation was unworkable. However, many geologists were relieved by Breuil's apparently detailed correlations describing which tool types belonged to which cultural stream. The whole edifice seemed to have a crisp scientific feel to it. But this belied a very profound problem with the basics of the system. Breuil never really provided precise definitions. Identification was based on experience and intuition, in other words, it was contextually subjective. The ambiguities in the system promoted by the most powerful prehistorian in the world are nicely highlighted by a story recounted by Desmond Collins:

> Lacaille showed Breuil some Levallois flakes from the Middle Thames area and Breuil proceeded to attribute each one to a stated Levallosian stage . . . Lacaille . . . showed him the same flakes a few years later. Breuil attributed them again, but with entirely different results. When this was pointed out he replied wittily, 'Ah! But science has advanced since then!'
>
> (Collins 1986: 36)

The 'idea' of a Clactonian was important to the scholars of the 1920s and 1930s because it exactly fitted expectations. Breuil used it as the root for many of his culture streams. The Clactonian was simple and crude; it was precisely the kind of acorn great oaks could grow from. This probably lies behind Breuil's insistence on its being a flake-based industry rather than a core tool one. Choppers would be difficult to explain away – there was little evidence for internal evolution within this category of artefact. They were not present in the flake-based Mousterian. The fact that replacement theory, and progressive incremental evolution in material culture were still part of these schemes makes it quite clear that social Darwinism still underpinned 1930s interpretation. A superb example of this is given in the following quote:

> During the Palaeolithic periods some tools and weapons decreased in numbers, while others greatly increased. The alteration of dominant form was attended by the gradual evolution from one style to another, which provides a most interesting instance of descent with modification.
>
> (Dewey 1932: 40)

It will be recalled that it was during the 1930s that the fledgling science of genetics vindicated natural selection as the mechanism behind Mendelian inheritance (Mayr 2001). This must have provided a considerable vote of confidence for the broadest applications of Darwin's views.

So, by the 1930s, the concept of a habitual non-biface-making tradition was firmly rooted into the consciousness of British and European prehistorians. A considerable public relations opportunity for the Clactonian was afforded by the first International Congress of Prehistoric and Proto-historic Sciences, held in London in 1932. Both Warren and Henry Dewey gave papers promoting the Clactonian to the assembled prehistorians of the world. The idea of the Clactonian was far too useful a concept to question, even had prevailing method and theory allowed any latitude for dissent. With each new variation on Breuil's scheme that appeared (Breuil 1939, and Table 10.5), the conceptual necessity of the Clactonian became ever more deeply ingrained. No doubt this was especially true for British prehistorians since it was the only indigenous pre-modern human culture the British had – a poor show for a nation who ruled so much of the globe.

The new-found importance of the Clactonian prompted a new phase of investigations into Clactonian sites, but now collecting was no longer good enough. The order of the day was controlled excavation with the recovery of artefacts and fauna under strict conditions. The main events of the 1930s are outlined in the Table 10.6. In this new phase of home-grown British fieldwork and interpretation, the internationalist views of Breuil were downplayed in favour of more locally significant sequences. In 1936, a critically important paper was published by William King and Kenneth Oakley. It attempted to establish an integrated chrono-stratigraphic sequence

Table 10.6 Selective overview of Lower Palaeolithic work in the 1930s as relevant to the Clactonian

Date	Collecting activities	Excavation	Interpretative
1934	Collecting activities by many people	Oakley and Leakey dig at Jaywick Sands Louis Leakey at Rickson's Pit	
1935	Alvan Marston finds 1st piece Swanscombe skull	New Clactonian site dug by T. T. Paterson at	
1936	Alvan Marston finds 2nd piece Swanscombe skull	Barnham St Gregory	Major reinterpretation of Thames stratigraphy by King and Oakley
1937		Molly Cotton digs for Swanscombe Committee at Barnfield	Jaywick Sands published with locally significant Clactonian interpretation
1938	Collecting activities by many people		Swanscombe Committee report published
1939			Breuil's revised Somme Valley chrono-stratigraphic cultural sequence

for the whole of the Lower and Middle Thames Valley, combining archaeology with other lines of evidence.

The sequence was in part derived from Kenneth Oakley's excavations at Jaywick Sands, Clacton, with Mary Leakey in 1934 (Oakley and Leakey 1937). It was the insights from the Jaywick Sands excavations that led to the assignment of formal stage names to the various Clactonian deposits. The sequence is presented in Table 10.7. The Swanscombe Lower Gravels contained some elements of Clactonian I, the glacially striated material of Chandler. Also present in the Lower Gravels were unstriated cores and flakes, Chandler's fresh series. These were identified as Clactonian IIa which was contemporary with the gravel and ancestral to the slightly more refined Clactonian IIb of Jaywick Sands and Warren's foreshore collections from the West Cliff and Lion Point. The site of High Lodge, near Mildenhall in Suffolk had very advanced-looking scrapers associated with cores and flakes but no handaxes. Oakley considered this to be an advanced form of Clactonian, and labelled it Clactonian III. Other sites that would be placed in Clactonian III were Stoke Newington in London, and Caddington in Bedfordshire (White 2000).

Notice that Table 10.7 has a Clactonian IV. It is not mentioned elsewhere in the 1937 paper, and I have never seen another reference to it. It is almost certainly a stage that was required by the sequence but for which no evi-

Table 10.7 Kenneth Oakley's sequence for cultural development within the Clactonian, proposed in 1937, mapped on to Breuil's scheme for the Levallois and the Acheulean

	Mousterian	Levallosian VI–VII
Acheulean VI–VII	Clactonian IV	Levalloisian III–V
Acheulean III–V	Clactonian III	Levallosian I–II
Acheulean III (France only)	Clactonian IIB	Proto-Levalloisian
Acheulean II	Clactonian IIA	
Acheulean I–II	Clactonian I	
Abbevillean	Clactonian I ?	

Note: Notice how the requirement of having comparable stages in independently evolving cultural streams results in a possible lengthening of the period of Clactonian I, and the insertion of a Clactonian IV.

dence existed, you couldn't have an empty period in an evolving cultural branch – just like nature, culture history abhorred a vacuum. I wonder what the archaeologists of the day thought of it; it is a good example of inherent difficulties in the whole culture-history paradigm being apparent at the time. The influence of the 1936 King and Oakley paper, and the 1937 Oakley and Leakey paper, cannot be over-emphasised. The same is true of Kenneth Oakley himself. In the 1930s, this scientist and archaeologist based in the British Museum (Natural History) at South Kensington was a rising star – he would become the British equivalent of the Abbé Breuil. He championed the Clactonian, and like Breuil he too believed it to be a flake-based culture.

Two important events gave a further impetus to the idea of an independent Clactonian culture. The first was the discovery of a new Clactonian site at Barnham St Gregory in Suffolk. It was excavated by T. T. Paterson from Cambridge, whom Dennell (1990) suggests was a confirmed fan of the Abbé. If this is so, he certainly felt no compunction to follow his lead. Paterson's PhD thesis (Paterson 1942) and other publications (1940–41; 1940; 1945) promoted a unique interpretation of parallel phyla and the independent Clactonian culture stream. Even though Paterson promoted his own individualistic take on culture-history, the power of the common assumptions of the day were evident in the reliance on social Darwinism, cultural fusions, and time-progressive cultural development, all used to underpin the system. The second big boost to the Clactonian, albeit an indirect one, was the discovery of a partial skull in Barnfield Pit, Swanscombe. On 29 June 1935, Alvan T. Marston, a dentist and diligent amateur collector from Clapham in London, had found a hominin occipital bone (back of the skull) in the Upper Middle Gravels (Figure 3.7). In 1936, he found a second portion of the skull, a left parietal (side) which refitted to the occipital (see Figure 1.9). The discovery of these two portions of the Swanscombe Skull focused the attention of the world on the Barnfield Pit, on its stratigraphic sequence, and on its archaeological succession (McNabb 1996a).

At Marston's request, an academic committee was formed by the Royal Anthropological Institute to study the skull and the archaeology of the site. The names of the members of the Swanscombe Committee included many of the most noted scientists of the day and the report itself set the official British party line on the stratigraphy of Swanscombe and the Lower Palaeolithic for the next 30 years (Swanscombe Committee 1938). Here Oakley's influence was never more apparent. He was the principal organiser of the project. The age of the skull, its broader geological context, and the lithic industries of the Barnfield Pit were all set into the framework he established with his 1936 and 1937 papers.

Conclusion

Throughout this chapter I have made a point of trying to show how theoretical beliefs constantly manipulated the perception of the Clactonian. The one theme that persisted throughout the first half of the century was the progressive nature of change and its relation to the passage of time. There was an inevitability to progress. It was rooted in a social Darwinist view of life. I have argued elsewhere (McNabb 1996a) that this acted as a *conceptual lock* which influenced all thinking on Lower Palaeolithic cultural interpretation. Given the circularity created by the intimate link between method and theory, it is not surprising that this conceptual lock held a powerful control over Palaeolithic archaeologists of the day. The Clactonian as a non-handaxe culture was exactly what most of the later Palaeolithic cultures needed at the root of their developmental trees. The conceptual lock provided no latitude to criticise the status of the Clactonian. If it wasn't a culture, then what else could it be? The orthodoxy of the day only allowed for cultural interpretations. Culture-history quite clearly reflected the broader political and social undercurrent of the times, particularly those concerned with racial and ethnic differences; after all, the Clactonian as a cultural construct was about difference.

11

COMING OF AGE IN THE BRAVE NEW WORLD

The Clactonian from the 1950s to the present

[T]heory is always, and must be, coloured by social and psychological biases of surrounding culture; we have no access to utterly objective observation or universally unambiguous knowledge.

(Gould 1996: 420)

Introduction

As the armies of the Soviet Union from the east, and the Allies from the west, made their way across Nazi-held Europe, the full scale of the fascist extermination programme was revealed to a horrified world. Death camp after death camp told the same story. But it was not only the Jews who were targeted for destruction. Anyone who did not fit the Nazi criteria of racial and social purity was eligible for extermination: gypsies, intellectuals, Slavic and other East European peoples, Catholics, those deemed mentally ill. At Nuremburg it became apparent just how much science and academia had contributed to the intellectual justification underpinning racial purity. Deeply implicated was the *Ahnenerbe* (Pringle 2006), the SS Ancestral Heritage foundation which had employed respected archaeologists to establish the deep roots of Aryan ethnic culture and racial distinctiveness.

Central to this ideology was the kind of social Darwinism that had been the foundation on which Prehistoric culture-history was predicated. The Nazi machine subverted archaeology and anthropology to show that race and society were one, and that indigenous Aryan cultural progress was an inevitable result of innate superiority. In post-war archaeology the result of this was a backlash against culture-history and the whole project of using archaeology to establish difference. Although the concept of progressive gradualism was still present in post-war Palaeolithic archaeology, the writing of cultural histories that documented an inevitable progression towards Darwinian-like perfection fell out of favour.

The late 1940s and early 1950s were a period of profound political and social change rooted in a deep uncertainty about the times and the future. Like the First World War, the Second had been a source of technological innovation. The post-war era saw an explosion of scientific achievement and, more so than ever before, the incorporation of such progress into the everyday lives of ordinary people. This was the first phase of the mass-communications revolution. In 1945, the jet engine was a novelty, but in just 15 years it would be mundane. Ever more powerful rockets would initiate the space age by 1957; televisions, refrigerators, and washing machines would be common by 1960; this was the era when people began to accept the labour-saving electric gadget. As television became more common, it brought the world into people's homes. Science and invention could now be seen to be working for the direct benefit of ordinary lives.

It is unlikely that the optimism of the post-war American middle classes (Trigger 1989) was shared by their British and European counterparts. The physical and economic infra-structure of American society had not been bombed out of existence as it had in Europe. Politically, this was a difficult era as science also fuelled the upwardly spiralling arms race between East and West. If the Cold War suddenly turned hot, most Europeans were only too aware that any land battles would be fought on European, not American, soil. Europe would face a new kind of holocaust. If the 1940s produced the first scientific generation, they grew up in the 1950s against a background of gloom and uncertainty. Science fiction is often used as a weathervane to reflect the mood of the times. The sci-fi movies of the 1950s were a catalogue of themes on the premise of Earth invaded/destroyed/threatened/doomed. Often the proliferation of atomic weaponry was the cause of the planet's troubles; doom merchants cheerfully predicted the end of the world.

Other changes were in the air too. The immediate post-war period saw an upsurge in nationalism and in popular movements dedicated to winning freedom for indigenous peoples from imperial control. The spirit of independence was abroad. With the exception of America, the victors of the Second World War emerged with their economies shattered and unemployment high. The cost of victory had been expensive and the allies owed vast debts to America. To use an old saying, in the new world order, the New World gave the orders. Little wonder that indigenous peoples in the colonies of the French and British Empires sensed their time was coming.

The post-war era – the 1940s and 1950s

In 1951, Hazzledine Warren published his definitive paper on the flint assemblage from Clacton-on-Sea. It was based on a lecture he gave to the Geologists' Association in 1950 on receipt of its prestigious Henry Stopes Medal. This was in recognition of a lifetime's achievement in geology and Palaeolithic archaeology and it was a singular honour. Much of the paper reaffirmed many of his earlier opinions. He maintained his belief that the

Clactonian was a nodule tool/core tool assemblage type and not merely a flake and core-based one as Breuil and Oakley still believed. But there were changes now. The big rolled and striated flakes formerly attributed to the Clactonian I phase were now just big rolled flakes, and the whole question of progressive development within the Clactonian had been dropped. He also questioned the uniqueness of the concept of the typical Clactonian flake advocated by Breuil. These were the features of any hard hammer-struck flake. Baden-Powell (1949) made the same argument but from an experimental perspective.

Part of the reason for Warren's insistence on nodule tools as deliberately made tools, was his rather unique view on what represented a flake core. Cores, he believed, were only characterised by parallel flaking. This is illustrated in Figure 11.1 (see also Chapter 12). Cores could also be worked by different sequences of parallel flaking which cross-cut each other (Warren 1932; 1934; 1951). What he called his nodule tools and chopping tools were made by alternate flaking (Figure 10.2), so they had an acute flaking angle and consequently they looked very different – very intentional. Parallel flaking produced angles between the platform and the flaking face that were wide and did not look like the cutting edge of a tool.

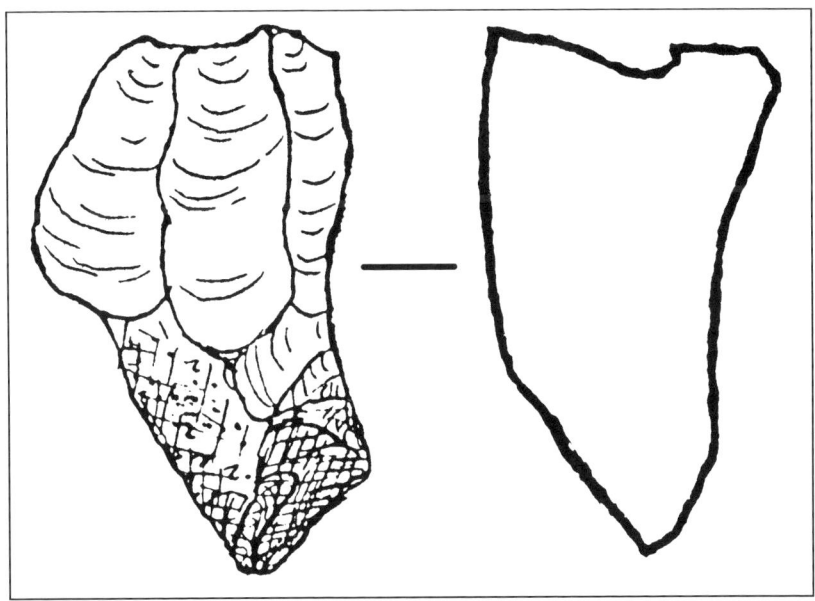

Figure 11.1 A core from Clacton-on-Sea as published by Hazzledine Warren.

Note: Note the three parallel scars, and more obtuse flaking angle, that for Warren distinguished this artefact from a deliberately made core-tool as in Figure 10.2. Used with permission.

Other changes in archaeological thinking had given Warren's views on the Clactonian a major boost, changes which he must have found deeply satisfying. In 1948, the American Hallam L. Movius Jnr published a monograph (Movius 1948b) on the Palaeolithic cultures of South-East Asia. This work was to establish the presence of a chopper/chopping tool culture zone east of a particular line that became known as the Movius Line. To the east were cultures which did not make handaxes, only chopping tools. To the west of this was the Acheulean culture area. Here, the main tool type made was the handaxe. This gave non-handaxe industries a global perspective. In 1951, Louis Leakey published the first volume of his Olduvai Gorge researches. The significance of this was it traced a *single and unbroken evolution* from chopping tools in the basal sediments of Olduvai Gorge into the Abbevillean and then the Acheulean, which subsequently underwent its own gradual development and refinement.

The interpretive sequence was an interesting mix of old and new ideas. The sequence was unilinear, it showed internal progressive development and was consequently rooted in progressive gradualism. But at the same time it rejected parallel phyla paying no heed to the Eurocentric interpretation Breuil and his supporters were advocating (Leakey 1934; 1951). What made Leakey's work believable was that he could demonstrate the whole developmental sequence from beginning to end *in the successive layers of one site*. He was also arguing that the pre-Abbevillean phase was very old indeed. He dated the initial Acheulean phases to the early Mindel. So, the internal evolution from chopping tools to Abbevillean handaxes to Acheulean handaxes must have been very much older again. Nothing quite comparable had been seen at a European site. One highly contentious implication of all this was that Africa was the home of tool-making hominins, reviving an original prediction by Darwin (1879) which had fallen out of fashion.

Warren was quick to seize on the implications of this, as his 1950 lecture shows. Leakey had been promoting these ideas for many years (see, for example, Leakey 1934) but the Second World War had delayed publication of the work at Olduvai (Dennell 1990). Warren allied the Clactonian squarely with the pebble tool cultures to the east of the Movius Line. Insightfully, he provided an explanation for the differences between the Clactonian and the Asian chopping tools. To the east of the Movius line, knappers had to use rounded river cobbles made from hard rock types. The Clacton knappers had to adapt to the irregularly shaped flint nodules found in European rivers. Warren (as usual) was many years ahead of his contemporaries in arguing that raw material could affect assemblage character. Explanations of this kind would only become a major part of research agendas during the last two decades of the twentieth century. Curiously, nobody really questioned what this outpost of the great chopper–chopping tool tradition was doing at the very western edge of the Old World.

The effect of Leakey's Olduvai volume is difficult for us to gauge today, though of course his views were not accepted by everyone. (The scandal of his divorce from the daughter of a Cambridge professor, and subsequent marriage to Mary Nichol, undoubtedly set many of the British archaeological establishment against him. He had dug in the lower gravels at Rickson's Pit, Swanscombe, in 1934, and found a Clactonian assemblage, but his work was never published and was rarely mentioned by other British archaeologists.) The Olduvai Gorge sequence would have been theoretically unacceptable to many European scholars as it cut to the very heart of Eurocentrism. In the years prior to the First World War, many scholars believed implicitly that Europe was the home of the human race. This in part explains the ready acceptance of Piltdown by the English scientific community. What could be more sensible than the origin of Europeans in Sussex? By the end of the 1930s debate had begin to polarise between those like Leakey who followed Darwin in advocating an African home for genus *Homo*, and those who advocated an Asian origin. So serious a possibility was this latter, that the American Museum of Natural History financed the Roy Chapman Andrews expeditions during the 1920s, with the express aim of finding evidence of the cradle of humanity in central Asia (Gallenkamp 2001). Leakey's discoveries provided powerful support for the Africanists.

At least Eurocentrics could take comfort from the fact that it was in Europe that the major advances in cultural evolution had subsequently been played out. The evolving parallel phyla and their hybridisation into new cultural lineages appeared to prove that quite clearly. But then Leakey's research questioned this too. His ideas reflected broader doubts concerning the older European-based ideas: 'it is doubtful if the seven stages of Acheulian recognised in the Somme are precisely applicable to the sequences found in other parts of N.W. Europe' (Oakley 1952: 285) or, more forcefully:

> After some twenty years of trial it is, however, probably fair to say that few investigators would care to rely on the wide validity of the distinctions proposed by Breuil, as a criterion of date. Indeed the whole question of the recognition of typological development of handaxes seems to have relapsed into extreme uncertainty.
>
> (West and McBurney 1954: 145)

Unlike the pre-war generation, whose debates had been designed to reinforce the status quo of the age (Dennell 1990), no such confidence in the times, or its socially validated theoretical orthodoxy existed in the 1950s. William Watson published his influential guide to the British Museum stone tool collections in 1956. In it he discounted the idea of progressive evolution in biface form within the Acheulean. But he nevertheless did assert 'The Abbeville-Acheulean culture begins in Europe in the Gunz/Mindel interglacial' (Watson 1956: 31).

There was new interest in the Clactonian, too. In 1957, John Wymer published a new Clactonian site at Little Thurrock, Essex. He had excavated at the site in 1954. It was one that his father had discovered in 1911. Like Smith and Dewey, Bertram Wymer had not known what to make of the cores and flakes he had found in the gravels at the site.

Science too was catching up with the Clactonian. Kathleen Pike and Harry Godwin (Pike and Godwin 1953) published the results of their work at Clacton-on-Sea. They had taken samples from sediment cores drilled through the Estuarine Beds and the Upper Freshwater Beds and extracted pollen grains. This was described in more detail in Chapter 3, see Figures 3.2, 3.3 and Table 3.1. Building on the work of Pike and Godwin, and other work by Richard West at Hoxne (West 1956; West and McBurney 1954), unique pollen spectra were identified for four interglacial periods. They were given local names to reflect the type sites where the characteristic deposits were sampled – see Figure 3.3. Four interglacials need to have glaciations to separate them out, and these too were given local British names. In the 1950s, the glaciations were correlated with the European four glacial system of Penck and Brückner (1909; see Chapter 10 and Table 10.2), which was still the basis of almost all European Pleistocene glacial–interglacial chronology. As Figure 3.3 shows, the earliest glaciation in Europe, the Gunz, was not present in the British sequence, so the Anglian glaciation (at that time called the Lowestoft glaciation) was equated with the Mindel – the second European glacial phase. Pike and Godwin (1953) fitted all the Clacton sediments into the Hoxnian interglacial.

Palynology was seen as a powerful and independent method of identifying geological sediments and placing discontinuous bodies of sediment into a relative geo-chronological sequence. In this sense it took over from the archaeological stone tool/type-fossil approach of the 1930s. The Cambridge palynologists, such as Harry Godwin, Kathleen Pike and Richard West, were influential figures in an emerging new discipline – Quaternary Research.

The 1960s and the 1970s, the new wave

The 1960s saw the rise of the so-called New Archaeology promoted by Kent Flannery and Lewis Binford in the United States, and by David Clark and Colin Renfrew among others in Britain (Trigger 1989). Science and objectivity were the new order of the day. Material culture was no longer seen as a metaphor for historical development, nor would its mere description be acceptable as the goal for archaeology. Now the emphasis was on explaining the internal dynamics of population groups and the reasons for cultural change. Interpretation moved from the vertical to the horizontal, as spatial excavations revealed patterns in the organisation of hominin behaviour. Scientific objectivity was empowered by the use of newly developed and still revolutionary dating techniques which offered the potential for absolute chronologies to replace the relative chronologies of the type fossil approach. Palaeolithic archaeologists now studied assemblages, not just one tool type; they randomly sampled, measured their data, and tested their theoretical models with statistical analysis.

This 'new' or 'processual' archaeology reflected the changing spirit of the times. The 1960s were a radical celebration of difference for its own sake. There were new styles in music and fashion and an air of permissive liberalism. Science could work for the benefit of humanity, not just its destruction. Much of the science fiction of the time took on a more positive note. Television programmes like *Star Trek* took a message of cultural respect to the stars. This was the United Nations in space. In 1951, UNESCO had produced the global orthodoxy on race as a direct response to the Nazi ideology (Proctor 2003). *Star Trek*'s prime directive of non-interference was an obvious counter to America's unpopular war in Vietnam.

As the 1920s had done after the First World War, the 1960s championed a freedom won from the war-torn 1940s and the gloomy rebuilding of the 1950s. The Apollo space programme caught the mood of the period. With enough time, money, and 'kit', science could achieve anything. Processual-ists took it for granted that science was objective. It stood apart from any subjective influences that society could impose. Processual archaeologists sought truth in their measurements, so naturally enough they found it. Just as the culture-historians had never doubted that their methods revealed an accurate picture of the past, neither did the processualists in their brave new world.

Dennell (1990) sums up some of the changes in the study of the Lower Palaeolithic that the 1960s initiated. For France and especially for Britain, the end of empire had come. The post-war nationalist movements had reached critical mass. As the Europeans retreated from the world stage, the Americans stepped in to fill the vacuum. Dennell has described the 1960s as a decade of American research backed by American resources. The American prehistoric approach was rooted in cultural anthropology so there was an emphasis on trying to understand how societies worked. Big picture geo-chronological sequences which sought to reproduce the European framework in other parts of the world were equally a thing of the past:

> Questions asked since 1960 in early hominid studies have con-
> cerned primarily the roots of human behaviour as seen today . . . It
> is a moot point how many of these questions reflect the concerns of
> our age to the same extent as an interest in stability and continuity
> reflected those of the 1930s in France and Britain.
>
> (Dennell 1990: 556)

In fact, focus moved away from Europe as the centre of Lower Palaeolithic research and increasingly concentrated on Africa and in particular the work of Louis and Mary Leakey. Their Olduvai Gorge excavations were now funded by the American *National Geographic Magazine* (Morell 1995). In 1959, the fossil skull *Zinjanthropus* was found on what was interpreted as a primary context Oldowan occupation surface in the lowest bed of the Olduvai sequence. Utilising the relatively new Potassium/Argon dating technique, its age astonished the world. It was nearly 2 million years old. Perhaps as much as anything else this one discovery highlighted how parochial and out of place the European sequences were. The glamour factor contributed as well. Leakey dalmations, watching the excavation of a 2-million-year-old site under the hot African sun, held the popular attention longer than digging a small gravel section in Essex on a rainy day in March. The ease with which television brought such discoveries into everyday life only added to the glamour.

With the change in *Zeitgeist* came changes in methodology, in particular, in France. François Bordes and Maurice Bourgon (Bordes and Bourgon 1951) were developing a methodology that would require the study of all the retouched tools in an assemblage not just one or two signature types (Bordes 1961). They applied it to the French Middle Palaeolithic. It could accommodate variability without compromising culturally based understandings. Bordes argued that most assemblages shared the same tool types, but different social groups produced them in different proportions. It was the combination of specific proportions of certain classes of tool, and some of the flaking techniques used to make them, that provided assemblages with their unique and recognisable cultural signature. It could also be applied to Lower Palaeolithic stone tool assemblages as well. What is more, it could be applied anywhere (Bordes 1968; Coles and Higgs 1969). Because of the use of measurements, indices, and percentages, it had an objective feel to it. Not surprisingly, it was a huge hit. Bordes' final version of the methodology was published in 1961; Breuil died in August of the same year; Hazzledine Warren had died in 1958.

In the same year as Bordes published his final methodology, John Wymer published his investigations into the Pleistocene gravels at the site of Highlands Farm Pit, Caversham, near Henley-on-Thames (Wymer 1961). The site was discussed in Chapter 4. In the gravels of an abandoned channel of the Thames, the Caversham Channel, Wymer described a series of different stone tool industries which he was able to separate out into a chronological sequence on the basis of a comparison with the artefacts in Barnfield Pit, Swanscombe. This was a critical paper for its era. He proposed an archaeo-logical sequence that was culture based and typological in character, but with the addition of technological factors to help distinguish between the different assemblages. The sequence in the Caversham Channel is shown in the right-hand column of Table 11.1, with a selection of the other sites that

Table 11.1 John Wymer's (1961) chrono-stratigraphic sequence for the British Lower Palaeolithic and the place of Highlands Farm Pit within it

Phases of the British Palaeolithic	Barnfield Pit	Rickson's Pit	Baker's Hole	Worthington Smith's sites in NE London	Iver/Hillingdon	Highlands Farm Pit in the Caversham Channel
Late Levalloisian					Grey brickearth with Levallois. Similar to Acton in London	
Early Levalloisian		? In Barnfield Upper Loam equivalent	Workshop buried by Coombe Rock	From 'floors' in brickearth	In red brickearth comparable to NE London	
Late Middle Acheulean. Soft hammer finished ovates, S twists, tranchets, and cordiforms	Upper Loam (handaxes overlain by the Upper Loam, and within it)	In Barnfield Upper Loam equivalent, and gravel below it		On top of gravel overlain by brickearths	In gravels	Present throughout same gravels as below
Middle Acheulean. Pointed handaxes	Middle Gravels (both units)			At base of gravel deposits, pointed handaxes		
Early Acheulean?						Crude small stone struck handaxes in same gravels
Clactonian	Lower Gravels	Lowest gravels				Distributed throughout the gravels

Source: From data in Wymer 1961, based on selected stratified sites as interpreted by Wymer.

Wymer believed contributed to the broader Palaeolithic sequence. In effect, Wymer was using sites in the Lower Thames Valley as a stratigraphic reference sequence, and using this to place sites elsewhere into a relative chrono-stratigraphic framework. The principle would have been very familiar to earlier workers.

At the base of the Barnfield sequence was the Clactonian in the Lower Gravels. This was the earliest industry in the Thames Valley. It was overlain by Acheulean industries. The Clactonian was therefore the earliest stone tool industry in Britain. It contained no bifaces and Wymer argued that the overlying Acheulean did not contain many chopping tools or chopper-cores, as he re-labelled them. In a sense, this was a blend of Breuil and Bordes, and it was an approach that was typical of the period. The Middle Gravels at Barnfield contained what he termed a Middle Acheulean identified on typological and technological grounds. Of interest was a possible Early Acheulean?, deliberately written with a query; but it had not actually been seen in a stratified British site. The whole sequence was a *mélange* of ideas drawn from the interpretative 'ether' of the time. The sequence was progressive but Wymer did not invoke the parallel phyla and social Darwinism of earlier decades.

One other significant feature of this paper was that at no time did it attempt to contextualise the Clactonian in terms of its broader global significance. I once asked Wymer what, during the 1960s, he thought the Clactonian was. He replied, 'I don't think we really knew, we just thought it was different.' In fact, the New Archaeology presented the British Lower Palaeolithic with a dilemma. Its aims were to explain how societies organised themselves, and to evaluate the nature of culture change. Later prehistoric archaeology had a variety of evidences to draw from; burials and grave goods, pottery, monuments, and an absolute chronology. The Lower Palaeolithic had only its stone tools, most in secondary context. In effect, it was almost forced to continue the project of identifying and describing cultural differences, while searching for a truly objective chrono-stratigraphic framework that would allow social interpretations.

This interpretative vacuum is nicely illustrated in the following example. In 1964, the Royal Anthropological Institute published a monograph on the Barnfield Pit (Ovey 1964). There was much new and important work on molluscs and fauna, and John Wymer's Middle Gravels excavations from the 1950s were reported. But the chrono-stratigraphic sequence within which it was embedded was the King and Oakley sequence of 1936. In fact, the geology chapter (among others) was lifted in its entirety from the 1938 Swanscombe Committee report and transplanted into the 1964 monograph.

The late 1960s and early 1970s were a productive time for Clactonian studies and for the British Lower Palaeolithic in general. Derek Roe had begun his monumental study of British handaxe assemblages in 1961, which was published in 1968 (Roe 1964; 1968). He characterised handaxes by a morpho-metric approach which emphasised three-dimensional form as well as the two-dimensional outline that was the stuff of typologists. The method didn't concentrate on individual artefacts, it considered the variability present in an assemblage of handaxes. His methodology became the standard way of representing handaxe data. Wymer published the results of many years of research in an equally monumental work on the Palaeolithic succession of the Lower Thames Valley (Wymer 1968).

At the Barnfield Pit, John d'Arcy Waechter of the London Institute of Archaeology, began a five-year excavation programme, concentrating on the Clactonian in the Lower Gravels. He also demonstrated that the Lower Loams were far from archaeologically sterile; in 1970, the Lower Loam knapping floor was discovered (Waechter *et al.* 1970; Conway *et al.* 1996). Because of the lack of any diagnostic tool forms Waechter hesitated to label the knapping floor Clactonian but other workers had little compunction in doing so.

There had been further excavations at Little Thurrock earlier in the decade (Snelling 1964), and Suzanne Palmer had described a possible Clactonian industry at Purfleet (Palmer 1975; Wymer 1985). In 1969, John Wymer and Ronald Singer excavated at the Golf Course site, Clacton-on-Sea, funded by the University of Chicago (Singer *et al.* 1973). This was part of a large programme of American/Chicago-funded palaeoanthropological research that led to excavations at Clacton (1969–70; Wymer and Singer 1970), Hoxne (1972–74 and 1978; Singer *et al.* 1993), and Barnham St Gregory (1979; Wymer 1985). This same research programme had already conducted work in Southern Africa, exemplifying Dennell's comment that this was a time of American-generated research underwritten by American funding.

Further pollen work had refined the chronological sub-divisions of the Hoxnian interglacial (Turner 1970), and a comprehensive review of molluscan data at Swanscombe allowed Michael Kerney (1971) to place the Swanscombe deposits within various sub-divisions of the Hoxnian. Now the Clactonian had precise chronological boundaries confirmed by two independent lines of environmental evidence – pollen and molluscs. It was evident that the Clactonian at Clacton and Swanscombe pre-dated the Acheulean at Hoxne, whose position in the interglacial had been also been fixed by pollen analysis (Turner and Kerney 1971; see Table 3.1). This was powerful independent support for the stratigraphic sequences at Swanscombe and Barnham St Gregory. By the early 1970s the British Clactonian was fitting comfortably into a very consistent story.

This emerging orthodoxy was empowered by research in Europe. By the end of the 1960s, many scholars accepted that eastern Europe represented a region dominated by non-handaxe assemblages. Sites like Vértesszölös in Hungary were frequently cited in support of this. There appeared to be a discontinuous presence in western Europe too. In addition to Clacton and Swanscombe, there were sites like Le Vallonet in France (see Figure 1.7; Lumley *et al.* 1963; Kretzoi and Vértes 1965; Bordes 1968; Collins 1969; Coles and Higgs 1969). The chopping tool tradition and the biface tradition were seen as two distinct but contemporary cultural phenomena whose relationship to hominins (and each other) was undetermined. These were not parallel phyla but two contemporary cultural blocks, something akin to the political situation of the post-war era with its ideological walls separating the Communist East from the capitalist West. The existence of the chopping tool 'eastern bloc' and its occasional western European outliers was a strong socio-psychological stimulus for maintaining the notion of an independent Clactonian.

In 1974, John Wymer gave the Stopes Memorial lecture to the Geologists' Association, and it was published in their proceedings the same year. He chose as his title 'Clactonian and Acheulean industries in Britain: their chronology and significance' (Wymer 1974). It was an apposite moment to review the subject. The paper included an exposition on the power of pollen analysis as a chrono-stratigraphic tool. He used his own excavations at Clacton and Hoxne, and Waechter's excavations at Swanscombe, see Table 3.1. He argued that there was no convincing evidence for any human occupation of Britain prior to the Anglian glaciation. The earliest hominin occupation of Britain occurred during some warmer spell within the late Anglian. These hominins were the makers of the flint tools found in the gravels at the Golf Course site at Clacton.

The Hoxnian interglacial was thought to have begun c. 220,000 years ago, and the Clactonian was present from the very beginning of the interglacial in the marl at the Golf Course. The Lower Loams at Swanscombe fitted into the Early Temperate phase of the Hoxnian; the Lower Gravels were more difficult to pinpoint. The Lower Freshwater Beds at Clacton were dated to pollen zone Ho IIb. No evidence existed of the Clactonian continuing after this time.

The big picture conclusions were clear. For Wymer, the temporal separation between the Clactonian and the earliest Acheulean was only a brief pollen sub-phase. This led Wymer to posit the possibility of direct replacement of the former by the latter so sudden was the disappearance. The Clactonian was a simplistic industry. Not only did it lack bifaces, but it lacked any evidence of standardised tools. Wymer was clear about many of the difficulties involved in pollen analyses such as poor samples, gaps in the sequences, contradictions with other lines of biological evidence, and the very real concern that the floral successions of each interglacial were not as diagnostic as claimed. Nevertheless it offered a consistent and coherent picture, and it fitted the expectations of the times. As in 1961, Wymer did not attempt to associate the Clactonian with other non-biface assemblages in Europe. Its significance, and where it made sense, were purely local.

In December 1979, the journal *Current Anthropology* published a comprehensive attack on the status of the Clactonian as an independent culture. The piece was written by a doctoral student of Ronald Singer from Chicago University, Milla Y. Ohel (Ohel 1979a). Ohel's contention was that Clactonian sites were merely preparatory areas where Acheulean knappers came to collect suitable raw material for roughing out handaxes and then take them away for finishing elsewhere. Some core working and flake tool manufacture were carried out at these sites, but they were largely quarrying and roughing out localities for hand axe makers. This was not the first time the Clactonian had been questioned as a discrete entity as one of the commentators on the paper, K. J. Narr noted (1979), he had questioned it as early as 1953, but this was the first time such a concept had been published in English and in a journal which reached a global audience. In retrospect, Ohel's work was a classic piece of New Archaeology attribute analysis. His interpretations were well grounded in empirical data. He saw technological similarities in knapping practices with the Acheulean, and identified Acheulean elements in Clactonian assemblages.

A number of archaeologists and anthropologists commented on the paper, and an analysis of this is quite instructive. Comments covered technological, methodological and chronological issues. British Palaeolithic archaeologists were not on the whole impressed. Comments ranged from polite disagreement to being openly scathing. Other commentators were more varied in their appraisal. Ohel, in his reply (Ohel 1979b), counted six who favoured his interpretations, three who didn't, and three who were non-committal. By my reckoning, on the basis of those who did clearly state their views, there were two in favour, four dead set against, and six who sat on the fence. When I began my studies on the Clactonian in the early 1980s people would still get hot under the collar at the mention of this paper. But on two points Ohel made a lasting contribution. His data showed that Clactonian assemblages which had been collected earlier in the century had a clear bias towards larger artefacts. Excavated assemblages showed a much greater range of artefact sizes. Second, the attributes of Clactonian flakes which Breuil had espoused in the 1930s were nothing more than the features of hard hammer percussion. Others had already said this, but Ohel was the first to bring a battery of empirical data from excavated assemblages to demonstrate it beyond doubt.

Despite the objections to it, Ohel's (1979a) was a great paper. It was based on original observations, which supported a new and dynamic interpretation, and it forced the British Lower Palaeolithic community to confront many of its basic assumptions. A generation of students knew about Milla Ohel and the Clactonian from endless essay and exam questions, and the paper was still being talked about a decade or more later. Most archaeologists including myself would not support Ohel's overall conclusions nowadays, but the seed of cultural doubt had been planted.

The 1980s to the present

During the 1980s, post-processualism began to make its mark in archae-ology. Most of the theoretical developments driving the new philosophy were, as usual, a result of research in later prehistory. Post-processualists emphasised those aspects of culture that the New Archaeologists avoided because they were unquantifiable. Cultures were the collective sum of indi-viduals pursuing private agendas. The clues to human behaviour were not in patterned regularity, but in the idiosyncratic personal meanings that people drew from the cultural signals around them. Archaeology was really about the different ideas in people's heads. Measuring and quantifying would never reveal a culture's inner workings:

> The most novel and far reaching contribution of post processual archaeology has been Ian Hodder's (1982) irrefutable ethno-archaeological demonstration that material culture inverts and dis-torts, as well as reflects, social organisation and hence plays a more active role in social process than was hitherto believed.
>
> (Trigger 1995: 449)

Post-processual thinking has made relatively little impact on British Lower Palaeolithic archaeology – as yet.

This period began with the publication of Derek Roe's *Lower and Middle Palaeolithic Periods in Britain* (Roe 1981b). Roe's work was rooted in the 1960s New Archaeology and took as its starting point the Barnfield Pit's sequence of stratified industries. The 1981 book replaced Wymer's 1968 volume as the standard text for the British Lower and Middle Palaeolithic.

In my opinion, there are three main themes to post-1970s research that can be said to have had a direct impact upon the Clactonian:

1   Developments in geo-chronology.
2   The acceptance of the value of multidisciplinary fieldwork.
3   The move to more behavioural and social interpretations.

Geo-chronology

The 'official' geo-chronological framework used in Britain during the 1970s and early 1980s was Mitchell *et al.* (1973) which was the basis for Figure 3.3. This was a sequence based exclusively on terrestrial sediments and pollen analysis. Many geologists were unhappy with this framework. British depositional sequences are erosion dominated. Sedimentation on land is seldom continuous, and erosion can remove part or all of a sedi-mentary unit; whole phases of a depositional sequence can be missing from a site. During the 1970s, pollen bio-stratigraphy had seemed to provide a way of placing different sedimentary units, at different sites, into a single regional chronological sequence.

But during the 1960s and 1970s, Pleistocene geo-chronologists began to look more to the marine record. The deep sea cores contained a record of mostly continuous sedimentation in certain favoured areas of the ocean bed, and so potentially a more complete record of the world's climate than any terrestrial sequence. I have described these in more detail in Chapter 2, see Figures 2.1 and 2.2. But the question was, how to relate these data to the terrestrial sequence? In Britain, this was done on the basis of two extreme events in the land-based record. The Ipswichian interglacial (called the Eemian on the Continent) was a warm high sea-level interglacial according to geological and faunal evidence, and this was equated with MIS 5.5. The Anglian glaciation, known to be the most severe and most extensive (at least in Britain) fitted with MIS 12. So these two major climatic events were used to anchor the terrestrial sequence within the more complete marine one.

The interglacial after the Anglian, the Hoxnian (see Figure 3.3 and Table 3.1), was equated with MIS 11. The framework thus established is shown in Figure 11.2. Straightaway there was a problem. In the traditional pollen-based sequence there was one glaciation between the Hoxnian (MIS 11) and the Ipswichian (MIS 5.5). But the deep sea core record indicated there were three glaciations (MIS 10, 8, 6) and two interglacials (MIS 9 and 7) to be fitted in here. In other words, the climate of the Middle Pleistocene had been a lot more complicated than the terrestrial sequences were suggesting. There were other problems too. The Cromerian, the pre-Anglian interglacial was actually a long and complicated period according to the mammal evidence from sites in East Anglia. This was described in more detail at the start of Chapter 4. Should all of this complexity really be shoe-horned into one interglacial – MIS 13?

Geo-chronologists were experimenting with the quantities of amino acids that occur in the shells of molluscs. Professor D. Q. Bowen of Aberystwyth University and his colleagues (Bowen et al. 1989) saw an opportunity of applying this dating technique to the sediments of the British Pleistocene record. He published his first 'big picture' version in 1989 in the journal Nature. It is shown in Figure 11.3. It provided strong support for the more complicated pattern of climate suggested by the DSC. Bowen et al. were able to place individual Palaeolithic sites into specific MI stages, in particular, the interglacials MIS 13, 11, 9, 7 and 5.5. There was consistency too. Swanscombe and Clacton which should have been in the interglacial immediately following the Anglian, fitted into MIS 11, while Ipswichian ratios matched MIS 5.5. But there were problems. The site of Hoxne, whose pollen signature had defined the Hoxnian, and which should have been MIS 11, turned out to be MIS 9. Moreover, the handaxe site of Waverley Wood in the English Midlands appeared in stage 15, dating the earliest occupation of

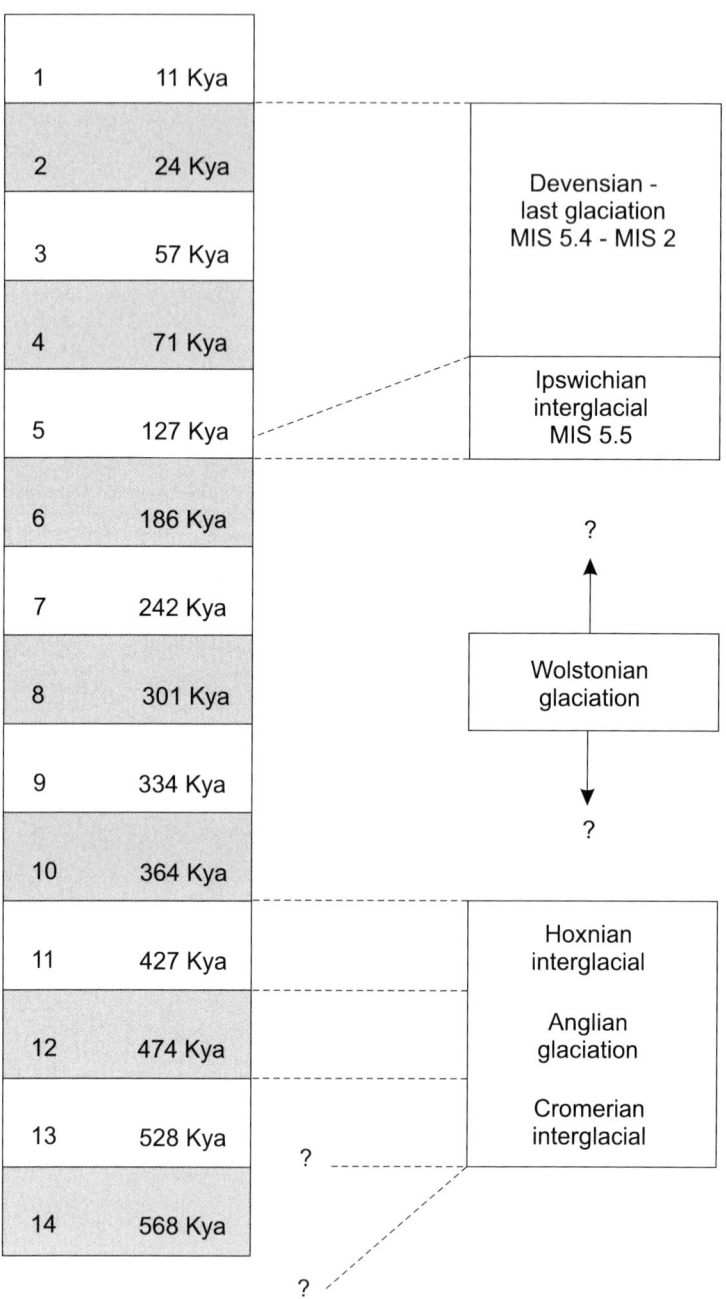

Figure 11.2 The difficulty in correlating the simpler pollen-based terrestrial chrono-stratigraphic sequence, with the more complicated marine isotope sequence.

Note: See Figure 1.5. Interglacials shaded.

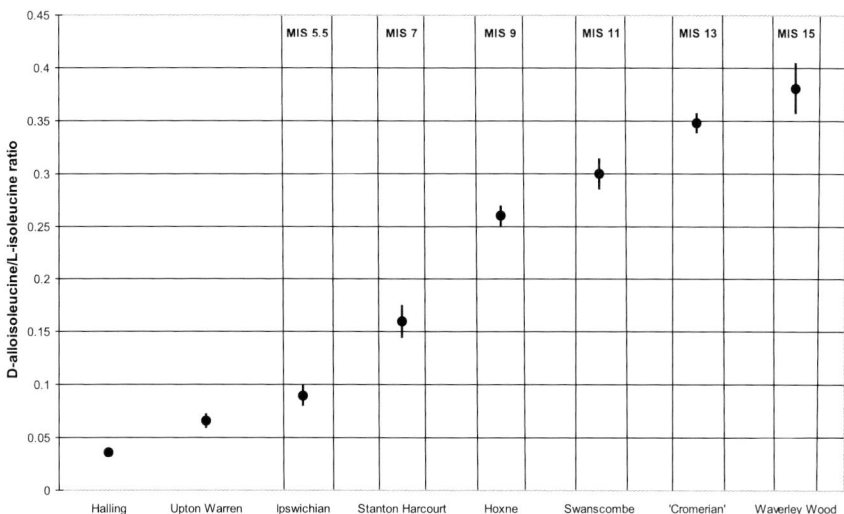

Figure 11.3 D. Q. Bowen et al.'s amino-acid (AA) dating results based on mollusc shells from British Middle Pleistocene interglacial sites.

Note: The AA ratios gave a relative chronological sequence (vertical scale) which was then fitted into the MIS sequence.

Source: Data from Bowen et al. (1989).

Britain to something like 600 kya. In the late 1980s, this was considered far too old to be plausible. These problems sparked a fierce debate (Ashton et al. 1994, and West and Gibbard 1994 for a good example of this).

There was one other knock-on effect arising from the Bowen et al. paper, and it had a profound effect on Lower Palaeolithic archaeology. At the beginning of the decade the Hoxnian was commonly thought to date to c. 220–250 kya. By the end of the 1980s, Clactonian sites in MIS 11 were considered about 400 kya. This was a direct result of the increasing engagement with the MI sequence. What is more, Bowen and colleagues had used mollusc samples from a number of Clactonian sites. Sediments that contained Clactonian artefacts were seen to contribute to this new perspective. I suspect it came as more of a shock to archaeologists than to their colleagues in Quaternary sciences. But it underscored the vital role to be played by multidisciplinary research.

The increasing importance of multidisciplinary fieldwork

Two sites in the 1980s were important in influencing the opinions of British Lower Palaeolithic archaeologists. Boxgrove in Sussex is now famous. It has Britain's oldest hominin remains (Roberts et al. 1994), and is one of the most impressive primary context occupation sites known anywhere in the world (Pitts and Roberts 1997), see Chapter 4. In addition to the perfectly preserved knapping scatters, there was a wealth of faunal remains, especially small mammals. In some respects these were more important than the archaeology!

The small mammals were telling a very complicated story, the modern implications of which were reviewed in Chapters 2 and 4. At Boxgrove the small mammals indicated a pre-Anglian date for the site. Initially there was resistance to this. It was hard to believe that a site with such incredible preservation could be that old. But what was even more surprising was the nature of the archaeology. The handaxes were ovates, made with an exceptional degree of skill; they were thin, refined, symmetrical, and finished with soft hammers. In many cases they had tranchet blows at their tips. They were similar to others in the Hoxnian Middle Acheulean of Wymer and Roe. However, the small mammal evidence was unequivocal; the site was older than the Anglian glaciation.

The second site to complicate matters in this decade was High Lodge, in Suffolk. The site had been known since the last century and there were all sorts of problems attached to the stratigraphy. The modern interpretation was discussed in Chapter 4. Here, I will only refer to the historical controversy surrounding the site. This is summarised in Table 11.2. There was an assemblage of flakes, cores, and very well-made scrapers from the clays, which lacked any evidence of biface making. In 1962, Gail Sieveking of the British Museum began a six-year excavation programme at the site, but the results only made things worse! The geologists were saying it was a pre-Anglian site, while the archaeologists were saying it was much younger.

The real problem were the scrapers. Typologically, i.e. visually, they were well made and regular in appearance. They looked like typical Mousterian scrapers made by Neanderthals in the Later Middle Palaeolithic. On the other hand, the clays contained a tooth from a species of rhinoceros which was associated with the Cromerian. Geologically it looked as if the clays were older than the till, but somehow had ended up above them. The problems were similar to Boxgrove; an early context at odds with later-looking archaeology. Because there were so many contradictions, High Lodge remained unpublished throughout the 1960s and 1970s. The exception was a brief note in the journal *Nature* (Anonymous 1968) which claimed that the British Museum excavation had proved the lower and upper tills to be Wolstonian (locally called the Gipping glaciation) in age, and that the core, flake, and scraper industry had been made during an interstadial in that glaciation. This was a clear example of archaeological typology driving the interpretation of geological sediments. The Mousterian-like scrapers simply could not be pre-Anglian.

In 1988, Jill Cook of the British Museum led a team with archaeologist Nick Ashton and geologists Simon Lewis and Jim Rose (Ashton *et al.*

Table 11.2 Schematic overview of various interpretations of the chrono-stratigraphic and archaeological sequence at High Lodge

Geological sequence	Archaeological sequence	Traditional interpretation of the culture historians	Alternative mid-twentieth-century interpretations	1960s British Museum interpretation	Modern interpretation
Upper till				Gipping (=Wolstonian)	Not a till – a late Anglian debris flow
Sands and gravels	Handaxes	Acheulean phases later in date than Clactonian III	Earlier Acheulean deposited over the Mousterian by solifluction from sides of valley	Acheulean	Outwash from Anglian glacial melt. Handaxes were planed off the same flood plain as the cores and flakes
Clays	Cores, flakes and well made scrapers and flake tools	Clactonian III	Mousterian	'Proto-Mousterian' – ancestral to the Mousterian	Pre-Anglian Bytham river flood plain remnant. Frozen by Anglian cold conditions and scooped up into glacier
Lower till				Gipping (=Wolstonian)	Anglian glacial moraine

1992a) back to the site. They were able to demonstrate that the clays with their cores, flake tools, and scrapers were indeed earlier than the lower till (see Chapter 4). So were the bifaces from the gravels. Many of these were refined ovates.

The lessons of Boxgrove and High Lodge were clear and they flagged a critical issue. Appearances can be deceptive. Technologically and typologically advanced-looking artefacts were not necessarily more recent in age. Crude or simple artefacts need not be chronologically early. In hindsight we can see that these traditional assumptions had maintained a powerful hold over the archaeological mindset. Although Lower Palaeolithic archaeology had always relied heavily on geology, and latterly on palynology and faunal studies, I get the impression that the Quaternary sciences had always played second fiddle to the archaeology in the minds of most archaeologists. Their role was to clarify the background against which the archaeology was played out. Indeed, while the archaeological project had been focused on stone tool cultures, geologists and environmental scientists were mostly on board to help with the dating. These had not been truly multidisciplinary collaborations.

Throughout the middle and late 1980s the all too evident benefits from a closer relationship between Lower Palaeolithic archaeology and the Quaternary environmental scientists, led to a number of multidisciplinary field projects. Nick Ashton of the British Museum, together with Simon Lewis, a quaternary geologist, and Simon Parfitt, a mammal specialist, began a five-year excavation programme at Paterson's old Clactonian site at Barnham (Ashton et al. 1998). In 1995, the same team began a five-year programme of excavations at the Acheulean site of Elveden. Other multidisciplinary collaborations have been equally productive, such as that between archaeologist Francis Wenban-Smith and geologist Martin Bates, in the growing area of developer-funded Pleistocene archaeology and research.

By engaging with a battery of Pleistocene environmental sciences Mark White has demonstrated the potential for big picture archaeological interpretations emplaced within a multidisciplinary framework. The work also relies heavily on the researches of Danielle Schreve, a mammal specialist. White reviewed the geological context and assemblage integrity of the sites traditionally classified as Clactonian, suggesting that two others be added to the corpus. These were the lower gravels from Cuxton, and the lower gravels from Bluelands and Greenlands Pits at Purfleet (see Chapters 5 and 6; White 2000; White and Schreve 2000). The importance of these two sites was that they extended the temporal range of the Clactonian, suggesting it was present in late MIS 10 and early MIS 9, as well as in MIS 11. The validity of these claims was thoroughly reviewed in Chapter 3. The Clactonian was seen against the movement of fauna and hominins backwards and forwards across the Kent–Artois plateau in response to shifts in climate and sea level. During glacial climates, when the ice margins moved south, Britain would have been abandoned and migration would have been via the emergent land bridge as global sea levels dropped. In interglacials, peninsular Britain became an island cut off from the European mainland by rising sea levels. White argued that in MIS 11 and 9 the earliest re-occupation of Britain was by Clactonian hunters. Acheulean occupation was always later in the interglacial.

Behavioural and social interpretations

Enormous advances in archaeological method and theory were made during the 1970s and 1980s by American research teams in East Africa. Continuing with the New Archaeology's commitment to spatial excavation, primary context living floors were being excavated which reflected the spatial organisation of hominin behaviour. These were then set into broader studies of Lower and Middle Pleistocene landscape use (e.g. Isaac 1977; Isaac and Isaac 1997). Detailed multidisciplinary studies revealed the taphonomic history (all the natural process that affect artefacts and bones after deposition) of these sites. Archaeologists believed they could distinguish between a site which showed natural disturbance patterns, and those with stone and bone associations which reflected hominin behaviours. This greatly empowered hominin behavioural reconstructions.

With only a few sites in primary context in Britain, behavioural interpretations of this type were all but impossible. As studies on the Clactonian showed, the British research agenda remained more descriptive than interpretative.

In 1994, Steven Mithen published one of the first theoretically informed and behaviourally orientated interpretations of the Clactonian (Mithen 1994). It took a wholly new approach. It drew on analogies from primate research and engaged with theoretical debates on the role of social learning. His argument was that Clactonian sites tended to be in forested environments where modern primate research had suggested that learning was relatively private and individualistic. Acheulean sites tended to be in open environments. Here hominin group sizes would be larger and social pressures would be greater generating higher degrees of regularity in behaviour. This would be reflected in much more intense social learning which would impose greater regularity on what and how material culture was made. This was why the Acheulean knappers made standardised tools like handaxes, while the Clactonian cores and flakes lacked any real imposed regularity. Nick Ashton and I wrote a reply to this paper (McNabb and Ashton 1995) pointing out that a number of Acheulean sites were in forested environments, and that the degree of variability seen in Clactonian cores was replicated in Acheulean cores because they were actually knapped in the same way.

Neither side accepted the other's point of view (Mithen 1995). In my opinion, the most important contribution Mithen's paper made was to require Clactonian and Acheulean scholars to face up to the fact that these hominins were social animals. This outlook had been singularly lacking in Clactonian studies up to that point. In showing how the traditional Lower Palaeolithic data set (tool assemblages and secondary context sites) could be made to contribute to new kinds of interpretation, using non-traditional approaches, Mithen broadened the Clactonian debate considerably.

My own work throughout the 1980s concentrated on examining the theoretical and methodological reasons for believing in a distinct Clactonian assemblage type and its interpretation as a cultural tradition. I concluded that there were no good grounds to consider it a distinctive phenomenon. I argued Clactonian sites reflected situationally flexible behaviours, and the few handaxes that were present in these assemblages were sufficient to deny their status as non-handaxe assemblages. Unfortunately, I was never able to explain away the time depth present in the accumulations at Swanscombe and Clacton. With hindsight, this seriously undermined my position.

Since the late 1980s, there have been a number of attempts to blend the types of social interpretations proposed by Mithen with the increasingly sophisticated data emerging from multidisciplinary fieldwork. Landscape-scale behavioural interpretations were attempted by Nick Ashton and colleagues at Barnham and Elveden. These were discussed in more detail in Chapter 5. Ashton's changing resource availability model, while not quite as socially orientated as Mithen's, does address at a basic level the ability of hominin society to adapt its patterns of tool behaviour to meet new circumstances. Socially grounded behaviour is therefore not immutable.

In recent years there has been a return to interpretations of the Clactonian that promote a purely cultural agenda. Although not stated explicitly, in my opinion this underpins the ideas promoted by Mark White described above. Those of Wenban-Smith (1998) explicitly addresses the social learning issue. He argued that over time cultures change – random cultural drift – in some instances losing aspects of their behavioural repertoire, and in others acquiring, or re-acquiring them. He posited that the critical difference between the Clactonian and the Acheulean was the soft hammer thinning technology that goes into the making of a biface. Such a trait could, over time, be lost by a group of Middle Pleistocene hominins. The Clactonian was a result of hominin groups becoming isolated in Britain in the early post-Anglian. There would be no shortage of river gravels available for making tools. In these circumstances handaxe-making hominins would adapt to an *ad hoc* core and flake technology. Later on in the interglacial, as bankside flint gravels became covered by mature rivers depositing finer sediments, there would be a need to maximise the life span and potential of available resources. Consequently there would be a return to biface using, and in time the re-invention of soft hammer thinning. In this interpretation, strong lines of social learning reinforce and sustain practical/strategic choices.

Conclusion

Does a goldfish really know it lives in a bowl? Are any of us really aware of the subtle influences our own times impose on us? Probably not. Post-processual dialogues have been hugely important in the past 20 years, in making us aware of the socially constituted nature of knowledge and the varying degrees of subjectivity that can be present in science. Once again, science fiction provides a window on society and what passes for the socially based nature of knowledge. The politically correct *Star Trek* of the 1980s was very much concerned with the rights of individuals and cultural groups, and was appropriate to the Clinton era's belief in the moral responsibility of American economic power. *Star Trek Deep Space Nine* in the 1990s projected a darker vision. After the mid-1990s this gave way to a *Star Trek* whose characters regularly meddled in the affairs of other cultures. The justifications were always expediency and necessity: a pre-emptive defence in which the ends were justified by the times. On a weekly basis, the military officers in *Stargate SG1* sought out new alien cultures and persuaded them of the benefits of an American-led alliance against a powerful enemy. *Star Trek Enterprise* saw the iconic space ship invade alien territory after an unprovoked attack on the Earth. The righteousness of their cause provided a moral safe house for questionable acts perpetrated in the name of strategic necessity. The parallel with the post-9/11 era is not difficult to see. How different peoples relate to each other and ultimately understand each other, is conditioned by the *Zeitgeist*. Science and popular culture are mirrors of their times – so is archaeology.

   In this chapter and the last, I have tried to show just why stone tool assemblages in secondary context were privileged with cultural explanations. Even today these explanations persist. The power of history to influence the supposedly more objective interpretations of the twenty-first century appears as strong as it ever was. A Clactonian assemblage type and assemblage tradition does exist, but what other options are there to understand it other than cultural ones?

12

THE CONTENTIOUS STONES

Introduction

In this chapter I will look in detail at aspects of the manufacture of stone tools in the Clactonian and Acheulean. Although I will briefly introduce the subject of knapping, I do not intend this chapter to be a detailed introduction to stone tool manufacture. I shall only concentrate on those aspects of knapping directly relevant to the Clactonian.

My aims in this chapter are twofold. First, to introduce and critique the older interpretations of Clactonian knapping, and dispel once and for all, any vestiges of the belief that Clactonian knappers were somehow inferior to Acheulean ones. Second, by applying a new framework of analysis, I will highlight just what similarities and differences there really are between the Clactonian and the Acheulean.

What is knapping?

All stone tools fashioned or shaped by hominins are knapped. The term itself comes from the Dutch, and means to flake, snap or break (Lord 1993). Here I will use the term to indicate the deliberate fracture of stone with a particular end product in mind. The breakage follows a specific methodology already known to produce the desired result, consequently it can be said to be enacted in a structured manner. This is a very British usage. In America, prehistorians tend to favour the term flaking which they apply in the same way. I will alternate between both terms. French archaeologists have a very strict concept of the process of making a stone tool, and they apply specific terms to specific stages within this framework. For example, French prehistorians use the word 'debitage' to imply the process of working a block of raw material, debitage is therefore seen as an action. What results from that action are various debitage products (Inizan *et al.* 1992). However, in the Anglo-American terminology debitage is often used to describe anything that comes off a core – flakes, broken flakes, chips, shatter fragments, etc. (see

Inizan *et al.* 1992; Debénath and Dibble 1994, for introductions to this aspect).

For the sake of simplicity, the following descriptions only apply to flint, which is the raw material most widely used in the British Lower and Earlier Middle Palaeolithic. But readers should be aware that a wide variety of rock types were used by Palaeolithic knappers.

There are only a few basic ways in which blocks of flint can be modified. The first is by *percussion*, which is the physical act of striking something. Direct percussion involves hitting a block of flint with a hammer of some description. British Lower and Earlier Middle Palaeolithic knapping was exclusively a product of direct percussion (as far as we know). Hard hammer direct percussion involves hitting the block of flint with a stone cobble or pebble that is at least as hard, or usually harder, than the flint itself. Most modern flint knappers carry a variety of quartzite pebbles recovered from river gravels or beaches for this purpose. This type of *percussor* is called a *hammer stone*. But it is clear that other rock types could have been used just as easily (Bradley and Sampson 1986). Experiments carried out by Francis Wenban-Smith (1989) at the site of Boxgrove, proved that the Palaeolithic knappers could have used rolled flint beach cobbles and even cortical flint cobbles as hammers. At a number of Lower and Earlier Middle Palaeolithic sites hard hammer percussors have been found, such as at Swanscombe and Little Thurrock, and Frindsbury, Figure 12.1, and since Wenban-Smith's experiments, hard hammers have been found at Boxgrove made from nodules of the local flint (Pitts and Roberts 1997).

When you modify a block of flint using hard hammer direct percussion, you transform the block itself into a *core*. That portion of the block/core you have detached is called a *flake*. On the surface of the core will be an outline of the shape of the flake you have just detached, this is called a *flake scar*. Evidence of previous flake detachments will also be present on the core, represented as a series of other flake scars; more recent ones will truncate older ones, see Figure 1.2.

Flakes detached by hard hammer direct percussion have diagnostic features which identify this mode of knapping and these are shown in Figure 12.2. They are known as *hard hammer percussion features* (Ohnuma and Bergman 1982). On the flake is a butt, this is a remnant of the flat surface on the core that the knapper struck with the hammer stone – on the core this is called the *striking platform* (see Figure 12.3A). On the flake's butt is a *point of percussion* (Figure 12.2), and directly underneath on the ventral surface is a *cone of percussion*. These are physical after-effects of the impact of the hammer stone deforming the surface of the flint (Cottrell and Kamminga 1987). The *ventral* face is the inside surface of the flake. It is the break surface, and represents the plane down which the force of the hammer stone's impact travelled to detach the flake from the core. Just below the cone of percussion there is often a *bulb of percussion* (Figure 12.2). This convexity is another

Figure 12.1 Hammer stones from Frindsbury. Upper two are quartzite pebbles with patches of percussion damage. Lower one is flint with extensive percussion damage.

result of the deforming force of the blow as it travelled through the flint. It is not present on every flake. Radiating out from the point and cone of percussion are a series of concentric *ripple marks* which represent the actual passage of the wave of force as it travelled through the flint, detaching the flake. Combined, the cone of percussion, the bulb (when present), and the concentric ripple marks, help to identify the ventral face of a flake.

The outside face of the flake is called the *dorsal* surface (Figure 12.2). Often it has *cortex*, a remnant of the chalky outer crust that develops on flint nodules while still embedded in the chalk. Just like a core, the dorsal surface of a flake will also have flake scars which will have concentric ripple marks. This is because the dorsal surface of the flake once represented part of the outer face of the core before the flake itself was detached. This is shown in Figure 12.3A. As with the flake scars on cores, any flake scars on the dorsal surface of a flake will have negative percussion features, to correspond with the positive (i.e. protruding) percussion features on the ventral surface of flakes, Figure 12.3A.

Both the ventral face of a flake, and a flake scar on a core will have an *axis of percussion*, see Figure 12.2. This is a line drawn through the centre of the

306

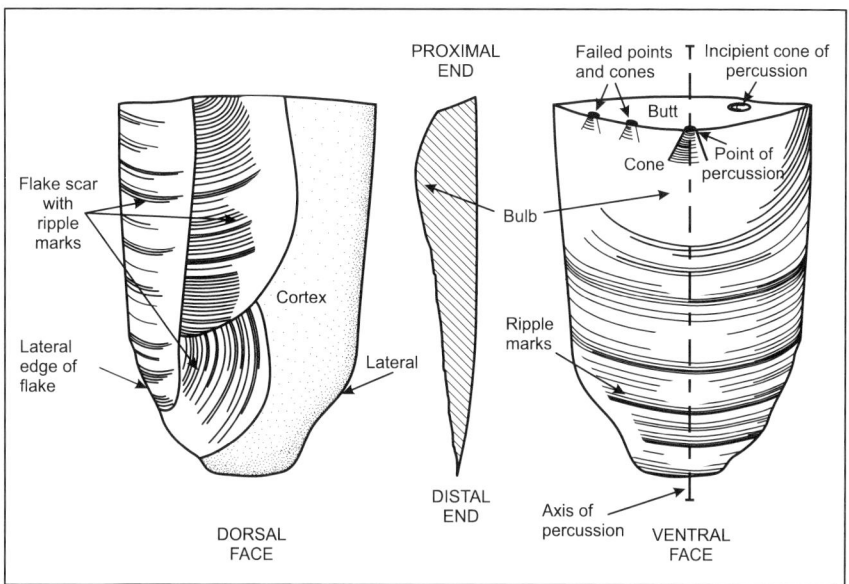

Figure 12.2 Hard hammer percussion features on a flake.

point/cone of percussion, and extended down the face of the ventral face or flake scar. It indicates the direction the wave of force took as it moved through the flint. That end of a flake's ventral face with the point/cone of percussion (or the corresponding negative percussion features on flake scars on cores) is called the *proximal* end. The opposite is the *distal* end. The two side edges of flakes or flake scars are the *lateral* edges.

Often (but not always) hard hammer percussion produces quite thick flakes, and the corresponding flake scars on the cores are deep. This is because this method of percussion punches the flake out from the surface of the flint.

Soft hammer direct percussion is identical to the hard hammer variety in the type of action involved. However, the percussor used is made of a softer organic material such as bone, wood, or antler. The type of force initiated by a softer percussor is known as a bending force. Rather than develop a crack (i.e. begin the formation of a cone of percussion) directly underneath the point of contact with the hammer, the fracture will begin somewhat away from the impact point, see Figure 12.3B (Cottrell and Kamminga 1987). These types of hammer produce a very different kind of flake (see Figure 1.1B), with the characteristic features of percussion being much more muted on soft hammer flakes. Cones are more diffused, if present at all, and points of percussion tend not to develop. These are termed *soft hammer percussion features*. In general, soft hammer flakes are much thinner.

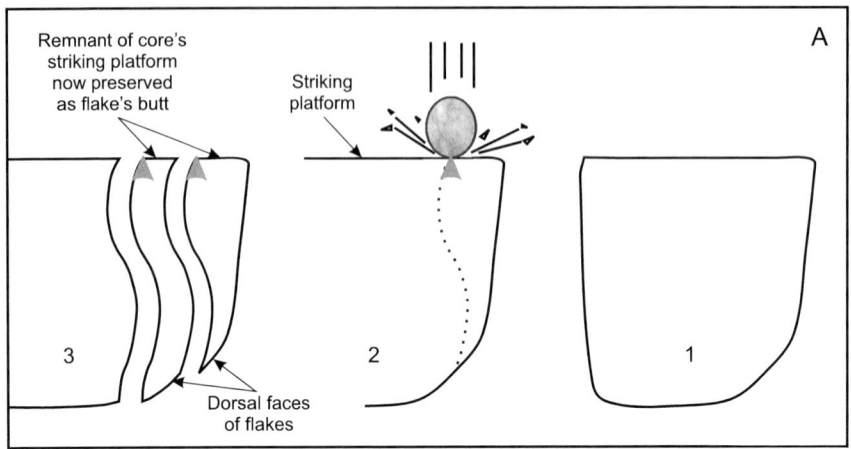

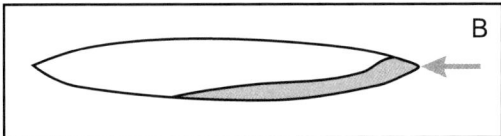

Figure 12.3 A: Flaking with a hard hammer in non-marginal mode. The negative and positive percussion features, relative to the dorsal and ventral faces of the flakes are indicated. B: handaxe thinning in marginal mode.

In many, but by no means all cases, the muted percussion features are accompanied by a pronounced lip between the butt and the ventral face.

Soft hammer direct percussion is very often used for making specific kinds of stone tool, where the knapper does not want to take deep biting removals from the surface of the flint. In the British Lower Palaeolithic this applies to the thinning and shaping of a biface rough-out which had been initially prepared with a hard hammer. Soft hammer direct percussion is therefore a characteristic of the Acheulean. Utilising the soft hammer, and striking on the edge of a biface rough-out (Figure 12.3B), the knapper can remove a controlled volume of flint from either face of the piece. This is termed flaking in *marginal mode* (as opposed to hard hammer core working which is flaking in *non-marginal mode*, Figure 12.3A). Lower Palaeolithic soft hammers have been discovered at Boxgrove where they date to c. 500 kya (Pitts and Roberts 1997). Several hammers in bone and antler have now been excavated from the site, and one still has microscopic flint chips embedded in the surface left there from thinning a biface half a million years ago. Although many Lower Palaeolithic handaxes were thinned and shaped using soft hammers, it is important to remember that not all were.

Traditional interpretations of Clactonian knapping technology

I think most Lower Palaeolithic archaeologists would nowadays agree that the traditional percussion features that were used by Breuil (Chapters 10 and 11) as hallmarks of Clactonian technology were not really diagnostic of any cultural approach to knapping. They simply reflected flaking with a hard hammer (Baden-Powell 1949; McNabb 1992a).

The criteria the culture historians used for recognising Clactonian flakes were very prominent percussion features and high (obtuse) flaking angles (see below). These were considered the result of knapping in a particular way, namely the block-on-block or direct anvil technique. It was an approach that was thought to be simpler and cruder than Acheulean flaking techniques. As described in the last two chapters, the Abbé Breuil was one of the most vociferous of those who felt that the Clactonian could be identified on the presence of flakes with these features.

Milla Ohel (1979a) posited that the culture historical perception of the Clactonian was in part related to analysing selectively collected assemblages, especially those from Clacton and Swanscombe (see Chapter 11). The collected assemblages contained artefacts that were larger on average than their counterparts in excavated assemblages. This is clear from Figure 12.4; here the excavated Clacton localities of Jaywick Sands and the Golf Course are compared with Warren's collected assemblage from Lion Point. In addition, the assemblage excavated by Waechter from the Lower Gavels at Swanscombe is compared to that collected by R.H. Chandler from the same deposit. The differences in flake size between the excavated and collected assemblages are quite clear. From the size of pieces in the Chandler collection it is not surprising that many researchers considered this assemblage to be somewhat earlier in date (Clacton IIa, see Chapter 10, and especially Table 10.7) than that at Clacton-on-Sea (Clacton IIb). The larger flakes and cores must have accentuated preconceptions of crudity and simplicity (Ohel 1979a). In his earlier writings Warren (1932) considered the style of flaking at Swanscombe much more robust than at Clacton – this is why.

The traditional Clactonian percussion features

The percussion features that classically identified Clactonian flakes were shown in Figure 12.2. They were prominent cones and bulbs of percussion, with a clear point of percussion on a large flake butt. It is important to remember that the majority of archaeologists in the middle part of the last century believed that the hominins responsible for the Acheulean only made handaxes, they didn't knapp cores for flakes. In all cases the presence of well-developed percussion features on largish flakes with big butts only served to reinforce the impression of technological simplicity.

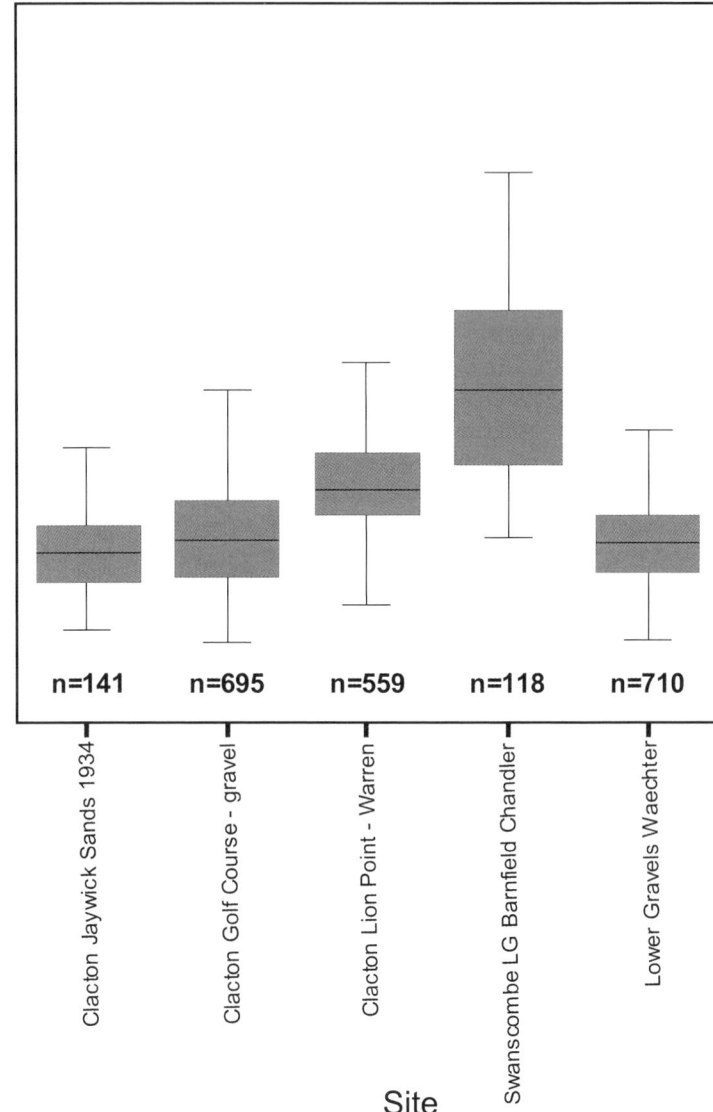

Figure 12.4 Boxplots of lengths of flakes from various assemblages in Clacton and Swanscombe.

Breuil (1932) made a point of identifying evidence for technical incompetence on Clactonian flakes. He noted examples of double or triple percussion cones. These are when a knapper has had several attempts to remove a flake before finally succeeding. In each case a percussion cone has developed within the flint at the point of each strike – but the flake did not detach. When the flake finally did come off, the failed percussion cones appeared to one side of the successful one. As miss-hits they were interpreted as a reflection of a poor appreciation of the angle between the striking platform and the flaking face, or, in other words, bad knapping. Examples are shown in Figure 12.2. Breuil also identified incipient percussion cones on flake butts. These were the bruises left on the surface of the striking platform when struck by a hammer stone but no flake comes off. They are part of the same process that results in double and triple percussion cones, and were also taken as evidence of a poor understanding of how to flake. Examples are also shown in Figure 12.2.

Data comparing the occurrence of these features in Acheulean and Clactonian sites are presented in Table 12.1. It makes two important points. There is a range of variation present that cross-cuts assemblage type. Second, Lion Point appears more Clactonian than any other Clactonian assemblage. As a selected assemblage it is a caricature of what culture historians

Table 12.1 Occurrence of single and multiple percussion cones on hard hammer flakes in non-biface/Clactonian, and biface/Acheulean assemblages

Assemblage type	Observed sample of flakes	Developed percussion cones (%)	Double percussion cones (%)	Triple percussion cones (%)	Diffused percussion cones (not thinning flakes) (%)
Non-biface assemblages					
Barnham	185	88.65	3.78	0.54	7.03
Lion Point	654	90.83	5.66	0.46	3.06
Golf Course	539	86.64	3.90	0.19	9.28
Jaywick	88	89.77	1.14	0	9.09
Little Thurrock	73	87.67	0	0	12.33
Swanscombe	398	83.09	6.26	0.42	10.23
Biface assemblages					
Bowman's Lodge	280	92.14	0.71	0	7.14
Elveden	50	84.00	0	0	16.00
Hoxne L. I.	73	83.56	0	0	16.44
Round Green	108	70.37	1.85	0	27.78
With simple prepared cores					
Frindsbury	256	96.09	0.78	0	3.13

Notes: A simple prepared core/Earlier Middle Palaeolithic assemblage is included for comparison. Developed = single cone, other cone types as stated. Barnham (industries A–E) and Elveden represent data from Paterson excavations; Hoxne L.I. represents Lower Industry West Cutting; Little Thurrock represents Bridgland excavation data; Swanscombe represents Lower Gravels and Lower Loam combined. Details presented in text.

expected it to be. The same will be seen for Chandler's Lower Gravels collection, only more so.

In fact, there is no need to think of such features as always reflecting bad knapping. Double and triple percussion cones, and incipient cones, may be the result of using too light a hammer stone (Newcomer, in Waechter *et al.* 1970), or too light a blow with the hammer. They can even result from having a worn hammer stone so that the area of contact between percussor and striking platform is greater than normal and the effect of the impact is diffused. On cores the size of some of those in the Chandler and Warren collections, it is surprising that there are not more such features. Considerable strength would have been required to detach flakes from such large nodules. Table 12.1 makes it clear that these are background noise in any hard hammer flaked assemblage, so the larger the sample, the more examples of accidents there should be.

The large size of the butt on so-called Clactonian flakes is also quickly dealt with. The data are shown in Figure 12.5. Notice how large the flake butts from Lion Point and the Chandler collection are when compared to those in excavated assemblages. Also the groupings along the line show no division into handaxe vs non-handaxe assemblages. Ohel came to a similar conclusion (1979a).

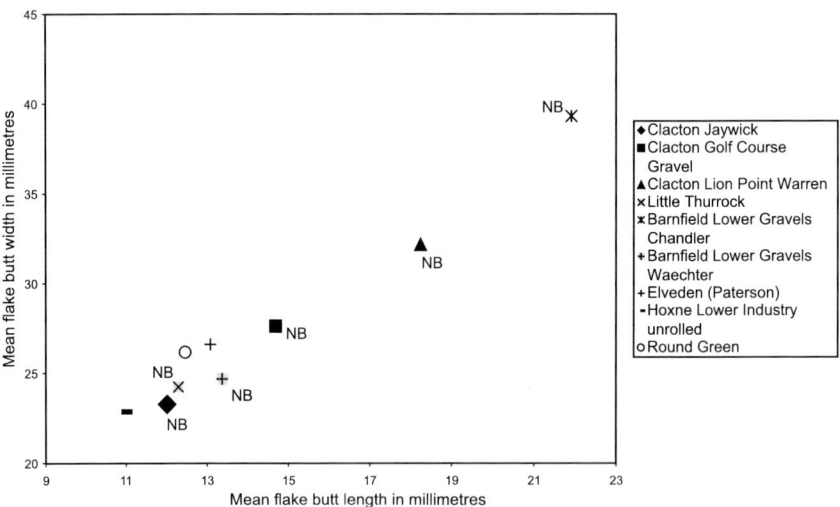

Figure 12.5 Comparison of flake butt size (length and width) from Clactonian and Acheulean assemblages.

Note: NB = non-biface.

The traditional Clactonian flaking angles

This aspect of lithic analysis acquired an almost mythical status during the middle half of the last century. Clactonian flakes had high flaking angles, and those from the Acheulean handaxe industries had much lower or more acute angles. Wide flaking angles were interpreted as a reflection of the inability to control flaking to any great extent – usually a result of flaking using an anvil. However, flake type played an important part in the rational for measurement. The bottom line here was that culture-historical preconceptions were influencing the kind of flakes that were being measured in these analyses.

Breuil and other culture-historians compared hard hammer Clactonian flakes, with Acheulean soft hammer thinning flakes. Not surprisingly, they found a big difference in the flaking angles; compare Figure 12.3A with 12.3B. Because thinning flakes were the culturally diagnostic debitage of handaxe makers, and hard hammer flakes were the culturally diagnostic debitage of the Clactonian, the two could be legitimately compared – they were the signatures of different knapping traditions. But this culturally sanctioned perception was a false one and it led to inappropriate comparisons. In effect, culture historians were not comparing like with like.

The favourite flaking angle to measure was the internal flaking angle, the IFA, see Figure 12.6. This was the angle between the flake's butt and the ventral surface. Hazzledine Warren presented his own measurements of the IFA in his seminal Clactonian paper (Warren 1951: Table 1), using the

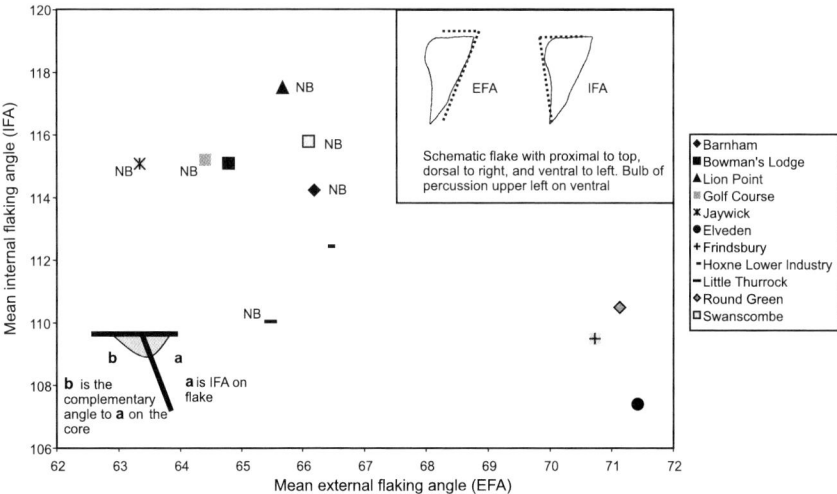

Figure 12.6 Flaking angles on flakes from Clactonian and Acheulean assemblages. Angles measured in degrees. Data drawn from Table 12.6.

Note: NB = non-biface.

median as a measure of central tendency. (He usually presented his data in terms of the angle on the core rather than that on the flake itself, i.e. he subtracted his measurement of the internal flaking angle on the flake from 180° to give the complementary angle on the core, angle **b** in Figure 12.6.) His site data are reproduced in the left-hand column of Table 12.2. The data have been reconverted to represent the angles on the flakes. The more 'advanced' assemblages clearly have lower IFAs. In the right-hand columns I have included the data from ten Lower Palaeolithic sites, and one possible Earlier Middle Palaeolithic site in order to compare with the data used by Warren. No division into handaxe vs non-handaxe groups is possible. This is because the flakes from these Acheulean sites are all from hard hammer core working. In other words like is now being compared with like. Today we know that many Acheulean handaxe assemblages do contain variable elements of hard hammer core working, and as will be shown below, their cores are

Table 12.2 The median value for the internal flaking angle for flakes from a series of Lower Palaeolithic assemblages

Warren's data from 1951	Median degree for IFA	Non-biface/ Clactonian sites	Biface/Acheulean sites	With simple prepared cores sites
	107		Elveden	
	108			
	109			
	110			Frindsbury
Clacton III. Assortment of handaxe thinning flakes	111			
	112			
	113	Little Thurrock		
	114		Hoxne L.I. Round Green	
	115	Barnham		
	116		Bowman's Lodge	
Swanscombe	117			
	118	Lion Point Golf Course Swanscombe		
Clacton	119	Jaywick		

Notes: Median values with a decimal place over 0.5 rounded up to next whole number. A simple prepared core/Earlier Middle Palaeolithic assemblage is included for comparison. Barnham (industries A–E) and Elveden represent data from Paterson excavations; Hoxne L.I. represents Lower Industry West Cutting; Little Thurrock represents Bridgland excavation data; Swanscombe represents Lower Gravels and Lower Loam combined. Details presented in text.

flaked in an identical manner to those from Clactonian sites. It is not surprising then that there is an overlap in flaking angles between handaxe and non-handaxe sites. In reality, the flaking angles merely reflect the natural variability inherent in hard hammer percussion.

To my mind, measuring the IFA always seemed a curious choice. Not every successful flake detachment will necessarily leave an angle between the striking platform and the flaking face that is suitable for continued flaking. A better angle is the external flaking angle, the EFA, see Figure 12.6. Since it is naturally present on all successful flakes it represents the relationship between striking platform and flaking face *as chosen by the knapper*. To reinforce the point that these flaking angles just sample the range of variability present in hard hammer flaking, the IFA and EFA have been plotted against each other in Figure 12.6. These data, based on the mean, show no persistent division between the Clactonian and Acheulean assemblages. Once more, Lion Point seems to be more 'Clactonian' than any of the other assemblages (see also Ohel 1979a).

But I would like to emphasise one point here. Flaking angles were the 'hard data' of the 1930s and 1940s. It is easy with hindsight to scoff at the culture-historians. But most were honest researchers who believed emphatically that these diagnostic criteria of cultural difference were genuine and self-evident. Their only real crime as archaeologists was that they were products of their age, no more and no less than that.

Interpretations of core shape

Another important assumption in the culture historian's world-view was that the shape of an artefact was deliberate. This was especially important for cores because many archaeologists believed them to be purposefully made as tools. Actually, the shape of a core reflects a number of different factors. The key one is the point at which the knapper *chooses* to stop flaking. One or two removals can change the shape of a core dramatically. As such, we should investigate core shape to determine whether distinctive shapes commonly reoccur in different Clactonian assemblages. This might indicate deliberate manufacture.

To explore core shape I will use an old methodology that I developed for this purpose. It is explained in Figure 12.7. It was a precursor to the methodology used in this book, which is outlined in the next section, but is less flexible (it is drawn from McNabb 1992a). However, for the purposes of examining core shape it will suffice.

Figure 12.8 displays the data for core shape presented as percentages. It is very clear from Figure 12.8 that the degree of variability within each assemblage type is quite marked, and no Clactonian or Acheulean assemblage-type pattern is present. Even the three Clacton localities show very clear differences when compared to each other. The higher incidence of

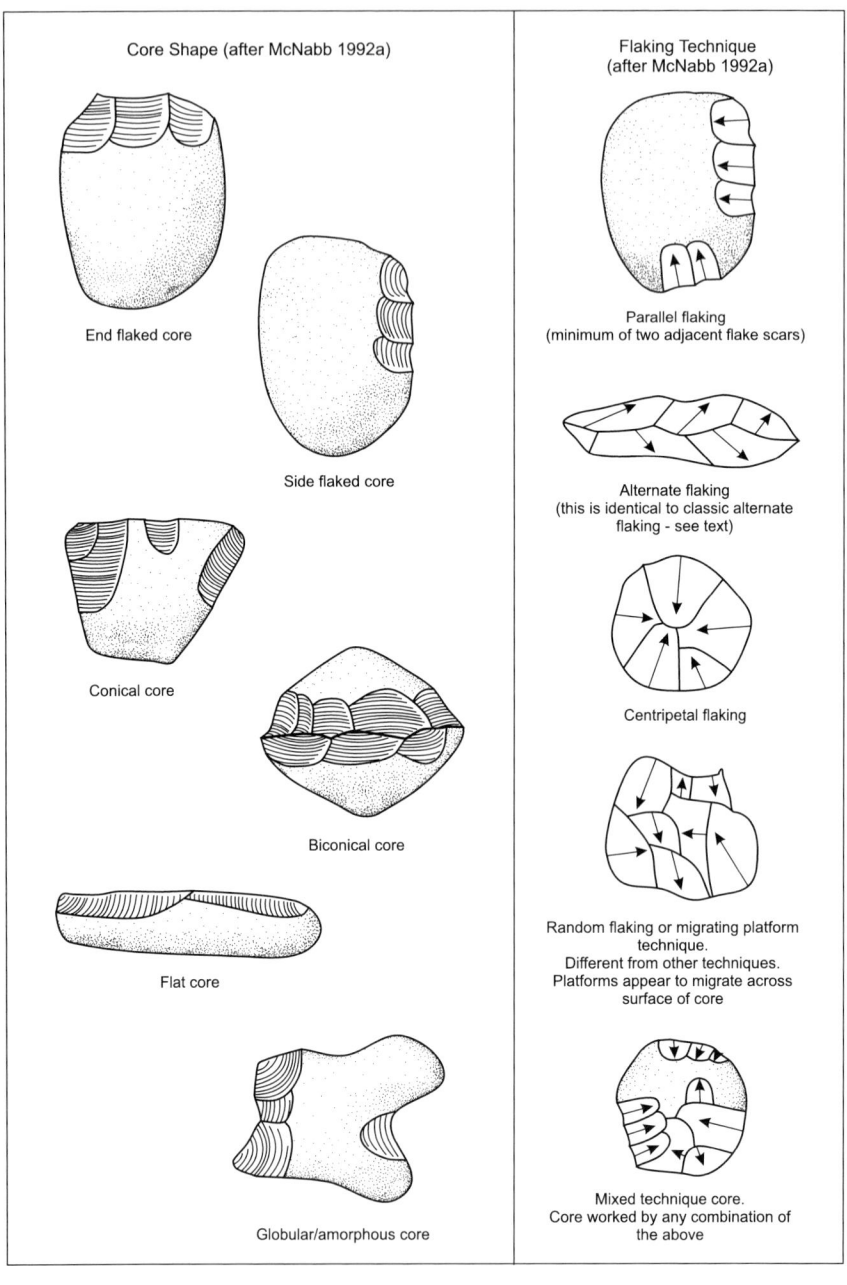

Figure 12.7 Core shape and flaking technique from a previous system of interpretation developed by the author.

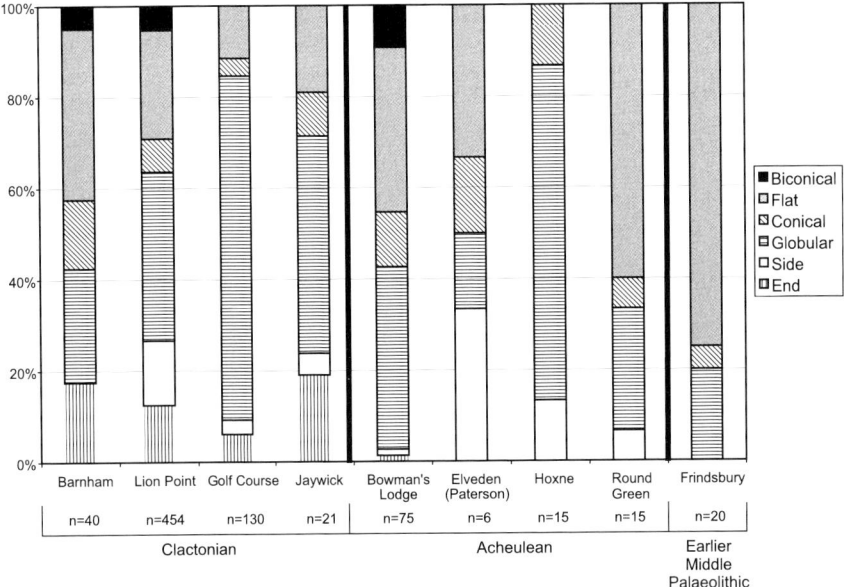

Figure 12.8 Frequency of occurrence of different core shapes in Clactonian and Acheulean assemblages.

cores worked down one side of the block at Lion Point probably reflects a collecting bias on the part of Hazzledine Warren – this morphology would have approximated his side-chopper group.

The higher percentage of cores worked at one end might also reflect a collecting bias, i.e. retaining those pieces that looked like end choppers. However, Barnham, the Golf Course, and Jaywick are all excavated sites – every artefact would have been kept. Perhaps we could invoke raw material character to explain this? They are all fluvial gravel sites where *rounded cobbles* would be more common. What would be easier than to knapp one end of a rounded clast in order to make a few flakes? – the fortuitous result would be an end chopper. This is not convincing either. The evidence from the sites (data not presented) shows that relatively few rounded cobbles were knapped. Irregular flint nodules were the commonest blank for core working. For the moment, the high incidence of end struck cores on flint nodules in the Clactonian sites remains a puzzle.

Unfortunately the very low sample size for the Acheulean does not lend itself to meaningful comparisons. There may be two examples in these data where we can see raw material type directly influencing core shape. Round Green and Frindsbury both have large numbers of flat cores. In the case of the former site, it is located in a clay-with-flints region (the Chiltern Hills) where thermally shattered slab-like blocks are common (personal observation; Smith 1916; White 1997). Frindsbury, a possible early expression of Levallois technology with simple prepared cores (White and Ashton 2003), is situated in a periglacially disturbed chalk area of northern Kent. Slab-like nodules and frost-shattered tabular flints may well have been common here too. Apart from these two examples there is no immediate relationship between core shape and raw material apparent in these data.

If core shape on excavated sites is not satisfactorily explained by raw materials, then what about knapping techniques? Do certain ways of flaking produce certain core shapes more frequently than others? Could cultural biases in knapping be reflected in the occurrence of specific core shapes? The methodology, again based on an older system of interpretation, is explained in Figure 12.7. These data are presented in Table 12.3. It is evident that all of the core shapes could be produced by almost all of the knapping techniques. This is reinforced by the high numbers of cores worked by a mixture of techniques and which successfully produced every one of the core shapes. So there is no real reason to believe that specific techniques consistently produced specific morphologies. This provides strong circumstantial evidence in support of the side and end flaked core morphologies not being knapped as pre-conceived chopping tools. The variety of techniques applied to their manufacture strongly suggests that their shapes are arbitrary stopping points in a flaking sequence (McNabb 1992a).

Table 12.3 Comparing the relationship between core shape and flaking technique as outlined in McNabb (1992a)

Core shape	Parallel flaking	Random flaking	Alternate flaking	Centripetal flaking	Mixture of techniques	Indeterminate
Knapped at one end	18	27	5	0	8	18
	0	1	0	0	0	0
Knapped along one side	6	20	6	0	19	18
	2	3	0	0	1	0
Globular/shapeless	44	113	3	4	90	32
	4	22	0	0	23	1
Conical	7	12	0	0	21	6
	4	4	0	0	5	1
Flat	22	48	2	7	42	21
	3	24	2	6	16	2
Biconical	0	4	0	0	16	6
	0	2	1	0	4	0

Notes: The figures in the cells refer to frequency counts. The upper left corner gives the frequency for non-biface assemblages. The lower right corner gives the frequency for biface assemblages. The non-biface assemblages used for this table were, Barnham (industries A–E Paterson excavation), Lion Point, Golf Course site, Jaywick. The biface assemblages were Bowman's Lodge, Elveden (Paterson excavation), Hoxne Lower Industry, Round Green. Frindsbury, a possible Earlier Middle Palaeolithic assemblage, was included with the biface assemblages.

318

A framework for describing assemblages in the British Lower and Earlier Middle Palaeolithic

The system described below was developed in order to facilitate comparisons between different assemblages of stone tools based on the presence, absence, and proportion of certain types of lithic artefact. The framework itself is shown in Table 12.4. It is meant only as a first filter, intended to establish the presence of variability and then describe its character. The framework is not intended as a detailed analytical tool designed to highlight the intricacies of hominin behaviour. For this, more detailed methodologies would be necessary, ones which were specifically orientated towards the particular research question the analyst was asking.

The framework is divided into two sections. Flaked pieces are artefacts which have been shaped by flaking and consequently have had their volume reduced by the detachment of flakes. This is also known as façonnage (White and Pettitt 1995). Detached pieces represent the product of that process. These are debitage products in the French sense of the word. Some detached pieces may have been accidental while others were the intended end-product.

The flaked pieces are divided into two groups. The cores which are here taken to be waste products, and the bifacially shaped pieces which are the intended end products. Three approaches to flaking are described below. All cores and bifacially shaped pieces will be knapped using these approaches. The cores can be grouped on the presence, absence, or combination of each of these approaches.

Approaches to flaking

British Middle Pleistocene knappers employed three basic ways of flaking (Ashton and McNabb 1996a; 1996b): alternate flaking, parallel flaking and single removals. These approaches represent the simplest way of detaching flakes from blocks of stone. This, however, does not mean they are simplistic, rather, they are efficient and effective ways of either reducing volume or of shaping it. In fact, it is difficult to see how else flakes could be systematically removed. These approaches underpin all structured knapping and as such they cannot be considered culturally diagnostic. They are likely to have been re-invented on a number of occasions (Rolland 1981; White 2000).

Alternate flaking

This is the most complicated form of flaking. It involves turning the blank over and using the proximal ends of the flake scars just created as platforms for the next removal or set of removals:

- Simple alternate flaking (Figure 12.9A). This involves detaching one or

Table 12.4 A framework for stone tool assemblages from the British Lower and Earlier Middle Palaeolithic

Flaked pieces		Detached pieces	
Cores	Bifacially shaped pieces	Unretouched	Retouched/utilised

Flaked pieces		Detached pieces	
Cores	**Bifacially shaped pieces**	**Unretouched**	**Retouched/utilised**
A. Generic non-PCT cores. No maintained flaking face and no fixed perimeter • Alternate (A1) • Mixture of episodes of alternate and parallel (A2) • Parallel either from 1 platform (A3) or multiple platforms (A4) • Single/multiple episodes of single (A5) • Mixture of any of above (A6) • Other generic non-PCT (A7) B. Non-PCT cores. A fixed perimeter only. • Dominated by centripetal alternate – biconical (B1) • Dominated by centripetal alternate – discoid (B2) • Other (B3) C. Cores knapped by Prepared Core Technology (PCT). A fixed perimeter related to a single maintained flaking face. Detachments parallel the fixed perimeter. • Radial (C1) • Convergent (C2) • Parallel/laminar (C3) • Simple prepared cores (C3a; after Ashton and White) • Other (C4) D. Cores knapped from a fixed platform. The flaking face is not pre-prepared to the same extent as in C, or maintained. Successive removals create the flaking face. • Laminar. Prismatic or conical, unipolar or bipolar (D1)	• Classic bifaces (E1) • Classic cleavers (E2) • Non-classic bifaces (E3) • Rough-outs (E4) • Bifacially shaped chopping tools (E5) • Other (E6)	• Chips (=< 20 mm maximum length – F1) • Chunks (F2) • Core fragments (F3) • Unbroken hard hammer flakes Toth types 1–6 (F4-F9) • Broken hard hammer flakes (F10) • Soft hammer/ thinning flakes (F11) • Debitage associated with PCT cores (C1–C4) and/or their preparation (F12) • Debitage associated with laminar cores (D1) and/or their preparation (F13) • Other debitage (F14) Levallois flakes and blades • Radial (G1) • Convergent (G2) • Laminar Non-pointed blades/ flake blades (G3) Pointed blades/flake blades (G4) Pointed laminar but cannot tell if made by convergent or laminar methods (G5)	• Denticulated edge (H1) • Denticulated scraper (H2) • Side scraper – any form (H3) • End or transverse scraper (H4) • Flake with scraper retouch (H5) • Scraper used as a wedge (H6) • Retouched point *sensu* awl (H7) • Retouched point *sensu* projectile or weapon point (H8) • Retouched notch (H9) • Retouched – non-diagnostic (H10) • Flaked flake or flaked flake spall (H11) • Multiple tool (H12) • Unretouched flake used as a wedge (H13) • Utilised flake with no retouch (H14)

more flakes on one face of the blank/core, and then turning the piece over and detaching one or more flakes from the proximal ends of the flake scar(s) just created. If the piece is turned only once, it is called simple alternate flaking. Simple alternate flaking can represent an episode of flake removals in its own right, or it can lead on to complex alternate flaking.

• *Complex alternate flaking* (Figure 12.9B). This strategy is similar to simple alternate. However, after the core has been turned once and knapped again, the core is turned *at least* once more, and the proximal ends of

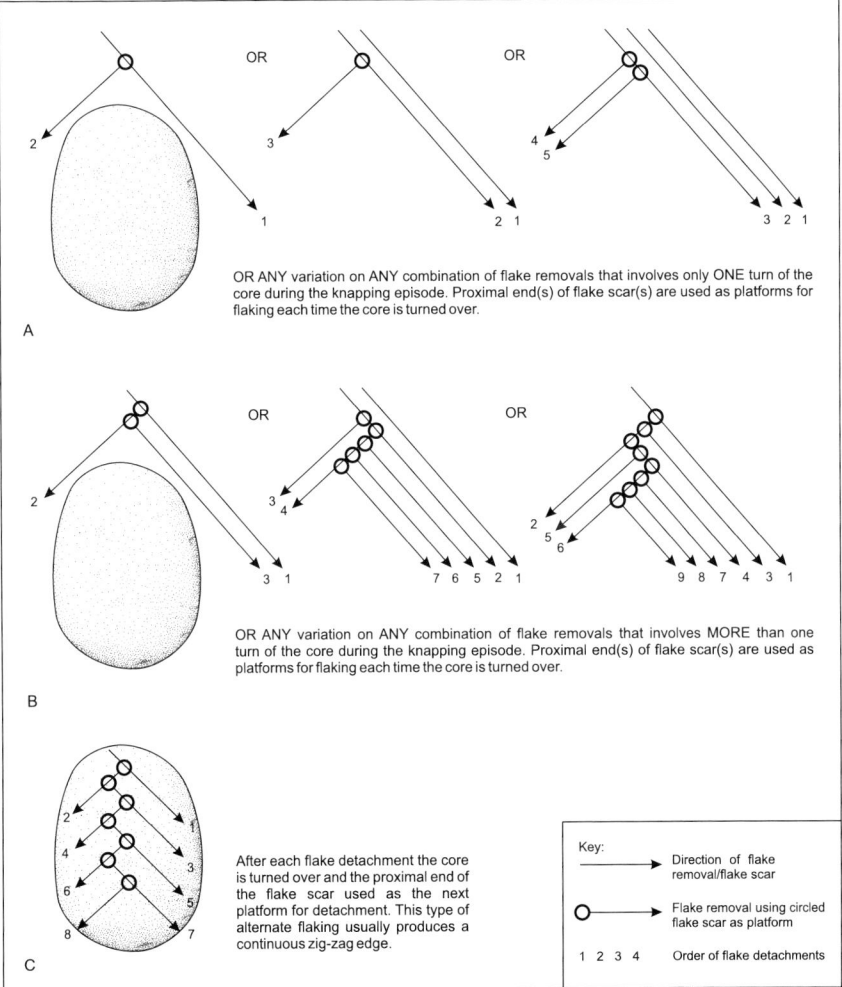

Figure 12.9 Three variations on the theme of alternate flaking. A: Simple alternate flaking. B: Complex alternate flaking. C Classic alternate flaking.

the last flake scar or scars then become the platforms for the next set of removals. In theory complex alternate flaking can involve any number of turns, although in practice three or four are usually the maximum.

- *Classic alternate flaking* (Figure 12.9C). This strategy involves many turns of the core (at least a minimum of three must be present). After *each* flake removal, the blank is turned over and that flake scar is used as a platform for the next detachment. The sequence thus involves: detach a flake, turn over, detach a flake, turn over, detach a flake, turn over, etc. A sequence of classic alternate flaking often creates an edge with a pronounced zigzag appearance.

Parallel flaking

This approach involves a series of three or more flake removals (in earlier versions of this it was two – Ashton and McNabb 1996b), whose axes of percussion must be parallel to each other (Figure 12.10A). The platform from which the parallel sequence is struck may be a flake scar or a natural/ cortical surface. The parallel flakes may be taken from two or more contiguous platforms of a different nature (e.g. one cortical, the other a flake scar). So long as there are three or more scars whose axes of percussion parallel each other, it does not matter what the nature of the platform is, it is assumed the parallel removals are part of the same episode. In practice, the platform is usually one flake scar or two adjacent ones.

When the striking platform is a flake scar, you should only identify a sequence of parallel flaking if the striking platform is the lateral edge, or distal edge of a flake scar. Why? If the striking platform is one or more proximal ends of flake scars, you cannot discount the possibility of the parallel scars being part of a sequence of alternate flaking.

Single removals

These represent cores which either have one flake scar, a number of discrete isolated flake scars, or have been extensively knapped but have one or more flake scars isolated from any other episodes of flaking (Figure 12.10B). In this last case scars may only be identified as single removals if their platforms are the lateral or distal edges of flake scars. As with parallel flaking, this way you can be sure they were not part of sequences of alternate flaking.

The episodic nature of flaking a core

All Lower Palaeolithic cores are knapped episodically. Each episode is a distinct run of one of the approaches to flaking just described. A core is knapped by a combination of episodes. For example, in its final stages a core might be worked by two separate episodes of alternate flaking and one

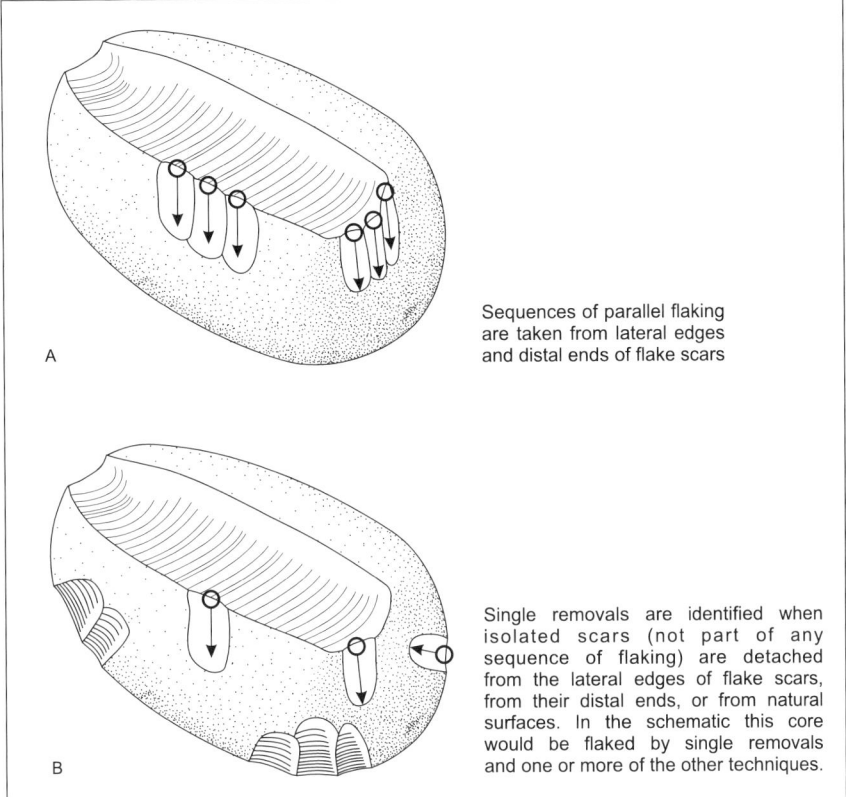

Sequences of parallel flaking
are taken from lateral edges
and distal ends of flake scars

Single removals are identified when
isolated scars (not part of any
sequence of flaking) are detached
from the lateral edges of flake scars,
from their distal ends, or from natural
surfaces. In the schematic this core
would be flaked by single removals
and one or more of the other techniques.

Figure 12.10 Schematic illustrations showing parallel flaking (A) and single removals (B).

of parallel. Or it may be worked by one episode of parallel, or several episodes of parallel. The clearest episodes of flaking on a core are almost always the last to be knapped – this is why they are the best preserved and the easiest to read. A core is usually knapped by a number of flaking episodes which overprint each other as the core gets smaller. So the interpretation of a core is actually that of the last few episodes of flaking in its life history.

What really determines which knapping techniques are applied to a core is the interplay between platform suitability (i.e. size) and the angle between the *flaking face* and the platform. The flaking face is the face below the striking platform from which flakes will be detached. Broad platforms set at a wide angle to the flaking face will usually be knapped by parallel flaking. Poorer angles and smaller platforms usually result in alternate flaking. A knapper will continue with one approach if it is continuing to produce flakes. When a run of detachments comes to an end, the knapper hunts for another place on the core that will sustain a new episode of flaking. The knapper will choose a location on the core that will allow the most flakes to be removed. The choice of which flaking technique to use is entirely dependent on what will suit that part of the core. This is why formal knapping techniques are not invariably applied. They are simple and effective approaches to the problem of reducing volume and of making flakes.

How do you read a sequence of flaking in order to identify an episode of alternate, parallel, or single flaking?

The identification of individual sequences/episodes of flaking is based on the following:

- Identification of the final scar in a sequence of flake removals. This is usually the most complete scar.
- Identification of its negative proximal end, and then the platform used to detach it from.
- This platform/scar is then traced to its point of origin, and the scar or surface used as a platform for its detachment is located.
- The process is repeated until a chain or sequence of removals is identified, and the method of knapping revealed.
- This represents one isolated episode of flaking.
- The process is then repeated for every episode that can be discerned on the core.

There will always be flake scars that cannot be fitted into any sequences – usually they are remnants of earlier episodes partially obliterated by later flaking. Although such loose ends can be irritating, the analyst just has to accept this. The core is interpreted on the basis of the last few sequences that can be identified.

How the approaches to flaking were implemented by Palaeolithic knappers

Group A cores (see Table 12.4) have no prepared flaking face or maintained perimeter. Flakes are removed by the three approaches to flaking described above from anywhere on the surface of the core that is suitable for flaking. The cores are classified by which of the approaches, or combination thereof, have been applied to the detachment of flakes in the last stages of working the core (subtypes A1–A7). Notice I do not distinguish between different patterns of alternate flaking here. This system operates at the level of a first filter, recognition of the presence of alternate flaking is sufficient.

One shortcoming I have become aware of concerns two adjacent flakes whose axes of percussion are parallel. In earlier versions of the system, Nick Ashton and I (Ashton and McNabb 1996b) considered two parallel flake scars enough to identify parallel flaking. I have chosen to make the minimum number three as I feel this increases the likelihood of recognising the knapper's intent to flake in this way. But that leaves open the question of what to do with two adjacent flakes. I have been placing them either in the A6 mixed sub-group, or in the A7 other non-PCT sub-group as appropriate. This may be one of those instances where an analyst may wish to adapt or add a new category.

Group B cores (see Table 12.4) combine an element of shape in their definition. The reason for this is that the shape is a direct result of the method of flaking – predominantly alternate. Extending knapping, by any of the three methods of alternate flaking, around all or most of the circumference of a flint nodule, usually creates a clear margin around the core. Biconical and discoidal shapes are shown in cross-section in Figures 12.11A and 12.11B. In order for a core to be classified in group B, more than 60 per cent of its fixed margin must be a consequence of alternate flaking. In other words, it must clearly represent the dominant form of flaking applied to the core. These two shapes can be fortuitously produced by a mixture of the other approaches, in which case they are classified within group A.

Group C (see Table 12.4) represents cores worked by Levallois method/ PCT. This was introduced in earlier chapters and briefly explained in Chapter 7. This is a complicated subject with a lot of disagreement about how to define it. Important advances have been made by E. Boëda (1995, and references therein) and his work is essential for any detailed understanding of this technology. Good introductions are presented by Mellars (1996), Schlanger (1996), Chazan (1997), White and Pettitt (1995), and White and Ashton (2003). Varying approaches and interpretations are rehearsed in Dibble and Bar-Yosef (1995). At this level of

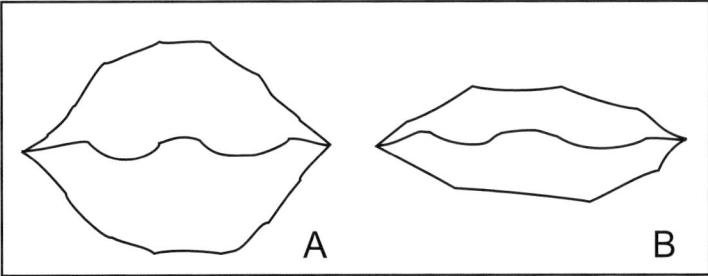

Figure 12.11 Schematic cross-section of cores knapped from a fixed margin (type B)

Note: The bi-conical core in Figure 12.11A has two high domes created by flaking from the fixed margin. The discoid in Figure 12.11B has much flatter upper and lower convexities created by flaking from the margin.

assemblage analysis, it is not necessary to go into great detail concerning the contrasting Levallois methods and end products. Group C recognizes five basic subdivisions, see Table 12.4 and Figure 7.1. For both the cores and their detached pieces (F12–13 and group G – see Table 12.4), recognition is based on planform and scar pattern. Group C cores are not present in the Clactonian, they only appear in the Earlier Middle Palaeolithic.

Group D (see Table 12.4) will not be discussed in any detail as this technology does not appear in the British Lower Palaeolithic, and its presence in the Earlier Middle Palaeolithic in Britain is disputed (e.g. at Crayford, see Chapter 7).

The results of analysing British Lower Palaeolithic cores (Groups A and B)

The data are presented in Table 12.5. Table 12.5 combines data from four excavated non-handaxe assemblages, and three excavated handaxe ones. It also presents the results for the frequency of the above knapping patterns from Clactonian assemblages that were selectively collected. All the sites are dated to MIS 11. The data are summarised in the line graph showing cumulative percentage in Figure 12.12.

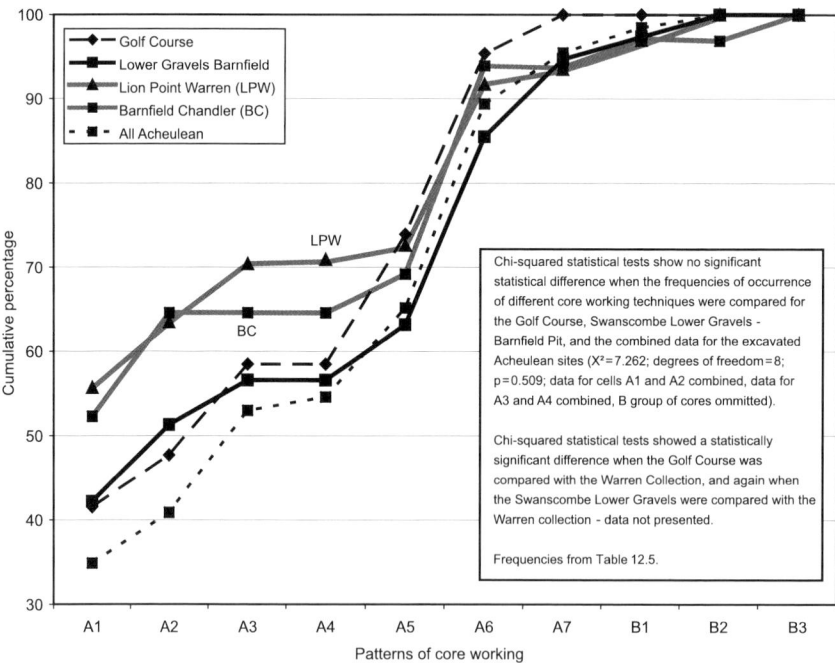

Figure 12.12 Comparison of the frequency of occurrence of the different types of core presented in Table 12.4.

Table 12.5 Data for patterns of core flaking as seen in a selection of Lower Palaeolithic non-biface and biface assemblages

Sites	A1	A2	A3	A4	A5	A6	A7	B1	B2	B3
Excavated non-biface/Clactonian assemblages										
Clacton – Jaywick Sands, gravel	11				3	6	1			
Clacton – Golf Course, gravel	27	4	7		10	14	3		1	
Little Thurrock – Wymer excavation	2	1			2	1				
Lower Gravels, Barnfield Pit, Swanscombe – Waechter excavation	32	7	4		5	17	7	2	2	
Selected (i.e. collected) Clactonian assemblages										
Clacton – Lion Point – Warren collection	128	18	16	1	4	44	4	8	7	
Lower Gravels, Barnfield Pit, Swanscombe – Chandler collection	34	8			3	16		2		2
Excavated biface/Acheulean assemblages										
Elveden BM excavations	14	2	4	1	5	9	1			
Lower Middle Gravels, Barnfield Pit, Swanscombe – Waechter excavations	4		1		1	3	1	1	1	
Hoxne Lower Industry, West Cutting, unrolled	5	2	3		1	4	2	1		

Note: For key to core types, see Table 2.4.

It is evident from the cumulative graph that the frequency of occurrence of the different knapping techniques in the excavated Clactonian sites and the three Acheulean sites (data combined because of smaller totals) follows a similar pattern. The two excavated Clactonian sites share similar numbers of cores worked only by alternate flaking (of any type – A1), with the Acheulean assemblages having fewer of these. There is a moderate increase of cores with parallel flaking (A2 and A3, slightly more so for the Acheulean sites indicated by the steeper gradient between A2 and A3), and all the excavated sites share a low incidence of cores flaked by multiple episodes of parallel flaking (A4 – indicated by the shallowness of the line between A3 and A4). The Barnfield Lower Gravels and the Acheulean sites share a similar frequency in the occurrence of cores worked by one or more episodes of single detachments (A5). The Golf Course differs here in having a much higher percentage of A5 (much steeper gradient on the graph). All the excavated sites share a high percentage of cores worked by a mixture of the approaches to flaking (A6). The presence of cores with a fixed perimeter is variable in all the excavated assemblages, and when present, these are infrequent.

Lion Point follows this pattern fairly closely, only really deviating from it in the lower frequency of A5 type cores. In fact, both of the selected (differentially collected) assemblages show a low incidence of these (minimal slope between A4 and A5). This may well reflect collecting bias as these artefacts may not have been recognised as cores by collectors. In the excavated Acheulean and Clactonian assemblages these types of core represent a small but persistent component (especially in the Golf Course).

So although we noted earlier that Lion Point may be quite different from excavated Clactonian assemblages in many respects, at least in the *pattern of flaking* present on cores, it broadly conforms to the observed pattern for other non-handaxe assemblages. The cores from Chandler's Barnfield Pit collection show some departure from this pattern. Cores worked by a combination of alternate and parallel flaking (A2) show an increase in frequency compared with the other sites, but then the two parallel flaking categories (A3 and A4) are not represented at all. Almost certainly this pattern reflects the selected character of the Chandler collection. I suspect it is much more heavily selected that the Warren collection from Lion Point.

Statistical tests support the broad comparability in core knapping between all the assemblages, irrespective of supposed cultural affiliations (Figure 12.12; McNabb and Ashton 1995). On the whole, there does not seem much of a difference in the flaking patterns between these eleven MIS 11 assemblages.

Group E Bifac... shaped pieces

This is the second group of artefacts ...rked by *façonnage* (White and Pettitt 1995) that can be thought of as deliberately flaked pieces.

Classic handaxes and cleavers (E1 and E2)

One of the most common and visually distinctive forms of deliberately shaped bifacial tool is the *biface* or *handaxe*. Bifaces remain the subject of much pointed study, but disagreement exists in virtually every aspect of their investigation; in classification (Roe 1968; Wymer 1985; McPherron 1995: 2ff.), in manufacturing technique (Newcomer 1971; Bradley and Sampson 1986), blank selection and influence (Wenban-Smith and Ashton 1998; White 1998a), function (Mitchell 1996), and in their cognitive and social significance (Kohn and Mithen 1999). As noted above for the purposes of the descriptive system set out in Table 12.4, it is only necessary to identify the presence of classic handaxes or cleavers in an assemblage (see Figure 1.1A for illustrations).

To qualify as a classic handaxe, both faces of the tool must be extensively modified by bifacial thinning and shaping, and the worked edges must reflect the imposition of shape through the application of this type of knapping. On occasion, a handaxe will have thinning and shaping applied to only one face. These are usually labelled unifaces. For the purposes of the system used here, these can be subsumed into the classic handaxe category so long as the imposition of shape by thinning is clear and unambiguous. A more detailed analysis of handaxes should follow one of the methodologies cited above.

Rough-outs (E4) and other bifacially shaped pieces (E6)

Rough-outs can be a difficult category of artefact to identify as they will usually lack any of the thinning or shaping that normally associates a flaked piece with the bifacially shaped group. They should be wide and fairly flat, and predominantly knapped by hard hammer. In reality, their identification is a subjective call; in handaxe assemblages, a large and flattish piece that the analyst does not consider a core is usually a rough-out.

In most large collections of bifaces there are a few bifacially worked artefacts that do not conform to any recognised category, these should be included in E6.

Non-classic handaxes (E3)

These were introduced in earlier chapters (see Figure 3.9). They represent artefacts which show a bare minimum of thinning and shaping, often confined to only one edge. They can be difficult to recognise as the thinning is in all probability casual and expedient, and they do not look like the more extensively thinned and shaped classic handaxes (Ashton and McNabb 1994). There is no attempt to impose any regularity on the outline. In some cases the bifacial working is merely designed to accentuate a section of naturally sharp edge.

They are an infrequent component of some Clactonian and Acheulean assemblages but not all. In my opinion, they are best explained by accepting that Middle Pleistocene hominin behaviour was complicated and situationally flexible.

Bifacially shaped chopping tools (E5)

One other bifacially shaped tool type needs to be described. These are artefacts which are made by bifacial thinning and shaping, but which have been given the label *chopping tools*. This term was originally applied by two nineteenth-century pioneers of Palaeolithic archaeology, Édouard Lartet and Henry Christy (1875; Ashton, pers. comm.; Ashton *et al.* 1992b), to a morphologically distinctive group of artefacts with only one cutting edge made by careful bifacial thinning and shaping. The opposite edge was usually thick and either unflaked or only roughly flaked, and was thought to be the hand grip. In cross-section, these pieces were wedge-shaped. Typologically they were sometimes called tea cosy forms or segmental choppers, some were thinned with a soft hammer (in Acheulean assemblages), while others were made with a hard hammer but still showed careful attention to bifacial working and regularity on the shaped working edge. They all shared a common concept, a single convex working edge that was the result of purposeful bifacial thinning and shaping. Whether these artefacts were conceived of as handaxes with only one cutting edge, or something different is not clear. At any rate, they represent a small but distinctive component of some stone tool assemblages.

But the term chopping tool gradually came to be applied to another class of artefact. In this second usage it described a tool were there was no attempt at shaping. The flaking was still applied to one end or side of a nodule but now it lacked the appearance of carefully imposed form. Looking down onto the working edge, it was a zig-zag, a result of the intersection of flake scars knapped by alternate flaking. When viewed in planform, the flaked portion was almost always irregular in outline. There was usually an unflaked part opposite the 'working edge' which was the hand grip.

These were the tools that Hazzledine Warren and Chandler thought of when they used the term chopping tool.

Just when the term chopping tool came to be applied to this variant alone is not known. Worthington Smith figures chopping tools of this latter description in his classic book *Man the Primeval Savage* (Smith 1894: Figure 157), and in his earlier descriptions of the knapping floor at Stoke Newington, London (Smith 1884). Hazzledine Warren certainly referred to this later meaning in his earliest publications on the Clactonian (Warren 1922; 1924a). From this time on, British archaeology used the label chopping, tool to refer to this second type of artefact. In my opinion, all of these chopping tools (*sensu* Warren) are cores. While some may have been used as occasional heavy duty tools (Keeley 1980), the majority are wholly unsuitable for this kind or activity (Ashton *et al.* 1992b; McNabb 1992a). They certainly lack the characteristic damage that experimental pieces acquire when chopping bone or wood (McNabb 1992a). I have subsumed them all into the various sub-categories of group A on Table 12.4.

The term chopping tool (E5) is only retained for the bifacially shaped convex-edged examples described above (*sensu* Lartet and Christy). Examples are illustrated in Figure 12.13, from the Acheulean site of Bowman's Lodge, and from near the base of the Lower Gravels at the Barnfield Pit, Swanscombe. The examples demonstrate that these artefacts can occur on occasion in any Lower Palaeolithic assemblage. They serve to reinforce the point made above about non-classic handaxes, that tool behaviour was subtle and situationally variable, and boxing it into cultural either/or interpretations may obscure important ambiguities.

Cores and shaped bifacial tools used for other purposes

Although cores are here considered waste products, a number of them appear to serve other functions after they were knapped. Although it is a not a common feature, a number of cores at various sites appear to have been used as hammer stones. On their unknapped surfaces, or sometimes on their flake scars, there are clusters of incipient percussion cones. They indicate that the core was either used to hit something, or it was hit by something else. This has been reported on cores in the Lower Gravels at Swanscombe (Chandler 1928–29) and at Little Thurrock (Snelling 1964). A similar feature has been noted on a small number of bifaces from Swanscombe (Wymer 1958; 1964) and from Boxgrove (Roberts *et al.* 1997). Again these observations remind us that our modern tendency to pigeonhole and objectify is probably more of a reflection on ourselves than on *Homo heidelbergensis*.

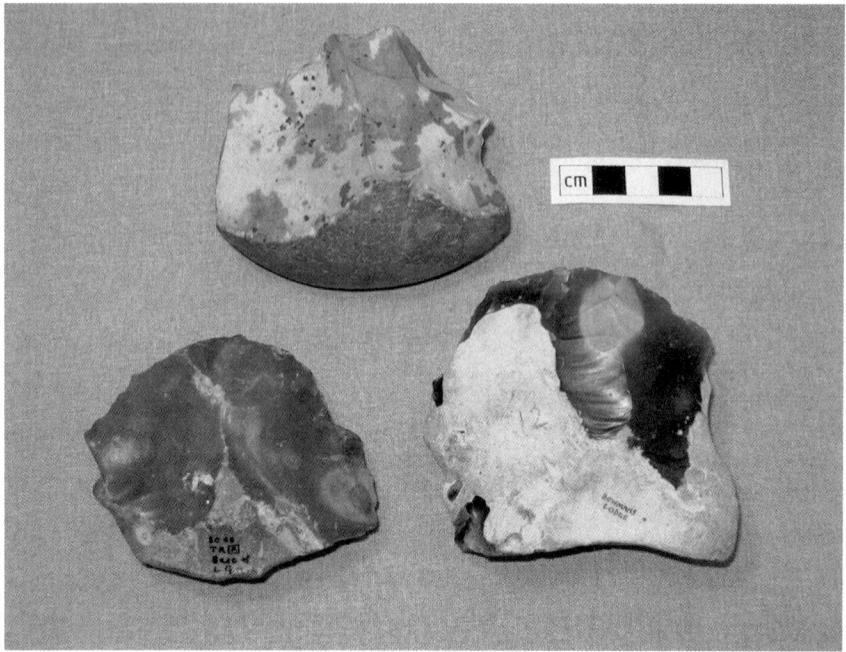

Figure 12.13 Chopping tools. Bottom right, chopping tool, *sensu* Lartet and Christie, from Acheulean site of Bowman's Lodge. Top chopping tool, *sensu* Warren, also from Bowman's Lodge. Bottom left, chopping tool, *sensu* Lartet and Christy, base Lower Gravels, Barnfield Pit, Swanscombe.

Group F Detached pieces

These artefacts represent the bi-products of *façonnage*, i.e. they are the result of flaking cores and bifacially shaped pieces. These are the products of debitage as the French would understand it, or often just described as debitage in the English speaking world. There are six heuristic groupings:

1   the unmodified or unused bi-products of flaking non-PCT cores (F3–10);
2   the unmodified or unused bi-products of thinning and shaping handaxes (F11);
3   the unmodified or unused bi-products of flaking PCT cores or blade cores (F12–F13);
4   the unretouched end products of flaking PCT/type C cores. These are combined together in group G;
5   the unmodified or unused bi-products of knapping flint that could result from making anything (F1–F2, F14);
6   detached pieces which have been modified by retouch into tools

332

(group H). In principle, these can be made on any of the above five groups, but in practice retouched tools are usually made on flakes.

Only those detached pieces relevant to the Clactonian and Acheulean will be discussed below.

Group F Detached pieces which are unretouched and unutilised

Chips (F1) should be the most common form of debitage on any undisturbed in-situ archaeological site where knapping has taken place. To class as a chip, a fragment of stone must be less than 2 cms in maximum length. Experimental studies make it clear that these can represent up to 80 per cent or more of the debitage on an in-situ site (Schick 1986). They are the first category of artefacts to be removed from a site by water flow, and only a small percentage would be recovered from a secondary context site. Chunks (F2) represent angular or cuboid shaped pieces which have no flake scars. They are usually the result of spontaneous shatter and breakage during knapping. Core fragments (F3) are identical to chunks, but flake scars or their remnants are clearly present (Field 1999). They can occur while knapping any flaked piece.

Broken hard hammer flakes (F10) are present in almost all assemblages where hard hammer core working or handaxe making has occurred. Their inclusion in analytical work should be approached with caution depending on what research questions the analyst is posing. Unbroken flakes are categorised following the scheme suggested by Nick Toth (1985). Flakes with wholly cortical dorsal faces and cortex on the butt are labelled F4 (Toth type 1); those with some cortex on the dorsal and the butt are F5 (Toth type 2); some cortex on the butt and none on the dorsal are F6 (Toth type 3); no cortex on the butt, and the dorsal completely cortical F7 (Toth type 4); some cortex on dorsal but none on the butt F8 (Toth type 5); no cortex at all F9 (Toth type 6). More detailed analysis of non-PCT debitage is provided in Ashton and McNabb (1996a; 1996b). In any analysis of debitage there will always be a number of detached pieces that defy interpretation. These should be included within F14.

In Figure 12.4, size data for Clactonian flakes were presented. Figure 12.14 presents further data on this, comparing an index of the mean volume of flakes with that of cores. In this case the data help to clarify information on the physical context of individual assemblages described in Chapter 3.

The atypical nature of the selected assemblages is re-emphasised for Lion Point, as is the exceptional size of the cores and flakes from Chandler's Lower Gravel collection. The artefacts from Little Thurrock and Jaywick Sands were described in Chapter 3 as having been recovered from the gravel at the margins of their respective channels. Artefacts at these two secondary

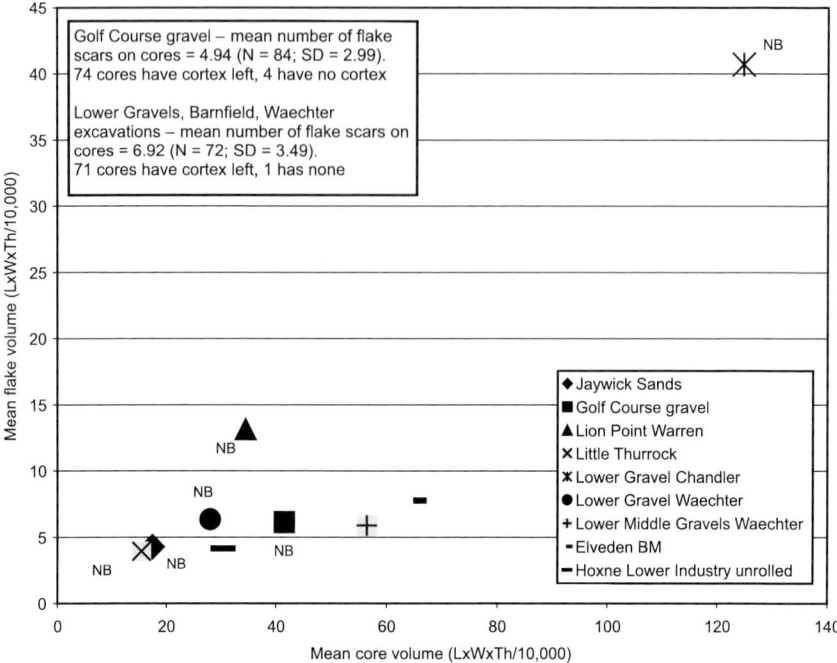

Figure 12.14 Comparison of the mean volume (as a proxy for size) for cores and flakes from a variety of Clactonian and Acheulean assemblages. An arbitrary correction factor of 10,000 was included in the calculation of volume in order to make the final data simpler to comprehend.

Note: NB = non-biface.

context sites came to rest in the shallow water close to the bank where transport energy was lower. Figure 12.14 clearly supports this, the two sites have the smallest cores and flakes and are very similar to each other in size. This reinforces my concern about interpreting Little Thurrock as a Clactonian site – it is difficult to demonstrate time depth for any assemblage in such a context.

The flakes from the Golf Course site at Clacton and the Lower Gravels at Swanscombe are similar in size, but the cores at the former site are bigger on average. The cores at the Golf Course also showed fewer flake scars that those in the Lower Gravels. Perhaps the nodules at the Golf course site were a little larger than those at Swanscombe necessitating less knapping. In Chapter 3 it was suggested that the Golf Course site represented a mixture of primary and secondary context material on the surface of a gravel bar near the river bank.

The larger size of the cores in the Swanscombe Lower Middle Gravels (Acheulean) may reflect a similar situation. Here artefacts were made on the flint from gravel bars in a braided river. A variety of clast sizes may well have been available, as on the bar's surface at the Golf Course. The size of the Elveden cores will reflect the derivation of these artefacts from the lag gravel which was used as a source of raw material by the handaxe makers at this site (Ashton et al. 2005).

The results for flake type from a selection of sites are presented in Figure 12.15. The two Clactonian sites are very similar to each other. The basic pattern appears to be a predominance of partially cortical flakes with no cortex on the butt (F8), lower quantities of wholly non-cortical flakes (F9), and flakes with some cortex on the butt and the dorsal face (F5). I suggest this would be the expected pattern in a large sample of flakes generated by the flaking techniques detailed above. Secondary context assemblages, with a large enough flake sample, should also reflect this pattern (e.g. Lower Gravels). The reason is they will be sampling any number of 'sites' along a river bank whose flake population will repeat this distribution. Even the collected assemblage from Lion Point approaches this pattern (data not presented). Although the Acheulean sample is smaller, frequency of occurrence is not dissimilar to that seen in the smaller Clactonian sites. At least for this limited data set, the results of the analysis of flakes supports the conclusions drawn from the cores, namely that there was no difference in the way Clactonian and Acheulean knappers flaked their cores (McNabb 1992a; McNabb and Ashton 1995).

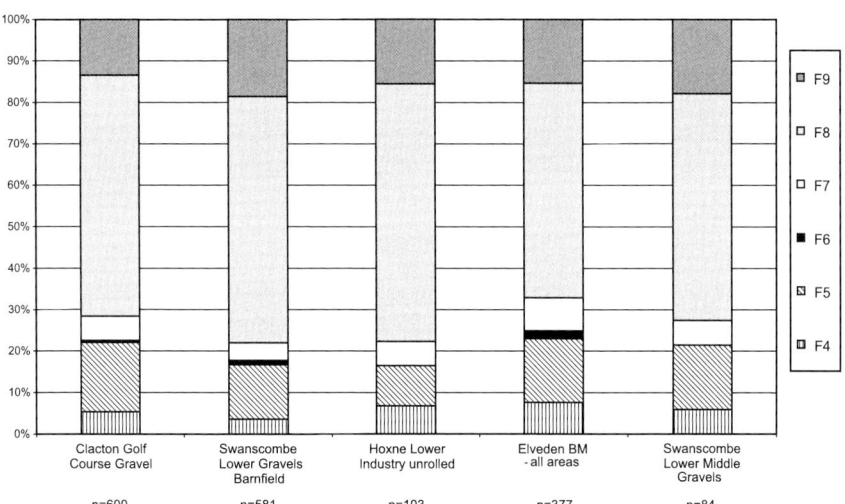

F4/Toth type 1 - cortex on butt and dorsal fully cortical; F5/Toth type 2 - cortex on butt and dorsal partially cortical;
F6/Toth type 3 - cortex on butt and dorsal has no cortex; F7/Toth type 4 - no cortex on butt, dorsal fully cortical;
F8/Toth type 5 - no cortex on butt, dorsal partially cortical; F9/Toth type 6 - no cortex on butt, dorsal has no cortex

Figure 12.15 Comparison of the frequency of occurrence of different hard hammer flake types (based on presence and location of cortex) from a selection of Clactonian and Acheulean assemblages.

Group H Detached pieces – retouched and utilised

> To retouch is to shape, sculpt, or transform a product of debit-
> age into a tool . . . Retouch is the trace left by this action
> (Tixier 1974: 19)

A formal terminology describing where retouch is found and what it looks like is an important staring point for any detailed study of retouch (Inizan *et al.* 1992). There are a number of different classifications for describing the retouched tools themselves. The most widely used is still that of Bordes (1961; Debénath and Dibble 1994). It has been applied to British Lower Palaeolithic assemblages but has not found wide acceptance. There are two reasons. Retouched tools represent quite a small component of British assemblages, and the Bordes system should have a minimum of one hundred retouched tools to be really effective. Second, it is overly complicated and so its relevance to the British Middle Pleistocene record is limited. The retouched element in British Lower Palaeolithic assemblages is, in my opinion, very conservative, only a few types more often than not dominated by flaked flakes (see Bisson 2000, for other problems). This situation may be compounded by traditional research directions. Britain Lower Palaeolithic studies tended to focus on handaxes.

In Table 12.6, the retouched tools from selected Lower Palaeolithic assemblages are listed. They are described below under three separate headings depending on which form of edge the retouching produces.

Unevenly retouched edges

The retouch produces a ragged edge or it is localised on an edge. The retouch is a series of small multiple contiguous removals.

Denticulated edge (H1)

The definition follows commonly accepted understandings of this edge morphology (Debénath and Dibble 1994). The retouch produces a length of uneven, saw-toothed, or scalloped-looking edge. The edge profile looks ragged. The retouching is semi-continuous down the length of an edge.

Denticulated scrapers (H2)

These are similar to H1. To qualify as a denticulated scraper the retouch must be continuous along the whole length of an edge. The blank should be large, and usually larger than H1. While the distinction between H1 and H2 is maintained here, it can be rather arbitrary, especially on smaller flake blanks. Analysts can adapt or abandon the category as required.

Table 12.6 Totals for retouch in selected Clactonian and Acheulean assemblages

| | Clactonian sites in MIS 11, apart from Little Thurrock which dates to the MIS 10/9 transition | | | | | | Acheulean sites from MIS 11 | | |
| | Clacton-on-Sea | | | Swanscombe – Barnfield Pit | | Little Thurrock (Wymer + Bridgland) | Elveden (BM all areas) | Swanscombe – Barnfield Pit Lower Middle Gravels | Hoxne Lower Industry unrolled |
	Jaywick Sands	Golf Course gravel	Lion Point (Warren)	Lower Gravels (Chandler)	Lower Gravels (Waechter)				
H1 Denticulate	1		3						
H2 Denticulated scraper			3						
H3 Side scraper			2	2	2		1	2	3
H4 End scraper		2	6	1		1			1
H5 Flake with scraper retouch	2	1					2		
H6 Scraper used as wedge									
H7 Retouched point – awl									
H8 Retouched point – weapon									
H9 Retouched notch		5	2		2	3	2	1	
H10 Retouch, non-diagnostic	1	10	2		4	2	2	1	4
H11 Flaked flake or spall	6	57	56	8	69	12	4	4	8
H12 Multiple tool	1	8	5		2	1	3	1	1
H13 Flake wedge		1							2
H14 Utilised flake		3							1

Note: Retouched tool types follow system described in Table 12.4.

Ordinary/retouched notches (H9)

These follow the definition of Bordes (1961) and Debénath and Dibble (1994). These are localised concavities on the edge of a flake that have been made by non-invasive multiple retouch scars.

A word of warning concerning notches and denticulates. There is a growing concern that edge morphologies of this character can be made by wholly natural means, either by sediment pressure pushing down on a fragile flake edge, or forcing it up against an adjacent stone (personal observation at Barnham). Alternatively, they may be created by rock fall and roof collapse in caves. It is possible that animal trampling can reproduce these edges too (Miller 1982; Arnold 1991). Analysts should pay careful attention to the context within which these tools occur before identifying them as genuine tools.

Irregular or non-diagnostic retouched pieces (H10)

In a number of assemblages it was noted that certain flakes had been used as blanks for retouching, but that the retouch was never very extensive. These pieces did not fit comfortably into the other classes of retouched artefact. These were grouped under the neutral label of irregular retouched pieces. Usually the retouch is very localised on an edge.

Evenly retouched edges

Semi-continuous or continuous retouch produces an edge with an even profile.

Scrapers (H3)

These are among the most familiar of all retouched tools. A semi-continuous or continuous length of edge is retouched. The edge profile is smooth. An example is shown in Figure 1.3. Although the retouch can be located any-where, it is usually on the dorsal face. It must be emphasised that many scrapers do not resemble idealised forms, and the degree of variability present in this group can be considerable. In the Bordes system, scrapers are divided into a number of sub-categories based on position of retouch, the shape of the edge, and how many edges are retouched. Here all such examples are subsumed into one broad category – H3.

There is one aspect of these tools that may be important. In the Warren collection from Clacton Lion Point, there are a number of unambiguous scrapers with quite abrupt retouch (steep, nearly at right angles). A small number are also present in the older collections from the Lower Gravels Swanscombe. I have never seen any such scrapers in Acheulean assemblages, where the edge angle between the dorsal and ventral faces is lower (nearer 45° – semi-abrupt). This may be a real difference between the two assemblage types, but it would require more rigorous testing to establish this.

End scrapers (H4)

Scraper retouch is applied to a long and fairly narrow flake. They are distinguished from other scrapers because the retouch is confined to the narrow distal end of the flake and (as defined here) is not found on the lateral edges. They are not common, and it is a moot point whether or not they should be classified separately from scrapers.

Wedge scrapers (H6)

These represent pieces which would be classified as scrapers, but in addition to the scraper retouch on one edge, the opposite edge shows evidence of the characteristic battering damage associated with being struck with a hammer. The damage is identical to that noted for flakes that have been used as wedges (H13, see below), and is described in more detail below. This indicates that in some assemblages scrapers were used as wedges in the same way big unretouched flakes were. It would be fascinating to know whether or not they were deliberately made to be used as wedge scrapers, or simply chosen from discarded tools because both edges were appropriate for the new task.

With scraper retouch (H5)

A number of tools have short lengths of scraper-like retouch which occupy only a part of the edge. The retouch is not continuous enough to classify the piece as a scraper, but it does not disrupt the profile of the edge sufficient to be classified with the uneven-edged tools (e.g. H10).

Retouched points (H7 and H8)

Two specific varieties are defined here. Those were the retouching forms a point and the tool resembles a piercer or awl, and those were the point resembles a weapon tip. In the former (*sensu* awl, H7), the retouch produces a narrow elongated point. In the latter (*sensu* weapon tip, H8), a sharp point is created by unifacial or bifacial retouch at the tip and down both of its convergent edges. The tip of H8 will be flatter and broader than that of H7. In the Bordes system these would be retouched Levallois points or Mousterian points.

Very few convincing examples of H7 have been identified in the British Lower Palaeolithic, and no convincing examples of H8 have ever been found. However, H8 are present in the British Earlier Middle Palaeolithic.

Sharp edged tools

These pieces demonstrate single localised removals or the use of un-retouched sharp edges.

Flaked flakes (H11)

These represent a group of artefacts which can be quite diverse in appearance. A flaked flake is just what the name implies. It is a flake that has been flaked again (Ashton *et al.* 1991), see Figure 1.3. One or more removals can be detached from anywhere on the edge of a flake, and on either face. Included in this category are the pieces described in the Bordes system as Clactonian notches, a concavity created by a single detachment. Typologically they are quite distinctive in appearance, but I would argue this visual distinctiveness is a result of the location of the removal. Any flake removed from the lateral or distal edge of a bigger flake, on its dorsal face, will usually leave a wide short flake scar. Technologically they are no different from any removal taken off from any other part of a bigger flake – they just look more purposeful. It is often suggested that some of these flaked flakes (Clactonian notch variety) could be used for wood working, a bit like a modern spoke-shave (Oakley 1972).

Flaked flake spalls (H11)

The flake that comes off when you knap a bigger flake is called a flaked flake spall. They come in all shapes and sizes. Those from the Clactonian notch variety are typically short (length paralleling the flaking axis) and wide, semi-circular in planform, and the IFA is wide.

Are flaked flakes tools or cores?

This is an intriguing question and it is made more difficult to answer because there are clear indications in the archaeological record that they are both. The problem is that we can only classify them on morphology and technique of manufacture. One reason for imagining flaked flakes as cores may be that the larger spalls guarantee a razor-sharp edge around the whole length of the flake apart from the butt which is easy to hold. However, this is not the only possibility. Some flaked flake spalls are deliberately modified by further flaking into other tools. Just to muddy the waters even more, some become flaked flakes – when another spall is removed from the first spall's edge!

A quick and dirty way of deciding whether you think they are cores or flake tools could be the clear presence of a ventral surface. If easily recognisable, then classify the piece as a flaked flake. If the ventral has been almost completely flaked away, or so little is present that identification is difficult, then it probably should be included with the cores. The flaked flake phenomenon is another example of the dangers of typological pigeon holing.

Unretouched flakes and flake wedges (H14 and H13)

Unretouched flakes (H14) are considered tools if microwear, residue analysis, or any macroscopic evidence of edge damage suggest that the un-retouched edge has been used in some way. Microwear (Keeley 1980) has demonstrated a wide range of activities were carried out using unretouched flake edges. Flake wedges (H13) are similar to the wedge scrapers (H6) described above except that in this case an un-retouched edge is used as the business end of the tool. They are identified by a characteristic battering damage on the opposite edge. This takes the form of long invasive flake scars, a result of hammering either with wood, or more likely antler. The damage is similar to that described by Barton (1986; see also Bordes 1971). Keeley (1980) found evidence of this activity preserved as microwear at both Acheulean and Clactonian sites.

Multiple tools (H12)

These are a small but significant part of many British Lower Palaeolithic assemblages. Two different types of retouched tool appear on the same blank. They cannot be considered as any form of re-tooling to continue the same job as the two edge forms are very different. Although any combination is possible, in practice it is usually a flaked flake accompanied by another retouched edge type.

Analysis of the retouched data

The data for retouched tools are presented in Table 12.6, and in Figure 12.16. There are a number of points which emerge from Table 12.6. Quantitatively, Clactonian sites appear to have more retouched tools than do Acheulean ones, but how much this pattern reflects the larger size of the Clactonian assemblages remains to be assessed. There are low retouched tool counts in some of the smaller secondary context Clactonian assemblages, matching the patterns seen in the Acheulean ones.

Qualitatively, two patterns may be worth further consideration, albeit cautiously. The first is the predominance of flaked flakes, which even in the smaller assemblages, are always the most frequently occurring retouched tool type (McNabb 1992a). The second pattern is the predominance of the sharp-edged tool component in the Clactonian assemblages as opposed to a larger shaped edge component (even or otherwise) in the Acheulean

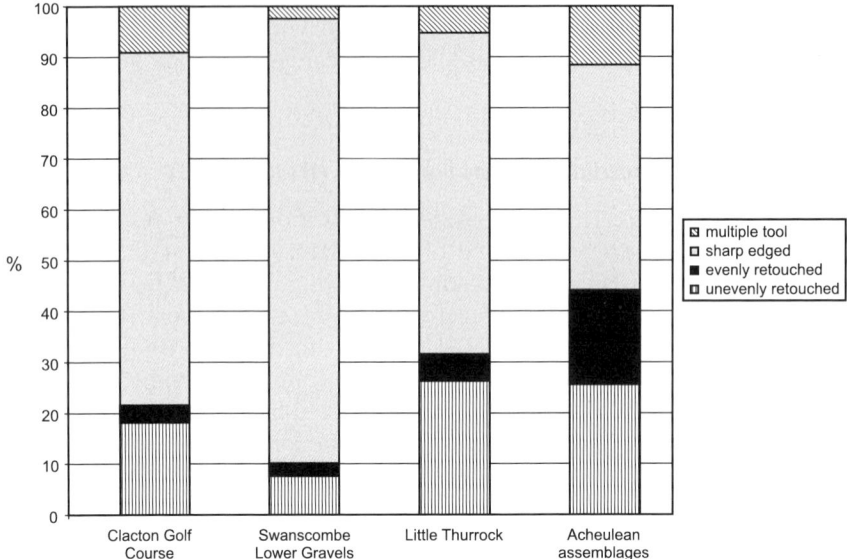

Figure 12.16 Comparison of the frequency of occurrence of different groups of retouched tools from a selection of Clactonian and Acheulean assemblages.

assemblages, see Figure 12.16. Here we can utilise for our own purposes one of the arguments for an independent Clactonian; namely that in a large secondary context site the assemblage will reflect the range of behaviours practiced in the vicinity over a period of time. I would like to propose that the high incidence of flaked flakes/sharp-edged tools in the Clactonian assemblages may well be a genuine reflection of the importance of this type of edge morphology at these locations.

Another pattern we may explore is the presence of activity-specific sites. Here, one activity, or a small number of related ones were practised. These are the jewel in the crown for Palaeolithic researchers as they directly connect us with specific hominin behaviours. They are recognised either by their primary context status (or nearly so), and/or their distinctive tool signatures. There are few such sites in the British Lower Palaeolithic. In Table 12.7, data on two are presented.

The Lower Loam knapping floor was discussed in Chapters 3 and 5. It was a primary context activity location, possibly dedicated to one activity, the butchery of a single deer carcass. The most significant of the retouched tools is a multiple tool. In this case, a large flake blank that has been used as a flaked flake and as a wedge. I have already suggested (Chapter 5) that this big, unretouched flake wedge was used to sever the neck vertebrae of the deer. Removing the head with its magnificent wrack of antlers would have

Table 12.7 A comparison of the retouched components from the Acheulean Upper Industry at Hoxne, and the Lower Loam knapping floor, Barnfield Pit, Swanscombe

	Frequency of retouched pieces from sub-units of Hoxne Upper Industry							Swanscombe Barnfield Pit Lower Loam Knapping Floor
	Archaeological layer 7	Archaeological layer 7a	Archaeological layer 7b	Archaeological layer 6	Archaeological layer 6x	Archaeological layer 6b	Total for Upper Industry	
H1 Denticulate	1				2		3	1
H2 Denticulated scraper								
H3 Scraper	5	2		4	32	10	53	
H4 End scraper								
H5 Flake with scraper retouch	2					2	4	
H6 Scraper used as wedge	2					3	5	
H7 Retouched point – awl								
H8 Retouched point – weapon								
H9 Retouched notch								
H10 Retouch, non-diagnostic								2
H11 Flaked flake or spall	5					1	6	3
H12 Multiple tool	4	2			2		8	1
H13 Flake wedge								
H14 Utilised flake	1						1	

Notes: Archaeological layer 7 at Hoxne was the equivalent of Geological Bed 5 (Singer et al. 1993), with artefacts in primary or near primary context, see Figure 5.10. Artefacts came from different levels within the deposit, but there was a scraper rich concentration at the top. Archaeological layer 6 at Hoxne was the equivalent of Geological Bed 6, a coarse sandy gravel. This unit directly overlay the colluvium, and artefacts within its base may well have been derived from this latter unit. The Lower Loam knapping floor, Conway et al. (1996), was a primary context locality with extensive refitting

made it much easier to butcher the carcass. No other significant bones were found on the knapping floor. As a whole the knapping floor, which was extensively excavated, shows a complete absence of evenly shaped retouched edges. For a single activity horizon it actually shows very little retouch at all. This example reminds us of the situationally flexible nature of activities distributed throughout the landscape.

Hoxne provides a different example of situational variability. The Upper Industry at Hoxne is an Acheulean MIS 11 assemblage (Ashton *et al.* n.d.). It was discussed in Chapter 5. The Upper Industry is distributed across six depositional sub-units (Singer *et al.* 1993). Cores, hard hammer and soft hammer flakes, handaxes and rough-outs are present throughout the Upper Industry as a whole. It is a moot point whether this represents a series of temporally separate hominin occupations, or one assemblage disturbed by a number of subsequent minor depositional events. Whichever is the case, the assemblage signature is a strong one, concentrating on scrapers which occur in a wide variety of types. Scrapers have been used as wedges as well, and it may be significant that flakes used as wedges were not present in the assemblage. (Although I cannot prove it, I believe that some of the retouch present in the Hoxne Lower Industry and shown in Table 12.6 is not proper retouch at all, but damage from using unretouched flakes as wedges, or in some other way that involved battering or hammering. Keeley (1980) identified a number of flakes in the Lower Industry that he also associated with this activity on the basis of microwear. If such an activity is present in the Lower Industry using sharp flake edges, and present in the stratigraphically higher Upper Industry but now using scrapers as wedges, then an intriguing behavioural pattern may be present.)

The material from archaeological layer 7 is the only material from the Upper Industry that can be considered *in situ*, and the numbers of evenly retouched pieces (9) are almost the equivalent of the sharp edged pieces (10), see Table 12.7. But once again, small totals may well be affecting the picture. This makes it all the more frustrating that the much larger frequencies in the overlying archaeological layer 6 come from a secondary context assemblage. There is no way of proving that they were derived from the underlying brown colluvial loam (though the use of scrapers as wedges as opposed to sharp-edged flakes is suggestive, in my opinion). The marked use of wedges at Hoxne, and the strong scraper frequency identify a locality in the landscape where a specific activity was being followed which had its own particular retouched tool pattern. I wonder if we will ever know what it was?

Conclusions for stone tools assemblages in the British Lower Palaeolithic

What is the technology and tool typology of the British Lower Palaeolithic telling us?

Other than the manufacture of bifaces I do not believe there is a single shred of convincing evidence to establish culturally specific knapping strategies. The same applies to overall tool behaviour.

This should not be so surprising, but I made too much out of this when I was younger. I used it to suggest that the Clactonian did not exist – this was very premature. The approaches to core flaking described are simple and effective ways of knapping stone and it would be hard to make any retouched tools other than those described above. No wonder there is little meaningful difference between the core, flake, and retouched tool elements in different Lower Palaeolithic assemblages.

Nevertheless, subtle differences do seem to be present between the two assemblage types. For the moment I will cautiously propose that sharp-edged tools are more common in non-biface assemblages. It is quite possible that this reflects location, since the Clactonian sites all sit on top of river gravels in the bottoms of valleys. Or in other words, at locations with so much good quality raw material to hand, a minimum effort strategy was all that was required.

It is also tempting to argue that there are more evenly shaped retouched edges in Acheulean assemblages, but sample size may be influencing our perception of the pattern. More sites and larger assemblages will be necessary to test this idea. The few primary context Acheulean assemblages we have may well be dedicated to specific activities, and not reflect the full range, or proportion of occurrence, of retouched tools present in the Acheulean repertoire. Unambiguous scrapers, with long continuous lengths of retouch, do seem are rare on Clactonian sites. When present, they are very steeply retouched unlike their Acheulean counterparts. Are the scraper wedges at Hoxne, and the flake wedges at Swanscombe, culturally different ways of doing the same job?

What is clear is that there are a few basic retouched forms that re-occur throughout the British Lower Palaeolithic record irrespective of assemblage type. They appear to be adaptable to most situations. In this sense they are no different from the core knapping techniques. I deeply suspect that all hominin tool behaviour, and especially that of retouched tool behaviour, was governed by expediency enhanced by a generalised tool kit that could be applied anywhere. This plasticity manifested itself in a situationally flexible approach. In effect, the tool kit was governed by the principle of equifinality; many means were possible to achieve one end, while many ends could be achieved by the same means. None of our primary context activity sites seem to represent places where hominins stayed for any real length of time. What we do have are places where hominins came, made and used things, and then left. The signal from these is clear – tool behaviour is limited, episodic, and transient. Get the job done and move on. The few exceptions to this may be the sites with hearths which are discussed in the next chapter. But even so, are these only overnight stops?

13

HOW WELL BEHAVED WAS
HOMO HEIDELBERGENSIS?

Introduction

In this chapter I will pose a question. Is there anything outside of the material culture of *Homo heidelbergensis* that will help us determine whether the Clactonian assemblage type should be considered a cultural tradition? Or in other words, what else is there that would persuade us that *Homo heidelbergensis*, in the later British Middle Pleistocene, was a truly cultural animal? Situational differences notwithstanding, the previous chapter has demonstrated that there is little in the material culture record that can help.

For well over a century anthropologists have struggled with the concept of culture, what it is, and how to define and describe it in all its manifestations. I think it is fair to say there is no agreement as yet. A recent introductory text had this to say about modern human culture: 'it would not be going too far to describe the whole concept of society as a set of shared symbols' (Hendry 1999: 83). In this kind of interpretation, society is an invisible web of common understandings and shared meanings. The threads that bind it together are individuals and their social relationships with others (either one to one, or one to many). Some of those relationships will be manifest in material things, like goods or physical structures. Sometimes those relationships will be present in ritualised acts. In such cases the individuals' relationship with the group may be expressed through the performance of a rite, or highlighted by its context. Most relationships of this nature will involve public symbols of some sort (*sensu* Hendry). In other cases the relationships between individuals and cultural institutions will be private and more ephemeral.

A great deal of anthropological fieldwork has also shown that culture (used hereafter to mean the sum of all those common understandings) does not perpetuate itself in a linear way. A generation does not simply recreate the relationships of its predecessors; culture is not dumped *en masse* on the next generation. For example, on the Polynesian atoll of Pucapuca, there are a wealth of legends and stories handed down from the ancestors (Borofsky 1987). They concern many aspects of Pucapucan society and work on a number of different levels. When different interviewees were asked to repeat these stories they were unable to agree on many of the details, although most got the gist of the different stories right. A similar thing was seen in learning the skills of boat building on the island (ibid.). There was no formal instruction where techniques and end products followed a blueprint to ensure conformity. Learning was a casual affair, emplaced within a social context (lots of drinking coffee, chatting, and smoking cigarettes); knowledge was acquired solely by observation, there was no direct instruction at all. Similar practices are noted by Ingold (2000) in other parts of the world. The lesson here is simple. For many non-literate human societies (but obviously not all) the shared common understandings that form the web of culture are not rigidly fixed (Palmer et al. 2005, and references therein), and over time will change. For example, a ritual may persist over many generations, as will the idea of why it is important to perform it, but the precise sequence of actions and their individual meanings may change substantially. Intergenerational cultural transmission is thus more of a sliding of the details than a fixed linear transmission. Knowledge handed down from the ancestors will always be open to interpretation.

In the field of primate cultural studies there have been similar conclusions. Cultural traditions in chimpanzee societies are not grafted onto the next generation, and there is significant variability between individuals in a group as to what they learn, how it is transmitted, and how well individuals accept new information: 'culture is not a thing, but a set of processes' (Boesch and Tomasello 1998: 603). And again:

> [C]ulture is not monolithic ... within one population there are many possible social conditions and lines of dissemination through which individuals may be exposed to particular behavioural practices within communities ... there are many different types of social learning processes by means of which individuals may acquire these behavioural practices, and these different learning processes lead to different cultural traditions with different properties over time.
>
> (ibid.: 592)

Any cultural explanation of the Clactonian that argues for a type of social learning that is an unvarying institutionalised template would appear to contradict the reality of cultural transmission. But was Homo heidelbergensis' social world so very different from our own, or our chimpanzee cousins?

The social environment: three different models of hominin sociality

The above feeds into some basic and unresolved discussions about the nature of culture and its relationship to the individual in Palaeolithic archaeology (see papers in Gamble and Porr 2005, for different views on this subject). For some researchers, culture is a pre-existing phenomenon – a given. You are born into it and it will condition who and what you are, and how you act. The individual has very little freedom of expression. For other researchers, culture is re-created on a day-to-day basis and individuals have the power to preferentially alter and subvert their social world through their actions. For yet another group of investigators, the significant control on behaviour is fixed at the genetic level; individuals have very little control over who they are. It's the old nature vs nurture debate and it's a long way from being settled (see Ingold 2000, and Pinker 2002, for summaries and contrasting views, and Hopkinson and White 2005, for a brief history of these arguments as applied to Palaeolithic culture). But just what would pass for cultural knowledge in pre-modern human society? How would individuals relate to each other in a social sense?

There are four ways to think of hominins:

1   more human than animal;
2   more animal than human;
3   a bit of both;
4   an animal, but one that was totally unique. Pre-modern humans were the products of ecologies and habitats for which no viable analogues now exist. Their behavioural adaptations were equally unique and we can only project inappropriate modern human or modern animal behavioural responses on to them.

My guess is that most Palaeolithic archaeologists prefer the third option. The more I think about it, I suspect it is the fourth that is nearer the mark. Just how much of the present can we project into the past?

There are very few models explaining hominin society. Throughout the greater part of the last century most people thought of it in terms of tribes or bands spending most of their time hunting. François Bordes (1968; 1972) certainly seemed to have envisaged Neanderthals that way. There is a review of the history of social interpretation in the Palaeolithic in Gamble (1999: 9ff.), especially of the role played by anthropological and ecological analogy.

There are three models of hominin society that apply to the British Lower Palaeolithic which I will briefly describe. I have selected these three as they seem to me to offer the most hope of exploring the relationship between individuals and their broader social context.

The first is the 'Social Brain' hypothesis of Robin Dunbar and colleagues (Dunbar 1998; 2003; 2004, and references therein). This treats hominins as more animal than human, and sets them firmly within the context of primate studies. Many primates, hominins included, will congregate in large groups as a defence against predators. There is safety in numbers. But there is a downside to this. The bigger the group, the greater the stress there is on the individual. This can take many forms; greater competition at feeding time, greater competition for mates, violent encounters with rivals, etc. To offset this, individuals make alliances with one another, or forge social partnerships as part of coalitions:

> Coalitions are functionally crucial to individuals within these groups because they enable the animals to minimize the levels of harass-ment and competition that they inevitably suffer when living in close proximity to others. Coalitions essentially allow primates to manage a fine balancing act between keeping other individuals off their backs while at the same time avoiding driving them away altogether and thereby losing the benefits for which the groups formed in the first place.
>
> (Dunbar 1998: 186)

So these coalitions are ways of managing social stress. However, this too has its downside. You have to invest a lot of time in maintaining those alliances with members of your coalition or core group. This means balancing a large number of social relationships. Maintaining all these social relations, or in other words, becoming a skilled social player, takes a lot of computing power in the brain.

One of the pillars of the Social Brain hypothesis concerns itself with how individuals use information about themselves and others and manipulate it to their own advantage. Individuals reflect on themselves and their actions, and they also understand that others do the same (called a theory of mind – ToM). They attempt to read another mind's intent, and then act on that interpretation in order to preferentially advance themselves in relation to the intent of that other individual. This is where all that computing power comes in. The bigger the group, the more of this mental gymnastics that will have to go on. Dunbar (2003) suggests that the *disproportionate size of the human brain has evolved over time as a direct result of living in large and stressful social groups*. Animals with large mean group sizes tend to have larger neocortical volume, and the neocortex is that part of the brain which deals with social relationships, among other things. Figure 13.1 shows Dunbar's hypothesis. Group size increases over time as different hominin species respond to the challenges of their social and physical environments. Neocortex volume increases proportionately. Clearly this is not a theory that specifically deals with hominin culture, it is more a hypothesis about the potential for ever

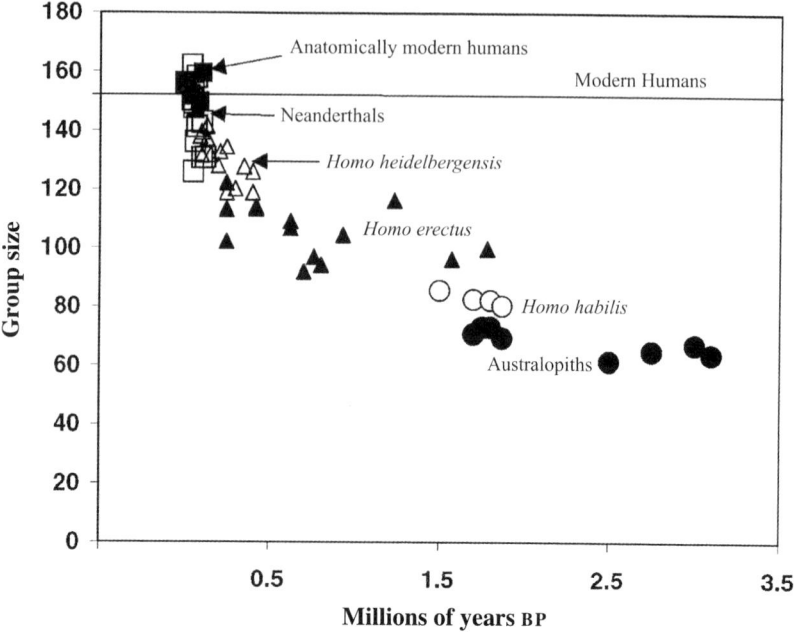

Figure 13.1 Comparison of estimated group size for different hominin groups as predicted by the Social Brain hypothesis.

Note: Full details in Dunbar (2003). Horizontal line indicates modern human average of about 150 people. Used with permission.

increasing complexity in individual social relations over time – but then this is the very stuff that societies are made of.

One prediction of the theory is that Homo heidelbergensis should have a limited linguistic capability. The reason is that as group sizes increases, it is necessary to spend more time reinforcing your relationship with core group/coalition partners. In effect, you have to spend more time grooming with them. Dunbar and colleagues suggest that for a predicted maximum group size of 120–140 individuals for H. heidelbergensis, some 30–40 per cent of the day would have to be spent in social grooming within the smaller core group. This is an enormous investment of time away from feeding. Some form of reinforcing mechanism would have been essential to maintain effective social relations at the same time as investing effort in the essential activities of daily life. Language is the only possible mechanism by which to do this. Language can allow you to do a number of different things at once: reinforce bonds, exchange news, feed, co-ordinate your activities and set plans in motion. By contrast, social grooming is a time-consuming one-to-one activity, but language, as a substitute for social grooming, can be done on a one-to-many basis. It represents a release from the limitations of immediacy. But for Homo heidelbergensis fully grammatical language, able to deal with complicated abstractions, is not implied in this scenario. Perhaps it took the form of a number of vowel or consonant sounds understood to represent physical objects, with some simple concepts to convey intended actions. Even this would greatly enhance the potential for group co-operative behaviour of the kind that I will suggest below. I will return to the Social Brain hypothesis later in this chapter.

The second theory is the theory of hominin culture promoted by Clive Gamble (1993a; 1999) which, on the other hand, strikes me as casting hominins in the role of more human than animal, this is more an anthropological theory than an ethological one. It differs somewhat from that of Dunbar in that it provides a more active role for hominins to create their social lifestyles, and it deals specifically with individual social relations. Nevertheless, the two interpretations do complement each other. Dunbar's is a top-down theory suggesting that there are cognitive constraints to what can be done, whilst Gamble's is a bottom-up theory describing just what can be done within those constraints.

Individuals create society through their day-to-day interactions as discrete actors. An individual literally *performs* society into being through visible actions. Actions, like making tools, bringing resources to a place, hunting skills, etc., all of these are social performances. Walking or stalking game, knapping or butchering an animal, are other examples. The specific character and social relevance of these movements are learnt by individuals as they grow up within a group. Why would visible gesture be so important? The reason is that in a non-linguistic society, or even one with a rudimentary language, visible action and display will be important in conveying messages to other group members. Visible display is the only other way of projecting a message. All these actions are comfortable through their familiarity, and this provides them with a powerful social resonance. Their constant repetition provides the social glue that binds and reinforces relations between individuals. In this sense, visible action is the equivalent of social grooming or language in Dunbar's model.

Action takes place at *locales* where individuals meet and bring resources. Familiar routines enacted in familiar places link individuals to each other and to these location as well. Furthermore, locales were connected by paths and tracks down which hominins and their material resources travel. Gamble argues that a hominin's understanding of the world and its resources was conditioned by these pathways linking one familiar place to the next. The physical world thus becomes a landscape of familiarity that is constantly being reinforced by repetitive acts carried out within it.

This familiar landscape, which Gamble calls the landscape of habit (1999, or local hominid network in earlier versions of the theory) is a product of hominin movement down the paths and tracks. Archaeologically, it can be accessed through the transfer of raw materials down these tracks. In practice, this means identifying the variety of different rock types used to make tools at a site and then determining their source. Modern ethnographic data suggest that local in this context can mean anything between 40 km and 100 km. Figure 13.2 shows some of the major sources from which different rock types were used at the Caune de l'Arago in south-east France. This site was discussed in Chapter 8 and raw material usage for retouched tools shown in Figure 8.3. Lucy Wilson (1988) noted that local for this site meant the river gravels literally outside the cave, while exotic could represent anywhere within a 65 × 30 km area. In Gamble's terms, this would be their landscape of habit accessed by well-known trails through the area, and along which they carried the different rock types from a large number of different sources, more than a hundred in the case of Arago (ibid.).

Gamble extends the theory to argue that although Lower Palaeolithic individuals created society through their relations with others in their

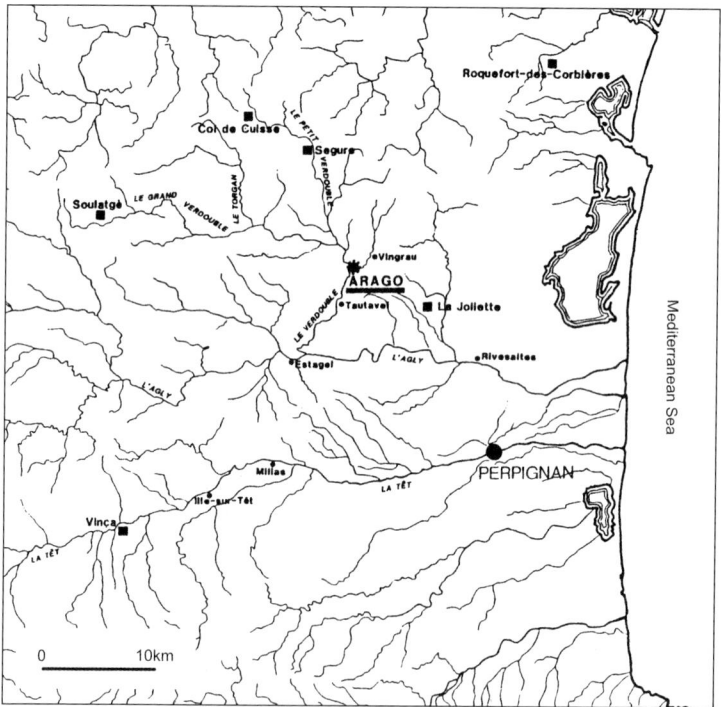

Figure 13.2 The local catchment area for the Caune de l'Arago. This would be the hominin's landscape of habit according to Gamble's model. The drainage pattern gives some idea of the complexity of the local terrain.

Note: Used with permission.

352

group, there was no extension of this outside of that group. Strangers from other groups in the area were to be avoided and discouraged – the familiar was comfortable, but the unfamiliar was not. The social networks could not be expanded to take in new groups. It was a face-to-face society, hence the comfort in the repetitive and familiar character of visual action. A set of reassuringly familiar actions in one group would be strange to the members of a different group. Unlike modern humans there were no mechanisms for extending individual or group social relations outwards, artefacts could not stand in the place of people and take on the symbolic role of tokens and messages sent to far-off places. In Gamble's phrase (1998), there was no release from proximity in Homo heidelbergensis society. While Gamble is right to emphasise the importance of visibility of action, I wonder, would the mere repetitious character of everyday activities be enough to bind a group together? Surely something more concrete would be necessary to take the place of grooming with its endorphin-enriched sense of well-being and security?

Third, in 1999, Stephen Mithen added a new component to his theory on the Clactonian (Kohn and Mithen 1999; Mithen 1994) which was briefly described in Chapter 11. To summarise, he had stated that the Acheulean was a product of strong intergenerational social learning. It stemmed from the increased social pressures resulting from living in large groups in predominantly open landscapes. Standardisation in the making and appearance of material culture would be an inevitable consequence. This was why, as a concept, the handaxe was so formalised, and why so many handaxes also looked the same. However, intergenerational social learning among the forest dwelling Clactonian groups was much weaker. Here, where potential danger from predators was much lower, social groups were more fragmented. There was less of a tendency to standardise as a result of a much greater emphasis on individual trial and error learning. Hence the lack of any evidently standardised tools in the Clactonian.

Marek Kohn and Steve Mithen (1999; Kohn 1999) proposed a mechanism that explained why some hominin groups could come to lose their knowledge of handaxes and why other groups continued to make them. In effect, how certain Acheulean populations could become Clactonian. The mechanism was sexual selection. This concept was originally formulated by Charles Darwin and operates alongside of natural selection. Sexual selection concerns individual mate choice. This is usually females selecting the fittest males in a group to breed with. The word fittest here is used in the genetic sense, the higher the quality of your genes, the genetically fitter you are. Individuals with superior genetic qualities will demonstrate them through some form of visual cue (Miller 1999; 2001). There are two ways in which an individual can advertise its fitness. One is by having certain physical traits that signal superiority (indicator theory). The second is through acts of display that are so impressive that a potential mate is convinced that such acts could only be produced by a clearly superior individual.

Kohn and Mithen argued that the finished forms of handaxes, as well as the act of making them, come into the latter category. Or put another way, handaxes and their manufacture are cultural acts which represent individuals displaying in mate competition. The handaxes are a proxy for genetic fitness levels. In this sense the theory nicely blends social anthropology with evolutionary theory – *it provides an explanation as to why visibility in social practice was so important.* The inference for society is that there was keen inter-male rivalry. A well-produced handaxe, confidently and expertly knapped, with an aesthetically pleasing finish, which was also bilaterally symmetrical, would be a powerful statement about the individual who made it. It would say they were skilful, confident, experienced, knowledgeable, dextrous, and physically well co-ordinated. All these would be useful skills in negotiating one's place in the social group, finding a mate, and in the all-important cooperative act of obtaining food through hunting. The better finished the axe, the stronger the message about its maker (Kohn 1999, for a good review of all these arguments).

How was all this linked to the Clactonian? They argued that in a forested environment the character of sexual selection changed. These environments have food and other resources spread out evenly throughout the forest. Predators are fewer and escape and evasion easier – you just climb a tree. A different social pattern develops, as does a different pattern in mate choice and in inter-male competition. There would be no need for the elaborate and costly act of making a handaxe. Why costly? While knapping, you are not paying attention to your surroundings, so you could be exposing yourself to predators. Handaxes could prove costly in other ways too. There was always the chance you might have an off day and knapp badly, thus affecting your social standing. In enclosed environments with females making choices about their potential mates on other criteria, handaxes in time would drop out of a group's body of inherited knowledge. The result would be the Clactonian.

It is an interesting theory and one that places H. *heidelbergensis* in the more animal than human camp, describing a social pattern best understood in ethological terms. There are problems with the model. Not the least of which is the secure presence of handaxe industries at Barnham, Elveden and Beeches Pit (Chapter 5) within the Early Temperate phase of MIS 11, or in other words within a time of extensive forest. Additionally, I believe the question of a lack of standardisation in Clactonian assemblages is illusory, a product of modern archaeologists making inappropriate value judgements. While handaxes were not present at Clactonian sites, this did not mean that what was left in the tool box was not standardised. If we refer to the retouched tool types in Table 12.4, and their occurrence in the Clactonian assemblages in Table 12.6, we can immediately see that the same tools are made time and again at all the sites. Now these may not have the value added factor that archaeologist like to invest handaxes with, but all these tools show *conceptual standardisation* which is every bit as formal as the concept of a biface. As such, they too are learned concepts. Side scrapers, for example, show both conceptual standardisation as well as physical stand-ardisation, and there is as much variability between individual examples as there is between many of the bifaces in a single handaxe assemblage (see below). I am afraid I can't accept the opinion that the Clactonian is a non-standardised assemblage type.

How much physical standardisation is present in handaxes is also open to debate. Even a brief examination of the handaxes in most Acheulean assemblages will show that there is quite a degree of variability present in shape and finish (archaeological reports tend to cherry-pick the most aesthetic for illustration). How is this explained? There are two reasons, according to Kohn and Mithen. Males would tend to put much greater effort into making superior-looking handaxes when females were around. The rest of the time they would make less aesthetic ones. In the meantime females would be making more practical handaxes. So combined, these two factors would generate intra-assemblage variability over time. These are intriguing suggestions. The archaeological record is frustratingly contra-dictory as usual. For example, at Boxgrove in MIS 13 (Roberts and Parfitt 1999) there are two clear traits: most of the handaxes are well made, and most look more or less the same. The trouble is at this site there isn't that much variability – and there should be at least some; some individuals have to outperform others. In the MIS 11 Middle Gravels at Swanscombe, there is nothing but variability (Wymer 1964). At the primary context Acheulean site at Round Green, in the Chiltern Hills (Smith 1916; White 1997), there is an assemblage which is, in all probability, the result of a one-off stop by handaxe makers. The site was collected by Worthington Smith. The bifaces are all well made, but the degree of variability in outline shape is quite astonishing, see Figure 13.3. Beeches Pit (Gowlett 2005), Figure 13.4, shows the same variability in handaxe shape.

The importance of visibility – display behaviour, and messages in material culture

Two out of the three interpretations of Palaeolithic society discussed above emphasise the concept of visible display in constructing social relations. I believe this is an important point. However, to use this concept to explain some of the structure in hominin society we would need to know whether or not hominins were able to both send out social signals, as well as receive and understand them correctly. After all, this is display with a socially learned communal significance.

The regression equations of the Social Brain hypothesis suggest a possible

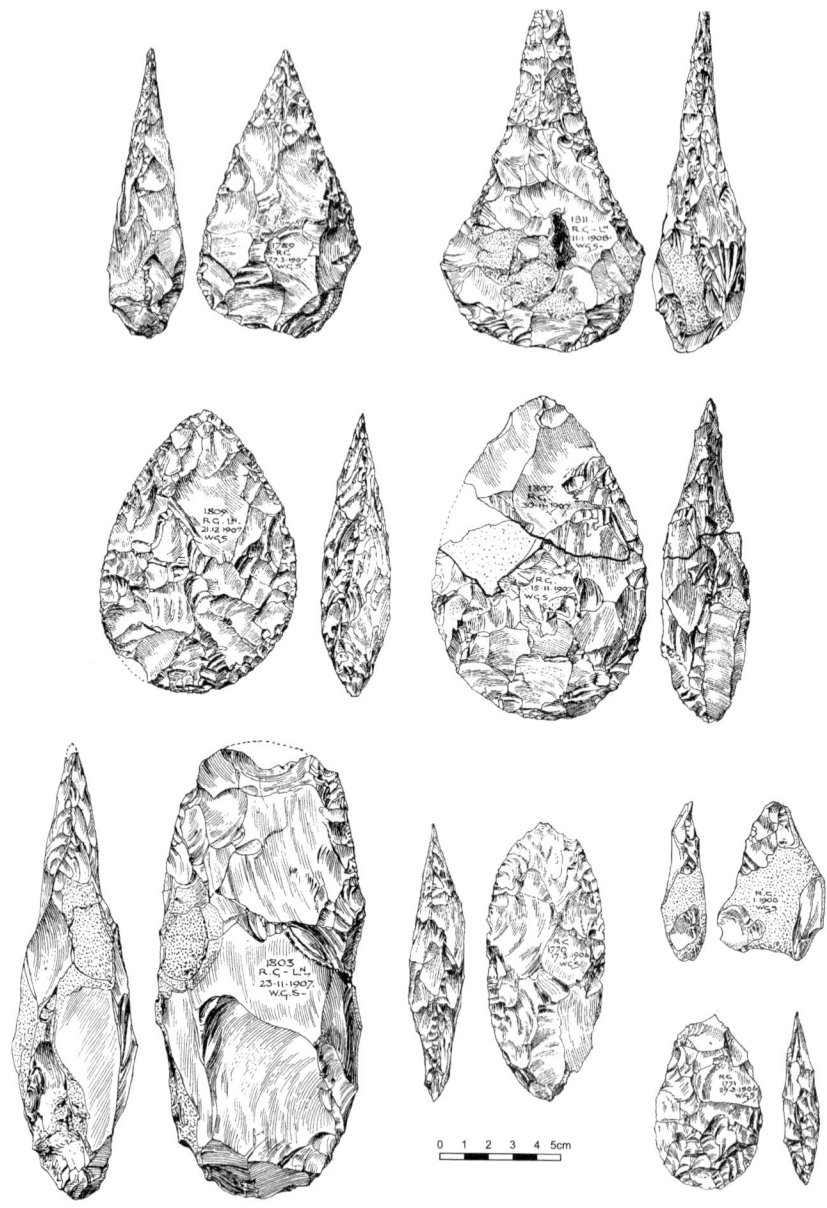

Figure 13.3 Handaxes from Round Green.

Note: Used with permission

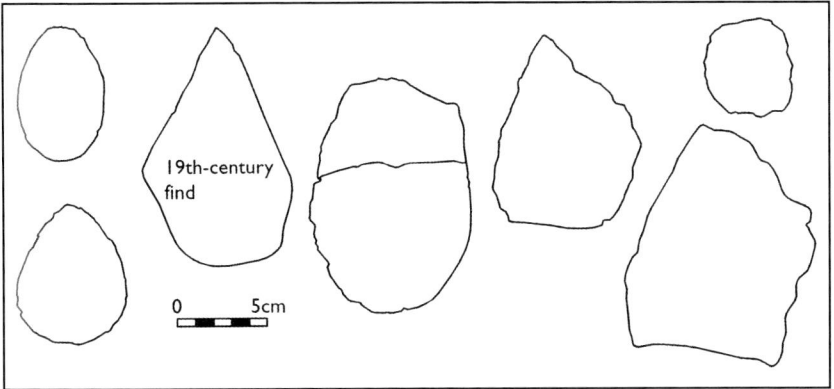

Figure 13.4 Outline diagram of variability in handaxe shape from Beeches Pit.

Note: Used with permission.

window on this. It concerns two interrelated concepts; theory of mind (ToM was briefly introduced above), and intensionality (spelt with an 's' by philosophers of mind).

ToM is a much discussed idea that stems from primate research. An animal has the ability to reflect on itself and its own actions. It understands that another of its kind can do the same. But it has no way of really knowing this for certain. In effect, what the animal does is take its 'model' of its own mind, and project that onto the other animal, and then assume that the other animal is capable of appreciating its own actions as well as those of others. As I described above, this ToM underpins the cognitive mechanisms that allow individuals to appreciate social situations and act on that information. It is central to the Social Brain hypothesis.

The second important concept concerns orders or levels of intensionality. This is an animal's ability to project ToM through a social group that contains a number of different individuals, and to comprehend/predict the belief states (intentions) of others in the group. But more than this, you have to be able to link these individuals together in a cognitive chain. You are conscious that each individual in the chain is capable of appreciating that all the others in the chain also hold a belief state about everyone else. The more individuals you factor in, the higher the level of intensionality. To cope with this takes a lot of computing power in the brain. This would be a very important skill for an animal with a stressful social life, and it would be especially important in staying onside with your core group. Levels of intensionality are explained in Table 13.1. In Figure 13.5, the idea has been adapted to material culture to show what levels of intensionality would be necessary for material culture to be able to carry a socially significant message. In other words, what level of intensionality would you need

357

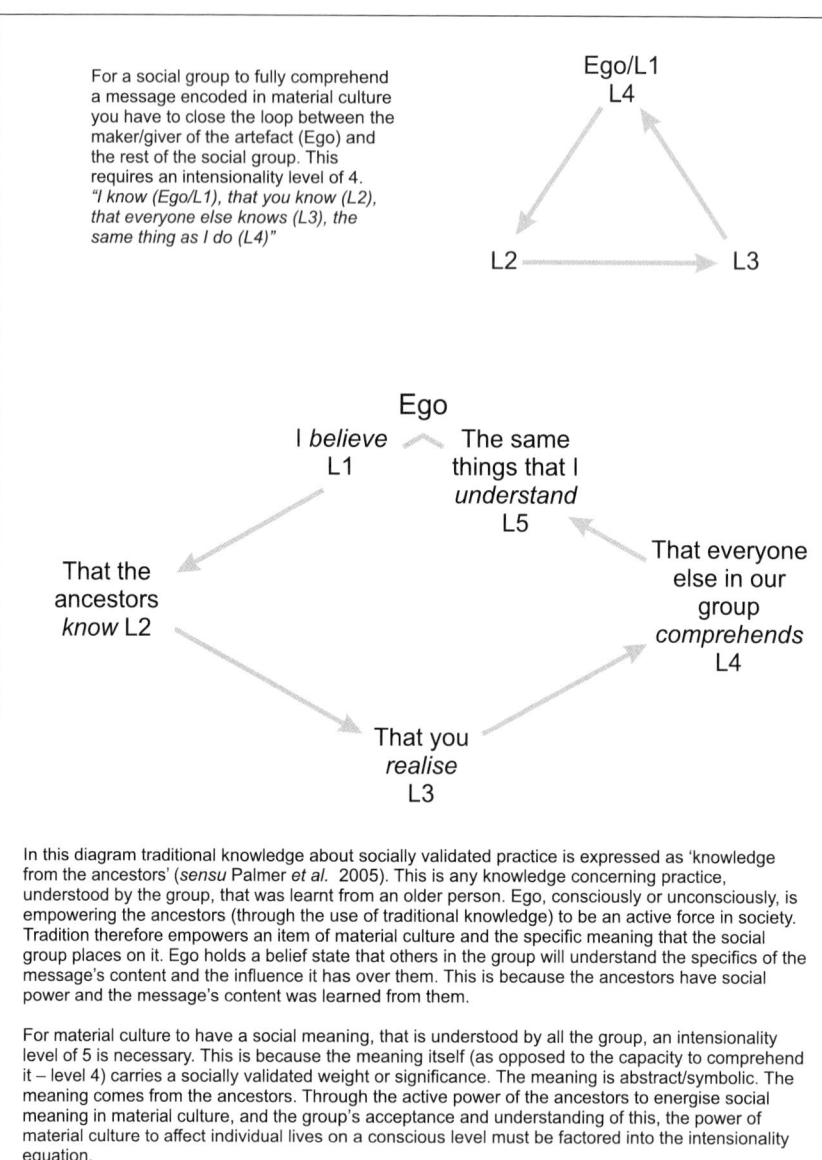

For a social group to fully comprehend a message encoded in material culture you have to close the loop between the maker/giver of the artefact (Ego) and the rest of the social group. This requires an intensionality level of 4.
"*I know (Ego/L1), that you know (L2), that everyone else knows (L3), the same thing as I do (L4)*"

Ego/L1
L4

L2 ——————————→ L3

Ego

I *believe*
L1

The same things that I *understand*
L5

That the ancestors *know* L2

That everyone else in our group *comprehends*
L4

That you *realise*
L3

In this diagram traditional knowledge about socially validated practice is expressed as 'knowledge from the ancestors' (*sensu* Palmer *et al.* 2005). This is any knowledge concerning practice, understood by the group, that was learnt from an older person. Ego, consciously or unconsciously, is empowering the ancestors (through the use of traditional knowledge) to be an active force in society. Tradition therefore empowers an item of material culture and the specific meaning that the social group places on it. Ego holds a belief state that others in the group will understand the specifics of the message's content and the influence it has over them. This is because the ancestors have social power and the message's content was learned from them.

For material culture to have a social meaning, that is understood by all the group, an intensionality level of 5 is necessary. This is because the meaning itself (as opposed to the capacity to comprehend it – level 4) carries a socially validated weight or significance. The meaning is abstract/symbolic. The meaning comes from the ancestors. Through the active power of the ancestors to energise social meaning in material culture, and the group's acceptance and understanding of this, the power of material culture to affect individual lives on a conscious level must be factored into the intensionality equation.

Figure 13.5 An attempt to relate concepts of intensionality, as a proxy measure of cognitive potential, with the projected symbolic/abstract capability (as seen in non-utilitarian social meanings placed on items of material culture) of *Homo heidelbergensis* as suggested by the Social Brain hypothesis.

Table 13.1 Orders of intensionality as expressed by philosophers of mind

1st order intensionality	2nd order intensionality	3rd order intensionality	4th order intensionality	5th order intensionality
I *believe*	That Bryn *supposes*	That Debby *believes*	That Jane *thinks*	That Helena *understands something*
	Necessary for a full ToM Arguably achieved by chimpanzees		Most human adults can operate at intensionality levels 4 and 5	
	Achieved by human children of c. 4 years of age	Most literature operates at 3rd and 4th levels of intensionality as the author requires the readers to accept the belief states of interacting characters – see below		Necessary for religion to be sustained as a communal enterprise
Joseph Conrad, the author of *Heart of Darkness intended*	His readers to *believe*	That his hero Marlow had come to *realise*	That Mr Kurtz *supposed* that the jungle had revealed his primordial self	

Note: Orders of intensionality concern belief states, here in italics. The higher the order of intensionality the more belief states an individual can hold in his or her head, all linked in a sequential chain. The lowest row is an example of how intensionality can be developed through literature, following Dunbar's example.

Source: Constructed from data in Dunbar 2004.

not only to broadcast a message through something that you made, but to know that others in your group could understand it? Figure 13.5 asserts that a purely functional understanding would require level 2. This is considered the minimum for a full ToM and is arguably achieved by some apes. Monkeys are only believed to achieve level 1.5 (Dunbar 2004). In my opinion, for material culture to carry a mutually comprehensible social signal, hominins must have had a minimum intensionality level of 4.

The regression equations of the Social Brain hypothesis, based on pre-dicted group size related to neocortex volume, can be applied to the prediction of levels of intensionality for different hominin species (Dunbar 2004). Figure 13.6 shows the results of this. *Homo erectus/ergaster* achieves a

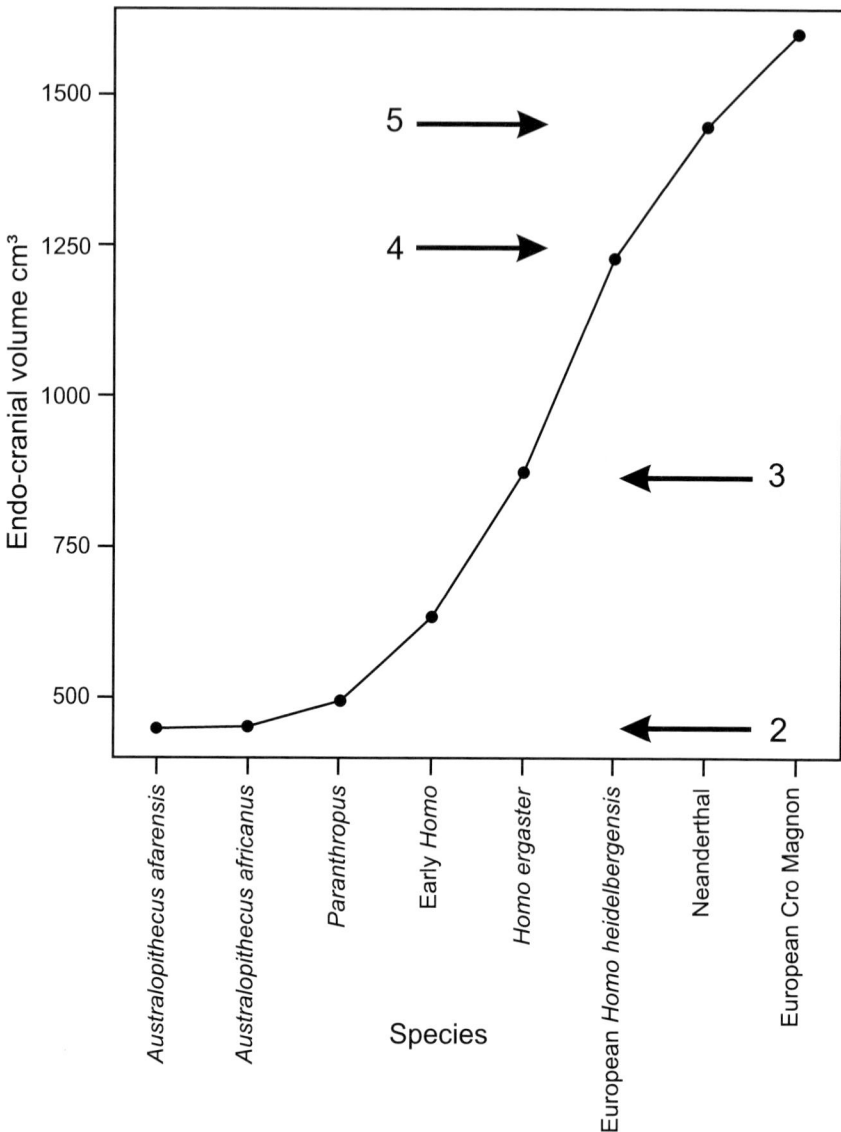

Figure 13.6 Levels of intensionality for different hominin species as predicted by the Social Brain hypothesis.

Note: Mean endo-cranial volume is a proxy measure of brain size. *A. afarensis* based on 2 specimens; *A. africanus* based on 6 specimens. *Paranthropus* based on 7 specimens. Early *Homo* in Africa (*H. habilis sensu lato*) based on 7 specimens. *H. ergaster* based on 5 specimens. *H. heidelbergensis* based on 5 specimens. Neanderthals based on 11 specimens. *H. sapiens* based on 1 specimen. Arrows indicate levels of intensionality as predicted by the Social Brain hypothesis for the species indicated. A diagram like this only indicates trends at the coarsest scale of analysis.

Source: Data from Dunbar (2004) and Aiello and Dean (1990).

level of about 3, while *Homo heidelbergensis* achieves an intensionality of 4. It is only with level 5 that fully grammatical language is able to operate, so not surprisingly, the manipulation of abstraction through metaphor and symbolism is only possible at level 5. This is the level that most modern adult humans operate at. Dunbar (2004) asserts that fully modern culture is only possible with a level 5 order of intensionality.

So according to these data, and my interpretation of it in relation to material culture, *Homo heidelbergensis* would at least have had the *potential* to have generated a socially resonant message. At the very least, it would have had the potential to engage in acts of visual display whose learned social significance (as opposed to a biological or instinctual significance) would be interpretable to the remainder of the group. What does this imply? Potentially, a cultural animal which could sustain a socially learned tradition and pass it on the next generation.

However, having the potential to encode meaning in material culture is one thing, but realising it and *sustaining* at a group level is quite a different matter. This is what the last part of Figure 13.5 is suggesting. A complicated socially significant message, that is learned and then passed on, has a tradition within the group. In Figure 13.5, this time depth is expressed as knowledge from the ancestors – it represents any cultural information that came from those who have gone before (*sensu* Palmer *et al.* 2005). In my opinion, to build such traditional knowledge into a group's common understanding, and then sustain it over time, will require an intensionality level of 5, in other words, beyond that of *Homo heidelbergensis*.

With an intensionality level of 5, it is not surprising that modern humans habitually encode messages into the things they make. We are able to understand and manipulate abstraction on both conscious and unconscious levels. We also make aesthetic and personal value judgements based on these abstractions. I suspect that while *physical display could carry social meaning at level 4, material culture with a socially resonant meaning, could only operate at intensionality level 5*. In my opinion *Homo heidelbergensis* was unable to project the significance of physical and bodily behaviour onto material culture. The tool kits described in the last chapter were merely that, tools for getting the job done. Even handaxes did not carry any deeper social significance.

In an extension of the Social Brain hypothesis, Louise Barrett and colleagues (Barrett *et al.* 2003) have added an important new dimension to this theory of hominin social relations. The complexities in group living are interpreted through the metaphor of the market place drawn from the world of business:

> The theory of biological markets views animals as traders engaged in a mutually beneficial exchange of commodities. Individuals within a biological market attempt to maximize 'profit' (in terms of fitness) by selecting social partners that offer the best value, with

361

an exchange rate set by the supply and demand of the commodity in question.

(Barrett et al. 2003: 494)

Just as commodities in the business world change their value with shifts in the market, so individual social relations can change with circumstances. Alliances with individuals or with coalitions could become socially dis-advantageous if partners or groups suffered reversals in fortunes. A skilled social player would need to be tracking changes in the social market place and re-negotiating (trading) his or her position constantly. Barrett et al. then go a stage further. Most primate (human and non-human) societies follow the fission-fusion pattern. Larger social groups will break up into smaller ones and disperse for a variety of situationally specific reasons. The time spent in fission can vary from a few hours to much longer. When the different groups coalesce again it would be distinctly advantageous for individuals to have retained their understanding of the power politics surrounding various group members, and quickly assess any new devel-opments that have occurred in the meantime: 'In such systems individuals must be able to represent mentally individuals that are not present and to retain and manipulate information about them for substantial periods of time' (ibid.: 495). This is the shifting commodities market of hominin social relations. Recognising the absence of an individual is important because it can affect one's judgement of the 'commercial value' of those that remain. Barrett and colleagues also suggest that what is important here is a sense of time. Being able to predict the reactions of individuals in the future (the future state of the market), and what their reactions will be to situations that have arisen during their absence, would be a critical cognitive faculty. What these researchers describe as the ability to represent the 'self and others' in different 'spatio-temporal locations', seems to me to be a key requirement for a hominin who was engaged in communal survival, particularly if hunting or pro-active scavenging was essential to that survival. We are in fact discussing a limited understanding of the passage of time, and one's own self conscious place in it (at least in terms of an individual's perceived goals). It also suggests to me that memory may have been under intense selective pressure within the social environment.

Martin Porr (2005) adds a further element to this. He suggests that the kill site would have been a particularly intense political arena. In terms of Barrett et al.'s metaphor, this would be the floor of the stock exchange. The sharing out of meat after the kill would have been a socially tense time. Who would get what, how much, and why? Who was involved in the kill? and importantly, who wasn't but should be kept sweet with a portion of meat?

In at the kill

Focusing attention on the carcass site (Porr 2005) is an important contribution that can be developed further. Individuals or coalitions would use this as a stage for display, for coalition building/re-inforcing, or for changing individual allegiances. Challenges for power could be made and shifts in the social market place rapidly effected, and all observed by other members of the group at the kill site. Where better to advertise through display the hunting prowess of an individual, or hunting coalition, than at the very locus of individual/group success? The same for a carcass won from other carnivores by competitive scavenging. Either way, a carcass would be a place with a powerful social resonance as it would ensure another few days of life for the group.

I would like to suggest that one of the most important core groups in H. *heidelbergensis* society was the hunting/scavenging coalition. Prowess in the hunt, co-operative abilities, proficiency at tool-making and using, all these could be broadcast through the hunting or scavenging coalition around a carcass. It could also be an arena for mate choice where display after success would be at its most effective.

I would also like to suggest that such contextually empowered situational display is a better explanation for the importance of visual action than the comfort to be derived from repeating familiar rhythms. The common thread that would unite the various situations would be inter-personal and inter-coalition competition. The social significance of visual display, in such a competitive market, would be more than apparent to a hominin with the cognitive capacity suggested by level 4 intensionality.

Having this intensionality level would, at the very least, suggest a certain awareness of the consequences of the choices individuals made (Robin Dunbar, pers. comm.). Being able to consciously evaluate the actions of 'self and others', in a variety of spatio-temporal locations, if only to a limited extent, would also be a powerful asset to negotiating individual social success (Figure 13.7). Additionally, memory, and Barrett *et al.*'s suggestion of a limited awareness of time, would enhance a social player's effectiveness. I believe that by the time of *Homo heidelbergensis* the main arena of selection on behaviour had moved out of the natural world, and into the social world. A hominin with level 4 intensionality, and the capacities just described, would be able to evaluate its decisions, and in particular assess the consequences of those decisions. This would influence mate choice and coalition/core group membership.

I will speculate that it is possible that some non-heritable characteristics (behaviours that have no genes and so cannot be reproduced by gene copying) can be carried into the next generation as they are intimately associated with heritable qualities. Mate choice may have revolved around physical traits such as strength and physique, stamina, perhaps physical

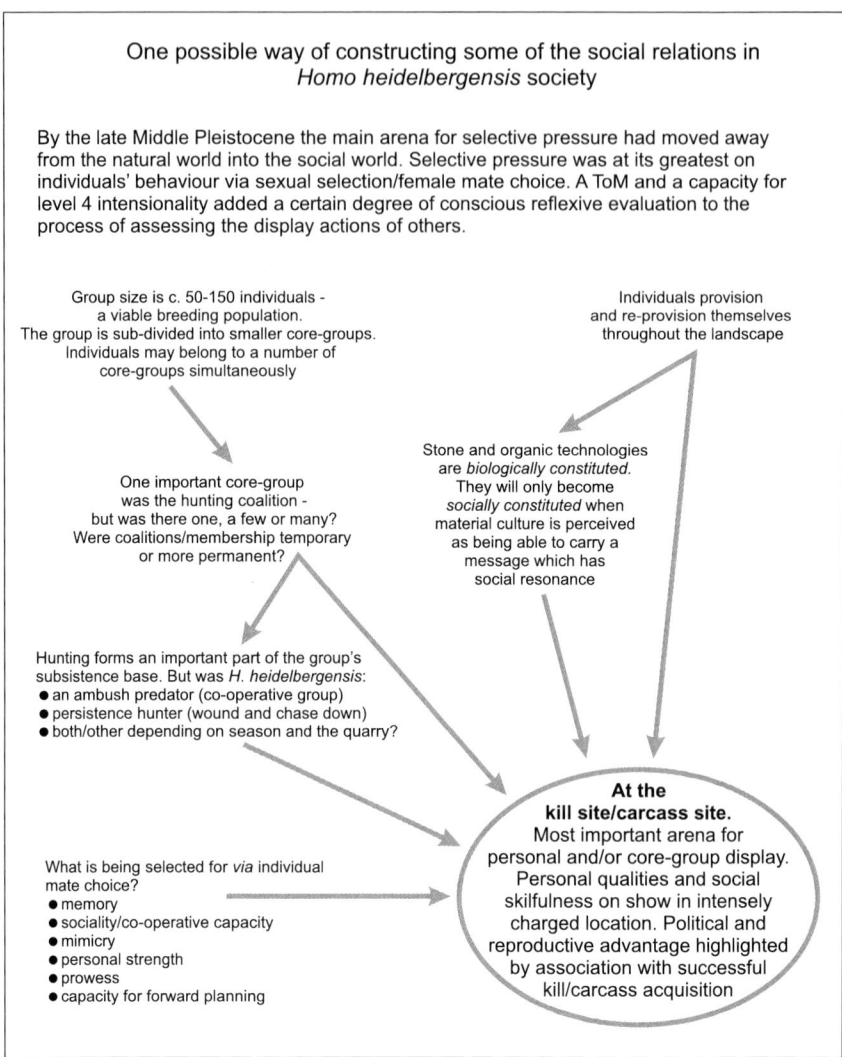

Figure 13.7 A selection of the significant aspects of Middle Pleistocene hominin social life, and how they might inter-relate when viewed through the filter of competitive inter-personal and inter-coalition display behaviour.

dexterity, and memory too if these were heritable qualities. However, these choices were made in a social context, by individuals who were responding to contextually empowered competitive display. Some of the individual qualities that enhanced heritable fitness, would have been socially significant ones as well. In effect, it was the social context that validated the physical/heritable traits by gifting them with social and reproductive significance. Consequently, the *statistical propensity* for non-heritable behaviours appearing in a group might increase over time. Even the limited reflexive quality suggested by level 4 intensionality, would add a significant social element to sexual selection and the process of making choices.

I have summarised some of these ideas in Figure 13.7 in the context of situational display by individuals and/or coalitions. Of course, I am speculating with *all* of this, but I would not be surprised if at least some of this did not approach the reality of past behaviours.

The visibility of action argued for in Gamble, and Mithen and Kohn's work, is perfectly compatible with a commodities market Social Brain interpretation of hominin society as postulated by Louise Barrett and her colleagues. It is not so much that visible action provided the social glue for individual relations, rather inter-personal competitive display provided the fabric against which different types of individual social relations were sown together.

Learning and tradition in *Homo heidelbergensis* society

Above I suggested that a key element in *Homo heidelbergensis* society was situationally empowered inter-personal/inter-coalition competitive display. I also suggested that the Social Brain hypothesis supported the idea that H. *heidelbergensis* could potentially sustain a socially learned tradition of behaviour on an inter-generational time scale. However, I also hypothesised that this was restricted to socially validated physical behaviour because H. *heidelbergensis* could not impose abstract meanings onto material culture, and then perpetuate them over time.

What about the Clactonian? How would such an explanation for social relations help in establishing whether or not the Clactonian assemblage type can also be considered as a cultural tradition? The key to determining this is in identifying its patterns of social learning. We have already noted that modern humans do not repeat the knowledge of preceding generations without putting their own spin on it. The quote from Boesch and Tomasello at the beginning of this chapter established the potential for a social group to contain many different patterns of learning – lineages of knowledge. Social knowledge, like genetic inheritance, undergoes copying errors, and individuals would be exposed to a number of them. Such a viewpoint seems inherently more realistic than the simple rolling over from one generation to the next of an unvarying set of practices – the endless repetition of institutionalised templates of action and end product.

The problem for the Clactonian is its lack of a tool form which archaeologists believe would reflect social learning. The cores, flakes and flake tools that it shares with the Acheulean have never been seen as unique social signatures because they represent the everyday knife–fork–spoon technology of all Lower Palaeolithic assemblages. If we wish to explore social learning in the Lower Palaeolithic, we are forced to concentrate on the biface with its clearly imposed shape.

Do handaxes, as potential indicators of inter-generational transmission, reveal anything about knowledge transmission, particularly in the sense of a society imposing its orthodoxy on what is learned? Not surprisingly the data are sparse, but Foxhall Road (Chapter 5; White and Plunkett 2004) does provide a very important clue:

> Cluster A at Foxhall Road comprises 11 complete handaxes. These can be divided into three groups of almost identical handaxes: a trio of beautiful twisted ovates, a pair of almond shaped ovates (limandes) and a pair of small untwisted ovates. The remaining four handaxes can also be divided into two pairs, although the similarities are less pronounced. We have interpreted this area as a small group focus, perhaps a hearth, to which finished artefacts were imported and around which five or so hominids sat and engaged in practical and social activities.
>
> (White and Plunkett 2004: 159)

White and Plunkett argue that this diversity of forms, at one small Acheulean campfire, reveals the presence of individuals with their own styles of knapping. Each hominin was responsible for a different set of similarly shaped handaxes. This robustly contradicts the existence of one institutionalised template whose form all young hominins would be conditioned to reproduce. White and Plunkett take their argument further: 'The style developed by young hominids probably depended more on their role model(s) than a collective pattern, the choice of model predicated on interpersonal relationships and social identities' (ibid.: 160). I would argue that each individual was a product of a different core-group from within a larger social aggregation. Lines of knowledge transfer were evidently different in each core-group, reflected in the different handaxe shapes that the hominins brought to the fireside. In Figure 13.7 I have suggested mimicry was a skill that was under strong social selective pressure. Mimicking a role model, and directly copying those in your core-group might be one way of perpetuating a distinctive learning tradition in the sense used by Boesch and Tomasello. Foxhall Road may have been a camping spot for a hunting coalition. Since there were a number of clusters found by Nina Layard at Foxhall Road, perhaps the hunting coalition was a large one. Then, again, perhaps this was the larger social group camping after one of its hunting coalitions successful kills. We will never know.

There are other sites which may support this type of scenario. Figure 13.4 presented the range of handaxe shapes at Beeches Pit, some of which were directly associated with the hearths. There is evidently no single shape template at work there. Figure 13.3 showed a selection from Round Green.

The diversity in shape is clear. The twisted ovate and the broken handaxe that has been refitted could almost be the product of one knapper. Even within the variable sameness of handaxe shape at Boxgrove there are pairs of handaxes at the waterhole location that look as if they were made by the same knapper (Matt Pope, pers. comm.).

All of the above leads me to believe that in the Acheulean, handaxes reflect lines of inter-generational learning that were organised around core groups. How fixed membership of these groups was, is anyone's guess. Individuals may have left to join other core groups at particular times in their lives. Hunting coalitions may have been one type of permanent core group, alternatively they may have been temporary alliances made by individuals from other core groups for the purposes of acquiring meat. This engages with the fission and fusion pattern that Barrett and colleagues described above, and could explain the diversity we see in handaxe shape at in-situ sites. As White and Plunkett have argued, an individual would not be restricted to making one handaxe shape for the whole of their lives, they would adapt as circumstances required (time pressure, raw material availability and quality), but they suggest knappers would always return to a limited set of possibilities. I would posit that the range of possibilities was constrained by what the knappers had learned from their role models in their earliest core group. A propensity for copying and mimicry represented the primary mechanism by which traditions in handaxe form were established and maintained. The limited set of possibilities in handaxe shape available to young apprentice knappers within their core group would represent that core groups body of knowledge from the ancestors. The broader social group that comprised the Foxhall Road Acheulean society would have been made up of many such core groups with many lineages of ancestral knowledge.

As the reader will be aware, none of this directly helps us with the Clactonian. The nature of Acheulean social relations which I speculate on here would apply equally to the Clactonian. However, without an item of material culture, whose form could vary around a series of limited possibilities, and so reflect distinct intra-community traditions of learning, recognising the nature of social learning in the Clactonian is all but impossible.

Projecting the social world into the natural environment

Many animals change their surroundings by artificially shaping them: the Bower Bird's nest, the hyaena's den, the chimp's sleeping platform. How much of this is genetically programmed, and how much is a product of learning through living in a social group is a matter of fierce debate (for example, contrast the views of Ingold 2000; Morris 2003; and Pinker

2002). Worthington Smith (Smith 1884; 1894), at the Acheulean site of Stoke Newington in north London, found masses of decayed vegetable matter on a palaeo-land surface. He suggested that these remains of the fern *Osmunda regalis* may have been collected together by hominins for bedding at sleeping places. This is by no means impossible, but is this a truly cultural act? Is it different from a chimp's nest? Is it a product of learned behaviour? Primatologists (Chimpanzee Cultures n.d.; Waal 2001: 31) identify truly cultural acts in primate societies as possessing the following three qualities:

- The actions are not the product of genetic inheritance which would mean all members of a species do those actions everywhere in exactly the same way. You would expect natural barriers which isolate groups to ensure that if two separate populations of the same species engage in a specific act, each has its own 'take' on it. If it could be shown that the two different approaches were the product of learned behaviour, these would be cultural acts.
- If distinct populations live in similar ecological niches, the environment cannot be shown to have channelled behaviour into similar pathways, i.e. forced upon each population a similar solution.
- It has to be independently demonstrated that the animals in that group are capable of learning by observing others and then transmitting that knowledge. But as readers will by now be aware, being able to tell any of this from the Middle Pleistocene archaeological record is proving difficult.

Box 13.1 summarises claims for cultural acts in the British Lower and Earlier Middle Palaeolithic that might approach these three criteria.

Box 13.1 The evidence for the built environment in the British Lower and Earlier Middle Palaeolithic, and a selection of notable European examples

- *Dwelling structures – huts.* No evidence for huts has ever been discovered in the British Lower or Earlier Middle Palaeolithic, and evidence for them elsewhere is limited. Henry de Lumley (Lumley 1969) identified a hut like structure on the foreshore at the site of Terra Amata, Nice, on the French Mediterranean coast. But subsequent refitting of the lithics by Paolo Villa (1983) showed that artefacts from that level could be conjoined with artefacts from other stratigraphically different levels. So the hut itself was in fact a misinterpretation of a number of discreet smaller features that belonged to different levels. Proper circular huts were claimed at

Bilzingsleben (Mania 1991; Mania 1995). Workshop zones were also associated with these structures as were anvil stones. Gamble (1999) however makes the point that the shelters are composed of a relatively small number of large elements, with smaller stones and bone flakes filling the gaps in between. Without extensive refitting it is difficult to know the rationale the excavators chose in deciding which pieces were part of the constructed walls, and which belonged to the background scatter of material on the surface. Gamble presents an alternative explanation for the oval structures. They are the root bowls of collapsed trees around which hominin occupation and activity took place.

- *Cobble platforms or pavements.* These are a curious feature of some Palaeolithic sites. They represent flat surfaces comprised of deliberately emplaced blocks of stone or cobbles. The explanation is usually that the surrounding sediment was wet or damp, and the so-called paved surface was an attempt to raise activity off this by creating an artificial floor. In some cases it is suggested that because such a platform would be uncomfortable to walk on, skins and hides would be spread over it. But how would such a practice work? Neanderthal examples are reviewed by Mellars (1996). At Bilzingsleben (Mania 1991; Mania and Mania 2005), a portion of a large area in front of the so-called hut structures was designated as a paved zone. The paving itself was composed of bone, stone, teeth, antler fragments and wood fragments, pressed into the loess soil. The fragments were small, the majority under 10 cm in length, with little evidence of any overlap of objects. It is unclear whether this spread of small fragmentary material is a deliberately created feature, or is perhaps due to the redistribution of activity debris when the surface was buried by more sediment. At Hoxne, the excavators (Singer *et al.* 1993; Wymer 1985) postulated a possible pavement in the late MIS 11 Upper Industry. The feature was formed of natural cobbles. Photographs show that the individual clasts are quite dispersed, and there is no evidence of packing of the stones together. The excavators themselves were not particularly convinced. The only other feasible example from Britain is from the Lower Loam at Swanscombe. In 1970 an area of flint pebbles and cobbles was recovered during the excavation. It is a small area, and the cobbles were not very densely packed. Perhaps this was the residue of a flood event that disturbed the otherwise quiet bankside setting. For the moment, interpretation of the Lower Loam pebble complex should remain in a suspense account.
- *Walls and windbreaks.* There is no evidence for these in the British Lower Palaeolithic, but their presence is suggested on a number of European sites. The most visually distinctive is that from Bilzingsle-

ben. This is a stone alignment more than anything else (Mania 1991). The 5 m-long feature is composed of blocks of shelly limestone and travertine laid out at regular 25–30 cm intervals. The two ends are each marked by an elephant tusk, suggested by the excavator to be from the same animal.

- Stone and bone clusters. In Britain these have only been reported from the MIS 11 Acheulean site at Hoxne (Singer et al. 1993; Wymer 1983). There were twelve stone clusters in the Lower Industry, West Cutting. They comprised cobbles, flint artefacts and broken bones (also flecks of charcoal). They were less than a metre in diameter, and appeared to run in a line demarcating one edge of the archaeological scatter (Wymer 1983). The excavators interpreted them as the remains of bags in-filled with debris so that they could serve as weights, possibly for fishing traps. In the Upper Industry there were four clusters of smashed bone. They formed tight discreet groups, just as the stone clusters did in the Lower Industry. These too were tentatively interpreted as the residue of disintegrated bags or containers. The bones were the remains of skulls and vertebrae, and may have been from a single animal in each case. What ever their explanation, a natural accumulation appears difficult to sustain.

Hearths

Hearths could represent good evidence for the existence of social learning. There is no hearth-building gene that we know of, and given the nature of fire, it is unlikely that it would be immediately apparent to all hominins everywhere that this would make a useful tool. The concept of fire as a manageable resource can only be a culturally learned phenomenon.

The concept of a hearth is intimately tied up with how social relations are interpreted. Hearths are places to sit and exchange news and ideas, make and repair tools, discuss the day's hunt, and make plans for the future. At the fireside, rituals can be practised, and acts redolent with social meaning can be performed. The hearth would take on an important conceptual focus in the process of establishing and maintaining social relations between individuals. Gamble (1993b; Stringer and Gamble 1993) argues that modern humans literally create societies around hearths; coalitions and core groups would be formed, maintained, and manipulated around the fireside. The social landscape of Homo sapiens was one of strangers and distant allies bound together in extended networks. So a carefully constructed hearth with a fire pit and retaining wall of stones, signals individuals contributing and sharing in a communal society.

Despite over a century of research, and the examination of thousands of sites, the evidence for constructed hearths in the Middle Pleistocene is sparse, but then a lot of these sites are secondary context. Moreover, a hearth does not need to be constructed. Not all modern humans will dig a shallow pit for the fire and surround it with stones to keep the embers within. Could pre-modern humans have had control over fire and not built 'proper' hearths? Many years ago François Bordes claimed this was so (Bordes 1972). In the Acheulean levels at Pech de l'Azé II he claimed there was evidence of fires simply lit on the cave floor, others had a shallow pit scooped out for the fire but no retaining wall of stones. Yet others did appear to have stones deliberately emplaced around the fire. James (1989) reviewed the evidence for fire at pre-modern human sites through-out the world. Almost all of it was contested or open to competing explanations. Since James's and Gamble's articles were published, little data have emerged to change those conclusions. At the major British Lower Palaeolithic sites of Barnham (Ashton et al. 1998), Elveden (Ashton et al. 2005), Hoxne (Singer et al. 1993) and Boxgrove (Roberts and Parfitt 1999), there is not a whiff of smoke! The same for Caddington (Sampson 1978; Smith 1894), Round Green, and the other Chiltern Hills sites (White 1997).

There have been two important discoveries in Britain in recent years, and one in Germany that are changing our perspective on this. We have already discussed the probable MIS 11 site at Foxhall Road, where ready-made handaxes were brought to a sheltered location and where a fire was lit. White and Plunkett (2004) believe no more than five individuals were present around the cluster A hearth. Conclusively proving this was a hearth is no longer possible, but there seems no reason to doubt it. There is a localised patch of discoloured sediment, a ring of artefacts around one side of it, and what appears to be a burnt artefact.

The other British site is the MIS 11 site of Beeches Pit (see Chapter 5; Gowlett 2005; Gowlett and Hallos 2000). Here Acheulean knappers occu-pied the margins of small channels or ponds. At both of the archaeological areas on the site, localised patches of burnt sediment were present that also contained burnt artefacts. Detailed analysis remains to be done on these hearths, but their localised position adjacent to stream channels, limited spatial extent, and the presence of burnt artefacts, which refit to un-burnt ones located around the outside edge of the burnt area, do suggest they are hearths. One of these archaeological areas represents a multiple burning event. Two hearths have been lit at different times on the same slope (Gowlett 2006). Such a highly localised pattern would be difficult to reproduce in a natural situation.

Similarly, localised patches of burning at Schöningen in Lower Saxony, Germany, also suggest deliberately laid fires without any evidence of formal hearth construction. Schöningen was discussed in Chapter 8. It appears to be a lakeside kill and butchery site, so perhaps the fire was for cooking, or for help in warding off rival predators.

At other sites there are suggestions of hearths but in some cases the evidence is less clear. At the Colombanien site of Ménez Drégan (Hallegouet *et al.* 1992, see Chapter 8), hearths are present in three levels (it is difficult to see how small burning patches could occur naturally on the marine littoral if they were not anthropogenic). Further east there are claims for fire at a number of sites (Svoboda 1989), for example, at Bilzingsleben (Mania and Mania 2005; but see Gamble 1999 and below), and Vértesszölös (Kretzoi and Vértes 1965; Valoch 1995), and on the Mediterranean shore at Terra Amata, Nice (Lumley 1969; Villa 1983).

Noel Boaz and Russell Ciochon (2004) have argued that hominins at the famous site of Zhoukoudian (the 'Peking Man' site) did manipulate fire but only had a partial control over it. These hominins were not H. *heidelbergensis*, these were H. *erectus*, a species that survived longer in Asia than anywhere else. At Zhoukoudian, they were broadly contemporary with the Clactonian and Acheulean in Britain, and they too used a non-handaxe tool kit, probably because the locally available quartz was not conducive to making handaxes. Boaz and Ciochon argue that H. *erectus* used fire mainly as a defence mechanism for fending off predators at night, and for chasing hyaenas out of the Zhoukoudian cave in order to scavenge off the kills in their dens. To use Boaz and Ciochon's phrase, they only used fire as an ecological tool. The implication is that they had learned to manipulate naturally occurring fire, but not to start it themselves.

A similar interpretation is proposed for Beeches Pit by Gowlett (2006). The stratigraphically separated hearths at Beeches were a result of hominins bringing fire in anew each time. Much social energy and a division of labour would be required to maintain it over extended periods of time. But once it went out, that was it. A new source (lightning strike/natural brush fire) would be required. Gowlett notes that fire is a high risk strategy. It brings many benefits, but when it goes out and there is no way to rekindle it, then it is accompanied by a high cost too.

One important aspect of fire is its use in a defensive role. Gowlett notes that the optimum locations for hominin fire use were caves and by the sides of watercourses. These are the very locations where hominins would be at risk from other hunting predators, especially at night. Fire used in this way, as an ecological tool, would indeed be an adaptive behaviour without precedent in the natural world. This would certainly fit the fourth way of thinking about hominins that I proposed at the beginning of this chapter.

Although the evidence is sparse, it seems clear that at least some H. *heidelbergensis* groups in Middle Pleistocene Britain had mastered fire. I believe we may take the learnt knowledge of how to manipulate naturally occurring fire as good evidence for the existence of a socially learned tradition. The knowledge may not have been shared by all H. *heidelbergensis* groups.

Conclusion

I will now return to the question posed at the beginning of this chapter. I do not believe that there is anything in the behavioural repertoire of *Homo heidelbergensis* that helps us to identify the Clactonian as a cultural tradition – an assemblage type with time depth, whose character is a result of a specific pattern of socially transmitted inter-generational learning. There are a number of behavioural traits that I have not dealt with, such as the evidence for hunting and subsistence behaviours, and raw material/artefact transport behaviour (see Hallos 2005, for a full discussion on this), preferring to restrict discussion to the question of how society was constructed.

I was searching for any proof that archaeological traditions or lineages of socially transferable knowledge existed in Middle Pleistocene hominin society. I believe such evidence does exist. Using fire as an ecological tool is a cultural act and one that would have to depend on pre-existing know-ledge within a group. The use of fire will not come naturally to an animal. The Foxhall Road evidence suggests intra-group lineages of learnt practice that did not reflect one group-wide cultural signature. Much of the vari-ability in handaxe shape seen at *in-situ* Acheulean sites reflects this in my opinion. The very stone tools themselves imply cultural acts and socially learned skills.

How does this help us with the Clactonian? Can any of the above help us to interpret the Clactonian as a body of culturally transmitted knowledge? Sadly, I do not think it can. It is clear that *Homo heidelbergensis* was a cultural animal which could perpetuate a number of lineages of knowledge within core groups, and larger parent groups, but proving that in the Clactonian seems, for the moment, to be impossible. We are back to square one.

EPILOGUE

But the wilderness had found him out early, and had taken on
him a terrible vengeance for the fantastic invasion. I think it
had whispered to him things about himself which he did not
know, things of which he had no conception till he took
council with this great solitude – and the whisper proved
irresistibly fascinating.

(Conrad 1973: 83)

In the last chapter I reviewed some of the main theories about how society
was constructed in the Middle Pleistocene, and the social context of inter-
generational knowledge transmission. A fission–fusion pattern has been
suggested for hominin society as a whole. A hominin social group would
be a fusion of individual sub-groups which would contain their own lineages
of knowledge passed down through the sub-group. Temporary alliances,
such as hunting coalitions, or perhaps winter foraging groups, would unite
members of different sub-groups together on a short term basis. I also
suggested that an important element in hominin social organisation was
individual self-preferment developed through the medium of personal
display. Individuals' social fitness (and the effectiveness of their personal
prowess display behaviour) would be enhanced through the context of
coalition/group competitive display. Co-operative coalition success would
reflect well on the individual. Selection on behaviour was firmly focused in
the social world; individual mate choice, through sexual selection, was the
driver. Mate choice was made on physical and social prowess. Material
culture, including handaxes, carried no social significance – as yet.

This is a far cry from the simple notion that a hominin group represented a single cohesive social entity where the young would all learn the
same thing and practise it in the same way. A normative view of cultural
transmission, where knowledge and practice are simply parachuted into
the next generation, has been shown to be inappropriate. What was learned,
and how it was learned, were intimately tied up with the nature of how

374

societies were constructed. Cultural knowledge is not a discrete entity handed from one individual to the next like a game of pass the parcel. It is like air, individuals move through it, absorb it, change it, and are in turn changed by it.

This view of *Homo heidelbergensis* society should apply to both Clactonian and Acheulean groups, except that it can't. There is a methodological conundrum here, as irresolvable as that described in the first chapter, and like that example, this is wholly a product of normative cultural thinking. The power of historical tradition, outlined in Chapters 10 and 11, has gifted the handaxe with a deep interpretative significance. In the foregoing pages we have been able to explore social construction through it. What in the Clactonian material culture repertoire allows us to do this? Nothing! Are the end flaked nodules described in Chapter 12 socially significant? I do not think so. Or the few abruptly retouched scrapers, or the higher frequency of sharp-edged flake tools? No. Nothing else about the Clactonian appears distinctive. Perhaps as much as anything, this one fact leads me to doubt our ability to properly interpret the Clactonian in its physical context. I still cannot explain away the time depth inherent in the sequences at Barnfield Pit, Rickson's Pit and at the Golf Course, but the above discussion convinces me that simple cultural explanations are not enough.

At the beginning of this book I made it clear I had no startling new interpretation that would finally settle the Clactonian question, even after a quarter of a century of researching it. I wish I did. Middle Pleistocene *Homo* was a truly unique creature. Its evolution was shaped by a physical and social world that has no viable analogues today. Its life was as complicated in its world, as ours is today in our own. Simple either/or dichotomies and cultural interpretations that we inherit from the founders of the discipline will not help us unravel that complexity. The simplicity of what the Clactonian really is, as described in Chapter 12, easily lends itself to a normative view of culture, but it is a mistake to think of it this way. Its invariance was not a product of limited channels of social learning. Its invariance was a reflection of the mechanical properties of flint. I believe hominin behaviour was situationally variable, and the simplicity of the material culture belied its effectiveness in a variety of different situations.

As I said, I do not have an answer to the Clactonian question, but whatever it ultimately is, presupposing there is one, I suspect it will surprise us all.

BIBLIOGRAPHY

Aiello, L. C. and Dean, C. (1990) *An Introduction to Human Evolutionary Anatomy*. London: Academic Press.

Aldhouse-Green, S. (1998) The Archaeology of Distance: Perspectives from the Welsh Palaeolithic. In Ashton, N., Healy, F. and Pettitt, P. (eds) *Stone Age Archaeology: Essays in Honour of John Wymer*. The Lithic Studies Society Occasional Paper 6; Oxford: Oxbow Books, pp. 137–145.

Aldhouse-Green, S. (2001) The Colonisations and Visitations of Wales by Neanderthals and Modern Humans in the Later Pleistocene. In Anderson, A., Lilley, I. and O'Connor, S. (eds) *Histories of Old Ages: Essays in Honour of Rhys Jones*. Canberra: Pandus Books, pp. 225–235.

Allen, L. G. and Gibbard, P. L. (1993) Pleistocene Evolution of the Solent River of Southern England. *Quaternary Science Reviews* 12: 503–528.

Amiot, C. (1993) Analyse Technologique de l'Industrie Lithique de Montsaugeon (Haute-Marne). *Paléo* 5: 83–109.

Andrews, P., Cook, J., Currant, A. and Stringer, C. (ed.) (1999) *Westbury Cave: The Natural History Museum Excavations, 1976–1984*. Bristol: Western Academic and Specialist Press.

Anonymous (1902) *A Guide to the Antiquities of the Stone Age in the Department of British and Mediaeval Antiquities*. London: Trustees of the British Museum.

Anonymous. (1913) Report on Excavations by Smith and Dewey. *Proceedings of the Society of Antiquaries of London* 25: 117–119.

Anonymous (1914) Report on Excavations by Smith and Dewey. *Proceedings of the Society of Antiquaries of London* 26: 154–155.

Anonymous (1968) High Lodge Palaeolithic Industry. *Nature* 220: 1065–1066.

Antoine, P., Lautridou, J. P. and Laurent, P. (2000) Long-Term Fluvial Archives in N. W. France: Response of the Seine and Somme Rivers to Tectonic Movements, Climatic Variations and Sea-Level Changes. *Geomorphology* 33: 183–207.

Antoine, P., Coutard, J. P., Gibbard, P. L., Hallegouet, B., Lautridou, J. P. and Ozouf, J-C. (2003) The Pleistocene Rivers of the English Channel Region. *Journal of Quaternary Science* 18: 227–243.

Antoñanzas, R. L. and Bescós, G. C. (2002) The Gran Dolina Site (Lower to Middle Pleistocene, Atapuerca, Burgos, Spain): New Palaeoenvironmental Data Based on the Distribution of Small Mammals. *Palaeogeography, Palaeoclimatology, Palaeoecology* 186: 311–334.

Arnold, K. (1991) Experimental Archaeology and the Denticulate Mousterian. *Papers from the Institute of Archaeology* 2: 2–7.

Ascenzi, A., Biddittu, I., Cassoli, P. F., Segre, A. G. and Segre-Naldini, E. (1996) A Calvarium of Late *Homo erectus* from Ceprano, Italy. *Journal of Human Evolution* 31: 409–423.

Ashton, N. (2001) One Step Beyond: Flint Shortage above the Goring Gap: the Example of Wolvercote. In Milliken, S. and Cook, J. (eds) *A Very Remote Period Indeed*. Oxford: Oxbow Books, pp. 199–206.

Ashton, N., Bowen, D. Q. and Lewis, S. G. (1994) Reply. *Journal of the Geological Society, London* 152: 571–574.

Ashton, N., Cook, J. and Rose, J. (eds) (1992a) *High Lodge: Excavations by G. de G. Sieveking 1962–1968 and J. Cook 1988*. London: British Museum Press.

Ashton, N., Dean, P. and McNabb, J. (1991) Flaked Flakes: What, Where, When and Why? *Lithics* 12: 1–11.

Ashton, N., Jacobi, R. and White, M. J. (2003) The Dating of Levallois Sites in West London. *Quaternary Newsletter* 99: 25–32.

Ashton, N. and Lewis, S. G. (2002) Deserted Britain: Declining Populations in the British Late Middle Pleistocene. *Antiquity* 76: 388–396.

Ashton, N., Lewis, S. G. and Parfitt, S. (eds) (1998) *Excavations at the Lower Palaeolithic Site at East Farm, Barnham, 1989–1994*. Occasional Papers British Museum 125. London: Trustees of the British Museum.

Ashton, N., Lewis, S. G. and Parfitt, S. A. (n.d.) Intra-MIS 11 Climatic Variability in the UK: New Evidence from Hoxne. in prep.

Ashton, N., Lewis, S. G., Parfitt, S. A., Candy, I., Keen, D. H., Kemp, R., Penckman, K., Thomas, G., Whittaker, J. and White, M. J. (2005) Excavations at the Lower Palaeolithic Site at Elveden, Suffolk, UK. *Proceedings of the Prehistoric Society* 71: 1–61.

Ashton, N. and McNabb, J. (1994) Bifaces in Perspective. In Ashton, N. and David, A. (eds) *Stories in Stone*. The Lithic Studies Society Occasional Paper 4. Oxford: The Lithics Studies Society, pp. 182–191.

Ashton, N. and McNabb, J. (1996a) The Flint Industries from the Waechter Excavations. In Conway, B., McNabb, J. and Ashton, N. (eds) *Excavations at Barnfield Pit, Swanscombe, 1968–72*. Occasional Papers British Museum 94. London: Trustees of the British Museum, pp. 201–236.

Ashton, N. and McNabb, J. (1996b) Appendix 1. In Conway, B., McNabb, J. and Ashton, N. (eds) *Excavations at Barnfield Pit, Swanscombe, 1968–1972*. Occasional Papers British Museum 94. London: Trustees of the British Museum, pp. 241–245.

Ashton, N., McNabb, J. and Parfitt, S. A. (1992b) Choppers and the Clactonian: A Re-investigation. *Proceedings of the Prehistoric Society* 58: 21–28.

Austin, L. (1994) Life and Death of a Boxgrove Biface. In Ashton, N. and David, A. (eds) *Stories in Stone*. The Lithic Studies Society Occasional Paper 4. Oxford: The Lithic Studies Society, pp. 119–125.

Avery, B. W., Bullock, P., Catt, J. A., Rayner, J. H. and Weir, A. H. (1982) Composition and Origin of Some Brickearths on the Chiltern Hills, England. *Catena* 9: 153–174.

Baden-Powell, D. (1949) Experimental Clactonian Technique. *Proceedings of the Prehistoric Society* 15: 38–41.

Barrett, L., Henzi, P. and Dunbar, R. (2003) Primate Cognition: from 'What Now?' to 'What If?' *Trends in Cognitive Science* 7: 494–497.

Barton, N. (1986) Experiments with Long Blades from Sproughton, near Ipswich, Suffolk. In Roe, D. A. (ed.) *Studies in the Upper Palaeolithic of Britain*. Oxford: British Archaeological Reports International Series 296, pp. 129–141.

Bar-Yosef, O. (1994) The Lower Palaeolithic of the Near East. *Journal of World Prehistory* 8: 211–265.

Bar-Yosef, O. and Belfer-Cohen, A. (2001) From Africa to Eurasia: Early Dispersals. *Quaternary International* 75: 19–28.

Bar-Yosef, O. and Goren-Inbar, N. (1993) *The Lithic Assemblages of 'Ubeidiya: A Lower Palaeolithic Site in the Jordan Valley*. Jerusalem: The Hebrew University of Jerusalem.

Bates, M. R. (1993) Quaternary Aminostratigraphy in Northwestern France. *Quaternary Science Reviews* 12: 793–809.

Bates, M. R. (2001) The Meeting of the Waters: Raised Beaches and River Gravels of the Sussex Coastal Plain/Hampshire Basin. In Wenban-Smith, F. F. and Hosfield, R. (eds) *Palaeolithic Archaeology of the Solent River*. The Lithic Studies Society Occasional Paper 7. London: The Lithic Studies Society, pp. 27–45.

Bates, M. R., Lambrick, G., Welsh, K. and White, M. J. (1998) Evaluation of Palaeolithic Deposits at Purfleet, Essex. *Lithics* 19: 72–87.

Bermúdez de Castro, J. M., Arsuaga, J. L., Carbonell, E., Rosas, A., Martínez, I. and Mosquera, M. (1997) A Hominid from the Lower Pleistocene of Atapuerca Spain: Possible Ancestor to Neandertals and Modern Humans. *Science* 276: 1392–1395.

Bermúdez de Castro, J. M., Martinón-Torres, M., Carbonell, E., Sarmiento, S., Rosas, A., van der Made, J. and Lozano, M. (2004) The Atapuerca Sites and their Contribution to the Knowledge of Human Evolution in Europe. *Evolutionary Anthropology* 13: 25–41.

Bietti, A. and Castorina, G. (1992) Clactonian and Acheulean in the Italian Lower Palaeolithic: A Re-Examination of Some Industries of Valle Giumentina (Pescara, Italy). *Quaternaria Nova* 11: 41–59.

Bischoff, J. L., Shamp, D. D., Aramburu, A., Arsuaga, J. L., Carbonell, E. and Bermúdez de Castro, J. M. (2003) The Sima de los Huesos Hominids Date to beyond U/Th Equilibrium (>350 kyr) and Perhaps to 400–500 kyr: New Radiometric Dates. *Journal of Archaeological Science* 30: 275–280.

Bishop, M. J. (1974) A Preliminary Report on the Middle Pleistocene Mammal Bearing Deposits of Westbury-sub-Mendip, Somerset. *Proceedings of the University of Bristol Spelaeological Society* 13: 301–318.

Bisson, M. S. (2000) Nineteenth-Century Tools for Twenty-First Century Archaeology? Why the Middle Palaeolithic Typology of François Bordes must be Replaced. *Journal of Archaeological Method and Theory* 7: 1–48.

Boaz, N. T. and Ciochon, R. L. (2004) *Dragon Bone Hill: An Ice Age Saga of Homo erectus*. Oxford: Oxford University Press.

Boëda, E. (1995) Levallois: A Volumetric Construction, Methods, a Technique. In Dibble, H. L. and Bar-Yosef, O. (eds) *The Definition and Interpretation of Levallois Technology*. Madison, WI: Prehistory Press, pp. 41–68.

Boesch, C. and Tomasello, M. (1998) Chimpanzee and Human Cultures. *Current Anthropology* 39: 591–604.

Bordes, F. (1961) *Typologie du Paléolithique Ancien et Moyen*. Bordeaux: Delmas.

Bordes, F. (1968) *The Old Stone Age*. London: Weidenfeld and Nicolson.

Bordes, F. (1971) Essai de Préhistoire Expérimentale: Fabrication d'un Épieu de

Bois. In Ecole Pratique des Hautes Études (ed.) *Mélanges de Préhistoire, d'Archéocivilisation, et d'Ethnologie Offerts à André Varagnac*. (Ecole Pratique des Hautes Études VIème Section, Centre de Recherches Historiques.) Paris: SEVPEN. pp. 69–73.

Bordes, F. (1972) *A Tale of Two Caves*. London: Harper and Row.

Bordes, F. and Bourgon, M. (1951) Le Complex Mousterien: Mousteriens, Levalloisien, et Tayacien. *L'Anthropologie* 55: 1–23.

Boreham, S. and Gibbard, P. L. (1995) Middle Pleistocene Hoxnian Stage Interglacial Deposits at Hitchin, Hertfordshire, England. *Proceedings of the Geologists' Association* 106: 259–270.

Borofsky, R. (1987) *Making History: Pukapukan and Anthropological Constructions of Knowledge*. Cambridge: Cambridge University Press.

Bosinski, G. (1995) The Earliest Occupation of Europe: Western Central Europe. In Roebroeks, W. and van Kolfschoten, T. (eds) *The Earliest Occupation of Europe: Proceedings of the European Science Foundation Workshop at Tautavel (France), 1993. Analecta Praehistorica Leidensia* 27. Leiden: University of Leiden, pp. 103–128.

Bowen, D. Q., Hughes, S., Sykes, G. A. and Miller, G. H. (1989) Land–Sea Correlations in the Pleistocene Based on Isoleucine Epimerization in Non-Marine Molluscs. *Nature* 340: 49–51.

Bradley, B. and Sampson, C. G. (1986) Analysis by Replication of Two Acheulean Artefact Assemblages. In Bailey, G. N. and Callow, P. (eds) *Stone Age Prehistory*. Cambridge: Cambridge University Press. pp. 29–45.

Bradley, R. S. (1999) *Paleoclimatology: Reconstructing Climates of the Quaternary*. 2nd edn. London: Academic Press.

Breuil, H. (1912) Les Subdivisions du Paléolithique Supérieur et leur Significance. *Congrès International d'Anthropologie et d'Archéologie Préhistoriques*. Compte Rendue, Session 14: 165–238.

Breuil, H. (1926) Palaeolithic Industries from the Beginning of the Rissian to the Beginning of the Würmian Glaciation. *Man* 26: 176–179.

Breuil, H. (1932) Les Industries a Éclats du Paléolithique Ancien, 1. Le Clactonien. *Préhistoire* 1: 125–190.

Breuil, H. (1939) The Pleistocene Succession in the Somme Valley. *Proceedings of the Prehistoric Society* 5: 33–38.

Breuil, H. and Koslowski, L. (1931) Études de Stratigraphie Paléolithique dans le Nord de la France, la Belgique et l'Angleterre. *L'Anthropologie* 41: 449–488.

Breuil, H. and Koslowski, L. (1932) Études de Stratigraphie Paléolithique dans le Nord de la France, la Belgique et l'Angleterre. *L'Anthropologie* 42: 27–47, 291–314.

Breuil, H. and Koslowski, L. (1934) Études de Stratigraphie Paléolithique dans le Nord de la France, la Belgique et l'Angleterre. *L'Anthropologie* 44: 249–290.

Breuil, H. and Zbyszewski, G. (1942–1945) Contribution à l'Étude des Industries Paléolithiques du Portugal et de Leurs Rapports avec la Géologie du Quaternaire. *Comunicações dos Serviços Geológicos de Portugal* 23 and 26: Lisboa.

Briant, R. M., Bates, M. R., Schwenninger, J-L. and Wenban-Smith, F. F. (2006) An Optically Stimulated Luminescence Dated Middle to Late Pleistocene Fluvial Sequence from the Western Solent Basin, Southern England. *Journal of Quaternary Science* 21: 507–523.

Bridgland, D. R. (1988) The Pleistocene Fluvial Stratigraphy and Palaeogeography of Essex. *Proceedings of the Geologists' Association* 99: 291–314.

Bridgland, D. R. (1994) *Quaternary of the Thames*. London: Chapman and Hall.

Bridgland, D. R. (1995) The Quaternary Sequence of the Eastern Thames Basin: Problems of Correlation. In Bridgland, D. R., Allen, P. and Haggart, B. A. (eds) *The Quaternary of the Lower Reaches of the Thames: Field Guide*. Durham: Quaternary Research Association, pp. 35–54.

Bridgland, D. R. (2001) The Pleistocene Evolution and Palaeolithic Occupation of the Solent River. In Wenban-Smith, F. F. and Hosfield, R. (eds) *Palaeolithic Archaeology of the Solent River*. The Lithics Studies Society Occasional Paper 7. London: Lithics Studies Society, pp. 15–25.

Bridgland, D. R. (2003) The Evolution of the River Medway, SE England, in the Context of Quaternary Palaeoclimate and the Palaeolithic Occupation of NW Europe. *Proceedings of the Geologists' Association* 114: 23–48.

Bridgland, D. R., Allen, P., Currant, A., Gibbard, P. L., Lister, A., Preece, R. C., Robinson, J. E., Stuart, A. J. and Sutcliffe, A. J. (1988) Report of Geologists' Association Field Meeting in North-East Essex, May 22nd–24th, 1987. *Proceedings of the Geologists' Association* 99: 315–333.

Bridgland, D. R., Allen, P. and Haggart, B. A. (eds) (1995a) *The Quaternary of the Lower Reaches of the Thames: Field Guide*. Durham: Quaternary Research Association.

Bridgland, D.R., Antoine, P., Limondin-Lozouet, N., Santisteban, J.I., Westaway, R. and White, M.J. (2006) The Palaeolithic Occupation of Europe as Revealed by Evidence from the Rivers: Data from IGCP 449. *Journal of Quaternary Science* 21: 437–455.

Bridgland, D. R. and D'Olier, B. (1995) The Pleistocene Evolution of the Thames and Rhine Drainage Systems in the Southern North Sea Basin. In Preece, R.C. (ed.) *Island Britain: A Quaternary Perspective*. Geological Society of London Special Publication 96. London: Geological Society of London, pp. 27–45.

Bridgland, D. R., Field, M. H., Holmes, J. A., McNabb, J., Preece, R. C., Selby, I., Wymer, J., Boreham, S., Irving, B., Parfitt, S. A. and Stuart, A. J. (1999) Middle Pleistocene Interglacial Thames-Medway Deposits at Clacton-on-Sea, England: Reconsideration of the Biostratigraphical and Environmental Context of the Type Clactonian Palaeolithic Industry. *Quaternary Science Reviews* 18: 109–146.

Bridgland, D. R. and Harding, P. (1984) Palaeolithic Artefacts from the Gravels of the Hoo Peninsula. *Archaeologia Cantiana* 101: 41–55.

Bridgland, D. R. and Harding, P. (1993) Middle Pleistocene Thames Terrace Deposits at Globe Pit, Little Thurrock, and their Contained Clactonian Industry. *Proceedings of the Geologists' Association* 104: 263–283.

Bridgland, D. R. and Harding, P. (1995) Lion Pit Tramway Cutting, West Thurrock (TQ 598783). In Bridgland, D. R., Allen, P. and Haggart, B. A. (eds) *The Quaternary of the Lower Reaches of the Thames: Field Guide*. Durham: Quaternary Research Association, pp. 217–230.

Bridgland, D. R., Keen, D. H., Schreve, D. C. and White, M. J. (1998) Chislet, Wear Farm Pit (TR 224650). In Murton, J. B., Whiteman, C. A., Bates, M. R., Bridgland, D. R., Long, A. J., Roberts, M. B. and Waller, M. P. (eds) *The Quaternary of Kent and Sussex: Field Guide*. Durham: Quaternary Research Association, pp. 44–50.

Bridgland, D. R., Lewis, S. G. and Wymer, J. (1995b) Middle Pleistocene Stratigraphy and Archaeology around Mildenhall and Icklingham, Suffolk: Report on the Geologists' Association Field Meeting, 27 June, 1992. *Proceedings of the Geologists' Association* 106: 57–69.

Bridgland, D. R., Maddy, D. and Bates, M. R. (2004) River Terrace Sequences: Templates for Quaternary Geochronology and Marine-Terrestrial Correlation. *Journal of Quaternary Science* 19: 203–218.

Bridgland, D. R., Patrick, A., Peter, A., Austin, L., Irving, B., Parfitt, S. A., Preece, R. C. and Tipping, R. M. (1995c) Purfleet Interglacial Deposits: Bluelands and Greenlands Quarries (TQ 569586). In Bridgland, D. R., Allen, P. and Haggart, B. A. (eds) *The Quaternary of the Lower Reaches of the Thames: Field Guide.* Durham: Quaternary Research Association, pp. 167–184.

Bridgland, D. R., Preece, R. C., Roe, H. M., Tipping, R. M., Coope, G. R., Field, M. H., Robinson, J. E., Schreve, D. C. and Crowe, K. (2001) Middle Pleistocene Interglacial Deposits at Barling, Essex, England: Evidence for a Longer Chronology for the Thames Terrace Sequence. *Journal of Quaternary Science* 16: 813–840.

Bridgland, D. R. and Schreve, D. C. (2001) River Terrace Formation in Synchrony with Long-Term Climatic Fluctuation: Examples from Southern Britain. In Maddy, D., Macklin, M. and Woodward, J. (eds) *River Basin Sediments Systems: Archives of Environmental Change.* Rotterdam: Balkema, pp. 229–248.

Bridgland, D. R., Schreve, D. C., Allen, P. and Keen, D. H. (2003) Key Middle Pleistocene Localities of the Lower Thames: Site Conservation Issues, Recent Research, and Report of a Geologists' Association Excursion, 8 July, 2000. *Proceedings of the Geologists' Association* 114: 211–225.

Bristow, C. R., Freshney, E. C. and Penn, I. E. (1991) *Geology of the Country Around Bournemouth.* Memoir of the Geological Survey. London: HMSO.

Brodrick, A. H. (1963) *The Abbé Breuil: Prehistorian.* London: Hutchinson and Co. Ltd.

Bronowski, J. (1973) *The Ascent of Man.* London: British Broadcasting Corporation.

Brown, J. (1838) Discovery of a Large Pair of Fossil Horns in Essex. *Magazine of Natural History. New Series.* 2: 163–164.

Brown, J. (1840) Notice of a Fluvio-Marine Deposit Containing Mammalian Remains Occurring in the Parish of Little Clacton on the Essex Coast. *Magazine of Natural History. New Series* 4: 197–201.

Brown, J. A. (1887) *Palaeolithic Man in N.W. Middlesex.* London: McMillan and Company.

Brühl, E. (2003) The Small Flint Tool Industry from Bilzingsleben-Steinrinne. In Burdukiewicz, J.M. and Ronen, A. (eds) Lower Palaeolithic Small Tools in Europe and the Levant. Oxford: British Archaeological Reports. International Series 1115. pp. 49–63.

Burchell, J. P. T. (1934) Fresh Facts Relating to the Boyn Hill Terrace of the Lower Thames Valley. *Antiquaries Journal* 14: 163–166.

Burdukiewicz, J.M. and Ronen, A. (eds) (2006). *Lower Palaeolithic Small Tools in Europe and the Levant.* Oxford: British Archaeological Reports. International Series 1115.

Bury, H. (1933) The Plateau Gravels of the Bournemouth Area. *Proceedings of the Geologists' Association* 44: 314–335.

Byrne, L. (2004) Lithic Tools from Arago Cave, Tautavel (Pyrénées-Orientales, France): Behavioural Continuity or Raw Material Determinism During the Middle Pleistocene. *Journal of Archaeological Science* 31: 351–364.

Calkin, J. B. and Green, J. F. N. (1949) Palaeoliths and Terraces near Bournemouth. *Proceedings of the Prehistoric Society* 15: 21–37.

Campbell, J. and Sampson, C. G. (1971) *A New Analysis of Kent's Cavern, Devonshire, England.* Oregon: University of Oregon Anthropological Papers 3.

Carbonell, E., Bermúdez de Castro, J. M., Arsuaga, J. L., Díez, J. C., Rosas, A., Cuenca-Bescós, G., Sala, R., Mosquera, M. and Rodriguez, P. (1995) Lower Pleistocene Hominids and Artefacts from Atapuerca-TD6 (Spain). *Science* 269: 826–830.

Carbonell, E., Bermúdez de Castro, J. M., Arsuaga, J. L., Allue, E., Bastir, M., Benito, A., Caceres, I., Canals, T., Díez, J. C., van der Made, J., Mosquera, M., Ollé, A., Pérez-González, A., Rodríguez, J., Rodríguez, X. P., Rosas, A., Rosell, J., Sala, R., Vallverdú, J. and Vergés, J. M. (2005) An Early Pleistocene Hominin Mandible from Atapuerca-TD6, Spain. *Proceedings of the National Academy of Sciences of the USA* 102: 5674–5678.

Carbonell, E. and Rodriguez, X. P. (1994) Early Middle Pleistocene Deposits and Artefacts in the Gran Dolina Site (TD4) of the 'Sierra de Atapuerca' (Burgos, Spain). *Journal of Human Evolution* 26: 291–311.

Carreck, J. N. (1976) Pleistocene Mammalian and Molluscan Remains from 'Taplow' Terrace Deposits at West Thurrock, Near Grays, Essex. *Proceedings of the Geologists' Association* 87: 83–92.

Chambers, J. C. (2003) Like a Rolling Stone? The Identification of Fluvial Transportation Damage Signatures on Secondary Context Bifaces. *Lithics* 24: 66–77.

Chandler, R. H. (1916) The Implements and Cores of Crayford. *Proceedings of the Prehistoric Society of East Anglia* 2: 240–248.

Chandler, R. H. (1928–29) On the Clactonian Industry of Swanscombe. *Proceedings of the Prehistoric Society of East Anglia* 6: 79–116.

Chandler, R. H. (1931) Preliminary Notice: Types of Clactonian Implements at Swanscombe. *Proceedings of the Prehistoric Society of East Anglia* 6: 377–378.

Chandler, R. H. (1932) The Clactonian Industry and Report of Field Meeting at Swanscombe (II). *Proceedings of the Geologists' Association* 43: 70–72.

Chandler, R. H. (1942) Reply to Bull (1942). *Proceedings of the Geologists' Association* 53: 21.

Chandler, R. H. and Leach, A. L. (1912) On the Dartford Heath Gravel and on a Palaeolithic Implement Factory. *Proceedings of the Geologists' Association* 23: 102–111.

Chazan, M. (1997) Redefining Levallois. *Journal of Human Evolution* 33: 719–735.

Chimpanzee Cultures. n.d. http://chimp.st-and.ac.uk/cultures3/default.htm.

Clark, J. D. (1994) The Acheulean Industrial Complex in Africa and Elsewhere. In Corruccini, R. S. and Ciochon, R. L. (eds) *Integrative Paths to the Past. Paleoanthropological Advances in Honor of F. Clark Howell*. Englewood Cliffs, NJ: Prentice Hall, pp. 451–469.

Clarke, R. J. (2000) A Corrected Reconstruction and Interpretation of the *Homo erectus* Calvaria from Ceprano, Italy. *Journal of Human Evolution* 39: 433–442.

Clayton, K. (2000) The Landform Changes Brought about by the Anglian Glaciation. In Lewis, S. G., Whiteman, C. A. and Preece, R. C. (eds) *The Quaternary of Norfolk and Suffolk: Field Guide*. Durham: Quaternary Research Association, pp. 55–60.

Coles, J. M. and Higgs, E. S. (1969) *The Archaeology of Early Man*. London: Faber and Faber.

Collins, D. (1969) Culture Traditions and Environment of Early Man. *Current Anthropology* 10: 267–316.

Collins, D. (1978) *Early Man in West Middlesex*. London: HMSO.

Collins, D. (1986) *Palaeolithic Europe: A Theoretical and Systematic Study*. Tiverton: Clayhanger Books.

Coltorti, M., Feraud, G., Marzoli, A., Peretto, C., Ton-That, T., Voinchet, P., Bahain, J. J., Minelli, A. and Thun Hohenstein, U. (2005) New ^{40}Ar/^{39}Ar, Stratigraphic and

Palaeoclimatic Data on Isernia La Pineta Lower Palaeolithic Site. *Quaternary International* 131: 11–22.

Conrad, J. ([1902]1973) *Heart of Darkness*. Harmondsworth: Penguin.

Conroy, G. C. (2005) *Reconstructing Human Origins*. 2nd edn. London: W.W Norton and Co.

Conway, B. (1970) Reply to West 1969. *Proceedings of the Geologists' Association* 81: 177–179.

Conway, B. (1996a) Bifaces in a Clactonian Context at Little Thurrock, Grays, Essex. *Lithics* 16: 41–46.

Conway, B. (1996b) The Geology Outside the National Nature Reserve, 1968–1972. In Conway, B., McNabb, J. and Ashton, N. (eds) *Excavations at Barnfield Pit, Swanscombe, 1968–1972*. Occasional Papers British Museum 94. London: Trustees of the British Museum, pp. 67–89.

Conway, B. (1996c) The Stratigraphy and Chronology of the Pleistocene Deposits of Barnfield Pit, Swanscombe. In Conway, B., McNabb, J. and Ashton, N. (eds) *Excavations at Barnfield Pit, Swanscombe, 1968–1972*. Occasional Papers British Museum 94. London: Trustees of the British Museum. pp. 117–136.

Conway, B., McNabb, J. and Ashton, N. (eds) (1996) *Excavations at Barnfield Pit, Swanscombe, 1968–1972*. Occasional Papers British Museum 94. London: Trustees of the British Museum.

Cook, J. (1986) A Blade Industry from Stoneham's Pit, Crayford. In Collcutt, S. (ed.) *The Palaeolithic of Britain and its Nearest Neighbours: Recent Trends*. Sheffield: Department of Archaeology and Prehistory, University of Sheffield, pp. 16–19.

Cook, J. and Jacobi, R. (1998) Observations on the Artefacts from the Breccia at Kent's Cavern. In Ashton, N., Healy, F. and Pettitt, P. (eds) *Stone Age Archaeology: Essays in Honour of John Wymer*. The Lithic Studies Society Occasional Paper 6. Oxford: Oxbow Books, pp. 77–89.

Cook, J., Stringer, C., Currant, A., Schwarcz, H. and Wintle, A. G. (1982) A Review of the Chronology of the European Middle Pleistocene Hominid Record. *Yearbook of Physical Anthropology* 25: 19–65.

Cook, W. H. and Killick, J. R. (1922–1924) On the Discovery of a Flint Working Site of Palaeolithic Date in the Medway Valley at Rochester, Kent, with Notes on the Drift-Stages of the Medway. *Proceedings of the Prehistoric Society of East Anglia* 4: 133–149.

Coope, G. R. (2006) Insect Faunas Associated with Palaeolithic Industries from Five Sites of Pre-Anglian Age in Central England. *Quaternary Science Reviews* 25: 1738–1754.

Cottrell, B. and Kamminga, J. (1987) The Formation of Flakes. *American Antiquity* 52: 675–708.

Cruse, R. J., Bridgland, D. R., Callow, P., Currant, A., Hubbard, R., N.L.B., Debenham, N. C. and Bowman, S. G. E. (1987) Further Investigation of the Acheulean Site at Cuxton. *Archaeologia Cantiana* 104: 39–81.

Currant, A. (1989) The Quaternary Origins of the Modern British Mammal Fauna. *Biological Journal of the Linnean Society* 38: 23–30.

Currant, A. (1996) Notes on the Mammalian Remains from Barnfield Pit, Swanscombe. In Conway, B., McNabb, J. and Ashton, N. (eds) *Excavations at Barnfield Pit, Swanscombe, 1968–1972*. Occasional Papers of the British Museum 94. London: Trustees of the British Museum. pp. 163–167.

Currant, A. and Jacobi, R. (2001) A Formal Mammalian Biostratigraphy for the Late Pleistocene of Britain. *Quaternary Science Reviews* 20: 1707–1716.

Dale (1913) Reply to Smith and Dewey. *Proceedings of the Society of Antiquaries of London* 25: 121.

Daniel, G. (1975) *A Hundred and Fifty Years of Archaeology*. London: Duckworth.

Darwin, C. (1879) *The Descent of Man, and Selection in Relation to Sex*. 2nd edn. London: John Murray. Reprint published by Penguin Classics in 2004.

Davies, W. and Charles, R. (eds) (1999) *Dorothy Garrod and the Progress of the Palaeolithic*. Oxford: Oxbow Books.

Davis, P. and Walker, A. (1996) The Footprint Surfaces at Barnfield Pit, Swanscombe: The Results of Analysis of a Potential Human Footprint. In Conway, B., McNabb, J. and Ashton, N. (eds) *Excavations at Barnfield Pit, Swanscombe, 1968–1972*. Occasional Papers British Museum 94. London: Trustees of the British Museum, pp. 169–185.

Debénath, A. and Dibble, H. L. (1994) *Handbook of Palaeolithic Typology. Vol. 1. Lower and Middle Palaeolithic of Europe*. Philadelphia, PA: University Museum, University of Pennsylvania.

Dennell, R. (1990) Progressive Gradualism, Imperialism and Academic Fashion: Lower Palaeolithic Archaeology in the 20th Century. *Antiquity* 64: 549–558.

Dewey, H. (1930) Palaeolithic Thames Deposits. *Proceedings of the Prehistoric Society of East Anglia* 6: 147–155.

Dewey, H. (1932) The Palaeolithic Deposits of the Lower Thames Valley. *Quarterly Journal of the Geological Society of London* 88: 35–54.

Dewey, H. (1959) Palaeolithic Deposits of the Thames at Dartford Heath and Swanscombe, North Kent. In Shephard-Thorn, E. R. (ed.) Privately Circulated Ms of the 1959 Henry Stopes Memorial Lecture. Geologists' Association.

Dewey, H. and Smith, R. A. (1925) Flints from the Sturry Gravels, Kent. *Archaeologia* 24: 117–136.

Dibble, H. L. and Bar-Yosef, O. (eds) (1995) *The Definition and Interpretation of Levallois Technology*. Madison, WI: Prehistory Press.

Dines, H. (1928) The Palaeolithic Site at Bapchild, Near Sittingbourne. *Transactions of the South Eastern Union of Scientific Societies* 5: 100–107.

Dines, H. (1929) The Flint Industries of Bapchild. *Proceedings of the Prehistoric Society of East Anglia* 6: 12–26.

Dobosi, V. (2003) Changing Environment – Unchanged Culture at Vértesszölös, Hungary. In Burdukiewicz, J.M. and Ronen, A. (eds) Lower Palaeolithic Small Tools in Europe and the Levant. Oxford: British Archaeological Reports. International Series 1115. pp. 101–111.

Domínguez-Rodrigo, M., Pickering, T. R., Semaw, S. and Rogers, M. J. (2005) Cutmarked Bones from Pliocene Archaeological Sites at Gona, Afar, Ethiopia: Implications for the Function of the World's Oldest Stone Tools. *Journal of Human Evolution* 48: 109–121.

Draper, J. C. (1951) Stone Industry from Rainbow Bar, Hants. *Archaeological Newsletter* 3: 147–149.

Dunbar, R. (1998) The Social Brain Hypothesis. *Evolutionary Anthropology* 6: 178–190.

Dunbar, R. (2003) The Social Brain: Mind, Language, and Society in Evolutionary Perspective. *Annual Review of Anthropology* 32: 163–181.

Dunbar, R. (2004) *The Human Story*. London: Faber and Faber.

Evans, J. (1872) *The Ancient Stone Implements, Weapons, and Ornaments of Great Britain*. London: Longmans, Green, Reader, and Dyer.

Evans, J. (1897) *The Ancient Stone Implements, Weapons, and Ornaments of Great Britain*. 2nd edn. London: Longmans, Green, and Co.

Falguères, C. and Bahain, J. J. (1997) U-Series and ESR Dating of Teeth from Acheulean and Mousterian Levels at La Micoque (Dordogne, France). *Journal of Archaeological Science* 24: 537–545.

Field, A. S. (1999) An Analytical and Comparative Study of the Earlier Stone Age Archaeology of the Sterkfontein Valley. Unpublished MSc thesis, University of the Witwatersrand, Johannesburg.

Frere, J. (1800) Flint Weapons Discovered at Hoxne in Suffolk. *Archaeologia* 13: 204–205.

Gabunia, L., Antón, S. C., Lordkipanidze, D., Vekua, A., Justus, A. and Swisher, C. C. (2001) Dmanisi and Dispersal. *Evolutionary Anthropology* 10: 159–170.

Gabunia, L. and Vekua, A. (1995) A Plio-Pleistocene Hominid from Dmanisi, East Georgia, Caucasus. *Nature* 373: 509–512.

Gabunia, M. (2000) On Ancient Man in the Volcanic Mountainous Region of South Georgia. In Lordkipanidze, D., Bar-Yosef, O. and Otte, M. (eds) *Early Humans at the Gates of Europe: Proceedings of the First International Symposium Dmanisi, Tbilisi, (Georgia) September 1998*. Liège: Etudes et Recherches Archéologiques de l'Université de Liège 92, pp. 43–47.

Gallenkamp, C. (2001) *Dragon Hunter*. London: Penguin Books.

Gamble, C. (1986) *The Palaeolithic Settlement of Europe*. Cambridge: Cambridge University Press.

Gamble, C. (1993a) Exchange, Foraging and Local Hominid Networks. In Scarre, C. and Healy, F. (eds) *Trade and Exchange in Prehistoric Europe*. Oxford: Oxbow Books, pp. 35–44.

Gamble, C. (1993b) *Timewalkers: The Prehistory of Global Colonisation*. Cambridge, MA: Harvard University Press.

Gamble, C. (1998) Palaeolithic Society, and the Release from Proximity: A Network Approach to Intimate Relations. *World Archaeology* 29: 426–449.

Gamble, C. (1999) *The Palaeolithic Societies of Europe*. Cambridge: Cambridge University Press.

Gamble, C. and Porr, M. (eds) (2005) *The Hominid Individual in Context*. Abingdon: Routledge.

Gibbard, P. L. (1979) Middle Pleistocene Drainage in the Thames Valley. *Geological Magazine* 116: 35–44.

Gibbard, P. L. (1985) *The Pleistocene History of the Middle Thames Valley*. Cambridge: Cambridge University Press.

Gibbard, P. L. (1995) Palaeogeographical Evolution of the Lower Thames. In Bridgland, D. R., Allen, P. and Haggart, B. A. (eds) *The Quaternary of the Lower Reaches of the Thames: Field Guide*. Durham: Quaternary Research Association, pp. 5–34.

Gibbard, P. L. and Lewin, J. (2002) Climate and Related Controls on Interglacial Fluvial Sedimentation in Lowland Britain. *Sedimentary Geology* 151: 187–210.

Gibert, J., Gibert, Ll., Ferràndez-Canyadell, C., Iglesias, A. and González, F. (2001) Venta Micena, Barranco León-5 and Fuentenueva-3: Three Archaeological Sites in the Early Pleistocene Deposits of Orce, South-East Spain. In Milliken, S. and

Cook, J. (eds) *A Very Remote Period Indeed: Papers on the Palaeolithic Presented to Derek Roe.* Oxford: Oxbow Books, pp. 144–152.

Gibert, J., Gibert, Ll., Iglesias, A. and Maestro, E. (1998) Two Oldowan Assemblages in the Plio-Pleistocene Deposits of the Orce Region, Southeast Spain. *Antiquity* 72: 17–25.

Gibert, Ll., Scott, G. and Ferràndez-Cañadell, C. (2006) Evaluation of the Olduvai Subchron in the Orce Ravine (SE Spain): Implications for Plio-Pleistocene Mammal Biostratigraphy and the Age of the Orce Archaeological Sites. *Quaternary Science Reviews* 25: 507–525.

Gibert, W. H., White, T. D. and Asfaw, B. (2003) Homo erectus, Homo ergaster, Homo 'cepranensis,' and the Daka Cranium. *Journal of Human Evolution* 45: 255–259.

Goren-Inbar, N. and Saragusti, I. (1996) An Acheulean Biface Assemblage from Gesher Benot Ya'aqov, Israel: Indications of African Affinities. *Journal of Field Archaeology* 23: 15–30.

Gould, S. J. (1984) *The Mismeasure of Man.* New York: W.W. Norton.

Gould, S. J. (1996) The First Unmaking of Nature. In Gould, S. J. (ed.) *Dinosaur in a Haystack.* London: Penguin Books, pp. 415–426.

Gould, S. J. (2000) Above All, Do No Harm. In Gould, S. J. (ed.) *The Lying Stones of Marrakech.* London: Jonathan Cape, pp. 299–314.

Gowlett, J. A. J. (2005) Seeking the Palaeolithic Individual in East Africa and Europe During the Lower-Middle Pleistocene. In Gamble, C. and Porr, M. (eds) *The Hominid Individual in Context.* Abingdon: Routledge, pp. 50–67.

Gowlett, J. A. J. (2006) The Early Settlement of Northern Europe: Fire History in the Context of Climate Change and the Social Brain. *C. R. Palevol* 5: 299–310.

Gowlett, J. A. J. and Hallos, J. (2000) Beeches Pit: Overview of the Archaeology. In Lewis, S. G., Whiteman, C. A. and Preece, R. C. (eds) *The Quaternary of Norfolk and Suffolk. Field Guide.* Durham: Quaternary Research Association, pp. 197–206.

Green, C. P. (1988) The Palaeolithic Site at Broom, Dorset, 1932–1941: From the Record of C.E. Bean Esq. F.S.A. *Proceedings of the Geologists' Association* 99: 173–180.

Green, C. P., Branch, N. P., Coope, G. R., Field, M. H., Keen, D. H., Wells, J. M., Schwenninger, J.-L., Preece, R. C., Schreve, D. C., Canti, M. G. and Gleed-Owen, C. P. (2006) Marine Isotope Stage 9 Environments of Fluvial Deposits at Hackney, North London, UK. *Quaternary Science Reviews* 25: 89–113.

Green, J. F. N. (1947) Some Gravels and Gravel-Pits in Hampshire and Dorset. *Proceedings of the Geologists' Association* 58: 128–143.

Green, S. H. (ed.) (1984) *Pontnewydd Cave: A Lower Palaeolithic Hominid Site in Wales: The First Report.* Cardiff: National Museum of Wales.

Green, S. H. (1988) Pontnewydd Cave: The Selection of Raw Materials for Artefact-Manufacture and the Question of Natural Damage. In MacRae, R. J. and Moloney, N. (eds) *Non-Flint Stone Tools and the Palaeolithic Occupation of Britain.* Oxford: British Archaeological Reports. British Series 189. pp. 223–232.

Hack, B. (1998) Stone Tools from Rainbow Bar, Hill Head. *Proceedings of the Hampshire Field Club and Archaeological Society* 53: 219–232.

Hack, B. (1999) More Stone Tools from Rainbow Bar, Hill Head. *Proceedings of the Hampshire Field Club and Archaeological Society* 54: 163–171.

Hack, B. (2000) Rainbow Bar: Some Observations and Thoughts. *Lithics* 21: 36–44.

Hack, B. (2004) Rainbow Bar, Hill Head: An Update. *Hampshire Field Club and Archaeological Society Newsletter* 42: 28–29.

Hack, B. (2005) Rainbow Bar, Hill Head: Final Thoughts. *Hampshire Field Club and Archaeological Society Newsletter* 43: 2.

Hallegouet, B., Hinguant, S., Gebhardt, A. and Monnier, J. L. (1992) Le Gisment Paléolithique Inférieur de Ménez-Drégan 1 (Plouhinec, Finistère): Premiers Résultats des Fouilles. *Bulletin de la Société Préhistorique Française* 89: 77–81.

Hallos, J. (2005) '15 Minutes of Fame': Exploring the Temporal Dimension of Middle Pleistocene Lithic Technology. *Journal of Human Evolution* 49: 155–179.

Hamblin, R. J. O. and Moorlock, B. S. P. (1995) The Kesgrave and Bytham Sands and Gravels of Eastern Suffolk. *Quaternary Newsletter* 77: 17–31.

Hardaker, T. (2003) Some Thoughts on a Stray Upper Thames Handaxe. *Lithics* 24: 21–31.

Hardaker, T. and MacRae, R. J. (2000) A Lost River and Some Palaeolithic Surprises: New Quartzite Finds from Norfolk and Oxfordshire. *Lithics* 21: 52–59.

Harding, P., Bridgland, D. R., Keen, D. H. and Rogerson, R. (1992) A Palaeolithic Site Rediscovered at Biddenham, Bedfordshire. *Bedfordshire Archaeology* 19: 87–90.

Harding, P., Gibbard, P. L., Lewin, J., Macklin, M. G. and Moss, E. (1987) The Transport and Abrasion of Flint Handaxes in a Gravel-Bed River. In Sieveking, G. d. G. and Newcomer, M. H. (eds) *The Human Uses of Flint and Chert: Proceedings of the Fourth International Flint Symposium.* Cambridge: Cambridge University Press, pp. 115–126.

Hawkes, C. F. C. (1943) Two Palaeoliths from Broom, Dorset. *Proceedings of the Prehistoric Society* 9: 48–52.

Hawking, S. (1988) *A Brief History of Time.* London: Bantam.

Hendry, J. (1999) *An Introduction to Social Anthropology: Other People's Worlds.* Basingstoke: Palgrave.

Hinton, M. A. C. and Kennard, A.S. (1905) The Relative Ages of the Stone Implements of the Lower Thames Valley. *Proceedings of the Geologists' Association* 19: 76–100.

Hodder, I. (1982) *Symbols in Action: Ethnoarchaeological Studies of Material Culture.* Cambridge: Cambridge University Press.

Hopkinson, T. and White, M. J. (2005) The Acheulean and the Handaxe: Structure and Agency in the Palaeolithic. In Gamble, C. and Porr, M. (eds) *The Hominid Individual in Context.* Abingdon: Routledge. pp. 13–28.

Hopson, P. H., Aldiss, D. T. and Smith, A. (1996) *Geology of the Country Around Hitchin (Sheet 221): Memoir of the Geological Survey.* London: HMSO.

Horton, A., Keen, D. H., Field, M. H. and Robinson, J. E. (1992) The Hoxnian Interglacial Deposits at Woodston, Peterborough. *Philosophical Transactions of the Royal Society of London Series B* 338: 131–164.

Horton, A., Worssam, B. C. and Whittow, J. B. (1981) The Wallingford Fan Gravels. *Philosophical Transactions of the Royal Society London. Series B* 293: 215–255.

Hosfield, R. (2005) Individuals among Palimpsest Data. In Gamble, C. and Porr, M. (eds) *The Hominid Individual in Context.* Abingdon: Routledge, pp. 220–243.

Hosfield, R. and Chambers, J. C. (2002) The Lower Palaeolithic Site of Broom: Geoarchaeological Implications of Optical Dating. *Lithics* 23: 33–42.

Hosfield, R. and Chambers, J. C. (2003) Flake Modifications during Fluvial Transportation: Three Cautionary Tales. *Lithics* 24: 57–65.

Hosfield, R. and Chambers, J. C. (2005a) River Gravels and Flakes: New Experiments in Site Formation, Stone Tool Transportation and Transformation. In Fansa, M.

(ed.) *Experimentelle Archäologie in Europa, Bilanz 2004, Heft 3.* Oldenburg: Isensee Verlag, pp. 57–74.

Hosfield, R. and Chambers, J. C. (2005b) Pleistocene Geochronologies for Fluvial Sedimentary Sequences: an Archaeologist's Perspective. *Journal of Quaternary Science* 20: 285–296.

Hosfield, R. and Terry, R. (2000) Renewed Excavations: Broom Palaeolithic Sites. *Lithics* 21: 3–8.

Howard, A. J. and Knight, D. (2004) The Pleistocene Background. In Knight, D. and Howard, A. J. (eds) *Trent Valley Landscapes.* Kings Lynn: Heritage Marketing and Publications Ltd, pp. 9–29.

Hubbard, R. N. L. B. (1982) The Environmental Evidence from Swanscombe and its Implications for Palaeolithic Archaeology. In Leach, P. (ed.) *Archaeology in Kent to A.D. 1500.* London: Council for British Archaeology, pp. 3–7.

Hubbard, R. N. L. B. (1996) The Palynological Studies from the Waechter Excavations. In Conway, B., McNabb, J. and Ashton, N. (eds) *Excavations at Barnfield Pit, Swanscombe, 1968–1972.* Occasional Papers of the British Museum 94. London: Trustees of the British Museum, pp. 191–199.

Hutchinson, J. N. (1998) Survey of the Interglacial Chalk Cliff and Associated Debris at Black Rock, Brighton. In Murton, J. B., Whiteman, C. A., Bates, M. R., Bridgland, D. R., Long, A. J., Roberts, M. B. and Waller, M. P. (eds) *The Quaternary of Kent and Sussex: Field Guide.* Durham: Quaternary Research Association, pp. 135–146.

Ingold, T. (2000) *The Perception of the Environment: Essays in Livelihood, Dwelling and Skill.* London: Routledge.

Inizan, M-L., Roche, H. and Tixier, J. (eds) (1992) *Technology of Knapped Stone.* Préhistoire de la Pierre Taillée. Vol. 3. Lille: CREP.

Isaac, G. L. (1977) *Olorgesailie: Archaeological Studies of a Middle Pleistocene Lake Basin in Kenya.* Chicago: University of Chicago Press.

Isaac, G. L. and Isaac, B. (eds) (1997) *Koobi Fora Research Project.* Vol. 5. *Plio-Pleistocene Archaeology.* Oxford: Clarendon Press.

James, S. R. (1989) Hominid Use of Fire in the Lower and Middle Pleistocene. *Current Anthropology* 30: 1–26.

Jaubert, J. and Servelle, C. (1996) L'Acheuléen dans le Bassin de la Garonne (Région Midi-Pyrénées): Etat de la Question et Implications. In Tuffreau, A. (ed.) *L'Acheuléen dans l'Ouest de l'Europe.* Lille: Centre d'Etudes et de Recherches Préhistoriques Université des Sciences et Technologies de Lille. Publications du CERP, 4, pp. 77–108.

Jones, R. L. and Keen, D. H. (1993) *Pleistocene Environments in the British Isles.* London: Chapman and Hall.

Keeley, L. H. (1980) *Experimental Determination of Stone Tool Uses.* Chicago: University of Chicago Press.

Keen, D. H. (1990) Significance of the Record Provided by Pleistocene Fluvial Deposits and their Included Molluscan Fauna for Palaeoenvironmental Reconstruction and Stratigraphy: Case Studies from the English Midlands. *Palaeogeography, Palaeoclimatology, Palaeoecology* 80: 25–34.

Keen, D. H. (2001) Towards a Late Middle Pleistocene Non-Marine Molluscan Biostratigraphy for the British Isles. *Quaternary Science Reviews* 20: 1657–1665.

Keen, D. H., Coope, G. R., Jones, R. L., Field, M. H., Griffiths, H. I., Lewis, S. G. and

Bowen, D. Q. (1997) Middle Pleistocene Deposits at Frog Hall Pit, Stretton-on-Dunsmore, Warwickshire, English Midlands, and their Implications for the Age of the Type Wolstonian. *Journal of Quaternary Science* 12: 183–208.

Keen, D. H., Hardaker, T. and Lang, A. T. O. (2006) A Lower Palaeolithic Industry from the Cromerian (MIS 13) Baginton Formation of Waverley Wood and Wood Farm Pits, Bubbenhall, Warwickshire, UK. *Journal of Quaternary Science* 21: 457–470.

Kennard, A. S. (1904) Notes on a Palaeolith from Grays, Essex. *Essex Naturalist* 13: 112–113.

Kennard, A. S. (1916) The Pleistocene Succession in England. *Proceedings of the Prehistoric Society of East Anglia* 2: 249–267.

Kennard, A. S. (1944) The Crayford Brickearths. *Proceedings of the Geologists' Association* 55: 121–169.

Kenworthy, J. W. (1898) Untitled Note. *Essex Naturalist* 10: 406.

Kerney, M. P. (1971) Interglacial Deposits in Barnfield Pit, Swanscombe, and their Molluscan Fauna. *Journal of the Geological Society of London* 127: 69–86.

King, W. B. R. and Oakley, K. P. (1936) The Pleistocene Succession in the Lower Parts of the Thames Valley. *Proceedings of the Prehistoric Society* 2: 52–76.

Klein, R. G. (1999) *The Human Career*. 2nd edn. Chicago: University of Chicago Press.

Kohn, M. (1999) *As We Know It: Coming to Terms with an Evolved Mind*. London: Granta Books.

Kohn, M. and Mithen, S. (1999) Handaxes: Products of Sexual Selection? *Antiquity* 73: 518–526.

Kozlowski, J. K. (2003) From Bifaces to Leafpoints. In Soressi, M. and Dibble, H. L. (eds) *Multiple Approaches to the Study of Bifacial Technologies*. Philadelphia, PA: University of Pennsylvania, Museum of Archaeology and Anthropology, pp. 149–164.

Kretzoi, M. and Vértes, L. (1965) Upper Biharian (Intermindel) Pebble-Industry Occupation Site in Western Hungary. *Current Anthropology* 6: 74–87.

Lang, A. T. O. and Keen, D. H. (2003) A Further Andesite Handaxe from Waverley Wood Quarry, Warwickshire. *Lithics* 24: 32–36.

Lang, A. T. O. and Keen, D. H. (2005) Hominid Colonisation and the Lower and Middle Palaeolithic of the West Midlands. *Proceedings of the Prehistoric Society* 71: 63–83.

Lartet, E. and Christy, H. (1875) *Reliquae Aquitanicae*. London: Williams and Norgate.

Laville, H., Rigaud, J. P. and Sackett, J. (1980) *Rock Shelters of the Perigord*. London: Academic Press.

Layard, N. F. (1912) Animal Remains from the Railway Cutting at Ipswich. *Proceedings of the Suffolk Institute of Archaeology* 14: 59–68.

Layard, N. F. (1920) The Stoke Bone-Bed, Ipswich. *Proceedings of the Prehistoric Society of East Anglia* 3: 210–219.

Leach, A. L. (1913) On Buried Channels in the Dartford Heath Gravel. *Proceedings of the Geologists' Association* 24: 337–344.

Leakey, L. S. B. (1934) The Oldoway Culture Sequence. *Proceedings of the First International Congress of Prehistoric and Protohistoric Sciences. London, August 1–6 1932.* 73.

Leakey, L. S. B. (1951) *Olduvai Gorge*. Cambridge: Cambridge University Press.

Leakey, M. D. (1971) *Olduvai Gorge: Excavations in Beds I and II 1960–1963*. Cambridge: Cambridge University Press.

Lee, J. R., Rose, J., Hamblin, J. O. and Moorlock, B. S. P. (2004) Dating the Earliest

Lowland Glaciation of Eastern England: A Pre-MIS 12 Early Middle Pleistocene Happisburgh Glaciation. *Quaternary Science Reviews* 23: 1551–1566.

Lewis, S. G. (1998) Quaternary Stratigraphy and Lower Palaeolithic Archaeology of the Lark Valley, Suffolk. In Ashton, N., Healy, F. and Pettitt, P. (eds) *Stone Age Archaeology: Essays in Honour of John Wymer*. The Lithics Studies Society Occasional Paper 6. Oxford: Lithics Studies Society and Oxbow Books, pp. 43–51.

Lewis, S. G., Ashton, N., Parfitt, S. A. and White, M. J. (2000) Hoxne, Suffolk (TM 176769). In Lewis, S. G., Whiteman, C. A. and Preece, R. C. (eds) *The Quaternary of Norfolk and Suffolk: Field Guide*. Durham: Quaternary Research Association, pp. 149–153.

Lisiecki, L. (2005) http://www.lorraine-lisiecki.com/stack.html.

Lisiecki, L. and Raymo, M. E. (2005) A Pliocene-Pleistocene Stack of 57 Globally Distributed Benthic delta[18] O records. *Paleoceanography* 20. PA1003. doi10.1029/2004PA001071: 1–17.

Lord, J. W. (1993) *The Nature and Subsequent Uses of Flint. Vol. 1. The Basics of Lithic Technology*. John Lord. ISBN No: 0 9521356 0 4.

Lordkipanidze, D., Vekua, A., Ferring, R., Rightmire, G. P., Agustí, J., Kiladze, G., Mouskhelishvili, A. and Nioradze. (2005) Anthropology: The Earliest Toothless Hominin Skull. *Nature* 434: 717–718.

Lowe, J. J. and Walker, M. J. C. (1997) *Reconstructing Quaternary Environments*. Harlow: Pearson Prentice Hall.

Lumley, H. de (1969) A Palaeolithic Camp Site at Nice. *Scientific American* 220: 42–50.

Lumley, H. de (1975) Cultural Evolution in France in its Palaeoecological Setting During the Middle Pleistocene. In Butzer, K. W. and Isaac, G. Ll. (eds) *After the Australopithecines*. The Hague: Mouton, pp. 745–808.

Lumley, H. D., Grégoire, S., Barsky, D., Batalla, G., Bailon, S., Belda, V., Briki, D., Byrne, L., Desclaux, E., Guenouni, K. E., Fournier, A., Kacimi, S., Lacombat, F., Lumley, M. A. d., Moigne, A. M., Moutoussamy, J., Paunescu, C., Perrenoud, C., Pois, V., Quiles, J., Rivals, F., Roger, T. and Testu, A. (2004) Habitat et Mode de Vie des Chasseurs Paléolithiques de la Caune de l'Arago (600,000–400,000 Ans). *L'Anthropologie* 108: 159–184.

Lumley, H. de, Gugnère, S., Barral, L. and Pascal, R. (1963) La Grotte du Vallonet Roquebrune Cap-Martin (A-M). *Bulletin du Musée d'Anthropologie Préhistorique de Monaco* 10.

McManus, J. F., Oppo, D. W. and Cullen, J. L. (1999) A 0.5 Million-Year Record of Millennial-Scale Climate Variability in the North Atlantic. *Science* 283: 971–975.

McNabb, J. (1989) Sticks and Stones: A Possible Experimental Solution to the Question of How the Clacton Spear Point was Made. *Proceedings of the Prehistoric Society* 55: 251–257.

McNabb, J. (1992a) The Clactonian: British Lower Palaeolithic Flint Technology in Biface and Non-Biface Assemblages. Unpublished PhD thesis, University of London.

McNabb, J. (1992b) The Cutting Edge, Bifaces in the Clactonian. *Lithics* 13: 4–10.

McNabb, J. (1996a) Through the Looking Glass: An Historical Perspective on Archaeological Research at Barnfield Pit, Swanscombe, ca. 1900–1964. In Conway, B., McNabb, J. and Ashton, N. (eds) *Excavations at Barnfield Pit, Swanscombe, 1968–1972*. Occasional Papers of the British Museum 94. London: Trustees of the British Museum, pp. 31–51.

McNabb, J. (1996b) More from the Cutting Edge: Further Discoveries of Clactonian Bifaces. *Antiquity* 70: 428–436.

McNabb, J. (1998) The History of Investigations at East Farm Pit, Barnham. In Ashton, N., Lewis, S. G. and Parfitt, S. A. (eds) *Excavations at the Lower Palaeolithic Site at East Farm, Barnham, Suffolk, 1989–1994*. Occasional Papers of the British Museum 125. London: Trustees of the British Museum, pp. 5–12.

McNabb, J. (2000) Boxgrove (Review Article). *Antiquity* 74: 439–441.

McNabb, J. (2005) Hominins and the Early-Middle Pleistocene Transition: Evolution, Culture and Climate in Africa and Europe. In Head, M. J. and Gibbard, P. L. (eds) *Early-Middle Pleistocene Transitions: The Land-Ocean Evidence*. London: Geological Society. Special Publications 247, pp. 287–304.

McNabb, J. (2006) The Palaeolithic. In Cooper, N. J. (ed.) *The Archaeology of the East Midlands: An Archaeological Resource Assessment and Research Agenda*. Leicester Archaeology Monograph 13. Leicester: University of Leicester Archaeology Services, School of Archaeology and Ancient History, University of Leicester, pp. 11–43.

McNabb, J. and Ashton, N. (1995) Thoughtful Flakers. *Cambridge Archaeological Journal* 5: 289–298.

McNabb, J., Felder, P. J., Kinnes, I. and Sieveking, G. (1996) An Archive Report on Recent Excavations at Harrow Hill, Sussex. *Sussex Archaeological Collections* 134: 21–37.

McPherron, S. P. (1995) A Re-Examination of the British Biface Data. *Lithics* 16: 47–63.

MacRae, R. J. (1988) The Palaeolithic of the Upper Thames and its Quartzite Implements. In MacRae, R. J. and Moloney, N. (eds) Oxford: British Archaeological Reports. British Series 189, pp. 123–154.

Maddy, D. and Bridgland, D. R. (2000) Accelerated Uplift Resulting from Anglian Glacioisostatic Rebound. *Quaternary Science Reviews* 19: 1581–1588.

Maddy, D., Bridgland, D. R. and Green, C. P. (2000) Crustal Uplift in Southern England: Evidence from the River Terrace Records. *Geomorphology* 33: 167–181.

Maddy, D., Bridgland, D. R. and Westaway, R. (2001) Uplift-Driven Valley Incision. *Quaternary International* 79: 23–36.

Maddy, D., Green, C. P., Lewis, S. G. and Bowen, D. Q. (1995) Pleistocene Geology of the Lower Severn Valley, U.K. *Quaternary Science Reviews* 14: 209–222.

Maddy, D. and Lewis, S. G. (1991) The Pleistocene Deposits at Snitterfield, Warwickshire. *Proceedings of the Geologists' Association* 102: 289–300.

Maddy, D., Lewis, S. G. and Green, C. P. (1991) A Review of the Stratigraphic Significance of the Wolvercote Terrace of the Upper Thames Valley. *Proceedings of the Geologists' Association* 102: 217–225.

Mallol, C. (1999) The Selection of Lithic Raw Materials in the Lower and Middle Pleistocene Levels TD6 and TD10A of Gran Dolina (Sierra de Atapuerca, Burgos, Spain). *Journal of Anthropological Research* 55: 385–407.

Mania, D. (1991) The Zonal Division of the Lower Palaeolithic Open-Air Site Bilzingsleben. *Anthropologie* 29: 17–24.

Mania, D. (1995) The Earliest Occupation of Europe: the Elbe-Salle Region. In Roebroeks, W. and van Kolfschoten, T. (eds) *The Earliest Occupation of Europe: Proceedings of the European Science Foundation Workshop at Tautavel (France), 1993*. Analecta Praehistorica Leidensia 27. Leiden: University of Leiden, pp. 85–101.

Mania, D. and Mania, U. (2005) The Natural and Socio-Cultural Environment of

Homo erectus at Bilzingsleben, Germany. In Gamble, C. and Porr, M. (eds) *The Hominid Individual in Context*. Abingdon: Routledge, pp. 98–114.

Manzi, G. (2004) Human Evolution at the Matuyama-Brunhes Boundary. *Evolutionary Anthropology* 13: 11–24.

Manzi, G., Mallegni, F. and Ascenzi, A. (2001) A Cranium for the Earliest Europeans: Phylogenetic Position of the Hominid from Ceprano, Italy. *Proceedings of the National Academy of Sciences of the USA* 98: 10011–10016.

Marshall, G. D. (2001) The Broom Pits: A Review of Research and a Pilot Study of Two Acheulean Biface Assemblages. In Wenban-Smith, F. F. and Hosfield, R. (eds) *Palaeolithic Archaeology of the Solent River*. The Lithics Studies Society Occasional Paper 7. London: Lithics Studies Society, pp. 77–84.

Marston, A. T. (1937) The Swanscombe Skull. *Journal of the Royal Anthropological Institute* 67: 339–406.

Marston, A. T. (1942) Flint Industries of the High Terrace at Swanscombe. *Proceedings of the Geologists' Association* 53: 106.

Marston, A. T. (1996) Appendix 2. An Additional Note on the Stratigraphy of the Barnfield Deposits by A.T.M. Marston, December 1937. In Conway, B., McNabb, J. and Ashton, N. (eds) *Excavations at Barnfield Pit, Swanscombe, 1968–1972*. Occasional Papers of the British Museum 94. London: Trustees of the British Museum, pp. 247–253.

Matskevich, Z., Goren-Inbar, N. and Gaudzinski, S. (2001) A Newly Identified Acheulean Handaxe Type at Tabun Cave: The Faustkeilblätter. In Milliken, S. and Cook, J. (eds) *A Very Remote Period Indeed*. Oxford: Oxbow Books, pp. 120–132.

Mayr, E. (2001) *What Evolution Is*. London: Weidenfeld and Nicolson.

Meijer, T. and Preece, R. C. (1995) Malacological Evidence Relating to the Insularity of the British Isles During the Quaternary. In Preece, R. C. (ed.) *Island Britain: A Quaternary Perspective*. London: Geological Society. Special Publications 96, pp. 89–110.

Mellars, P. (1974) The Palaeolithic and Mesolithic. In Renfrew, C. (ed.) *British Prehistory: A New Outline*. London: Duckworth.

Mellars, P. (1996) *The Neanderthal Legacy*. Princeton, NJ: Princeton University Press.

Miller, G. (1999) Sexual Selection for Cultural Displays. In Dunbar, R., Knight, C. and Power, C. (eds) *The Evolution of Culture: An Interdisciplinary View*. Edinburgh: Edinburgh University Press.

Miller, G. (2001) *The Mating Mind*. London: Vintage.

Miller, R. (1982) Pseudo-Tools Created by Livestock from Halawa, Syria. *Journal of Field Archaeology* 9: 281–283.

Milliken, S. (1999) The Earliest Occupation of Italy. *Accordia Research Papers. Accordia Research Institute, University of London*. Vol. 7, 1997–1998: 7–36.

Milliken, S. (2001) Acheulean Handaxe Variability in Middle Pleistocene Italy: A Case Study. In Milliken, S. and Cook, J. (eds) *A Very Remote Period Indeed*. Oxford: Oxbow Books, pp. 160–173.

Mitchell, G. F., Penny, L. F., Shotton, F. W. and West, R. G. (1973) *A Correlation of the Quaternary Deposits in the British Isles* – Geological Society of London, Special Report 4. London: Geological Society of London.

Mitchell, J. C. (1996) Studying Biface Butchery at Boxgrove: Roe Deer Butchery with Replica Handaxes. *Lithics* 16: 64–69.

Mithen, S. (1994) Technology and Society During the Middle Pleistocene: Hominid

Group Size, Social Learning and Industrial Variability. *Cambridge Archaeological Journal* 4: 3–32.

Mithen, S. (1995) A Reply (Reply to McNabb and Ashton 1995). *Cambridge Archaeological Journal* 5: 298–301.

Moir, J. R., Hopwood, A. T., Baden-Powell, D. F. W., Kennard, A. S. and Ovey, C. D. (1939) Excavations at Brundon, Suffolk (1935–1937). *Proceedings of the Prehistoric Society* 5: 1–32.

Moncel, M. H. (1996) L'Industrie Lithique d'Orgnac 3 (Ardèche-France): Technologie et Outillage. In Tuffreau, A. (ed.) *L'Acheuléen dans l'Ouest de l'Europe.* Centre d'Etudes et de Recherches Préhistoriques Université des Sciences et Technologies de Lille. Lille: Publications du CERP, 4, pp. 109–114.

Moncel, M. H. (2003) Some Observations on Microlithic Assemblages in Central Europe During Lower and Middle Palaeolithic Kulna and Předmostí II (Czech Republic), Vértesszölös and Tata (Hungary). In Burdukiewicz, J. M. and Ronen, A. (eds) *Lower Palaeolithic Small Tools in Europe and the Levant.* Oxford: British Archaeological Reports, pp. 169–187.

Moncel, M. H., Gaillard, C. and Combier, J. (2001) The Lower Palaeolithic Industry from Azé Cave (Saône et Loire) France: A Case Study of an Assemblage Without any Handaxes. *Proceedings of the Prehistoric Society* 67: 174–193.

Moncel, M. H., Moigne, A. M. and Combier, J. (2005) Pre-Neanderthal Behaviour During Isotopic Stage 9 and the Beginning of Stage 8. New Data Concerning Fauna and Lithics in the Different Occupation Levels of Orgnac 3 (Ardèche, South-East France): Occupation Types. *Journal of Archaeological Science* 32: 1283–1301.

Monnier, J. L. (1996) Acheuléen et Industries Archaïques dans le Nord-Ouest de la France. In Tuffreau, A. (ed.) *L'Acheuléen dans l'Ouest de l'Europe.* Centre d'Etudes et de Recherches Préhistoriques Université des Sciences et Technologies de Lille. Lille: Publications du CERP, 4, pp. 145–153.

Monnier, J. L. and Molines, N. (1993) Le 'Columbanien': un Facies Régional du Paléolithique Inferieur sur le Littoral Armoricano-Atlantique. *Bulletin de la Société Préhistorique Française* 90: 283–294.

Moore, J. and Desmond, A. (2004) *Introduction to 'The Descent of Man' by Charles Darwin.* London: Penguin Classics.

Morell, V. (1995) *Ancestral Passions.* New York: Simon and Schuster.

Morris, S. C. (2003) *Life's Solution.* Cambridge: University of Cambridge Press.

Movius, H. (1948a) Tyacian Man from the Cave of Fontéchevade (Charente). *American Anthropologist* 50: 366–367.

Movius, H. (1948b) The Lower Palaeolithic Cultures of South-Eastern and Eastern Asia. *Transactions of the American Philosophical Society* 38: 329–420.

Murton, J. B., Whiteman, C. A., Bates, M. R., Bridgland, D. R., Long, A. J., Roberts, M. B. and Waller, M. P. (eds) (1998) *The Quaternary of Sussex and Kent: Field Guide.* Durham: Quaternary Research Association.

Mussi, M. (1995) The Earliest Occupation of Europe. In Roebroeks, W. and van Kolfschoten, T. (eds) *The Earliest Occupation of Europe: Proceedings of the European Science Foundation Workshop at Tautavel (France), 1993. Analecta Praehistorica Leidensia* 27. Leiden: University of Leiden, pp. 27–49.

Narr, K. J. (1979) Comment on Ohel. *Current Anthropology* 20: 717.

Navarro, B. M., Turq, A., Ballester, J. A. and Oms, O. (1997) Fuente Nueva-3 (Orce,

Granada, Spain) and the First Human Occupation of Europe. *Journal of Human Evolution* 33: 611–620.

Newcomer, M. H. (1971) Some Quantitative Experiments in Handaxe Manufacture. *World Archaeology* 3: 85–94.

Newcomer, M. H. (1984) Flaking Experiments with Pontnewydd Raw Materials. In Green, S. H. (ed.) *Pontnewydd Cave: A Lower Palaeolithic Hominid Site in Wales: The First Report*. Cardiff: National Museum of Wales, pp. 153–158.

Newton, W. M. (1901) Kent: Flint Implements. *Man* 1: 81–82.

Oakley, K. P. (1939) Part I: Geology and Palaeolithic Studies. In Oakley, K. P., Rankine, W. F. and Lowther, W. G. (eds) *A Survey of the Prehistory of the Farnham District (Surrey), Prepared for the Surrey Archaeological Society*. Guilford: Surrey Archaeological Society, pp. 3–58.

Oakley, K. P. (1947) Early Man in Hertfordshire. *Transactions of the Hertfordshire Natural History Society* 22: 247–256.

Oakley, K. P. (1952) Swanscombe Man. *Proceedings of the Geologists' Association* 63: 271–300.

Oakley, K. P. (1959) The Life and Work of Samuel Hazzledine Warren, F.G.S. *Essex Naturalist* 30: 1–5.

Oakley, K. P. (1972) *Man the Tool Maker*. 6th edn. London: British Museum (Natural History).

Oakley, K. P., Andrews, P., Keeley, L. H. and Clark, J. D. (1977) A Reappraisal of the Clacton Spearpoint. *Proceedings of the Prehistoric Society* 43: 13–30.

Oakley, K. P. and Leakey, M. (1937) Report on Excavations at Jaywick Sands, Essex (1934). *Proceedings of the Prehistoric Society* 3: 217–260.

Oakley, K. P. and Newcomer, M. H. (1978) Notes on Palaeolithic Flakes from Ilford. *Proceedings of the Prehistoric Society* 44: 435–439.

O'Connor, A. (2003) The Making of the British Early Palaeolithic, 1880–1960. Unpublished PhD, University of Durham.

Ohel, M. Y. (1979a) The Clactonian: An Independent Complex or an Integral Part of the Acheulean? *Current Anthropology* 20: 685–713.

Ohel, M. Y. (1979b) Reply. *Current Anthropology* 20: 719–722.

Ohel, M. Y. (1982) Is Barnham Indeed Clactonian? *Praehistorische Zeitschrift* 57: 181–200.

Ohel, M. Y. and Lechevalier, C. (1979) The 'Clactonian' of Le Havre and its Bearing on the English Clactonian. *Quartär* 29/30: 85–103.

Ohnuma, K. and Bergman, C. (1982) Experimental Studies in the Determination of Flaking Mode. *Bulletin of the Institute of Archaeology, London* 19: 161–170.

Oms, O., Parés, J. M., Martínez-Navarro, B., Agustí, J., Toro, I., Martínez-Fernández, G. and Turq, A. (2000) Early Human Occupation of Western Europe: Palaeomagnetic Dates for Two Palaeolithic Sites in Spain. *Proceedings of the National Academy of Sciences of the USA* 97: 10666–10670.

Otte, M. (2003) Palaeolithic Micro-Industries: Value and Significance. In Burdukiewicz, J. M. and Ronen, A. (eds) *Lower Palaeolithic Small Tools in Europe and the Levant*. Oxford: British Archaeological Reports. International Series 1115, pp. 223–233.

Ovey, C. D. (ed.) (1964) *The Swanscombe Skull: A Survey of Research on a Pleistocene Site*. Occasional Paper Royal Anthropological Institute 20. London: Royal Anthropological Institute.

Palmer, C. T., Coe, K. and Wadley, R. L. (2005) On Tools and Traditions. *Current Anthropology* 46: 459–460.

Palmer, S. (1975) A Palaeolithic Site at North Road, Purfleet, Essex. *Transactions of the Essex Archaeological Society* 7: 1–13.

Parés, J. M., Pérez-González, A., Rosas, A., Benito, A., Bermúdez de Castro, J. M., Carbonell, E. and Huguet, R. (2006) Matuyama-Age Lithic Tools from the Sima del Elefante Site, Atapuerca (Northern Spain). *Journal of Human Evolution* 50: 163–169.

Parfitt, S. A. (2005) A Butchered Bone from Norfolk: Evidence for Very Early Human Presence in Britain. *Archaeology International* 8: 14–17.

Parfitt, S. A., Barendregt, R. W., Breda, M., Candy, I., Collins, M. J., Coope, G. R., Durbidge, P., Field, M. H., Lee, J. R., Lister, A., Mutch, R., Penkman, K. E. H., Preece, R. C., Rose, J., Stringer, C., Symmons, R., Whittaker, J., Wymer, J. and Stuart, A. J. (2005) The Earliest Record of Human Activity in Northern Europe. *Nature* 438: 1008–1012.

Parfitt, S. A., Owen, F. and Keen, D. H. (1998) Pleistocene Stratigraphy, Vertebrates and Mollusca, Black Rock, Brighton. In Murton, J. B., Whiteman, C. A., Bates, M. R., Bridgland, D. R., Long, A. J., Roberts, M. B. and Waller, M. P. (eds) *The Quaternary of Kent and Sussex: Field Guide*. Durham: Quaternary Research Association, pp. 146–150.

Parfitt, S. A., Pitts, M., Stuart, A. J., Stringer, C. and Preece, R. C. (2006) Pakefield: A Weekend to Remember. *British Archaeology* January/February 2006: 19–27.

Paterson, T. T. (1937) Studies on the Palaeolithic Succession in England. *Proceedings of the Prehistoric Society* 3: 87–135.

Paterson, T. T. (1940) Geology and Early Man. *Nature* 146: 12f and 49f.

Paterson, T. T. (1940–41) On a World Correlation of the Pleistocene. *Transactions of the Royal Society of Edinburgh* 60: 373–425.

Paterson, T. T. (1942) Lower Palaeolithic Man in the Cambridge District. Unpublished PhD thesis. University of Cambridge.

Paterson, T. T. (1945) Core, Culture and Complex in the Old Stone Age. *Proceedings of the Prehistoric Society* 11: 1–19.

Paterson, T. T. and Fagg, B. E. B. (1940) Studies on the Palaeolithic Succession in England, no. II. *Proceedings of the Prehistoric Society* 6: 1–29.

Penck, A. and Brückner, E. (1909) *Die Alpen im Eiszeitalter*. Leipzig: Tachnitz.

Picton, H. (1912) Observations on the Bone Bed at Clacton. *Proceedings of the Prehistoric Society of East Anglia* 1: 158–159.

Pike, K. and Godwin, H. (1953) The Interglacial at Clacton-on-Sea, Essex. *Quarterly Journal of the Geological Society of London* 108: 261–272.

Pinker, S. (2002) *The Blank Slate: The Modern Denial of Human Nature*. London: The Penguin Group.

Piperno, M., Lefèvre, D., Raynal, J.-P. and Tagliacozzo, A. (1998) Notarchirico. An Early Middle Pleistocene Site in the Venosa Basin. *Anthropologie* 36: 85–90.

Pitts, M. and Roberts, M. (1997) *A Fairweather Eden*. London: Century Books.

Pope, M. and Roberts, M. (2005) Observations on the Relationship Between Palaeolithic Individuals and Artefact Scatters at the Middle Pleistocene Site of Boxgrove, UK. In Gamble, C. and Porr, M. (eds) *The Hominid Individual in Context*. Abingdon: Routledge, pp. 81–97.

Porr, M. (2005) The Making of the Biface and the Making of the Individual. In

Gamble, C. and Porr, M. (eds) *The Hominid Individual in Context*. Abingdon: Routledge, pp. 68–80.

Posnansky, M. (1963) The Lower and Middle Palaeolithic Industries of the English Midlands. *Proceedings of the Prehistoric Society* 29: 357–394.

Preece, R. C. (2001) Molluscan Evidence for Differentiation of Interglacials within the 'Cromerian Complex'. *Quaternary Science Reviews* 20: 1643–1656.

Preece, R. C., Bridgland, D. R., Lewis, S. G., Parfitt, S. A. and Griffiths, H. I. (2000) Beeches Pit, West Stow, Suffolk (TL798719). In Lewis, S. G., Whiteman, C. A. and Preece, R. C. (eds) *The Quaternary of Norfolk and Suffolk: Field Guide*. Durham: Quaternary Research Organisation, pp. 185–195.

Preece, R. C., Gowlett, J. A. J., Parfitt, S. A., Bridgland, D. R. and Lewis, S. G. (2006) Humans in the Hoxnian: Habitat, Context and Fire Use at Beeches Pit, West Stow, Suffolk, UK. *Journal of Quaternary Science* 21: 485–496.

Preece, R. C. and Parfitt, S. A. (2000) The Cromer Forest-Bed Formation: New Thoughts on an Old Problem. In Lewis, S. G., Whiteman, C. A. and Preece, R. C. (eds) *The Quaternary of Norfolk and Suffolk: Field Guide*. Durham: Quaternary Research Association, pp. 1–27.

Preece, R. C. and Parfitt, S. A. (n.d.) *The Earliest Human Occupation of Northern Europe: New Evidence from Southern Britain*. Paper Presented at Q.R.A. Annual Discussion Meeting on the Palaeolithic Occupation of Europe, January 2005.

Pringle, H. (2006) *The Master Plan: Himmler's Scholars and the Holocaust*. London: Fourth Estate.

Proctor, C. J., Berridge, P., Bishop, M. J., Richards, D. A. and Smart, P. L. (2005) Age of Middle Pleistocene Fauna and Lower Palaeolithic Industries from Kent's Cavern, Devon. *Quaternary Science Reviews* 24: 1243–1252.

Proctor, C. J. and Smart, P. L. (1989) A New Survey of Kent's Cavern. *Proceedings of the University of Bristol Spelaeological Society* 18: 422–429.

Proctor, R. N. (2003) Three Roots of Human Recency. Molecular Anthropology, the Refigured Acheulean, and the UNESCO Response to Auschwitz. *Current Anthropology* 44: 213–239.

Querol, M. A. and Santonja, M. (1983) *El Yacimiento de Cantos Trabajados de El Aculadero (Puerto de Santa Maria, Cádiz)*. E.A.E: Ministerio de Cultura, p. 130.

Raposo, L. and Santonja, M. (1995) The Earliest Occupation of Europe: The Iberian Peninsula. In Roebroeks, W. and Van Kolfschoten, T. (eds) *The Earliest Occupation of Europe: Proceedings of the European Science Foundation Workshop at Tautavel (France), 1993*. *Analecta Praehistorica Leidensia* 27. Leiden: University of Leiden, pp. 7–21.

Reid, C. (1897) The Palaeolithic Deposits at Hitchin and their Relation to the Glacial Epoch. *Proceedings of the Royal Society of London* B287: 535–570.

Rigaud, J. P. and Texier, J. P. (1981) A Propos des Particularités Techniques et Typologiques du Gisment des Tares, Commune de Sourzac (Dordogne). *Bulletin de la Société Préhistorique Francaise* 78: 109–117.

Rightmire, G. P. (1998) Human Evolution in the Middle Pleistocene: The Role of *Homo heidelbergensis*. *Evolutionary Anthropology* 6: 218–227.

Rightmire, G. P., Lordkipanidze, D. and Vekua, A. (2006) Anatomical Description, Comparative Studies and Evolutionary Significance of the Hominin Skulls from Dmanisi, Republic of Georgia. *Journal of Human Evolution* 50: 115–141.

Roberts, M. B. and Parfitt, S. A. (eds) (1999) *Boxgrove: A Middle Pleistocene Hominid Site at Eartham Quarry, Boxgrove, West Sussex*. London: English Heritage.

Roberts, M. B., Parfitt, S. A., Pope, M. I., Wenban-Smith, F. F., Macphail, R. I., Locker, A. and Stewart, J. R. (1997) Boxgrove, West Sussex: Rescue Excavations of a Lower Palaeolithic Landsurface (Boxgrove Project B, 1989–91). *Proceedings of the Prehistoric Society* 63: 303–358.

Roberts, M. B., Stringer, C. and Parfitt, S. A. (1994) A Hominid Tibia from Middle Pleistocene Sediments at Boxgrove, UK. *Nature* 369: 311–313.

Roe, D. A. (1964) The British Lower and Middle Palaeolithic: Some Problems, Methods of Study and Preliminary Results. *Proceedings of the Prehistoric Society* 30: 245–267.

Roe, D. A. (1968) British Lower and Middle Palaeolithic Handaxe Groups. *Proceedings of the Prehistoric Society* 34: 1–82.

Roe, D. A. (1981a) Amateurs and Archaeologists: Some Early Contributions to British Palaeolithic Studies. In Evans, J. D., Cunliffe, B. and Renfrew, C. (eds) *Antiquity and Man: Essays in Honour of Glyn Daniel*. London: Thames and Hudson, pp. 214–220.

Roe, D. A. (1981b) *The Lower and Middle Palaeolithic Periods in Britain*. London: Routledge and Kegan Paul.

Roe, D. A. (1995) The Orce Basin (Andalucía, Spain) and the Initial Palaeolithic of Europe. *Oxford Journal of Archaeology* 14: 1–12.

Roe, D. A. (2001) Some Earlier Palaeolithic Find-Spots of Interest in the Solent Region. In Wenban-Smith, F. F. and Hosfield, R. (eds) *Palaeolithic Archaeology of the Solent River*. The Lithic Studies Society Occasional Paper 7. London: The Lithics Studies Society, pp. 47–56.

Roe, D. A. (2003) No Stone Unturned: A Look at the Study of Stone Tools in Early Prehistory. *Lithics* 24: 37–56.

Roe, H. M. (1999) Late Middle-Pleistocene Sea-Level Change in the Southern North Sea: the Record from Eastern Essex, UK. *Quarternary International* 55: 115–128.

Roebroeks, W. (2001) Hominid Behaviour and the Earliest Occupation of Europe: An Exploration. *Journal of Human Evolution* 41: 437–461.

Roebroeks, W., Conard, N. J. and van Kolfschoten, T. (1992) Dense Forests, Cold Steppes, and the Palaeolithic Settlement of Northern Europe. *Current Anthropology* 33: 551–586.

Roebroeks, W. and van Kolfschoten, T. (1995) The Earliest Occupation of Europe: A Reappraisal of Artefactual and Chronological Evidence. In Roebroeks, W. and van Kolfschoten, T. (eds) *The Earliest Occupation of Europe: Proceedings of the European Science Foundation Workshop at Tautavel (France), 1993. Analecta Praehistorica Leidensia* 27. Leiden: University of Leiden, pp. 298–308.

Rolland, N. (1981) The Interpretation of Middle Palaeolithic Variability. *Man* 16: 15–42.

Rolland, N. (1986) Recent Findings from La Micoque and Other Sites in South-Western and Mediterranean France: Their Bearing on the 'Tyacian' Problem and Middle Palaeolithic Emergence. In Bailey, G. N. and Callow, P. (eds) *Stone Age Prehistory*. Cambridge: Cambridge University Press, pp. 121–151.

Ron, H. and Levi, S. (2001) When Did Hominids First Leave Africa? New High-Resolution Magnetostratigraphy from the Erk El-Ahmar Formation, Israel. *Geology* 29: 887–890.

Ron, H., Porat, N., Ronen, A., Tchernov, E. and Horwitz, L. K. (2003) Magneto-stratigraphy of the Evron Member – Implications for the Age of the Middle Acheulean Site of Evron Quarry. *Journal of Human Evolution* 44: 633–639.

Rose, J., Lee, J. A., Candy, I. and Lewis, S. G. (1999) Early and Middle Pleistocene River Systems in Eastern England: Evidence from Leet Hill, Southern Norfolk, England. *Journal of Quaternary Science* 14: 347–360.

Rose, J., Moorlock, B. S. P. and Hamblin, J. O. (2001) Pre-Anglian Fluvial and Coastal Deposits in Eastern England: Lithostratigraphy and Palaeoenvironments. *Quaternary International* 79: 5–22.

Sahnouni, M., Hadjouis, D., Made, J. v. d., Derradji, A., Canals, A., Medig, M., Belahrech, H., Harichane, Z. and Rabhi, M. (2002) Further Research at the Oldowan Site of Ain Hanech, North-Eastern Algeria. *Journal of Human Evolution* 43: 925–937.

Sainty, J. E. and Watson, A. Q. (1944) Palaeolithic Implements from Southacre. *Norfolk Archaeologist* 28: 183–186.

Sampson, C. G. (ed.) (1978) *Paleoecology and Archaeology of an Acheulean Site at Caddington, England.* Dallas, TX: Department of Anthropology, Southern Methodist University.

Santonja, M. and Villa, P. (1990) The Lower Palaeolithic of Spain and Portugal. *World Prehistory* 4: 45–94.

Saragusti, I. and Goren-Inbar, N. (2001) The Biface Assemblage from Gesher Benot Ya'aqov, Israel: Illuminating Patterns in 'Out of Africa' Dispersal. *Quaternary International* 75: 85–89.

Saville, A. (1988) The Waite Collection of Palaeolithic Quartzites from the Nuneaton Area of Warwickshire. In MacRae, R. J. and Moloney, N. (eds) *Non-Flint Stone Tools and the Palaeolithic Occupation of Britain.* British Archaeological Reports, British Series 189. Oxford: British Archaeological Reports, pp. 67–88.

Schick, K. D. (1986) *Stone Age Sites in the Making.* British Archaeological Reports, International Series 319. Oxford: British Archaeological Reports.

Schlanger, N. (1996) Understanding Levallois: Lithic Technology and Cognitive Archaeology. *Cambridge Archaeological Journal* 6: 231–254.

Schreve, D. C. (2001) Differentiation of the British Late Middle Pleistocene Interglacials: The Evidence from Mammal Biostratigraphy. *Quaternary Science Reviews* 20: 1577–1582.

Schreve, D. C. (2004a) The Mammalian Fauna of Barnfield Pit, Swanscombe, Kent. In Schreve, D. C. (ed.) *The Quaternary Mammals of Southern and Eastern England.* London: Quaternary Research Association, pp. 29–48.

Schreve, D. C. (2004b) The Mammalian Fauna of the Penultimate (MIS 7) Interglacial in the Thames Valley. In Schreve, D. C. (ed.) *The Quaternary Mammals of Southern and Eastern England.* London: Quaternary Research Association, pp. 69–79.

Schreve, D. C. and Bridgland, D. R. (2002) Correlation of English and German Middle Pleistocene Fluvial Sequences Based on Mammalian Biostratigraphy. *Netherlands Journal of Geosciences/Geologie en Mijnbouw* 81: 357–373.

Schreve, D. C., Bridgland, D. R., Allen, P., Blackford, J. J., Gleed-Owen, C. P., Griffiths, H. I., Keen, D. H. and White, M. J. (2002) Sedimentology, Palaeontology, and Archaeology of Late Middle Pleistocene River Thames Terrace Deposits at Purfleet, Essex, UK. *Quaternary Science Reviews* 21: 1423–1464.

Scott, K. and Buckingham, C.M. (2001) A River Runs Through It: A Decade of Research at Stanton Harcourt. In Milliken, S. and Cook, J. (eds) *A Very Remote Period Indeed.* Oxford: Oxbow Books, pp. 206–213.

Shakesby, R. A. and Stephens, N. (1984) The Pleistocene Gravels of Axe Valley. *Report of the Transactions of the Devon Association for the Advancement of Science* 116: 77–88.

Shipman, P. (2001) *The Man Who Found the Missing Link*. London: Weidenfeld and Nicolson.

Shotton, F. W. (1953) The Pleistocene Deposits of the Area Between Coventry, Rugby and Leamington, and their Bearing on the Topographic Development of the Midlands. *Philosophical Transactions of the Royal Society London. Series B* 237: 209–260.

Shotton, F. W. and Wymer, J. (1989) Handaxes of Andesitic-Tuff from Beneath the Standard Wolstonian Succession in Warwickshire. *Lithics* 10: 1–6.

Singer, R., Gladfelter, B. G. and Wymer, J. (eds) (1993) *The Lower Palaeolithic Site at Hoxne, England*. Chicago: Chicago University Press.

Singer, R., Wymer, J., Gladfelter, B. G. and Wolff, R. G. (1973) Excavation of the Clactonian Industry at the Golf Course, Clacton-on-Sea, Essex. *Proceedings of the Prehistoric Society* 39: 6–74.

Smith, K. A. (1995) Mammal Fossils and a Possible Water Hole and Pathway from the Nene Valley, Northampton, U.K. *Quaternary Newsletter* 75: 36–44.

Smith, R. A. (1911a) A Palaeolithic Industry at Northfleet, Kent. *Archaeologia* 62: 515–532.

Smith, R. A. (1911b) *A Guide to the Antiquities of the Stone Age in the Department of British and Mediaeval Antiquities*. London: Trustees of the British Museum.

Smith, R. A. (1931) *The Sturge Collection of Flints*. London: Trustees of the British Museum.

Smith, R. A. (1933) Implements from High Level Gravel Near Canterbury. *Proceedings of the Prehistoric Society of East Anglia* 7: 165–170.

Smith, R. A. and Dewey, H. (1913) Stratification at Swanscombe: Report on Excavations Made on Behalf of the British Museum and H.M. Geological Survey. *Archaeologia* 64: 177–204.

Smith, R. A. and Dewey, H. (1914) The High Terrace of the Thames: Report on Excavations Made on Behalf of the British Museum and H.M. Geological Survey in 1913. *Archaeologia* 65: 187–212.

Smith, W. G. (1884) On a Palaeolithic Floor at North-East London. *Journal of the Anthropological Institute* 13: 357–384.

Smith, W. G. (1894) *Man the Primeval Savage*. London: Stanford.

Smith, W. G. (1916) Notes on the Palaeolithic Floor near Caddington. *Archaeologia* 67: 49–74.

Snelling, A. J. R. (1964) Excavations at the Globe Pit, Little Thurrock, Grays, Essex. *Essex Naturalist* 31: 199–208.

Solomon, J. D. (1933) The Implementiferous Gravels of Warren Hill. *Journal of the Royal Anthropological Institute* 63: 101–110.

Spencer, F. (1990) *Piltdown: A Scientific Forgery*. London: Natural History Museum Publications.

Spurrell, F. J. C. (1880a) On the Discovery of the Place Where Palaeolithic Implements Were Made at Crayford. *Quarterly Journal of the Geological Society of London* 336: 544–548.

Spurrell, F. J. C. (1880b) On Implements and Chips from the Floor of a Palaeolithic Workshop. *Archaeological Journal* 38: 294–299.

Spurrell, F. J. C. (1883) Palaeolithic Implements Found in West Kent. *Archaeologia Cantiana* 15: 89–103.

Stopes, H. (1899) On the Discovery of *Neritina Fluviatilis* with a Pleistocene Fauna and

Worked Flints in High Terrace Gravels of the Thames Valley. *Journal of the Royal Anthropological Institute* 29: 302–303.

Straw, A. (1996) The Quaternary Record of Kent's Cavern: A Brief Reminder and Update. *Quaternary Newsletter* 80: 17–25.

Stringer, C. and Gamble, C. (1993) *In Search of the Neanderthals: Solving the Puzzle of Human Origins*. London: Thames and Hudson.

Stuart, A. J. (1982) *Pleistocene Vertebrates in the British Isles*. London: Longman.

Stuart, A. J. and Lister, A. M. (2001) The Mammalian Faunas of Pakefield/Kessingland and Corton, Suffolk, UK: Evidence for a New Temperate Episode in the British Early Middle Pleistocene. *Quaternary Science Reviews* 20: 1677–1692.

Sturge, W. A. (1908) Presidential Address. *Proceedings of the Prehistoric Society of East Anglia* 1: 9–16.

Svoboda, J. (1987) Lithic Industries of the Arago, Vértesszölös, and Bilzingsleben Hominids: Comparison and Evolutionary Interpretation. *Current Anthropology* 28: 219–227.

Svoboda, J. (1989) Middle Pleistocene Adaptations in Central Europe. *Journal of World Prehistory* 3: 33–70.

Swanscombe Committee (1938) Report on the Swanscombe Skull. Prepared by the Swanscombe Committee of the Royal Anthropological Institute. *Journal of the Royal Anthropological Institute* 68: 17–98.

Tappen, M., Adler, D. S., Ferring, C. R., Gabunia, M., Vekua, A. and Swisher, C. C. (2002) Akhalkalaki: The Taphonomy of an Early Pleistocene Locality in the Republic of Georgia. *Journal of Archaeological Science* 29: 1367–1391.

Tavoso, A. (1976) Les Civilisations du Paléolithique Inférieur des Pyrénées et du Bassin de la Garonne. In Lumley, H. de (ed.) *La Préhistoire Française*. Paris: C.N.R.S., pp. 893–898.

Tchernov, E., Horwitz, L. K., Ronen, A. and Lister, A. (1994) The Faunal Remains from Evron Quarry in Relation to Other Lower Palaeolithic Hominid Sites in the Southern Levant. *Quaternary Research* 42: 328–339.

Tester, P. J. (1951) Palaeolithic Flint Implements from the Bowman's Lodge Gravel Pit, Dartford Heath. *Archaeologia Cantiana* 63: 122–134.

Tester, P. J. (1965) An Acheulean Site at Cuxton. *Archaeologia Cantiana* 80: 30–60.

Tester, P. J. (1976) Further Consideration of the Bowman's Lodge Industry. *Archaeologia Cantiana* 91: 29–39.

Tester, P. J. (1985) Clactonian Flints from Rickson's Pit, Swanscombe. *Archaeologia Cantiana* 100: 15–28.

Texier, J. P. and Bertran, P. (1993) New Palaeoenvironmental and Chronostratigraphic Interpretation of the Palaeolithic Site of La Micoque (Dordogne) – Archaeological Implications. *Comptes Rendus de l'Académie des Sciences Série II* 316: 1611–1617.

Thieme, H. (1997) Lower Palaeolithic Hunting Spears from Germany. *Nature* 385: 807–810.

Thieme, H. (2005) The Lower Palaeolithic Art of Hunting. In Gamble, C. and Porr, M. (eds) *The Hominid Individual in Context*. Abingdon: Routledge, pp. 115–132.

Thomas, G. N. (2001) Late Middle Pleistocene Biostratigraphy in Britain: Pitfalls and Possibilities in the Separation of Interglacial Sequences. *Quaternary Science Reviews* 20: 1621–1630.

Tixier, J. (1974) *Glossary for the Description of Stone Tools*. New York: Washington State University.

Toth, N. (1985) The Oldowan Reassessed: A Close Look at Early Stone Artefacts. *Journal of Archaeological Science* 12: 101–20.

Treacher, M. S., Arkell, J. W. and Oakley, K. P. (1948) On the Ancient Channel Between Caversham and Henley, Oxfordshire, and its Contained Implements. *Proceedings of the Prehistoric Society* 14: 126–154.

Trigger, B. (1989) *A History of Archaeological Thought*. Cambridge: Cambridge University Press.

Trigger, B. (1995) Expanding Middle-Range Theory. *Antiquity* 69: 449–458.

Tuffreau, A. (1971) Les Anciennes Industries de la Pointe-Aux-Oies à Wimereux. In Tuffreau, A. (ed.) *Quelques Aspects du Paléolithique dans le Nord de la France (Nord et Pas-de-Calais)*. Numéro Spécial du Bulletin de la Société de Préhistoire du Nord, Bulletin 8. Amiens: Musée de Picardie, pp. 15–18.

Tuffreau, A. and Antoine, P. (1995) The Earliest Occupation of Europe: Continental Northwestern Europe. In Roebroeks, W. and van Kolfschoten, T. (eds) *The Earliest Occupation of Europe: Proceedings of the European Science Foundation Workshop at Tautavel (France), 1993. Analecta Praehistorica Leidensia* 27. Leiden: University of Leiden, pp. 147–159.

Tuffreau, A., Lammotte, A. and Marcy, J. L. (1997) Land-Use and Site Function in Acheulean Complexes of the Somme Valley. *World Archaeology* 29: 225–241.

Turner, A. (1992) Large Carnivores and Earliest European Hominids: Changing Determinants of Resources Availability During the Lower and Middle Pleistocene. *Journal of Human Evolution* 22: 109–126.

Turner, C. (1970) The Middle Pleistocene Deposits at Marks Tey, Essex. *Philosophical Transactions of the Royal Society London. Series B* 257: 373–440.

Turner, C. (1985) Problems and Pitfalls in the Application of Palynology to Pleistocene Archaeological Sites in Western Europe. In Renault-Mskovsky, J., Bui, T. M. and Girard, M. (eds) *Actes des Journées du 25, 26, 27 Janvier 1984*. Paris: Editions du Centre National de la Recherché Scientifique, pp. 347–373.

Turner, C. and Kerney, M. P. (1971) Appendix: A Note on the Age of the Freshwater Beds of the Clacton Channel. *Journal of the Geological Society of London* 127: 87–93.

Valoch, K. (1995) The Earliest Occupation of Europe: Eastern Central and South-eastern Europe. In Roebroeks, W. and van Kolfschoten, T. (eds) *The Earliest Occupation of Europe: Proceedings of the European Science Foundation Workshop at Tautavel (France), 1993. Analecta Praehistorica Leidensia* 27. Leiden: University of Leiden, pp. 67–84.

van Ripper, A. B. (1993) *Men Among the Mammoths: Victorian Science and the Discovery of Human Antiquity*. Chicago: University of Chicago Press.

Ventris, P. A. (1996) Hoxnian Interglacial Freshwater and Marine Deposits in Northwest Norfolk, England and their Implications for Sea-Level Reconstruction. *Quaternary Science Reviews* 15: 437–450.

Villa, P. (1983) *Terra Amata and the Middle Pleistocene Archaeological Record of Southern France*. University of California Publications in Anthropology 13. Berkeley: University of California.

Villa, P. (2001) Early Italy and the Colonization of Western Europe. *Quaternary International* 75: 113–130.

Waal, F. de (2001) *The Ape and the Sushi Master*. London: The Penguin Press.

Waechter, J. de A. (1973) The Late Middle Acheulean Industries in the Swanscombe Area. In Strong, D. E. (ed.) *Archaeological Theory and Practice*. London: Seminar Press, pp. 67–86.

Waechter, J. de A., Newcomer, M. H. and Conway, B. (1970) Swanscombe 1970. *Proceedings of the Royal Anthropological Institute of Great Britain and Ireland for 1970*, pp. 43–64.

Walker, M. (2005) *Quaternary Dating Methods*. Chichester: John Wiley and Sons, Ltd.

Warren, S. H. (1911) On a Palaeolithic (?) Wooden Spear. *Quarterly Journal of the Geological Society of London* 67: xcix.

Warren, S. H. (1912) Palaeolithic Remains from Clacton-on-Sea, Essex. *Essex Naturalist* 17: 15.

Warren, S. H. (1922) The Mesvinian Industry of Clacton-on-Sea, Essex. *Proceedings of the Prehistoric Society of East Anglia* 3: 1–6.

Warren, S. H. (1923) The *Elephas-Antiquus* Bed of Clacton-on-Sea. *Quarterly Journal of the Geological Society of London* 79: 634–619.

Warren, S. H. (1924a) The Elephant Bed of Clacton-on-Sea. *Essex Naturalist* 21: 32–40.

Warren, S. H. (1924b) Pleistocene Classifications. *Proceedings of the Geologists' Association* 35: 265–282.

Warren, S. H. (1926) The Classification of the Lower Palaeolithic with Especial Reference to Essex. *The South-Eastern Naturalist* 31: 38–50.

Warren, S. H. (1932) The Palaeolithic Industries of the Clacton and Dovercourt Districts. *Essex Naturalist* 24: 1–29.

Warren, S. H. (1934) The Palaeolithic Industry of Clacton-on-Sea. *Proceedings of the First International Congress of Prehistoric and Protohistoric Sciences. London, August 1–6 1932*, pp. 69–70.

Warren, S. H. (1951) The Clacton Flint Industry: A New Interpretation. *Proceedings of the Geologists' Association* 62: 107–135.

Warren, S. H. (1955) The Clacton (Essex) Channel Deposits. *Quarterly Journal of the Geological Society of London* 111: 287–307.

Watson, W. (1956) *Flint Implements*. London: Trustees of the British Museum.

Wenban-Smith, F. F. (1989) The Use of Canonical Variates for Determination of Biface Manufacturing Technology at Boxgrove Lower Palaeolithic Site and the Behavioural Implications of this Technology. *Journal of Archaeological Science* 16: 17–26.

Wenban-Smith, F. F. (1995) The Ebbsfleet Valley, Northfleet (Baker's Hole) (TQ 615735). In Bridgland, D. R., Allen, P. and Haggart, B. A. (eds) *The Quaternary of the Lower Reaches of the Thames: Field Guide*. Durham: Quaternary Research Association, pp. 147–164.

Wenban-Smith, F. F. (1998) Clactonian and Acheulean Industries in Britain: Their Chronology and Significance Reconsidered. In Ashton, N., Healy, F. and Pettitt, P. (eds) *Stone Age Archaeology: Essays in Honour of John Wymer*. The Lithics Studies Society Occasional Paper 6. Oxford: Oxbow Books, pp. 90–97.

Wenban-Smith, F. F., Allen, P., Bates, M. R., Parfitt, S. A., Preece, R. C., Stewart, J. R., Turner, C. and Whittaker, J. (2006) The Clactonian Elephant Butchery Site at Southfleet Road, Ebbsfleet, UK. *Journal of Quaternary Science* 21: 471–483.

Wenban-Smith, F. F. and Ashton, N. (1998) Raw Material and Lithic Technology. In Ashton, N., Lewis, S. G. and Parfitt, S. A. (eds) *Excavations at the Lower Palaeolithic Site at East Farm, Barnham, Suffolk 1989–1994*. Occasional Papers of the British Museum 125. London: Trustees of the British Museum, pp. 237–244.

Wenban-Smith, F. F. and Bridgland, D. R. (2001) Palaeolithic Archaeology at the

Swan Valley Community School, Swanscombe, Kent. *Proceedings of the Prehistoric Society* 67: 219–259.

Wenban-Smith, F. F. and Hosfield, R. (eds) (2001) *Palaeolithic Archaeology of the Solent River*. The Lithics Studies Society Occasional Paper 7. London: The Lithics Studies Society.

Wessex Archaeology (1992) *Region 3 (The Upper Thames Valley, the Kennet Valley) and Region 5 (The Solent Drainage System): Southern Rivers Palaeolithic Project Report 1*. Salisbury: Wessex Archaeological Trust.

Wessex Archaeology (1994) *Region 6 (Sussex Raised Beaches) and Region 2 (Severn River): Southern Rivers Palaeolithic Project Report 3*. Salisbury: Wessex Archaeological Trust.

Wessex Archaeology (1996) *Region 7 (Thames) and Region 10 (Warwickshire Avon): English Rivers Palaeolithic Project Report 5*. Salisbury: Wessex Archaeological Trust.

Wessex Archaeology (1997) *Region 8 (East Anglian Rivers) and Region 11 (Trent Drainage): English Rivers Palaeolithic Project Report 3*. Salisbury: Wessex Archaeological Trust.

West, R. G. (1956) The Quaternary Deposits at Hoxne, Suffolk. *Philosophical Transactions of the Royal Society London. Series B* 239: 265–356.

West, R. G. (1969) Pollen Analysis from Interglacial Deposits at Aveley and Grays, Essex. *Proceedings of the Geologists' Association* 80: 271–282.

West, R. G. (1980) *The Pre-Glacial Pleistocene of the Norfolk and Suffolk Coasts*. Cambridge: Cambridge University Press.

West, R. G. and Gibbard, P. L. (1994) Discussion on Excavations at the Lower Palaeolithic Site at East Farm, Barnham, Suffolk. *Journal of the Geological Society, London* 152: 570–571.

West, R. G. and McBurney, C. M. B. (1954) The Quaternary Deposits at Hoxne, Suffolk, and their Archaeology. *Proceedings of the Prehistoric Society* 20: 131–154.

Westaway, R., Bridgland, D. R. and Mishra, S. (2003) Rheological Differences Between Archaean and Younger Crust Can Determine Rates of Quaternary Vertical Motions Revealed by Fluvial Geomorphology. *Terra Nova* 15: 287–298.

Westaway, R., Bridgland, D. R. and White, M. (2006) The Quaternary Uplift History of Central Southern England: Evidence from the Terraces of the Solent River System and Nearby Raised Beaches. *Quaternary Science Reviews* 25: 2212–2250.

Westaway, R., Maddy, D. and Bridgland, D. R. (2002) Flow in the Upper Continental Crust as a Mechanism for the Uplift of South-East England, Constraints from the Thames Terrace Record. *Quaternary Science Reviews* 21: 559–603.

White, C. (1995) La Grotte du Vallonet: Evidence of Early Hominid Activity or Natural Processes. *Lithics* 16: 70–77.

White, M. J. (1997) The Earlier Palaeolithic Occupation of the Chilterns (Southern England): Re-assessing the Sites of Worthington G. Smith. *Antiquity* 71: 912–931.

White, M. J. (1998a) On the Significance of Acheulean Biface Variability in Southern Britain. *Proceedings of the Prehistoric Society* 64: 15–44.

White, M. J. (1998b) Palaeolithic Archaeology of the Stour Terraces. In Murton, J. B., Whiteman, C. A., Bates, M. R., Bridgland, D. R., Long, A. J., Roberts, M. B. and Waller, M. P. (eds) *The Quaternary of Kent and Sussex: Field Guide*. Durham: Quaternary Research Association, pp. 50–52.

White, M. J. (1998c) Twisted Ovates in the British Lower Palaeolithic. In Ashton, N., Healy, F. and Pettitt, P. (eds) *Stone Age Archaeology: Essays in Honour of John Wymer*. The Lithics Studies Society Occasional Paper 6. Oxford: Oxbow Books, pp. 98–104.

White, M. J. (2000) The Clactonian Question: On the Interpretation of Core-and-Flake Assemblages in the British Lower Palaeolithic. *Journal of World Prehistory* 14: 1–63.

White, M. J. and Ashton, N. (2003) Lower Palaeolithic Core Technology and the Origins of the Levallois Method in North-Western Europe. *Current Anthropology* 44: 598–609.

White, M. J. and Jacobi, R. (2002) Two Sides to Every Story. *Bout Coupé* Handaxes Revisited. *Oxford Journal of Archaeology* 21: 109–133.

White, M. J., Mitchell, J., Bridgland, D. R. and McNabb, J. (1998) Rescue Excavations at an Acheulean Site at Southend Road, South Woodford, London Borough of Redbridge, E18 (TQ407905). *The Archaeological Journal* 155: 1–21.

White, M. J. and Pettitt, P. (1995) Technology of Early Palaeolithic Western Europe: Innovation, Variability, and a Unified Framework. *Lithics* 16: 27–40.

White, M. J. and Plunkett, S. (eds) (2004) *Miss Layard Excavates: A Palaeolithic Site at Foxhall Road, Ipswich, 1903–1905*. Liverpool: Western Academic and Specialist Press.

White, M. J. and Schreve, D. C. (2000) Insular Britain – Peninsula Britain: Palaeo-geography, Colonisation and Settlement History of Lower Palaeolithic Britain. *Proceedings of the Prehistoric Society* 66: 1–28.

White, M. J., Scott, B. and Ashton, N. (2006) The Early Middle Palaeolithic in Britain: Archaeology, Settlement History and Human Behaviour. *Journal of Quaternary Science* 21: 525–541.

Whittaker, K., Beasley, M., Bates, M. R. and Wenban-Smith, F. F. (2004) The Lost Valley. *British Archaeology* 74: 22–27.

Wilson, L. (1988) Petrography of the Lower Palaeolithic Tool Assemblage of the Caune de l'Arago (France). *World Archaeology* 19: 376–387.

Wood, B. A. and Richmond, B. G. (2000) Human Evolution: Taxonomy and Paleobiology. *Journal of Anatomy* 197: 19–60.

Wymer, J. J. (1956) Palaeoliths from Gravel of the Ancient Channel Between Caversham and Henley at Highlands near Henley. *Proceedings of the Prehistoric Society* 22: 29–36.

Wymer, J. J. (1957) A Clactonian Flint Industry at Little Thurrock, Grays, Essex. *Proceedings of the Geologists' Association* 68: 159–177.

Wymer, J. J. (1958) Localised Battering on Handaxes. *Archaeological Newsletter* 6: 139.

Wymer, J. J. (1961) The Lower Palaeolithic Succession in the Thames Valley and the Date of the Ancient Channel Between Caversham and Henley, Oxon. *Proceedings of the Prehistoric Society* 27: 1–27.

Wymer, J. J. (1964) Excavations at Barnfield Pit, 1955–1960. In Ovey, C. D. (ed.) *The Swanscombe Skull: A Survey of Research on a Pleistocene Site*. Royal Anthropological Institute Occasional Paper 20. London: Royal Anthropological Institute, pp. 19–60.

Wymer, J. J. (1968) *Lower Palaeolithic Archaeology in Britain*. London: John Baker Publishers Ltd.

Wymer, J. J. (1974) Clactonian and Acheulean Industries in Britain: Their Chronology and Significance. *Proceedings of the Geologists' Association* 85: 391–421.

Wymer, J. J. (1976) The Interpretation of Palaeolithic Cultural and Faunal Material Found in Pleistocene Sediments. In Davidson, D. A. and Shackley, M. L. (eds) *Geoarchaeology*. London: Duckworth, pp. 327–334.

Wymer, J. J. (1983) The Lower Palaeolithic Site at Hoxne. *Proceedings of the Suffolk Institute of Archaeology* 35: 169–189.

Wymer, J. J. (1985) *Palaeolithic Sites of East Anglia*. Norwich: Geo Books.

Wymer, J. J. (1994) The Lower Palaeolithic Period in the London Region. *Transactions of the London and Middlesex Archaeological Society* 42: 1–15.

Wymer, J. J. (1999) *The Lower Palaeolithic Occupation of Britain*. Salisbury: Trust for Wessex Archaeology.

Wymer, J.J. (2001) Palaeoliths in a Lost Pre-Anglian Landscape. In Milliken, S. and Cook, J. (eds) *A Very Remote Period Indeed*. Oxford: Oxbow Books, pp. 174–179.

Wymer, J. J. and Singer, R. (1970) The First Season of Excavations at Clacton-on-Sea, Essex, England: A Brief Report. *World Archaeology* 2: 12–16.

INDEX

407

Related titles from Routledge

Archaeology Coursebook, 2nd Edition
An Introduction to Study Skills, Topics and Methods
Jim Grant, Sam Gorin and Neil Fleming

This fully updated and revised new edition of the bestselling title *The Archaeology Coursebook* is a guide for students studying archaeology for the first time. Including new methods and case studies in this second edition, it provides pre-university students and teachers, as well as undergraduates and enthusiasts, with the skills and technical concepts necessary to grasp the subject.

Specially designed to assist learning it:

- introduces the most commonly examined archaeological methods, concepts, and themes, and provides the necessary skills to understand them
- explains how to interpret the material students may meet in examinations and how to succeed with different types of assignments and exam questions
- supports study with case studies, key sites, key terms, tasks and skills development
- illustrates concepts and commentary with over 200 photos and drawings of excavation sites, methodology and processes, tools and equipment
- contains new material on British pre-history and the Roman Empire; new case studies, methods, examples, boxes, photographs and diagrams; as well as updates on examination changes for pre-university students.

A book no archaeology student should be without.

Hb: 0–415–36076–5
Pb: 0–415–36077–3

Available at all good bookshops
For ordering and further information please visit:
www.routledge.com

Related titles from Routledge

Archaeology: An Introduction
Fourth Edition
Kevin Greene

'The best one-stop introduction to archaeology.' – *Mick Aston, University of Bristol, Time Team*

This substantially updated fourth edition of the highly popular, and comprehensive *Archaeology: An Introduction* is aimed at all beginners in the subject. In a lucid and accessible style Kevin Greene takes the reader on a journey which covers history, techniques and the latest theories. He explains the discovery and excavation of sites, outlines major dating methods, gives clear explanations of scientific techniques, and examines current theories and controversies.

This fourth edition constitutes the most extensive reshaping of the text to date. New features include:

- A completely new user-friendly text design with initial chapter overviews and final conclusions, key references for each chapter section, an annotated guide to further reading, a glossary, refreshed illustrations, case studies and examples, bibliography and full index

- A new companion website built for this edition providing hyperlinks from contents list to individual chapter summaries which in turn link to key websites and other material

- An important new chapter on current theory emphasizing the richness of sources of analogy or interpretation available today.

Archaeology: An Introduction will interest students and teachers at pre-university and undergraduate level as well as enthusiastic general readers of archaeology. The stimulating coverage of the history, methods, science and theory of archaeology make this a book which has a life both within and beyond the academy.

Hb: 0–415–23354–2
Pb: 0–415–23355–0

Available at all good bookshops
For ordering and further information please visit:
www.routledge.com

Related titles from Routledge

Archaeology
The Key Concepts
Edited by Colin Renfrew and Paul Bahn

Clearly written, and easy to follow, *Archaeology: The Key Concepts* collates entries written specifically by specialists in their field. Each entry offers a definition of the term, its origins and development, and all the major figures involved in the area.

The entries include:

- thinking about landscape
- archaeology of cult and religion
- cultural evolution
- concepts of time
- urban societies
- the Antiquity of Man
- archaeology of gender
- feminist archaeology
- experimental archaeology
- multiregional evolution.

Accessibly written for even beginner students, with guides to further reading and extensive cross-referencing, this book is a superb guide for anyone studying, teaching, or with any interest in archaeology.

Hb: 0–415–31757–6
Pb: 0–415–31758–4

Available at all good bookshops
For ordering and further information please visit:
www.routledge.com

Related titles from Routledge

Iron Age Communities in Britain, Fourth Edition
An Account of England, Scotland and Wales from the Seventh Century BC until the Roman Conquest
Barry Cunliffe

Praise for earlier editions:

'This is an important and original book, dealing not simply with Iron Age archaeology, but with the very foundations of British society.' – *Colin Renfrew, The Guardian*

'This is an occasion for celebration ... the book is readable, abundantly illustrated and has full bibliographic references. Its severest critic should give it a resounding welcome.' – *New Scientist*

'Excellent ... it shows a true historian's mastery of archaeological material.' – *Sunday Times*

Since its first publication in 1971, Barry Cunliffe's monumental survey has established itself as a classic of British archaeology. This fully revised fourth edition maintains the qualities of the earlier editions, whilst taking into account the significant developments that have moulded the discipline in recent years. Barry Cunliffe here incorporates new theoretical approaches, technological advances and a range of new sites and finds, ensuring that *Iron Age Communities in Britain* remains the definitive guide to the subject.

ISBN10: 0–415–34779–3 (hbk)
ISBN13: 978–0–415–34779–2 (hbk)

Available at all good bookshops
For ordering and further information please visit:
www.routledge.com

Related titles from Routledge

Objects
Reluctant Witness to the Past
Chris Caple

Objects provides nine detailed case studies to provide a brilliantly clear and comprehensible guide to the different methods and approaches (cultural, scientific and technical) which can and have been used to study ancient artefacts.

From the Bayeux Tapestry to small medieval brass pins, Chris Caple's integral text deals with a full range of materials, from medieval wooden doors to Saxon jewellery, and clearly and simply explains key scientific techniques, technology, anthropological jargon and historical approaches.

Key demonstrations include:

- how information from objects builds into a picture of the ancient society that made and used them
- the commonly used scientific techniques for object analysis
- how and why object typologies work
- how cultural and economic factors as well as the material properties influence what objects are made of
- how simple observation of an object can build its biography.

Revealing answers to crucial questions such as: Can DNA be obtained from objects? Why do people x-ray ancient artefacts? And can you determine the source of metal objects from their trace elements? *Objects* is an absolutely essential text for students of archaeology, museum studies and conservation.

ISBN10: 0–415–30588–8 (hbk)
ISBN10: 0–415–30589–6 (pbk)

ISBN13: 978–0–415–30588–4 (hbk)
ISBN13: 978–0–415–30589–1 (pbk)

Available at all good bookshops
For ordering and further information please visit:
www.routledge.com

THE BRITISH LOWER PALAEOLITHIC

This introductory text is a fresh and original introduction to social themes in Palaeolithic archaeology which teaches the ability to reconstruct ancient lifestyles from the building blocks of data research and theory. Through an exploration of the Clactonian, a stone tool culture of the period and central research issue, it provides a useful and accessible study course in archaeological methods, aims, knowledge and understanding.

John McNabb's unique approach uses the Clactonian as a vehicle to illustrate just how a case study can enrich our understanding of the period by clearly expounding his research and analysis. Here, he takes as a central theme the issue of whether early hominins organised themselves into societies as we understand them and draws fascinating conclusions about the intricacies of ancient human behaviour, which, he argues, was as complex as our own.

Drawing on over 20 years' experience as a specialist in the field, McNabb provides a valuable overview of the most recent developments in the field as he analyses data from a wide variety of disciplines, including archaeology, climatology, palaeontology, geology, evolutionary psychology, environmental and biological disciplines and dating techniques.

John McNabb is the Director of the Centre for the Archaeology of Human Origins at the University of Southampton; his research interests are focused on the construction of social relations, as seen through material culture, in pre-modern humans. He is a Fellow of the British Academy's 'From Lucy to Language: The Social Brain' project and is a member of the National Ice Age Network.

THE BRITISH LOWER PALAEOLITHIC

Stones in contention

John McNabb

Routledge
Taylor & Francis Group

LONDON AND NEW YORK

First published 2007
by Routledge
2 Park Square, Milton Park, Abingdon, Oxon OX14 4RN

Simultaneously published in the USA and Canada
by Routledge
270 Madison Ave, New York, NY 10016

Routledge is an imprint of the Taylor & Francis Group, an informa business

© 2007 John McNabb

Typeset in Joanna by
RefineCatch Limited, Bungay, Suffolk
Printed and bound in Great Britain by
Antony Rowe Ltd, Chippenham, Wiltshire

British Library Cataloguing in Publication Data
A catalogue record for this book is available from the British Library

Library of Congress Cataloging in Publication Data
A catalog record for this book has been requested

ISBN10: 0–415–42727–4 (hbk)
ISBN10: 0–415–42728–2 (pbk)

ISBN13: 978–0–415–42727–2 (hbk)
ISBN13: 978–0–415–42728–9 (pbk)

THIS BOOK IS DEDICATED TO ROGER JACOBI, NICK
ASHTON, JOHN GOWLETT AND CLIVE GAMBLE, FOR
DIFFERENT REASONS. THANK YOU.
IT IS ESPECIALLY DEDICATED TO JOHN WYMER AND
DAVID KEEN WHO BOTH DIED BEFORE I HAD THE
CHANCE TO THANK THEM. YOU ARE MUCH MISSED.